W9-AAC-211

The Heart of CATHOLICISM

Essential Writings of the Church from St. Paul to John Paul II

Compiled and Edited by
Theodore E. James, Ph.D.

Our Sunday Visitor Publishing Division
Our Sunday Visitor, Inc.
Huntington, Indiana 46750

Faith, children: To Ted, Jr.; Nick; Bill; Frank; J.P.; and Faith, Jr.; to their spouses, Helen; Mary Ellen; Carol; Stephanie; Beverly; and Roger; and to the grandchildren, Ted III; Mark; Nicholas; Tristan; Billy; Elizabeth; Brendan; and Charlotte.

LC: 96-70433
ISBN: 0-87973-806-5

Printed in the United States of America

Cover design by Monica Watts

806

Contents

Part IV: Additional Clarifications of Catholicism

Part V: Philosophical Perspectives and Basic Mysticism

Part VI: Devotional Classics

Part VII: Practice of Basic Catholic Teachings

Foreword

The search for truth, like that for goodness and beauty, has occupied the minds of men and women for centuries. Truth has been seen as an elusive reality, either too ethereal or ideal to be comprehended by our faulty mortal faculties or too relative to our circumstances and contemporary lifestyle to be universal. The Gospel of John captures this tension in the exchange between Pontius Pilate and Christ. Pilate took the relativist view of truth when he sneered "What is truth?" in reply to Christ's statement:

"The reason I was born, the reason why I came into the world, is to testify to the truth. Anyone committed to the truth hears my voice."

Christ has intrigued and baffled men and women for centuries, since He is himself Truth incarnate. What does this mean, that Truth, uncircumscribed and beyond human comprehension, is now come among us as a man? The unknowable is now known and seen and heard, not in image and shadow, as Plato would have, but as one like ourselves, in our own world, circumstances, and conditions. This Truth speaks to the heart of the human person, as John Henry Newman phrased it, "*Cor ad cor loquitur*" (Heart to heart).

The Roman Catholic Church has spoken for centuries of this Truth and its transforming power in creation. From the moment of Pentecost to the present, the Church has recorded, taught and clarified the message of Christ, rephrasing and deepening its own understanding of Christ's words in order to make it more intelligible to men and women of every time and place. "*Cor ad cor loquitur*," the Truth of Christ, Christ himself, who continues to touch the hearts of men and women through His Church in order to transform them for all eternity.

The Heart of Catholicism, edited by Dr. Theodore E. James, is a collection of Church writings which exemplify the teachings of the Church throughout its history. Beginning with excerpts from the New Testament, the collection presents the writings of the Church Fathers and early councils, those of the great Catholic reformers, mystics, and teachers down to the popes, bishops, and saints of our own century.

For those who have never studied or even read the Church's teachings, this volume provides an enlightening and refreshing collection. The Church's teachings throughout the centuries provide a clear explanation of the reality of God, His creation, humankind as created in His image, His redemptive love, and His continuing work of sanctification of the world through His Church. These truths form the heart of the writings of some of the greatest minds of the centuries: the Apostles Peter, Paul, James and John, Clement of Rome, Cyril of Alexandria, Basil the Great and Gregory of Nyssa, John Chrysostom, Ambrose and Augustine, Benedict, Bernard of Clairvaux, Thomas Aquinas, Bonaventure, Ignatius of Loyola, Teresa of Ávila and John of the Cross, Francis de Sales, John Henry Newman, Popes Leo XIII, Pius XII, and Paul VI. All have written about God, His relationship to the world and to us, His image, in language and terms familiar to men and women of their times in order to express more clearly the transforming Truth of God.

This is a collection for all Christians interested in the teachings of the Church, either from an academic perspective or as an instrument to enrich their personal and spiritual lives.

The teachings of the Church, either in Scripture, from the Fathers, or from the spiritual writers throughout the ages, have served as the source of nourishment for my own spiritual life, from my days in the seminary, as a priest, and today as a bishop of the Church. This is a splendid collection which I highly recommend to you, and I hope that it will serve to deepen your own faith in the Lord and in His Church.

Christ said, "the truth will set you free." It is not an unattainable truth, but one that is near to us, given flesh through the Church and its teachings. The Truth is Christ himself, come into the world to transform us and to share with us His personal, eternal life, "*cor ad cor loquitur*."

The Most Reverend Edward M. Egan
Bishop of Bridgeport

General Introduction

The contents of this volume are presented as being those writings which are considered to present, explain, and/or defend the traditional teachings and practices of the Catholic Church.

The main purpose for the selection is to show that the teachings and practices of the contemporary Catholic Church, as presented and defended by its official Magisterium and clarified by the Congregation for the Doctrine of the Faith, are essentially the same as those originally presented in the New Testament and repeated again and again in ensuing historical periods as the circumstances required.

The contents are presented in a format that may appeal to anyone interested in knowing what are the basic teachings and practices of the Roman Catholic Church concerning a variety of topics in the areas of belief and practices or, if one prefers, in the areas of faith and morals.

It is hoped that the reader will be helped to understand what has been and really is the Catholic teaching on such topics as the Trinity and Unity of God, the Incarnation of the Second Person of the Trinity, the historical Jesus, Papal Infallibility, the basis of the authority of the Magisterium, the traditional teaching on the nature and value of the Mass as sacrifice and *agape* banquet, the seven Sacraments, the sacramentals, human sexuality, contraception, abortion, infanticide, euthanasia, celibacy, etc.

Because of the limitations of space, not all pertinent writings can be included. Those that have been selected are chosen because they are judged to be most suitable to carry out the main purpose. They illustrate the fact that the word "classic" was traditionally used to signify the most important and most valuable in any class of things and, hence, can be associated with the basic writings of Catholicism.

The rationale of this collection is to include those writings of those individuals who have been accepted during their lifetime and in subsequent times as reliable witnesses of the essential characteristics of the Catholic Church: unity of doctrine, holiness of life, universality of application, and apostolic continuity.

It is essential to the present compilation to emphasize what other collections of readings have not considered as their purpose, namely, the source of the teachings and practice of Catholicism in the New Testament and the traditional reiteration and application of such by those explicitly aware of the need to reemphasize them because of external and internal dissent or misunderstanding of the contents.

One who reads these documents will be in a position to understand some of the background for an objective evaluation of the activities of the Magisterium, the official teaching authority of the Catholic Church, in criticizing the statements of those theologians who dissent from the traditional official statement of matters concerning Catholic faith and morals. As is well known, there have been individuals and groups following them such as Gnostics, Monarchians, Donatists, Manichaeans, Arians, Pelagians, Nestorians, Monophysites, Materialists, Modernists, Historicists, and Secular Humanists who have been the occasion for the re-presentation and defense of Catholic teachings and practices from the time of the New Testament down to our own.

The documents in this collection are not presented as historical, or philosophical, or theological, or sociopsychological, or any other kind of *interpretation* of the teachings of the Catholic Church that are found in the writings in this volume. The purpose is to present the statements of the content of that teaching as found in the New Testament and in the subsequent documents in the various periods of the development of the Catholic Church down to the present day, so that it is clear to an unbiased reader that what is taught by the Magisterium at various times and in various places is authentic Catholic teaching. A subsidiary purpose is to collect evidence to show that what some theologians at various times have claimed to be the doctrine and practices of the Catholic Church, which should be taught and practiced today, do not really coincide with the statements approved by the Magisterium exercising its authoritative role down through the ages as the depository of the classical presentation of Catholic teaching and practices.

Theodore E. James, Ph.D.

Part I
Classical Beginnings

Introduction

These writings are selected passages from the New Testament and the *Teaching of the Twelve Apostles* (*Didache*), selected letters of the Apostolic Fathers, and an allegorical presentation of the nature and value of penance.

The period covered is from the beginning of Christianity to the third quarter of the second century A.D. These writings are expository in form. The teachings and practices of Catholicism are presented in simple prose without a great amount of the kind of defense that tends to predominate in the Apologies of Part II.

There are many other authors besides these herein who present and explain the classical teachings and practices of Catholicism, such as Barnabas, who may have been a companion of St. Paul; Tertullian and Minucius Felix, the African Fathers; and Irenaeus, who stresses against the Gnostics that "the true *gnosis* is the teaching of the twelve Apostles" and that no one can be both a gnostic and a Christian. In the Christian tradition, he asserts that God created all other things out of nothing and that each man is essentially a living and rational being with a strictly individual soul endowed with free will. In the Pauline tradition Irenaeus stresses that there is one God Whose existence is naturally known from a consideration of His works.

Chapter 1 • The Person and Teachings of Jesus

In this section are presented the teachings of and about Jesus that are found in the "Good News" of Matthew, Mark, Luke, and John, which are fundamental classics in the Catholic tradition.

Beginning with John's Gospel the emphasis is on the divine nature of Jesus as the Word of God Who became man and is the source of the power to make all who believe in Him to be children of God. Jesus manifested His divine nature and personality by many miracles, beginning with the marriage feast of Cana. Luke, Matthew, and Mark incorporate in their version of the Good News other instances of the divinity of Jesus as well as of His humanity. There are many instances of miracles worked by Jesus to show His compassion for those ill in body and mind or suffering from the loss of a dear one, as in the case of the daughter of Jairus, of the son of the widow of Naim, and of Lazarus. Jesus healed the deaf, the dumb, the blind as well as those suffering from other physical and mental handicaps. The promise of the institution of the Eucharist as the Body and Blood of Christ and the fulfillment of that promise at the Last Supper is an essential classical teaching of Catholicism. The account of the Resurrection highlights the most basic of Catholic teachings.

Lack of space does not permit the inclusion in this section of many instances in John for the basis of the sacramental teachings; in Luke for the stress on the fact that Jesus prayed in a social way before major events in His life, such as at His baptism, prior to the choice of the Apostles, His transfiguration, His passion, and on the cross; in Mark to illustrate the character and personality of the Messiah and to establish a basis for the most important question — "Who do you say that I am? — and its answer — "You are the Christ, the Son of the Living God"; in Matthew for the emphasis on the destruction of sin, hope of salvation, redemptive function of Jesus' passion and death as part of the new covenant.

The active role of the Holy Spirit in the life of the Catholic Church is promised by Jesus in the Gospels, dramatically fulfilled in the Pentecostal accounts of the Acts, as well as in the development of the teachings of Jesus in the Letters of Peter, James, John, Paul, Clement, Ignatius of Antioch, Polycarp, in the *Didache*, Fragments of Papias, and The Shepherd of Hermas to refer to just a few.

> In the beginning was the Word, and the Word was with God, and the Word was God.
>
> The same was in the beginning with God.

All things were made by him: and without him was made nothing that was made.

In him was life, and the life was the light of men. . . .

He came unto his own, and his own received him not.

But as many as received him, he gave them power to be made the sons of God, to them that believe in his name.

Who are born, not of blood, nor of the will of the flesh, nor of the will of man, but of God.

And the Word was made flesh, and dwelt among us, (and we saw his glory, the glory as it were of the only begotten of the Father,) full of grace and truth. . . .

No man hath seen God at any time: the only begotten Son who is in the bosom of the Father, he hath declared him.

John 1:1-18 (some verses omitted)

. . . Jesus came from Nazareth, in the region of Galilee, and John baptized him in the Jordan. As soon as Jesus came up out of the water he saw heaven opening and the Spirit coming down on him like a dove. And a voice came from heaven: "Your are my own dear Son. I am well pleased with you."

Mark 1:9-11

. . . There was a marriage in Cana of Galilee: and the mother of Jesus was there.

And Jesus also was invited, and his disciples, to the marriage.

And the wine failing, the mother of Jesus saith to him: "They have no wine."

And Jesus saith to her: "Woman, what is that to me and to thee? my hour is not yet come."

His mother said to the waiters: "Whatsoever he shall say to you, do ye."

Now there were set there six waterpots of stone, according to the manner of the purifying of the Jews, containing two or three measures apiece.

Jesus saith to them: "Fill the waterpots with water." And they filled them up to the brim.

And Jesus saith to them: "Draw out now, and carry to the chief steward of the feast." And they carried it.

And when the chief steward had tasted the water made wine, and knew not whence it was, but the waiters knew who had drawn the water, the chief steward called the bridegroom.

And said to him: "Every man at first sets forth good wine, and when men have well drunk, then that which is worse. But you have kept the good wine until now."

This beginning of miracles did Jesus in Cana of Galilee; and manifested his glory, and his disciples believed in him.

John 2:1-11

For God so loved the world, as to give his only begotten Son; that whosoever believe in him, may not perish, but may have life everlasting.

For God sent not his Son into the world to judge the world, but that the world may be saved by him.

John 3:16-17

And it came to pass, when he was in a certain city, behold a man full of leprosy, who seeing Jesus, and falling on his face, besought him, saying: "Lord, if you wilt, you can make me clean."

And stretching forth his hand, he touched him, saying: "I will. Be cleansed." And immediately the leprosy departed from him.

And he charged him that he should tell no man, but, go, show himself to the priest, and offer for thy cleansing according as Moses commanded, for a testimony to them.

But the fame of him went abroad the more, and great multitudes came together to hear, and to be healed by him of their infirmities.

Luke 5:12-15

And it came to pass on a certain day, as he sat teaching, that there were also Pharisees and doctors of the law sitting by, that were come out of every town of Galilee, and Judea and Jerusalem: and the power of the Lord was to heal them.

And behold, men brought in a bed a man, who had the palsy: and they sought means to bring him in, and to lay him before him.

And when they could not find by what way they might bring him in, because of the multitude, they went up upon the roof, and let him down through the tiles with his bed into the midst before Jesus.

Whose faith when he saw, he said: "Man, your sins are forgiven."

And the scribes and Pharisees began to think, saying: "Who is this who speaks blasphemies? Who can forgive sins, but God alone?"

And when Jesus knew their thoughts, answering, he said to them: "What is it you think in your hearts?"

"Which is easier to say, your sins are forgiven", or to say; "Arise and walk?"

But that you may know that the Son of man has power on earth to forgive sins, (he saith to the sick of the palsy,) I say to thee, "Rise, take up thy bed, and go into thy house."

And immediately rising up before them, he took up the bed on which he lay; and he went away to his own house, glorifying God.

And all were astonished; and they glorified God. And they were filled with fear, saying: "We have seen wonderful things today."

Luke 5:17-26

And it came to pass afterwards that he went into a city that is called Naim; and there went with him his disciplines and a great multitude.

And when he came nigh to the gate of the city, behold a dead man was carried out, the only son of his mother; and she was a widow: And a great multitude of the city was with her.

Whom when the Lord had seen, being moved with mercy towards her, he said to her: "Weep not."

And he came near and touched the bier. And they that carried it, stood still. And he said: "Young man, I say to arise."

And he that was dead, sat up, and began to speak. And he gave him to his mother.

And there came a fear upon them all: and they glorified God, saying: "A great prophet is risen up among us: and, God hath visited his people."

Luke 7:11-16

Thus therefore shall you pray: "Our Father who art in heaven, hallowed be thy name.

Thy kingdom come. Thy will be done on earth as it is in heaven.

Give us this day our supersubstantial bread.

And forgive us our debts, as we also forgive our debtors.

And lead us not into temptation. But deliver us from evil. Amen."

Matthew 6:9-13

And after six days Jesus taketh with him Peter and James and John, and leadeth them up into an high mountain apart by themselves, and was transfigured before them.

And his garments became shining and exceeding white as snow, so as no fuller upon earth can make white.

And there appeared to them Elias with Moses; and they were talking with Jesus.

And Peter answering, said to Jesus: "Rabbi, it is good for us to be here: and let us make three tabernacles, one for thee, and one for Moses, and one for Elias."

For he knew not what he said for they were struck with fear.

And there was a cloud overshadowing them and a voice came out of the cloud, saying: "This is my most beloved son; hear ye him."

And immediately looking about, they saw no man anymore, but Jesus only with them.

And as they came down from the mountain, he charged them not to tell any man what things they had seen, till the Son of man shall be risen again from the dead.

Mark 9:1-8

And the Pharisees coming to him asked him: "Is it lawful for a man to put away his wife?" tempting him.

But he, answering, saith to them: "What did Moses command you?"

Who said: "Moses permitted to write a bill of divorce, and to put her away."

To whom Jesus, answering, said: "Because of the hardness of your heart he wrote you that precept.

"But from the beginning of the creation, God made them male and female.

"For this cause a man shall leave his father and mother; and shall cleave to his wife.

"And they two shall be in one flesh. Therefore now they are not two, but one flesh.

"What therefore God hath joined together, let no man put assunder."

And in the house again his disciples asked him concerning the same thing.

And he saith to them: "Whosoever shall put away his wife and marry another, committeth adultery against her.

"And if the wife shall put away her husband, and be married to another, she committeth adultery."

Mark 10:2-12

"Amen, amen, I say unto you: He that believes in me has everlasting life. I am the bread of life.

"This is the bread which comes down from heaven; that if any man eat of it, he may not die.

"I am the living bread which came down from heaven.

"If any man eat of this bread, he shall live for ever; and the bread that I will give is my flesh, for the life of the world."

The Jews therefore strove among themselves, saying: "How can this man give us his flesh to eat?"

Then Jesus said to them: "Amen, amen, I say unto you: Except you eat the flesh of the Son of man, and drink his blood, you shall not have life in you.

"He that eats my flesh, and drinks my blood, has everlasting life. and I will raise him up in the last day.

"For my flesh is meat indeed: and my blood is drink indeed.

"He that eats my flesh, and drinks my blood, abides in me, and I in him.

"As the living Father has sent me, and I live by the Father; so he that eats me, the same also shall live by me."

John 6:47-58

And Jesus came into the quarters of Cesarea Philippi: and he asked his disciples, saying: "Who do men say that the Son of man is?"

But they said: "Some John the Baptist, and other some Elias, and others Jeremias, or one of the prophets."

Jesus saith to them: "But who do you say that I am?"

Simon Peter answered and said: "Thou art Christ, the Son of the living God."

And Jesus, answering, said to him: "Blessed art thou, Simon Bar-Jona: because flesh and blood hath not revealed it to thee, but my Father who is in heaven.

"And I say to thee: That thou art Peter; and upon this rock I will build my church, and the gates of hell shall not prevail against it.

"And I will give to thee the keys of the kingdom of heaven, whatsoever thou shalt bind upon earth, it shall be bound also in heaven: and whatsoever thou shalt loose on earth, it shall be loosed also in heaven."

Then he commanded his disciples, that they should tell no one that he was Jesus the Christ.

Matthew 16:13-20

And the day of the unleavened bread came, on which it was necessary that the pasch should be killed.

And he sent Peter and John, saying: "Go, and prepare for us the pasch, that we may eat."

Luke 22:7, 8

And when the hour was come, he sat down, and the twelve apostles with him.

And he said to them: "With desire I have desired to eat this pasch with you, before I suffer.

"For I say to you, that from this time I will not eat it, till it be fulfilled in the kingdom of God."

Luke 22:14-16

And taking bread, he gave thanks, and broke; and gave to them saying: "This is my body which is given for you. Do this for commemoration of me."

In like manner the chalice also, after he had supped, saying: "This is the chalice, the new testament in my blood which shall be shed for you."

Luke 22:7-8, 19-20

"A new commandment I give unto you: That you love one another, as I have loved you, that you also love one another.

"By this shall all men know that you are my disciples, if you have love one for another."

John 13:34, 35

"If you love me, keep my commandments.

"And I will ask the Father, and he shall give you another Paraclete, that he may abide with you forever.

"The Spirit of truth, whom the world cannot receive, because it does not see him, or know him: but you shall know him; because he shall abide with you, and shall be in you."

John 13:34, 35

"The Paracete, the Holy Spirit, whom the Father will send in my name, he will teach you all things, and bring all things to your mind, whatsoever I shall have said to you."

John 14:26

"This is my commandment, that you love one another as I have loved you.

"Greater love than this no man hath, that a man lay down his life for his friends."

John 15:12-13

"Master, which is the great commandment in the law?"

Jesus said to him. "Thou shalt love the Lord thy God with thy whole heart, and with thy whole soul, and with thy whole mind.

"This is the greatest and the first commandment.

"And the second is like to this: Thou shalt love thy neighbor as thyself.

"On these two commandments depend the whole law and the prophets."

Matthew 22:36-40

Then therefore Pilate delivered Jesus to them to be crucified. And they took Jesus, and led him forth.

And bearing his own cross, he went forth to that place which is called Calvary, but in Hebrew Golgotha.

Where they crucified him, and with him two others, one on each side, and Jesus in the midst.

And Pilate wrote a title also: and he put it upon the cross. And the writing was: JESUS OF NAZARETH, THE KING OF THE JEWS.

John 19:16-19

On the first day of the week, Mary Magdalene came early, when it was yet dark, unto the sepulchre: and she saw the stone taken away from the sepulchre.

She ran, therefore, and came to Simon Peter, and to the other disciple whom Jesus loved, and said to them: "They have taken away the Lord out of the sepulchre, and we know not where they have laid him."

Peter therefore went out, and that other disciple, and they came to the sepulchre.

And they both ran together, and that other disciple, did outrun Peter, and came first to the sepulchre.

And when he stooped down, he saw the linen cloths lying: but yet he went not in.

Then came Simon Peter, following him, and went into the sepulchre, and saw the linen cloths lying.

And the napkin that had been about his head, not lying with the linen clothes, but apart, wrapt up into one place.

Then that other disciple also went in, who came first to the sepulchre: and he saw, and believed.

For as yet they knew not the scripture, that he must rise again from the dead.

John 20:1-9

Now when it was late that same day, the first of the week, and the doors were shut, where the disciples were gathered together, Jesus came and stood in the midst, and said to them: "Peace be to you."

And when he had said this, he showed them his hands, and his side. The disciples therefore were glad, when they saw the Lord.

He said therefore to them again: "Peace be to you. As the Father has sent me, I also send you."

When he had said this, he breathed on them; and he said to them: "Receive the Holy Spirit.

"Whose sins you shall forgive, they are forgiven them: and whose sins you shall retain, they are retained."

Now Thomas, one of the twelve, who is called Didymus, was not with them when Jesus came.

The other disciples therefore said to him: "We have seen the Lord." But he said to them. "Except I shall see in his hands the print of the nails, and put my finger into the place of the nails, and put my hand into his side, I will not believe."

And after eight days, again his disciples were within, and Thomas with them. Jesus came, the doors being shut, and stood in the midst, and said: "Peace be to you."

Then he said to Thomas: "Put in thy finger hither, and see my hands, and bring hither thy hand and put it into my side; and be not faithless, but believing."

John 20:19-27

Thomas answered, and said to him: "My Lord, and my God."

Jesus said to him: "Because thou hast seen me, Thomas, thou hast believed: blessed are they that have not seen, and have believed."

John 20:28-29

And the eleven disciples went into Galilee, unto the mountain where Jesus had appointed them.

And seeing him they adored: but some doubted.

And Jesus, coming, spoke to them, saying: “All power is given to me in heaven and in earth.

Going therefore, teach ye all nations; baptizing them in the name of the Father, and of the Son, and of the Holy Spirit.

Teaching them to observe all things whatsoever I have commanded you: and behold I am with you all days, even to the consummation of the world.

Matthew 28:16-20

Many other signs also did Jesus in the sight of his disciples, which are not written in this book.

But these are written, that you may believe that Jesus is the Christ, the Son of God; and that believing you may have life in is name.

John 20:30-31

Chapter 2 • The Acts of the Apostles

In this section is a selected account of the events connected with the origin and early development of the Church. The basis of the selection is again devotional. The selections presented are typical and significant. The Acts cover the last days of Jesus, the Pentecostal vivification of the Church, the missionary activities of the Apostles (especially Peter and Paul), and the last days of Paul in Rome — the period from the coming of the Messiah to A.D. 62.

The former treatise I made, O Theophilus, of all things which Jesus began to do and to teach,

Until the day on which, giving commandments by the Holy Spirit to the apostles whom he had chosen, he was taken up.

To whom also he showed himself alive after his passion, by many proofs, for forty days appearing to them, and speaking of the kingdom of God.

And eating together with them, he commanded them, that they should not depart from Jerusalem, but should wait for the promise of the Father, which you have heard (saith he) by my mouth.

"For John indeed baptized with water, but you shall be baptized with the Holy Spirit not many days hence.

Acts 1:1-15

"You shall receive the power of the Holy Spirit coming upon you, and you shall be witnesses unto me in Jerusalem, and in all Judea, and Samaria, and even to the uttermost part of the earth."

And when he had said these things, while they looked on, he was raised up and a cloud received him out of their sight.

Acts 1:8-9

When the days of the Pentecost were accomplished, they were all together in one place:

And suddenly there came a sound from heaven, as of a mighty wind coming, and it filled the whole house where they were sitting.

And there appeared to them parted tongues as it were of fire, and it sat upon every one of them:

And they were all filled with the Holy Spirit, and they began to speak with divers tongues, according as the Holy Spirit gave them to speak.

Now there were dwelling at Jerusalem Jews, devout men, out of every nation under heaven.

And when this was noised abroad, the multitude came together, and were confounded in mind, because that every man heard them speak in his own tongue.

And they were all amazed, and wondered, saying: "Behold, are not all these, that speak, Galileans?

"And how have we heard, every man our own tongue wherein we were born?

"Parthians, and Medes, and Elamites, and inhabitants of Mesopotamia, Judea, and Cappadocia, Pontus and Asia,

"Phrygia, and Pamphylia, Egypt, and the parts of Libya about Cyrene, and strangers of Rome.

"Jews also, and proselytes, Cretes, and Arabians: we have heard them speak in our own tongues the wonderful works of God."

And they were all astonished, and wondered, saying one to another: "What meaneth this?"

Acts 2:1-12

But Peter standing up with the eleven, lifted up his voice and spoke to them:

". . . Ye men of Israel, hear these words: Jesus of Nazareth, a man approved of God among you, by miracles, and wonders, and signs, which God did by him in the midst of you, as you also know;

"This same being delivered up, by the determinate counsel and fore-knowledge of God, you by the hands of wicked men have crucified and slain.

"Whom God hath raised up, having loosed the sorrows of hell, as it was impossible that he should be holden by it."

Acts 2:14, 22-24

"This Jesus hath God raised again, whereof all we are witnesses.

"Being exalted therefore by the right hand of God, and having received of the Father the promise of the Holy Spirit, he hath poured forth this which you see and hear."

Acts 2:32-33

Now when they had heard these things, they had compunction in their heart, and said to Peter, and to the rest of the apostles: "What shall we do, men and brethren?"

But Peter said to them: "Do penance, and be baptized every one of you in the name of Jesus Christ, for the remission of your sins: and you shall receive the gift of the Holy Spirit."

. . . They therefore that received his word, were baptized; and there were added in that day about three thousand souls.

And they were persevering in the doctrine of the apostles, and in the communication of the breaking of bread, and in prayers.

Acts 2:37-38, 41-42

Chapter 3 • The Letters of St. Paul

The letters that were addressed to the widely scattered Christian communities of the first century and traditionally attributed to Paul of Tarsus make up a fundamental presentation of the doctrines of Catholicism. With a characteristic philosophical insight, these letters present these teachings, contrast them with the "wisdom" of the pagan world, defend their content, elucidate their rationale and divine guarantee, and exhort the members of the far-flung communities to persevere in their unity of faith, worship, and love. From these letters we can learn what the faith meant to their author, of the reality of the Church as a living witness to Jesus and of the essentials of the Christian doctrine. A similar witness is found in *The Faith of our Fathers*, the classic work of James Cardinal Gibbons.

Of all the matters emphasized in the letters of St. Paul, most outstanding is the unanimous acceptance of the doctrines taught by Jesus and handed down by the Apostles, and the unity in the catholicity of the Christian message: one for all. Fundamental to Paul's conception of the Christian teaching is the acceptance of the belief that all men are equally subject to sin. They are incapable of escaping this limitation by their own natural efforts; Jesus has become man in order to redeem all of us and call all of us to salvation in union with Him. A more concise contemporary summary of the fundamentals of Christianity is found in the *Credo* of Pope Paul VI.

For the purposes of this study, the letter to the Hebrews is being attributed to Paul.

To the Romans

Paul, a servant of Jesus Christ, called to be an apostle, separated unto the gospel of God. . . .

To the Greeks and to the barbarians, to the wise and to the unwise, I am a debtor.

For I am not ashamed of the gospel. For it is the power of God unto salvation to every one that believeth: to the Jew first and to the Greek.

For the justice of God is revealed therein from faith unto faith, as it is written: "The just man liveth by faith."

For the wrath of God is revealed from heaven against all ungodliness and injustice of those men that detain the truth of God in injustice:

Because that which is known of God is manifest in them. For God hath manifested it unto them.

For the invisible things of him, from the creation of the world, are clearly seen, being understood by the things that are made: his eternal power also, and divinity, so that they are inexcusable.

Because that, when they knew God, they have not glorified him as God, or given thanks; but became vain in their thoughts, and their foolish heart was darkened.

For professing themselves to be wise, they became fools. . . .

Wherefore God gave them up to the desires of their heart, unto uncleanness, to dishonor their own bodies among themselves.

Who changed the truth of God into lie and worshipped and served the creature rather than the Creator, who is blessed forever. Amen.

For this cause God delivered them up to shameful affections. For their women have changed the natural use into that use which is against nature.

And, in like manner, the men also, leaving the natural use of the women, have burned in their lusts one towards another, men with men working that which is filthy, and receiving in themselves the recompense which was due to their error.

And as they liked not to have God in their knowledge, God delivered them up to a reprobate sense, to do those things which are not convenient;

Being filled with all iniquity, malice, fornication, avarice, wickedness, full of envy, murder, contention, deceit, malignity, whisperers,

Detractors, hateful to God, contumelious, proud, haughty, inventors of evil things, disobedient to parents,

Foolish, dissolute, without affection, without fidelity, without mercy.

Who, having known the justice of God, did not understand that they who do such things, are worthy of death; and not only they that do them, but they also that consent to them that do them. . . .

But glory, and honor, and peace to everyone that worketh good, to the Jew first, and also to the Greek.

For there is no respect of persons with God.

For whosoever have sinned without the law, shall perish without the law; and whosoever have sinned in the law, shall be judged by the law.

For not the hearers of the law are just before God, but the doers of the law shall be justified.

For when the Gentiles, who have not the law, do by nature those things that are of the law; these, having not the law, are a law to themselves.

Who shew the work of the law written in their hearts, their conscience bearing witness to them: and their thoughts between themselves accusing or also defending one another.

In the day when God shall judge the secrets of men by Jesus Christ, according to my gospel. . . .

Romans 1:1, 14-22, 24-32; 2:10-16

Being justified therefore by faith, let us have peace with God, through our Lord Jesus Christ:

By whom also we have access through faith into this grace wherein we stand: and glory in the hope of the glory of the sons of God.

And not only so: but we glory also in tribulation, knowing that tribulation worketh patience. . . .

Wherefore as by one man sin entered into this world and by sin death; and so death passed upon all men, in whom all have sinned.

For until the law sin was in the world: but sin was not imputed, when the law was not.

But death reigned from Adam unto Moses, even over them also who have not sinned, after the similitude of the transgression of Adam, who is a figure of him who was to come. . . .

For I am delighted with the law of God according to the inward man:

but I see another law in my members, fighting against the law of my mind and captivating me in the law of sin that is in my members.

Unhappy man that I am, who shall deliver me from the body of this death?

The grace of God, by Jesus Christ our Lord. Therefore, I myself, with the mind, serve the law of God: but with the flesh, the law of sin. . . .

For the Spirit himself gives testimony to our spirit that we are the sons of God.

And if sons, heirs also, heirs indeed of God and joint heirs with Christ: yet so, if we suffer with him, that we may be also glorified with him.

For I reckon that the sufferings of this time are not worthy to be compared with the glory to come that shall be revealed in us.

Romans 5:1-3; 12-14; 7:22-25; 8:16-18

Now we know that for those who love God all things work together unto good, for those who, according to his purpose, are saints through his call.

For those whom he has foreknown he has also predestined to become conformed to the image of his Son, that he should be the firstborn among many brethren. And those whom he has predestined, them he has also called; and those whom he has called, them he has also justified, and those whom he has justified, them he has also glorified. . . .

Who shall separate us from the love of Christ? Shall tribulation, or distress, or persecution, or hunger, or nakedness, or danger, or the sword? Even as it is written,

"For thy sake we are put to death all the day long.
We are regarded as sheep for the slaughter" [Ps. 43:22].

Romans 8:28-30, 35-36

But in all these things we overcome because of him who has loved us. For I am sure that neither death, nor life, nor angels, nor principalities, nor things present, nor things to come, nor powers, nor height, nor depth, nor any other creature will be able to separate us from the love of God, which is in Christ Jesus our Lord. . . .

Oh, the depth of the riches of the wisdom and of the knowledge of God! How incomprehensible are his judgments and how unsearchable his ways! For

"Who has known the mind of the Lord,
or who has been his counsellor?
Or who has first given to him,
that recompense should be made him?" [Isa. 40:13].

Romans 8:37-39; 11:33-35

For from him and through him and unto him are all things. To him to be the glory forever, amen.

I exhort you therefore, brethren, by the mercy of God, to present your bodies as a sacrifice, living, holy, pleasing to God — your spiritual service. . . .

Render therefore to all men their dues. Tribute, to whom tribute is due: custom, to whom custom: fear, to whom fear, honor, to whom honor.

Owe no man any thing, but to love one another. For he that loveth his neighbor, hath fulfilled the law.

For Thou shalt not commit adultery; Thou shalt not kill; Thou shalt not steal; Thou shalt not bear false witness; Thou shalt not covet; and if there by any other commandment, it is comprised in this word, Thou shalt love thy neighbor as thyself.

The love of our neighbor worketh no evil. Love therefore is the fulfilling of the law.

Romans 11:36; 12:1; 13:7-10

First Letter to the Corinthians

Now I beseech you, brethren, by the name of our Lord Jesus Christ, that you all speak the same thing, and that there be no schisms among you, but that you be perfect in the same mind, and in the same judgment. . . .

We preach Christ crucified, unto the Jews indeed a stumbling block, and unto the Gentiles foolishness:

But unto them that are called, both Jews and Greeks, Christ the power of God, and the wisdom of God. . . .

For the foolishness of God is wiser than men and the weakness of God is stronger than men. . . .

But we speak the wisdom of God in a mystery, a wisdom which is hidden, which God ordained before the world, unto our glory. . . .

But, as it is written: That eye hath not seen, nor ear heard, neither hath it entered into the heart of man, what things God hath prepared for them that love him.

But to us God hath revealed them, by his Spirit for the Spirit searcheth all things, yea, the deep things of God. . . .

1 Corinthians 1:10, 23-25; 2:7-10

Avoid immorality. Any other sin a man commits does not affect his body; but the man who commits immorality sins against his own body. Don't you know that your body is the temple of the Holy Spirit, who lives in you, and was given to you by God? You do not belong to yourselves but to God; he bought you for a price. So use your bodies for God's glory.

Now, to deal with the matters you wrote about.

A man does well not to marry. But because there is so much immorality every man should have his own wife, and every woman should have her own husband. A man should fulfill his duty as a husband and a woman should fulfill her duty as a wife, and each should satisfy the other's needs. The wife is not the master of her own body, but the husband is; in the same way the husband is not the master of his own body, but the wife is. Do not deny yourselves to each other, unless you first agree to do so for a while, in order to spend your time in prayer; but then resume normal marital relations, to keep you from giving in to Satan's temptation because of your lack of self-control.

I tell you this not as an order, but simply as a permission. Actually I would prefer that all were as I am; but each one has the special gift that God has given him, one man this gift, another man that.

Now, I say this to the unmarried and to the widows: it would be better for you to continue to live alone, as I do. But if you cannot restrain your desires, go on and marry — it is better to marry than to burn with passion.

For married people I have a command, not my own but the Lord's: a wife must not leave her husband; if she does, she must remain single or else be reconciled to her husband; and a husband must not divorce his wife.

To the others I say (I, myself, not the Lord): if a Christian man has a wife who is an unbeliever and she agrees to go on living with him, he must not divorce her. And if a Christian woman is married to a man who is an unbeliever, and he agrees to go on living with her, she must not divorce him. For the unbelieving husband is made acceptable to God by being united to his wife, and the unbelieving wife is made acceptable to God by being united to her Christian husband. If this were not so, their children would be like pagan children; but as it is, they are acceptable to God. However, if the one who is not a believer wishes to leave the Christian partner, let it be so. In such cases the Christian partner, whether husband or wife, is free to act. God has called you to live in peace. How can you be sure, Christian wife, that you will not save your husband? Or how can you be sure, Christian husband, that you will not save your wife?

Each one should go on living according to the Lord's gift to him, and as he was when God called him. This is the rule I teach in all the churches. If a circumcised man has accepted God's call, he should not try to remove the marks of circumcision; if an uncircumcised man has accepted God's call, he should not get circumcised. Because being circumcised or not means nothing. What matters is to obey God's commandments. Every man should remain as he was when he accepted God's call. . . .

1 Corinthians 6:18-20; 7:1-20; 8:23-26

The chalice of benediction, which we bless, is it not the communion of the blood of Christ? And the bread, which we break, it is not the partaking of the body of the Lord? . . .

For I have received of the Lord that which also I delivered unto you, that the Lord Jesus, the same night in which he was betrayed, took bread.

And giving thanks, broke, and said: "Take ye and eat: this is my body which shall be delivered for you: this do for the commemoration of me."

In like manner also the chalice, after he had supped, saying: "This chalice is the new testament in my blood; this do ye, as often as you shall drink, for the commemoration of me.

For as often as you shall eat this bread, and drink the chalice, you shall shew the death of the Lord until he come. . . ."

1 Corinthians 10:16; 11:23-26

If I speak with the tongues of men and of angels, and have not charity, I am become as sounding brass, or a tinkling cymbal.

And if I should have prophecy and should know all mysteries and all knowledge, and if I should have all faith, so that I could remove mountains, and have not charity, I am nothing.

And if I should distribute all my goods to feed the poor, and if I should deliver my body to be burned, and have not charity, it profiteth me nothing.

Charity is patient, is kind, charity envieth not, dealeth not perversely, is not puffed up.

Is not ambitious, seeketh not her own, is not provoked to anger, thinketh no evil;

Rejoiceth not in iniquity, but rejoiceth with the truth;

Beareth all things, believeth all things, hopeth all things, endureth all things.

Charity never fadeth away. . . .

1 Corinthians 13:1-8

Now if Christ be preached that he arose again from the dead, how do some among you say that there is no resurrection of the dead?

But if there be no resurrection of the dead, then Christ is not risen again.

And if Christ be not risen again, then is our preaching vain and your faith is also vain.

Yea, and we are found false witnesses of God because we have given testimony against God, that he hath raised up Christ, whom he hath not raised up, if the dead rise not again.

For if the dead rise not again, neither is Christ risen again.

And if Christ be not risen again, your faith is vain for you are yet in your sins. . . .

But thanks be to God, who hath given us the victory through our Lord Jesus Christ.

1 Corinthians 15:12-17, 57

Second Letter to the Corinthians

Now the Lord is a Spirit and where the Spirit of the Lord is, there is liberty.

While we look not at the things which are seen, but at the things which are not seen. For the things which are seen are temporal; but the things which are not seen are eternal. . . .

(For we walk by faith, and not by sight.)

But all things are of God, who hath reconciled us to himself by Christ and hath given to us the ministry of reconciliation.

For God indeed was in Christ, reconciling the world to himself, not imputing to them their sins and he hath placed in us the word of reconciliation. . . .

2 Corinthians 3:17; 4:18; 5:7, 18-19

To the Galatians

For I give you to understand, brethren, that the gospel which was preached by me is not of man. For I did not receive it from man, nor was I taught it; but I received it by a revelation of Jesus Christ. . . .

But when it pleased him who from my mother's womb set me apart and called me by his grace, to reveal his Son in me, that I might preach him among the Gentiles, immediately, without taking counsel with flesh and blood, and without going up to Jerusalem to those who were appointed apostles before me, I retired into Arabia, and again returned to Damascus. . . .

For you are all the children of God through faith in Christ Jesus.

For all you who have been baptized into Christ, have put on Christ.

There is neither Jew nor Greek; there is neither slave nor freeman; there is neither male nor female. For you are all one in Christ Jesus. . . .

For you, brethren, have been called unto liberty: only make not liberty an occasion to the flesh, but by charity of the spirit serve one another. For all the law is fulfilled in one word, Thou shalt love they neighbor as thyself.

Galatians 1:11-12, 15-17; 3:26-28; 5:13-14

To the Ephesians

God chose us in Christ before the foundation of the world, that we should be holy and unspotted in his sight in charity.

Who hath predestinated us unto the adoption of children through Jesus Christ unto himself according to the purpose of his will;

Unto the praise of the glory of his grace, in which he hath graced us in his beloved Son.

In whom we have redemption through his blood, the remission of sins, according to the riches of his grace.

Which hath superabounded in us, in all wisdom and prudence.

Ephesians 1:4-8

For this cause I bow my knees to the Father of our Lord Jesus Christ.

Of whom all paternity in heaven and earth is named.

That he would grant you, according to the riches of his glory, to be strengthened by his Spirit with might unto the inward man.

That Christ may dwell by faith in your hearts; that being rooted and founded in charity,

You may be able to comprehend, with all the saints what is the breadth, and length, and height, and depth,

To know also the charity of Christ, which surpasseth all knowledge, that you may be filled unto all the fullness of God.

Ephesians 3:14-19

Wherefore putting away lying, speak ye the truth every man with his neighbor for we are members one of another.

Be angry, and sin not. Let not the sun go down upon your anger.

He that stole, let him now steal no more, but rather let him labor, working with his hands the thing which is good, that he may have something to give to him that suffereth need.

So also ought men to love their wives as their own bodies. He that loveth his wife, loveth himself.

Ephesians 4:25-28; 5:29

For no man ever hated his own flesh; but nourisheth and cherisheth it, as also Christ doth the church,

Because we are members of his body, of his flesh, and of his bones.

"For this cause shall a man leave his father and mother, and shall cleave to his wife as himself. . . . and let the wife fear her husband.

Ephesians 5:29-31, 33

Children, obey your parents in the Lord, for this is just.

Honor thy father and thy mother, which is the first commandment with a promise:

That it may be well with thee, and thou mayest be long lived upon earth.

And you, fathers, provoke not your children to anger; but bring them up in the discipline and correction of the Lord.

Ephesians 6:1-4

To the Philippians

For let this mind be in you, which was also in Christ Jesus:

Who being in the form of God, thought it not robbery to be equal with God:

But emptied himself, taking the form of a servant, being made in the likeness of men, and in habit found as a man.

He humbled himself, becoming obedient unto death even to the death of the cross.

For which cause God also hath exalted him, and hath given him a name which is above all names:

That in the name of Jesus every knee should bow of those that are in heaven, on earth, and under the earth:

And that every tongue should confess that the Lord Jesus Christ is in the glory of God the Father. . . .

Rejoice in the Lord always; again, I say, rejoice. . . .

I can do all things in him who strengthened me.

Philippians 2:5-11; 4:4, 13

To the Colossians

The son is the image of the invisible God, the firstborn of every creature. For in him were created all things in the heavens and on the earth, things visible and things invisible. . . .

All things have been created through and unto him, and he is before all creatures, and in him all things hold together. Again, he is the head of his body, the Church; he, who is the beginning, the firstborn from the dead, that in all things he may have the first place. For it has pleased God the Father that in him all his fullness should dwell, and that through him he should reconcile to himself all things, whether on the earth or in the heavens, making peace through the blood of his cross.

Colossians 1:15-20

Beware lest any man cheat you by philosophy, and vain deceit; according to the tradition of men, according to the elements of the world, and not according to Christ:

For in him dwelleth all the fullness of the Godhead corporeally. . . .

All whatsoever you do in word or in work, do all in the name of the Lord Jesus Christ, giving thanks to God the Father by him.

Colossians 2:8-9; 3:17

First Letter to the Thessalonians

Therefore, we also give thanks to God without ceasing because, that when you had received of us the word of the hearing of God, you received it not as the word of men, but (as it is indeed) the word of God, who worketh in you that have believed. . . .

For you know what precepts I have given to you by the Lord Jesus.

For this is the will of God, your sanctification, that you should abstain from fornication;

That everyone of you should know how to possess his vessel in sanctification and honor.

Not in the passion of lust, like the Gentiles that know not God:

And that no man overreach, nor circumvent his brother in business: because the Lord is the avenger of all these things, as we have told you before, and have testified.

For God hath not called us unto uncleanliness, but unto sanctification.

Therefore, he that despiseth these things, despiseth not man, but God, who also hath given his holy Spirit in us.

1 Thessalonians 2:13; 4:2-8

To Timothy

I desire therefore first of all that supplications, prayers, intercessions and thanksgivings be made for all men.

For kings, and for all that are in high stations that we may lead a quiet and a peaceable life in all piety and chastity.

For this is good and acceptable in the sight of God our Savior,

Who will have all men to be saved, and to come to the knowledge of the truth.

For there is one God and one mediator of God and men, the man Christ Jesus. . . .

1 Timothy 2:1-5

Now the Spirit manifestly saith, that in the last times some shall depart from the faith, giving heed to spirits of error, and doctrines of devils, speaking lies in hypocrisy, and having their conscience seared, forbidding to marry, to abstain from meats, which God hath created to be received with thanksgiving by the faithful, and by them that have known the truth.

For every creature of God is good, and nothing to be rejected that is received with thanksgiving,

For it is sanctified by the word of God and prayer.

1 Timothy 4:1-5

If any man teach otherwise, and consent not to the sound words of our Lord Jesus Christ, and to that doctrine which is according to godliness,

he is proud, knowing nothing, but sick about questions and strifes of words from which arise envies, contentions, blasphemies, evil suspicions,

conflicts of men corrupted in mind, and who are destitute of the truth. . . .

The desire of money is the root of all evils, which some coveting have erred from the faith, and have entangled themselves in many sorrows.

1 Timothy 6:3-5, 10

Second Letter to Timothy

God has redeemed us and called us with a holy calling, not according to our works but according to his own purpose and the grace which was granted us in Christ Jesus before this world existed. . . . Hold to the form of sound teaching which you have heard from me in the faith and love which are in Christ Jesus. . . .

Avoid foolish and ignorant controversies, knowing that they breed quarrels. But the servant of the Lord must not quarrel, but be gentle towards all, ready to teach, patient, gently admonishing those who resist, in case God should give them repentance to know the truth, and they recover themselves from the snare of the devil, to whose will they are held captive.

2 Timothy 1:9, 13, 23-26

All Scripture is inspired by God and useful for teaching, for reproving, for correcting, for instructing in justice; that the man of God may be perfect, equipped for every good work.

2 Timothy 3:16-17

For there will come a time when they will not endure the sound doctrine but, having itching ears, will heap up to themselves teachers according to their own lusts. And they will turn away their hearing from the truth and turn aside rather to fables. . . .

2 Timothy 4:3-4

To Titus

For a bishop must be without crime, as the steward of God: not proud, but given to hospitality, gentle, sober, just, holy, continent, embracing that faithful word which is according to doctrine, that he may be able to exhort in sound doctrine, and to convince the gainsayers.

For there are many disobedient, vain talkers, and seducers, who must be reproved, who subvert whole houses, teaching things which they ought not, for filthy lucre's sake. . . .

All things are clean to the clean, but to them that are defiled, and to unbelievers, nothing is clean: but both their mind and their conscience are defiled.

They profess that they know God, but in their works they deny *him*; being abominable, and incredulous, and to every good work reprobate. . . .

But speak thou the things that become sound doctrine.

Titus 1:7-11, 15; 2:1

To the Hebrews

God, who, at sundry times and in divers manners, spoke in time past to the fathers by the prophets, last of all, in these days hath spoken to us by his Son, whom he hath appointed heir of all things, by whom also he made the world.

Who being the brightness of his glory, and the figure of his substance, and upholding all things by the word of his power, making purgation of sins, sitteth on the right hand of the majesty on high.

Hebrews 1:1-3

Now faith is the substance of things to be hoped for, the evidence of things that are not seen; for by it the men of old had testimony borne to them. By faith we understand that the world was fashioned by the word of God: and thus things visible were made out of things invisible.

Hebrews 11:1-3

Remember your superiors, who spoke to you the word of God. Consider how they ended their lives, and imitate their faith. Jesus Christ is the same, yesterday and today, yes, and forever.

Do not be led away by various and strange doctrines. For it is good to make steadfast the heart by grace, not by foods in which those who walked found no profit.

Hebrews 13:7-9

Chapter 4 • The Letters of Sts. James, Peter, and John: The Apostles' Creed

The Letter of James, the first bishop of Jerusalem, has been traditionally designated as "catholic" in the sense that it was addressed to all those of the twelve tribes of the dispersion who accepted the Good News of Christianity. Yet these brethren are seriously tried by the temptations of the world, the flesh, and the devil, and by the persecution of the unbelievers. James urges them to persevere in faith; he advises them that their faith is tested by trial. "Take courage because he who conquers and remains steadfast will receive the crown of everlasting life."

Two basic issues are developed. In the controversy between faith and works, James emphasizes the preeminence of works. He does not rule out the value and necessity of faith but insists that faith without works is dead. By works a man is justified and not by faith alone. The other problem concerns the value of the individual. As far as Christianity is concerned, all men are brothers: "Love thy neighbor" is a basic axiom, and this means a love of charity whereby one performs good works to help anyone in need, especially the poor.

In this Letter we find an account of the practice of administering the sacrament of the sick and an exhortation to confession of sins. The Letter ends with the statement that "he who causes a sinner to be converted from the error of his way, shall save his soul from death and shall cover a multitude of sins."

The First Letter of Peter is a masterpiece of brevity. In it are summed up the fundamentals of Christianity, the bases of the faith, and the results of a life lived according to the principles of Jesus. Especially appropriate is his advice concerning a respect for authority on every level and irrespective of the worthiness of the individual in the position of authority. Like Paul he emphasized the proper respect and mutual regard of husbands and wives. "Let wives be subject to their husbands. . . . Ye husbands . . . giving honor to the female as to the weaker vessel and as to the co-heirs of the grace of life." He ends the letter by exhorting all to be of *one* mind, lovers of the brotherhood, merciful, modest, and humble. "But before all things have a constant mutual charity among yourselves for charity covereth a multitude of sins." In the Second Letter he reminds the faithful of the promise that they will be made partakers of the divine nature. He, like James, counsels the doing of good works to ensure their calling and election. He himself has made known the power and presence of Jesus Christ, having been an eyewitness to his majesty. He warns them to be on their guard against false prophets and lying teachers who shall bring in sects of perdition that will be widely acclaimed and popular with the misinformed: "Take heed lest being led aside by the error of the unwise you fall from your own steadfastness."

The three Letters of John emphasize the twofold law of love of God and neighbor. He insists that he has seen with his own eyes, heard with his own ears, and handled with his own hands the Word of life. From Jesus he has the knowledge that "God is light" — all men have sinned and all have been cleansed by the blood of the Son of God. To preserve truth within ourselves, we should keep the commandments, especially the commandment of love of neighbor: "He that loveth his brother, abideth in the light." Avoid the concupiscences of the world, of the flesh, and of the eyes, and the pride of life. "Behold what manner of charity the Father hath bestowed upon us that we should be called and should be the sons of God." We know the love of God for us because He laid down his life for us; we should lay down our lives for the brethren.

In addition to the practical exhortations to love of God and neighbor John is a witness to the basic doctrines of Catholicism concerning the Trinity, Incarnation, Redemption, and Eternal Salvation. These doctrines are found again and again in the great writings of Catholicism, especially in the *Credo* of Pope Paul VI. The Apostles' Creed is quite simply a classic expression of Catholic belief.

The Catholic Letter of St. James the Apostle

Let no man when he is tempted, say that he is tempted by God. For God is not a tempter of evils, and he tempteth no man.

But every man is tempted by his own concupiscence, being drawn away and allured.

Then when concupiscence has conceived, it brings forth sin. But sin, when it is completed, begets death.

Do not err therefore, my dearest brethren.

Every best gift, and every perfect gift, is from above, coming down from the Father of lights, with whom there is no change, nor shadow of alteration.

James 1:13-17

What shall it profit, my brethren, if a man say he hath faith, but hath not works? Shall faith be able to save him?

James 2:14

But wilt thou know, O vain man, that faith without works is dead?

James 2:20

Do you see that by works a man is justified, and not by faith only?

James 2:24

For even as the body without the spirit is dead, so also faith without works is dead. . . .

Is any man sick among you? Let him bring in the priests of the church, and let them pray over him, anointing him with oil in the name of the Lord.

And the prayer of faith shall save the sick man and the Lord shall raise him up and if he be in sins, they shall be forgiven him.

James 2:26; 5:14-15

My brethren, if any of you err from the truth, and one convert him he must know, that he who causeth a sinner to be converted from the error of his way, shall save his soul from death, and shall cover a multitude of sins.

James 5:19-20

First Letter of St. Peter the Apostle

If you invoke as Father him who, without respect of persons, judgeth according to every one's work, converse in fear during the time of your sojourning here,

Knowing that you were not redeemed with corruptible things as gold or silver, from your vain conversation of the tradition of your fathers,

but with the precious blood of Christ, as of a lamb unspotted and undefiled, Foreknown indeed before the foundation of the world, but manifested in the last times for you,

Who through him are faithful in God, who raised him up from the dead, and hath given him glory, that your faith and hope might be in God.

Purifying your souls in the obedience of charity, with a brotherly love, from a sincere heart love one another earnestly,

Being born again not of corruptible seed, but incorruptible, by the word of God who haveth and remaineth for ever.

For all flesh is as grass; and all the glory thereof as the flower of grass. The grass is withered, and the flower thereof is fallen away.

But the word of the Lord endureth forever. And this is the word which by the gospel hath been preached unto you.

1 Peter 1:17-25

Be ye subject therefore to every human creature for God's sake whether it be to the king as excelling

or to governors as sent by him for the punishment of evildoers, and for the praise of the good;

for so is the will of God, that by doing well you may put to silence the ignorance of foolish men;

as free, and not as making liberty a cloak for malice, but as the servants of God.

Honor all men. Love the brotherhood. Fear God. Honor the king.

1 Peter 2:13-17

In like manner also let wives be subject to their husbands, so that even if any do not believe the word, they may without word be won through the behavior of their wives, observing reverently your chaste behavior. Let not theirs be the outward adornment of braiding the hair, or of wearing gold, or of putting on robes; but let it be the inner life of the heart, in the imperishableness of a quiet and gentle spirit, which is of great price in the sight of God. For after this manner in old times the holy women also who hoped in God adorned themselves, while being subject to their husbands. . . .

Husbands, likewise dwelling with them according to knowledge, giving honor to the female as to the weaker vessel, and as to the co-heirs of the grace of life that your prayers be not hindered.

And in fine, be all of one mind, having compassion one of another, being lovers of the brotherhood, merciful, modest, humble. . . .

But before all things have a constant mutual charity among yourselves for charity covereth a multitude of sins.

1 Peter 3:1-5, 7-8; 4:8

Second Letter of St. Peter the Apostle

We have not followed cunningly devised fables, when we made known to you the power and presence of our Lord Jesus Christ: but having been made eyewitness of his majesty.

For, he received from God the Father honor and glory; this voice coming down to him from the excellent glory, This is my beloved Son in whom I am well pleased, hear ye him.

And this voice we heard brought from heaven, when we were with him on the holy mount.

And we have the more firm prophetical word, whereunto you do well to attend, as to a light that shineth in a dark place, until the day dawn, and the day star arise in your hearts, understanding this first, that no prophecy of scripture is made by private interpretation.

For prophecy came not by the will of man at any time but the holy men of God spoke inspired by the Holy Spirit.

2 Peter 1:16-21

The First Epistle of St. John the Apostle

That which was from the beginning, which we have heard, which we have seen with our eyes, which we have looked upon, and our hands have handled, of the word of life:

For the life was manifested; and we have seen and do bear witness, and declare unto you for life eternal, which was with the Father and hath appeared to us:

That which we have seen and have heard, we declare unto you, that you also may have fellowship with us, and our fellowship may be with the Father, and with his Son Jesus Christ.

And these things we write to you, that you may rejoice, and your joy may be full.

1 John 1:1-4

Love not the world, nor the things which are in the world. If any man love the world, the charity of the Father is not in him.

For all that is in the world is the concupiscence of the flesh, and the concupiscence of the eyes, and the pride of life, which is not of the Father, but is of the world.

And the world passeth away, and the concupiscence thereof. But he that doth the will of God, abideth forever.

1 John 2:15-17

Behold what manner of charity the Father hath bestowed upon us, that we should be called; and should be the sons of God. Therefore, the world knoweth not us, because it knew not him.

Dearly beloved, we are now the sons of God and it hath not yet appeared what we shall be. We know that, when he shall appear, we shall be like to him because we shall see him as he is.

1 John 3:1-3

For this is the charity of God, that we keep his commandments and his commandments are not heavy.

1 John 5:3

The Second Letter of St. John the Apostle

Whosoever revolts and continues not in the doctrine of Christ, hath not God. He that continues in the doctrine, the same has both the Father and the Son.

If any man come to you, and bring not this doctrine, receive him not into the house nor say to him, God speed you.

For he that says unto him, God speed you, communicates with his wicked works.

2 John 9-11

The Third Letter of St. John the Apostle

Dearly beloved, follow not that which is evil, but that which is good. He that doth good is of God; he that doth evil hath not seen God.

3 John 11

The Apostles' Creed

I believe in God, the Father almighty, Creator of heaven and earth; and in Jesus Christ, His only Son, our Lord; who was conceived by the Holy Spirit, born of the Virgin Mary, suffered under Pontius Pilate, was crucified, died, and was buried. He descended into hell; the third day he arose again from the dead; he ascended into heaven, sits at the right hand of God, the Father almighty; whence he shall come to judge the living and the dead. I believe in the Holy Spirit, the holy Catholic Church, the communion of saints, the forgiveness of sins, the resurrection of the body, and life everlasting. Amen.

Traditional, Second Century A.D.

Chapter 5 • St. Clement of Rome: Letters

The First Letter of Clement is noteworthy for many reasons. It is not only a summary of the fundamental doctrines and practices of the Church during the pontificate of the fourth pope (A.D. 88-97), but is of capital importance as an historical document attesting to the fact that the Bishop of Rome was accorded doctrinal and jurisdictional primacy throughout the Church. Clement, by his intervention into the doctrinal and administrative problems of the Church at Corinth, gives witness to the accepted prerogative of the Pope to pronounce authoritative decisions in discussions which threaten to divide Christians. It is quite clear from the letter that the elders of Corinth had petitioned Rome for a decision in these matters. In spite of the heated opposition between the warring factions at Corinth, the Church there accepted the decisions of Pope Clement on the doctrinal and administrative problems and, as a result, unity of belief and practice was restored.

Though the Second Letter of Clement may be considered by some as spurious, it is included in this collection because it is a clear and unequivocal witness to certain basic teachings of Catholicism, especially regarding the explicit statement that "when we were not He called us and willed that out of nothing we should attain real existence."

The First Letter to the Corinthians

The church of God which sojourns at Rome to the church of God sojourning at Corinth, to them that are called and sanctified by the will of God, through our Lord Jesus Christ: Grace unto you, and peace, from Almighty God through Jesus Christ, be multiplied.

We have been somewhat tardy in turning our attention to the points respecting which you consulted us and especially to that shameful and detestable sedition, utterly abhorrent to the elect of God, which a few rash and self-confident persons have kindled to such a pitch of frenzy, that your venerable and illustrious name, worthy to be universally loved, has suffered grievous injury.

For you did all things without respect of persons, and walked in the commandments of God, being obedient to those who had the rule over you, and giving all fitting honor to the presbyters among you. . . .

Wherefore let us give up vain and fruitless cares, and approach to the glorious and venerable rule of our holy calling. Let us attend to what is good, pleasing, and acceptable in the sight of Him who formed us. Let us look steadfastly to the blood of Christ, and see how precious that blood is to God, which, having been shed for our salvation, has set the grace of repentance before the whole world. . . .

Let us therefore, brethren, be of humble mind, laying aside all haughtiness, and pride, and foolishness, and angry feelings and let us act according to that which is written (for the Holy Spirit saith, "Let not the wise man glory in his wisdom, neither let the mighty man glory in his might, neither let the rich man glory in his riches but let him that glorieth glory in the Lord, in diligently seeking Him, and doing judgment and righteousness"), being especially mindful of the words of the Lord Jesus which He spake, teaching us meekness and long-suffering. For thus He spoke: "Be ye merciful, that ye may obtain mercy; forgive, that it may be forgiven to you; as ye do, so shall it be done unto you; as ye judge, so shall ye be judged; as ye are kind, so shall kindness be shown to you with what measure ye mete, with the same it shall be measured to you."

Wherefore, having so many great and glorious examples set before us, let us turn again to the practice of that peace which from the beginning was the mark set before us; and let us look steadfastly to the Father and Creator of the universe, and cleave to His mighty and surpassingly great gifts and benefactions of peace. Let us contemplate Him with our understanding, and look with the eyes of our soul to His long-suffering will. Let us reflect how free from wrath He is towards all His creation.

Let us consider, beloved, how the Lord continually proves to us that there shall be a future resurrection, of which He has rendered the Lord Jesus Christ the first fruits by raising Him from the dead.

And we, too, being called by His will in Christ Jesus, are not justified by ourselves, nor by our own wisdom, or understanding, or godliness, or works which we have wrought in holiness of heart; but by the faith through which, from the beginning, Almighty God has justified all men; to whom be glory for ever and ever. Amen.

What shall we do, then, brethren? Shall we become slothful in well-doing, and cease from the practice of love? God forbid that any such course should be followed by us! But rather, let us hasten with all energy and readiness of mind to perform every good work. For the Creator and Lord of all Himself rejoices in His works, for by His infinitely great power He established the heavens, and by His incomprehensible wisdom He adorned them. He also divided the earth from the water which surrounds it, and fixed it upon the immovable foundation of His own will. The animals also which are upon it He commanded by His own word into existence. So likewise, when He had formed the sea, and the living creatures which are in it. He enclosed them within their proper bounds by His own power. Above all, with His holy and undefiled hands He formed man, the most excellent of His creatures, and truly great through intelligence — the express likeness of His own nature. For God spoke thus: Let us make man according to our image and likeness; and God made man, male and female and having finished these things, He approved them, and blessed them, and said, "Increase and multiply." We see, then, how all righteous men have been adorned with good works, and how the Lord Himself, adorning Himself with His works, rejoiced. Having therefore such an example, let us without delay accede to His will, and let us work the work of righteousness with our whole strength. . . .

How blessed and wonderful, beloved, are the gifts of God! Life in immortality, splendor in righteousness, truth in perfect confidence, faith in assurance, self-control in holiness! And all these fall under the cognizance of our understandings now; what then shall those things be which are prepared for such as wait for Him? The Creator and Father of all worlds, the Most Holy, alone knows their amount and their beauty. Let us therefore earnestly strive to be found in the number of those that wait for Him, in order that we may share in His promised gifts. But how, beloved, shall this be done? If our understanding be fixed by faith towards God; if we earnestly seek the things which are pleasing and acceptable to Him; if we do the things which are in harmony with His blameless will; and if we follow the way of truth, casting away from us all unrighteousness and iniquity, along with all covetousness, strife, evil practices, deceit, whispering, and evil-speaking, all hatred of God, pride and haughtiness, vainglory and ambition. For they that do such things are hateful to God; and not only they that do them, but also those that take pleasure in them that do them.

Let us then, men and brethren, with all energy act the part of soldiers, in accordance with His holy commandments. Let us consider those who serve under our generals, with what order, obedience, and submissiveness they perform the things which are commanded them. All are not prefects, nor commanders of a thousand, nor of a hundred, nor of fifty, nor the like, but each one in his own rank performs the things commanded by the king and the generals. The great cannot subsist without the small, nor the small without the great. There is a kind of mixture in all things, and thence arises mutual advantage. Let us take our body for an example.

Let our whole body, then, be preserved in Christ Jesus; and let every one be subject to his neighbor, according to the special gift bestowed upon him. Let the strong not despise the weak, and let the weak show respect unto the strong. Let the rich man provide for the wants of the poor; and let the poor man bless God, because He hath given him one by whom his need may be supplied. Let the wise man display his wisdom, not by mere words, but through good deeds. Let the humble not bear testimony to himself, but leave witness to be borne to him by another. Let him that is pure in the flesh not grow proud of it, and boast, knowing that it was another who bestowed on him the gift of continence. Let us consider, then, brethren, of what matter we were made — who and what manner of beings we came into the world, as it were out of a sepulcher, and from utter darkness. He who made us and fashioned us, having prepared His bountiful gifts for us before we were born, introduced us into His world. Since, therefore, we receive all these things from Him, we ought for everything to give Him thanks; to Whom be glory for ever and ever. Amen. . . .

The apostles have preached the gospel to us from the Lord Jesus Christ; Jesus Christ has done so from God. Christ therefore was sent forth by God, and the apostles by Christ.

You are fond of contention, brethren, and full of zeal about things which do not pertain to salvation. Look carefully into the Scriptures, which are the true utterances of the Holy Spirit. Observe that nothing of an unjust or counterfeit character is written in them. There you will not find that the righteous were cast off by men who themselves were holy. The righteous were indeed persecuted, but only by the wicked. They were cast into prison, but only by the unholy; they were stoned, but only by transgressors; they were slain, but only by the accursed, and such as had conceived an unrighteous envy against them. Exposed to such sufferings, they endured them gloriously.

Why do we divide and tear in pieces the members of Christ, and raise up strife against our own body, and have reached such a height of madness as to forget that "we are members one of another"? Remember the words of our Lord Jesus Christ, how He said, "Woe to that man by whom offenses come! It were better for him that he had never been born, than that he should cast a stumbling-block before one of my elect. Yea, it were better for him that a millstone should be hung about his neck, and he should be sunk in the depths of the sea, than that he should cast a stumbling-block before one of my little ones" [cf. Matt. 18:6, Mark 9:42; Luke 17:1-2]. Your schism has subverted the faith of many, has discouraged many, has given rise to doubt in many, and has caused grief to us all. And still your sedition continueth.

Let us therefore, with all haste, put an end to this state of things; and let us fall down before the Lord, and beseech Him with tears, that He would mercifully be reconciled to us, and restore us to our former seemly and holy practice of brotherly love.

Let him who has love in Christ keep the commandments of Christ. Who can describe the blessed bond of the love of God? What man is able to tell the excellence of its beauty, as it ought to be told? The height to which love exalts is unspeakable. Love unites us to God. Love covers a multitude of sins. Love beareth all things, is long-suffering in all things. There is nothing base, nothing arrogant in love. Love admits of no schisms: love gives rise to no seditions: love does all things in harmony. By love have all the elect of God been made perfect; without love nothing is well-pleasing to God. In love has the Lord taken us to Himself.

On account of the love He bore us, Jesus Christ our Lord gave His blood for us by the will of God; His flesh for our flesh, and His soul for our souls.

Who then among you is noble-minded? Who compassionate? Who full of love? Let him declare, "If on my account sedition and disagreement and schisms have arisen, I will depart, I will go away whithersoever you desire, and I will do whatever the majority commands; only let the flock of Christ live on terms of peace with the presbyters set over it." He that acts thus shall procure to himself great glory in the Lord; and every place will welcome him. For "the earth is the Lord's, and the fullness thereof" [cf. Psalms 24]. These things they who live a godly life, that is never to be repented of, both have done and always will do.

The Second Letter

Brethren, it is fitting that you should think of Jesus Christ as of God as the Judge of the living and the dead. And it does not become us to think lightly of our salvation; for if we think little of Him, we shall also hope but to obtain little from Him. For He called us when we were not, and willed that out of nothing we should attain a real existence.

Since, then, He has displayed so great mercy towards us and especially in this respect, that we who are living should not offer sacrifices to gods that are dead, or pay them worship, but should attain through Him to the knowledge of the true Father, whereby shall we show that we do indeed know Him, but by denying Him through whom this knowledge has been attained: For He himself declares, "Whosoever shall confess me before men, him will I confess before my Father." This, then, is our reward if we shall confess Him by whom we have been saved. But in what way shall we confess Him? By doing what He says, and not transgressing His commandments, and by honoring Him not with our lips only, but with all our heart and all our mind.

Therefore, brethren, let us confess Him by our works, by loving one another, by not committing adultery, or speaking evil of one another, or cherishing envy; but being content, compassionate, and good. We ought also to sympathize with one another, and not be avaricious. By such works let us confess Him, and not by those that are of an opposite kind. And it is not fitting that we should fear men, but rather God.

And consider, brethren, that the sojourning in the flesh in this world is but brief and transient, but the promise of Christ is great and wonderful, even the rest of the kingdom to come, and of life everlasting. By what course of conduct, then, shall we attain these things, but by leading a holy and righteous life, and by deeming these worldly things as not belonging to us, and not fixing our desire upon them? For if we desire to possess them, we fall away from the path of righteousness.

As long, therefore, as we are upon earth, let us practice repentance, for we are as clay in the hand of the artificer. So let us also, while we are in this world, repent with our whole heart of the evil deeds we have done in the flesh, that we may be saved by the Lord, while we have yet an opportunity of repentance. For after we have gone out of the world, no further power of confessing or repenting will there belong to us. Wherefore, brethren, by doing the will of the Father, and keeping the flesh holy, and observing the commandments of the Lord, we shall obtain eternal life.

Let us therefore serve God with a pure heart, and we shall be righteous; but if we do not serve Him, because we believe not the promise of God, we shall be miserable.

Let us expect, therefore, hour by hour, the kingdom of God in love and righteousness, since we know not the day of the appearing of God.

Attributed to St. Clement of Rome

Chapter 6 • *Didache*: The Teaching of the Twelve Apostles

There is considerable discussion concerning the date of this document, which was quoted near the close of the first century of the Christian era, disappeared in the fourteenth century, and was rediscovered in a Greek manuscript and published in 1883. It is included here at the end of the first century as a summary of the teachings and practices of the Christian community at the close of the apostolic age. As a manual of religious practices regarding the moral conduct of life and liturgical functions, it presents the role of baptism, confession, and the Eucharist in great detail. It is another classic document attesting to the unity of doctrine and worship found in the church. It is interesting to note that the practice of abortion is considered to be murder of the child.

Chapter 1. The Two Ways: The First Commandment

There are two ways, one of life and one of death; but a great difference between the two ways. The way of life, then, is this: First, thou shalt love God who made thee; second, thy neighbor as thyself, and all things whatsoever thou wouldst should not occur to you, thou also to another do not do. And of these sayings the teaching is this: bless them that curse you, and pray for your enemies, and fast for them that persecute you. For what thanks is there if you love them that love you? Do not also the Gentiles do the same? But do you love them that hate you and you shall not have an enemy. Abstain from fleshy and worldly lusts. . . . Happy is he that gives according to the commandment, for he is guiltless.

Chapter 2. The Second Commandment: Gross Sin Forbidden

The second commandment of the Teaching: Thou shalt not commit murder, thou shalt not commit adultery, thou shalt not commit paederasty, thou shalt not commit fornication, thou shalt not steal, thou shalt not practice magic, thou shalt not practice witchcraft, thou shalt not murder a child by abortion nor kill that which is begotten, thou shalt not covet the things of thy neighbor, thou shalt not forswear thyself, thou shalt not bear false witness, thou shalt not speak evil, thou shalt bear no grudge. Thou shalt not be double-minded nor double-tongued for to be double-tongued is a snare of death. Thy speech shall not be false, nor empty, but fulfilled by deed. Thou shalt not be covetous, nor rapacious, nor a hypocrite, nor evil disposed, nor haughty. Thou shalt not take evil counsel against thy neighbor. Thou shalt not hate any man; but some thou shalt love more than they own life.

Chapter 3. Other Sins Forbidden

My child, flee from every evil thing, and from every likeness of it. Be not prone to anger, for anger leadeth the way to murder; neither jealous, nor quarrelsome, nor of hot temper; for out of all these murders are engendered. My child, be not a lustful one; for lust leadeth the way to fornication; neither a filthy talker, nor of lofty eye; for out of all these adulteries are engendered. My child, be not an observer of omens, since it leadeth the way to idolatry; neither an enchanter, nor an astrologer, nor a purifier, nor be willing to look at these things; for out of all these idolatry is engendered. My child, be not a liar, since a lie leadeth the way to theft; neither money-loving nor vainglorious, for out of all these thefts are engendered. My child, be not a murmurer, since it leadeth the way to blasphemy; neither self-willed nor evil-minded, for out of all these blasphemies are engendered. But be thou meek, since the meek shall inherit the earth. Be long-suffering and pitiful and guileless and gentle and good and always trembling at the words which thou hast heard. Thou shalt not exalt thyself, nor give over-confidence to thy soul. Thy soul shall not be joined with lofty ones, but with just and lowly ones shall it have its intercourse. The workings that befall thee receive as good, knowing that apart from God nothing cometh to pass.

Chapter 4. Various Precepts

My child, him that speaketh to thee the word of God remember night and day; and thou shalt honor him as the Lord; for in the place whence lordly rule is uttered, there is the Lord. And thou shalt seek out day by day the faces of the saints, in order that thou mayest rest upon their words. Thou shalt not long for division, but shalt bring those who contend to peace. Thou shalt judge righteously, thou shalt not respect persons in reproving for transgressions. Thou shalt not be undecided whether it shall be or no. Be not a stretcher forth of the hands to receive and a drawer of them back to give. If thou hast aught, through thy hands thou shalt give ransom for thy sins. Thou shalt not hesitate to give, nor murmur when thou givest; for thou shalt know who is the good repayer of the hire. Thou shalt not turn away from him that is in want, but thou shalt share all things with thy brother, and shalt not say that they are thine own; for if ye are partakers in that which is immortal, how much more in things which are mortal? Thou shalt not remove thy hand from thy son or from thy daughter, but from their youth shalt teach them the fear of God. Thou shalt not enjoin aught in thy bitterness upon thy bondman or maidservant, who hope in the same God, lest ever they shall fear not God who is over both; for he cometh not to call according to the outward appearance, but unto them whom the Spirit hath prepared. And ye bondmen shall be subject to your masters as to a type of God, in modesty and fear. Thou shalt hate all hypocrisy and everything which is not pleasing to the Lord. Do thou in no wise forsake the commandments of the Lord; but thou shalt keep what thou has received, neither adding thereto nor taking away therefrom. In the church thou shalt acknowledge thy transgressions, and thou shalt not come near for thy prayer with an evil conscience. This is the way of life.

Chapter 5. The Way of Death

And the way of death is this: First of all it is evil and full of curse: murders, adulteries, lusts, fornications, thefts, idolatries, magic arts, witchcrafts, rapines, false witnessings, hypocrisies, double-heartedness, deceit, haughtiness, depravity, self-will, greediness, filthy talking, jealousy, overconfidence, loftiness, boastfulness; persecutors of the good, hating truth, loving a lie, not knowing a reward for righteousness, not cleaving to good nor to righteous judgment, watching not for that which is good but for that which is evil; from whom meekness and endurance are far, loving vanities, pursuing requital, not pitying a poor man, not laboring for the afflicted, not knowing Him that made them, murderers of children, destroyers of the handiwork of God, turning away from him that is in want, afflicting him that is distressed, advocates of the rich, lawless judges of the poor, utter sinners. Be delivered, children, from all these.

Chapter 6. Against False Teachers, and Food Offered to Idols

See that no one cause thee to err from this way of the Teaching, since apart from God it teacheth thee. For if thou art able to bear all the yoke of the Lord, thou wilt be perfect; but if thou art not able, what thou art able that do. And concerning food, bear what thou art able; but against that which is sacrificed to idols be exceedingly on the guard; for it is the service of dead gods.

Chapter 7. Concerning Baptism

And concerning baptism, thus baptize ye: Having first said all these things, baptize into the name of the Father, and of the Son, and of the Holy Spirit, in living water. But if thou have not living water, baptize into other water: and if thou canst not in cold, in warm. But if thou have not either, pour out water thrice upon the head into the name of Father and Son and Holy Spirit. But before the baptism let the baptizer fast and the baptized, and whatever others can; but thou shalt order the baptized to fast one or two days before.

Chapter 8. Concerning Fasting and Prayer (The Lord's Prayer)

But let not your fasts be with the hypocrites, for they fast on the second and fifth day of the week; but do ye fast on the fourth day and the Preparation (Friday). Neither pray as the hypocrites, but as the Lord commanded in His Gospel, thus pray; Our Father who art in heaven, hallowed be Thy name. Thy kingdom come. Thy will be done as in heaven, so on earth. Give us to-day our daily (needful) bread, and forgive us our debt as we also forgive our debtors. And bring us not into temptation, but deliver us from the evil one (or, evil); for Thine is the power and the glory for ever. Thrice in the day thus pray.

Chapter 9. The Thanksgiving (Eucharist)

Now concerning the Thanksgiving (Eucharist), thus give thanks. First, concerning the cup: We thank thee, our Father, for the holy vine of David Thy servant, which Thou madest known to us through Jesus Thy Servant; to Thee be the glory forever. And concerning the broken *bread*: We thank Thee, our Father, for the life and knowledge which Thou madest known to us through Jesus Thy Servant; to Thee be the glory forever. Even as this broken bread was scattered over the hills, and was gathered together and became one, so let Thy church be gathered together from the ends of the earth into Thy kingdom: for Thine is the glory and the power through Jesus Christ forever. But let no one eat or drink of your Thanksgiving (Eucharist), but they who have been baptized into the name of the Lord; for concerning this also the Lord hath said, Give not that which is holy to the dogs.

Chapter 10. Prayer After Communion

But after ye are filled, thus give thanks: We thank Thee, holy Father, for Thy holy name which Thou didst cause to tabernacle in our hearts, and for the knowledge and faith and immortality, which Thou madest known to us through Jesus Thy Servant; to Thee be the glory for ever. Thou, Master almighty, didst create all things for Thy name's sake; Thou gavest food and drink to men for enjoyment, that they might give thanks to Thee; but to us

Thou didst freely give spiritual food and drink and life eternal through Thy Servant. Before all things we thank Thee that Thou art mighty; to Thee be the glory forever. Remember, Lord, Thy Church, to deliver it from all evil and to make it perfect in Thy love, and gather it from the four winds, sanctified for Thy kingdom which Thou hast prepared for it; for Thine is the power and the glory forever. Let grace come, and let this world pass away. Hosanna to the God (Son) of David! If any one is holy, let him come; if any one is not so, let him repent. Maranatha, Amen. But permit the prophets to make Thanksgiving as much as they desire.

Chapter 11. Concerning Teachers, Apostles, and Prophets

Whosoever, therefore, cometh and teacheth you all these things that have been said before, receive him. But if the teacher himself turn and teach another doctrine to the destruction of this, hear him not; but if he teach so as to increase righteousness and the knowledge of the Lord, receive him as the Lord. But concerning the apostles and prophets, according to the decree of the Gospel, thus do. Let every apostle that cometh to you be received as the Lord. But he shall not remain except one day; but if there be need, also the next; but if he remain three days, he is a false prophet. And when the apostle goeth away, let him take nothing but bread until he lodgeth; but if he ask money, he is a false prophet. And every prophet that speaketh in the Spirit ye shall neither try nor judge; for every sin shall be forgiven, but this sin shall not be forgiven. But not every one that speaketh in the Spirit is a prophet; but only if he hold the ways of the Lord. Therefore from their ways shall the false prophet and the prophet be known. And every prophet who ordereth a meal in the Spirit eateth not from it, except indeed he be a false prophet; and every prophet who teacheth the truth, if he do not what he teacheth, is a false prophet. And every prophet, proved true, working unto the mystery of the Church in the world, yet not teaching *others*: to do what he himself doeth, shall not be judged among you, for with God he hath his judgment; for so did also the ancient prophets. But whoever saith in the Spirit, Give me money, or something else, ye shall not listen to him; but if he saith to you to give for others' sake who are in need, let no one judge him.

Chapter 12. Reception of Christians

But let every one that cometh in the name of the Lord be received, and afterward ye shall prove and know him; for ye shall have understanding right and left. If he who cometh is a wayfarer, assist him as far as ye are able; but he shall not remain with you, except for two or three days, if need be. But if he willeth to abide with you, being an artisan, let him work and eat; but if he hath no trade, according to your understanding see to it that, as a Christian, he shall not live with you idle. But if he willth not so to do, he is a Christ-monger. Watch that ye keep aloof from such.

Chapter 13. Support of Prophets

But every true prophet that willeth to abide among you is worthy of his support. So also a true teacher is himself worthy, as the workman, of his support. Every first-fruit, therefore, of the products of wine-press and threshing-floor, of oxen and of sheep, thou shalt take and give to the prophets, for they are your high priests. But if ye have not a prophet, give it to the poor. If thou makest a batch of dough, take the first-fruit and give according to the commandment. So also when thou openest a jar of wine or of oil, take the first-fruit and give it to the prophets; and of money (silver) and clothing and every possession, take the first-fruit, as it may seem good to thee, and give according to the commandment.

Chapter 14. Christian Assembly on the Lord's Day

But every Lord's day do ye gather yourselves together, and break bread, and give thanksgiving after having confessed your transgressions, that your sacrifice may be pure. But let no one that is at variance with his fellow come together with you until they be reconciled, that your sacrifice may not be profaned. For this is that which was spoken by the Lord: In every place and time offer to me a pure sacrifice; for I am a great King, saith the Lord, and my name is wonderful among the nations.

Chapter 15. Bishop and Deacons; Christian Reproof

Appoint, therefore, for yourselves, bishops and deacons worthy of the Lord, men meek, and not lovers of money, and truthful and proved; for they also render to you the service of prophets and teachers. Despise them not therefore, for they are your honored ones, together with the prophets and teachers. And reprove one another, not in anger, but in peace, as ye have it in the Gospel; but to every one that acts amiss against another, let no one speak, nor let him hear aught from you until he repent. But your prayers and alms and all your deeds so do, as ye have it in the Gospel of our Lord.

Chapter 16. Watchfulness; The Coming of the Lord

Watch for your life's sake. Let not your lamps be quenched, nor your loins unloosed; but be ye ready, for ye know not the hour in which our Lord cometh. [But often shall ye come together, seeking the things that are befitting to your souls: for the whole time of your faith will not profit you if ye be not made perfect in the last time.] For in the last days false prophets and corrupters shall be multiplied, and the sheep shall be turned into wolves, and love shall be turned into hate; for when lawlessness increaseth, they shall hate and persecute and betray one another and then shall appear the world-deceiver as Son of God, and shall do signs and wonders, and the earth shall be delivered into his hands, and he shall do iniquitous things which have never yet come to pass since the beginning. Then shall the creation of men come into the fire of trial and many shall be made to stumble and shall perish; but they that endure in their faith shall be saved from under the curse itself. And then shall appear the signs of the truth; first, the sign of an outspreading in heaven; then the sign of the sound of the trumpet, and the third, the resurrection of the dead; yet not of all, but as it is said: The Lord shall come and all His saints with Him. Then shall the world see the Lord coming upon the clouds of heaven.

All selections from the *Didache* are taken from the *Ante-Nicene Fathers, Translations of the Writings of the Fathers Down to A.D. 325*,
The Reverend Alexander Roberts, D.D. and
James Donaldson, LL.D., editors,
American Reprint of the Edinburgh Edition,
Volume VII, New York: The Christian Literature Company, 1888

Chapter 7 • St. Ignatius of Antioch: Letters

Of all the writings attributed to Ignatius, third bishop of Antioch, the seven presented here are now generally considered to be authentic. Little is known of his personal history beyond the fact that he was martyred by being thrown to the beasts in Rome in the latter part of the reign of the Emperor Trajan (A.D. 98-117).

In these writings we have an explicit presentation of the doctrines of the Trinity, Incarnation, Redemption, and Eucharist. Ignatius insists on the primacy of the See of Rome and the hierarchy of bishops, priests, and deacons. The bishop is Christ living in the midst of the faithful: "There where the Bishop is, there is his Church even as where Jesus Christ is, there is the Catholic Church." "Catholic" is considered by some to be found in these Letters for the first time in Christian Literature. He refers to the practice of virginity and the religious quality of marriage. In fact, his Letters constitute an authentic witness to doctrinal and liturgical orthodoxy in the second century.

The Letter to the Ephesians

Ignatius, who is also called Theophorus, to the church which is at Ephesus, in Asia, deservedly most happy, being blessed in the greatness and fullness of God the Father, and predestinated before the beginning of time, that it should be always for an enduring and unchangeable glory, being united and elected through the true passion by the will of the Father, and Jesus Christ, our God: Abundant happiness through Jesus Christ, and His undefiled grace.

I do not issue orders to you, as if I were some great person. For though I am bound for the name [of Christ], I am not yet perfect in Jesus Christ. For now I begin to be a disciple, and I speak to you as fellow-disciples with me. For it was needful for me to have been stirred up by you in faith, exhortation, patience, and long-suffering. But inasmuch as love suffers me not to be silent in regard to you, I have therefore taken upon me first to exhort you that you would all run together in accordance with the will of God. For even Jesus Christ, our inseparable life, is the manifested will of the Father; as also bishops, settled everywhere to the utmost bounds of the earth, are so by the will of Jesus Christ.

Wherefore it is fitting that ye should run together in accordance with the will of your bishop, which thing also you do. For your justly renowned presbytery, worthy of God, is fitted as exactly to the bishop as the strings are to the harp. Therefore in your concord and harmonious love, Jesus Christ is sung. And do ye, man by man, become a choir, that being harmonious in love, and taking up the song of God in unison, you may with one voice sing to the Father through Jesus Christ, so that He may both hear you, and perceive by your works that you are indeed the members of His Son. It is profitable, therefore, that you should live in an unblamable unity, that thus you may always enjoy communion with God.

For if I, in this brief space of time, have enjoyed such fellowship with your bishop — I mean not of a mere human, but of a spiritual nature — how much more do I reckon you happy who are so joined to him as the church is to Jesus Christ, and as Jesus Christ is to the Father, that so all things may agree in unity! Let no man deceive himself: if any one be not within the altar, he is deprived of the bread of God. For if the prayer of one or two possesses such power, how much more that of the bishop and the whole church! He, therefore, that does not assemble with the church, has even by this manifested his pride, and condemned himself. For it is written, "God resisteth the proud." Let us be careful, then, not to set ourselves in opposition to the bishop, in order that we may be subject to God.

It is manifest, therefore, that we should look upon the bishop even as we would upon the Lord Himself. And indeed Onesimus himself greatly commends your good order in God, that ye all live according to the truth, and that no sect has any dwelling-place among you. Nor, indeed, do ye hearken to any one rather than to Jesus Christ speaking in truth.

For some are in the habit of carrying about the name of Jesus Christ in wicked guile, while yet they practice things unworthy of God whom you must flee as would wild beasts. For they are ravening dogs, who bite secretly, against whom you must be on your guard, inasmuch as they are men who can scarcely be cured. There is one Physician who is possessed both of flesh and spirit; both made and not made; God existing in flesh; true life in death; both of Mary and of God; first passible and then impassible, — even Jesus Christ our Lord.

Let not then any one deceive you, as indeed you are not deceived, inasmuch as you are wholly devoted to God. For since there is no strife raging among you which might distress you, you are certainly living in accordance with God's will.

Nevertheless, I have heard of some who have passed on from this to you, having false doctrine, whom you did not suffer to sow among you, but stopped your ears, that you might not receive those things which were sown by them, as being stones of the temple of the Father, prepared for the building of God the Father, and drawn up on high by the instrument of Jesus Christ, which is the cross, making use of the Holy Spirit as a rope, while your faith was the means by which you ascended, and your love the way which led up to God. You therefore, as well as all your fellow-travellers, are God-bearers, temple-bearers, Christ-bearers, bearers of holiness, adorned in all respects with the commandments of Jesus Christ in whom also I exult that I have been thought worthy, by means of this epistle, to converse and rejoice with you, because with respect to your Christian life you love nothing but God only.

I entreat I may always be a partaker, that I may be found in the lot of the Christians of Ephesus, who have always been of the same mind with the apostles through the power of Jesus Christ.

Take heed, then, often to come together to give thanks to God, and show forth His praise. For when you assemble frequently in the same place, the powers of Satan are destroyed, and the destruction at which he aims is prevented by the unity of your faith. Nothing is more precious than peace, by which all war, both in heaven and earth, is brought to an end.

None of these things is hid from you, if you perfectly possess that faith and love towards Christ Jesus which are the beginning and the end of life.

For the beginning is faith, and the end is love. Now these two, being inseparably connected together, are of God, while all other things which are requisite for a holy life follow after them. No man [truly] making a profession of faith sins; nor does he that possesses love hate any one. The tree is made manifest by its fruit, so those that profess themselves to be Christians shall be recognized by their conduct. For there is not now a demand for mere profession, but that a man be found continuing in the power of faith to the end.

Do not err, my brethren. Those that corrupt families shall not inherit the kingdom of God. If, then, those who do this as respects the flesh have suffered death, how much more shall this be the case with any one who corrupts by wicked doctrine the faith of God, for which Jesus Christ was crucified! Such an one becoming defiled [in this way], shall go away into everlasting fire, and so shall every one that hearkens unto him.

For this end did the Lord suffer the ointments to be poured upon His head, that He might breathe immortality into His church. Be not you anointed with the bad odour of the doctrine of the prince of this world; let him not lead you away captive from the life which is set before you. And why are we not all prudent, since we have received the knowledge of God, which is Jesus Christ? Why do we foolishly perish, not recognizing the gift which the Lord has of a truth sent to us?

Let my spirit be counted as nothing for the sake of the cross, which is a stumbling-block to those that do not believe, but to us salvation and life eternal. "Where is the wise man? where the disputer?" Where is the boasting of those who are styled prudent?

For our God, Jesus Christ, was, according to the appointment of God, conceived in the womb by Mary, of the seed of David, but by the Holy Spirit He was born and baptized, that by His passion He might purify the water.

Now the virginity of Mary was hidden from the prince of this world, as was also her offspring, and the death of the Lord; three mysteries of renown, which were wrought in silence by God. How, then, was He manifested to the world? A star shone forth in heaven above all the other stars, the light of which was inexpressible, while its novelty struck men with astonishment. And all the rest of the stars, with the sun and moon, formed a chorus to this star, and its fight was exceedingly great above them all. And there was agitation felt as to whence this new spectacle came, so unlike to everything else [in the heavens]. Hence every kind of magic was destroyed, and every bond of wickedness disappeared; ignorance was removed, and the old kingdom abolished, God himself being manifested in human form for the renewal of eternal life. And now that took a beginning which had been prepared by God. Henceforth all things were in a state of tumult, because He meditated the abolition of death.

If Jesus Christ shall graciously permit me through your prayers, and if it be His will, I shall, in a second little work which I will write to you, make further manifest to you [the nature of] the dispensation of which I have begun [to treat], with respect to the new man, Jesus Christ, in His faith and in His love, in His suffering and in His resurrection. Especially [will I do this] if the Lord make known to me that you come together man by man in common through grace, individually, in one faith, and in Jesus Christ, who was of the seed of David according to the flesh, being both the Son of man and the Son of God, so that ye obey the bishop and the presbytery with an undivided mind, breaking one and the same bread, which is the medicine of immortality, and the antidote to prevent us from dying, but [which causes] that we should live forever in Jesus Christ.

My soul be for yours and theirs whom, for the honor of God, you have sent to Smyrna; whence also I write to you, giving thanks unto the Lord, and loving Polycarp even as I do you. Remember me, as Jesus Christ also remembered you. Pray you for the church which is in Syria, whence I am led bound to Rome, being the last of the faithful who are there, even as I have been thought worthy to be chosen to show forth the honor of God. Farewell in God the Father, and in Jesus Christ, our common hope.

To the Magnesians

It is fitting, then, not only to be called Christians, but to be so in reality. . . .

For as there are two kinds of coins, the one of God, the other of the world, and each of these has its special character stamped upon it, [so is it also here.] The unbelieving are of this world; but the believing have, in love, the character of God the Father by Jesus Christ, by whom, if we are not in readiness to die in His passion, His life is not in us.

As therefore the Lord did nothing without the Father, being united to Him, neither by himself nor by the apostles, so neither do you anything without the bishop and presbyters. Neither endeavour that anything appear reasonable and proper to yourselves apart; but being come together into the same place, let there be one prayer, one supplication, one mind, one hope, in love and in joy undefiled. There is one Jesus Christ, than whom nothing is more excellent.

Therefore, having become His disciples, let us learn to live according to the principles of Christianity. For whosoever is called by any other name besides this, is not of God.

Be ye subject to the bishop, and to one another, as Jesus Christ to the Father, according to the flesh, and the apostles to Christ, and to the Father, and to the Spirit; that so there may be a union both fleshly and spiritual.

To the Trallians

I therefore, yet not I, out of love of Jesus Christ, entreat you that ye use Christian nourishment only, and abstain from herbage of a different kind; I mean heresy. For those [that are given to this] mix up Jesus Christ with their own poison, speaking things which are unworthy of credit, like those who administer a deadly drug in sweet wine, which he who is ignorant of does greedily take, with a fatal pleasure, leading to his own death.

Be on your guard, therefore, against such persons. And this will be the case with you if you are not puffed up, and continue in intimate union with Jesus Christ our God, and the bishop, and the enactments of the apostles. He that is within the altar is pure, but he that is without is not pure; that is, he who does anything apart from the bishop, and presbyter, and deacons, such a man is not pure in his conscience.

Stop your ears, therefore, when any one speaks to you at variance with Jesus Christ, who was descended from David, and was also of Mary; who was truly born, and did eat and drink. He was truly persecuted under Pontius Pilate; He was truly crucified, and [truly] died, in the sight of beings in heaven, and on earth, and under the earth. He was also truly raised from the dead, His Father quickening Him even as after the same manner His Father will so raise up us who believe in Him by Christ Jesus, apart from whom we do not possess the true life.

To the Romans

Suffer me to become food for the wild beasts, through whose instrumentality it will be granted me to attain to God. I am the wheat of God, and let me be ground by the teeth of the wild beasts, that I may be found the pure bread of Christ. Rather entice the wild beasts, that they may become my tomb, and may leave nothing of my body; so that when I have fallen asleep [in death], I may be no trouble to any one. Then shall I truly be disciple of Christ, when the world shall not see so much as my body. Entreat Christ for me, that by these instruments I may be found a sacrifice [to God].

I desire the bread of God, the heavenly bread, the bread of life, which is the flesh of Jesus Christ, the Son of God, who became afterwards of the seed of David and Abraham; and I desire the drink of God, namely His blood, which is incorruptible love and eternal life.

To the Philadelphians

Take ye heed, then, to have but one Eucharist. For there is one flesh of our Lord Jesus Christ, and one cup to [show forth] the unity of His blood; one altar; as there is one bishop, along with the presbytery and deacons, my fellow-servants: that so, whosoever you do, you may do it according to [the will of] God.

But the Spirit proclaimed these words: Do nothing without the bishop; keep your bodies as the temples of God; love unity, avoid divisions; be the followers of Jesus Christ, even as He is of His Father.

I therefore did what belonged to me, as a man devoted to unity. For where there is division and wrath, God doth not dwell. To all them that repent, the Lord grants forgiveness, if they turn in penitence to the unity of God, and to communion with the bishop.

To the Smyrnaeans

I glorify God, even Jesus Christ, who has given you such wisdom. For I have observed that you are perfected in an immovable faith, as if you were nailed to the cross of our Lord Jesus Christ, both in the flesh and in the spirit, and are established in love through the blood of Christ, being fully persuaded with respect to our Lord, that He was truly of the seed of David according to the flesh, and the Son of God according to the will, and power of God; that He was truly born of a virgin, was baptized by John, in order that all righteousness might be fulfilled by Him; and was truly, under Pontius Pilate and Herod the tetrach, nailed [to the cross] for us in His flesh. Of this fruit we are by His divinely-blessed passion, that He might set up a standard for all ages, through His resurrection, to all His holy and faithful [followers], whether among Jews or Gentiles, in the one body of His church.

Now, He suffered all these things for our sakes, that we might be saved. And He suffered truly, even as also He truly raised up himself.

Let no man do anything connected with the church without the bishop. Let that be deemed a proper Eucharist, which is [administered] either by the bishop, or by one to whom he has entrusted it. Wherever the bishop shall appear, there let the multitude [of the people] also be; even as, wherever Jesus Christ is, there is the catholic church. It is not lawful without the bishop either to baptize or to celebrate a love-feast; but whatsoever he shall approve of, that is also pleasing to God, so that everything that is done may be secure and valid.

To Polycarp

Be sober as an athlete of God: the prize set before thee is immortality and eternal life of which thou are also persuaded to all things may my soul be for thine, and my bonds also, which thou hast loved.

Flee evil arts; but all the more discourse in public regarding them. Speak to my sisters, that they love the Lord, and be satisfied with their husbands both in the flesh and spirit. In like manner also, exhort my brethren, in the name of Jesus Christ, that they love their wives, even as the Lord the church. But it becomes both men and women who marry to form their union with the approval of the bishop, that their marriage may be according to God, and not after their own lust. Let all things be done to the honour of God.

All selections from *The Letters of Ignatius* are taken from *The Ante-Nicene Fathers, Translations of The Writings of the Fathers Down to A.D. 325,*
The Reverend Alexander Roberts, D.D. and
James Donaldson, LL.D., editors,
Volume I, Buffalo: The Christian Literature Publishing Company, 1887

8 • St. Polycarp: Letters; *The Encyclical of the Church at Smyrna*

Little is known of the bishop of Smyrna outside of the fact that he wrote this Letter to the Philippians, was the teacher of Irenaeus, and lived during the second century. He was said to have heard John the Apostle preaching at Ephesus and to have been appointed by John to his see at Smyrna. He received at least one letter from Ignatius of Antioch, and made a trip to Rome to consult with Pope Anicetus (155-166).

The Encyclical Letter of the Church at Smyrna gives a vivid account of the life, teaching, and reputation of Polycarp. This document is a classic example of the many accounts of the martyrdom of revered witnesses to the teaching and practices of the early Christians.

To the Philippians

Polycarp, and the presbyters with him, to the church of God sojourning at Philippi: Mercy to you, and peace from God Almighty, and from the Lord Jesus Christ, our Saviour, be multiplied.

I have greatly rejoiced with you in our Lord Jesus Christ, because you have followed the example of true love as displayed by God, and have accompanied, as became you, those who were bound in chains, the fitting ornaments of saints, and which are indeed the diadems of the true elect of God and our Lord; and because the strong root of your faith, spoken of in days long gone by, endureth even until now, and bringeth forth fruit to our Lord Jesus Christ, who for our sins suffered even unto death, but "whom God raised from the dead, having loosed the bands of the grave."

"Wherefore, girding up your loins," "serve the Lord in fear" and truth, as those who have forsaken the vain, empty talk and error of the multitude, and "believed in Him who raised up our Lord Jesus Christ from the dead, and gave Him glory," and a throne at His right hand. . . . But He who raised Him up from the dead will raise up us also, if we do His will, and walk in His commandments, and love what He loved, keeping ourselves from all unrighteousness, covetousness, love of money, evil-speaking, false-witness;" not rendering evil for evil, or railing for railing," or blow for blow, or cursing for cursing, but being mindful of what the Lord said in His teaching: "Judge not, that ye be not judged; forgive, and it shall be forgiven unto you; be merciful, that ye may obtain mercy, with what measure ye mete, it shall be measured to you again": and once more, "Blessed are the poor and those that are persecuted from righteousness' sake, for theirs is the kingdom of God."

Teach the widows to be discreet as respects the faith of the Lord, praying continually for all, knowing that they are the altar of God, that He clearly perceives all things, and that nothing is hid from Him, neither reasonings, nor reflections, nor any one of the secret things of the heart.

In like manner should the deacons be blameless before the face of His righteousness, as being the servants of God and Christ, and not of men. They must not be slanderers, double-tongued, or lovers of money, but temperate in all things, compassionate, industrious, walking according to the truth of the Lord, who was the servant of all. If we please Him in this present world, we shall receive also the future world, according as He has promised to us that He will raise us again from the dead, and that if we live worthily of Him, "we shall also reign together with Him," provided only we believe. In like manner, let the young also be blameless in all things, being especially careful to preserve purity, and keeping themselves in, as with a bridle, from every kind of evil. For it is well that they should be cut off from the lusts that are in the world, since "every lust warrant against the spirit;" and "neither fornicators, nor effeminate, nor abusers of themselves with mankind, shall inherit the kingdom of God." Wherefore, it is needful to abstain from all these things, being subject to the presbyters and deacons, as unto God and Christ. The virgins also must walk in a blameless and pure conscience.

And let the presbyters be compassionate and merciful to all, bringing back those that wander, visiting all the sick, and not neglecting the widow, the orphan, or the poor, but always "providing for that which is becoming in the sight of God and men;" abstaining from all wrath, respect of persons, and unjust judgment; keeping far off from all covetousness, not quickly crediting an evil report against any one, not severe in judgment, as knowing that we are all under a debt of sin.

"For whosoever does not confess that Jesus Christ has come in the flesh, is antichrist"; and whosoever does not confess the testimony of the cross, is of the devil; and whosoever perverts the oracles of the Lord to his own lusts, and says that there is neither a resurrection nor a judgment, he is the first-born of Satan. Wherefore, forsaking the vanity of many, and their false doctrines, let us return to the word which has been handed down to us from the beginning.

I exhort you all, therefore, to yield obedience to the word of righteousness, and to exercise all patience, such as ye have seen set before your eyes, not only in the case of the blessed Ignatius, and Zosimus, and Rufus, but also in others among yourselves, and in Paul himself, and the rest of the apostles.

The Encyclical Letter of the Church at Smyrna

The church of God which sojourns at Smyrna, to the church of God sojourning in Philomelium, and to all the congregations of the holy and catholic church in every place: Mercy, peace, and love from God the Father, and our Lord Jesus Christ, be multiplied.

We have written to you, brethren, as to what relates to the martyrs, and especially to the blessed Polycarp, who put an end to the persecution, having, as it were, set a seal upon it by his martyrdom. For almost all the events that happened previously to this one, took place that the Lord might show us from above a martyrdom becoming the gospel. For he waited to be delivered up, even as the Lord had done, that we also might become his followers, while we look not merely at what concerns ourselves, but have regard also to our neighbors. For it is the part of a true and well-founded love, not only to wish one's self to be saved, but also all the brethren.

All the martyrdoms, then, were blessed and noble which took place according to the will of God. And truly, who can fail to admire their nobleness of mind, and their patience, with that love towards their Lord which they displayed? — who, when they were so torn with scourges, that the frame of their bodies, even to the very inward veins and arteries, was laid open, still patiently endured, while even those that stood by pitied and bewailed them. But they reached such a pitch of magnanimity, that not one of them let a sigh or a groan escape them; thus proving to us all that those holy martyrs of Christ, at the very time when they suffered such torments, were absent from the body, or rather, that the Lord then stood by them, and communed with them. And, looking to the grace of Christ, they despised all the torments of this world, redeeming themselves from eternal punishment by the suffering of a single hour. For this reason the fire of their savage executioners appeared cool to them. For they kept before their view escape from that fire which is eternal and never shall be quenched, and looked forward with the eyes of their heart to those good things which are laid up for such as endure; things "which ear hath not heard, nor eye seen, neither have entered into the heart of man," but were revealed by the Lord to them, inasmuch as they were no longer men, but had already become angels, and, in like manner, those who were condemned to the wild beasts endured dreadful tortures, being stretched out upon beds full of spikes and subjected to various other kinds of torments, in order that, if it were possible, the tyrant might, by their lingering tortures, lead them to a denial [of Christ].

The most admirable Polycarp, when he first heard that he was sought for, was in no measure disturbed, but resolved to continue in the city. However, in deference to the wish of many, he was persuaded to leave it. He departed, therefore, to a country house not far distant from the city. There he stayed with a few [friends], engaged in nothing else night and day than praying for all men, and for the churches throughout the world, according to his usual custom. And while he was praying, a vision presented itself to him three days before he was taken; and, behold, the pillow under his head seemed to him on fire. Upon this, turning to those that were with him he said to them prophetically, "I must be burnt alive."

His pursuers then, along with horsemen, went forth at supper-time on the day of the preparation, with their usual weapons, as if going out against a robber. And being come about evening [to the place where he was], they found him lying down in the upper room of a certain little house, from which he might have escaped into another place; but he refused, saying, "The will of God be done." So when he heard that they were come, he went down and spake with them. And as those that were present marvelled at his age and constancy, some of them said, "Was so much effort made to capture such a venerable man?" Immediately then, in that very hour, he ordered that something to eat and drink should be set before them, as much indeed as they cared for, while he besought them to allow him an hour to pray without disturbance. And on their giving him leave, he stood and prayed, being full of the grace of God, so that he could not cease for two full hours, to the astonishment of them that heard him, insomuch that many began to repent that they had come forth against so godly and venerable an old man.

Now, as Polycarp was entering into the stadium, there came to him a voice from heaven, saying, "Be strong, and show thyself a man, O Polycarp!" No one saw who it was that spoke to him; but those of our brethren who were present heard the voice. And when he came near, the proconsul asked him whether he was Polycarp. On his confessing that he was [the proconsul] sought to persuade him to deny [Christ], saying, "Have respect to thy old age," and other similar things, according to their custom, [such as], "Swear by the fortune of Caesar; repent, and say, Away with the atheists." But Polycarp, gazing with a stem countenance on all the multitude of the wicked heathen then in the stadium, and waving his hand towards them, while with groans he looked up to heaven, said "Away with the atheists." Then, the proconsul urging him, and saying, "Swear, and I will set thee at liberty, reproach Christ'; Polycarp declared, "Eighty and six years have I served Him, and He never did me any injury: how then can I blaspheme my King and my Saviour?"

"Hear me declare with boldness, I am a Christian. And if you wish to learn what the doctrines of Christianity are, appoint me a day, and thou shalt hear them." The proconsul replied, "Persuade the people." But Polycarp said, "To thee I have thought it right to offer an account of my faith; for we are taught to give all due honor (which entails no injury upon ourselves) to the powers and authorities which are ordained of God. But as for these, I do not deem them worthy of receiving any account from me."

The proconsul said to him, "I will cause thee to be consumed by fire, seeing thou despisest the wild beasts, if thou wilt not repent." But Polycarp said, "Thou threatenest me with fire which burneth for an hour, and after a little is extinguished, but art ignorant of the fire of the coming judgment and of external punishment, reserved for the ungodly. But why tarriest thou? Bring forth what thou wilt."

The proconsul was astonished, and sent his herald to proclaim in the midst of the stadium thrice, "Polycarp has confessed that he is a Christian." This proclamation having been made by the herald, the whole multitude both of the heathen and Jews, who dwelt at Smyrna, cried out with uncontrollable fury, and in a loud vice, "This is the teacher of Asia, the father of the Christians, and the overthrower of our gods, he who has been teaching many not to sacrifice, or to worship to gods. . . ." Then it seemed good to them to cry out with one consent, that Polycarp should be burnt alive. For thus it behoved the vision which was revealed to him in regard to his pillow to be fulfilled, when, seeing it on fire as he was praying, he turned about and said prophetically to the faithful that were with him, "I must be burnt alive."

This, then, was carried in effect with greater speed than it was spoken, the multitudes immediately gathering together wood and fagots out of the shops and baths; the Jews especially, according to custom, eagerly assisting them in it. And when the funeral pile was ready, Polycarp, lay aside all his garments. Immediately then they surrounded him with those substances which had been prepared for the funeral pile. But when they were about also to fix him with nails, he said, "Leave me as I am; for he that giveth me strength to endure the fire, will also enable me, without your securing me by nails, to remain without moving in the pile."

And he, placing his hands behind him, and being bound like a distinguished ram taken out of a great flock for sacrifice, and prepared to be an acceptable burnt-offering unto God, looked up to heaven, and said, "O Lord God Almighty, the Father of Thy beloved and blessed Son Jesus Christ, by whom we have received the knowledge of thee, the God of angels and powers, and of every creature, and of the whole race of the righteous who live before thee, I give thee thanks that Thou has counted me worthy of this day and this hour, that I should have a part in the number of Thy martyrs, in the cup of thy Christ, to the resurrection of eternal life, both of soul and body, through the incorruption (imparted) by the Holy Ghost. Among whom may I be accepted this day before Thee as a fat and acceptable sacrifice, according as Thou, the ever-truthful God, hast fore-ordained, hast revealed beforehand to me, and now hast fulfilled. Wherefore also I praise Thee for all things, I bless Thee, I glorify Thee, along with the everlasting and heavenly Jesus Christ, Thy beloved Son, with whom, to Thee, and the Holy Ghost, be glory both now and to all coming ages. Amen."

When he had pronounced this amen, and so finished his prayer, those who were appointed for the purpose kindled the fire. And as the flame blazed forth in great fury, we, to whom it was given to witness it, beheld a great miracle, and have been preserved that we might report to others what then took place. For the fire, shaping itself into the form of an arch, like the sail of a ship when filled with the wind, encompassed as by a circle the body of the martyr. And he appeared within not like flesh which is burnt, but as bread that is baked, or as gold and silver glowing in a furnace. Moreover, we perceived such a sweet odour coming from the pile, as if frankincense or some such precious spices had been smoking there.

The centurion then, seeing the strife excited by the Jews, placed the body in the midst of the fire, and consumed it. Accordingly, we afterwards took up his bones, as being more precious than the most exquisite jewels, and more purified than gold, and deposited them in a fitting place, whither, being gathered together, as opportunity is allowed us, with joy and rejoicing, the Lord shall grant us to celebrate the anniversary of his martyrdom, both in memory of those who have already finished their course and for the exercising and preparation of those yet to walk in their steps.

Now, the blessed Polycarp suffered martyrdom on the second day of the month just begun, the seventh day before the Calends of May, on the great Sabbath, at the eighth hour. He was taken by Herod, Philip the Trallian being high priest, Statius Quadratus being proconsul, but Jesus Christ being King forever, to whom be glory, honor, majesty, and an everlasting throne, from generation to generation. Amen.

All selections from "The Encyclical Letter of the Church at Smyrna"
concerning the martyrdom of the Holy Polycarp are taken from
Ante-Nicene Fathers,
Translation of the Writings of the Fathers Down to A.D. 325,
The Reverend Alexander Roberts, D.D. and James Donaldson, LL.D., editors,
Volume I, Buffalo: The Christian Literature Publishing Company, 1887

Chapter 9 • The Fragments of Papias

Papias was bishop of the church in Heirapolis in Phygia in central Asia Minor. Little is known of him except what is contained in these fragments, which are included because they demonstrate the historical continuity of the Good News of Christianity. Papias is a second-century witness to the existence and authenticity of the Gospels of Mark and Matthew, and the Letters of John and Peter. He is explicit in attesting to the existence of a large body of tradition concerning the verbal teaching and customary practices of the early Christian communities.

Fragments of Papias

The writings of Papias in common circulation are five in number, and these are called an Exposition of the Oracles of the Lord. Irenaeus makes mention of these as the only works written by him, in the following words: "Now testimony is borne to these things in writing by Papias, an ancient man, who was a hearer of John, and a friend of Polycarp, in the fourth of his books; for five books were composed by him." Thus wrote Irenaeus. Moreover, Papias himself, in the introduction to his books, makes it manifest that he was not himself a hearer and eyewitness of the holy apostles; but he tells us that he received the truths of our religion from those who were acquainted with them [the apostles] in the following words:

But I shall not be unwilling to put down, along with my interpretations, whatsoever instructions I received with care at any time from the elders, and stored up with care in my memory, assuring you at the same time of their truth. For I did not, like the multitude, take pleasure in those who spoke much, but in those who taught the truth; nor in those who related strange commandments, but in those who rehearsed the commandments given by the Lord to faith, and proceeding from truth itself. If, then, any one who had attended on the elders came, I asked minutely after their sayings -- what Andrew or Peter said, or what was said by Philip, or by Thomas, or by James, or by John, or by Matthew, or by any other of the Lord's disciples: which things Aristion and the presbyter John, the disciples of the Lord, say. For I imagined that what was to be got from books was not so profitable to me as what came from the living and abiding voice.

As the presybters say, then, those who are deemed worthy of an abode in heaven shall go there, others shall enjoy the delights of Paradise, and others shall possess the splendor of the city; for everywhere the Saviour will be seen, according as they shall be worthy who see Him. But that there is this distinction between the habitation of those who produced an hundred-fold, and that of those who produce sixty-fold, and that of those who produce thirty-fold; for the first will be taken up into the heavens, the second class will dwell in Paradise, and the last will inhabit the city; and that on this account the Lord said, "In my Father's house are many mansions:" for all things belong to God, who supplies all with a suitable dwelling-place, even as His word says, that a share is given to all by the Father, according as each one is or shall be worthy. And this is the couch in which they shall decline who feast, being invited to the wedding. The presbyters, the disciples of the apostles, say that this is the gradation and arrangement of those who are saved, and that they advance through steps of this nature; and that, moreover, they ascend through the Spirit to the Son, and through the Son to the Father; and that in due time the Son will yield up His work to the Father, even as it is said by the apostle. "For He must reign till He hath put all enemies under His feet. The last enemy that shall be destroyed is death." For in the times of the kingdom the just man who is on the earth shall forget to die." But when He saith all things are put under Him, it is manifest that He is excepted which did put all things under Him. And when all things shall be subdued unto Him, than shall the Son also Himself be subject unto Him that put all things under Him, that God may be in all."

It may also be worthwhile to add to the statements of Papias already given, other passages of his in which he relates some miraculous deeds, stating that he acquired the knowledge of them from tradition. We must now point out how Papias relates that he had received a wonderful narrative from the daughters of the Apostle Philip. For he relates that a dead man was raised to life in his day. He also mentions another miracle relating to Justus, surnamed Barsabas, how he swallowed a deadly poison, and received no harm, on account of the grace of the Lord. The same person, moreover, has set down other things as coming to him from unwritten tradition, amongst these some strange parables and instructions of the Saviour, and some other things of a more fabulous nature. Amongst these he says that there will be a millennium after the resurrection from the dead, when the personal reign of Christ will be established on this earth. He moreover hands down, in his own writing, other narratives given by the previously mentioned Aristion of the Lord's sayings, and the traditions of the presbyter John. For information on these points, we can merely refer our readers to the books themselves; but now, to the extracts already made, we shall add, as being a matter of primary importance, a tradition regarding Mark who wrote the Gospel, which he [Papias] has given in the following words: And the presbyter said this. Mark, having become the interpreter of Peter, wrote down accurately whatsoever he remembered. It was not, however, in exact order that he related the saying or deeds of Christ. For he neither heard the Lord nor accompanied Him, but afterwards, as I said, he accompanied Peter, who accommodated his instructions to the necessities [of his bearers], but with no intention of giving a regular narrative of the Lord's sayings. Wherefore Mark made no mistake in thus writing some things as he remembered them. For of one thing he took especial care, not to omit anything he had heard, and not to put anything, fictitious into the statements. [This what is related by Papias regarding Mark; but with regard to Matthew he has made the following statements:] Matthew put together the oracles [of the Lord] in the Hebrew language, and each one interpreted them as best he could. [The same person uses proofs from the First Epistle of John, and from the Epistle of Peter in like manner. And he also gives another story of a woman who was accused of many sins before the Lord, which is to be found in the Gospel according to the Hebrews.]

With regard to the inspiration of the book (Revelation), we deem it superfluous to add another word: for the blessed Gregory Theologus and Cyril, and even men of still older date, Papias, Irenaeus, Methodius, and Hippolytus, bore entirely satisfactory testimony to it.

Taking occasion from Papias of Merapohs, the illustrious, a disciple of the apostle who leaned on the bosom of Christ, and Clemens, and Pantaenus the priest of [the church] of the Alexandrians, and the wise Ammonius, the ancient and first expositors, who agreed with each other, who understood the work of the six days as referring to Christ and the whole church.

(1.) Mary, the mother of the Lord; (2.) Mary, the wife of Cleophas or Alpheus, who was the mother of James the bishop and apostle, and of Simon and Thaddeus, and of one Joseph; (3.) Mary Salome, wife of Zebedee, mother of John the evangelist and James; (4.) Mary Magdalene. These four are found in the Gospel. James and Judas and Joseph were sons of an aunt (2) of the Lord's. James also and John were sons of another aunt (3) of the Lord's. Mary (2), mother of James the less and Joseph, wife of Alpheus, was the sister of Mary, the mother of the Lord, whom John names of Cleophas, either from her father or from the family of the clan, or for some other reason. Mary Salome (3) is called Salome either from her husband or her village. Some affirm that she is the same as Mary of Cleophas, because she had two husbands.

All selections taken from "Fragments of Papias" are from
Ante-Nicene Fathers,
Translations of the Writings of the Fathers Down to A.D. 325,
The Reverend Alexander Roberts, D.D. and James Donaldson, LL.D., editors,
Volume I, Buffalo: The Christian Literature Publishing Company, 1887

Chapter 10 • *The Shepherd of Hermas*

Although there has been considerable debate about the identity of the author of this allegorical presentation of the basic theology of repentance current in the Christian communities around A.D. 150, it is certain that the work was very popular during the second, third, and fourth centuries. Many considered it an excellent introduction to the Christian way of life. It indicates very well the form and content of a book which appealed to the people of the time and which many preferred to the more "realistic" defenses of Christian dogmas. In the work as a whole we find, in addition to the main theme of penance, a belief in one God, love of truth, chastity, and the sanctity of marriage, detachment from the things of this world, the need to give alms to the poor, the need to pray for our benefactors, the value of good works, and the necessity for confident prayer.

The Shepherd of Hermas
VISION FIRST

He who had brought me up, sold me to one Rhode in Rome. Many years after this I recognized her, and I began to love her as a sister. Some time after, I saw her bathe in the river Tiber; and I gave her my hand, and drew her out of the river. The sight of her beauty made me think with myself, "I should be a happy man if I could but get a wife as handsome and good as she is." This was the only thought that passed through me: this and nothing more. A short time after this, as I was walking on my road to the villages, and magnifying the creatures of God, and thinking how magnificent, and beautiful, and powerful they are, I fell asleep. And the Spirit carried me away, and took me through a pathless place, through which a man could not travel, for it was situated in the midst of rocks; it was rugged and impassable on account of water. Having passed over this river, I came to a plain. I then bent down on my knees, and began to pray to the Lord, and to confess my sins. And as I prayed, the heavens were opened, and I see the woman whom I had desired saluting me from the sky, and saying, "Hail, Hermas!" And looking up to her, I said, "Lady, what doest thou here?" And she answered me, "I have been taken up here to accuse you of your sins before the Lord." "Lady,' said I, "are you to be the subject of my accusation?" "No," said she; "but hear the words which I am going to speak to you. God, who dwells in the heavens, and made out of nothing the things that exist, and multiplied and increased them on account of His holy church, is angry with you for having sinned against me." I answered her, "Lady, have I sinned against you? How? Why do you falsely accuse me of this wickedness and impurity?" With a smile she replied to me, "The desire of wickedness arose within your heart. Is it not your opinion that a righteous man commits sin when an evil desire arises in his heart? There is sin in such a case, and the sin is great," said she, "for the thoughts of a righteous man should be righteous. But such as entertain wicked thoughts in their minds are bringing upon themselves death and captivity; and especially is this the case with those who set their affections on this world, and glory in their riches, and look not forward to the blessings of the life to come."

After she had spoken these words, the heavens were shut. I was overwhelmed with sorrow and fear, and said to myself, "If this sin is assigned to me, how can I be saved, or how shall I propitiate God in regard to my sins, which are of the grossest character?" While I was thinking over these things, and discussing them in my mind, there came up an old woman, arrayed in a splendid robe, and with a book in her hand; and she sat down alone, and saluted me, "Hail, Hermas!" And in sadness and tears I said to her, "Lady, hail!" And she said to me, "Why are you downcast, Hermas? for you were wont to be patient and temperate, and always smiling. Why are you so gloomy, and not cheerful?" I answered her and said, "O Lady, I have been reproached by a very good woman, who says that I sinned against her." And she said, "Far be such a deed from a servant of God. But perhaps a desire after her has arisen within your heart. Such a wish, in the case of the servants of God, produces sin. For it is a wicked and horrible wish in an all-chaste and already well-tried spirit to desire an evil deed.

"But God is not angry with you on account of this, but that you may convert your house, which have committed iniquity against the Lord, and against you, their parents. And although you love your sons, yet did you not warn your house, but permitted them to be terribly corrupted. Cease not therefore to admonish your sons; for I know that, ff they will repent with all their heart, they will be enrolled in the Books of Life with the saints." Having ended these words, she said to me, "Do you wish to hear me read?" I say to her, "Lady, I do." "Listen then, and give ear to the glories of God." "Lo, the God of powers, who by His invisible strong power and great wisdom has created the world, and by His glorious counsel has surrounded His creation with beauty, and by His strong word has fixed the heavens and laid the foundations of the earth upon the waters, and by His own wisdom and providence has created His holy church, which He has blessed, lo! He removes the heavens and the mountains, the hills and the seas, and all things become plain to His elect, that He may bestow on them the blessing which He has promised them, with much glory and joy, if only they shall keep the commandments of God which they have received in great faith."

VISION FIFTH

Concerning the commandments

After I had been praying at home, and had sat down on my couch, there entered a man of glorious aspect, dressed like a shepherd. And straightway he sat down beside me, and I said to him, "Who are you? "I," said he, "am that shepherd to whom you have been entrusted." "Do not be confounded, but receive strength from the commandments which I am going to give you. For I have been sent," said he, "to show you again all the things which you saw before, especially those of them which are useful to you. First of all, then, write down my commandments and similitudes, and you will write the other things as I shall show you. For this purpose," said he, "I command you to write down the commandments and similitudes first, that you may read them easily, and be able to keep them."

COMMANDMENT FIRST

On faith in God

First of all, believe that there is one God who created and finished all things, and made all things out of nothing.

COMMANDMENT SECOND

On avoiding evil-speaking, on giving alms in simplicity

First, then, speak evil of no one, nor listen with pleasure to any one who speaks evil of another. But if you listen, you will partake of the sin of him who speaks evil, if you believe the slander which you hear; for believing it, you will also have something to say against your brother. Thus, then, will you be guilty of the sin of him who slanders. For slander is evil and an unsteady demon. It never abides in peace, but always remains in discord. Keep yourself from it, and you will always be at peace with all.

COMMANDMENT THIRD

On avoiding falsehood

Again he said to me, "Love the truth, and let nothing but truth proceed from your mouth, that the spirit which God has placed in your flesh may be found truthful before all men; and the Lord, who dwelleth in you, will be glorified, because the Lord is truthful in every word, and in Him is no falsehood. They therefore who lie deny the Lord, and rob Him, not giving back to Him the deposit which they have received. For they received from Him a spirit free from falsehood.

COMMANDMENT FOURTH

On putting one's wife away, for adultery

"I charge you," said he, "to guard your chastity, and let no thought enter your heart of another man's wife, or of fornication, or of similar iniquities; for by doing this you commit a great sin. But if you always remember your own wife, you will never sin. For if this thought enter your heart, then you will sin; and if, in like manner, you think other wicked thoughts, you commit sin." I said to him, "Sir, permit me to ask you a few questions." "Say on," said he. And I said to him, "Sir, if any one has a wife who trusts in the Lord, and if he detect her in adultery, does the man sin if he continue to live with her?" And he said to me, "As long as he remains ignorant of her sin, the husband commits no transgression in living with her. But if the husband know that his wife has gone astray, and if the woman does not repent, but persists in her fornication, and yet the husband continues to live with her, he also is guilty of her crime, and a sharer in her adultery." And I said to him, "What then, sir, is the husband to do, if his wife continue in her vicious practices?" And he said, "The husband should put her away, and remain by himself. But if he put his wife away and marry another, he also commits adultery." And I said to him, "What if the woman put away should repent, and wish to return to her husband: shall she not be taken back by her husband?" And he said to me, "Assuredly. If the husband do not take her back, he sins, and brings a great sin upon himself, for he ought to take back the sinner who has repented. But not frequently. For there is but one repentance to the servants of God. In case, therefore, that the divorced wife may repent, the husband ought not to marry another, when his wife has been put away. In this matter man and woman are to be treated exactly in the same way.

And I said to him, "I should like to continue my questions." "Speak on," said he. And I said, "I heard, sir, some teachers maintain that there is no other repentance than that which takes place, when we descended into the water and received remission of our former sins,' He said to me, "That was sound doctrine which you heard; for that is really the case. For he who has received remission of his sins ought not to sin any more, but to live in purity. Since, however, you inquire diligently into all things, I will point this also out to you, not as giving occasion for error to those who are to believe, or have lately believed, in the Lord. For those who have now believed, and those who are to believe, have not repentance for their sins; but they have remission of their previous sins. For to those who have been called before these days, the Lord has set repentance. For the Lord knowing the heart, and foreknowing all things, knew the weakness of men and the manifold wiles of the devil, that he would inflict some evil on the servants of God, and would act wickedly towards them. The Lord, therefore, being merciful, has had mercy on the work of His hand, and has set repentance for them; and He has entrusted to me power over this repentance. And therefore I say to you, that if any one is tempted by the devil, and sins after that great and holy calling in which the Lord has called His people to everlasting life, he has opportunity to repent but once. But if he should sin frequently after this, and then repent, to such a man his repentance will be of no avail; for with difficulty will he live." And I said, "Sir, I feel that life has come back to me in listening attentively to these commandments; for I know that I shall be saved, if in future I sin no more." And he said, "You will be saved, you and all who keep these commandments."

COMMANDMENT FIFTH

Of sadness of heart, and of patience

"Be patient," said he, "and of good understanding, and you will rule over every wicked work, and you will work all righteousness. For if you be patient, the Holy Spirit that dwells in you will be pure. He will not be darkened by any evil spirit, but, dwelling in a broad region, he will rejoice and be glad; and with the vessel in which he dwells he will serve God in gladness, having great peace within himself. But if any outburst of anger take place forthwith the Holy Spirit, who is tender, is straitened, not having a pure place, and He seeks to depart. For he is choked by the vile spirit, and cannot attend on the Lord as he wishes, for anger pollutes him. For the Lord dwells in long-suffering, but the devil in anger."

"Hear now," said he, "how wicked is the action of anger, and in what way it overthrows the servants of God by its action, and turns them from righteousness. But it does not turn away those who are full of faith, nor does it act on them, for the power of the Lord is with them. It is the thoughtless and doubting that it turns away. Now this patience dwells with those who have complete faith. But anger is foolish, and fickle, and senseless. Now, of folly is begotten bitterness, and of bitterness anger, and of anger frenzy. This frenzy, the product of so many evils, ends in great and incurable sin. . . . Wherefore do you depart from that most wicked spirit anger, and put on patience, and resist anger and bitterness, and you will be found in company with the purity which is loved by the Lord."

COMMANDMENT SIXTH

How to recognize the two spirits attendant on each man, and how to distinguish the suggestions of the one from those of the other

"I gave you," he said, "directions in the first commandment to attend to faith, and fear, and self-restraint. Trust you, therefore, the righteous, but put no trust in the unrighteous. For the path of righteousness is straight, but that of unrighteousness is crooked. But walk in the straight and even way, and mind not the crooked."

"Hear now," said he, "in regard to faith. There are two angels with a man — one of righteousness, and the other of iniquity. The angel of righteousness is gentle and modest, meek and peaceful. When, therefore, he ascends into your heart, forthwith he talks to you of righteousness, purity, chastity, contentment, and of every righteous deed and glorious virtue. Trust him, then, and his works. Look now at the works of the angel of iniquity. First, he is wrathful, and bitter, and foolish, and his works are evil, and ruin the servants of God. When, then, he ascends into your heart, know him by his works. When anger comes upon you, or harshness, know that he is in you; and you will know this to be the case also, when you are attacked by a longing after many transactions, and the richest delicacies, and drunken revels, and divers luxuries, and things improper, and by a hankering after women, and by overreaching, and pride, and blustering, and by whatever is like to these. When these ascend into your heart, know that the angel of iniquity is in you. Now that you know his works, depart from him, and in no respect trust him, because his deeds are evil, and unprofitable to the servants of God. These, then, are the actions of both angels."

COMMANDMENT SEVENTH

On fearing God, and not fearing the devil

"Fear," said he, "the Lord, and keep His commandments. For if you keep the commandments of God, you will be powerful in every action, and every one of your actions will be incomparable. For, fearing the Lord, you will do all things well. This is the fear which you ought to have, that you may be saved. But fear not the devil; for, fearing the Lord, you will have dominion over the devil, for there is no power in him. Fear, therefore, the deeds of the devil, since they are wicked, for, fearing the Lord, you will not do these deeds, but will refrain from them. For fears are of two kinds: for if you do not wish to do that which is evil, fear the Lord, and you will not do it; but, again, if you wish to do that which is good, fear the Lord, and you will do it. Wherefore the fear of the Lord is strong, and great, and glorious."

COMMANDMENT EIGHTH

We ought to shun that which is evil, and do that which is good

"Restrain yourself in regard to evil, and do it not; but exercise no restraint in regard to good, but do it. For if you exercise restraint in the doing of good, you will commit a great sin; but if you exercise restraint, so as not to do that which is evil, you are practicing great righteousness. Restrain yourself, therefore, from all iniquity, and do that which is good." "What, sir," say I, "are the evil deeds from which we must restrain ourselves?" "Hear," says he: "from adultery and fornication, from unlawful revelling, from wicked luxury, from indulgence in many kinds of food and the extravagance of riches, and from boastfulness, and haughtiness, and insolence, and lies, and backbiting, and hypocrisy from the remembrance of wrong, and from all slander. These are the deeds that are most wicked in the life of men. From all these deeds, therefore, the servant of God must restrain himself. For he who does not restrain himself from these, cannot live to God. Listen, then, to the deeds that accompany these." "Are there, sir," said I, "any other evil deeds?" "There are," says he; "and many of them, too, from which the servant of God must restrain himself — theft, lying, robbery, false witness, overreaching, wicked lust, deceit, vain glory, boastfulness, and all other vices like to these." "Do you not think that these are really wicked?" "Exceedingly wicked in the servants of God."

"But listen," says he, "to the things in regard to which you have not to exercise self-restraint, but which you ought to do. Restrain not yourself in regard to that which is good, but do it." ". . . First of all there is faith, then fear of the Lord, love, concord, words of righteousness, truth, patience. Than these, nothing is better in the life of men. Then there are the following attendant on these: helping widows, looking after orphans and the needy, rescuing the servants of God from necessities, being hospitable — for in hospitality good-doing finds a field — never opposing any one, being quiet, having fewer needs than all men, reverencing the aged, practicing righteousness, watching the brotherhood, bearing insolence, being long-suffering, encouraging those who are sick in soul, not casting those who have fallen into sin from the faith, but turning them back and restoring them to peace of mind, admonishing sinners, not oppressing debtors and the needy, and if there are any other actions like these. Do these seem to you good?" says he. "For what, sir," say I, "is better than these?" "Walk then in them," says he, "and restrain not yourself from them, and you will live to God."

COMMANDMENT NINTH

Prayer must be made to God without ceasing and with unwavering confidence

He says to me, "Put away doubting from you, and do not hesitate to ask of the Lord, saying to yourself, 'How can I ask of the Lord and receive from Him, seeing I have sinned so much against Him?' Do not thus reason with yourself. . . . For He is not like men, who remember evils done against them; but He himself remembers not evils, and has compassion on His own creature. Cleanse, therefore, your heart from all the vanities of this world, and from the words already mentioned, and ask of the Lord and you will receive all. But if you doubt in your heart, you will receive none of your requests. But those who are perfect in faith ask everything, trusting in the Lord; and they obtain, because they ask nothing doubting, and not being double-souled. For every double-souled man, even if he repent, will with difficulty be saved. Cleanse your heart, therefore, from all doubt, and put on faith, because it is strong, and trust God that you will obtain from Him all that you ask. And if at any time, after you have asked of the Lord, you are slower in obtaining your request [than you expected], do not doubt because you have not soon obtained the request of your soul; for invariably it is on account of some temptation or some sin of which you are ignorant that you are slower in obtaining your request. Wherefore do not cease to make the request of your soul, and you will obtain it.

COMMANDMENT TENTH

Of grief, and not grieving
the Spirit of God which is in us

"Those who have never searched for the truth, nor investigated the nature of the Divinity, but have simply believed, when they devote themselves to and become mixed up with business, and wealth, and heathen friendships, and many other actions of this world, do not perceive the parables of Divinity; for their minds are darkened by these actions, and they are corrupted and become dried up. Those, on the other hand, who have the fear of God, and search after Godhead and truth, and have their hearts turned to the Lord, quickly perceive and understand what is said to them, because they have the fear of the Lord in them. For where the Lord dwells, there is much understanding. Cleave, then, to the Lord, and you will understand and perceive all things."

COMMANDMENT ELEVENTH

The Spirit and prophets to be tried by their works;
also of the two kinds of spirit

First, he who has the Divine Spirit proceeding from above is meek, and peaceable, and humble, and refrains from all iniquity and the vain desire of his world, and contents himself with fewer wants than those of other men, and when asked he makes no reply; nor does he speak privately, nor when man wishes the spirit to speak does the Holy Spirit speak, but it speaks only when God wishes it to speak. When, then, a man having the Divine Spirit comes into an assembly of righteous men who have faith in the Divine Spirit, and this assembly of men offers up prayer to God, then the angel of the prophetic Spirit, who is destined for him, fills the man; and the man being filled with the Holy Spirit, speaks to the multitude as the Lord wishes. Thus, then, will the Spirit of Divinity become manifest. Whatever power therefore comes from the Spirit of Divinity belongs to the Lord. Hear, then," says he, "in regard to the spirit which is earthly, and empty and powerless, and foolish. First, the man who seems to have the Spirit exalts himself, and wishes to have the first seat, and is bold, and impudent, and talkative, and lives in the midst of many luxuries and many other delusions, and takes rewards for his prophesy; and if he does not receive rewards, he does not prophesy. Can, then, the Divine Spirit take rewards and prophesy? It is not possible that the prophet of God should do this, but prophets of this character are possed by an earthly spirit. . . . Hear, then, the parable which I am to tell you. Take a stone, and throw it to the sky, and see if you can touch it. Or again, take a squirt of water and squirt into the sky, and see if you can penetrate the sky." "How, sir," say I, "can these things take place? For both of them are impossible." "As these things," says he, "are impossible, so also are the earthly spirits powerless and pithless. But look, on the other hand, at the power which comes from above. Hail is of the size of a very small grain, yet when it falls on a man's head how much annoyance it gives him! Or, again, take the drop which falls from a pitcher to the ground, and yet it hollows a stone. You see, then, that the smallest things coming from above have great power when they fall upon the earth. Thus also is the Divine Spirit, which comes from above, powerful. Trust, then, that Spirit, but have nothing to do with the other."

COMMANDMENT TWELFTH

On the twofold desire. The commandments of God can be kept, and believers ought not to fear the devil

He says to me, "Put away from you all wicked desire, and clothe yourself with good and chaste desire; for clothed with this desire you will hate wicked desire, and will rein yourself in even as you wish. For wicked desire is wild, and is with difficulty tamed. . . ." "What then, sir," say I, "are the deeds of wicked desire which deliver men over to death? Make them known to me, and I will refrain from them." "Listen, then, to the works in which evil desire slays the servants of God.

"Foremost of all is the desire after another's wife or husband, and after extravagance, and many useless dainties and drinks, and many other foolish luxuries; for all luxury is foolish and empty in servants of God. These, then, are the evil desires which slay the servants of God. . . . Put you on, then, the desire of righteousness; and arming yourself with the fear of the Lord, resist them. For the fear of the Lord dwells in good desire.

If you serve good desire, and be subject to it, you will gain the mastery over evil desire, and make it subject to you even as you wish."

"I should like to know," say I, "in what way I ought to serve good desire." "Hear," says he: "You will practice righteousness and virtue, truth and the fear of the Lord, faith and meekness, and whatsoever excellences are like to these. Practicing these, you will be a well-pleasing servant of God, and you will live to Him; and every one who shall serve good desire, shall live to God." I say to him, "Sir, these commandments are great, and good, and glorious, and fitted to gladden the heart of the man who can perform them. But I do not know if these commandments can be kept by man, because they are exceeding hard." He answered and said to me, "If you lay it down as certain that they can be kept, then you will easily keep them, and they will not be hard. But if you come to imagine that they cannot be kept by any man, then you will not keep them. Now I say to you, If you do not keep them, but neglect them, you will not be saved, nor your children, nor your house, since you have already determined for yourself that these commandments cannot be kept by man."

"But I, the angel of repentance, say to you, Fear not the devil; for I was sent," says he, "to be with you who repent with all your heart, and to make you strong in faith. Trust God, then, ye who on account of your sins have despaired of life, and who add to your sins and weight down your life; for if ye return to the Lord with all your heart, and practice righteousness the rest of your days, and serve Him according to His will, He will heal your former — sins, and you will have power to hold away over the works of the devil. But as to the threats of the devil, fear them not at all, for he is powerless as the sinews of a dead man. Give ear to me, then, and fear Him who has all power, both to save and destroy, and keep His commandments, and ye will live to God." I say to him, "Sir, I am now made strong in all the ordinances of the Lord, because you are with me; and I know that you will crush all the power of the devil, and we shall have rule over him, and shall prevail against all his works. And I hope, sir, to be able to keep all these commandments which you have enjoined upon me, the Lord strengthening me." "You will keep them," says he, "if your heart be pure towards the Lord; and all will keep them who cleanse their hearts from the vain desires of this world, and they will live to God."

All selections taken from "The Pastor of Hermas" are from
Ante-Nicene Fathers,
Translations of the Writings of the Fathers Down to A.D. 325,
The Reverend Alexander Roberts, D.D. and James Donaldson, LL.D., editors,
Volume II, Buffalo: The Christian Literature Publishing Company, 1887

Part II
Early Clarification of Catholic Teachings

Introduction

The point of view here shifts somewhat to the literary form of an Apology, a defense of Catholic teachings and practices against the criticisms and persecution of anti-Christian civil and religious authorities.

In the *Letter to Diognetus* we find a criticism of the worship of the man-made images "made of stone, brass, wood, silver, iron, and earthenware" that were considered as gods by the Greeks in spite of the fact that being destitute of sense and intelligence, they are really inferior to people. The main part of the Letter is a concise, clear, and comprehensive presentation and explanation of the basic beliefs that distinguish the Christians from the others with whom they live. The letter is an outstanding example of the continuity of Catholic teachings of faith and morals with the classics of the first section.

Justin Martyr, also called "the philosopher," gives another example of the apology form. Along with the other Greek apologists of the second century A.D., he holds that Greek philosophy prepared the way for the Christian religion and that, although the Christian religion did not need philosophy, philosophy could be a useful instrument for the explanation of Christian beliefs. Clement of Alexandria especially agreed.

Aristides of Athens and Tatian demonstrate the existence of God from the order in the world; Athenagoras and Theophilus use the contingency of things as a basis for the same conviction; Aristides also uses motion as a starting point; Justin uses the basic Platonic idea of the community of many perfections in the one absolute perfection. Adding God as the absolute first cause (Creator) of the world, they give a clear presentation of what was later called the five ways of Thomas Aquinas for proving the existence of God. They emphasize that one can learn about the eternal and invisible attributes of God from the contemplation of the created, visible things of experience — as related by Paul in his Letter to the Romans. The infinity of God is not emphasized probably because the current Greek word for infinity was *apeiron*, which the philosophers used to refer to what is infinite in the sense of having no positive characteristics, not qualified in any positive way, capable of being formed into anything.

Human souls are considered as directly created by God and endowed with liberty, freedom of choice. Justin, as well as others, emphasizes that, though people have free choice, that does not mean that every choice is morally good; some choices are morally bad because they oppose the nature of man and God and the fundamental laws of the Church. All forms of moral relativism and moral subjectivism are explicitly opposed.

The Apologists are witnesses to the existence of the Gospels of Matthew, Mark, Luke, and John with frequent references to certain statements in the Gospels to substantiate what they present. They also show that they were familiar with many of the ideas and writings of the philosophers before Plato — including Socrates, and those of Plato and Aristotle, the Stoics, Epicureans, and Skeptics, all of whom are mentioned by name. The same is true of Clement of Alexandria and others of the same time.

Lactantius, the Christian Cicero, is impressive, along with Cyprian, for his emphasis on the unity of the Church as regards the belief of its members and of the Magisterium, centered worldwide in the bishop of Rome and geographically in the local bishops and the consilium of all bishops. This appears in the Councils convened to decide on the appropriate formulas of the teachings of the Church.

Chapter 11 • Letter to Diognetus

Nothing is known about the author of this letter or about the time of its composition or about the Diognetus to whom it was addressed, other than the author's claim to having been "a disciple of the Apostles" and "a teacher of the Gentiles." If this Diognetus is the same as the tutor of Marcus Aurelius (A.D. 121-180), we may have a definite bit of information for putting it in this place just before Justin Martyr. From internal evidence there could be a well-founded conjecture that it is one of the many extant examples of the classic Apologies so numerous in the second and third centuries.

The Letter is noteworthy for many reasons. There is no doubt but that the author is a well-educated and cultured Hellene. He gives evidence of a broad and well-founded acquaintance with Greek and Roman philosophy. He is among those who work out a harmonious relationship between faith and reason at this time, and he naturally and smoothly presents rational evidence for the clarification of many theological points. Gerald G. Walsh, S.J., considered him "a fervent Christian filled with Pauline convictions, a humanist who had achieved a remarkable harmony of supernatural faith and charity, with a highly cultivated intelligence, literary taste, conscience, and social sense. The calm and clarity of his thought reveal a master of logic, the deep convictions of a serious thinker, the eloquence of a trained rhetorician, the breadth of mind and warmth of heart, the poise of an educated gentleman." The Letter is a useful vehicle to serve as a transition to the more sophisticated documents of the second part of our collection.

Since I see thee, most excellent Diognetus, exceedingly desirous to learn the mode of worshiping God prevalent among the Christians, and inquiring very carefully and earnestly concerning them, what God they trust in, and what form of religion they observe, so as all to look down upon the world itself, and despise death, while they neither esteem those to be gods that are reckoned such by the Greeks, nor hold to the superstition of the Jews; and what is the affection which they cherish among themselves; and why, in fine, this new kind or practice [of piety] has only now entered into the world, and not long ago; I cordially welcome this thy desire.

Come, then, after you have freed yourself from all prejudices possessing your mind, and laid aside what you have been accustomed to, as something apt to deceive you, and being made, as if from the beginning, a new man, inasmuch as, according to your own confession, you are to be the hearer of a new [system of] doctrine; come and contemplate, not with your eyes only, but with your understanding, the substance and the form of those whom ye declare and deem to be gods. Is not one of them a stone similar to that on which we tread? Is not a second brass, in no way superior to those vessels which are constructed for our ordinary use? Is not a third wood, and that already rotten? Is not a fourth silver, which needs a man to watch it, lest it be stolen? Is not a fifth iron, consumed by rust? Is not a sixth earthenware, in no degree more valuable than that which is formed for the humblest purposes? Are not all these of corruptible matter? Was not every one of them, before they were formed by the arts of these [workmen] into the shape of these [gods], each in its own way subject to change? Are they not all deaf? Are they not blind? Are they not without life? Are they not destitute of feeling? Are they not incapable of motion? Are they not all liable to rot? Are they not all corruptible? These things ye call gods; these ye serve; these ye worship; and ye become altogether like to them. For this reason ye hate the Christians, because they do not deem these to be gods. But do not ye yourselves, who now think and suppose [such to be gods], much more cast contempt upon them than they [the Christians do]? Do ye not much more mock and insult them, when ye worship those that are made of stone and earthenware, without appointing any person to guard them; but those made of silver and gold ye shut up by night, and appoint watchers to look after them by day, lest they be stolen? And by those gifts which ye mean to present to them, do ye not, if they are possessed of sense, rather punish [than honor] them? But if, on the other hand, they are destitute of sense, ye convict them of this fact, while ye worship them with blood and the smoke of sacrifices. But not a single human being will, unless compelled to it, endure such treatment, since he is endowed with sense and reason. A stone, however, readily bears it, seeing it is insensible. Certainly you do not show [by your conduct] that he [your God] is possessed of sense.

And next, I imagine that you are most desirous of hearing something on this point, that the Christians do not observe the same forms of divine worship as do the Jews. The Jews, then, if they abstain from the kind of service above described, and deem it proper to worship one God as being Lord of all, [are right], but if they offer Him worship in the way which we have described, they greatly err. For while the Gentiles, by offering such things to those that are destitute of sense and hearing, furnish an example of madness; they, on the other hand, by thinking to offer these things to God as if He needed them, might justly reckon it rather an act of folly than of divine worship. For He that made heaven and earth, and all that is therein, and gives to us all the things of which we stand in need, certainly requires none of those things which He Himself bestows on such as think of furnishing them to Him. But those who imagine that, by means of blood, and the smoke of sacrifices and burnt-offerings, they offer sacrifices [acceptable] to Him, and that by such honors they show Him respect — these, by supposing that they can give anything to Him who stands in need of nothing, appear to me in no respect to differ from those who studiously confer the same honor on things destitute of sense, and which therefore are unable to enjoy such honors.

For the Christians are distinguished from other men neither by country, nor language, nor the customs which they observe. For they neither inhabit cities of their own, nor employ a particular form of speech, nor lead a life which is marked out by any singularity. The course of conduct which they follow has not been devised by any speculation or deliberation of inquisitive men; nor do they, like some, proclaim themselves the advocates of any merely human doctrines. But, inhabiting Greek as well as barbarian cities, according as the lot of each of them had determined, and following the customs of the natives in respect to clothing, food, and the rest of their ordinary conduct, they display to us their wonderful and confessedly striking method of life. They dwell in their own countries, but simply as sojourners. As citizens, they share in all things with others, and yet endure all things as if foreigners. Every foreign land is to them as their native country, and every land of their birth as a land of strangers. They marry, as do all [others]; they beget children; but they do not destroy their offspring. They have a common table, but not a common bed. They are in the flesh, but they do not live after the flesh. They pass their days on earth, but they are citizens of heaven. They obey the prescribed laws, and at the same time surpass the laws by their lives. They love all men, and are persecuted by all. They are unknown and condemned; they are put to death, and restored to life. They are poor, yet make many rich; they are in lack of all things, and yet abound in all; they are dishonored, and yet in their very dishonor are glorified. They are evil spoken of, and yet are justified; they are reviled, and bless; they are insulted, and repay the insult with honor; they do good, yet are punished as evil-doers. When punished, they rejoice as if quickened into life; they are assailed by the Jews as foreigners, and are persecuted by the Greeks; yet those who hate them are unable to assign any reason for their hatred.

To sum up all in one word — what the soul is in the body, that the Christians in the world. The soul is dispersed through all the members of the body, and Christians are scattered through all the cities of the world. The soul dwells in the body, yet is not of the body; and Christians dwell in the world, yet are not of the world. The visible soul is guarded by the visible body, and Christians are known indeed to be in the world, but their godliness remains visible. The flesh hates the soul, and wars against it, though itself suffering no injury, because it is prevented from enjoying pleasures; the world also hates the Christians, though in no wise injured, because they abjure pleasures. The soul loves the flesh that hates it, and [loves also] the members; Christians likewise love those that hate them. The soul is imprisoned in the body, yet preserves that very body; and Christians are confined in the world as in a prison, and yet they are the preservers of the world. The immortal soul dwells in a mortal tabernacle; and Christians dwell as sojourners in corruptible [bodies], looking for an incorruptible dwelling in the heavens. The soul, when but ill-provided with food and drink, becomes better; in like manner, the Christians, though subjected day by day to punishment, increase the more in number. God has assigned them this illustrious position, which it were unlawful for them [to] forsake.

For, as I said, this was no mere earthly invention which was delivered to them, nor is it a mere human system of opinion, which they judge it right to preserve so carefully, nor has a dispensation of mere human mysteries been committed to them, but truly God himself, who is almighty, the Creator of all things, and invisible, has sent from heaven, and placed among men, [Him who is] the truth, and the holy and incomprehensible Word, and has firmly established Him in their hearts. He did not, as one might have imagined, send to men any servant, or angel, or ruler, or any one of those who bear sway over earthly things, or one of those to whom the government of things in the heavens has been entrusted, but the very Creator and Fashioner of all things — by whom He made the heaven, — by whom he enclosed the sea within its proper bounds — whose ordinances all the stars faithfully observe — from whom the sun has received the measure of his daily course to be observed — whom the moon obeys, being commanded to shine in the night, and whom the stars also obey, following the moon in her course; by whom all things have been arranged, and placed within their proper limits, and to whom all are subject — the heavens and the things that are therein, the earth and the things that are therein, the sea and the things that are therein — fire, air, and the abyss — the things which are in the heights, the things which are in the depths, and the things which lie between. This [messenger] He sent to them. Was it then, as one might conceive, for the purpose of exercising tyranny, or of inspiring fear and terror? By no means, but under the influence of clemency and meekness. As a king sends his son, who is also a king, so sent He Him; as God He sent Him; as to men He sent Him; as a Saviour He sent Him, and as seeking to persuade, not to compel us; for violence has no place in the character of God. As calling us He sent Him, not as vengeful pursuing us; as loving us He sent Him, not as judging us. For He will yet send Him to judge us, and who shall endure His appearing?. . . Do you not see them exposed to wild beasts, that they may be persuaded to deny the Lord, and yet not overcome? Do you not see that the more of them that are punished, the greater becomes the number of the rest? This does not seem to be the work of man: this is the power of God; these are the evidences of His manifestation.

For, who of men at all understood before His coming what God is? Do you accept of the vain and silly doctrines of those who are deemed trustworthy philosophers? of whom some said that fire was God, calling that God to which they themselves were by and by to come; and some water; and others some other of the elements formed by God. But if any one of these theories be worthy of approbation, every one of the rest of created things might also be declared to be God. But such declarations are simply the startling and erroneous utterances of deceivers; and no man has either seen Him, or made Him known, but He has revealed himself. And He has manifested Himself through faith, to which alone it is given to behold God. For God, the Lord and Fashioner of all things, who made all things, and assigned them their several positions, proved Himself not merely a friend of people, but also long-suffering [in His dealings with them]. Yea, he was always of such a character, and still is, and will ever be, kind and good, and free from wrath, and true, and the only one who is [absolutely] good; and He formed in His mind a great and unspeakable conception, which He communicated to His Son alone. As long, then, as

He held and preserved His own wise counsel in concealment, He appeared to neglect us, and to have no care over us. But after He revealed and laid open, through His beloved Son, the things which had been prepared from the beginning. He conferred every blessing all at once upon us, so that we should both share in His benefits, and see and be active [in His service]. Who of us would ever have expected these things? He was aware, then, of all things in His own mind, along with His Son, according to the relation subsisting between them.

As long then as the former time endured, He permitted us to be borne along by unruly impulses, being drawn away by the desire of pleasure and various lusts. This was not that He at all delighted in our sins, but that He simply endured them; nor that He approved the time of working iniquity which then was, but that He sought to form a mind conscious of righteousness, so that being convinced in that time of our unworthiness of attaining life through our own works, it should now, through the kindness of God, be vouchsafed to us; and having made it manifest that in ourselves we were unable to enter into the kingdom of God, we might through the power of God be made able. But when our wickedness had reached its height, and it had been clearly shown that its reward, punishment, and death, was impending over us and when the time had come which God had before appointed for manifesting His own kindness and power, how the one love of God, through exceeding regard for men, did not regard us with hatred, nor thrust us away, nor remember our iniquity against us, but showed great long-suffering, and bore with us, He himself took on Him the burden of our iniquities, He gave His own Son as a ransom for us, the holy One for transgressors, the blameless One for the wicked, the righteous One for the unrighteous, the incorruptible One for the corruptible, the immortal One for them that are mortal. For what other thing was capable of covering our sins than His righteousness? By what other one was it possible that we, the wicked and ungodly, could be justified, than by the only Son of God? O sweet exchange! O searchable operation! O benefits surpassing all expectation! that the wickedness of many should be hid in a single righteous One, and that the righteousness of One should justify many transgressors! Having therefore convinced us in the former time that our nature was unable to attain to life, and having now revealed the Savior who is able to save even those things which it was [formerly] impossible to save, by both these facts He desired to lead us to trust in His kindness, to esteem Him our Nourisher, Father, Teacher, Counselor, Healer, our Wisdom, Light, Honor, Glory, Power, and Life, so that we should not be anxious concerning clothing and food.

If you also desire [to possess] this faith, you likewise shall receive first of all the knowledge of the Father. For God has loved people, on whose account He made the world, to whom He rendered subject all the things that are in it, to whom He gave reason and understanding, to whom alone He imparted the privilege of looking upwards to himself whom He formed after His own image, to whom He sent His only begotten Son, to whom He has promised a kingdom in heaven, and will give it to those who have loved Him. And when you have attained this knowledge, with what joy do you think you will be filled? Or, how will you love Him who has first so loved you? And if you love Him, you will be an imitator of His kindness. And do not wonder that a man may become an imitator of God. He can, if he is willing. For it is not by ruling over his neighbors, or by seeking to hold the supremacy over those that are weaker, or by being rich, and showing violence towards those that are inferior, that happiness is found; nor can any one by these things become an imitator of God. But these things do not at all constitute His majesty. On the contrary he who takes upon himself the burden of his neighbor; he who, in whatsoever respect he may be superior, is ready to benefit another who is deficient; he who, whatsoever things he has received from God, by distributing these to the needy, becomes a god to those who receive [his benefits]: he is an imitator of God. Then thou shalt see, while still on earth, that God in the heavens rules over [the universe]; then thou shalt begin to speak the mysteries of God; then shalt thou both love and admire those that suffer punishment because they will not deny God; then shalt thou condemn the deceit and error of the world when thou shalt know what it is to live truly in heaven, when thou shalt despise that which is here esteemed to be death, when thou shalt fear what is truly death, which is reserved for those who shall be condemned to the eternal fire, which shall afflict those even to the end that are committed to it. Then shalt thou admire those who for righteousness' sake endure the fire that is but for a moment, and shalt count them happy when thou shalt know [the nature of] that fire.

I do not speak of things strange to me, nor do I aim at anything consistent with right reason; but having been a disciple of the apostles, I am become a teacher of the Gentiles. I minister the things delivered to me to those that are disciples worthy of the truth. For who that is rightly taught and begotten by the loving Word, would not seek to learn accurately the things which have been clearly shown by the Word to His disciples, to whom the Word being manifested has revealed them, speaking plainly [to them], not understood indeed by the unbelieving, but conversing with the disciples, who, being esteemed faithful by Him acquired a knowledge of the mysteries of the Father? For which reason He sent the Word, that He might be manifested to the world; and He, being despised by the people [of the Jews], was, when preached by the apostles, believed in by the Gentiles. This is He who was from the beginning, who appeared as if new, and was found old, and yet who is ever born afresh in the hearts of the saints. This is He who, being from everlasting, is today called the Son; through whom the church is enriched, and grace, widely spread, increases in the saints, furnishing understanding, revealing mysteries, announcing times, rejoicing over the faithful, giving to those that seek, by whom the limits of faith are not broken through, nor the boundaries set by the fathers passed over. Then the fear of the law is changed, and the grace of the prophets is known, and the faith of the gospels is established, and the tradition of the apostles is preserved, and the grace of the church exults; which grace if you grieve not, you shall know those things which the Word teaches, by whom He wills, and when He pleases. For whatever things we are moved to utter by the will of the Word commanding us, we communicate to you with pains, and from love of the things that have been revealed to us.

When you have read and carefully listened to these things, you shall know what God bestows on such as rightly love Him, being made [as ye are] a paradise of delight, presenting in yourselves a tree bearing all kinds of produce and flourishing well, being adorned with various fruits. For in this place the tree of knowledge and the tree of life have been planted; but it is not the tree of knowledge that destroys — it is disobedience that proves destructive. Nor truly are those words without significance which are written, how God from the beginning planted the tree of life in the midst of paradise, revealing through knowledge the way to life, and when those who were first formed did not use this [knowledge] properly, they were, through the fraud of the serpent, stripped naked. For neither can life exist without knowledge, nor is knowledge secure without life. Wherefore both were planted close together. The apostle, perceiving the force [of this conjunction], and blaming that knowledge which, without true doctrine, is admitted to influence life, declares, "Knowledge puffeth up, but love edifieth." For he who thinks he knows anything without true knowledge, and such as is witnessed to by life, knows nothing, but is deceived by the serpent, as not loving life. But he who combines knowledge with fear, and seeks after life, plants in hope, looking for fruit. Let your heart by our wisdom; and let your life be true knowledge inwardly received. Bearing this tree and displaying its fruit, thou shalt always gather in those things which are desired by God, which the serpent cannot reach, and to which deception does not approach; nor is Eve then corrupted, but is trusted as a virgin; and salvation is manifested, and the apostles are filled with understanding, and the passover of the Lord advances, and the choirs are gathered together, and are arranged in proper order, and the Word rejoices in teaching the saints — by whom the Father is glorified: to whom be glory forever. Amen.

All selections taken from the "Letter to Diognetus" are from
The Writings of the Apostolic Fathers,
Translated by Drs. Robert Donaldson and E. Crombie,
Edinburgh: T. & T. Clark, 1867

Chapter 12 • Justin Martyr: *The Second Apology*; Irenaeus: *Against Heresies*

Historians are agreed that Justin was born in Flavia Neapolis (Nablûs) in Samaria, ca. A.D. 100-110, of pagan and Greco-Roman parents. He received an excellent education and traveled widely in search of the philosophy of life. He attended the schools of the Stoics, Aristotelians, Pythagoreans, and Platonists. The latter attracted him most, and actually the teaching of the Platonists served as a basis for his conversion to Catholicism, which he terms "the only certain and useful philosophy." He is said to have settled in Rome and to have opened a school devoted to philosophy. One of his pupils was Tatian. He was decapitated by order of Rusticus the Prefect of Rome, ca. A.D. 165. Of the works attributed to Justin, the two *Apologies* and *Dialogue with Trypho* are generally accepted as authentic. The excerpts from the *Second Apology* are presented as a classic example of the early apologetic Christian literature.

In all his printings Justin shows his indebtedness to Greek philosophy, especially Platonic. He was among those who worked out at this time a satisfactory relationship between Christian theology and philosophy and thereby avoided falling into the errors of Gnosticism. Unlike the author of the *Letter to Diognetus*, Justin is unsure about the appropriate philosophical terms to apply to the Triune God and to the relationship between the Persons of that Trinity, or to the soul and its relationship to the body on the one hand and the Spirit of God on the other. He is a good witness to the fundamental difficulties encountered by the educated converts of the second and third centuries when they tried to express in philosophical terms the basic dogmas of their faith.

The short excerpt from the lengthy treatise of Irenaeus (A.D. 126/40-202), Bishop of Lyons, *Against Heresies*, is included because of its emphasis on the traditional "marks" or characteristics associated with the Catholic Church — i.e., that it is "one, holy, catholic, and apostolic." Irenaeus traces the successors of St. Peter in an unbroken line down to Eleutherius. Hence we know that this section of the treatise was composed between A.D. 175 and 189, while Eleutherius was Pope.

The Second Apology for the Christians to Antoninus Pius

Even the deeds that were done yesterday and the day before in our city by Urbicus, O Romans, and those which in like manner are unreasonably perpetrated by your governors in all parts, compel me to frame this composition of argument, in behalf of us. But in order that the very cause of the whole thing that Urbicus did may be made plain to you, I will relate all that was done.

A certain woman had a husband who was intemperate, she herself also formerly being intemperate. But when she knew the doctrines of Christ, she was brought to self-control; and endeavored to persuade her husband to the same, relating these doctrines, and teaching him that there would be a future punishment in eternal fire, for all who did not govern their lives by moderation and right reason. But he continued in the same excesses, and by his conduct alienated his wife from him; when her husband went into Alexandria, and was said to be acting worse, she, that she might not be a partaker in his sins and impieties, by remaining in her connection with him, and continuing to share his table and his bed, gave him what you call the bill of divorce, and was separated. But this good and admirable husband, when she had parted from him against his will, laid an accusation against her, declaring that she was a Christian. And she addressed a petition to you, O Emperor, praying that she might first be permitted to arrange her affairs, and then, after they were set in order, she would defend herself on the subject of the accusation, and you granted her petition. Her former husband then, being now unable to reply to her, turned in the following manner on a certain Ptolemaeus, who was her teacher in the Christian doctrines, whom Urbicus punished; he persuaded the centurions who threw Ptolemaeus into prison, to take him, and ask him this single question alone: Was he a Christian? And Ptolemaeus, who was a lover of truth, and no wise disposed to be a deceiver or falsifier, confessed himself to be a Christian; on which the centurion caused him to be put in bonds, and confined him for a long time in the prison. At last, when he came before Urbicus, he was likewise asked this same question only, if he were a Christian. And he again, knowing the blessings he had derived through the doctrine of Christ, confessed the school of divine virtue. . . . And when Urbicus commanded him to be led away to execution, a certain Lucius, who was also himself a Christian, seeing the decision that was thus unreasonably given, said to Urbicus, "What is the reason of your punishing this man, who is neither an adulterer, nor a fornicator, nor a murderer, nor a thief, nor a robber, and who is not convicted of having committed any offense whatever, but who confesses himself to bear the name of a Christian? You judge not, O Urbicus, in such a manner as becomes the Emperor Pius, or the Philosopher the son of Caesar, or the sacred Senate." He gave no other reply to Lucius than merely this: "You yourself also appear to me to be such a one"; and, when Lucius answered: "Certainly I am"; he commanded him also, in turn, to be led away. . . . And some other third person coming up, was in like manner condemned to punishment.

I also expect to be entrapped by some of those whom I have mentioned, and to be affixed to the stake, even perhaps by Crescens, that lover of noise and boasting: for it is not fit to term the man a lover of wisdom, who accuses us in public of what he knows nothing of; as if Christians were atheists, and wicked persons; acting thus to gain the grace and favor of the deluded multitude. For if he attacks us with studying the doctrines of Christ, he is utterly wicked, and far worse than the common people, who often take care not to speak about subjects they do not understand, and bear false witness. Or, if he have read them, and have not understood the sublimity of their contents; or have understood it, and acts thus that he may not be suspected of being a Christian; he is far more base and utterly depraved, as being a slave to popular and senseless opinion and fear. For I wish you to know, that I proposed and asked him certain questions of [this kind] both to ascertain, and to prove, that he really knows nothing, and that I speak truth. If these disputations have not been reported to you, I am ready to repeat my questions again even in your presence, and it would even be a deed worthy of you as Emperor. But, if my questions and his answers are known to you, you must see that he knows nothing of our customs, or, if he knows them, that he does not dare to speak of them as Socrates would have done, through fear of his hearers: proving himself not a lover of Wisdom, as I have already said, but a lover of vainglory, who values not that admirable saying of Socrates, that no man should be honored before the truth; but it is impossible for a Cynic, who asserts the End to be indifferent, to know any good but indifference.

But, lest any one should say to us, Do you all then destroy yourselves, and go at once to God, and give us no trouble! I will tell you why we do not so; and why, when we are interrogated, we fearlessly confess. We have been taught that God made not the world for nothing, but for the human race; and we have said that He takes pleasure in those who imitate His own perfections, and is displeased with those who prefer evil, whether in word or in deed. If then we should all destroy ourselves, we are the cause, as far as in us lies, why no one would be born and instructed in the doctrines of God: or even that the human race should cease to exist; and if we act thus, even we ourselves do what is contrary to the will of God. But, when we are interrogated, we do not deny, because we are conscious of nothing evil in ourselves, but account it wicked not in all things to speak the truth, which we also know to be pleasing to God; and we also now desire to disabuse you of an unfair prejudice.

But if the idea should occur to any one, that, if we confess God to be our helper, we should not, as we say, be mastered and persecuted by the wicked; I will answer this also; God, Who made the whole world, having subjected the things on earth to man, and arranged the heavenly bodies for the increase of fruits, and the changes of seasons, and laid down a divine law for these, which He is also seen to have created for man, delivered the care of man, and of things under heaven, to the Angels whom He appointed over them.

The proper name for the Father of all things, Who is unbegotten, there is none. For whoever is called by a name, has the person older than himself who gives him that name. But the terms Father, and God, and Creator, and Lord, and Master, are not names, but terms of address derived from His benefits and His works. But His Son, Who alone is properly called Son, the Word, Who was before all things, and Who was with Him, and was begotten, when in the beginning through Him He created and ordered all things, is called Christ, as He was anointed; and by Him God set all things in order, and this name itself contains an unknown signification; as also the title God is not a name, but the notion which is implanted in the nature of man, of a thing which can hardly be explained. But Jesus has the name and signification both of Man and of Saviour; for He was even made Man as I have said, and born according to the will of God and the Father, for those who believe in Him.

Hence, God also refrains from causing the confusion and destruction of the whole world . . . because of the race of the Christians, which He knows to be in nature the cause of its preservation. Otherwise it would be no longer possible for you to execute, and be urged to, such things as you do by evil demons; but the fire of judgment would descend, and utterly dissolve all things; just as formerly the waters of the flood left no one, but only him, with his family, who is called by us Noah, and by you Deucalion; from whom, again, such multitudes were born, of whom some were evil, and others good. So we also affirm, that there will be the conflagration; but not like that of the Stoics according to the theory of the change of all things into one another, which appears a most degrading notion. Neither is it by fatality that men do or endure what takes place; but each does well, or ill, by his choice; and by the activity of evil demons it is that the good, as Socrates and the like, are persecuted and imprisoned: but Sardanapalus, and Epicurus, and the like, appear to flourish in plenty and splendor. But the Stoics, not understanding this, declare that all things happen by the compulsion of fatality. But, because God in the beginning created the race of men, with free will, they will justly suffer in eternal fire the penalty of whatever they have done amiss; for it is the nature of every such creature to be capable of vice and of virtue, nor would any of them be praiseworthy if it had not the power of being turned toward either. And men everywhere who have been legislators or philosophers according to right reason, shew this from their directions to do one thing, and to abstain from another; and the Stoics in their system of morals hold the same principles in great honor; so that you may see that in their doctrine of principles, and incorporeals, they do not succeed well; for if they say that the actions of men are done by fatality, they will either assert that God is nothing but what undergoes change and alteration, and is ever resolved into the same elements; and will appear to have a comprehension only of things corruptible, and to say that God Himself both in part and in whole comes into every kind of vice; or, that virtue and vice are nothing; which is opposed to every sound idea, and reason, and mind.

And those who followed the doctrines of the Stoics, since they were admirable in their ethical system, as were also the poets in some respects, because of the seed of that reason which is implanted in the whole race of man, were, we know, both hated and put to death.

But that no one may repeat what is said by those who are considered Philosophers, that what we say about the wicked being punished in eternal fire, is a mere boast, and a bugbear; and that it is through fear, and not for the sake of what is good, and pleasurable, that we would have men live virtuously; I will briefly reply to this, that if it be not so, there is no God; or if there is one, He cares not for men; and virtue and vice are nothing; and, as I have said, the lawgivers punish unjustly those who transgress their good ordinances. But since they are not unjust, and their Father teaches them by the Word to do the same thing as himself, they who agree with them are not unjust. But should any one instance the different laws which are found among men, and say that with some this is thought to be good, and that to be evil, and with others what the former thought evil, is held to be good, and what they thought to be good is held to be evil; let him listen to what I will also reply to this. The true Word, when He came, showed that not all opinions, nor all doctrines, were good; but that some were bad, and others were good; so that I will declare the same and like things even to such men as these, and they shall be uttered at more length if need be.

Our doctrines, then, appear to be more sublime than all human teaching, because Christ Who appeared for us was made the whole rational being, both body, and reason, and soul: for all that the philosophers and legislators at any time declared, or discovered aright, they accomplished according to their portion of discovery and contemplation of the Word; but as they did not know all the properties of the Word, which is Christ, they often said things that were even contrary to themselves. And they who were born before Christ as to His Humanity, when they endeavored to examine and confute things by reason, were dragged before the judgment-seats as wicked men, and busybodies. He who was more active in this than all of them, Socrates, was accused of the same things as we are; for they said that he introduced new gods, and did not acknowledge those whom the city considered as gods. He, in fact, expelled from the polity the evil demons, and such as did what the Poets described; and he taught men to reject Homer, and the other Poets; and he exhorted them to gain the knowledge of the God Who was unknown to them, by the investigation of reason; saying, "It is not easy to discover the Father and Creator of all things, nor when discovered is it safe to declare Him to all." This however our Christ did through His own power. For no one trusted in Socrates so as to die for this doctrine. But in Christ, Who was known even to Socrates in part (for He was, and is, the Word, Who is in every one, and Who foretold all things that were about to come to pass, both by the Prophets, and by himself also; when He was made of like passions with us, and taught these things), not only philosophers and grammarians put their faith, but even handicraftsmen, and such as were wholly uneducated, despising reputation, and fear, and death; for it is the power of the Ineffable Father which does this, and not the powers of human reason.

Nor should we be slain, nor would wicked men and devils be stronger than we, were it not that to every man that is born, it is also appointed to die; hence when we pay that debt, we give thanks. And here I think it good and opportune to insert this extract from Xenophon, for the benefit of Crescens, and those who are as senseless as him. Xenophon says, that Hercules, as he came to a place where three roads met, found Virtue and Vice, who appeared to him in the form of women; and that Vice, in a luxurious and sensual garb, and with a countenance made alluring by such means, and being instantly captivating to the sight, promised Hercules, that if he would be her follower, she would always take care that he should pass his life amidst pleasure, and decked with the most brilliant ornaments, and such as she herself then wore: and that Virtue, who had a homely mien, and vest, said, If you will obey me, you shall adorn yourself with no brief and perishable decoration or beauty, but with everlasting and beautiful ornaments. And we are sure that everyone who eschews those things which appear good, and prefers those which are considered difficult and unaccountable, gains happiness: for Vice, as a disguise of her own actions, assuming the properties which appertain to Virtue, and which are really good, through imitation of what is incorruptible (for she has nothing that is incorruptible, nor can she produce such), leads captive the low-minded among men, putting her own evil habits on virtue. But they who understand the things that belong to that which is truly good, are also uncorrupted in virtue; which every sensible person ought to think of Christians, and of the athletes, and of all who do such things as the Poets relate of those who are honored as gods; drawing his conclusion from the fact, that death, even when we could escape it, is held by us in contempt.

For I myself, when I took pleasure in the doctrines of Plato, and heard the Christians slandered, seeing them to be fearless of death, and of everything else that was thought dreadful, considered that it was impossible that they should live in wickedness and sensuality: for, who that was a sensualist, or licentious, and thought human flesh to be good food, would welcome death, that he might be deprived of his enjoyments, and not endeavor, by every means, always to continue his present life, and to escape the officers; not to speak of denouncing himself to death? This also then have the evil demons, through the agency of certain wicked men, caused to be done; for when they had killed some, to serve the false accusations which they bring against us, they dragged our domestics, or children, or wives to the torture, and compelled them by dreadful torments to admit those fabulous rites which they themselves openly perform; of which, as we have no concern with them, we make no account; having the Unbegotten and Ineffable God as a witness of our thoughts and actions. For why did we not publicly confess even these things to be good, and prove them to be divine philosophy; saying, that when we kill a man, we celebrate the mysteries of Saturn; and that, when we take our fill of blood (as it is said of us), we imitate what you do to the idol that you honor, on which is sprinkled the blood not only of irrational animals, but even of men? For through him who is the most illustrious and noble among you, you make the libation of the blood of those who are put to death. And why, when you imitate Jupiter, and the other gods, in your sodomitical practices, and your shameless connections with women, do you urge in your defense the writings of Epicurus and the Poets? But when we persuade you to avoid these practices, and those who thus acted, with their imitators; as I have even now taken pains to do in these pages; we are attacked by you in various ways. But for this we care not, for we know that God is a just observer of all things. I would that we now had someone to mount a high rostrum, and cry with a loud voice: "Shame, shame, on you, that ye charge what yourselves do openly on these innocent persons; even attributing to them things that apply to yourselves, and your gods; but with which they have no concerns whatever. Alter your ways, learn moderation."

For I myself, when I discovered the evil disguise which was thrown around the divine doctrines of Christians to deter others from them, laughed, both at the authors of these falsehoods, and their disguise, and the popular opinion; and I confess that I both prayed, and strove with all my might, to be found a Christian; not because the doctrines of Plato are entirely different from those of Christ, but because they are not in all respects like them; no more in fact are those of the others, the Stoics, for example, and poets, and prose writers; for each seeing, through a part of the Seminal Divine Words, that which was kindred to those, discoursed rightly. But they who contradict them on more important points, appear not to have possessed the hidden wisdom and the knowledge which cannot be spoken against. Whatever all men have uttered aright, then, belongs to us Christians; for we worship and love, next to God, the Word which is from the Unbegotten and Ineffable God: for it was even for us that He was made Man, that He might be a partaker of our very sufferings, and bring us healing. For all writers through the engrafted seed of the Word, which was planted in them, were able to see the truth darkly; for the seed and imitation of a thing, which is given accordingly to capability, is one thing, and the thing itself of which the communication and imitation are given according to His grace, is another.

I entreat you then to be pleased to subscribe your judgment, and publish this little book, that our customs may be explained to others as well as yourselves, so that these things may be known to men, and that they may have the power of being freed from erroneous opinions and ignorance of good, who are at present subject by their own fault to punishment, that what I have said may be made known: because it is in the nature of man to know good and evil, and because in condemning us, whom they know not, of such actions as they term shameful, while they take pleasure in gods who do such, and, even now, require the like from men; in punishing us, as if we did such things, with death or chains, or some other like infliction, they condemn themselves. Hence there is no need of other judges.

And I have held in utter contempt the doctrine of the wicked and deceitful Simon of my own nation, and if you subscribe this work, I will unmask him to them all, that they may, if possible, change their opinion; for it is on this account alone that I have composed this treatise. Our doctrines, however, are not to a sane judgment shameful, but they surpass all human wisdom. If not so, they are at least unlike those of the Sotadist, the Philaenidians, the dancers, the Epicureans, and other like doctrines of the Poets, with which when enacted and written, all are allowed to acquaint themselves. I will now conclude, having done what I can, and prayed that all men may in every land be vouchsafed the truth. May you too, in a manner worthy of piety and philosophy, decide for your own sake with justice.

Irenaeus
Against Heresies
BOOK I, CHAPTER X

Unity of the faith of the church throughout the whole world

The church, though dispersed throughout the whole world, even to the ends of the earth, has received from the apostles and their disciples this faith: [She believes] in one God, the Father Almighty, Maker of heaven, and earth, and the sea, and all things that are in them; and in one Christ Jesus, the Son of God, who became incarnate for our salvation; and in the Holy Spirit, who proclaimed through the prophets the dispensations of God, and the advents, and the birth from a virgin, and the passion, and the resurrection from the dead, and the ascension into heaven in the flesh of the beloved Christ Jesus, our Lord, and His [future] manifestation from heaven in the glory of the Father "to gather all things in one," and to raise up anew all flesh of the whole human race, in order that to Christ Jesus, our Lord, and God, and Saviour, and King, according to the will of the invisible Father, "every knee should bow, of things in heaven, and things in earth, and things under the earth, and that every tongue should confess" to Him, and that He should execute just judgment towards all; that He may send "spiritual wickedness," and the angels who transgressed and became apostates, together with the ungodly, and unrighteous, and wicked, and profane among men, into everlasting fire; but may, in the exercise of His grace, confer immortality on the righteous, and holy, and those who have kept His commandments, and have persevered in His love, some from the beginning [of their Christian course], and others from [the date of] their repentance, and may surround them with everlasting glory.

As I have already observed, the church, having received this preaching and this faith, although scattered throughout the whole world, yet, as if occupying but one house, carefully preserves it. She also believes these points [of doctrine] just as if she had but one soul, and one and the same heart, and she proclaims them, and teaches them, and hands them down, with perfect harmony, as if she possessed only one mouth. For, although the languages of the world are dissimilar, yet the import of the tradition is one and the same. For the churches which have been planted in Germany do not believe or hand down anything different, nor do those in Spain, nor those in Gaul, nor those in the East, nor those in Egypt, nor those in Libya, nor those which have been established in the central regions of the world. But as the sun, that creature of God, is one and the same throughout the whole world, so also the preaching of the truth shineth everywhere, and enlightens all men that are willing to come to a knowledge of the truth. Nor will any one of the rulers in the churches, however highly gifted he may be in point of eloquence, teach doctrines different from these (for no one is greater than the Master); nor, on the other hand, will he who is deficient in power of expression inflict injury on the tradition. For the faith being ever one and the same, neither does one who is able at great length to discourse regarding it, make any addition to it, nor does one, who can say but little, diminish it.

It does not follow because men are endowed with greater and less degrees of intelligence, that they should therefore change the subject-matter [of the faith] itself, and should conceive of some other God besides Him who is the

Framer, Maker, and Preserver of this universe (as if He were not sufficient for them), or of another Christ, or another Only-begotten. But the fact referred to simply implies this, that one may [more accurately than another] bring out the meaning of those things which have been spoken in parables, and accommodate them to the general scheme of the faith; and explain [with special clearness] the operation and dispensation of God connected with human salvation; and show that God manifested long suffering in regard to the apostasy of the angels who transgressed, as also with respect to the disobedience of men; and set forth why it is that one and the same God has made something temporal and some eternal, some heavenly and others earthly; and understand for what reason God, though invisible, manifested himself to the prophets not under one form, but differently to different individuals; and show why it was that more covenants than one were given to mankind; and teach what was the special character of each of these covenants; and search out for what reason "God hath confused every man in unbelief, that He may have mercy upon all," and gratefully describe on what account the Word of God became flesh and suffered; and relate why the advent of the Son of God took place in these last times, that is, in the end, rather than in the beginning [of the world]; and unfold what is contained in the Scripture concerning the end [itself], and things to come; and not be silent as to how it is that God has made the Gentiles, whose salvation was despaired of, fellow-heirs, and of the same body, and partakers with the saints; and discourse how it is that "this mortal body shall put on immortality, and this corruptible shall put on incorruption": and proclaim in what sense [God] says, "That is a people who was not a people; and she is beloved who was not beloved"; and in what sense He says that "more are the children of her that was desolate, than of her who possessed a husband." For in reference to these points, and others of a like nature, the apostle exclaims: "Oh! the depth of the riches both of the wisdom and knowledge of God; how unsearchable are His judgments, and His ways past finding out!" But the [superior skill spoken of] is not found in this, that anyone should, beyond the Creator and Framer [of the world], conceive of the Enthymesis of an erring Aeon, their mother and his, and should thus proceed to such a pitch of blasphemy; nor does it consist in this, that he should again falsely imagine, as being above this [fancied being], a Pleroma at one time supposed to contain thirty, and at another time an innumerable tribe of Aeons, as these teachers who are destitute of truly divine wisdom maintain; while the Catholic church possesses one and the same faith throughout the whole world, as we have already said.

IRENAEUS
Against Heresies
BOOK III, CHAPTER III

A refutation of the heretics, from the fact that, in the various churches, a perpetual succession of bishops was kept up

It is within the power of all, therefore, in every church, who may wish to see the truth, to contemplate dearly the tradition of the apostles manifested throughout the whole world; and we are in a position to reckon up those who were by the apostles instituted bishops in the churches, and [to demonstrate] the successions of these men to our own times; those who neither taught nor knew of anything like what these [heretics] rave about. For if the apostles had known hidden mysteries, which they were in the habit of imparting to "the perfect" apart and privily from the rest, they would have delivered them especially to those to whom they were also committing the churches themselves. For they were desirous that these men should be very perfect and blameless in all things, whom also they were leaving behind as their successors, delivering up their own place of government to these men; which men, if they discharged their functions honestly, would be a great boon [to the church], but if they should fall away, the direst calamity.

Since, however, it would be very tedious, in such a volume as this, to reckon up the successions of all the churches, we do put to confusion all those who, in whatever manner, whether by an evil self-pleasing, by vainglory, or by blindness and perverse opinion, assemble in unauthorized meetings; [we do this, I say,] by indicating that tradition derived from the apostles, of the very great, the very ancient, and universally known church founded and organized at Rome by the two most glorious apostles, Peter and Paul; as also [by pointing out] the faith preached to men, which comes down to our time by means of the successions of the bishops. For it is a matter of necessity that every church should agree with this church, on account of its pre-eminent authority, that is, the faithful everywhere, inasmuch as the apostolical tradition has been preserved continuously by those [faithful men] who exist everywhere.

The blessed apostles, then, having founded and built up the church, committed into the hands of Linus the office of the episcopate. Of this Linus, Paul makes mention in the Epistles to Timothy. To him succeeded Anacletus; and after him, in the third place from the apostles, Clement was allotted the bishopric. This man, as he had seen the blessed apostles, and had been conversant with them, might be said to have the preaching of the apostles still echoing [in his ears], and their traditions before his eyes. Nor was he alone [in this], for there were many still remaining who had received instructions from the apostles. In the time of this Clement, no small dissension having occurred among the brethren at Corinth, the church in Rome despatched a most powerful letter to the Corinthians, exhorting them to peace, renewing their faith, and declaring the tradition which it had lately received from the apostles, proclaiming the one God, omnipotent, the Maker of heaven and earth, the Creator of man. From this document, whosoever chooses to do so, may learn that He, the Father of our Lord Jesus Christ, was preached by the churches, and may also understand the apostolical tradition of the church, since this epistle is of older date than these men who are now propagating falsehood, and who conjure into existence another god beyond the Creator and the Maker of all existing things. To this Clement there succeeded Evaristus. Alexander followed Evaristus; then, sixth from the apostles, Sixtus was appointed; after him Telesphorus, who was gloriously martyred; then Hyginus; after him, Pius; then after him, Anicetus. Soter having succeeded Anicetus, Eleutherius does now, in the twelfth place from the apostles, hold the inheritance of the episcopate. In this order, and by this succession, the ecclesiastical tradition from the apostles, and the preaching of the truth, have come down to us. And this is most abundant proof that there is one and the same vivifying faith, which has been preserved in the church from the apostles until now, and handed down in truth.

But Polycarp, also was not only instructed by apostles, and conversed with many who had seen Christ, but was also, by apostles in Asia, appointed bishop of the church in Smyrna, whom I also saw in my early youth, for he tarried [on earth] a very long time, and, when a very old man, gloriously and most nobly suffering martyrdom, departed this life, having always taught the things which he had learned from the apostles, and which the church has handed down, and which alone are true. To these things all the Asiatic churches testify, as do also those men who have succeeded Polycarp down to the present time — a man who was of much greater weight, and a more steadfast witness of truth than Valentinus, and Marcion, and the rest of the heretics. He it was who, coming to Rome in the time of Anicetus, caused many to turn away from the aforesaid heresies to the church of God, proclaiming that he had received this one and sole truth from the apostles — that, namely, which is handed down by the church. There are also those who heard from him that John, the disciple of the Lord, going to bathe at Ephesus, and perceiving Cerinthus within, rushed out of the bath-house without bathing, exclaiming, "Let us fly, lest even the bath-house fall down, because Cerinthus, the enemy of the truth, is within." And Polycarp himself replied to Marcion, who met him on one occasion, and said, "Dost thou know me?" "I do know thee, the first-born of Satan." Such was the horror which the apostles and their disciples had against holding even a verbal communication with any corrupters of the truth; as Paul also says, "A man that is an heretic, after the first and second admonition, reject; knowing that he that is such is subverted, and sinneth, being condemned of himself."

Selections from "The Second Apology" are from
The Writings of the Apostolic Fathers,
Translated by Drs. Robert Donaldson and E. Crombie.
Edinburgh: T. & T. Clark, 1867

Selections from "Irenaeus Against Heresies" are from
Ante-Nicene Fathers,
Translations of the Writings of the Fathers Down to A.D. 325,
The Reverend Alexander Roberts, D.D. and James Donaldson, LL.D., editors,
Volume I, Buffalo: The Christian Literature Publishing Company, 1887

Chapter 13 • Tatian: Address to the Greeks

Tatian tells us in the conclusion of this treatise that he was an Assyrian, but we have no definite information about the dates of his life. He was educated as a Greek rhetorician, traveled, and studied philosophy in all the current schools, and came to Rome to study under Justin. He was influenced by Gnosticism, especially of the kind proclaimed by Valentinus, later founding or revivifying the sect of the Encratites, which proscribed marriage and prescribed abstinence from meat and wine. He went so far as to substitute water for wine in the Eucharistic celebration. The excerpt presented here are good examples of Christian orthodoxy struggling with the difficult task of reconciling philosophy with the theological deposit of faith. It shows the errors into which one could be tempted to fall due to the influence of Gnosticism. He does, however, give a clear presentation of the unity of God, creation of the world, the doctrine of the Logos resurrection (though he is confused about the nature and immortality of the human soul), fall of man, freedom of will, and the reasons for his conversion.

Tatian's Address to the Greeks

CHAPTER IV

Man is to be honoured as a fellow-man; God alone is to be feared — He who is not visible to human eyes, nor comes within the compass of human art. Only when I am commanded to deny Him, will I not obey, but will rather die than show myself false and ungrateful. Our God did not begin to be in time: He alone is without beginning, and He himself is the beginning of all things. God is a spirit, not pervading matter, but the Maker of material spirits, and of the forms that are in matter; He is invisible, impalpable, being himself the Father of both sensible and invisible things. Him we know from His creation, and apprehend His invisible power by His works. I refuse to adore that workmanship which He has made for our sakes. The sun and moon were made for us: how, then, can I adore my own servants?

CHAPTER V

The doctrine of the Christians as to the creation of the world

God was in the beginning; but the beginning, we have been taught, is the power of the Logos. For the Lord of the universe, who is himself the necessary ground (υπόστασις) of all being, inasmuch as no creature was yet in existence was alone; but inasmuch as He was all power, himself the necessary ground of things visible and invisible, with Him were all things; with Him, by Logos-power (δύναμις), the Logos himself also, who was in Him, subsists. And by His simple will the Logos springs forth; and the Logos, not coming forth in vain, becomes the first-begotten work of the Father. Him (the Logos) we know to be the beginning of the world. But He came into being by participation, not by abscission; for what is cut off is separated from the original substance, but that which comes by participation, making its choice of function, does not render him deficient from whom it is taken. For just as from one torch many fires are lighted, but the light of the first torch is not lessened by the kindling of many torches, so the Logos, coming forth from the Logos-power of the Father, has not divested of the Logos-power Him who begat Him. I myself, for instance, talk, and you hear; yet, certainly, I who converse do not become destitute of speech (λόγος) by the transmission of speech, but by the utterance of my voice I endeavour to reduce to order the unarranged matter in your minds. And as the Logos, begotten in the beginning, begat in turn our world, having first created for himself the necessary matter, so also I, in imitation of the Logos, being begotten again, and having become possessed of the truth, am trying to reduce to order the confused matter which is kindred with myself. For matter is not, like God, without beginning, nor, as having no beginning, is of equal power with God; it is begotten, and not produced by any other being, but brought into existence by the Framer of all things alone.

CHAPTER VI

Christians' belief in the resurrection

And on this account we believe that there will be a resurrection of bodies after the consummation of all things; not, as the Stoics affirm, according to the return of certain cycles, the same things being produced and destroyed for no useful purpose, but a resurrection once for all, when our periods of existence are completed, and in consequence solely of the constitution of things under which men alone live, for the purpose of passing judgment upon them. Nor is sentence upon us passed by Minos or Rhadamanthus, before whose decease not a single soul, according to the mythic tales, was judged; but the Creator, God himself, becomes the arbiter. And, although you regard us as mere triflers and babblers, it troubles us not, since we have faith in this doctrine. For just as, not existing before I was born, I knew not who I was, and only existed in the potentiality (υπόστασις) of fleshly matter, but being born, after a former state of nothingness, I have obtained through my birth a certainty of my existence; in the same way, having been born, and through death existing no longer, and seen no longer, I shall exist again, just as before I was not, but was afterwards born. Even though fire destroy all traces of my flesh, the world receives the vaporized matter; and though dispersed through rivers and seas, or torn in pieces by wild beasts, I am laid up in the storehouses of a wealthy Lord. And, although the poor and the godless know not what is stored up, yet God the Sovereign, when he pleases, will restore the substance that is visible to Him alone to its pristine condition.

CHAPTER VII

For the heavenly Logos, a spirit emanating from the Father and a Logos from the Logos-power, in imitation of the Father who begat Him made man an image of immortality, so that, as incorruption is with God, in like manner, man, sharing in a part of God, might have the immortal principle also. The Logos, too, before the creation of men, was the Framer of angels. And each of these two orders of creatures was made free to act as it pleased, not having the nature of good, which again is with God alone, but is brought to perfection in men through their freedom of choice, in order that the bad man may be justly punished, having become depraved through his own fault, but the just man be deservedly praised for his virtuous deeds, since in the exercise of his free choice he refrained from transgressing the will of God.

CHAPTER XXIX

Account of Tatian's conversion

Wherefore, having seen these things, and moreover also having been admitted to the mysteries, and having everywhere examined the religious rites performed by the effeminate and the pathic, and having found among the Romans their Latiarian Jupiter delighting in human gore and the blood of slaughtered men, and Artemis not far from the great city sanctioning acts of the same kind, and one demon here and another there instigating to the perpetration of evil — retiring by myself, I sought how I might be able to discover the truth. And, while I was giving my most earnest attention to the matter, I happened to meet with certain barbaric writings, too old to be compared with the opinions of the Greeks, and too divine to be compared with their errors; and I was led to put faith in these by the unpretending cast of the language, the inartificial character of the writers, the foreknowledge displayed of future events, the excellent quality of the precepts, and the declaration of the government of the universe as centered in one Being. And, my soul being taught of God, I discerned that the former class of writings lead to condemnation, but that these put an end to the slavery that is in the world, and rescue us from a multiplicity of rulers and ten thousand tyrants, while they give us, not indeed what we had not before received, but what we had received but were prevented by error from retaining.

CHAPTER XXXV

Tatian speaks as any eyewitness

The things which I have thus set before you I have not earned at second hand. I have visited many lands; I have followed rhetoric, like yourselves; I have fallen in with many arts and inventions; and finally, when sojourning in the city of the Romans, I inspected the multiplicity of statues brought thither by you: for I do not attempt, as is the custom with many, to strengthen my own views by the opinions of others, but I wish to give you a distinct account of what I myself have seen and felt. So, bidding farewell to the arrogance of Romans and the idle talk of Athenians, and all their ill-connected opinions, I embraced our barbaric philosophy. I began to show how this was more ancient than your institutions, but left my task unfinished, in order to discuss a matter which demanded more immediate attention; but now it is time I should attempt to speak concerning its doctrines. Be not offended with our teaching, nor undertake an elaborate reply filled with trifling and ribaldry, saying, "Tatian, aspiring to be above the Greeks, above the infinite number of philosophic inquirers, has struck out a new path, and embraced the doctrines of Barbarians." For what grievance is it, that men manifestly ignorant should be reasoned with by a man of like nature with themselves? Or how can it be irrational, according to your own sophist, to grow old always learning something?

CHAPTER XLII

Concluding statement as to the author

These things, 0 Greeks, I Tatian, a disciple of the barbaric philosophy, have composed for you. I was born in the land of the Assyrians, having been first instructed in your doctrines, and afterwards in those which I now undertake to proclaim. Henceforward, knowing who God is and what is His work, I present myself to you prepared for an examination concerning my doctrines, while I adhere immovably to that mode of life which is according to God.

Selections from Tatian are from
Ante-Nicene Christian Library,
Reverend Alexander Roberts, D.D. and James Donaldson, LL.D.,
Volume III, Edinburgh: T. & T. Clark, 1867

Chapter 14 • Theophilus to Autolycus

As Tatian was in Rome, Theophilus of Antioch (second century A.D.) was a representative witness to the doctrines of Christianity in the regions of the other most important Christian area during the last quarter of the second century. In an introductory chapter of his letter to Autolycus, we catch glimpses of the great mystical tradition stretching from John the Apostle to the Pseudo-Areopagite and John Scotus Erigena, to St. Bonaventure and St. Thomas Aquinas, to the Brothers of the Common Life, and to St. Teresa of Ávila and St. John of the Cross. This is integrated very well with the fundamental doctrines of the nature of God, that the attributes of God are known from His works. This excerpt is noteworthy for the explicit example it gives of the tradition which compares the doctrines of Christianity with the teachings of the philosophers and poets of Greece. The emphasis is placed on the fact that the teachings of the great Greek poets and philosophers confirm the teachings of the prophets.

BOOK I
CHAPTER III
Nature of God

You will say, then, to me, "Do you, who see God, explain to me the appearance of God." Hear, 0 man. The appearance of God is ineffable and indescribable, and came to be seen by eyes of flesh. For in glory He is incomprehensible, in greatness unfathomable, in height inconceivable, in power incomparable, in wisdom unrivalled, in goodness inimitable, in kindness unutterable. For if I say He is Light, I name but His own work; if I call Him Word, I name but His sovereignty; if I call Him Mind, I speak but of His wisdom; if I say He is Spirit, I speak of His breath; if I call Him Wisdom, I speak of His offspring; if I call Him Strength, I speak of His sway; if I call Him Power, I am mentioning His activity; if Providence, I but mention His goodness; if I call Him Kingdom, I but mention His glory; if I call Him Judge, I speak of Him as being just; if I call Him Father, I speak of all things as being from Him; if I call Him Fire, I but mention His anger. You will say, then, to me, "Is God angry?" Yes; He is angry with those who act wickedly but He is good, and kind, and merciful, to those who love and fear Him; for He is a chastener of the godly, and father of the righteous; but he is a judge and punisher of the impious.

CHAPTER IV

Attributes of God

And He is without beginning, because He is unbegotten; and He is unchangeable, because He is immortal. And He is called God [θεός] on account of His having placed [τεθεικέναι] all things on security afforded by himself; and on account of [θέειν], for θέειν means running, and moving, and being active, and nourishing, and foreseeing, and governing, and making all things alive. But he is Lord because He rules over the universe; Father, because he is before all things; Fashioner and Maker, because He is creator and maker of the universe; the Highest, because of His being above all; and Almighty, because He himself rules and embraces all. For the heights of heaven, and the depths of the abysses, and the ends of the earth, are in His hand, and there is no place of His rest. For the heavens are His work, the earth is His creation, the sea is His handiwork; man is His formation and His image; sun, moon, and stars are His elements, made for signs, and seasons, and days, and years, that they may serve and be slaves to man; and all things God has made out of things that were not into things that are, in order that through His works His greatness may be known and understood.

CHAPTER V

The Invisible God perceived through His works

For as the soul in man is not seen, being invisible to men, but is perceived through the motion of the body, so God cannot indeed be seen by human eyes, but is beheld and perceived through His providence and works. For, in like manner, as any person, when he sees a ship on the sea rigged and in sail, and making for the harbour, will no doubt infer that there is a pilot in her who is steering her; so we must perceive that God is the governor [pilot] of the whole universe, though He be not visible to eyes of flesh, since He is incomprehensible. For if a man cannot look upon the sun, though it be a very small heavenly body, on account of its exceeding heat and power, how shall not a mortal man be much more unable to face the glory of God, which is unutterable? For as the pomegranate, with the rind containing it, has within it many cells and compartments which are separated by tissues, and has also many seeds dwelling in it, so the whole creation is contained by the spirit of God, and the containing spirit is along with the creation contained by the hand of God. As, therefore, the seed of the pomegranate, dwelling inside cannot see what is outside the rind, itself being within; so neither can man, who along with the whole creation is enclosed by the hand of God, behold God. Then again, an earthly king was believed to exist, even though he be not seen by all, for he was recognized by his laws and ordinances, and authorities, and forces, and statutes; and are you unwilling that God should be recognized by His works and mighty deeds?

BOOK II
CHAPTER IV

Absurd opinions of the philosophers concerning God

Some of the philosophers of the Porch say that there is no God at all; or, if there is, they say that He cares for none but himself; and these views the folly of Epicurus and Chrysippus has set forth at large. And others say that all things are produced without external agency, and that the world is uncreated, and that nature is eternal, and have dared to give out that there is no providence of God at all, but maintain that God is only each man's conscience. But Plato and those of his school acknowledge indeed that God is uncreated, and the Father and Maker of all things; but then they maintain that matter as well as God is uncreated, and aver that it is coeval with God. But if God is uncreated and matter uncreated, God is no longer, according to the Platonists, the Creator of all things, nor, so far as their opinions hold, is the monarchy of God established. And further, as God, because He is uncreated, is also unalterable; so if matter, too, were uncreated, it also would be unalterable, and equal to God; for that which is created is mutable and alterable. But the power of God is manifested in this, that out of things that are not He makes whatever He pleases; just as the bestowal of life and motion is the prerogative of no other than God alone. But God has this property in excess of what man can do, in that He makes a work, endowed with reason, life, sensation. As, therefore, in all these respects God is more powerful than man, so also in this; that out of things that are not He creates and has created things that are, and whatever He pleases, as He pleases.

CHAPTER VIII

Faith required in all matters

But you do not believe that the dead are raised. When the resurrection shall take place, then you will believe, whether you will or no; and your faith shall be reckoned for unbelief, unless you believe now. And why do you not believe? If, the husbandman trusts the earth, and the sailor the boat, and the sick the physician, will you not place confidence in God, even when you hold so many pledges at His hand? For first He created you out of nothing and brought you into existence.

CHAPTER IX

The prophets inspired by the Holy Ghost

But men of God carrying in them a holy spirit and becoming prophets, being inspired and made wise by God, became God-taught, and holy, and righteous. Wherefore they were also deemed worthy of receiving this reward, that they should become instruments of God, and contain the wisdom that is from Him, through which wisdom they uttered both what regarded the creation of the world and all other things.

BOOK III
CHAPTER IX

Christian doctrine of God and His law

Now we also confess that God exists, but that He is one, the creator, and maker, and fashioner of this universe; and we know that all things are arranged by His providence, but by Him alone. And we have learned a holy law; but we have as lawgiver Him who is really God, who teaches us to act righteously, and to be pious, and to do good. And concerning piety He says, "Thou shalt have no other gods before me. Thou shalt not make unto thee any graven image, or any likeness of anything that is in heaven above, or that is in the earth beneath, or that is in the water under the earth: thou shalt not bow down thyself to them, nor serve them: for I am the Lord thy God." And of doing good he said: "Honour thy father and thy mother; that it may be well with thee, and that thy days may be long in the land which I the Lord God give thee." Again, concerning righteousness: "Thou shalt not commit adultery. Thou shalt not kill. Thou shalt not steal. Thou shalt not bear false witness against thy neighbour. Thou shalt not covet thy neighbour's wife, thou shalt not covet thy neighbour's house, nor his land, nor his man-servant, nor his maidservant, nor his ox, nor his beast of burden, nor any of his cattle, nor anything that is thy neighbour's. Thou shalt not wrest the judgment of the poor in his cause. From every unjust matter keep thee far. The innocent and righteous thou shalt not slay; thou shalt not justify the wicked; and thou shalt not take a gift, for gifts blind the eyes of them that see and pervert righteous words."

CHAPTER XIII

Of chastity

And concerning chastity, the holy word teaches us not only not to sin in act, but not even in thought, not even in the heart to think of any evil, nor looking on another man's wife with our eyes to lust after her. And the voice of the gospel teaches still more urgently concerning chastity, saying: "Whosoever looketh on a woman who is not his own wife, to lust after her, hath committed adultery with her already in his heart." "And he that marrieth," says [the gospel], "her that is divorced from her husband, committeth adultery; and whosoever putteth away his wife, saving for the cause of fornication, causeth her to commit adultery." Because Solomon says: "Can a man take fire in his bosom, and his clothes not be burned? Or can one walk upon hot coals, and his feet not be burned? So he that goeth in to a married woman shall not be innocent."

CHAPTER XIV

Of loving our enemies

And the gospel says: "Love your enemies, and pray for them that despitefully use you. For if ye love them who love you, what reward have ye? This do also the robbers and the publicans."

CHAPTER XV

The innocence of the Christians defended

Consider, therefore, whether those who teach such things can possibly live indifferently, and be commingled in unlawful intercourse, or, most impious of all, eat human flesh, especially when we are forbidden so much as to witness shows of gladiators, lest we become partakers and abettors of murders. But neither may we see the other spectacles, lest our eyes and ears be defiled, participating in the utterances there sung. For if one should speak of cannibalism, in these spectacles the children of Thyestes and Tereus are eaten; and as for adultery, both in the case of men and of gods, whom they celebrate in elegant language for honours and prizes, this is made the subject of their dramas. But far be it from Christians to conceive any such deeds; for with them temperance dwells, self-restraint is practised, monogamy is observed, chastity is guarded, iniquity exterminated, sin extirpated, righteousness exercised, law administered, worship performed, God acknowledged: truth governs, grace guards, peace screens them; the holy word guides, wisdom teaches, life directs, God reigns. Therefore, though we have much to say regarding our manner of life, and the ordinances of God, the maker of all creation, we yet consider that we have for the present reminded you of enough to induce you to study these things, especially since you can now read [our writings] for yourself, that as you have been fond of acquiring information, you may still be studious in this direction also.

Selections from "Theophilus to Autolycus" are from
Ante-Nicene Fathers, Fathers of the Second Century,
American Edition edited by A. Cleveland Coxe, D.D.
Volume II, Buffalo: The Christian Literature Publishing Company, 1887

Chapter 15 • Clement of Alexandria: *Paidagogos*; *Stromata*

Clement is reputed to have been the third Head of the Catechetical School at Alexandria. He is said to have been born at Athens ca. A.D. 150 and to have been converted to Christianity at an early age. Like so many others of that time and after, he traveled quite extensively in search of a body of teaching which would satisfy the insatiable desire he had for truth and happiness. He was impressed by the teaching presented in the School of Alexandria, and remained there until forced to flee by the persecution of Septimius Severus. He died in 215/216.

Clement's three great works —*Discourse of Exhortation to the Greeks (Protrepticos), The Instructor (Paidagogos),* and *Miscellanies or Tapestries (Stromata)* — constitute an extraordinary introduction to Christianity. In these works Clement shows his breadth and depth of knowledge of the fundamentals of Christianity as well as of Greek and Roman philosophy and literature. He, like the author of the *Letter to Diognetus*, is a cultured gentleman employing his wealth of knowledge of pagan learning in the service of Christianity. He claims that all ancient learning, but especially philosophy, is an excellent preparation for the "Good News." Philosophy is also the handmaiden of theology. Greek philosophy and the law of Moses are like two streams which unite to form Christianity. The liberal arts serve philosophy; philosophy serves Divine Wisdom (doctrines of the Church). Clement opposed the Gnostics by stressing the equality of every Christian with regard to salvation after baptism. His view of secular literature and philosophy is an elaboration of the Pauline one, and it received explicit and systematic theological concretization in the *Summa Theologiae* of St. Thomas Aquinas.

BOOK I
CHAPTER VII

Who the instructor is, and respecting his instruction

Since all of us are by Scripture called children; and not only so, but that we who have followed Christ are figuratively called babes; and that the Father of all alone is perfect, for the Son is in Him, and the Father is in the Son; it is time for us in due course to say who our Instructor is.

He is called Jesus. Sometimes He called himself a shepherd, and says, "I am the good Shepherd." According to a metaphor drawn from shepherds, who lead the sheep, is hereby understood the Instructor, who leads the children — the Shepherd who tends the babes. For the babes are simple, being figuratively described as sheep." And they shall all," it is said, "be one flock, and one shepherd." The Word, then, who leads the children to salvation, is appropriately called *the Instructor*. Now piety is instruction, being the learning of the service of God, and training in the knowledge of the truth, and right guidance which leads to heaven. And the word "instruction" is employed variously. For there is the instruction of him who is led and learns, and that of him who leads and teaches; and there is, thirdly, the guidance itself; and fourthly, what is taught, as the commandments enjoined.

Now the instruction which is of God is the right direction of truth to the contemplation of God, and the exhibition of holy deeds in everlasting perseverance.

The Instructor guides the children to a saving course of conduct, through solicitude for us; and, in general, whatever we ask in accordance with reason from God to be done for us, will happen to those who believe in the Instructor.

Your Instructor is the holy God Jesus, the Word, who is the guide of all humanity. The loving God himself is our Instructor.

When He speaks in His own person, He confesses himself to be the Instructor: "I am the Lord thy God, who brought thee out of the land of Egypt." Who, then, has the power of leading in and out? Is it not the Instructor? This was He who appeared to Abraham, and said to him, "I am thy God, be accepted before Me," and in a way most befitting an instructor, forms him into a faithful child, saying, "And be blameless; and I will make My covenant between Me and thee, and thy seed."

The same who is instructor is judge, and judges those who disobey Him; and the loving Word will not pass over their transgression in silence. He reproves, that they may repent. For "the Lord willeth the repentance of the sinner rather than his death." See the care, and wisdom, and power of the Instructor: "He shall not judge according to opinion, nor according to report; but He shall dispense judgment to the humble, and reprove the sinners of the earth."

BOOK III
CHAPTER I

On the true beauty

It is then, as appears, the greatest of all lessons to know one's self. For if one knows himself, he will know God; and knowing God, he will be made like God, not by wearing gold or long robes, but by well-doing, and by requiring as few things as possible.

Now, God alone is in need of nothing, and rejoices most when He sees us bright with the ornament of intelligence; and then, too, rejoices in him who is arrayed in chastity, the sacred stole of the body. Since then the soul consists of three divisions; the intellect, which is called the reasoning faculty, is the inner man, which is the ruler of this man that is seen. And that one, in another respect, God guides. But the irascible part, being brutal, dwells near to insanity. And appetite, which is the third department, is many-shaped above Proteus, the varying sea god, who changed himself now into one shape, now into another, and it allures to adulteries, to licentiousness, to seductions.

Passions break out, pleasures overflow; beauty fades, and falls quicker than the leaf on the ground, when the amorous storms of lust blow on it before the coming of autumn, and is withered by destruction. For lust becomes and fabricates all things, and wishes to cheat, so as to conceal the man. But that man with whom the Word dwells does not alter himself, does not get himself up: he has the form which is of the Word; he is made like to God; he is beautiful; he does not ornament himself; his is beauty, the true beauty, for it is God; and that man becomes God, since God so wills.

There is, too, another beauty of men — love. "And love," according to the apostle, "suffers long, and is kind; envieth not; vaunteth not, itself, is not puffed up."

STROMATA BOOK I
CHAPTER V

Philosophy the handmaid of theology

Accordingly, before the advent of the Lord, philosophy was necessary to the Greeks for righteousness. And now it becomes conducive to piety; being a kind of preparatory training to those who attain to faith through demonstration. "For thy foot," it is said, "will not stumble, if thou refer what is good, whether belonging to the Greeks or to us, to Providence." For God is the cause of all good things; but of some primarily, as of the Old and the New Testament; and of others by consequence, as philosophy. Perchance, too, philosophy was given to the Greeks directly and primarily, till the Lord should call the Greeks. For this was a schoolmaster to bring "the Hellenic mind," as the law, the Hebrews, "to Christ." Philosophy, therefore, was a preparation, paving the way for him who is perfected in Christ.

We are admonished to use indeed, but not to linger and spend time with, secular culture. For what was bestowed on each generation advantageously, and at seasonable times, is a preliminary training for the word of the Lord. "For already some men, ensnared by the charms of handmaidens, have despised their consort philosophy, and have grown old, some of them in music, some in geometry, others in grammar, the most in rhetoric." "But as the encyclical branches of study contribute to philosophy, which is their mistress; so also philosophy itself co-operates for the acquisition of wisdom. For philosophy is the study of wisdom, and wisdom is the knowledge of things divine and human; and their causes." Wisdom is therefore queen of philosophy, as philosophy is of preparatory culture. For if philosophy "professes control of the tongue, and the belly, and the parts below the belly, it is to be chosen on its own account. But it appears more worthy of respect and preeminence, if cultivated for the honour and knowledge of God."

We merely therefore assert here, that philosophy is characterized by investigation into truth and the nature of things (this is the truth of which the Lord himself said, "I am the truth"); and that, again, the preparatory training for rest in Christ exercises the mind, rouses the intelligence, and begets an inquiring shrewdness, by means of the true philosophy, which the initiated possess, having found it, or rather received it, from the truth itself.

CHAPTER VI

The benefit of culture

The readiness acquired by previous training conduces much to the perception of such things as are requisite; but those things which can be perceived only by mind are the special exercise for the mind. In such studies, therefore, the soul is purged from sensible things, and is excited, so as to be able to see truth distinctly.

Again, God has created us naturally social and just; whence justice must not be said to take its rise from implantation alone. But the good imparted by creation is to be conceived of as excited by the commandment; the soul being trained to be willing to select what is noblest.

But as we say that a man can be a believer without learning, so also we assert that it is impossible for a man without learning to comprehend the things which are declared in the faith. But to adopt what is well said, and not to adopt the reverse, is caused not simply by faith, but by faith combined with knowledge. But if ignorance is want of training and of instruction, then teaching produces knowledge of divine and human things. But just as it is possible to live rightly in penury of this world's good things, so also in abundance. And we avow, that at once with more ease and more speed will one attain to virtue through previous training. But it is not such as to be unattainable without it; but it is attainable only when they have learned, and have had their senses exercised. We must be conversant with the art of reasoning, for the purpose of confuting the deceitful opinions of the sophists. Well and felicitously, therefore, does Anaxarchus write in his book respecting "kingly rule." Erudition benefits greatly and hurts greatly him who possesses it; it helps him who is worthy, and injures him who utters readily every word, and before the whole people. It is necessary to know the measure of time, for this is the end of wisdom.

CHAPTER IX

Human knowledge necessary for the understanding of the scriptures

Some, who think themselves naturally gifted, do not wish to touch either philosophy or logic; nay more, they do not wish to learn natural science. They demand bare faith alone, as if they wished, without bestowing any care on the vine, straightway to gather clusters from the first.

CHAPTER XX

In what respect philosophy contributes to the comprehension of divine truth

As many men drawing down the ship, cannot be called many causes, but one cause consisting of many — for each individual by himself is not the cause of the ship being drawn, but along with rest — so also philosophy, being the search for truth, contributes to the comprehension of truth; not as being the cause of comprehension, but a cause along with other things, and cooperator, perhaps also a joint cause. And as the several virtues are causes of the happiness of one individual; so while truth is one, many things contribute to its investigation. But its discovery is by the Son. If then we consider, virtue is, in power, one. But it is the case, that when exhibited in some things, it is called prudence, in others temperance, and in others manliness or righteousness. By the same analogy, while truth is one — geometry there is the truth of geometry; in music, that of music; and in the right philosophy, there will be Hellenic truth. But that is the only authentic truth, unassailable, in which we are instructed by the Son of God.

And each, whether it be virtue or truth, called by the same name, is the cause of its own peculiar effect alone; and from the blending of them arises a happy life. For we are not made happy by names alone, when we say that a good life is happiness, and that the man who is adorned in his soul with virtue is happy. But if philosophy contributes remotely to the discovery of truth, by reaching, by diverse essays, after the knowledge which touches close on the truth, the knowledge possessed by us, it aids him who aims at grasping it, in accordance with the Word, to apprehend knowledge.

And if, for the sake of those who are fond of fault-finding, we must draw a distinction, by saying that philosophy is a concurrent and cooperating cause of true apprehension, being the search for truth, then we shall avow it to be a preparatory training for the enlightened man (τοῦγνωστικοῦ); not assigning as the cause that which is but the joint-cause; nor as the upholding cause, what is merely cooperative; nor giving to philosophy the place of a *sine qua non*. Since almost all of us, without training in arts and sciences, and the Hellenic philosophy, and some even without learning at all, through the influence of a philosophy divine and barbarous, and by power, have through faith received the word concerning God, trained by self-operating wisdom. But that which acts in conjunction with something else, being of itself incapable of operating by itself, we describe as cooperating and concausing, and say that it becomes a cause only in virtue of its being a joint-cause, and receives the name of cause only in respect of its concurring with something else, but that it cannot by itself produce the right effect.

Although at one time philosophy justified the Greeks, not conducting them to that entire righteousness to which it is ascertained to cooperate, as the first and second flight of steps help you in your ascent to the upper room, and the grammarian helps the philosopher. Not as if by its abstraction, the perfect Word would be rendered incomplete, or truth perish; since also sight, and hearing, and the voice contribute to truth, but it is the mind which is the appropriate faculty for knowing it. But of those things which co-operate, some contribute a greater amount of power; some, a less. Perspicuity accordingly aids in the communication of truth, and logic in preventing us from falling under the heresies by which we are assailed. But the teaching, which is according to the Saviour, is complete in itself and without defect, being "the power and wisdom of God"; and the Hellenic philosophy does not, by its approach, make the truth more powerful; but rendering powerless the assault of sophistry against it, and frustrating the treacherous plots laid against the truth, is said to be the proper "fence and wall of the vineyard." And the truth which is according to faith is as necessary for life as bread; while the preparatory discipline is like sauce and sweetmeats. And the Scripture has expressly said, "The innocent will become wiser by understanding, and the wise will receive knowledge." "And he that speaketh of himself," said the Lord, "seeketh his own glory; but He that seeketh His glory that sent Him is true, and there is no unrighteousness in Him."

BOOK II
CHAPTER XIX

The true gnostic is an imitator of God, especially in beneficence

He is the Gnostic, who is after the image and likeness of God, who imitates God as far as possible, deficient in none of the things which contribute to the likeness as far as compatible, practicing self-restraint and endurance, living righteously, reigning over the passions, bestowing of what he has as far as possible, and doing good both by word and deed.

Now Plato the philosopher, defining the end of happiness, says that it is likeness to God as far as possible; whether concurring with the precept of the law (for great natures that are free of passions somehow hit the mark respecting the truth, as the Pythagorean Philo says in relating the history of Moses), or whether instructed by certain oracles of the time, thirsting as he always was for instruction. For the law says, "Walk after the Lord your God, and keep my commandments."

For the law calls assimilation following; and such a following to the utmost of its power assimilates. "Be," says the Lord, "merciful and pitiful, as your heavenly Father is pitiful." Thence also the Stoics have laid down the doctrine, that living agreeably to nature is the end, fitly altering the name of God into nature; since also nature extends to plants, to seeds, to trees, and to stones. It is therefore plainly said, "Bad men do not understand the law; but they who love the law fortify themselves with a wall."

We are taught that there are three kinds of friendship; and that of these the first and the best is that which results from virtue, for the love that is founded on reason is firm; that the second and intermediate is by way of recompense, and is social, liberal, and useful for life; for the friendship which is the result of favour is mutual.

And the third and last *we* assert to be that which is founded on intimacy; others, again, that it is that variable and changeable form which rests on pleasure.

The divine law, while keeping in mind all virtue, trains man especially to self-restraint, laying this as the foundation of the virtues; and disciplines us beforehand to the attainment of self-restraint by forbidding us to partake of such things as are by nature fat, as the breed of swine, which is full-fleshed. For such a use is assigned to epicures.

If, then, we are to exercise control over the belly, and what is below the belly, it is clear that we have of old heard from the Lord that we are to check lust by the law.

And this will be completely effected, if we unfeignedly condemn what is the fuel of lust: I mean pleasure.

CHAPTER XXIII
On marriage

Since pleasure and lust seem to fall under marriage, it must also be treated of. Marriage is the first conjunction of man and woman for the procreation of legitimate children.

We ask if we ought to marry; which is one of the points, which are said to be relative. For some must marry, and a man must be in some condition, and he must marry someone in some condition. For everyone is not to marry, nor always. But there is a time in which it is suitable, and a person for whom it is suitable, and an age up to which it is suitable. Neither ought everyone to take a wife, nor is it every woman one is to take, nor always, nor in every way, nor inconsiderately. But only he who is in certain circumstances, and such an one and at such time as is requisite, and for the sake of children, and one who is in every respect similar, and who does not by force or compulsion love the husband who loves her.

Let us briefly follow the history. Plato ranks marriage among outward good things, providing for the perpetuity of our race, and handing down as a torch a certain perpetuity to children's children. Democritus repudiates marriage and the procreation of children, on account of the many annoyances thence arising, and abstractions from more necessary things. Epicurus agrees, and those who place good in pleasure, and in the absence of trouble and pain. According to the opinion of the Stoics, marriage and the rearing of children are a thing indifferent; and according to the Peripatetics, a good.

In a word, these, following out their dogmas in words, became enslaved to pleasure; some using concubines, some mistresses, and the most youths.

But they who approve of marriage say, Nature has adapted us for marriage, as is evident from the structure of our bodies, which are male and female. And they constantly proclaim that command, "Increase and replenish." And though this is the case, yet it seems to them shameful that man, created by God, should be more licentious than the irrational creatures, which do not mix with many licentiously, but with one of the same species, such as pigeons and ringdoves, and creatures like them. Furthermore, they say, "The childless man fails in the perfection which is according to nature, not having substituted his proper successor in his place. For he is perfect that has produced from himself his like, or rather, when he sees that he has produced the same; that is, when that which is begotten attains to the same nature with him who begat."

Now that the Scripture counsels marriage, and allows no release from the union, is expressly contained in the law, "Thou shalt not put away thy wife, except for the cause of fornication," and it regards as fornication, the marriage of those separated while the other is alive.

"He that taketh a woman that has been put away," it is said, "committeth adultery; and if one puts away his wife, he makes her an adulteress," that is, compels her to commit adultery. And not only is he who puts her away guilty of this, but he who takes her, by giving to the woman the opportunity of sinning; for did he not take her, she would return to her husband.

The marriage, then, that is consummated according to the word, is sanctified, if the union be under subjection to God, and be conducted "with a true heart, in full assurance of faith, having hearts sprinkled from an evil conscience, and the body washed with pure water, and holding the confession of hope; for He is faithful that promised." And the happiness of marriage ought never to be estimated either by wealth or beauty, but by virtue.

For with perfect propriety Scripture has said that woman is given by God as "a help" to man. It is evident, then, in my opinion, that she will charge herself with remedying, by good sense and persuasion, each of the annoyances that originate with her husband in domestic economy. And if he do not yield, then she will endeavor, as far as possible for human nature, to lead a sinless life; whether it be necessary to die, in accordance with reason, or to live; considering that God is her helper and associate in such a course of conduct, her true defender and Savior both for the present and for the future; making Him the leader and guide of all her actions, reckoning sobriety and righteousness her work, and making the favor of God her end. Gracefully, therefore, the apostle says in the Epistle to Titus, "that the elder women should be of godly behavior, should not be slanderers, not enslaved to much wine; that they should counsel the young women to be lovers of their husbands, lovers of their children, discreet, chaste, housekeepers, good, subject to their own husbands; that the word of God be not blasphemed." But rather, he says, "Follow peace with all men, and holiness, without which no man shall see the Lord."

BOOK VI
CHAPTER VII

What true philosophy is, and whence so called

As we have long ago pointed out, what we propose as our subject is not the discipline which obtains in each sect, but that which is really philosophy, strictly systematic Wisdom, which furnishes acquaintance with the things which pertain to life. And we define Wisdom to be certain knowledge, being a sure and irrefragable apprehension of things divine and human, comprehending the present, past, and future, which the Lord hath taught us, both by His advent and by the prophets. And it is irrefragable by reason, inasmuch as it has been communicated. And so it is wholly true according to [God's] intention, as being known through means of the Son. And in one aspect it is eternal, and in another it becomes useful in time. Partly it is one and the same, partly many and indifferent — partly perfect, partly incomplete.

This wisdom, then — rectitude of soul and of reason, and purity of life — is the object of the desire of philosophy, which is kindly and lovingly disposed towards wisdom, and does everything to attain it.

Now those are called philosophers, among us, who love Wisdom, the Creator and Teacher of all things, that is, the knowledge of the Son of God.

If, then, we assert that Christ himself is Wisdom, and that it was His working which showed itself in the prophets, by which the gnostic tradition may be learned, as He himself taught the apostles during His presence; then it follows that the *gnosis*, which is the knowledge and apprehension of things present, future, and past, which is sure and reliable, as being imparted and revealed by the Son of God, is wisdom.

And if, too, the end of the wise man is contemplation, that of those who are still philosophers aims at it, but never attains it, unless by the process of learning it receives the prophetic utterances which have been made known, by which it grasps both the present, the future, and the past — how they are, were, and shall be.

And the *gnosis* itself is that which has descended by transmission to a few, having been imparted unwritten by the apostles. Hence, then, knowledge or wisdom ought to be exercised up to the eternal and unchangeable habit of contemplation.

CHAPTER VIII

Philosophy is knowledge given by God

For Paul too, in the Epistles, plainly does not disparage philosophy; but deems it unworthy of the man who has attained to the elevation of the Gnostic, any more to go back to the Hellenic "philosophy," figuratively calling it "the rudiments of this world," as being most rudimentary, and a preparatory training for the truth. Wherefore also, writing to the Hebrews, who were declining again from faith to the law, he says, "Have ye not need again of one to teach you which are the first principles of the oracles of God, and are become such as have need of milk, and not of strong meat?" So also to the Colossians, who were Greek converts, "Beware lest any man spoil you by philosophy and vain deceit, after the tradition of men, after the rudiments of this world, and not after Christ," enticing them again to return to philosophy, the elementary doctrine.

And should one say that it was through human understanding that philosophy was discovered by the Greeks, still I find the Scriptures saying that understanding is sent by God.

Philosophy is not then false, though the thief and the liar speak truth, through a transformation of operation. Nor is sentence of condemnation to be pronounced ignorantly against what is said, on account of him who says it (which also is to be kept in view, in the case of those who are now alleged to prophesy); but what is said must be looked at, to see if it keep by the truth.

And in general terms, we shall not err in alleging that all things necessary and profitable for life came to us from God, and that philosophy more especially was given to the Greeks, as a covenant peculiar to them — being, as it is, a stepping-stone to the philosophy which is according to Christ.

For we now dare aver (for here is the faith that is characterized by knowledge) that such an one knows all things, and comprehends all things in the exercise of sure apprehension, respecting matters difficult for us, and really pertaining to the true gnosis such as were James, Peter, John, Paul, and the rest of the apostles. For prophecy is full of knowledge (*gnosis*), inasmuch as it was given by the Lord, and again explained by the Lord to the apostles. And is not knowledge (*gnosis*) an attribute of the rational soul, which trains itself for this, that by knowledge it may become entitled to immortality? For both are powers of the soul, both knowledge and impulse. And impulse is found to be a movement after an assent. For he who has an impulse towards an action, first receives the knowledge of the action, and secondly the impulse. Let us further devote our attention to this. For since learning is older than action (for naturally, he who does what he wishes to do learns it first; and knowledge comes from learning, and impulse follows knowledge; after which comes action); knowledge turns out the beginning and author of all rational action. So that rightly the peculiar nature of the rational soul is characterized by this alone; for in reality impulse, like knowledge, is excited by existing objects. And knowledge (*gnosis*) is essentially a contemplation of existences on the part of the soul, either of a certain thing or of certain things, and when perfected, of all together. Although some say that the wise man is persuaded that there are some things incomprehensible, in such wise as to have respecting them a kind of comprehension, inasmuch as he comprehends that things incomprehensible are incomprehensible; which is common, and pertains to those who are capable of perceiving little. For such a man affirms that there are some things incomprehensible.

Selections taken from *Paidagogos* and *Stromata* are from
Ante-Nicene Fathers, Fathers of the Second Century,
Alexander Roberts, D.D. and James Donaldson, LL.D., editors,z
Volume II, Buffalo: The Christian Literature Publishing Company, 1885

Chapter 16 • St. Cyprian: *On the Unity of the Church*

The treatise *On the City of the Church* is a typical example of a third-century presentation of the fundamental characteristic or mark of the Church by the bishop of Carthage (A.D. 248-58). He presents the apostolic and traditional concept of this unity, its foundation in authority, and the subtle forms of deviation from it. Cyprian's letters also bear eloquent testimony to his concern for the unity and harmony of the members of the Church. The unity of the Church is a participation in the Unity of God, which is locally expressed in the office of the Bishop and maintained throughout the Christian church by the unity of the episcopal authorities.

The Treatises of Cyprian

TREATISE I

On the Unity of the Church

Argument — On the occasion of the schism of Novatian, to keep back from him the Carthaginians, who already were not averse to him, on account of Novatus and some other presbyters of his Church, who had originated the whole disturbance, Cyprian wrote this treatise. And first of all, fortifying them against the deceits of these, he exhorts them to constancy, and instructs them that heresies exist because Christ, the head of the church, is not looked to, that the common commission first entrusted to Peter is contemned, and the one Church and the one Episcopate are deserted. Then he proves, as well by the scriptures as by the figures of the Old and New Testament, the unity of the church.

Satan has invented heresies and schisms, whereby he might subvert the faith, might corrupt the truth, might divide the unity. Those whom he cannot keep in the darkness of the old way, he circumvents and deceives by the error of a new way. He snatches men from the Church itself; and while they seem to themselves to have already approached to the light, and to have escaped the night of the world, he pours over them again, in their unconsciousness, new darkness; so that, although they do not stand firm with the Gospel of Christ, and with the observation and law of Christ, they still call themselves Christians, and, walking in darkness, they think that they have the light, while the adversary is flattering and deceiving, who, according to the apostle's word, transforms himself into an angel of light, and equips his ministers as if they were the ministers of righteousness, who maintain night instead of day, death for salvation, despair under the offer of hope, perfidy under the pretext of faith, antichrist under the name of Christ; so that, while they feign things like the truth, they make void the truth by their subtlety. This happens, beloved brethren, so long as we do not return to the source of truth, as we do not seek the head nor keep the teaching of the heavenly Master.

If any one consider and examine these things, there is no need for lengthened discussion and arguments. There is easy proof for faith in a short summary of the truth. The Lord speaks to Peter, saying, "I say unto thee, that thou art Peter; and upon this rock I will build my Church, and the gates of hell shall not prevail against it. And I will give unto thee the keys of the kingdom of heaven; and whatsoever thou shalt bind on earth shall be bound also in heaven, and whatsoever thou shalt loose on earth shall be loosed in heaven." And again to the same He says, after His resurrection, "Feed my sheep." And although to all the apostles, after His resurrection, He gives an equal power, and says, "As the Father hath sent me, even so send I you: Receive ye the Holy Spirit: Whose soever sins ye remit, they shall be remitted unto him; and whose soever sins ye retain, they shall be retained," yet, that He might set forth unity, He arranged by His authority the origin of that unity, as beginning from one. Assuredly the rest of the apostles were also the same as was Peter, endowed with a like partnership both of honour and power, but the beginning proceeds from unity. Which one Church, also, the Holy Spirit in the Song of Songs designated in the person of our Lord, and says, "My dove my spotless one, is but one. She is the only one of her mother, elect of her that bare her." Does he who does not hold this unity of the Church think that he holds the faith? Does he who strives against and resists the Church trust that he is in the Church, when moreover the blessed Apostle Paul teaches the same thing and sets forth the sacrament of unity, saying, "There is one body and one spirit, one hope of your calling, one Lord, one faith, one baptism, one God"?

And this unity we ought firmly to hold and assert, especially those of us that are bishops who preside in the Church, that we may also prove the episcopate itself to be one and undivided. Let no one deceive the brotherhood by a falsehood: let no one corrupt the truth of the faith by perfidious prevarication. The episcopate is one, each part of which is held by each one for the whole. The Church also is one, which is spread abroad far and wide into a multitude by an increase of fruitfulness.

Thus the Church, shone over with the light of the Lord, sheds forth her rays over the whole world, yet it is one light which is everywhere diffused, nor is the unity of the body separated. Whoever is separated from the Church is separated from the promises of the Church; nor can he who forsakes the Church of Christ attain to the rewards of Christ. He is a stranger; he is profane; he is an enemy. He can no longer have God for his Father, who has not the Church for his mother. If any one could escape who was outside the ark of Noah, then he also may escape who shall be outside of the Church. The Lord warns, saying "He who is not with me is against me, and he who gathereth not with me scattereth." He who breaks the peace and the concord of Christ, does so in opposition to Christ; he who gathereth elsewhere than in the Church, scatters the Church of Christ. The Lord says, "I and the Father are one," and again it is written of the Father, and of the Son, and of the Holy Spirit, "And these three are one." And does any one believe that this unity which thus comes from the divine strength and coheres in celestial sacraments, can be divided in the Church, and can be separated by the parting asunder of opposing wills? He who does not hold this unity does not hold God's law, does not hold the faith of the Father and the Son, does not hold life and salvation.

This sacrament of unity, this bond of a concord inseparably cohering, is set forth where in the Gospel the coat of the Lord Jesus Christ is not at all divided nor cut, but is received as an entire garment, and is possessed as an uninjured and undivided robe by those who cast lots concerning Christ's garment, who should rather put on Christ.

He cannot possess the garment of Christ who parts and divides the Church of Christ.

Who, then, is so wicked and faithless, who is so insane with the madness of discord that either he should believe that the unity of God can be divided, or should dare to rend it — the garment of the Lord — the Church of Christ? He himself in His Gospel warns us, and teaches, saying, "And there shall be one flock and one shepherd."

The Apostle Paul, moreover, urging upon us this same unity, beseeches and exhorts, saying, "I beseech you, brethren, by the name of our Lord Jesus Christ, that ye all speak the same thing, and that there be no schisms among you; but that ye be joined together in the same mind and in the same judgment." And again, he says, "Forbearing one another in love, endeavouring to keep the unity of the Spirit in the bond of peace." Do you think that you can stand and live if you withdraw from the Church, building for yourself other homes and a different dwelling?

Hence, heresies not only have frequently been originated, but continue to be so; while the perverted mind has no peace — while a discordant faithlessness does not maintain unity. But the Lord permits and suffers these things to be while the choice of one's own liberty remains, so that while the discrimination of truth is testing our hearts and our minds, the sound faith of those that are approved may shine forth with manifest light. The Holy Spirit forewarns and says by the apostle, "It is needful also that there should be heresies, that they which are approved may be made manifest among you." Thus the faithful are approved, thus the perfidious are detected, thus even here, before the day of judgment, the souls of the righteous and of the unrighteous are already divided, and the chaff separated from the wheat.

Nor let any deceive themselves by a futile interpretation, in respect of the Lord having said, "Whensoever two or three are gathered together in my name, there am I in the midst of them." Corrupters and false interpreters of the Gospel quote the last words, and lay aside the former ones, remembering part, and craftily suppressing part: as they themselves are separated from the Church, so they cut off the substance of one section. For the Lord, when He would urge unanimity and peace upon His disciples, said, "I say unto you, That if two of you shall agree on earth touching anything that ye shall ask, it shall be given you by my Father which is in heaven. For wheresoever two or three are gathered together in my name, I am with them," showing that most is given, not to the multitude, but to the unanimity of those that pray. "If," He says, "two of you shall agree on earth." He placed agreement first; He has made the concord of peace a prerequisite; He taught that we should agree firmly and faithfully. But how can he agree with anyone who does not agree with the body of the Church itself, and with the universal brotherhood? How can two or three be assembled together in Christ's name, who, it is evident, are separated from Christ and from His Gospel? For we have not withdrawn from them, but they from us; and since heresies and schisms have risen subsequently, from their establishment for themselves of diverse places of worship, they have forsaken the Head and Source of the Truth. The Lord in His Gospel, when He would direct the way of our hope and faith in a brief summary, said, "The Lord thy God is one God: and thou shalt love the Lord thy God with all thy heart, and with all thy soul, and with all thy strength. This is the first commandment; and the second is like unto it: Thou shalt love thy neighbour as thyself. On these two commandments hang all the law and the prophets." He taught, at the same time, love and unity by His instruction. He has included all the prophets and the law in two precepts. But what unity does he keep, what love does he maintain or consider, who, savage with the madness of discord, divides the Church, destroys the faith, disturbs the peace, dissipates charity, profanes the sacrament?

Does he think that he has Christ, who acts in opposition to Christ's priests, who separates himself from the company of His clergy and people? He bears arms against the Church, he contends against God's appointment. An enemy of the altar, a rebel against Christ's sacrifice, for the faith faithless, for religion profane, a disobedient servant, an impious son, a hostile brother, despising the bishops, and forsaking God's priests, he dares to set up another altar, to make another prayer with unauthorized words, to profane the truth of the Lord's offering by false sacrifices, and not to know that he who strives against the appointment of God, is punished on account of the daring of his temerity by divine visitation.

These, doubtless, they imitate and follow, who, despising God's tradition, seek after strange doctrines, and bring in teachings of human appointment, whom the Lord rebukes and reproves in His Gospel, saying, "Ye reject the commandments of God, that ye may keep your own tradition." This is a worse crime than that which the lapsed seem to have fallen into, who nevertheless, standing as penitent for their crime, beseech God with full satisfactions. In this case, the Church is sought after and entreated; in that case, the Church is resisted: here it is possible that there has been necessity; there the will is engaged in the wickedness; on the one hand, he who has passed has only injured himself; on the other, he who had endeavoured to cause a heresy or a schism has deceived many by drawing them with him. In the former, it is the loss of one soul; in the latter, the risk of many.

Certainly the one both understands that he has sinned, and laments and bewails it; the other, puffed up in his heart, and pleasing himself in his very crimes, separates sons from their Mother, entices sheep from their shepherd, disturbs the sacraments of God; and while the lapsed has sinned but once, he sins daily.

I indeed desire, beloved brethren, and I equally endeavour and exhort, that if it be possible, none of the brethren should perish, and that our rejoicing Mother may enclose in her bosom the one body of a people at agreement. Yet if wholesome counsel cannot recall to the way of salvation certain leaders of schisms and originators of dissensions, who abide in blind and obstinate madness, yet do you others, if either taken in simplicity, or induced by error, or deceived by some craftiness of misleading cunning, loose yourselves from the nets of deceit, free your wandering steps from errors, acknowledge the straight way of the heavenly road. The word of the witnessing apostle is: "We command you," says he, "in the name of our Lord Jesus Christ, that ye withdraw yourselves from all brethren that walk disorderly, and not after the tradition that they have received from us." And again he says, "Let no man deceive you with vain words; for because of these things cometh the wrath of God upon the children of disobedience. Be not ye therefore partakers with them." We must withdraw, nay rather must flee, from those who fall away, lest, while any one is associated with those who walk wickedly, and goes on in ways of error and of sin, he himself also, wandering away from the path of the true road, should be found in like guilt. God is one, and Christ is one, and His Church is one, and the faith is one, and the people is joined into a substantial unity of body by the cement of concord.

This unanimity formerly prevailed among the apostles; and thus the new assembly of believers, keeping the Lord's commandments, maintained its charity. Divine Scripture proves this, when it says, "But the multitude of them which believed were of one heart and of one soul." And again: "These all continued with one mind in prayer with the women, and Mary the mother of Jesus, and with His brethren." And thus they prayed with effectual prayers; thus, they were able with confidence to obtain whatever they asked from the Lord's mercy.

Selections from "The Treatises of Cyprian" are from
The Ante-Nicene Fathers, The Writings of the Fathers Down to A.D. 325,
Alexander Roberts, D.D. and James Donaldson, LL.D., editors,
Volume V, Buffalo: The Christian Literature Co., 1886

Chapter 17 • Lactantius: *On the Workmanship of God*

The work of Lactantius marks the period of the termination of the civil persecution of the Catholic Church and the beginning of the glorious period of the golden age of the fourth century. The writers of this era were less concerned with apologetics and more involved in the theoretical constructive formalization of the theology of the dogmas of the Church. Among other things Lactantius stresses the traditional idea that wisdom and the Christian religion are indeed distinct disciplines but that they cannot be separated: "neither is any religion to be undertaken without wisdom nor any wisdom to be approved without religion."The seven books entitled *Divinarum Institutiones* may be classified as a manual of theology. The short excerpts from the *De Opificio Dei* emphasizes that traducianism (the theological teaching that the human soul is passed on along with the body from the parents) cannot be a true account of the origin of the human soul, but that each human soul is created directly by God, Who is responsible for the conception and molding of the body, the breathing in of life, and the bringing forth in safety of whatever contributes to the preservation of man.

On The Workmanship of God

CHAPTER XIX

Of the soul, and it given by God

A question also may arise respecting this, whether the soul is produced from the father, or rather from the mother, or indeed from both. But I think that this judgment is to be formed as though in a doubtful matter. For nothing is true of these three opinions, because souls are produced neither from both nor from either. For a body may be produced from a body, since something is contributed from both; but a soul cannot be produced from souls, because nothing can depart from a slight and incomprehensible subject. Therefore the manner of the production of souls belongs entirely to God alone.

"In fine, we are all sprung from a heavenly seed, all have that same Father," as Lucretius says. For nothing but what is mortal can be generated from mortals. Nor ought to be deemed a father who in no way perceives that he has transmitted or breathed a soul from his own; nor, if he perceives it, comprehends in his mind when or in what manner that effect is produced.

From this it is evident that souls are not given by parents, but by one and the same God and Father of all, who alone has the law and method of their birth, since He alone produces them. For the part of the earthly parent is nothing more than with a sense of pleasure to emit the moisture of the body, in which is the material of birth, or to receive it; and to this work man's power is limited, nor has he any further power. Therefore men wish for the birth of sons, because they do not themselves bring it about. Everything beyond this is the work of God — namely, the conception itself, and the moulding of the body, and the breathing in of life, and the bringing forth in safety, and whatever afterwards contribute to the preservation of man: it is His gift that we breathe, that we live, and are vigorous. For, besides that we owe it to His bounty that we are safe in body, and that He supplies us with nourishment from various sources. He also gives to man wisdom, which no earthly father can by any means give; and therefore it often happens that foolish sons are born from wise parents, and wise sons from foolish parents, which some persons attribute to fate and the stars. But this is not now the time to discuss the subject of fate. It is sufficient to say this, that even if the stars hold together the efficacy of all things, it is nevertheless certain that all things are done by God, who both made and set in order the stars themselves. They are therefore senseless who detract this power from God, and assign it to His work.

He would have it, therefore, to be in our own power, whether we use or do not use this divine and excellent gift of God. For, having granted this, He bound man himself by the mystery of virtue, by which he might be able to gain life. For great is the power, great the reason, great the mysterious purpose of man; and if anyone shall not abandon this, nor betray his fidelity and devotedness, he must be happy; he, in short, to sum up the matter in few words, must of necessity resemble God. For he is in error whosoever judges of man by his flesh. For this worthless body with which we are clothed is the receptacle of man. For man himself can neither be touched, nor looked upon, nor grasped, because he has hidden within this body, which is seen. And if he shall be more luxurious and delicate in this life than its nature demands, if he shall despise virtue, and give himself to the pursuit of fleshly lusts, he will fall and be pressed down to the earth; but if (as his duty is) he shall readily and constantly maintain his position, which is right for him, and he has rightly obtained — if he shall not be enslaved to the earth, which he ought to trample upon and overcome, he will gain eternal life.

Selections from "On the Workmanship of God" from
Ante-Nicene Fathers, The Writings of the Fathers Down to A.D. 325,
Alexander Roberts, D.D. and James Donaldson, LL.D., editors,
Volume VII, New York: Charles Scribner's Sons, 1905

Part III
Arian and Other Unorthodox Beliefs Rejected

Introduction

During the period of the Council of Nicaea there are many Greek and Latin authors who emphasized the clarification of the language in which the basic beliefs of the Catholic Church are presented. The writings presented here exemplify the problems facing those authors and their orthodox solutions, in hymns, homilies, and philosophical and theological forms.

Arianism was one of the most widespread attacks on the Nicaean expression of the nature of Jesus Christ. Many of the early Christian writers spoke of the Son of God as being in some way subordinated to the Father, as Jesus himself seemed to assert on occasion. The expression "Son of Man" was interpreted to justify this point of view. However, if one emphasizes the symbolic use of the phrase as a personification of the Kingdom of God or of the person of the Messiah or of the Divine King and Judge, "the expression 'Son of Man' thus implies both the dignity of the Messiah and His humiliation: God's anointed passes through suffering and death to his dominion." The Arians, however, taught that the Son was not "consubstantial" with the Father but a creature in his own right. Athanasius, among the Greek ecclesiastical writers, became the great champion of orthodoxy against the Arians by virtue of his explanation of the Unity of the Trinity, the substantial identity of the Three Persons, and the Johannine statement that the Word became flesh in reality and not just in appearance.

This part includes some of the works of the Post-Nicaean Greek authors but omits famous ones such as Eusebius' *Preparation for the Gospels,* and *Demonstration of the Gospel*, and Gregory (the Theologian) Nazianzen's *Theological Orations* and *Letter on the Trinity.* St. Hilary, Bishop of Poitiers (ca. 353), was the Latin author who performed a role similar to that of Athanasius, as shown by his *De Trinitate (On the Trinity)*, also known as *On the Faith against the Arians (De fide adversus Arianos*).

Chapter 18 • St. Ephraim the Syrian: *The Pearl; Seven Hymns on the Faith*

St. Ephraim (c. 306-373 c.) was referred to by some of his friends as "The Harp of the Holy Spirit." He is famous for using hymns for the elucidation of exegetical, dogmatic, and ascetical themes, especially in his refutations of the Arians and Gnostics. He may have attended the Council of Nicaea. He was very devoted to the Blessed Virgin and is often mentioned as a witness to the Immacuate Conception of Mary. Pope Benedict XV declared him a Doctor of the Church.

HYMN I.

1. On a certain day a pearl did I take up, my brethren; I saw in it mysteries pertaining to the Kingdom; semblances and types of the Majesty; it became a fountain, and I drank out of it mysteries of the Son.

I put it, my brethren, upon the palm of my hand, that I might examine it: I went to look at it on one side, and it proved faces on all sides. I found out that the Son was incomprehensible, since He is wholly Light.

In its brightness I beheld the Bright One Who cannot be clouded and in its pureness a great mystery, even the Body of our Lord which is well-refined: in its undividedness I saw the Truth which is undivided.

It was so that I saw there its pure conception, — the Church, and the Son within her. The cloud was the likeness of her that bare Him, and her type the heaven, since there shone forth from her His gracious Shining.

I saw therein His trophies, and His victories, and His crowns. I saw His helpful and overflowing graces, and His hidden things with His revealed things.

2. It was greater to me than the ark, for I was astonied thereat: I saw therein folds without shadow to them because it was a daughter of light, types vocal without tongues, utterances of mysteries without lips, a silent harp that without voice gave out melodies.

The trumpet falters and the thunder matters; be not thou daring then; leave things hidden, take things revealed. Thou hast seen in the clear sky a second shower; the clefts of thine ears, as from the clouds, they are filled with interpretations.

And as that manna which alone filled the people, in the place of pleasant meats, with its pleasantnesses, so does this pearl fill me in the place of books, and the reading thereof, and the explanations thereof.

And when I asked if there were yet other mysteries, it had no mouth for me that I might hear from, neither any ears wherewith it might hear me. O thou thing without senses, whence I have gained new senses!

3. It answered me and said, "The daughter of the sea am I, the illimitable sea! And from that sea whence I came up it is that there is a mighty treasury of mysteries in my bosom! Search thou out the sea, but search not out the Lord of the sea!

"I have seen the divers who came down after me, when astonied, so that from the midst of the sea they returned to the dry ground; for a few moments they sustained it not. Who would linger and be searching on into the depths of the Godhead?

"The waves of the Son are full of blessings, and with mischiefs too. Have ye not seen, then, the waves of the sea, which if a ship should struggle with them would break her to pieces, and if she yield herself to them, and rebel not against them, then she is preserved? In the sea all the Egyptians were choked, though they scrutinized it not, and, without prying, the Hebrews too were overcome upon the dry land, and how shall ye be kept alive? And the men of Sodom were licked up by the fire, and how shall ye prevail?

"At these uproars the fish in the sea were moved,[1] and Leviathan also. Have ye then a heart of stone that ye read these things and run into these errors? O great fear that justice also should be so long silent!"[2]

4. "Searching is mingled with thanksgiving, and whether of the two will prevail? The incense of praise riseth along with the fume of disputation from the tongue, and unto which shall we hearken? Prayer and prying [come] from one mouth,[3] and which shall we listen to?

"For three days was Jonah a neighbor [of mine] in the sea: the living things that were in the sea were affrighted, [saying,] 'Who shall flee from God? Jonah fled, and ye are obstinate at your scrutiny of Him!' "

HYMN II.

1. Whereunto art thou like? Let thy stillness speak to one that hears; with silent mouth speak with us: for who so hears the stammerings of thy silence, to him thy type utters its silent cry concerning our Redeemer.

Thy mother is a virgin of the sea; though he took her not [to wife]: she fell into his bosom, though he knew her not; she conceived thee near him, though be did not know her. Do thou, that art a type, reproach the Jewish women that have thee hung upon them. Thou art the only progeny of all forms which art like to the Word on High, Whom singly the Most High begot. The engraven forms seem to be the type of created things above. This visible offspring of the invisible womb is a type of great things[4]. Thy goodly conception was without seed, and without wedlock was thy pure generation, and without brethren was thy single birth.

Our Lord had brethren and yet not brethren, since He was an Only-Begotten. O solitary one, thou type exact of the Only-Begotten! There is a type of thine in the crown of kings, (wherein) thou hast brothers and sisters.

Goodly gems are thy brethren, with beryls and unions as thy companions: may gold be as it were thy kinsman, may there be unto the King of kings a crown from thy well-beloved ones! When thou earnest up from the sea, that living tomb, thou didst cry out, Let me have a goodly assemblage of brethren, relatives, and kinsmen. As the wheat is in the stalk, so thou art in the crown with princes: and it is a just restoration to thee, as if of a pledge,[5] from that depth thou shouldest be exalted to a goodly eminence. Wheat the stalk bears in the field; thee the head of the king upon his chariot carries about.

O daughter of the water, who hast left sea, wherein thou wert born, and art gone up to the dry and, wherein thou art beloved: for men have loved and seized and adorned themselves with thee, like as they did that Offspring Whom the Gentiles loved and crowned themselves withal.

It is by the mystery of truth that Leviathan is trodden down of mortals: the divers put him off, and put on Christ. In the sacrament of oil did the Apostles[6] steal Thee away, and came up. They snatched their souls from his mouth, bitter as it was.

Thy Nature is like a silent lamb in its sweetness, of which if a man is to lay hold, he lifts it in a crucial form by its ears, as it was on Golgotha. He cast out abundantly all His gleams upon them that looked upon Him.

2. Shadowed forth in thy beauty is the beauty of the Son, Who clothed himself with suffering when the nails passed through Him. The awl passed in thee since they handled thee roughly, as they did His hands; and because He suffered He reigned, as by thy sufferings thy beauty increased.

And if they showed no pity upon thee, neither did they love thee: still suffer as thou mightest, thou hast come to reign! Simon Peter[7] showed pity on the Rock; whoso hath smitten it, is himself thereby overcome; it is by reason of Its suffering that Its beauty hath adorned the height and the depth.

HYMN III.

1. Thou dost not hide thyself in thy bareness, O pearl! With the love of thee is the merchant ravished also, for he strips off his garments; not to cover thee, [seeing] thy clothing is thy light, thy garment is thy brightness, O thou that art bared!

Thou art like Eve who was clothed with nakedness. Cursed be he that deceived her and stripped her and left her. The serpent cannot strip off thy glory. In the mysteries whose type thou art, women are clothed with Light in Eden.[8]

2. Very glistening are the pearls of Ethiopia, as it is written, Who gave thee to Ethiopia [the land] of black men.[9] He that gave light to the Gentiles, both to the Ethiopians and unto the Indians did His bright beams reach.

The eunuch of Ethiopia upon his chariot[10] saw Philip: the Lamb of Light met the dark man from out of the water. While he was reading, the Ethiopian was baptized and shone with joy, and journeyed on!

He made disciples and taught, and out of black men he made men white.[11] And the dark Ethiopic women[12] became pearls for the Son; He offered them up to the Father, as a glistening crown from the Ethiopians.

3. The Queen of Sheba[13] was a sheep[14] that had come into the place of wolves; the lamp of truth did Solomon give her, who also married[15] her when he fell away. She was enlightened and went away, but they were dark as their manner was.

The bright spark which went down home with that blessed [Queen], held on its shining amid the darkness, till the new Day-spring came. The bright spark met with this shining, and illumined the place.

4. There are in the sea divers fishes of many cubits, and with all their greatness they are very small; but by thy littleness the crown is made great, like as the Son, by whose littleness Adam was made great.

For the head is thy crown intended: for the eye thy beauty, for the ear thy goodliness. Come up from the sea, thou neighbor to the dry land, and come and sojourn by the [seat of] hearing. Let the ear love the word of life as it loveth thee!

In the ear is the word, and without it is the pearl. Let it as being warned by thee, by thee get wisdom, and be warned by the word of truth. Be thou its mirror: the beauty of the Word in thine own beauty shall it see: in thee it shall learn how precious is the Word on High! The ear is the leaf: the flesh is the tree, and thou in the midst of it are a fruit of light, and to the womb that brings forth Light, thou art a type that points.

Thee He used as a parable of that kingdom, O pearl! as He did the virgins that entered into it, five in number, clothed with the light of their lamps! To thee are those bright ones like, thou that art clad in light!

5. Who would give a pearl to the daughter of the poor? For when it hangs on her, it becomes her not. Gain without price that faith, all of which becomes all the limbs of men. But for no gold would a lady exchange her pearl.

It were a great disgrace if thou shouldst throw thy pearl away into the mire for nought!

In the pearl of time let us behold that of eternity; for it is in the purse, or in the seal, or in the treasury. Within the gate there are other gates with their locks and keys. Thy pearl hath the High One sealed up as taking account of all.

HYMN IV.

1. The thief gained the faith which gained him,[16] and brought him up and placed him in paradise. He saw in the Cross a tree of life; that was the fruit, he was the eater in Adam's stead.

The fool, who goes astray, grazes the faith, as it were an eye,[17] by all manner of questions. The probing of the finger blinds the eye, and much more doth that prying blind the faith.

For even the diver pries not into his pearl. In it do all merchants rejoice without prying into whence it came; even the king who is crowned therewith does not explore it.

2. Because Balaam was foolish, a foolish beast in the ass spoke with him, because he despised God Who spoke with him. Thee too let the pearl reprove ill the ass's stead.

The people that had a heart of stone, by a Stone He set at nought,[18] for lo, a stone hears words. Witness its work that has reproved them; and you, ye deaf ones, let the pearl reprove to-day.

With the swallow[19] and the crow did He put men to shame; with the ox, yea with the ass,[20] did He put them to shame; let the pearl reprove now, O ye birds and things on earth and things below.

3. Not as the moon does thy light fill or wane; the Sun whose light is greater than all, lo! of Him it is that a type is shadowed out in thy little compass. O type of the Son, one spark of Whom is greater than the sun!—

The pearl itself is full, for its light is full; neither is there any cunning worker who can steal from it; for its wall is its own beauty, yea, its guard also! It lacks not, since it is entirely perfect.

And if a man would break thee to take a part from thee, thou art like the faith which with the heretics perishes, seeing they have broken it in pieces and spoiled it: for is it any better than this to have the faith scrutinized?

The faith is an entire nature that may not be corrupted. The spoiler gets himself mischief by it: the heretic brings ruin on himself thereby. He that chases the light from his pupils blinds himself.

Fire and air are divided when sundered. Light alone, of all creatures, as its Creator, is not divided; it is not barren, for that it also begets without losing thereby.

4. And if a man thinks that thou art framed [by art] he errs greatly; thy nature proclaims that thou, as all stones, art not the framing of art; and so thou art a type of the Generation which no making framed.

Thy stone flees from a comparison with the Stone [which is] the Son. For thy own generation is from the midst of the deep, that of the Son of thy Creator is from the highest height; He is not like thee, in that He is like His Father.

And as they tell, two wombs bare thee also. Thou camest down from on high a fluid nature; thou camest up from the sea a solid body. By means of thy second birth thou didst show thy loveliness to the children of men.

Hands fixed thee, when thou wast embodied, into thy receptacles; for thou art in the crown as upon a cross, and in a coronet as in a victory; thou art upon the ears, as if to fill up what was lacking; thou extendest over all.

HYMN V.

1. O gift that camest up without price[21] with the diver! Thou laidest hold upon this visible light, that without price rises for the children of men: a parable of the hidden One that without price gives the hidden Dayspring!

And the painter too paints a likeness of thee with colors. Yet by thee is faith painted in types and emblems for colors, and in the place of the image by thee and thy colors is thy Creator painted.

O thou frankincense without smell, who breathest types from out of thee! thou art not to be eaten, yet thou givest a sweet smell unto them that hear thee! thou art not to be drunk, yet by thy story, a fountain of types art thou made unto the ears!

2. It is thou which art great in thy littleness, O pearl! Small is thy measure and little thy compass with thy weight; but great is thy glory: to that crown alone in which thou art there is none like.

And who hath not perceived of thy littleness, how great it is; if one despises thee and throws thee away, he would blame himself for his clownishness, for when he saw thee in a king's crown he would be attracted to thee.

3. Men stripped their clothes off and dived and drew thee out, pearl! It was not kings that put thee before men, but those naked ones who were a type of the poor and the fishers and the Galileans.

For clothed bodies were not able to come to thee; they came that were stript as children; they plunged their bodies and came down to thee; and thou didst much desire them, and thou didst aid them who thus loved thee.

Glad tidings did they give for thee: their tongues before their bosoms did the poor [fishers] open, and produced and showed the new riches among the merchants: upon the wrists of men they put thee as a medicine of life.

4. The naked ones in a type saw thy rising again by the sea-shore; and by the side of the lake they, the Apostles[22] of a truth, saw the rising again of the Son of thy Creator. By thee and by thy Lord the sea and the lake were beautified.

The diver came up from the sea and put on his clothing; and from the lake too Simon Peter came up swimming and put on his coat;[23] clad as with coats, with the love of both of you, were these two.

5. And since I have wandered in thee, pearl, I will gather up my mind, and by having contemplated thee, would become like thee, in that thou art all gathered up into thyself; and as thou in all times art one, one let me become by thee!

Pearls have I gathered together that I might make a crown for the Son in the place of stains which are in my members. Receive my offering, not that Thou art shortcoming; it is because of mine own shortcoming that I have offered it to Thee. Whiten my stains!

This crown is all spiritual pearls, which instead of gold are set in love, and instead of ouches in faith; and instead of hands, let praise offer it up to the Highest!

HYMN VI.

1. Would that the memory of the fathers would exhale from the tombs; who were very simple as being wise, and reverend as believing. They without cavilling searched for, and came to the right path.

He gave the law; the mountains melted away; fools broke through it. By unclean ravens He fed Elijah at the desert stream; and moreover gave from the skeleton honey unto Samson. They judged not, nor inquired why it was unclean, why clean.

2. And when He made void the sabbaths, the feeble Gentiles were clothed with health. Samson took the daughter of the aliens, and there was no disputing among the righteous; the prophet also took a harlot, and the just held their peace.

He blamed the righteous,[24] and He held up and lifted up [to view] their delinquencies: He pitied sinners,[25] and restored them without cost: and made low the mountains of their sins:[26] He proved that God is not to be arraigned by men, and as Lord of Truth, that His servants were His shadow; and whatsoever way His will looked, they directed also their own wills; and because Light was in Him,[27] their shadows were enlightened.

3. How strangely perplexed are all the heretics by simple things! For when He plainly foreshadowed this New Testament by that of the Prophets, those pitiable men rose, as though from sleep, and shouted out and made a disturbance. And the Way, wherein the righteous held straight on, and by their truths had gone forth therein, that [Way] have these broken[28] up, because they were besotted: this they left and went out of; because they pried, all evil searching, [yea,] an evil babbling led them astray.

They saw the ray: they made it darkness, that they might grope therein: they saw the jewel, even the faith: while they pried into it, it fell and was lost. Of the pearl they made a stone, that they might stumble upon it.

4. O Gift, which fools have made a poison! The People were for separating Thy beauteous root from Thy fountain, though they separated it not: [false] teachings estranged Thy beauty also from the stock thereof.

By Thee did they get themselves estranged, who wished to estrange Thee. By Thee the tribes were cut off and scattered abroad from out of Sion, and also the [false] teachings of the seceders.

Bring Thyself within the compass of our littleness, O Thou Gift of ours. For if love cannot find Thee out on all sides, it cannot be still and at rest. Make Thyself small, Thou Who art too great for all, Who comest unto all!

5. By this would those who wrangle against our Pearl be reproved; because instead of love, strife has come in and dared to essay to unveil thy beauty. It was not graven, since it is a progeny which cannot be interpreted.

Thou didst show thy beauty among the objects to show whereto thou art like, thou Pearl that art all faces. The beholders were astonied and perplexed at thee. The separatists separated thee in two, and were separated in two by thee, thou that art of one substance throughout.

They saw not thy beauty, because there was not in them the eye of truth. For the veil of prophecy, full as it was of the mysteries; to them was a covering of thy glistering faces: they thought that thou wast other [than thou art], O thou mirror of ours! and therefore these blind schismatics defiled thy fair beauty.

6. Since they have extolled thee too much, or have lowered thee too much, bring them to the even level. Come down, descend a little from that height of infidelity and heathendom; and come up from the depth of Judaism, though thou art in the Heaven.

Let our Lord be set between God and men![29] Let the Prophets be as it were His heralds! Let the Just One, as being His Father, rejoice! that Word it is which conquered both Jews and Heathens!

7. Come, Thou Gift of Holy Church, stay, rest in the midst of Her! The circumcised have troubled Thee, in that they are vain babblers, and so have the [false] doctrines in that they are contentious. Blessed be He that gave Thee a goodly company which bears Thee about!

In the covenant of Moses is Thy brightness shadowed forth: in the new covenant Thou dartest it forth: from those first Thy light shineth even unto those last. Blessed be He that gave us Thy gleam as well as Thy bright rays.

HYMN VII.

1. As in a race saw I the disputers, the children of strife, [trying] to taste fire, to see the air, to handle the light: they were troubled at the gleaming, and struggled to make divisions.

The Son, Who is too subtle for the mind, did they seek to feel: and the Holy Ghost Who cannot be explored, they thought to explore with their questionings. The Father, Who never at any time was searched out, have they explained and disputed of.

The sound form of our faith is from Abraham, and our repentance is from Nineveh and the house of Rahab,[30] and ours are the expectations of the Prophets,[31] ours of the Apostles.

2. And envy is from Satan: the evil usage of the evil calf is from the Egyptians.[32] The hateful sight of the hateful image of four faces is from the Hittites.[33] Accursed disputation, that hidden moth, is from the Greeks.

The bitter [enemy] read and saw orthodox teachings, and subverted them; he saw hateful things, and sowed them; and he saw hope, and he turned it upside down and cut it off. The disputation that he planted, lo! it has yielded a fruit bitter to the tooth.

3. Satan saw that the truth strangled him, and united himself to the tares,

and secreted his frauds, and spread his snares for the faith, and cast upon the priests the darts of the love of pre-eminence.

They made contests for the throne, to see which should first obtain it. There was that meditated in secret and kept it close: there was that openly combated for it: and there was that with a bribe crept up to it: and there was that with fraud dealt wisely to obtain it.

The paths differed, the scope was one, and they were alike. Him that was young, and could not even think of it, because it was not time for him; and him that was hoary and shaped out dreams for time beyond; all of them by his craftiness did the wicked one persuade and subdue. Old men, youths, and even striplings, aim at rank!

4. His former books did Satan put aside, and put on others: the People who was grown old had the moth and the worm devoured and eaten and left and deserted: the moth came into the new garment of the new peoples:

He saw the crucifers who were rejected and cast forth as strangers: he made of those of the household, pryers; and of worshippers, they became disputants. From that garment the moth gendered and wound it up and deposited it.

The worm gendered in the storehouse of wheat, and sat and looked on: and lo! the pure wheat was mildewed, and devoured were the garments of glory! He made a mockery of us, and we of ourselves, since we were besotted!

He showed tares, and the bramble shot up in the pure vineyard! He infected the flock, and the leprosy broke out, and the sheep became hired servants of his! He began in the People, and came unto the Gentiles, that he might finish.

5. Instead of the reed which the former people made the Son hold, others have dared with their reed[34] to write in their tracts that He is only a Son of man. Reed for reed does the wicked one exchange against our Redeemer, and instead of the coat of many colours,[35] wherewith they clothed Him, titles has he dyed craftily. With diversity of names he clothed Him; either that of a creature or of a thing made, when He was the Maker.

And as he plaited for Him by silent men speechless thorns that cry out, thorns from the mind has he plaited [now] by the voice, as hymns; and concealed the spikes amid melodies that they might not be perceived.[36]

6. When Satan saw that he was detected in his former [frauds]; that the spitting was discovered, and vinegar, and thorns, nails and wood, garments and reed and spear, which smote him, and were hated and openly known; he changed his frauds.

Instead of the blow with the hand, by which our Lord was overcome, he brought in distractions; and instead of the spitting, cavilling entered in; and instead of garments, secret divisions; and instead of the reed, came in strife to smite us on the face.

Haughtiness called for rage its sister, and there answered and came envy, and wrath, and pride, and fraud. They have taken counsel against our Redeemer as on that day when they took counsels at His Passion.

And instead of the cross, a hidden wood hath strife become; and instead of the nails, questionings have come in; and instead of hell, apostasy: the pattern of both Satan would renew again.

Instead of the sponge which was cankered with vinegar and wormwood, he gave prying, the whole of which is cankered with death. The gall which they gave Him did our Lord put away from Him; the subtle questioning, which the rebellious one hath given, to fools is sweet.

7. And at that time there were judges against them,[37] lo, the judges are, as it were, against us, and instead of a handwriting are their commands. Priests that consecrate crowns, set snares for kings.

Instead of the priesthood praying for royalty that wars may cease from among men, they teach wars of overthrow, which set kings to combat with those round about.

O Lord, make the priests and kings peaceful; that in one Church priests may pray for their kings, and kings spare those round about them; and may the peace which is within Thee become ours, Lord, Thou that art within and without all things![38]

Selected hymns and homilies of St. Ephraim the Syrian from
The Pearl: Seven Hymns on the Faith, translated by Reverend J. B. Morris, and
A Select Library of Nicene and Post-Nicene Fathers of the Christian Church,
Second Series, Volume XIII, Part II,
Grand Rapids: Wm. B. Eerdmans Publishing Company, n.d.

Notes

1. Hos. iv. 3; Zeph. i. 3.
2. Eccles. viii. II.
3. James iii. 10.
4. Pearls, he means, have their beauty by nature and so are like Christ; other stones must be graven and so are like created natures.
5. Job xli. 4; Ps. lxxi. 14.
6. See Note on Hymn V. 4 (below).
7. Cephas; *i.e.*, Rock.
8. *I.e.,* with the mysteries typified in the pearl, women are clothed with light at Baptism.
9. Job xxviii. 19 (Pesh.).
10. Acts viii. 27.
11. Jer. xiii. 23; Is. i. 18.
12. Ps. lxviii. 31.
13. I Kings x. 1.
14. Why St. E. contemplates the queen as a sheep appears from his remarks on the place. The following are a part of them: "It was not the fame of Solomon only, but also the Name of the Lord, which called to this queen, who sought to know the God of Solomon, who set out upon a dangerous long journey, and brought presents fit for a king. . . . Our Lord also extolled this queen in the Gospel, and praised her zealousness, when He rebuked the sluggishness of the Jews."
15. This was a tradition of the Jews, a tradition based in part on Canticles i. 5.
16. Luke xxii, 42.
17. Zech. ii. 8.
18. Matt. xxi. 42.
19. Jer. viii. 7.
20. Is. i. 3.
21. Is lv. 1.
22. The same word in Syriac means *naked* and *Apostle*.
23. John xxi. 7.
24. Hos. i. 2.
25. Matt. ix. 13.
26. Luke xviii. 9.
27. Cant. ii. 17.
28. *Or*, pierced — perhaps a word of intentionally uncertain meaning, so as to suit with "the way" in either sense of it.
29. I Tim. ii. 5.
30. On Josh. ii.9, *For I know that God hath delivered unto you the land*, etc., St. E. makes Rahab say, "This forty years is this land yours; and now it is that we might repent, that we have continued in it up to this day."
31. Gen. xv. 6.
32. The calf might be at once intended for a symbol of God, and also a copy from the worship of Apis.
33. Elsewhere (*Opp. Syr*. 11. 384) St. E. calls the Teraphim of Micah (Judges xviii. 2, 14) "the idol *with four faces*."
34. Reeds are used all over the East to write with.

35. St. E. assumes that the type of Joseph was fulfilled in Christ to the letter.
36. This alludes probably to Bardesanes, the existence of whose rhythmical compositions induced St. E to try and counteract them by orthodox ones of the same kind.
37. Luke xxiii. 14,15.
38. *I.e.,* omnipresent in space, but not limited by space.

Chapter 19 • The Nicene Creed

Here we have in summary form the essential beliefs of the Catholic Church. Originally formulated in A.D. 325, it was revised by the First Council of Constantinople in 381. The subsequent excerpts present the manifold expressions and explanations by fourth-century theologians of the basic doctrines of the Catholic Church expressed in this creed.

I believe in one God, the Father almighty, Maker of heaven and earth, and of all things visible and invisible. And in one Lord, Jesus Christ, the only-begotten Son of God. Born of the Father before all ages. God of God, light from light, true God from true God. Begotten, not made; of one being with the Father: by whom all things were made. Who for us men, and for our salvation came down from heaven.

And was made Flesh
by the Holy Spirit, of the Virgin
Mary: and was made Man.

He was also crucified for us, suffered under Pontius Pilate, and was buried. And on the third day He arose again, according to the Scriptures. And ascending into heaven, He sitteth at the right hand of the Father. And He shall come again with glory to judge the living and the dead: and of His kingdom there shall be no end. And in the Holy Spirit, the Lord and Giver of life, who proceedeth from the Father and the Son. Who together with the Father and the Son is no less adored and glorified: who spoke by the prophets. And in one, holy, catholic, and apostolic Church. I confess one baptism for the remission of sins. And I look for the resurrection of the dead. And the life of the world to come. Amen.

Chapter 20 • St. Athanasius: *The Incarnation of the Word of God; Statement of Faith*

Athanasius (297-373) is famous for his defense of the orthodox teaching of the Church concerning the Incarnation against the Arians. He was born in Alexandria, and was for a time a student of St. Anthony, Patriarch of the Cenobites, whose life he later wrote. It was at the Council of Nicaea that Athanasius defended the traditional teaching on the Incarnation and expressed it along the lines elaborated in the following excerpt. His life as bishop of Alexandria was disrupted by ceaseless controversies with the Arians and by physical exile from his see on five occasions. He was caught in the midst not only of theological controversies, but also of political intrigues occasioned by the particular religious beliefs of the civil authorities. When they were friendly to the Arians, Athanasius was exiled. When they were influenced by the orthodox believers, he was recalled. His stormy career did not prevent him from writing some very excellent polemical treatises in defense of Christian monotheism and against the Arians and Macedonians, in addition to the exemplary biography of St. Anthony.

The Incarnation of the Word of God

1. You are wondering, perhaps, for what possible reason, having proposed to speak of the Incarnation of the Word, we are at present treating of the origin of mankind. But this, too, properly belongs to the aim of our treatise. 2. For in speaking of the appearance of the Savior amongst us, we must needs speak also of the origin of men, that you may know that the reason of His coming down was because of us, and that our transgression called forth the loving-kindness of the Word, that the Lord should both make haste to help us and appear among men. 3. For of His becoming Incarnate we were the object, and for our salvation He dealt so lovingly as to appear and be born even in a human body. 4. Thus, then, God has made man, and willed that he should abide in incorruption; but men, having despised and rejected the contemplation of God, and devised and contrived evil for themselves (as was said in the former treatise), received the condemnation of death with which they had been threatened; and from thenceforth no longer remained as they were made, but were being corrupted according to their devices; and death had the mastery over them as king. For transgression of the commandment was turning them back to their natural state, so that just as they have had their being out of nothing, so also,

as might be expected, they might look for corruption into nothing in the course of time. 5. For if, out of a former normal state of non-existence, they were called into being by the Presence and loving-kindness of the Word, it followed naturally that when men were bereft of the knowledge of God and were turned back to what was not (for what is evil is not, but what is good is), they should, since they derive their being from God who IS, be everlastingly bereft even of being; in other words, that they should be disintegrated and abide in death and corruption. 6. For man is by nature mortal, inasmuch as he is made out of what is not; but by reason of his likeness to Him that is (and if he still preserved this likeness by keeping Him in his knowledge) he would stay his natural corruption, and remain incorrupt; as Wisdom says: "The taking heed to His laws in the assurance of immortality," but being incorrupt, he would live henceforth as God, to which I suppose the divine Scripture refers, when it says: "I have said ye are gods, and ye are all sons of the most High; but ye die like men, and fall as one of the princes."

For God has not only made us out of nothing; but He gave us freely, by the Grace of the Word, a life in correspondence with God. But men, having rejected things eternal, and, by counsel of the devil, turned to the things of corruption, became the cause of their own corruption in death, being, as I said before, by nature corruptible, but destined, by the grace following from partaking of the Word, to have escaped their natural state, had they remained good. For because of the Word dwelling with them, even their natural corruption did not come near them, as Wisdom also says: "God made man for incorruption, and as an image of His own eternity: but by envy of the devil death came into the world." But when this was come to pass, men began to die, while corruption thenceforward prevailed against them, gaining even more than its natural power over the whole race, inasmuch as it had, owing to the transgression of the commandment, the threat of the Deity as a further advantage against them. For even in their misdeeds men had not stopped short at any set limits; but gradually pressing forward, have passed on beyond all measure: having to begin with been inventors of wickedness and called down upon themselves death and corruption; while later on, having turned aside to wrong and exceeding all lawlessness, and stopping at no one evil but devising all manner of new evils in succession, they have become insatiable in sinning. For there were adulteries everywhere and thefts, and the whole earth was full of murders and plunderings. And as to corruption and wrong, no heed was paid to law, but all crimes were being practiced everywhere, both individually and jointly. Cities were at war with cities, and nations were rising up against nations, and the whole earth was rent with civil commotions and battles; each man vying with his fellows in lawless deeds. Nor were even crimes against nature far from them, but, as the Apostle and witness of Christ says: "For their women changed the natural use into that which is against nature: and likewise also the men, leaving the natural use of the women, burned in their lust one toward another, men with men working unseemliness, and receiving in themselves that recompense of their error which was meet."

For this cause, then, death having gained upon men, and corruption upon them, the race of man was perishing; the rational man made in God's image was disappearing, and the handiwork of God was in process of dissolution. For death, as I said above, gained from that time forth a legal hold over us, and it was impossible to evade the law, since it had been laid down by God because of the transgression, and the result was in truth at once monstrous and unseemly. For it were monstrous, firstly, that God, having spoken, should prove false — that, when once He had ordained that man, if he transgressed the commandment, should die the death, after the transgression man should not die, but God's word should be broken. For God would not be true, if, when He had said we should die, man died not. Again, it were unseemly that creatures once made rational, and having partaken of the Word, should go to ruin, and turn again toward non-existence by the way of corruption. For it were not worthy of God's goodness that the things He had made should waste away, because of the deceit practiced on men by the devil. Especially it was unseemly to the last degree that God's handicraft among men should be done away, either because of their own carelessness, or because of the deceitfulness of evil spirits. So, as the rational creatures were wasting and such works in course of ruin, what was God in His goodness to do? Suffer corruption to prevail against them and death to hold them fast? And where were the profit of their having been made, to begin with? For better were they not made, than once made, left to neglect and ruin. For neglect reveals weakness, and not goodness on God's part — if, that is, He allows His own work to be ruined when once He had made it — more so than if He had never made man at all. For if He had not made them, none could impute weakness; but once He had made them, and created them out of nothing, it were most monstrous for the work to be ruined, and that before the eyes of the Maker. It was, then, out of the question to leave men to the current of corruption; because this would be unseemly, and unworthy of God's goodness.

On the other hand there was the consistency of God's nature, not to be sacrificed for our profit. Were men, then, to be called upon to repent? But repentance cannot avert the execution of a law; still less can it remedy a fallen nature. We have incurred corruption and need to be restored to the Grace of God's Image. None could renew but He Who had created. He alone could recreate all, suffer for all, represent all to the Father.

But just as this consequence must needs hold, so, too, on the other side the just claims of God lie against it; that God should appear true to the law He had laid down concerning death. For it were monstrous for God, the Father of truth, to appear a liar for our profit and preservation. So here, once more, what possible course was God to take? To demand repentance of men for their transgression? For this one might pronounce worthy of God; as though, just as from transgression men have become set towards corruption, so from repentance they may once more be set in the way of incorruption. But repentance would, firstly, fail to guard the just claim of God. For He would still be none the more true, if men did not remain in the grasp of death; nor, secondly, does repentance call men back from what is their nature — it merely stays them from acts of sin. Now, if there were merely a misdemeanor in question, and not a consequent corruption, repentance were well enough. But if, when transgression had once gained a start, men became involved in that corruption which was their nature, and were deprived of the grace which they had, being in the image of God, what further step was needed? or what was required for such grace and such recall, but the Word of God, which had also at the beginning made everything out of nought?

For His it was once more both to bring the corruptible to incorruption, and to maintain intact the just claim of the Father upon all. For being the Word of the Father, and above all, He alone of natural fitness was both able to recreate everything, and worthy to suffer on behalf of all and to be ambassador for all with the Father.

For this purpose, then, the incorporeal and incorruptible and immaterial Word of God, comes to our realm, howbeit he was not far from us before. For no part of Creation is left void of Him: He has filled all things everywhere, remaining present with His own Father. But He comes in condescension to show loving-kindness upon us, and to visit us. And seeing the race of rational creatures in the way to perish, and death reigning over them by corruption; seeing, too, that the threat against transgression gave a firm hold to the corruption which was upon us, and that it was monstrous that before the law was fulfilled it should fall through: seeing, once more, the unseemliness of what was come to pass: that the things whereof He himself was Artificer were passing away: seeing further, the exceeding wickedness of men, and how by little and little they had increased it to an intolerable pitch against themselves: and seeing, lastly, how all men were under penalty of death: He took pity on our race, and had mercy on our infirmity, and condescended to our corruption and, unable to bear that death should have the mastery — lest the creature should perish, and His Father's handiwork in men be spent for nought — He takes unto himself a body, and that of no different sort from ours. For He did not simply will to become embodied, or will merely to appear. For if He willed merely to appear, He was able to effect His divine appearance by some other and higher means as well. But He takes a body of our kind, and not merely so, but from a spotless and stainless virgin, knowing not a man, a body clean and in very truth pure from intercourse of men. For being himself mighty, and Artificer of everything, He prepares the body in the Virgin as a temple unto himself, and makes it His very own as an instrument, in it manifested, and in it dwelling. And thus taking from our bodies one of like nature, because all were under penalty of the corruption of death He gave it over to death in the stead of all, and offered it to the Father — doing this, moreover, of His loving-kindness, to the end that, firstly, all being held to have died in Him, the law involving the ruin of men might be undone (inasmuch as its power was fully spent in the Lord's body, and had no longer holding-ground against men, his peers), and that, secondly, whereas men had turned toward corruption, He might turn them again toward incorruption and quicken them from death by the appropriation of His body and by the grace of the Resurrection, banishing death from them like straw from the fire.

For the Word, perceiving that no otherwise could the corruption of men be undone save by death as a necessary condition, while it was impossible for the Word to suffer death, being immortal, and Son of the Father; to this end He takes to himself a body capable of death, that it, by partaking of the Word Who is above all, might be worthy to die in the stead of all, and might, because of the Word which was come to dwell in it, remain incorruptible, and that thenceforth corruption might be stayed from all by the Grace of the Resurrection. Whence, by offering unto death the body He himself had taken, as an offering and sacrifice free from any stain, straightway He put away death from all His peers by the offering of an equivalent. For being over all, the Word of God naturally by offering His own temple and corporeal instrument for the life of all satisfied the debt by His death. And thus He, the incorruptible Son of God, being conjoined with all by a like nature, naturally clothed all with incorruption, by the promise of the Resurrection. For the actual corruption in death has no longer holding-ground against men, by reason of the Word, which by His one body has come to dwell among them. For now that He has come to our realm, and taken up his abode in one body among His peers, henceforth the whole conspiracy of the enemy against mankind is checked, and the corruption of death which before was prevailing against them is done away. For the race of men had gone to ruin, had not the Lord and Savior of all, the Son of God, come among us to meet the end of death.

Now in truth this great work was peculiarly suited to God's goodness. God the Word of the all-good Father did not neglect the race of men, His work, going to corruption; but, while He blotted out the death which had ensued by the offering of His own body, He corrected their neglect by His own teaching, restoring all that was man's by His own power.

And of this one may be assured at the hands of the Savior's own inspired writers, if one happen upon their writings, where they say: "For the love of Christ, constraineth us; because we thus judge, that if one died for all, then all died, and He died for all that we should no longer live unto ourselves, but unto Him Who for our sakes died and rose again," our Lord Jesus Christ. And, again: "But we behold Him, Who hath been made a little lower than the angels, even Jesus, because of the suffering of death crowned with glory and honor, that by the grace of God He should taste of death for every man." Then He also points out the reason why it was necessary for none other than God the Word himself to become incarnate; as follows: "For it became Him, for Whom are all things, and through Whom are all things, in bringing many sons unto glory, to make the Captain of their salvation perfect through suffering", by which words He means, that it belonged to none other to bring man back from the corruption which had begun, than the Word of God, Who had also made them from the beginning. And that it was in order to sacrifice for bodies such as His own that the Word himself also assumed a body, to this, also, they refer in these words: "Forasmuch then as the children are the sharers in blood and flesh, He also himself in like manner partook of the same, that through death He might bring to nought Him that had the power of death, that is, the devil; and might deliver them who, through fear of death, were all their lifetime subject to bondage." For by the sacrifice of His own body, He both put an end to the law which was against us, and made a new beginning of life for us, by the hope of resurrection which He has given us. For since from man it was that death prevailed over men, for this cause conversely, by the Word of God being made man has come about the destruction of death and the resurrection of life; as the man which bore Christ saith: "For since by man came death, by man came also the resurrection of the dead. For as in Adam all die, so also in Christ shall all be made alive" and so forth. For no longer now do we die as subject to condemnation; but as men who rise from the dead we await the general resurrection of all, "which in its own times He shall show," even God, Who has also wrought it, and bestowed it upon us. This then is the first cause of the Savior's being made man. But one might see from the following reasons also, that His gracious coming amongst us was fitting to have taken place.

God, Who has the power over all things, when He was making the race of men through His own Word, seeing the weakness of their nature, that it was not sufficient of itself to know its Maker, nor to get any idea at all of God, because while He was uncreated, the creatures had been made of nought, and while He was incorporeal, men had been fashioned in a lower way in the body, and because in every way the things made fell far short of being able to comprehend and know their Maker — taking pity, I say, on the race of men, inasmuch as He is good, He did not leave them destitute of the knowledge of Himself, lest they should find no profit in existing at all.

For what profit to the creatures if they knew not their Maker? or how could they be rational without knowing the Word (and Reason) of the Father, in Whom they received their very being? For there would be nothing to distinguish them from brute creatures if they had knowledge of nothing but earthly things. Nay, why did God make them at all, as He did not wish to be known by them?

Whence, lest this should be so, being good, He gives them a share in His own Image, our Lord Jesus Christ, and makes them after His own Image and after His likeness: so that by such grace perceiving the Image, that is, the Word of the Father, they may be able through Him to get an idea of the Father, and knowing their Maker, live the happy and truly blessed life. But men once more in their perversity having set at nought, in spite of all this, the grace given them, so wholly rejected God, and so darkened their soul, as not merely to forget their idea of God, but also to fashion for themselves one invention after another. For not only did they grave idols for themselves, instead of the truth, and honor things that were not before the living God, "and serve the creature rather than the Creator," but worst of all, they transferred the honor of God even to sticks and stones and to every material object and to men, and went even further than this, as we have said in the former treatise. So far indeed did their impiety go, that they proceeded to worship devils, and proclaimed them as gods, fulfilling their own lusts. For they performed, as was said above, offerings of brute animals, and sacrifices of men, as was meet for them, binding themselves down all the faster under their maddening inspirations. For this reason it was also that magic arts were taught among them, and oracles in divers places led men astray, and all men ascribed the influences of their birth and existence to the stars and to all the heavenly bodies, having no thought of anything beyond what was visible. And, in a word, everything was full of irreligion and lawlessness, and God alone, and His Word, was unknown, albeit He had not hidden himself out of men's sight, nor given the knowledge of himself in one way only; but had, on the contrary, unfolded it to them in many forms and by many ways.

Statement of Faith

We believe in one Unbegotten God, Father Almighty, maker of all things both visible and invisible, that hath His being from himself. And in one Only-begotten Word, Wisdom, Son, begotten of the Father without beginning and eternally; Word not pronounced nor mental, nor an effluence of the Perfect, nor a dividing of the impassible Essence, nor an issue; but absolutely perfect Son, living and powerful (Heb. iv. 12), the true Image of the Father, equal in honor and glory. For this, he says, 'is the will of the Father, that as they honor the Father, so they may honor the Son also' (Joh. v. 23): very God of very God, as John says in his general Epistles, 'And we are in Him that is true, even in His Son Jesus Christ: this is the true God and everlasting life' (I Joh. v. 20): Almighty of Almighty. For all things which the Father rules and sways, the Son rules and sways likewise: wholly from the Whole, being like the Father as the Lord says, 'he that hath seen Me hath seen the Father' (Joh. xiv. 9). But He was begotten ineffably and incomprehensibly, for 'who shall declare his generation?' (Isa. liii. 8). In other words, no one can. Who, when at the consummation of the ages (Heb. ix. 26), He had descended from the bosom of the Father, took from the undefiled Virgin Mary our humanity (ἄνθρωπον), Christ Jesus, whom He delivered of His own will to suffer for us, as the Lord saith: 'No man taketh My life from Me. I have power to lay it down, and have power to take it again' (Joh. x. 18). In which humanity He was crucified and died for us, and rose from the dead, and was taken up into the heavens, having been created as the beginning of ways for us (Prov. viii. 22), when on earth He shewed us light from out of darkness, salvation from error, life from the dead, and entrance to paradise, from which Adam was cast out, and into which he again entered by means of the thief, as the Lord said, 'This day shalt thou be with Me in paradise' (Luke xxiii. 43), into which Paul also once entered. [He shewed us] also a way up to the heavens, whither the humanity of the Lord, in which He will judge the quick and the dead, entered as precursor for us. We believe, likewise, also in the Holy Spirit that searcheth all things, even the deep things of God (I Cor. ii. 10), and we anathematise doctrines contrary to this.

For neither do we hold a Son-Father, as do the Sabellians, calling Him of one but not of the same essence, and thus destroying the existence of the Son. Neither do we ascribe the passible body which He bore for the salvation of the whole world to the Father. Neither can we imagine three Subsistences separated from each other, as results from their bodily nature in the case of men, lest we hold a plurality of gods like the heathen. But just as a river, produced from a well, is not separate, and yet there are in fact two visible objects and two names. For neither is the Father the Son, nor the Son the Father. For the Father is Father of the Son, and the Son, Son of the Father. For like as the well is not a river, nor the river a well, but both are one and the same water which is conveyed in a channel from the well to the river, so the Father's deity passes into the Son without flow and without division. For the Lord says, 'I came out from the Father and am come' (Jon. xvi. 28). But He is ever with the Father, for He is in the bosom of the Father, nor was ever the bosom of the Father void of the deity of the Son. For He says, 'I was by Him as one setting in order' (Prov. viii. 30). But we do not regard God the Creator of all, the Son of God, as a creature, or thing made, or as made out of nothing, for He is truly existent from Him who exists, alone existing from Him who alone exists, inasmuch as the like glory and power was eternally and conjointly begotten of the Father. For 'He that hath seen' the Son 'hath seen the Father' (Joh. xiv. 9). All things to wit were made through the Son; but He Himself is not a creature, as Paul says of the Lord: 'In Him were all things created, and He is before all' (Col. i. 16). Now He says not, 'was created' before all things, but 'is' before all things. To be created, namely, is applicable to all things, but 'is before all' applies to the Son only.

He is then by nature an Offspring, perfect from the Perfect, begotten before all the hills (Prov. viii. 25), that is before every rational and intelligent essence, as Paul also in another place calls Him 'first-born of all creation' (Col. i. 15).

But by calling Him First-born, He shew that He is not a Creature, but Offspring of the Father. For it would be inconsistent with His deity for Him to be called a creature. For all things were created by the Father through the Son, but the Son alone was eternally begotten from the Father, whence God the Word is 'first-born of all creation,' unchangeable from unchangeable. However, the body which He wore for our sakes is a creature: concerning which Jeremiah says, according to the edition of the seventy translators (Jer. xxxi. 22): 'The Lord created for us for a planting, a new salvation, in which salvation men shall go about' but according to Aquila the same text runs: 'The Lord created a new thing in woman.' Now the salvation created for us for a planting which is new, not old, and for us, not before us, is Jesus, Who in respect of the Savior was made man, and whose name is translated in one place Salvation, in another Savior. But salvation proceeds from the Savior, just as illumination does from the light. The salvation, then, which was from the Savior, being created new, did as Jeremiah says, 'create for us a new salvation,' and as Aquila renders: 'The Lord created a new thing in woman,' that is in Mary. For nothing new was created in woman, save the Lord's body, born of the Virgin Mary without intercourse, as also it says in the Proverbs in the person of Jesus: 'The Lord created me, a beginning of His ways for His works' (Prov. viii. 22). Now He does not say, 'created me before His works,' lest any should take the text of the deity of the Word.

Each text then which refers to the creature is written with reference to Jesus in a bodily sense. For the Lord's Humanity was created as 'a beginning of ways,' and He manifested it to us for our salvation. For by it we have our access to the Father. For He is the way (Joh. xiv. 6) which leads us back to the Father. And a way is a corporeal visible thing, such as is the Lord's humanity. Well, then, the Word of God created all things, not being a creature, but an offspring. For He created none of the created things equal or like unto himself. But it is the part of a Father to beget, while it is a workman's part to create. Accordingly, that body is a thing made and created, which the Lord bore for us, which was begotten for us, as Paul says, 'wisdom from God, and sanctification and righteousness, and redemption', while yet the Word was before us and before all Creation, and is, the Wisdom of the Father. But the Holy Spirit, being that which proceeds from the Father, is ever in the hands of the Father Who sends and of the Son Who conveys Him, by Whose means He filled all things. The Father possessing His existence from himself, begat the Son, as we said, and did not create Him, as a river from a well and as a branch from a root, and as brightness from a fight, things which nature knows to be indivisible; through Whom to the Father be glory and power and greatness before all ages, and unto all the ages of the ages. Amen.

Selections from St. Athanasius are from
A Select Library of Nicene & Post-Nicene Fathers of the Christian Church,
Edited by D. Schaff & H. Wace,
Volume IV, New York: The Christian Literature Company, 1892

Chapter 21 • St. Cyril of Jerusalem: *On the Ten Points of Doctrine*; *On the Mysteries*

Little is known of St. Cyril's (ca. 315-386) early life and education, which are supposed to have taken place at Jerusalem. In about 345 he was ordained; he probably gave his famous *Catechetical Instructions* to the catechumens at Jerusalem in 347/348. He was chosen to succeed Maximus as bishop there, and was exiled from his see on three occasions because of the opposition of the Arians. His instructions to those preparing for baptism contain an extraordinary treasure of Catholic teaching and practice. The second instruction concerns penance; the fourth is especially noteworthy for its synopsis of the ten points of doctrine; and the twenty-second lecture concerns the doctrines and practices relevant to the celebration of the Holy Eucharist.

LECTURE IV

On the Ten Points of Doctrine

Colossians ii. 8

Beware lest any man spoil you through philosophy and vain deceit, after the tradition of men, after the rudiments of the world, & c.

Vice mimics virtue, and the tares strive to be thought wheat, growing like the wheat in appearance, but being detected by good judges from the taste. *The devil also transfigures himself into an angel of light*; not that he may reascend to where he was, for having made his heart hard as an anvil, he has henceforth a will that cannot repent; but in order that he may envelop those who are living an Angelic life in a mist of blindness, and a pestilent condition of unbelief. Many wolves are going about *in sheeps' clothing*, their clothing being that of sheep, not so their claws and teeth: but clad in their soft side, and deceiving the innocent by their appearance, they shed upon them from their fangs the destructive poison of ungodliness. We have need therefore of divine grace, and of a sober mind, and of eyes that see, lest from eating tares as wheat we suffer harm from ignorance, and lest from taking the wolf to be a sheep we become his prey, and from supposing the destroying Devil to be a beneficent Angel we be devoured: for, as the Scripture saith, *He goeth about as a roaring lion, seeking whom he may devour.*

This is the cause of the Church's admonitions, the cause of the present instructions, and of the lessons which are read.

For the method of godliness consists of these two things, pious doctrines, and virtuous practice: and neither are the doctrines acceptable to God apart from good works, nor does God accept the works which are not perfected with pious doctrines. For what profit is it, to know well the doctrines concerning God, and yet to be a vile fornicator? And again, what profit is it, to be nobly temperate, and an impious blasphemer? A most precious possession therefore is the knowledge of doctrines: also there is need of a wakeful soul, since there are many that *make spoil through philosophy and vain deceit*. The Greeks on the one hand draw men away by their smooth tongue, for *money droppeth from a harlot's lips:* whereas they of the Circumcision deceive those who come to them by means of the Divine Scriptures, which they miserably misinterpret through *studying them from childhood to old age*, and growing old in ignorance. But the children of heretics, by *their good words and smooth tongue, deceive the hearts of the innocent*, disguising with the name of Christ as it were with honey the poisoned arrows of their impious doctrines: concerning all of whom together the Lord saith, Take *heed lest any man mislead you*. This is the reason for the teaching of the Creed and for expositions upon it.

But before delivering you over to the Creed, I think it is well to make use at present of a short summary of necessary doctrines; that the multitude of things to be spoken, and the long interval of the days of all this holy Lent, may not cause forgetfulness in the mind of the more simple among you; but that, having strewn some seeds now in a summary way, we may not forget the same when afterwards more widely tilled. But let those here present whose habit of mind is mature, and who have *their senses already exercised to discern good and evil*, endure patiently to listen to things fitted rather for children, and to an introductory course, as it were, of milk: that at the same time both those who have need of the instruction may be benefitted, and those who have the knowledge may rekindle the remembrance of things which they already know.

Of God

First then let there be laid as a foundation in your soul the doctrine concerning God; that God is One, alone unbegotten, without beginning, change, or variation; neither begotten of another, not having another to succeed Him in His life; who neither began to live in time, nor endeth ever: and that He is both good and just; that if ever thou hear a heretic say, that there is one God who is just, and another who is good, thou mayest immediately remember, and discern the poisoned arrow of heresy. For some have impiously dared to divide the One God in their teaching: and some have it that one is the Creator and Lord of the soul, and another of the body; a doctrine at once absurd and impious. For how can a man become the one servant of two masters, when our Lord says in the Gospels, *No man can serve two masters*? There is then Only One God, the Maker both of souls and bodies: One the Creator of heaven and earth, the Maker of Angels and Archangels: of many the Creator, but of One only the Father before all ages, of One only, His Only-begotten Son, our Lord Jesus Christ, by Whom He made *all things visible and invisible*.

This Father of our Lord Jesus Christ is not circumscribed in any place, nor is He less than the heaven; but *the heavens are the works of His fingers*, and *the whole earth is held in His grasp*; He is in all things and around all. Think not that the sun is brighter than He, or equal to Him: for He Who at first formed the sun must needs be incomparably greater and brighter. He foreknoweth the things that shall be, and is mightier than all, knowing all things and doing as He will; not being subject to any necessary sequence of events, nor to nativity, nor chance, nor fate; in all things perfect, and equally possessing every absolute form of virtue, neither diminishing nor increasing, but in mode and conditions ever the same; Who hath prepared punishment for sinners, and a crown for the righteous.

Seeing then that many have gone astray in divers ways from the One God, some having deified the sun, that when the sun sets they may abide in the night season without God; others the moon, to have no God by day; others the other parts of the world; others the arts; others their various kinds of food; others their pleasures; while some, made after women, have set up on high an image of a naked woman, and called it Aphrodite, and worshipped their own lust in a visible form; and others dazzled by the brightness of gold have deified it and the other kinds of matter; — whereas if one lay as a first foundation in his heart the doctrine of the unity of God, and trust to Him, he roots out at once the whole crop of the evils of idolatry, and of the error of the heretics; lay thou, therefore, this first doctrine of religion as a foundation in thy soul by faith.

Of Christ

Believe also in the Son of God, One and Only, our Lord Jesus Christ, Who was begotten God of God, begotten Life of Life, begotten Light of Light, Who is in all things like to Him that begat, Who received not His being in time, but was before all ages eternally and incomprehensibly begotten of the Father: The Wisdom and the Power of God, and His Righteousness personally subsisting: Who sitteth on the right hand of the Father before all ages.

For the throne at God's right hand He received not, as some have thought, because of His patient endurance, being crowned as it were by God after His Passion; but throughout His being, — a being by eternal generation, — He holds His royal dignity, and shares the Father's seat, being God and Wisdom and Power, as hath been said; reigning together with the Father, and creating all things for the Father, yet lacking nothing in the dignity of Godhead, and knowing Him that hath begotten Him, even as He is known of Him that hath begotten; and to, speak briefly, remember thou what is written in the Gospels, that none *knoweth the Son but the Father, neither knoweth any the Father save the Son.*

Further, do thou neither separate the Son from the Father, nor by making a confusion believe in a Son-Fatherhood; but believe that of One God there is One Only-begotten Son, who is before all ages God the Word; not the uttered word diffused into the air, nor to be likened to impersonal words; but the Word the Son, Maker of all who partake of reason, the Word Who heareth the Father, and himself speaketh. And on these points, should God permit, we will speak more at large in due season; for we do not forget our present purpose to give a summary introduction to the Faith.

Concerning His Birth of the Virgin

Believe then that this Only-begotten Son of God for our sins came down from heaven upon earth, and took upon Him this human nature of like passions with us, and was begotten of the Holy Virgin and of the Holy Ghost, and was made Man, not in seeming and mere show, but in truth; nor yet by passing through the Virgin as through a channel; but was of her made truly flesh, [and truly nourished with milk], and did truly eat as we do, and truly drink as we do. For if the Incarnation was a phantom, salvation is a phantom also. The Christ was of two natures, Man in what was seen, but God in what was not seen; as Man truly eating like us, for He had the like feeling of the flesh with us; but as

God raising him that had been dead four days; truly sleeping in the ship as Man, and walking upon the waters as God.

Of the Cross

He was truly crucified for our sins. For if thou wouldst deny it, the place refutes thee visibly, this blessed Golgotha, in which we are now assembled for the sake of Him who was here crucified; and the whole world has since been filled with pieces of the wood of the Cross. But He was crucified not for sins of His own, but that we might be delivered from *our* sins. And though as Man He was at the time despised *of men*, and was buffeted, yet He was acknowledged by the Creation as God: for when the sun saw his Lord dishonored, he grew dim and trembled, not enduring the sight.

Of His Burial

He was truly laid as Man in a tomb of rock; but rocks were rent asunder by terror because of Him. He went down into the regions beneath the earth, that thence also He might redeem the righteous. For, tell me, couldst thou wish the living only to enjoy His grace, and that, though most of them are unholy; and not wish those who from Adam had for a long while been imprisoned to have now gained their liberty? Esaias [Isaiah] the Prophet proclaimed with loud voice so many things concerning Him; wouldst thou not wish that the King should go down and redeem His herald? David was there, and Samuel, and all the Prophets, John himself also, who by his messengers said, *Art thou He that should come, or look we for another*? Wouldst thou not wish that He should descend and redeem such as these?

Of the Resurrection

But He who descended into the regions beneath the earth came up again; and Jesus, who was buried, truly rose again the third day. And if the Jews ever worry thee, meet them at once by asking thus: Did Jonah come forth from the whale on the third day, and hath not Christ then risen from the earth on the third day? Is a dead man raised to life on touching the bones of Elisha, and is it not much easier for the Maker of mankind to be raised by the power of the Father? Well then, He truly rose, and after He had risen was seen again of the disciples: and twelve disciples were witnesses of His Resurrection, who bare witness not in pleasing words, but contended even unto torture and death for the truth of the Resurrection. What then, shall *every word be established at the mouth of two or three witnesses*, according to the Scripture, and, though twelve bear witness to the Resurrection of Christ, art thou still incredulous in regard to His Resurrection?

Concerning the Ascension

But when Jesus had finished His course of patient endurance, and had redeemed mankind from their sins, He ascended again into the heavens, a cloud receiving Him up: and as He went up Angels were beside Him, and Apostles were beholding. But if any man disbelieves the words which I speak, let him believe the actual power of the things now seen. All kings when they die have their power extinguished with their life: but Christ crucified is worshipped by the whole world. We proclaim the Crucified, and the devils tremble now. Many have been crucified at various times; but of what other who was crucified did the invocation ever drive the devils away?

Let us, therefore, not be ashamed of the Cross of Christ; but though another hide it, do thou openly seal it upon thy forehead, that the devils may behold the royal sign and flee trembling far away. Make then this sign at eating and drinking, at sitting, at lying down, at rising up, at speaking, at walking: in a word, at every act. For He who was here crucified is in heaven above. If after being crucified and buried He had remained in the tomb, we should have had cause to be ashamed; but in fact, He who was crucified on Golgotha here, has ascended into heaven from the Mount of Olives on the East. For after having gone down hence into Hades, and come up again to us, He ascended again from us into heaven, His Father addressing Him, and saying, Sit *Thou on My right hand, until I make Thine enemies Thy footstool.*

Of Judgment to Come

This Jesus Christ who is gone up shall come again, not from earth but from heaven: and I say, "not from earth," because there are many Antichrists to come at this time from earth. For already, as thou hast seen, many have begun to say, *I am the Christ*: and the *abomination of desolation* is yet to come, assuming to himself the false title of Christ. But look thou for the true Christ, the Only-begotten Son of God, coming henceforth no more from earth, but from heaven, appearing to all more bright than any lightning and brilliancy of light, with angel guards attended, that He may judge both quick and dead, and reign in a heavenly, eternal kingdom, which shall have no end. For on this point also, I pray thee, make thyself sure, since there are many who say that Christ's Kingdom hath an end.

Of the Holy Spirit

Believe thou also in the Holy Spirit, and hold the same opinion concerning Him, which thou hast *received to hold* concerning the Father and the Son, and follow not those who teach blasphemous things of Him. But learn thou that this Holy Spirit is One, indivisible of manifold power; having many operations, yet not himself divided; Who knoweth the mysteries, Who searcheth *all things, even the deep things of God:* Who descended upon the Lord Jesus Christ in form as a dove; Who wrought in the Law and in the Prophets; Who now also at the season of Baptism sealeth thy soul; of Whose holiness also every intellectual nature hath need: against Whom if *any dare to blaspheme, he hath no forgiveness, neither in this world, nor in that which is to come*: "Who with the Father and the Son together" is honored with the glory of the Godhead: of Whom also *thrones, and dominions, principalities, and powers* have need. For there is One God, the Father of Christ: and One Lord Jesus Christ, the Only-begotten Son of the Only God; and One Holy Spirit, the sanctifier and deifier of all, Who spoke in the Law and in the Prophets, in the Old and in the New Testament.

Have thou ever in thy mind this seal, which for the present has been lightly touched in my discourse, by way of summary, but shall be stated, should the Lord permit, to the best of my power with the proof from the Scriptures. For concerning the divine and holy mysteries of the Faith, not even a casual statement must be delivered without the Holy Scriptures; nor must we be drawn aside by mere plausibility and artifices of speech. Even to me, who tell thee these things, give not absolute credence, unless thou receive the proof of the thing which I announce from the Divine Scriptures. For this salvation which we believe depends not on ingenious reasoning, but on demonstration of the Holy Scriptures.

Of the Soul

Next to the knowledge of this venerable and glorious and all-holy Faith, learn further what thou thyself art: that as man thou art of a two-fold nature, consisting of soul and body; and that, as was said a short time ago, the same God is the Creator both of soul and body. Know also that thou hast a soul self-governed, the noblest work of God, made after the image of its Creator: immortal because of God that gives it immortality; a living being, rational, imperishable, because of Him that bestowed these gifts: having free power to do what it willeth. For it is not according to thy nativity that thou sinnest, nor is it by the power of chance that thou committest fornication, nor, as some idly talk, do the conjunctions of the stars compel thee to give thyself to wantonness. Why dost thou shrink from confessing thine own evil deeds, and ascribe the blame to the innocent stars? Give no more heed, pray, to astrologers; for of these the divine Scripture saith, *Let the stargazers of the heaven stand up and save thee*, and what follows: Behold, *they all shall be consumed as stubble on the fire, and shall not deliver their soul from the flame.*

And learn this also, that the soul, before it came into this world, had committed no sin, but having come in sinless, we now sin of our free-will. Listen not, I pray thee, to any one perversely interpreting the words, *But if I do that which I would not*: but remember Him who saith, If *ye be willing, and hearken unto Me, ye shall eat the good things of the land: but if ye be not willing, neither hearken unto Me, the sword shall devour you*, etc.: and again, As *ye presented your members as servants to uncleanness and to iniquity unto iniquity, even so now present your members as servants to righteousness unto sanctification*. Remember also the Scripture, which saith, Even *as they did not like to retain God in their knowledge*: and, *That which may be known of God is manifest in them*: and again, *their eyes they have closed.* Also remember how God again accuseth them, and saith, Yet *I planted thee a fruitful vine, wholly true: how art thou turned to bitterness, thou the strange vine*?

The soul is immortal, and all souls are alike both of men and women; for only the members of the body are distinguished. There is not a class of souls sinning by nature, and a class of souls practicing righteousness by nature: but both act from choice, the substance of their souls being of one kind only, and alike in all. I know, however, that I am talking much, and that the time is already long: but what is more precious than salvation? Art thou not willing to take trouble in getting provisions for the way against the heretics? And wilt thou not learn the bypaths of the road, lest from ignorance thou fall down a precipice? If thy teachers think it no small gain for thee to learn these things, shouldst not thou the learner gladly receive the multitude of things told thee?

The soul is self-governed: and though the devil can suggest, he has not the power to compel against the will. He pictures to thee the thought of fornication: if thou wilt, thou acceptest it; if thou wilt not, thou rejectest. For if thou wert a fornicator by necessity, then for what cause did God prepare hell? If thou wert a doer of righteousness by nature and not by will, wherefore did God prepare crowns of ineffable glory? The sheep is gentle, but never was it crowned for its gentleness: since its gentle quality belongs to it not from choice but by nature.

Of the Body

Thou hast learned, beloved, the nature of the soul, as far as there is time at present: now do thy best to receive the doctrine of the body also. Suffer none of those who say that this body is no work of God: for they who believe that the body is independent of God, and that the soul dwells in it as in a strange vessel, readily abuse it to fornication. And yet what fault have they found in this wonderful body? For what is lacking in comeliness? And what in its structure is not full of skill? Ought they not to have observed the luminous construction of the eyes? And how the ears being set obliquely receive the sound unhindered? And how the smell is able to distinguish scents, and to perceive exhalations? And how the tongue ministers to two purposes, the sense of taste, and the power of speech? How the lungs placed out of sight are unceasing in their respiration of the air? Who imparted the incessant pulsation of the heart? Who made the distribution into so many veins and arteries? Who skillfully knitted together the bones with the sinews? Who assigned a part of the food to our substance, and separated a part for decent secretion, and hid away the unseemly members in more seemly places? Who when the human race must have died out, rendered it by a simple intercourse perpetual?

Tell me not that the body is a cause of sin. For if the body is a cause of sin, why does not a dead body sin? Put a sword in the right hand of one just dead, and no murder takes place. Let beauties of every kind pass before a youth just dead, and no impure desire arises. Why? Because the body sins not of itself, but the soul through the body. The body is an instrument, and, as it were, a garment and robe of the soul; and if by this latter it be given over to fornication, it becomes defiled: but if it dwell with a holy soul, it becomes a temple of the Holy Spirit. It is not I that say this, but the Apostle Paul hath said, *Know ye not, that your bodies are the temple of the Holy Spirit which is in you*? Be tender, therefore, of thy body as being a temple of the Holy Spirit. Pollute not thy flesh in fornication; defile not this thy fairest robe: and if ever thou hast defiled it, now cleanse it by repentance: get thyself washed, while time permits.

And to the doctrine of chastity let the first to give heed be the order of Solitaries [hermits] and of Virgins, who maintain the angelic life in the world; and let the rest of the Church's people follow them. For you, brethren, a great crown is laid up: barter not away a great dignity for a petty pleasure: listen to the Apostle speaking: Lest *there be any fornicator or profane person, as Esau, who for one mess of meat sold his own birthright*. Enrolled henceforth in the Angelic books for thy profession of chastity, see that thou be not blotted out again for thy practice of fornication.

Nor again, on the other hand, in maintaining thy chastity be thou puffed up against those who walk in the humbler path of matrimony. For as the Apostle saith, *Let marriage be had in honor among all, and let the bed be undefiled*. Thou too who retainest thy chastity, wast thou not begotten of those who had married? Because thou hast a possession of gold, do not on that account reprobate the silver, But let those also be of good cheer, who being married use marriage lawfully; who make a marriage according to God's ordinance, and not of wantonness for the sake of unbounded license; who recognize seasons of abstinence, that *they may give themselves unto prayer*; who in our assemblies bring clean bodies as well as clean garments into the Church; who have entered upon matrimony for the procreation of children, but not for indulgence.

Let those also who marry but once not reprobate those who have consented to a second marriage: for though continence is a noble and admirable thing, yet it is also permissible to enter upon a second marriage, that the weak may not fall into fornication. For it is good *for them*, saith the Apostle, if *they abide even as I. But if they have not continency, let them marry; for it is better to marry than to burn*. But let all the other practices be banished afar, fornication, adultery, and every kind of licentiousness: and let the body be kept pure for the Lord, that the Lord also may have respect unto the body. And let the body be nourished with food, that it may live, and serve without hindrance; not, however, that it may be given up to luxuries.

Concerning Meats

And concerning food let these be your ordinances, since in regard to meats also many stumble. For some deal indifferently with things offered to idols, while others discipline themselves, but condemn those that eat: and in different ways men's souls are defiled in the matter of meats, from ignorance of the useful reasons for eating and not eating. For we fast by abstaining from wine and flesh, not because we abhor them as abominations, but because we look for our reward; that having scorned things sensible, we may enjoy a spiritual and intellectual feast; and that having *now sown in tears we may reap in joy* in the world to come. Despise not therefore them that eat, and because of the weakness of their bodies partake of food: nor yet blame those who use *a little wine for their stomach's sake and their often infirmities*: and neither condemn the men as sinners, nor abhor the flesh as strange food; for the Apostle knows some of this sort, when he says: forbidding *to marry, and commanding to abstain from meats, which God created to be received with thanksgiving by them that believe*. In abstaining then from these things, abstain not as from things abominable, else thou hast no reward: but as being good things disregard them for the sake of the better spiritual things set before thee.

Guard thy soul safely, lest at any time thou eat of things offered to idols: for concerning meats of this kind, not only I at this time, but ere now Apostles also, and James the bishop of this Church, have had earnest care: and the Apostles and Elders write a Catholic epistle to all the Gentiles, that they should *abstain* first from *things offered to idols*, and then *from blood* also and *from things strangled*. For many men being of savage nature, and living like dogs, both lap up blood, in imitation of the manner of the fiercest beasts, and greedily devour things strangled. But do thou, the servant of Christ, in eating observe to eat with reverence. And so enough concerning meats.

Of Apparel

But let thine apparel be plain, not for adornment, but for necessary covering: not to minister to thy vanity, but to keep thee warm in winter, and to hide the unseemliness of the body: lest under pretense of hiding the unseemliness, thou fall into another kind of unseemliness by thy extravagant dress.

Of the Resurrection

Be tender, I beseech thee, of this body, and understand that thou wilt be raised from the dead, to be judged with this body. But if there steal into thy mind any thought of unbelief, as though the thing were impossible, judge of the things unseen by what happens to thyself. For tell me; a hundred years ago or more, think where wast thou thyself: and from what a most minute and mean substance thou art come to so great a stature, and so much dignity of beauty. What then? Cannot He who brought the non-existent into being, raise up again that which already exists and has decayed? He who raises the corn, which is sown for our sakes, as year by year it dies, — will He have difficulty in raising us up, for whose sakes that corn also has been raised? Seest thou how the trees stand now for many months without either fruit or leaves: but when the winter is past they spring up whole into life again as if from the dead: shall not we much rather and more easily return to life? The rod of Moses was transformed by the will of God into the unfamiliar nature of a serpent: and cannot a man, who has fallen into death, be restored to himself again?

Heed not those who say that this body is not raised; for it is raised: and Esaias is witness, when he says: The *dead shall arise, and they that are in the tombs shall awake*: and according to Daniel, Many *of them that sleep in the dust of the earth shall arise, some to everlasting life, and some to everlasting shame*. But though to rise again is common to all men, yet the resurrection is not alike to all for the bodies received by us all are eternal, but not like bodies by all: for the just receive them, that through eternity they may join the Choirs of Angels; but the sinners, that they may endure for ever the torment of their sins.

Of the Laver

For this cause the Lord, preventing us according to His loving-kindness, has granted repentance at Baptism, in order that we may cast off their chief — nay rather the whole burden of our sins, and having received the seal by the Holy Spirit, may be made heirs of eternal life. But as we have spoken sufficiently concerning the Laver the day before yesterday, let us now return to the remaining subjects of our introductory teaching.

Of the Divine Scriptures

Now these the divinely inspired Scriptures of both the Old and the New Testament teach us. For the God of the two Testaments is One, Who in the Old Testament foretold the Christ Who appeared in the New; Who by the Law and the Prophets led us to Christ's school. For *before faith came, we were kept in ward under the law*, and, *the law hath been our tutor to bring us unto Christ*. And if ever thou hear any of the heretics speaking evil of the Law or the Prophets, answer in the sound of the Savior's voice, saying, Jesus came *not to destroy the Law, but to fulfill it*. Learn also diligently, and from the Church, what are the books of the Old Testament, and what those of the New. And, pray, read none of the apocryphal writings: for what dost thou, who knowest not those which are acknowledged among all, trouble thyself in vain about those which are disputed? Read the Divine Scriptures, the twenty-two books of the Old Testament, these that have been translated by the Seventy-two Interpreters.

For after the death of Alexander, the King of the Macedonians, and the division of his kingdom into four principalities, into Babylonia, and Macedona, and Asia, and Egypt, one of those who reigned over Egypt, Ptolemy Philadelphus, being a king very fond of learning, while collecting the books that were in every place, heard from Demetrius Phalereus, the curator of his library, of the Divine Scriptures of the Law and the Prophets, and judged it much nobler, not to get the books from the possessors by force against their will, but rather to propitiate them by gifts and friendship and knowing that what is extorted is often adulterated, being given unwillingly, while that which is willingly supplied is freely given with all sincerity, he sent to Eleazar, who was then High Priest, a great many gifts for the Temple here at Jerusalem, and caused him to send him six interpreters from each of the twelve tribes of Israel for the translation. Then, further, to make experiment whether the books were Divine or not, he took precaution that those who had been sent should not combine among themselves, by assigning to each of the interpreters who had come his separate chamber in the island called Pharos, which lies over against Alexandria, and committed to each the whole Scriptures to translate. And when they had fulfilled the task in seventy-two days, he brought together all their translations, which they had made in different chambers without sending them one to another, and found that they agreed not only in the sense but even in words. For the process was no word-craft, nor contrivance of human devices: but the translation of the Divine Scriptures, spoken by the Holy Spirit, was of the Holy Spirit accomplished.

Of these read the two and twenty books, but have nothing to do with the apocryphal writings. Study earnestly these only which we read openly in the Church. Far wiser and more pious than thyself were the Apostles, and the bishops of old time, the presidents of the Church who handed down these books. Being therefore a child of the Church, trench thou not upon its statutes. And of the Old Testament, as we have said, study the two and twenty books, which, if thou art desirous of learning, strive to remember by name, as I recite them. For of the Law the books of Moses are the first five, Genesis, Exodus, Leviticus, Numbers, Deuteronomy. And next, Joshua the son of Nun, and the book of Judges, including Ruth, counted as seventh. And of the other historical books, the first and second books of the Kings are among the Hebrews one book; also the third and fourth one book. And in like manner, the first and second of Chronicles are with them one book; and the first and second of Esdras are counted one. Esther is the twelfth book; and these are the Historical writings. But those which are written in verses are five, Job, and the book of Psalms, and Proverbs, and Ecclesiastes, and the Song of Songs, which is the seventeenth book. And after these come the five Prophetic books: of the Twelve Prophets one book, of Isaiah one, of Jeremiah one, including Baruch and Lamentations and the Epistle; then Ezekiel, and the Book of Daniel, the twenty-second of the Old Testament.

Then of the New Testament there are the four Gospels only, for the rest have false titles and are mischievous. The Manichaeans also wrote a Gospel according to Thomas, which being tinctured with the fragrance of the evangelic title corrupts the souls of the simple sort. Receive also the acts of the Twelve Apostles; and in addition to these the seven Catholic Epistles of James, Peter, John, and Jude; and as a seal upon them all, and the last work of the disciples, the fourteen Epistles of Paul. But let all the rest be put aside in a secondary rank. And whatever books are not read in Churches, these read not even by thyself, as thou hast heard me say. Thus much of these subjects.

But shun thou every diabolical operation, and believe not the apostate Serpent, whose transformation from a good nature was of his own free choice: who can overpersuade the willing, but can compel no one. Also give heed neither to observations of the stars nor auguries, nor omens, nor to the fabulous divinations of the Greeks, Witchcraft, and enchantment, and the wicked practices of necromancy, admit not even to a hearing. From every kind of intemperance stand aloof, giving thyself neither to gluttony nor licentiousness, rising superior to all covetousness and usury. Neither venture thyself at heathen assemblies for public spectacles, nor ever use amulets in sicknesses; shun also all the vulgarity of tavern-haunting. Fall not away either into the sect of the Samaritans, or into Judaism: for Jesus Christ henceforth hath ransomed thee. Stand aloof from an observance of Sabbaths, and from calling any indifferent meats *common or unclean*. But especially abhor all the assemblies of wicked heretics; and in every way make thine own soul safe, by fastings, prayers, almsgivings, and reading the oracles of God; that having lived the rest of thy life in the flesh in soberness and godly doctrine, thou mayest enjoy the one salvation which flows from Baptism; and thus enrolled in the armies of heaven by God and the Father, mayest also be deemed worthy of the heavenly crowns, in Christ Jesus our Lord, to Whom be the glory for ever and ever. Amen.

LECTURE XXII

On the Mysteries, IV.

On the Body and Blood of Christ

I Cor. xi. 23

I received of the Lord that which also I delivered unto you, how that the Lord Jesus, in the night in which He was betrayed, took bread, etc.

Even of itself the teaching of the Blessed Paul is sufficient to give you a full assurance concerning those Divine Mysteries, of which having been deemed worthy, ye are become of *the same body* and blood with Christ. For you have just heard him say distinctly, *That our Lord Jesus Christ in the night in which He was betrayed, took bread, and when He had given thanks He brake it, and gave to His disciples, saying, Take, eat, this is My Body: and having taken the cup and given thanks, He said, Take, drink, this is My Blood.* Since then He himself declared and said of the Bread, *This is My Body*, who shall dare to doubt any longer? And since He has himself affirmed and said, *This is My Blood*, who shall ever hesitate, saying, that it is not His blood?

He once in Cana of Galilee, turned the water into wine, akin to blood, and is it incredible that He should have turned wine into blood? When called to a bodily marriage, He miraculously wrought that wonderful work; and *on the children of the bride-chamber*, shall He not much rather be acknowledged to have bestowed the fruition of His Body and Blood?

Wherefore with full assurance let us partake as of the Body and Blood of Christ: for in the figure of Bread is given to thee His Body, and in the figure of Wine His Blood; that thou by partaking of the Body and Blood of Christ, mayest be made of the same body and the same blood with Him. For thus we come to bear Christ in us, because His Body and Blood are distributed through our members; thus it is that, according to the blessed Peter, *we become partakers of the divine nature.*

Christ on a certain occasion discoursing with the Jews said, *Except ye eat My flesh and drink My blood, ye have no life in you.* They not having heard His saying in a spiritual sense were offended, and went back, supposing that He was inviting them to eat flesh.

In the Old Testament also there was show-bread; but this, as it belonged to the Old Testament, has come to an end; but in the New Testament there is Bread of heaven, and a Cup of salvation, sanctifying soul and body; for as the Bread corresponds to our body, so is the Word appropriate to our soul.

Consider therefore the Bread and the Wine not as bare elements, for they are, according to the Lord's declaration, the Body and Blood of Christ; for even though sense suggests this to thee, yet let faith establish thee. Judge not the matter from the taste, but from faith be fully assured without misgiving, that the Body and Blood of Christ have been vouchsafed to thee.

Also the blessed David shall advise thee the meaning of this, saying, *Thou hast prepared a table before me in the presence of them that afflict me*. What he says, is to this effect: Before Thy coming, the evil spirits prepared a table for men, polluted and defiled and full of devilish influence; but since Thy coming, 0 Lord, *Thou hast prepared a table before me*. When the man says to God, *Thou hast prepared before me a table*, what other does he indicate but that mystical and spiritual Table, which God hath prepared for us *over against*, that is, contrary and in opposition to, the evil spirits? And very truly; for that had communion with devils, but this, with God. *Thou hast anointed my head with oil*. With oil He anointed thine head upon thy forehead, for the seal which thou hast of God; that thou mayest be made *the engraving of the signed, Holiness unto God*. And *thy cup intoxicateth me, as very strong*. Thou seest that cup here spoken of, which Jesus took in His hand, and gave thanks, and said, *This is My blood, which is shed for many for the remission of sins*.

Therefore Solomon also, hinting at this grace, says in Ecclesiastes, *Come hither, eat thy bread with joy* (that is, the spiritual bread; *Come hither*, he calls with the call to salvation and blessing), *and drink thy wine with a merry heart* (that is, the spiritual wine); *and let oil be poured out upon thy head* (thou seest he alludes even to the mystic Chrism); *and let thy garments be always white, for the Lord is well pleased with thy works;* for before thou camest to Baptism, thy works were *vanity of vanities*. But now, having put off thy old garments, and put on those which are spiritually white, thou must be continually robed in white: of course we mean not this, that thou must be clad in the garments that are truly white and shining and spiritual, that thou mayest say with the blessed Esaias, *My soul shall be joyful in my God; for He that clothed me with a garment of salvation, and put a robe of gladness around me*.

Having learnt these things, and been fully assured that the seeming bread is not bread, though sensible to taste, but the Body of Christ; and that the seeming wine is not wine, though the taste will have it so, but the Blood of Christ; and that of this David sung of old, saying, *And bread strengthened man's heart, to make his face to shine with oil*, "strengthen thou thine heart," by partaking thereof as spiritual, and "make the face of thy soul shine." And so having it unveiled with a pure conscience, mayest thou *reflect as a mirror the glory of the Lord*, and proceed from *glory to glory*, in Christ Jesus our Lord: — To whom be honor, and might, and glory, for ever and ever. Amen.

LECTURE XXIII

On the Mysteries, V.

On the Sacred Liturgy and Communion I Pet. ii. 1

Wherefore putting away all filthiness,

and all guile, and evil speaking, etc.

By the loving-kindness of God ye have heard sufficiently at our former meetings concerning Baptism, and Chrism, and partaking of the Body and Blood of Christ; and now it is necessary to pass on to what is next in order, meaning today to set the crown on the spiritual building of your edification.

Ye have seen then the Deacon who gives to the Priest water to wash, and to the Presbyters who stand round God's altar. He gave it not at all because of bodily defilement; it is not that; for we did not enter the Church at first with defiled bodies. But the washing of hands is a symbol that ye ought to be pure from all sinful and unlawful deeds; for since the hands are a symbol of action, by washing them, it is evident, we represent the purity and blamelessness of our conduct. Didst thou not hear the blessed David opening this very mystery, and saying, *I will wash my hands in innocency, and so will I compass Thine Altar, 0 Lord*? The washing therefore of hands is a symbol of immunity from sin.

Then the Deacon cries aloud, "Receive ye one another; and let us kiss one another." Think not that this kiss is of the same character with those given in public by common friends. It is not such: but this kiss blends souls one with another, and courts entire forgiveness for them. The kiss therefore is the sign that our souls are mingled together, and banish all remembrance of wrongs. For this cause Christ said, *If thou art offering thy gift at the altar, and there rememberest that thy brother hath aught against thee, leave there thy gift upon the altar, and go thy way; first be reconciled to thy brother, and then come and offer thy gift*. The kiss therefore is reconciliation, and for this reason holy: as the blessed Paul somewhere cried, saying, *Greet ye one another with a holy kiss*; and Peter, *with a kiss of charity*.

After this the Priest cries aloud, "Lift up your hearts." For truly ought we in that most awful hour to have our heart on high with God, and not below, thinking of earth and earthly things. In effect therefore the Priest bids all in that hour to dismiss all cares of this life, or household anxieties, and to have their heart in heaven with the merciful God. Then ye answer, "We lift them up unto the Lord": assenting to it, by your avowal, but let no one come here, who could say with his mouth, "We lift up our hearts unto the Lord," but in his thoughts have his mind concerned with the cares of this life. At all times, rather, God should be in our memory; but if this is impossible by reason of human infirmity, in that hour above all this should be our earnest endeavor.

Then the Priest says, "Let us give thanks unto the Lord." For verily we are bound to give thanks, that He called us, unworthy as we were, to so great grace; that He reconciled us when we were His foes; that He vouch-safed to us the Spirit of adoption. Then ye say, "It is meet and right": for in giving thanks we do a meet thing and a right; but He did not right, but more than right, in doing us good, and counting us meet for such great benefits.

After this, we make mention of heaven, and earth, and sea; of sun and moon; of stars and all the creation, rational and irrational, visible and invisible; of Angels, Archangels, Virtues, Dominions, Principalities, Powers, Thrones; of the Cherubim with many faces: in effect repeating that call of David's, *Magnify the Lord with me*. We make mention also of the Seraphim, whom Esaias in the Holy Spirit saw standing around the throne of God, and with two of their wings veiling their face, and with twain their feet, while with twain they did fly, crying *Holy, Holy, Holy, is the Lord of Sabaoth*. For the reason of our reciting this confession of God, delivered down to us from the Seraphim, is this, that so we may be partakers with the hosts of the world above in their Hymn of praise.

Then having sanctified ourselves by these spiritual Hymns, we beseech the merciful God to send forth His Holy Spirit upon the gifts lying before Him; that He may make the Bread the Body of Christ, and the Wine the Blood of Christ; for whatsoever the Holy Spirit has touched, is surely sanctified and changed.

Then, after the spiritual sacrifice, the bloodless service, is completed, over that sacrifice of propitiation we entreat God for the common peace of the

Churches, for the welfare of the world; for kings; for soldiers and allies; for the sick; for the afflicted; and, in a word, for all who stand in need of succor we all pray and offer this sacrifice.

Then we commemorate also those who have fallen asleep before us, first Patriarchs, Prophets, Apostles, Martyrs, that at their prayers and intercessions God would receive our petition. Then on behalf also of the Holy Fathers and Bishops who have fallen asleep before us, and in a word of all who in past years have fallen asleep among us, believing that it will be a very great benefit to the souls, for whom the supplication is put up, while that holy and most awful sacrifice is set forth.

And I wish to persuade you by an illustration. For I know that many say, what is a soul profited, which departs from this world either with sins, or without sins, if it be commemorated in the prayer? For if a king were to banish certain who had given him offense, and then those who belong to them should weave a crown and offer it to Him on behalf of those under punishment, would he not grant a remission of their penalties? In the same way we, when we offer to Him our supplications for those who have fallen asleep, though they be sinners, weave no crown, but offer up Christ sacrificed for our sins propitiating our merciful God for them as well as for ourselves.

Then, after these things, we say that Prayer which the Savior delivered to His own disciples, with a pure conscience entitling God our Father, and saying, *Our Father, which art in heaven*. 0 most surpassing loving-kindness of God! On them who revolted from Him and were in the very extreme of misery has He bestowed such a complete forgiveness of evil deeds, and so great participation of grace, as that they should even call Him Father. *Our Father, which art in heaven*; and they also are a heaven who *hear the image of the heavenly*, in whom is God *dwelling and walking in them*.

Hallowed be Thy Name. The Name of God is in its nature holy, whether we say so or not; but since it is sometimes profaned among sinners, according to the words, *Through you My Name is continually blasphemed among the Gentiles*, we pray that in us God's Name may be hallowed; not that it comes to be holy from not being holy, but because it becomes holy in us, when we are made holy, and do things worthy of holiness.

Thy kingdom come. A pure soul can say with boldness, *Thy kingdom come*; for he who has heard Paul saying, *Let not therefore sin reign in your mortal body*, and has cleansed himself in deed, and thought, and word, will say to God, *Thy kingdom come*.

Thy will be done as in heaven so on earth. God's divine and blessed Angels do the will of God, as David said in the Psalm, *Bless the Lord, all ye Angels of His, mighty in strength, that do His pleasure.* So then in effect thou meanest this by thy prayer, "as in the Angels Thy will is done, so likewise be it done on earth in me, 0 Lord."

Give us this day our substantial bread. This common bread is not substantial bread, but this Holy Bread is substantial, that is, appointed for the substance of the soul. For this Bread *goeth not into the belly and is cast out into the draught*, but is distributed into thy whole system for the benefit of body and soul. But by *this day*, he means, "each day," as also Paul said, *While it is called to-day.*

And forgive us our debts as we also forgive our debtors. For we have many sins. For we offend both in word and in thought, and very many things we do worthy of condemnation; and *if we say that we have no sin*, we lie, as John says. And we make a covenant with God, entreating Him to forgive us our sins, as we also forgive our neighbors their debts. Considering then what we receive and in return for what let us not put off nor delay to forgive one another. The offenses committed against us are slight and trivial, and easily settled; but those which we have committed against God are great, and need such mercy as His only is. Take heed therefore, lest for the slight and trivial sins against thee thou shut out for thyself forgiveness from God for thy very grievous sins.

And lead us not into temptation, O Lord. Is this then what the Lord teaches us to pray, that we may not be tempted at all? How then is it said elsewhere, "a man untempted is a man unproved"; and again, *My brethren, count it all joy when ye fall into divers temptations*? But does perchance the entering into temptation mean the being overwhelmed by the temptation? For Temptation is, as it were, like a winter torrent difficult to cross. Those therefore who are not overwhelmed in temptations, pass through, shewing themselves excellent swimmers, and not being swept away by them at all; while those who are not such, enter into them and are overwhelmed. As for example, Judas having entered into the temptation of the love of money, swam not through it, but was overwhelmed and was strangled both in body and spirit. Peter entered into the temptation of the denial; but having entered, he was not overwhelmed by it, but manfully swam through and was delivered from the temptation. Listen again, in another place, to a company of unscathed saints, giving thanks for deliverance from temptation, *Thou, 0 God, hast proved us; Thou hast tried us by fire like as silver is tried. Thou broughtest us into the net; Thou layedst afflictions upon our loins. Thou hast caused men to ride over our heads; we went through fire and water; and thou broughtest us out into a place of rest*. Thou seest them speaking boldly in regard to their having passed through and not been pierced. *But Thou broughtest us out into a place of rest*; now their coming into a place of rest is their being delivered from temptation.

But deliver us from the evil. If *Lead us not into temptation* implied the not being tempted at all, He would not have said, *But deliver us from the evil*. Now evil is our adversary the devil, from whom we pray to be delivered. Then after completing the prayer thou sayest, *Amen*; by this *Amen*, which means "so be it," setting thy seal to the petitions of the divinely taught prayer.

After this the Priest says, "Holy things to holy men." Holy are the gifts presented, having received the visitation of the Holy Spirit; holy are ye also, having been deemed worthy of the Holy Spirit; the holy things therefore correspond to the holy persons. Then ye say, "One is Holy, One is the Lord, Jesus Christ." For One is truly holy, by nature holy; we too are holy, but not by nature, only by participation, and discipline, and prayer.

And after this ye hear the chanter inviting you with a sacred melody to the communion of the Holy Mysteries, and saying, *0 taste and see that the Lord is good*. Trust not the judgment to thy bodily palate; no, but to faith unfaltering; for they who taste are bidden to taste, not bread and wine, but the antitypical Body and Blood of Christ.

In approaching therefore, come not with thy wrists extended, or thy fingers spread; but make thy left hand a throne for the right, as for that which is to receive a King. And having hollowed thy palm, receive the Body of Christ, saying over it, *Amen*. So then after having carefully hallowed thine eyes by the touch of the Holy Body, partake of it; giving heed lest thou lose any portion thereof; for whatever thou losest, is evidently a loss to thee as it were from one of thine own members. For tell me, if any one gave thee grains of gold, wouldest thou not hold them with all carefulness, being on thy guard against losing any of them, and suffering loss? Wilt thou not then much more carefully keep watch, that not a crumb fall from thee of what is more precious than gold and precious stones?

Then after thou hast partaken of the Body of Christ, draw near also to the Cup of His Blood; not stretching forth thine hands, but bending, and saying with an air of worship and reverence, *Amen*, hallow thyself by partaking also of the Blood of Christ. And while the moisture is still upon thy lips, touch it with thine hands, and hallow thine eyes and brow and the other organs of sense. Then wait for the prayer, and give thanks unto God, who hath accounted thee worthy of so great mysteries.

Hold fast these traditions undefiled and, keep yourselves free from offense. Sever not yourselves from the Communion; deprive not yourselves, through the pollution of sins, of these Holy and Spiritual Mysteries. *And the God of peace sanctify you wholly; and may your spirit, and soul, and body be preserved entire without blame at the coming of our Lord Jesus Christ*; — To whom be glory and honor and might, with the Father and the Holy Spirit, now and ever, and world without end. Amen.

Selections from St. Cyril of Jerusalem are from *A Selected Library of Nicene and Post-Nicene Fathers of the Christian Church*, Second Series, Volume VII, New York: The Christian Literature Co., 1894

Chapter 22 • St. Basil the Great: *On the Use of Pagan Authors;* Letter Concerning the Difference Between οὐσία (substance) and ὑποστασις (person)

Basil (ca. 330-379) is an example of the thoroughly educated and cultured gentleman of the fourth century — a real "renaissance" man. He studied in the school of Caesarea, famous for the teaching of Origen, then at Constantinople, and later at Athens, where he was associated with Gregory of Nazianzus in the study of grammar, rhetoric, and philosophy. He was baptized in 357, ordained by Eusebius in 364, made bishop of Caesarea in Cappadocia in 370, and was actively engaged all his Christian life with the problems of the Church. He drew up a set of rules for the monastic life which have influenced all the rules of subsequent monastic groups, especially the Franciscans.

The treatise presented here shows the generally accepted Christian point of view in regard to the value of Greek literature and philosophy. Space does not permit the inclusion of his philosophical speculations on the origin and nature of the world as found in his classic *In Hexaemeron*. Letter 38 is a classic example of the traditional problem of understanding the Tri-unity of God. We see it occurring again and again in the writings of St. Augustine, St. Hilary of Poitiers, and Boethius.

On the Use of Pagan Authors

There are many things, 0 children, encouraging me to give you those counsels which I judge to be best, and which I believed would be useful to you receiving them. For the fact of my having attained the age which I have reached, and having been exercised by many affairs, and also of my having fairly partaken of the change in both *good and evil fortune*, which teaches all things, has made me experienced in human things, so that I am enabled to show, as it were, the safest way to those who have just chosen for themselves a course of life. . . .

Chapter II

We, my children, consider this human life to be nothing, to be absolutely nothing; nor do we think or call anything at all good which affords advantage to us for this life only. Wherefore we do not consider nobility of ancestors, nor strength of body, nor beauty, nor greatness, nor honor from all men, nor empire itself, nor anything that any one might mention, great, nor even worthy of prayer, nor do we regard those who have them, but we proceed higher with our hopes, and do all things as preparation for the other life. The things therefore, which are profitable to us for the other life, those, I say, we ought to love and pursue with all our strength; but that we should neglect, as worth nothing, those which do not reach it. But what this life is, and where, and how we are to love it, is a greater height than that I should reach it by this present effort. Nevertheless, saying this much, I have perhaps sufficiently shown to you, that if any one were to collect in his discourse, and heap into one, all the happiness that has been, since men have existed, he will find that it is not to be compared with the least portion of those blessings (of the other life), but that all of the advantages here below, are farther removed from the dignity of the least among those *in the future* life, than by how much a shadow and a dream are left behind by the realities. But rather, in order that I may use a more familiar example, by so much as the soul is more precious than the body, so great is the difference between both lives. But to this life, indeed, the sacred writings lead, instructing us through secret *meanings*; but so long as by reason of your age it is not possible for you to understand the depth of their meaning, let us exercise ourselves beforehand by the eye of the soul in other books which are not altogether different *from the Sacred Scriptures*, as in certain shadows and mirrors, imitating those who practice exercises in military tactics; who, when they have acquired experience in the movement of the hands and in leaping, derive gain in actual conflict from the sham battle. And certainly we ought to think, that the greatest contest of all is proposed for us, unto the preparation for which we must do and labor all in our power, and we must converse with poets and historians and rhetoricians, and with all men, from whom may be about to come some help for the care of our souls. If the indelible glory of virtue is to remain with us, once having initiated ourselves in the sciences external to those (the sacred sciences), will learn from them the sacred and secret teachings, and as those accustomed to see the sun in the water, we shall apply our eyes to the light itself.

Chapter III

If, therefore, the letters — *sacred and profane* — have any relationship to each other, the knowledge of them would be to the purpose for us: but if not, it would be no small advantage for the confirmation of the better learning, that, putting them opposite each other, we should learn their difference. To what, therefore, having compared each *of the courses* of instruction, can you find an image *to illustrate their difference?* Assuredly, as it is the proper virtue of a plant to abound with seasonable fruit, but, nevertheless, the leaves stirred upon its branches contribute a certain ornament; even so, truth is primarily the fruit of the soul; but it is not ungraceful that it should be clothed with the wisdom from without, as with certain leaves, affording a shade to the fruit, and not an unpleasing aspect. Wherefore Moses, he the very illustrious, whose name is greatest for, wisdom amongst all men, having been exercised in the learning of the Egyptians, is said to have thus come to the contemplation of Him who is. But similarly with him, and even in later times, it is said that the wise Daniel, having learned the wisdom of the Chaldeans in Babylon, then applied to the Divine teachings.

Chapter IV

But enough has been said to show that those external studies are not a useless thing. But how you are to partake of them is in turn to be said. In the first place, it is fit that you should not apply your minds to all things alike, *which are said* by the poets (in order to begin with those), since some are of every character in their writings; but when they relate to you the deeds or words of good men it is right to love them, and imitate them, and try to resemble them as much as possible; but when they come to wicked men by their description, it is right that you should fly those things, having stopped your ears not less than those say that Ulysses avoided the songs of the Sirens. For familiarity with corrupt words is a kind of way to the acts themselves. For which reason you must guard your souls with the utmost watchfulness, lest through the pleasure of the words we may unknowingly take any of the vicious *portions*, as those who receive poisons with honey. We, therefore, shall not praise the poets when they describe men who are revilers and scoffers, or those in love, or drunkards, nor when they measure glory by a well-filled table and dissolute songs. But, least of all, let us attend to them speaking concerning the gods, and especially when they speak of them as of many, and those not agreeing among themselves. For amongst them brother raises sedition against brother, and father against children, and those again have an implacable war against their parents. But the adulteries of the gods, and their amours, and their embraces in public, and those especially of the head and prince of all, Jupiter, such as any one would blush to mention concerning brute animals, those we shall leave to the people upon the stage.

But I have the very same things to say concerning the historians, and especially when they write for the sake of leading the minds of their students with them. And let us not imitate the rhetoricians with regard to lying. For neither in judicial proceedings, nor in other matters, is falsehood proper for us who have made choice of the straight and true path of life, *of us* to whom it has been commanded by the law not to litigate. But let us rather receive those writings of theirs by which they have praised virtue and condemned vice. For even as for all other creatures the enjoyment of flowers is that of their scent or their color, but it is for the bees to take honey also out of them; thus also in this department of letters, it is for us, not merely preserving the sweetness or pleasantness of those letters, to lay up for use in our souls some profit from them. We must therefore, partake of those writings completely after the example of the bees. For neither do they go to all flowers alike, nor do they endeavor to take away the whole substance from those flowers over which they fly, but having taken from them as much as is suitable for their work, bid goodbye to the remainder. And we, indeed, if we be wise, having taken as much as is proper to us and akin to truth, will pass over what is left. And as in culling the flowers of the rose bush, we avoid the thorns, in like manner, having gathered of those writings whatever is useful, let us guard against what is hurtful. It were fit, therefore, that from the beginning we should consider each of those studies, and fit it to its end, according to the Doric proverb, keeping the stone to the plumb line.

Chapter V

And since it is through virtue that we must reach our life, and since many things tending towards this are repeated by the poets, and many by the historians, and much more still by the philosophers, to such of those writings as bear that tendency, must we apply our minds in particular. For it is no small help that a certain familiarity and fellowship with virtue should be generated in the minds of the young, since studies of such matters are by nature unchangeable, being deeply engraven in their minds on account of their tenderness. What else are we to suppose that He said had in view when he made those verses which all sing, than this? Was it not that he should encourage the young to virtue? He says that at first the way leading to virtues is rough and difficult of access, and full of frequent sweat and labor, and arduous. For which reason it is not the lot of every one, either to approach it on account of its steepness, or when he has approached it, easily to reach the summit. But having once gained the top, it is given him to see how smooth and fair it is, and how easy and unobstructed, and more pleasant than that of the path which leads to vice,

which the same poet has said might at once be taken on account of its being adjoining. For he appears to me to have gone through those things doing nothing else than encouraging us to virtue, and inviting us all to be good, and that we should not turn away from our object, having been made too soft for labors. And, indeed, if any other poet has sung any thing similar to those leading to virtue, let us receive those writings as leading to the same object with us.

But, as I have heard from a man who was skilled in discovering the meaning of the poet, his entire poem is for Homer in praise of virtue, and with him everything that is not superfluous conduces to this end, but not least of all in those verses, in which he has represented the general of the Cephalonians, after he had been saved naked from shipwreck — first, indeed, when he was seen alone, to have inspired the princess with a feeling of modesty: so far was he from incurring shame when he was seen naked: for *the poet* represented him as clothed with virtue instead of with a garment: and next, to have been considered worthy of such honor by the Phaeadans that having discarded the luxury in which they were living, they all looked up to him and emulated him, and that no one of the Phaeacians at that time should have preferred anything than to be Ulysses, and this even though Ulysses was a man just saved from ship wreck. For in those things the interpreter of the meaning of the poet affirms that Homer crying out, only says, 0 men, you must attend to virtue, which swims out together with him who has been shipwrecked, and will exhibit him, naked as he is upon the strand, as more worthy of honor than the fortunate Phaeacians.

Virtue alone of all possessions is a thing that cannot be taken away, and remains with a man living and dead. Whence also Solon appears to me to say those things to the rich: "But we will not barter our virtue with those for riches; since the one (virtue) is always steadfast, but different men have human riches at different times." But nearly similar to those are the verses of Theognis, in which he says that God (whatever God he alludes to) weighs down the balance for men at different times in different directions: that at one time they are rich, but at another time have nothing.

And, indeed, the Chian sophist, somewhere in his writings, has reasoned matters germane to these, regarding virtue and vice. To whom, also, are we to apply our understanding, for the man is by no means contemptible. But his expression is somewhat to this effect, as far as I recollect the meaning of the man, for I do not know the words, unless that he spoke simply thus, without meter. That while Hercules was very young, and of about the age that you are now, while he was deliberating which of the two ways he should turn, whether that which leads through labors to virtue, or the easy way, two women came forward; but that those were virtue and vice, and that they, though silent, manifested by their dress the difference between them. For, that one was arrayed for beauty by the cosmetic art, and overflowed with luxury, and brought the entire swarm of pleasure hanging from her: and that she, therefore, showed those things, and promising more, endeavored to draw Hercules to herself. But that the other was thin, and squalid, and looked fixedly, and said such and such things of another kind, and promised nothing indolent, nothing sweet, but infinite sweat and labors, and dangers, over all land and sea. But that the reward of those things was to become a god, as his expression is, whom Hercules ended by going along with.

Chapter VI

And almost all of whom there is any mention, small or great, in connection with philosophy, have entered into the praise of virtue in their writings. Whom we are to obey and to try to illustrate their writings in our lives. For he who confirms in work that philosophy which amongst others extends only as far as words, "is wise, the others flutter as shadows." And it appears to me that this is almost similar *to the case*, as if, a picture representing a man of astonishing beauty, the man himself should be in fact such as the painter represented him on the tablets. Since, indeed, to praise virtue publicly in brilliant terms, and to spin out long speeches about it, but in private to prefer pleasure to moderation, and the possession of more *than others have*, to justice, is like, I should say, to those performing actors upon the stage, who oftentimes come forth as kings and dynasts, being neither kings nor dynasts, nor haply free men at all. Thus, a musician would not willingly endure that his lyre should be discordant, and the leader of a choir would not wish to have a choir which should not be quite in accord. Each one therefore will disagree with himself, and will not have a life conformable with his words, but he will say, according to Euripides: My tongue, indeed, has sworn, but my mind is unsworn: and he will prefer the appearing good to the being so. But this is the utmost limit of injustice, if any credit is to be given to Plato, to appear to be just while one is not so.

Chapter VII

Let us thus, therefore, receive those of the writings of the ancients which have arguments of honorable subjects; and since the strenuous acts of the ancient men are preserved for us either by the sequence of memory, or kept by the writing of poets or historians, let us not be destitute of help from hence either.

Chapter IX

What then shall we do? Some one may say. What else than to have care of our soul, the best attentions are to be given to the soul, having released her by philosophy from the fellowship which she has with the passions of the body, and at the same time rendering the body stronger than its passions, ministering to the belly the things necessary, not the things sweetest. But to take trouble about shaving and dresses beyond what is necessary, is the part either of the unfortunate or of the unjust, according to that saying of Diogenes. So that I say, that persons of this description should be as much ashamed to be and to be called a fop as to live in prostitution, or to plot against the marriage *vows* of others. For what is the difference to any one of sense whether he be clad in a fine texture, or wears a garment of the coarser materials, provided it want nothing for being a protection against cold and heat? But, in the same way, it is right that we should not furnish ourselves with other matters beyond what is necessary, nor take greater care of the body than is for the advantages of the soul. For it is no less reproach to a man who is really worthy of this designation to be a fop and a lover of his person, than to be disgracefully subject to any other vice. For, the applying all one's zeal so as that he may have his body most adorned, is the part of one who does not know himself, and does not understand the wise admonition by which we are told that the man is not merely that which is seen, but that there is need of some wisdom over and above, through which each of us, whoever he may be, will know himself. But the purification of the soul, in order that I may speak compendiously and sufficiently for you, is to spurn the pleasures coming to us through the senses, not to feast our eyes upon the absurd shows of the jugglers, nor upon the gaze of bodies which drive in the goad of pleasure, not to pour in through our ears the melody which corrupts the soul.

But I am ashamed to dissuade from mingling with the air all kinds of perfumes, which bring pleasure to the smell, or from daubing yourselves with unguents. But what should any one say concerning its not being right to hunt after the pleasures in the touch and in the taste, unless that they compel those who devote themselves to this pursuit, to live like beasts bowed downwards to the belly and to the parts beneath?

But, in one word, the whole body is to be neglected by him who does not intend to be buried in his pleasures as in mire, or so much indulgence is to be given to it by him as ought to be given by those who apply its service by philosophy, as Plato says, speaking things similar to those spoken by Paul, who admonishes that we ought to have no provision for the flesh unto matter of concupiscence.

For those who are careful of the body, so that it may be in the best condition, but neglect the soul which is in that body as of no value, how do they differ from those who work at *the manufacture* of instruments, but neglect the art which operates through those instruments? Since, therefore, this excessive care of the body is unprofitable to the body itself, and obstructive to the soul, it is manifest madness to subject oneself to, and to minister to it.

For what need shall we have of riches, despising the pleasures which come to us through the body? For whatever is over and above one's need, this will he despise so much the more as he has less need of it; but he will limit his need, not by pleasures, but by the necessities of nature. But we, when we think that human virtue is not sufficient for its own adornment, do we imagine that we do things deserving of less shame?

But shall we neglect riches, and despise the pleasures coming through the senses, and yet pursue flattery and adulation, and imitate the cunning and varied artifice of the fox of Archilochus? But there is nothing more to be avoided by the wise man than living for glory, and regarding the things that may appear praiseworthy to the multitude, and not to make right reason the leader of our life, so that even if it should be necessary to undergo ignominy and danger for the sake of virtue, we should not choose to reverse any of the things rightly decided. Since he now, indeed, praises justice amongst all who honor it, but by and by he will utter words the opposite to those, when he perceives that injustice is in favor, which is the way of flatterers. And as they say that the Polypous changes his color for *that of* the Earth which lies near him, so he changes his opinion according to the sentiments of those who may be with him.

Chapter X

But though we shall learn those things more clearly in our own (*sacred*) writings, we shall trace from the teaching without, as much of a certain sketch of virtue as will answer for the present. Nor let us become indolent because those things are difficult and requiring labor; but I *would exhort you*, that mindful of him who admonishes us, that each one should choose the best life, and expect that it would grow pleasing from habit, you should set your hands to the best *practices*.

LETTER XXXVIII

To his Brother Gregory, concerning the difference between οὐσία *and* ὑποστασις

Many persons, in their study of the sacred dogmas, failing to distinguish between what is common in the essence or substance, and the meaning of the hypostases, arrive at the same notions, and think that it makes no difference whether οὐσία or hypostasis be spoken of. The result is that some of those who accept statements on these subjects without any enquiry, are pleased to speak of "one hypostasis," just as they do of one "essence" or "substance"; while on the other hand those who accept three hypostases are under the idea that they are bound in accordance with this confession, to assert also, by numerical analogy, three essences or substances. Under these circumstances, lest you fall into similar error, I have composed a short treatise for you by way of memorandum. The meaning of the words, to put it shortly, is as follows:

Of all nouns the sense of some, which are predicated of subjects plural and numerically various, is more general; as for instance *man*. When we so say, we employ the noun to indicate the common nature, and do not confine our meaning to any one man in particular who is known by that name. Peter, for instance is no more *man*, than Andrew, John, or James. The predicate therefore being common, and extending to all the individuals ranked under the same name, requires some note of distinction whereby we may understand not man in general but Peter or John in particular.

Of some nouns on the other hand the denotation is more limited: and by the aid of the limitation we have before our minds not the common nature but a limitation of anything, having, so far as the peculiarity extends, nothing in common with what is of the same kind; as for instance, Paul or Timothy. For, in a word of this kind there is no extension to what is common in the nature;

there is a separation of certain circumscribed conceptions from the general idea, and expression of them by means of their names. Suppose then that two or more are set together, as, for instance, Paul, Silvanus, and Timothy, and that an enquiry is made into the essence or substance of humanity; no one will give one definition of essence or substance in the case of Paul, a second in that of Silvanus, and a third in that of Timothy; but the same words which have been employed in setting forth the essence or substance of Paul will apply to the others also. Those who are described by the same definition of essence or substance are of the same essence or substance when the inquirer has learned what is common, and turns his attention to the differentiating properties whereby one is distinguished from another, the definition by which each is known will no longer tally in all particulars with the definition of another, even though in some points it be found to agree.

My statement, then, is this. That which is spoken of in a special and peculiar manner is indicated by the name of the hypostasis. Suppose we say "a man." The indefinite meaning of the word strikes a certain vague sense upon the ears. The nature is indicated, but what subsists and is specially and peculiarly indicated by the name is not made plain. Suppose we say "Paul." We set forth, by what is indicated by the name, the nature subsisting.

This then is the hypostasis, or "*understanding*"; not the indefinite conception of the essence or substance, which, because what is signified is general, finds no "*standing*," but the conception which by means of the expressed peculiarities gives *standing* and circumscription to the general and uncircumscribed. It is customary in Scripture to make a distinction of this kind, as well in many other passages as in the History of Job. When proposing to narrate the events of his life, Job first mentions the common, and says "a man"; then he straightway particularizes by adding "a certain." As to the description of the essence as having no bearing on the scope of his work, he is silent, but by means of particular notes of identity, mentioning the place and points of character, and such external qualifications as would individualize, and separate from the common and general idea, he specifies the "certain man," in such a way that from name, place, mental qualities, and outside circumstances, the description of the man whose life is being narrated is made in all particulars perfectly clear. If he had been giving an account of the essence, there would not in his explanation of the nature have been any mention of these matters. The same moreover would have been the account that there is in the case of Bildad the Shuhite, and Zophar the Naamathite, and each of the men there mentioned. Transfer, then, to the divine dogmas the same standard of difference which you recognize in the case both of essence and of hypostasis in human affairs, and you will not go wrong. Whatever your thought suggests to you as to the mode of the existence of the Father, you will think also in the case of the Son, and in like manner too of the Holy Ghost. For it is idle to halt the mind at any detached conception from the conviction that it is beyond all conception. For the account of the uncreate and of the incomprehensible is one and the same in the case of the Father and of the Son and of the Holy Ghost. For one is not more incomprehensible and uncreate than another. And since it is necessary, by means of the notes of differentiation, in the case of the Trinity, to keep the distinction unconfounded, we shall not take into consideration, in order to estimate that which differentiates, what is contemplated in common, as the uncreate, or what is beyond all comprehension, or any quality of this nature; we shall only direct our attention to the enquiry by what means each particular conception will be lucidly and distinctly separated from that which is conceived of in common.

Now the proper way to direct our investigation seems to me to be as follows. We say that every good thing, which by God's providence befalls us, is an operation of the Grace which worketh in us all things, as the apostle says, "But all these worketh that one and the self same Spirit dividing to every man severally as he will." If we ask, if the supply of good things, which thus comes to the saints has its origin in the Holy Ghost alone, we are on the other hand guided by Scripture to the belief that of the supply of the good things which are wrought in us through the Holy Ghost, the Originator and Cause is the Only-begotten God; for we are taught by Holy Scripture that "All things were made by Him," and "by Him consist." When we are exalted to this conception, again, led by God-inspired guidance, we are taught that by that power all things are brought from non-being into being, but yet not by that power to the exclusion of origination. On the other hand there is a certain power subsisting without generation and without origination, which is the cause of the cause of all things. For the Son, by whom are all things, and with whom the Holy Ghost is inseparably conceived of, is of the Father. For it is not possible for any one to conceive of the Son if he be not previously enlightened by the Spirit. Since, then, the Holy Ghost, from Whom all the supply of good things for creation has its source, is attached to the Son, and with Him is inseparably apprehended, and has Its being attached to the

Father, as cause, from Whom also It proceeds; It has this note of Its peculiar hypostatic nature, that It is known after the Son and together with the Son, and that It has Its subsistence of the Father. The Son, Who declares the Spirit proceeding from the Father through Himself and with Himself, shining forth alone and by only-begetting from the unbegotten fight, so far as the peculiar notes are concerned, has nothing in common either with the Father or with the Holy Spirit. He alone is known by the stated signs. But God, Who is over all, alone has, as one special mark of His own hypostasis, His being Father, and His deriving His hypostasis from no cause; and through this mark He is peculiarly known. Wherefore in the communion of the substance we maintain that there is no mutual approach or intercommunion of those notes of indication perceived in the Trinity, whereby is set forth the proper peculiarity of the Persons delivered in the faith, each of these being distinctively apprehended by His own notes. Hence, in accordance with the stated signs of indication, discovery is made of the separation of the hypostases; while so far as relates to the infinite, the incomprehensible, the uncreate, the uncircumscribed, similar attributes, there is no variableness in the life-giving nature; in that, I mean, of Father, Son, and Holy Ghost, but in Them is seen a certain communion indissoluble and continuous. And by the same considerations, whereby a reflective student could perceive the greatness of any one of the (Persons) believed in the Holy Trinity, he will proceed without variation. Beholding the glory in Father, Son and Holy Ghost, his mind all the while recognizes no void interval wherein it may travel between Father, Son, and Holy Ghost, for there is nothing inserted between Them; nor beyond the divine nature is there anything so subsisting as to be able to divide that nature from itself by the interposition of any foreign matter. Neither is there any vacuum of interval, void of subsistence, which can make a break in the mutual harmony of the divine essence, and solve the continuity by the interjection of emptiness. He who perceives the Father, and perceives Him by himself, has at the same time mental perception of the Son; and he who receives the Son does not divide Him from the Spirit, but, in consecution, so far as order is concerned, in conjunction so far as nature is concerned, expresses the faith commingled in himself in the three together. He who makes mention of the Spirit alone, embraces also in this confession Him of whom He is the Spirit. And since the Spirit is Christ's and of God, as says Paul, then just as he who lays hold on one end of the chain pulls the other to him, so he who "draws the Spirit," as says the prophet, by His means draws to him at the same time both the Son and the Father. And if any one verily receives the Son, he will hold Him on both sides, the Son drawing towards him on the one His own Father, and on the other His own Spirit. For He who eternally exists in the Father can never be cut off from the Father, nor can He who worketh all things by the Spirit ever be disjoined from His own Spirit. Likewise moreover he who receives the Father virtually receives at the same time both the Son and the Spirit; for it is no wise possible to entertain the idea of severance or division, in such a way as that the Son should be thought of apart from the Father, or the Spirit be disjoined from the Son. But the communion and the distinction apprehended in Them are, in a certain sense, ineffable and inconceivable, the continuity of nature being never rent asunder by the distinction of the hypostases, nor the notes of proper distinction confounded in the community of essence. Marvel not then at my speaking of the same thing as being both conjoined and parted, and thinking as it were darkly in a riddle, of a certain new and strange conjoined separation and separated conjunction. Indeed, even in objects perceptible to the senses, any one who approaches the subject in a candid and uncontentious spirit, may find similar conditions of things.

Yet receive what I say as at best a token and reflection of the truth; not as the actual truth itself. For it is not possible that there should be complete correspondence between what is seen in the tokens and the objects in reference to which the use of tokens is adopted. Why then do I say that an analogy of the separate and the conjoined is found in objects perceptible to the senses? You have before now, in springtime, beheld the brightness of the bow in the cloud; the bow, I mean, which, in our common parlance, is called Iris, and is said by persons skilled in such matters to be formed when a certain moisture is mingled with the air, and the force of the winds expresses what is dense and moist in the vapor, after it has become cloudy, into rain. The bow is said to be formed as follows. When the sunbeam, after traversing obliquely the dense and darkened portion of the cloud formation, has directly cast its own orb on some cloud, the radiance is then reflected back from what is moist and shining, and the result is a bending and return, as it were, of the light upon itself. For the flame-like flashings are so constituted that if they fall on any smooth surface they are refracted on themselves; and the shape of the sun, which by means of the beam is formed on the moist and smooth part of the air, is round. The necessary consequence therefore is that the air adjacent to the cloud is marked out by means of the radiant brilliance in conformity with the shape of the sun's disc. Now this brilliance is both continuous and divided. It is of many colors; it is of many forms; it is insensibly steeped in the variegated bright tints of its dye; imperceptibly abstracting from our vision the combination of many colored things, with the result that no space, mixing or partaking within itself the difference of color, can be discerned either between blue and flame-colored, or between flame-colored and red, or between red and amber. For all the rays, seen at the same time, are far shining, and while they give no signs of their mutual combination, are incapable of being tested, so that it is impossible to discover the limits of the flame-colored or of the emerald portion of the light, and at what point each originates before it appears as it does in glory. As then in the token we clearly distinguish the difference of the colors, and yet it is impossible for us to apprehend by our senses any interval between them; so in like manner conclude. I pray you, that you may reason concerning the divine dogmas; that the peculiar properties of the hypostases, like colors seen in the Iris, flash their brightness on each of the Persons Whom we believe to exist in the Holy Trinity; but that of the proper nature no difference can be conceived as existing between one and the other, the peculiar characteristics shining, in community of essence, upon each. Even in our example, the essence emitting the many-colored radiance, and refracted by the sun beam, was one essence; it is the color of the phenomenon which is multiform. My argument thus teaches us, even by the aid of the visible creation, not to feel distressed at points of doctrine whenever we meet with questions difficult of solution, and when at the thought of accepting what is proposed to us, our brains begin to reel. In regard to visible objects experience appears better than theories of causation, and so in matters transcending all knowledge, the apprehension of argument is inferior to the faith which teaches us at once the distinction in hypostasis and the conjunction in essence. Since then our discussion has included both what is common and what is distinctive in the Holy Trinity, the common is to be understood as referring to the essence; the hypostasis on the other hand is the several distinctive sign.

It may however be thought that the account here given of the hypostasis does not tally with the sense of the Apostle's words, where he says concerning the Lord that He is "the brightness of His glory, and the express image of His person," for if we have taught hypostasis to be the conflux of the several properties; and if it is confessed that, as in the case of the Father something is contemplated as proper and peculiar, whereby He alone is known, so in the same way is it believed about the Only-begotten; how then does Scripture in this place ascribe the name of the hypostasis to the Father alone, and describes the Son as form of the hypostasis, and designated not by His own proper notes, but by those of the Father? For if the hypostasis is the sign of several existence, and the property of the Father is confined to the unbegotten being, and the Son is fashioned according to His Father's properties, then the term unbegotten can no longer be predicated exclusively of the Father, the existence of the Only-begotten being denoted by the distinctive note of the Father.

My opinion is, however, that in this passage the Apostle's argument is directed to a different end; and it is looking to this that he uses the terms "brightness of glory," and "express image of person." Whoever keeps this carefully in view will find nothing that clashes with what I have said, but that the argument is conducted in a special and peculiar sense. For the object of the apostolic argument is not the distinction of the hypostases from one another by means of the apparent notes; it is rather the apprehension of the natural, inseparable, and close relationship of the Son to the Father. He does not say "Who being the glory of the Father" (although in truth He is); he omits this as admitted, and then in the endeavor to teach that we must not think of one form of glory in the case of the Father and of another in that of the Son, He defines the glory of the Only-begotten as the brightness of the glory of the Father, and, by the use of the example of the light, causes the son to be thought of in indissoluble association with the Father. For just as the brightness is emitted by the flame, and the brightness is not after the flame, but at one and the same moment the flame shines and the light beams brightly, so does the Apostle mean the Son to be thought of as deriving existence from the Father, and yet the Only-begotten not to be divided from the existence of the Father by any intervening extension in space, but the caused to be always conceived of together with the cause. Precisely in the same manner, as though by way of interpretation of the meaning of the preceding cause, and with the object of guiding us to the conception of the invisible by means of material examples, he speaks also of "express image of person." For as the body is wholly in form, and yet the definition of the body and the definition of the form are distinct, and no one wishing to give the definition of the one would be found in agreement with that of the other; and yet, even if in theory you separate the form from the body, nature does not admit of the distinction, and both are inseparably apprehended; just so the Apostle thinks that even if the doctrine of the faith represents the difference of the hypostases as unconfounded and distinct, he is bound by his language to set forth also the continuous and as it were concert relation of the Only-begotten to the Father. And this he states not as though the Only-begotten had not also a hypostatic being, but in that the union does not admit of anything intervening between the Son and the Father, with the result that he, who with his soul's eyes fixes his gaze earnestly on the express image of the Only-begotten, is made perceptive also of the hypostasis of the Father. Yet the proper quality contemplated in them is not subject to change, nor yet to commixture, in such wise as that we should attribute either an origin of generation to the Father or an origin without generation to the Son, but so that if we could encompass the impossibility of detaching one from the other, the n one might be apprehended severally and alone, for, since the mere name implies the Father, it is not possible that any one should even name the Son without apprehending the Father.

Since then, as says the Lord in the Gospels he that hath seen the Son sees the Father also; on this account he says that the Only-begotten is the express image of His Father's person. That this may be made still plainer I will quote also other passages of the Apostle in which he calls the Son "the image of the invisible God," and again "image of His goodness"; not because the image differs from the Archetype according to the definition of indivisibility and goodness, but that it may be shewn that it is the same as the prototype, even though it be different. For the idea of the image would be lost were it not to preserve throughout the plain and invariable likeness. He therefore that has perception of the beauty of the image is made perceptive of the Archetype. So he, who has, as it were mental apprehension of the form of the Son, prints the express image of the Father's hypostasis, beholding the latter in the former, not beholding in the reflection the unbegotten being of the Father (for thus there would be complete identity and no distinction), but gazing at the unbegotten beauty in the Begotten. Just as he who in a polished mirror beholds the reflection of the form as plain knowledge of the represented face, so he, who has knowledge of the Son, through his knowledge of the Son receives in his heart the express image of the Father's Person. For all things that are the Father's are beheld in the Son, and all things that are the Son's are the Father's; because the whole Son is in the Father and has all the Father in himself. Thus the hypostasis of the Son becomes as it were form and face of the knowledge of the Father, and the hypostasis of the Father is known in the form of the Son, while the proper quality which is contemplated therein remains for the plain distinction of the hypostasis.

Selections from "On the Use of Pagan Authors" are from
The Fathers, Historians, and Writers of the Church,
W.B. Kelly, Dublin, 1864

Selections from the "Letter Concerning the Difference" are from
Nicene and Post-Nicene Fathers,
Volume VIII, New York: The Christian Literature Company, 1895

Chapter 23 • St. Gregory of Nyssa: *The Great Catechism*

St. Gregory (ca. 331-ca. 395), the younger brother of Basil, received a good education in the classics, rhetoric, and philosophy. Because of the influence of Gregory of Nazianzus he became a cleric, and in 371 was made bishop of Nyssa by his brother Basil. Like most of his orthodox contemporaries he was harassed by the Arians and exiled from his diocese. His writings are polemical, catechetical, ascetical, philosophical, and literary. Gregory is of great importance for his philosophical insights in defense of the Christian faith. His treatise *Against Eunomius* is a classical anti-Arian polemic, as is the work *On the Holy Spirit* and *On Not The Gods*. His *On the Making of Man* is a philosophico-theological treatment of the nature of man and his position in the Christian dispensation. A general summary of his thought is found in the quoted excerpt *The Great Catechism*, a typical synopsis of the belief and practice of the time. His use of analogy in acquiring knowledge about God is elaborated by Dionysius the Pseudo-Areopagite and St. Thomas Aquinas, among others.

The Great Catechism
Prologue

The presiding ministers of the "mystery of godliness" have need of a system in their instructions, in order that the Church may be replenished by the accession of such as should be saved through the teaching of the word of Faith being brought home to the hearing of unbelievers. Not that the same method of instruction will be suitable in the case of all who approach the word. The catechism must be adapted to the diversities of their religious worship with an eye, indeed, to the one aim and end of the system, but not using the same method of preparation in each individual case.

Should he say there is no God, then, from the consideration of the skillful and wise economy of the Universe he will be brought to acknowledge that there is a certain overmastering power manifested through these channels. If, on the other hand, he should have no doubt as to the existence of Deity, but should be inclined to entertain the presumption of a plurality of gods, then we will adopt against him some such train of reasoning as this: "Does he think Deity is perfect or defective?" and if, as is likely, he bears testimony to the perfection in the Divine nature, then we will demand of him to grant a perfection throughout in everything that is observable in that divinity, in order that Deity may not be regarded as a mixture of opposites, defect and perfection.

For if goodness, and justice, and wisdom, and power may be equally predicated of it, then also imperishability and eternal existence, and every orthodox idea would be in the same way admitted. As then all distinctive difference in any aspect whatever has been gradually removed, it necessarily follows that together with it a plurality of gods has been removed from his belief, the general identity round conviction to the Unity.

Chapter I

But since our system of religion is wont to observe a distinction of persons in the unity of the Nature, there is need again of a distinct technical statement in order to correct all error on this point.

For not even by those who are external to our doctrine is the Deity held to be without Logos. If, then, logic requires him to admit this eternal subsistence of God's Word, it is altogether necessary to admit also that the subsistence of that word consists in a living state. And since the nature of the Logos is reasonably believed to be simple, we are compelled to think that the Logos has an independent life, and not a mere participation of life. If, then, the Logos, as being life, lives, it certainly has the faculty of will. Moreover that such a will has also a capacity to act must be the conclusion of a devout mind.

And we must suppose that this will in its power to do all things will have no tendency to anything that is evil (for impulse towards evil is foreign to the Divine nature), but that whatever is good, this it also wishes, and, wishing, is able to perform, and, being able, will not fail to perform; but that it will bring all its proposals for good to effectual accomplishment. Now the world is good, and all its contents are seen to be wisely and skillfully ordered. All of them, therefore, are the works of the Word, of one who, while He lives and subsists, in that He is God's Word, has a will too, in that He lives; of one too who has power to effect what He wills, and who wills what is absolutely good and wise and all else that connotes superiority. Whereas, then, the world is admitted to be something good, and from what has been said the world has been shown to be the work of the Word, who both wills and is able to effect the good, this Word is other than He of whom He is the Word. For this, too, to a certain extent is a term of "relation," inasmuch as the Father of the Word must needs be thought of with the Word for it would not be word were it not a word of someone.

The Word of God by its self-subsistence is distinct from Him from whom is has its subsistence; and yet by exhibiting in itself those qualities which are recognized in God it is the same in nature with Him who is recognizable by the same distinctive marks.

Chapter II

As, then, by the higher mystical ascent from matters that concern ourselves to that transcendent nature we gain a knowledge of the Word, by the same method we shall be led on to a conception of the Spirit, by observing in our own nature certain shadows and resemblances of His ineffable power.

When we think of God's Word we do not deem the Word to be something unsubstantial, nor the result of instruction, nor an utterance of the voice, nor what after being uttered passes away, nor what is subject to any other condition such as those which are observed in our word, but to be essentially self-subsisting, with a faculty of will ever-working, all-powerful. The like doctrine have we received as to God's Spirit; we regard it as that which goes with the Word and manifests its energy, and not as a mere effluence of the breath.

But we conceive of it as an essential power, regarded as self-centered in its own proper person, yet equally incapable of being separated from God in Whom it is, or from the Word of God whom it accompanies, but as being, after the likeness of God's Word, existing as a person, able to will, self-moved, efficient, ever choosing the good, and for its every purpose having its power concurrent with its will.

Chapter III

And so one who severely studies the depths of the mystery, receives secretly in his spirit, indeed, a moderate amount of apprehension of the doctrine of God's nature, yet he is unable to explain clearly in words the ineffable depth of this mystery. For, in personality, the Spirit is one thing and the Word another, and yet again that from which the Word and Spirit is, another. But when you have gained the conception of what the distinction is in these, the oneness, again, of the nature admits not division, so that the supremacy of the one First Cause is not split and cut up into differing godships.

Chapter V

That there is, then, a Word of God, and a Breath of God, the Greek, with his "innate ideas," and the Jew, with his Scriptures, will perhaps not deny. But the dispensation as regards the Word of God, whereby He became man, both parties would perhaps equally reject, as being incredible and unfitting to be told of God.

Now in what has been previously said, the Word of God has been shown to be a power essentially and substantially existing, willing all good, and being possessed of strength to execute all its will; and, of a world that is good, this power appetitive and creative of good is the cause. If, then, the subsistence of the whole world has been made to depend on the power of the Word, an absolute necessity prevents us entertaining the thought of there being any other cause of the organization of the several parts of the world than the Word Himself, through whom all things in it passed into being. If any one wants to call Him Word, or Skill, or Power, or God, or anything else that is high and prized, we will not quarrel with him. For whatever word or name be invented as descriptive of the subject, one thing is intended by the expressions, namely the eternal power of God which is creative of things that are, the discoverer of things that are not, the sustaining cause of things that are brought into being, the foreseeing cause of things yet to be. This, then, whether it be God, or Word, or Skill, or Power, has been shown by inference to be the Maker of the nature of man, not urged to framing him by a necessity, but in the superabundance of love operating the production of such a creature. For needful it was neither His light should be unseen, nor His glory without witness, nor His goodness unenjoyed, nor that any other quality observed in the Divine nature should in any case lie idle, with none to share it or enjoy it. If, therefore, man comes to his birth upon these conditions, namely to be a partaker of the good things in God, necessarily he is framed of such a kind as to be adapted to the participation of such good. Thus, then, it was needful for man, born for the enjoyment of Divine good, to have something in his nature akin to that in which he is to participate.

In truth this has been shown in the comprehensive utterance of one expression, in the description of the cosmogony, where it is said that man was made "in the image of God."

For in this likeness, implied in the word image, there is a summary of all things that characterize Deity; and whatever else Moses relates, in a style more in the way of history, of these matters, placing doctrines before us in the form of a story, is connected with the same instruction.

But, perhaps, what has been said will be contradicted by one who looks only to the present condition of things, and thinks to convict our statement of untruthfulness, inasmuch as man is seen no longer under those primeval circumstances, but under almost entirely opposite ones. "Where is the Divine resemblance in the soul? Where the body's freedom from suffering? Where the eternity of life? Man is of brief existence, subject to passions, liable to decay, and ready both in body and mind for every form of suffering." By these and the like assertions, and by directing the attack against human nature, the opponent will think that he upsets the account that has been offered respecting man. But to secure that our argument may not have to be diverted from its course at any future stage, we will briefly discuss these points. That the life of man is at present subject to abnormal conditions is no proof that man was not created in the midst of good. For since man is the work of God, Who through His goodness brought this creature into being, no one could reasonably suspect that he, of whose constitution goodness is the cause, was created by his Maker in the midst of evil.

For He who made man for the participation of His own peculiar good, and incorporated in him the instincts for all that was excellent, in order that his desire might be carried forward by a corresponding movement in each case to its like, would never have deprived him of that most excellent and precious of all goods; I mean the gift implied in being his own master, and having a free will.

How can that nature which is under a yoke and bondage to any kind of necessity be called an image of a Master Being? Was it not, then, most right that that which is in every detail made like the Divine should possess in its nature a self-ruling and independent principle, such as to enable the participation of good to be the reward of its virtue? Whence, then, comes it, you will ask, that he who had been distinguished throughout with most excellent endowments exchanged these good things for the worse? The reason of this also is plain. No growth of evil had its beginning in the Divine will. Vice would have been blameless were it inscribed with the name of God as its maker and father. But the evil is, in some way or other, engendered from within, springing up in the will at that moment when there is a retrocession of the soul from the beautiful.

So, as long as the good is present in the nature, vice is a thing that has no inherent existence; while the departure of the better state becomes the origin of its opposite. Since, then, this is the peculiarity of the possession of a free will, that it chooses as it likes the thing that pleases it, you will find that it is not

God Who is the author of the present evils, seeing that He has ordered your nature so as to be its own master and free; but rather the recklessness that makes choice of the worse in preference to the better.

Chapter VI

But you will perhaps seek to know the cause of this error of judgment; for it is to this point that the train of our discussion tends. An argument such as the following we have received by tradition from the Fathers; and this argument is no mere mythical narrative, but one that naturally invites our credence. Of all existing things there is a twofold manner of apprehension, the consideration of them being divided between what appertains to intellect and what appertains to the senses; and besides these there is nothing to be detected in the nature of existing things, as extending beyond this division.

The world of thought is bodiless, impalpable, and figureless; but the sensible is, by its very name, bounded by those perceptions which come through the organs of sense.

Rather, owing to the Divine wisdom, there is an admixture and interpenetration of the sensible with the intellectual department, in order that all things may equally have a share in the beautiful, and no single one of existing things be without its share in that superior world. For this reason the corresponding locality of the intellectual world is a subtle and mobile essence, which, in accordance with its supramundane habitation, has in its peculiar nature large affinity with the intellectual part. Now, by a provision of the supreme Mind there is an intermixture of the intellectual with the sensible world, in order that nothing in creation may be thrown aside as worthless, as says the Apostle or be left without its portion of the Divine fellowship. On this account it is that the commixture of the intellectual and sensible in man is effected by the Divine Being, as the description of the cosmogony instructs us. . . .

Now this living being was man. In him, by an ineffable influence, the godlike beauty of the intellectual nature was mingled. But the question, how one who had been created for no evil purpose by Him who framed the system of the Universe in goodness fell away nevertheless, into this passion of envy, it is not a part of my present business minutely to discuss though it would not be difficult, and it would not take long, to offer an account to those who are amenable to persuasion. For the distinctive difference between virtue and vice is not to be contemplated as that between two actually subsisting phenomena; but as there is a logical opposition between that which is and that which is not, and it is not possible to say that, as regards subsistency, that which is not is distinguished from that which is, but we say that nonentity is only *logically* opposed to entity, in the same way also the word vice is opposed to the word virtue not as being any existence in itself, but only as becoming thinkable by the absence of the better.

As we say that blindness is logically opposed to sight, not that blindness has of itself a natural existence, being only a deprivation of a preceding faculty, so also we say that vice is to be regarded as the deprivation of goodness.

As, then, freedom from the agitation of the passions is the beginning and groundwork of a life in accordance with virtue, so the bias to vice generated by Envy is the constituted road to all these evils which have been since displayed. For when once he, who by his apostasy from goodness had begotten in himself this Envy, had received this bias to evil.

Chapter VII

Yet let no one ask, "How was it that, if God foresaw the misfortune that would happen to man from want of thought, He came to create him, since it was, perhaps, more to his advantage not to have been born than to be in the midst of such evils? "This is what they who have been carried away by the false teaching of the Manichees put forward for the establishment of their error, as thus able to show that the Creator of human nature is evil. For if God is not ignorant of anything that is, and yet man is in the midst of evil, the argument for the goodness of God could not be upheld; that is, if He brought forth into life the man who was to be in this evil. For if the operating force which is in accordance with the good is entirely that of a nature which is good, then this painful and perishing life, they say, can never be referred to the workmanship of the good, but it is necessary to suppose for such a life as this another author, from whom our nature derives its tendency to misery. Now all these and the like assertions seem to those who are thoroughly imbued with the heretical fraud, as with some deeply ingrained stain, to have a certain force from their superficial plausibility. But they who have a more thorough insight into the truth clearly perceive that what they say is unsound, and admits of speedy demonstration of its fallacy. In my opinion, too, it is well to put forward the Apostle as pleading with us on these points for their condemnation. In his address to the Corinthians he makes a distinction between the carnal and spiritual dispositions of souls; showing, I think, by what he says that it is wrong to judge of what is morally excellent, or, on the other hand, of what is evil, by the standard of the senses; but that, by withdrawing the mind from bodily phenomena, we must decide by itself and from itself the true nature of moral excellence and its opposite. "The spiritual man," he says, "judgeth all things." This, I think, must have been the reason of the invention of these deceptive doctrines on the part of those who propound them, viz. that when they define the good they have an eye only to the sweetness of the body's enjoyment, and so, because from its composite nature and constant tendency to dissolution that body is unavoidably subject to suffering and sicknesses, and because upon such conditions of suffering there follows a sort of sense of pain, they decree that the formation of man is the work of an evil deity. Since, if their thoughts had taken a loftier view, and, withdrawing their minds from this disposition to regard the gratifications of the senses, they had looked at the nature of existing things dispassionately, they would have understood that there is no evil other than wickedness. Now all wickedness has its form and character in the deprivation of the good; it exists not by itself, and cannot be contemplated as a substance. For no evil of any kind lies outside and independent of the will; but it is the non-existence of the good that is so denominated. Now that which is not has no substantial existence, and the Maker of that which has no substantial existence is not the Maker of things that have substantial existence. Therefore the God of things that are is external to the causation of things that are evil, since He is not the Maker of things that are non-existent. He Who formed the sight did not make blindness. He Who manifested virtue manifested not the deprivation thereof. He Who has proposed as the prize in the contest of a free will the guerdon of all good to those who are living virtuously, never, to please Himself, subjected mankind to the yoke of a strong compulsion, as if he would drag it unwilling, as it were his lifeless tool towards the right: But if, when the light shines very brightly in a clear sky, a man of his own accord shuts his eyelids to shade his sight, the sun is clear of blame on the part of him who sees not.

Chapter VIII

Nevertheless one who regards only the dissolution of the body is greatly disturbed, and makes it a hardship that this life of ours should be dissolved by death; it is, he says, the extremity of evil that our being should be quenched by this condition of mortality. Let him then observe through this gloomy prospect the excess of the Divine benevolence. He may by this perhaps, be the more induced to admire the graciousness of God's care for the affairs of man. To live is desirable to those who partake of life, on account of the enjoyment of things to their mind; since, if any one lives in bodily pain, not to be is deemed by such in one much more desirable than to exist in pain. Let us inquire, then, whether He Who gives us our outfit for living has any other object in view, than how we may pass our life under the fairest circumstances. Now since by a motion of our self-will we contracted a fellowship with evil and, owing to some sensual gratification, mixed up the evil with our nature like some deleterious ingredient spoiling the taste of honey, and, so, falling away from that blessedness which is involved in the thought of passionlessness, we have been viciously transformed — for this reason Man, like some earthen potsherd, is resolved again into the dust of the ground, in order to secure that he may part with the soil which he has now contracted, and that he may, through the resurrection, be reformed anew after the original pattern; at least if in this life that now is he has preserved what belongs to that image. . . .

This liability to death, then taken from the brute creation, was provisionally made to envelop the nature created for immortality. It enwrapped it externally, but not internally. It grasped the sentient part of man, but laid no hold upon the Divine image. This sentient part, however, does not disappear, but is dissolved. Disappearance is the passing away into non-existence, but dissolution is the dispersion again into those constituent elements of the world of which it was composed. But that which is contained in them perishes not, though it escapes the cognizance of our senses.

For as in regard to the flesh we pronounce the separation of the sentient life to be death, so in respect of the soul we call the departure of the real life death. While, then, as we have said before, the participation in evil observable both in soul and body is of one and the same character, for it is through both that the evil principle advances into actual working, the death of dissolution does not affect the soul. For how can that which is incompounded be subject to dissolution? But since there is a necessity that the defilements which sin has engendered in the soul as well should be removed thence by some remedial process, the medicine which virtue supplies has, in the life that now is, been applied to the healing of such mutilations as these. If, however, the soul remains unhealed, the remedy is dispensed in the life that follows this.

If, then, any one looks to the ultimate aim of the Wisdom of Him Who directs the economy of the universe, he would be very unreasonable and narrow-minded to call the Maker of man the Author of evil; or to say that He is ignorant of the future, or that, if He knows it and has made him, He is not uninfluenced by the impulse to what is bad. He knew what was going to be, yet did not prevent the tendency towards that which actually happened. That humanity, indeed, would be diverted from the good, could not be unknown to Him Who grasps all things by His power of foresight, and Whose eyes behold the coming equally with the past events. As, then, He had in sight the perversion, so He devised man's recall to good. Accordingly, which was the better way? — never to have brought our nature into existence at all, since He foresaw that the being about to be created would fall away from that which is morally beautiful; or to bring him back by repentance, and restore his diseased nature to its original beauty? But, because of the pains and sufferings of the body which are the necessary accidents of its unstable nature, to call God on that account the Maker of evil, or to think that He is not the Creator of man at all, in hopes thereby to prevent the supposition of His being theAuthor of what gives us pain — all this is an instance of that extreme narrow-mindedness which is the mark of those who judge of moral good and moral evil by mere sensation. Such persons do not understand that only is intrinsically good which sensation does not reach, and that the only evil is estrangement from the good. But to make pains and pleasures the criterion of what is morally good and the contrary, is a characteristic of the unreasoning nature of creatures in whom, from their want of mind and understanding, the apprehension of real goodness has no place. That man is the work of God, created morally noble and for the noblest destiny, is evident not only from what has been said, but from a vast number of other proofs; which, because they are so many, we shall here omit. But when we call God the Maker of man we do not forget how carefully at the outset we defined our position against the Greeks. It was there shown that the Word of God is a substantial and personified being, Himself both God and the Word; Who has embraced in Himself all creative power, or rather Who is every power with an impulse to all good; Who works out effectually whatever He wills by having a power concurrent with His will; Whose will and work is the life of all things that exist; by Whom, too, man was brought into being and adorned with the highest excellences after the fashion of Deity. But since that alone is unchangeable in its nature which does not derive its origin through creation, while whatever by the uncreated being is brought into existence out of what was nonexistent, from the very first moment that it begins to be, is ever passing through change, and if it acts according to its nature the change is ever to the better, but if it be diverted from the straight path, then a movement to the contrary succeeds — since I say, man was thus conditioned, and in him the changeable element in his nature had slipped aside to the exact contrary, so that this departure from the good introduced in its train every form of evil to match the good (as, for instance, on the defection of life there was brought in the antagonism of death; on the deprivation of light darkness supervened; in the absence of virtue vice arose in its place, and against every form of good might be reckoned a like number of opposite evils), by whom, I ask, was man, fallen by his recklessness into this and the like evil state (for it was not possible for him to retain even his prudence when he had estranged himself from prudence, or to take any wise counsel when he had severed himself from wisdom) — by whom was man to be recalled to the grace of his original state? To whom belonged the restoration of the fallen one, the recovery of the lost, the leading back the wanderer by the hand? To whom else than entirely to Him Who is the Lord of his nature? For Him only Who at the first had given the life was it possible, or fitting to recover it when lost. This is what we are taught and learn from the Revelation of the truth that God in the beginning made man and saved him when he had fallen.

Chapter IX

Concerning the incarnation of the Word, I deem it necessary first of all to remove our thoughts for a moment from the grossness of the carnal element, and to fix them on what is morally beautiful in itself, and on what is not, and on the distinguishing marks by which each of them is to be apprehended. No one, I think, who has reflected will challenge the assertion that, in the whole nature of things, one thing only is disgraceful, and that is vicious weakness; while whatever has no connection with vice is a stranger to all disgrace; and whatever has no mixture in it of disgrace is certainly to be found on the side of the beautiful; and what is really beautiful has in it no mixture of its opposite. Now whatever is to be regarded as coming within the sphere of the beautiful becomes the character of God. Either, then, let them show that there was viciousness in His birth, His bringing up, His growth, His progress to the perfection of His nature, His experience of death and return from death; or, if they allow that the aforesaid circumstances of His life remain outside the sphere of viciousness, they will perforce admit that there is nothing of disgrace in this that is foreign to viciousness. Since, then, what is thus removed from every disgraceful and vicious quality is abundantly shown to be morally beautiful, how can one fail to pity the folly of men who give it as their opinion that what is morally beautiful is not becoming in the case of God?

Chapter X

"But the nature of man," it is said, "is narrow and circumscribed, whereas the Deity is infinite. How could the infinite be included in the atom?" But who is it that says the infinitude of the Deity is comprehended in the envelopment of the flesh as if it were in a vessel? Not even in the case of our own life is the intellectual nature shut up within the boundary of the flesh.

If, then, the soul of man, although by the necessity of its nature it is transfused through the body, yet presents itself everywhere at will, what necessity is there for saying that the Deity is hampered by an environment of fleshly nature, and why may we not, by examples which we are capable of understanding, gain some reasonable idea of God's plan of salvation?. . .

What is there, then, to prevent our thinking of a kind of union or approximation of the Divine nature with humanity, and yet in this very approximation guarding the proper notion of Deity, believing as we do that, though the Godhead be in man, it is beyond all circumscription?

Chapter XI

Should you, however, ask in what way Deity is mingled with humanity, you will have occasion for a preliminary inquiry as to what the coalescence is of soul with flesh. But supposing you are ignorant of the way in which the soul is in union with the body, while we have reason to believe that the soul is something other than the body, because the flesh when isolated from the soul becomes dead and inactive, we have yet no exact knowledge of the method of the union, so in that other inquiry of the union of Deity with manhood, while we are quite aware that there is a distinction as regards degree of majesty between the Divine and the mortal perishable nature, we are not capable of detecting how the Divine and the human elements are mixed up together. The miracles recorded permit us not to entertain a doubt that God was born in the nature of man. But how — this, as being a subject unapproachable by the processes of reasoning, we decline to investigate.

Chapter XII

If a person requires proofs of God's having been manifested to us in the flesh, let him look at the Divine activities. For of the existence of the Deity at all one can discover no other demonstration than that which the testimony of those activities supplies.

Chapter XIII

But, it is said, to be born and to die are conditions peculiar to the fleshly nature. I admit it. . . .

Well, he who has recorded that He was born has related also that He was born of a Virgin. If, therefore, on the evidence stated, the fact of His being born is established as a matter of faith, it is altogether incredible, on the same evidence, that He was not born in the manner stated. For the author who mentions His birth adds also, that it was of a Virgin; and in recording His death bears further testimony to His resurrection from the dead. If, therefore, from what you are told, you grant that He both was born and died, on the same grounds you must admit that both His birth and death were independent of the conditions of human weakness — in fact, were above nature. The conclusion, therefore, is that He Who has thus been shown to have been born under supernatural circumstances was certainly Himself not limited by nature.

Chapter XIV

"Then why," it is asked, "did the Deity descend to such humiliation? Our faith is staggered to think that God, that incomprehensible, inconceivable, and ineffable reality, transcending all glory of greatness, wraps Himself up in the base covering of humanity, so that His sublime operations as well are debased by this admixture with the groveling earth."

Chapter XV

Even to this objection we are not at a loss for an answer consistent with our idea of God. You ask the reason why God was born among men.

If love of man be a special characteristic of the Divine nature, here is the reason for which you are in search, here is the cause of the presence of God among men. Our diseased nature needed a healer. Man in his fall needed one to set him upright. He who had lost the gift of life stood in need of a life-giver, and he who had dropped away from his fellowship with good wanted one who would lead him back to good. He who was shut up in darkness longed for the presence of the light. The captive sought for a ransomer, the fettered prisoner for some one to take his part, and for a deliverer he who was held in the bondage of slavery.

If, then, God is real and essential virtue, and no mere existence of any kind is logically opposed to virtue, but only vice is so; and if the Divine birth was not into vice, but into human existence; and if only vicious weakness is unseemingly and shameful — and with such weakness neither was God born, nor had it in His nature to be born — why are they scandalized at the confession that God came into touch with human nature, when in relation to virtue no contrariety whatever is observable in the organization of man? For neither Reason, nor Understanding, nor Receptivity for science, nor any other like quality proper to the essence of man, is opposed to the principle of virtue.

Chapter XX

It is, then, universally acknowledged that we must believe the Deity to be not only almighty, but just, and good, and wise, and everything else that suggests excellence.

If, then, it is fitting that all excellences should be combined in the views we have of God, let us see whether this Dispensation as regards man fails in any of those conceptions which we should entertain of Him. The object of our inquiry in the case of God is before all things the indications of His goodness. And what testimony to His goodness could there be more palpable then this, viz., His regaining to Himself the allegiance of one who had revolted to the opposite side, instead of allowing the fixed goodness of His nature to be affected by the variableness of the human will?

In what way, then, is wisdom contemplated in combination with goodness; in the actual events, that is, which have taken place? because one cannot observe a good purpose in the abstract; a purpose cannot possibly be revealed unless it has the light of some events upon it. Well, the things accomplished, progressing as they did in orderly series and sequence, reveal the wisdom and the skill of the Divine economy. And since, as has been before remarked, wisdom, when combined with justice, then absolutely becomes a virtue, but, if it be disjoined from it, cannot in itself alone be good, it were well moreover in this discussion of the Dispensation in regard to man, to consider attentively in the light of each other these two qualities; I mean, its wisdom and its justice.

Chapter XXI

What, then, is justice?

Now that we had voluntarily bartered away our freedom, it was requisite that no arbitrary method of recovery, but the one consonant with justice should be devised by Him Who in His goodness had undertaken our rescue. Now this method is in a measure this; to make over to the master of the slave whatever ransom he may agree to accept for the person in his possession.

His choosing to save man is a testimony of His goodness; His making the redemption of the captive a matter of exchange exhibits His justice, while the invention whereby He enabled the Enemy to apprehend that of which he was before incapable, is a manifestation of supreme wisdom.

Chapter XXIV

But possibly one who has given his attention to the course of the preceding remarks may inquire: "Wherein is the power of the Deity, wherein is the imperishableness of that Divine power, to be traced in the processes you have described?" In order, therefore, to make this also clear, let us take a survey of the sequel of the Gospel mystery, where that Power conjoined with Love is more especially exhibited. In the first place, then, that the omnipotence of the Divine nature should have had strength to descend to the humiliation of humanity, furnishes a clearer proof of that omnipotence than even the greatness and supernatural character of the miracles. For that something pre-eminently great should be wrought out by Divine power is, in a manner, in accordance with, and consequent upon, the Divine nature; nor is it startling to hear it said that the whole of the created world, and all that is understood to be beyond the range of visible things, subsists by the power of God, His will giving it existence according to His good pleasure. But this His descent to the humility of man is a kind of superabundant exercise of power, which thus finds no check even in directions which controvene nature.

Selections from "The Great Catechism" are from
Nicene and Post-Nicene Fathers,
Volume XIII, New York: The Christian Literature Company, 1894

Chapter 24 • St. John Chrysostom: *On Ephesians*

Born at Antioch of wealthy parents, St. John (344/347-407) studied rhetoric and philosophy as was the custom of the educated people of the time. John made a profound and thorough study of the Christian teachings, was baptized by Meletius, patriarch of Antioch, and became a priest in 386 and patriarch of Constantinople in 398. He, too, was opposed by the political and ecclesiastical intrigues of the Arians. John Chrysostom is famous for his practical rather than speculative approach to the problem of Christianity. His written works are *Letters* and *Homilies.* Two of his 112 homilies on the Epistles of St. Paul are presented here. The first is a classic exposition of the text concerning the relationship between husbands and wives; the second concerns the duties of children to their parents. Similar ideas are found in the encyclicals of Pius XI.

On Ephesians

"Wives, be in subjection unto your own husbands, as unto the Lord. For the husband is the head of the wife, as Christ also is the head of the Church, being Himself the Savior of the body. But as the Church is subject to Christ, so let the wives also be to their husbands in everything."

A certain wise man, setting down a number of things in the rank of blessings, set down this also in the rank of a blessing. "A wife agreeing with her husband." (Ecclus. [Sirach] xxv.i.) And elsewhere again he sets it down among blessings, that a woman should dwell in harmony with her husband. (Ecclus. xl. 23.) And indeed from the beginning, God appears to have made special provision for this union; and discoursing of the twain as one, He said thus, "Male and female created He them" (Gen. i.27); and again, "There is neither male nor female." (Gal. iii.28.) For there is no relationship between man and man so close as that between man and wife, if they be joined together as they should be.

For there is nothing which so welds our life together as the love of man and wife. For this many will lay aside even their arms, for this they will give up life itself. And Paul would never without a reason and without an object have spent so much pains on this subject, as when he says here, "Wives, be in subjection unto your own husbands, as unto the Lord." And why so? Because when they are in harmony, the children are well brought up, and the domestics are in good order, and neighbors, and friends, and relations enjoy the fragrance. But if it be otherwise, all is turned upside down, and thrown into confusion. And just as when the generals of an army are at peace one with another, all things are in due subordination, whereas on the other hand, if they are at variance, everything is turned upside down; so, I say, is it also here. Wherefore, saith he, "Wives, be in subjection unto your own husbands, as unto the Lord."

Yet how strange! for how then is it, that it is said elsewhere, "If one bid not farewell both to wife and to husband, he cannot follow me"? (Luke xiv. 26.) For if it is their duty to be in subjection "as unto the Lord," who saith He that they must depart from them for the Lord's sake? Yet their duty indeed it is, their bounden duty. But the word "as" is not necessarily and universally expressive of exact equality. He either means this "as knowing that ye are servants to the Lord"; (which, by the way, is what he says elsewhere, that, even though they do it not for the husband's sake, yet must they primarily for the Lord's sake;) or else he means, "when thou obeyest thy husband, do so as serving the Lord." For if he who resisteth these external authorities, those of governments, I mean, "withstandeth the ordinance of God" (Rom. xiii.2), much much more does she who submits not herself to her husband. Such was God's will from the beginning.

Let us take as our fundamental position then, that the husband occupies the place of the "head," and the wife the place of the "body."

Ver. 23, 24. Then, he proceeds with arguments and says that "the husband is the head of the wife, as Christ also is the head of the Church, being Himself the Savior of the body. But as the Church is subject to Christ, so let the wives be to their husbands in everything."

Then after saying, "The husband is the head of the wife, as Christ also is of the Church," he further adds, "and He is the Savior of the body." For indeed the head is the saving health of the body. He had already laid down beforehand for man and wife, the ground and provision of their love, assigning to each their proper place, to the one that of authority and forethought, to the other that of submission. As then, "the Church," that is, both husbands and wives, "is subject unto Christ, so also ye wives submit yourselves to your husbands, as unto God."

Ver. 25. "Husbands, love your wives, even as Christ also loved the Church."

Thou hast heard how great the submission; thou hast extolled and marvelled at Paul, how, like an admirable and spiritual man, he welds together our whole life. Thou didst well. But now hear what he also requires at thy hands; for again he employs the same example.

"Husbands," said he, "love your wives, even as Christ also loved the Church."

Thou hast seen the measure of obedience, hear also the measure of love. Wouldst thou have thy wife obedient unto thee, as the Church is to Christ? Take then thyself the same provident care for her, as Christ takes for the Church. Yea, even if it shall be needful for thee to give thy life for her, yea, and to be cut into pieces ten thousand times, yea, and to endure and undergo any suffering whatever — refuse it not.

But the partner of one's life, the mother of one's children, the foundation of one's every joy, one ought never to chain down by fear and menaces, but with love and good temper. For what sort of union is that, where the wife trembles at her husband? And what sort of pleasure will the husband himself enjoy, if he dwells with his wife as with a slave, and not as with a free-woman? yea, though thou shouldst suffer anything on her account, do not upbraid her; for neither did Christ do this.

Ver. 28. "Even so ought husbands to love their own wives," saith he, "as their own bodies."

What, again, means this? To how much greater a similitude, and stronger example has he come; and not only so, but also to one how much nearer and clearer, and to a fresh obligation. For that other one was of no very constraining force, for He was Christ, and was God, and gave Himself. He now manages his argument on a different ground, saying, "so ought men"; because the thing is not a favor, but a debt. Then, "as their own bodies." And why?

Ver. 29. "For no man ever hated his own flesh, but nourisheth and cherisheth it."

That is, tends it with exceeding care. And how is she his flesh? Hearken: Ver. 31. "For this cause shall a man leave his father and mother, and shall cleave to his wife, and the twain shall become one flesh."

Behold again a third ground of obligation; for he shows that a man leaving them that begat him, and from whom he was born, is knit to his wife; and that then the one flesh is, father, and mother, and the child, from the substance of the two commingled. For indeed by the commingling of their seeds is the child produced, so that the three are one flesh. Thus then are we in relation to Christ; we become one flesh by participation, and we much more than the child. And why and how so? Because so it has been from the beginning.

Ver. 32. "This is great mystery; but I speak in regard of Christ and of the Church."

Why does he call it a great mystery? That it was something great and wonderful, the blessed Moses, or rather God, intimated. For the present, however, saith he, I speak regarding Christ, that having left the Father, He came down and come to the Bride, and became one Spirit. "For he that is joined unto the Lord is one Spirit." (I Cor.vi.17) And well saith he, "it is a great mystery." And then as though he were saying, "But still nevertheless the allegory does not destroy affection", he adds.

Ver. 33. "Nevertheless do ye also severally love each one his own wife as himself; and let the wife see that she fears her husband."

For indeed, in very deed, a mystery it is, yea, a great mystery, that a man should leave him that gave him being, him that begat him, and that brought him up, and her that travailed with him and had sorrow, those that have bestowed upon him so many and great benefits, those with whom he has been in familiar intercourse, and be joined to one who was never even seen by him and who has nothing in common with him, and should honor her before all others. A mystery it is indeed.

The principle of love, however, he explains; that of fear he does not. And mark, how on that of love he enlarges, stating the arguments relating to Christ and those relating to one's own flesh, the words, "For this cause shall a man leave his father and mother." (Ver. 31.) Whereas upon those drawn from fear he forbears to enlarge. And why so? Because he would rather that this principle prevail, this, namely, of love, for where this exists, everything else follows of course, but where the other exists, not necessarily. For the man who loves his wife, even though she be not a very obedient one, still will bear with everything. So difficult and impracticable is unanimity, where persons are not bound together by that love which is founded in supreme authority; at all events, fear will not necessarily effect this. Accordingly, he dwells the more upon this, which is the strong tie. And the wife though seemingly to be the loser in that she was charged to fear, is the gainer, because the principal duty, love, is charged upon the husband. "But what," one may say, "if a wife reverence me not?" Never mind, thou are to love, fulfill thine own duty. For though that which is due from others may not follow, we ought of course to do our duty. This is an example of what I mean. He says, "submitting yourselves one to another in the fear of Christ." And what then if another submit not himself? Still obey thou the law of God. Just so, I say, is it also here. Let the wife at least, though she be not loved, still reverence notwithstanding, that nothing may lie at her door; and let the husband, though his wife reverence him not, still show her love notwithstanding, that he himself be not wanting in any point. For each has received his own.

This then is marriage when it takes place according to Christ, spiritual marriage, and spiritual birth, not of blood, nor of travail, nor of the will of the flesh. Such was the birth of Christ, not of blood, nor of travail. Such also was that of Isaac. Hear how the Scripture saith, "And it ceased to be with Sarah after the manner of women." (Gen. xviii. 11.) Yea, a marriage it is, not of passion, nor of the flesh, but wholly spiritual, the soul being united to God by a union unspeakable, and which He alone knoweth. Therefore he saith, "He that is joined unto the Lord is one spirit." (I Cor. vi. 17.) Mark how earnestly he endeavors to unite both flesh with flesh, and spirit with spirit. And where are the heretics? Never surely, if marriage were a thing to be condemned, would he have called Christ and the Church a bride and bridegroom; never would he have brought forward by way of exhortation the words, "A man shall leave his father and his mother"; and again have added, that it was "spoken in regard of Christ and of the Church."

Now why did he not say of the wife also, She shall be joined unto her husband? Why, I say, is this? Because he was discoursing concerning love, and was discoursing to the husband. For to her indeed he discourses concerning reverence, and says, "the husband is the head of the wife" (ver. 23), and again, "Christ is the Head of the Church." Whereas to him he discourses concerning love, and commits to him this province of love, and declares to him that which pertains to love, thus binding him and cementing him to her.

However, when thou hearest of "fear," demand that fear which becomes a free woman, not as though thou were exacting it of a slave. For she is thine own body; and if thou do this, thou reproachest thyself in dishonoring thine own body. And of what nature is this "fear"? It is the not contradicting, the not rebelling, the not being fond of the preeminence. It is enough that fear be kept within these bounds. But if thou love, as thou art commanded, thou wilt make it yet greater. Or rather it will not be any longer by fear that thou wilt be doing this, but love itself will have its effect.

Supply her with everything. Do everything and endure trouble for her sake. Necessity is laid upon thee.

But the word "flesh" has reference to love — and the word "shall cleave" has in like manner reference to love. For if thou shalt make her "holy and without blemish" everything else will follow. Seek the things which are of

God, and those which are of man will follow readily enough. Govern thy wife, and thus will the whole house be in harmony. Hear what Paul saith. "And if they would learn any thing, let them ask their own husbands at home." (I.Cor.xiv-35.) If we thus regulate our own houses, we shall be also fit for the management of the Church. For indeed a house is a little Church.

Thus it is possible for us by becoming good husbands and wives, to surpass all others.

MORAL. Let us then be very thoughtful both for our wives, and children, and servants; knowing that we shall thus be establishing for ourselves an easy government, and shall have our accounts with them gentle and lenient, and say, "Behold I, and the children which God hath given me." (Isa.viii.18.) If the husband command respect, and the head be honorable, then will the rest of the body sustain no violence. Now what is the wife's fitting behavior, and what the husband's, he states accurately, charging her to reverence him as the head, and him to love her as a wife; but how, it may be said, can these things be? That they ought indeed so to be, he has proved. But how they can be so, I will tell you. They will be so, if we will despise money, if we will look but to one thing only, excellence of soul, if we will keep the fear of God before our eyes. For what he says in his discourse to servants, "whatsoever any man doeth, whether it be good or evil, the same shall he receive of the Lord" (Eph.vi.8); this is also the case here. Love her therefore not for her sake so much as for Christ's sake. This, at least, he as much as intimates, in saying, "as unto the Lord." So then do everything, as in obedience to the Lord, and as doing everything for His sake.

This were enough to induce and to persuade us, and not to suffer that there should be any teasing and dissension. Let none be believed when slandering the husband to his wife; no, nor let the husband believe anything at random against the wife, nor let the wife be without reason inquisitive about his goings out and his comings in. No, nor on any account let the husband ever render himself worthy of any suspicion whatever. For what, tell me, what if thou shalt devote thyself on the day to thy friends, and give the evening to thy wife, and not even thus be able to content her, and place her out of reach of suspicion? Though thy wife complain, yet be not annoyed — it is her love, not her folly — they are the complaints of fervent attachment and burning affection, and fear.

And again, never call her simply by her name, but with terms of endearment, with honor, with much love. Honor her, and she will not need honor from others; she will not want the glory that comes from others, if she enjoys that which comes from thee. Prefer her before all, on every account, both for her beauty and her discernment, and praise her. Thou wilt thus persuade her to give heed to none that are without, but to scorn all the world except thyself. Teach her the fear of God, and all good things will flow from this as from a fountain, and the house will be full of ten thousand blessings. If we seek the things that are incorruptible, these corruptible things will follow. "For," saith He, "seek first His kingdom, and all these things shall be added unto you." (Matt.vi.33.) What sort of persons, think you, must the children of such parents be? What the servants of such masters? What all others who come near them? Will not they too eventually be loaded with blessings out of number? For generally the servants also have their characters formed after their master's, and are fashioned after their humors, love the same objects, which they have been taught to love, speak the same language, and engage with them in the same pursuits. If thus we regulate ourselves, and attentively study the Scriptures, in most things we shall derive instruction from them. And thus, shall be able to please God, and to pass through the whole of the present life virtuously, and to attain those blessings which are promised to those that love Him, of which God grant that we may all be counted worthy, through the grace and loving-kindness of our Lord Jesus Christ, with Whom, together with the Holy Spirit, be unto the Father, glory, power, and honor, now, and ever, through all ages. Amen.

Selections from "On Ephesians" are from
Nicene and Post-Nicene Fathers,
Volume XIII, New York: The Christian Literature Company, 1894

Chapter 25 • Anonymous Treatises

This section fittingly concludes with several anonymous treatises on a variety of Christian topics. They indicate the breadth of the concern of the writers of the times. The classic treatises of the fourth century covered a range of theoretical and practical questions that are still discussed in the Church in the twentieth century.

Justice Comprises All Other Virtues

Do not think that justice is a part of virtue, but consider that it is virtue complete and universal. Thus, Job also was just, having every virtue belonging to man, not indeed abstaining from this vice while subject to this other. Thus also we say that a balance is just which is even in every direction, not, indeed, if it be able to weigh gold fairly, but lead the reverse, but which affords equality in all kinds of matters. And thus Job was just, being fair in every respect. For he did not preserve this fairness in money matters merely, but in all things, never exceeding the right measure. Nor could any one have it to say that, in money matters, indeed, he cherished fairness, but that, in his conversation with his neighbor, he exceeded moderation, as any one proud and arrogant. For he avoided this with much care. For which reason also he said: "If I have despised to abide judgment with my man-servant or my maid-servant, when they had a controversy against me, or if as I was they were not likewise." But this also is an extreme injustice, to be haughty and arrogant. For, as we say that he is avaricious who wishes to secure the property of others, and is not content with his own means; even so, we say, that a man is haughty when he asks from his neighbor more services than those due to him; when any one stations himself in all honor, and dishonors another. But this comes not from elsewhere than from injustice.

Poverty and Covetousness

Do not consider poverty as anything dreadful, and it will not be dreadful. For this fear is not in the nature of the thing, but in the judgment of weak-souled men. On the contrary, I am ashamed that *I have need* to say so much on behalf of poverty, merely to show that it is nothing dreadful; for, if thou act in the spirit of philosophy, it will be to thee a spring of ten thousand advantages.

And if any one should offer to thee rule and political offices and wealth and luxury, and then having laid poverty before thee, should allow thee to take whichever thou shouldst wish, thou wouldst willingly snatch at poverty if thou didst know her beauty. And I know that many laugh when those things are said: but we are not disturbed. And we also ask you to bear with us, and you will quickly vote along with us. For to me it appears that poverty should be likened to some adorned and fair and comely maiden: but avarice, to a woman of bestial shape, to some Scylla or Hydra, and other such monsters framed by the mythologists. Do not produce for me those who accuse poverty, but also those who have been illustrious through her. Reared with her, Elias [Elijah] was carried off, through that blessed capture. With her Eliseus [Elisha] shone; with her, John, and all the apostles. But with the latter, Achab [Ahab], Jesabel [Jezabel], Giezi, Judas, Nero, and Caiphas were condemned.

But, if it seem fit, let us see not only those who have been illustrious in poverty, but let us consider the beauty itself of this maiden. For her eye is pure and transparent, and hath nothing turbid like that of avarice, now full of anger, now filled with pleasure, now disturbed by intemperance. But the eye of poverty is not such. It is mild, calm, looking sweetly upon all, gentle, pleasant, hating no one, turning away from no one. For where there is money, there is an occasion of enmity and of innumerable wars. Again, the mouth of the latter (avarice) is full of insults, of much haughtiness, of cursing, of deceit; but, of the former, on the contrary, the mouth is sound, full of constant thanksgivings, of blessing, and of kind speeches. But if thou desire to see the arrangement of her members, she is stately, and much better than wealth. But do not be surprised if many avoid her, for the foolish avoid every other virtue likewise. But the poor man, some one says, is insulted by the rich man. Again, thou dost mention to me an encomium of poverty. For who, tell me, is the happy man? He who insults or he who is insulted? Plainly he who is insulted and bears it bravely. Therefore, avarice encourages to insult, and poverty exhorts to endure.

Virtue Alone Confers Immortal Glory

Nothing makes a name immortal so much as the nature of virtue. The martyrs prove this, the relics of the apostles prove it, the recollection of those who have walked in virtue proves it. Many kings have founded cities and constructed ports, and having given their names to them, have departed: but they derived no advantage from it; they are passed over in silence and consigned to oblivion. But, the fisherman Peter, having done none of those things, since, however, he followed virtue, and took possession of the imperial city, shines beyond the sun, even after his death. But what thou dost is ridiculous and full of shame. For not only will these monuments not render thee splendid, but they will make thee ridiculous and will open the mouths of all. For thy buildings stand everywhere like pillars and trophies of thy covetousness, *of thy* covetousness, which might otherwise have been consigned to oblivion by time. "And man, when he was in honor, did not understand; he is compared to senseless beasts, and is become like to them." Here, the prophet thenceforward appears to me to complain that the rational animal, who has taken the supremacy upon Earth, has stooped himself to the vileness of irrational creatures, laboring in vain, planning things opposed to his salvation, pursuing vain glory, pursuing avarice, laboring at useless things. For virtue is the honor of man, and so likewise is the reasoning wisely about future things, and procuring all things for that *future* life, and the neglect of present things. For the life of irrational animals is shut up within the limits of the present life, but ours points to a better life, and one which has no end. But those who know nothing about the things to come are worse than the irrational animals.

Selections from "Anonymous Authors" are from
Nicene and Post-Nicene Fathers,
Volume XIII, New York: The Christian Literature Company, 1894

Part IV
Additional Clarifications of Catholicism

Introduction

The authors presented in this section employ several different literary forms in expounding and defending Western Catholic teachings and practices during the fourth and fifth centuries A.D.

St. Ambrose (whose works are included in the Migne compilation of *Latin Patrology*, Volumes 14-17) wrote an *Hexaemeron (Work of the Six Days: Genesis*), a *De fide (On the Faith*), a *De Incarnatione (On the Incarnation)*, a *De bono mortis (The Good of Death)*, and others, in addition to the selections in this part. One of his claims to fame is that he baptized St. Augustine, who had been deeply impressed by Ambrose's spiritual interpretations of the Scriptures. It is generally agreed that his point of view was more practical than theoretical.

Prudentius was one of many authors during this period who used the verse form to explain Catholic teachings by way of poems or lyrics for popular hymns — as did St. Nicetus of Remesiana, St. Paulinus of Nola, St. Ambrose, and St. Patrick, the patron saint of Ireland. Lack of space does not permit the inclusion of the many classical treatises of Catholicism by the writers in the Isle of Saints and Scholars.

Hilary of Poitiers, in addition to the use of hymns, wrote a lengthy prose explanation of the Trinity for the Christians of Gaul; he wrote it while in Phrygia, in exile because of his teachings against the Arians. In the *De Trinitate* he tells us about reading the statement of God recorded by Moses, "I am that I am," which he understood to refer to the absolute existence of God, which St. Thomas later considered to be the proper name of God. Hilary was also influenced by the prologue of the Gospel attributed to St. John concerning the identity of the Word with God and the Incarnation of the Word.

St. Jerome is well-known for his translation of the Bible into Latin. The Old Testament in part was translated from the Hebrew; the New Testament was translated from the Greek, for he was familiar with the many varying Latin texts and judged that the only procedure was to go back to the original Greek and correct the errors of the inaccurate translations. He is another witness to the accepted fact that Matthew was the first to write a gospel of Christ and that it was written in Hebrew characters, though it was subsequently translated into Greek or formed a basis for a Matthew gospel in Greek.

The lack of space does not permit the inclusion of more writings of St. Augustine. He was acquainted with many heretical sects, having been himself a Manichaean and familiar with the Gnostic teaching about salvation taught by Mani; then he became a skeptic, and later wrote *Contra Academicos (Against the Skeptics)*. In the *City of God* he shows that he is familiar with ancient and contemporary Greek and Roman philosophy. His works are found in sixteen volumes of the Migne compilation, *Patrologia Latina*.

The commonitories [admonitions] (*Instructions to Himself or Reminders*) of Vincent of Lerins became popular again in the nineteenth and early twentieth centuries because of his "General Rules for Distinguishing the Truth of the Catholic Faith from the Falsehood of Heretical Pravity," his advice about "What Is to Be Done if One or More Dissent from the Rest," and his "On Development in Religious Knowledge." John Henry Cardinal Newman in his essay on the latter was influenced by Vincent, as was Pope Pius X in his treatment of Modernism.

This part is fittingly concluded by the *Confiteor*.

Chapter 26 • St. Ambrose: *On the Resurrection*; Collected Poems

In this section we turn to the Latin ecclesiastical writers of the fourth century. Ambrose was born of Christian parents around A.D. 340 and educated at Rome, was one-time civil governor of Liguria and Aemilia, and was appointed by popular acclaim the bishop of Milan in 374. The preaching of Ambrose, one of the opponents of Arianism in the West, helped persuade St. Augustine to convert. Ambrose's homilies reveal a wide classical learning and acquaintance with Patristic literature. He was mainly concerned with the ethical aspects of Christianity. He wrote many hymns, and is considered the author of the plainsong called the Ambrosian Chant. The first excerpt is a typical example of early Christian teaching on the resurrection; the examples of the contents of the Christian poetry are presented in prose form.

On the Resurrection

The faith of the resurrection is drawn with more peculiar evidence from three *proofs*, in which all things are included: from reason, from the example of the universe, from the testimony of what has been done, because several have arisen. Because whereas our entire course of life is in the companionship of body and soul, and the resurrection contains either the reward of well-doing or the punishment of ill-doing, it is necessary that the body should arise, whose doing is examined; for how can the soul be called to judgment without the body, when an account has to be rendered concerning her own fellowship with the body?

Resurrection has been given to all things; but for this reason is it considered difficult, because it is not our deserving, but the gift of God. The first *principle*, therefore, *of* belief in the resurrection, is the course of the world and the condition of all things, the series of generations, the alternation of successions, the setting and rising of the signs (*of the Zodiac*), the setting of day and night; and their daily succession coming as it were to life again. The system also of the genital constitution of this earth could not exist *in the earth*, on any other condition than that the divine arrangement should renew by the nightly dew as much of its moisture, by which all earthly things are generated, as the heat of the sun in the day-time should cause to evaporate. For why must I speak of the fruits? Do they not appear to thee to set when they fall, and to rise when they bloom again? What has been sown rises again; what has been dead arises, and they are formed again into the same kinds and into the same species *(to which they originally belonged*). The earth first gave back those fruits, and in those our nature first imitated the appearance of the resurrection.

Why dost thou doubt that body arises from body? The grain is sown, the grain rises: the apple falls, the apple rises; but the grain is dressed with the flower and is clothed with the hull. "And this mortal must put on immortality, and this corruptible must put on incorruption." Immortality is the flower of the resurrection, incorruption is the flower of the resurrection. For what is more fruitful than perpetual repose? What is richer than lasting security? This is the manifold fruit, by whose increase the nature of men buds forth more prolific after death.

But thou dost wonder how things putrefied become solid, how things scattered unite, how things destroyed are renewed; thou dost not wonder how things dissolved by the warmth and pressure of the earth bloom again. For, indeed, by the cohesion also of the earth, things putrefied are dissolved, and when the sap of the genital soil has animated those hidden and dead *seeds* with a certain vital warmth, they exhale a certain spirit of the blooming herb. Then by degrees the stalk quickly raises the tender age of the growing ear, and nature like an attentive mother encloses it as it were in certain sheaths, lest the harsh frost wither it as it advances to maturity, and she protects it from the excessive heat of the sun, and she has also been wont to hedge round with a certain fence of beards, the grain itself just bursting as it were from its cradle, and by and by grown up, lest the rain should shake it out, or the breeze should scatter it, or the pecking of the smaller birds kill it.

Why, therefore, dost thou wonder if the earth restore the men whom she has taken, seeing that she vivifies, erects, clothes, protects, and defends whatever bodies of seeds she has received? Cease, therefore, to doubt that the *good* faith of the earth, which restores the seeds entrusted to her multiplied with a certain usurious interest, pays back also the deposit of the human race. For why am I to speak concerning the kind of trees which rise from a sown seed, and resuscitate with revived fertility the fruits which have been dissolved, and restore them to their old form and likeness, and transmit certain renewed bodies of trees through many ages; so that by lasting, they conquer centuries themselves? We see the grape-stone rot, and the vine arise *therefrom*: the graft is inserted and the tree revives. So that there is a divine Providence for the renewal of trees, and none for the renewal of men! And *is it to be believed that*

He who did not suffer those things to perish which He gave for the use of men, should suffer man to perish, whom He has made to His own likeness?

But it appears to thee incredible that the dead should live again. "Senseless man, that which thou sowest, does it not die first that it be quickened?" Sow any dry fruit, it is revived; but it has a sap. And our body has its blood, has its own moisture. This is the sap of our body. Whence that argument which I believe has been exploded, that some deny that a withered graft can ever revive, and endeavor to draw this circumstance to the prejudice *of the resurrection* of the flesh. For the flesh is not dry, in as much as all flesh is from the slime of the earth, and slime consists in moisture, and moisture is from the earth. Finally, many plants arise even in perpetual serenity and *(absence of rain)* and in dry and sandy soil, since the earth supplies moisture to herself. In the *case* of men, therefore, does the earth degenerate, which has been wont to regenerate all other things? Thus, it is not to be doubted that *the resurrection* is according to nature rather than against it for it is agreeable to nature that all things which were born rise again; it is contrary to nature that they perish.

Next follows that argument which for the most part disquiets the Gentiles — how it should come to pass that the earth should restore those whom the sea has engulfed, whom wild animals have torn, whom beasts have devoured. By which course of reasoning we must necessarily come to this, that the doubt is entertained not concerning the doctrine of the resurrection, but concerning a portion of it. For, let it be *taken for granted* that the bodies of those who have been torn do not rise again, the others rise again, nor is the resurrection destroyed, but a condition is exempted from it. Nevertheless, I wonder why they should think they ought to doubt concerning these, as if all things which come from the earth do not return to earth and are not resolved into earth. The water for the most part also throws up upon the neighboring shores whatever corpses of men the sea itself shall have sunk. Even if this were not so, *am I to* imagine that it would be difficult for God to collect what had been dispersed, to unite what had been scattered? to God, whom the world hearkens, whom the dumb elements obey, whom nature serves, as if it is not a greater miracle to animate the slime of the earth than to put it together?

Therefore, although thou believe not our resurrection by faith, although thou believe it not by example, thou art about to believe it by experience. And for the ripening of other fruits, such as the vine, the olive, and the various kinds of apples, the last period of the year is suitable, and for us also the consummation of the world, as it were the last part of the year, has prescribed a suitable age of resurrection. And the resurrection of the dead is properly in the consummation of the world, lest after the resurrection we should have to fall back into this evil world. For therefore did Christ suffer that He might free us from this evil world, lest the temptations of this world should again destroy us, and it would hurt us to be born again, if we were to be born again to sin.

Collected Poems

I

Splendor of the paternal glory, bringing forth light from light. Light of light and fountain of luster; day, illuminating the day; and true sun; glide into us, shining with perpetual brightness, and pour the beam of the Holy Spirit into our senses. Let us also invoke with our prayers the Father, the Father of eternal glory, the Father of powerful grace, that He may banish slippery guilt — that He may confirm our strenuous acts — that He may blunt the tooth of the envious — that He may make adverse circumstances prosperous, and may give the grace of enduring them. May He govern the mind in a chaste and faithful body; may faith glow with warmth; may it be ignorant of the poisons of fraud. Let Christ be our food, and let faith be our drink. Let us, joyful, drink the sober drunkenness of the Spirit. Let this day pass joyfully, so that modesty be our dawn — faith, as it were, our midday — and let our mind know no twilight. The dawn advances her course: let Christ advance with the dawn — the entire Son in the Father, and the entire Father in the Lord.

II

External glory of Heaven! Blessed hope of mortals! Only *Son* of the Heavenly Thunderer, and offspring of the chaste Virgin! give Thy right hand to those who are rising, that the sober mind may arise glowing, and may repay unto the praise of God the well-due thanks. The darkness of the night falls; the morning star, arisen, shine forth, announce the scattered light, the mist of the nights falls; let holy light illumine us, and remaining, let it drive away the night of the world from our senses, and preserve our breasts purified to the full end of time. Let faith, sought first of all, strike root into our inmost minds; next let hope rejoice along with her, than whom (*hope*) charity is greater.

III

O God, the Creator of all things, and Ruler of the firmament, clothing the day with comely light and the night with the favor of sleep, in order that repose may restore the relaxed limbs to the use of labor, and may soothe the wearied minds and relieve anxious cares. Singing our hymn, we pay our thanks, the day being now spent, and our prayers with supplications at the beginning of the night, in order that Thou mayest assist us, guilty as we are. Let the depths of the heart sing Thee in concert; let the tuneful voice echo Thee; let chaste affection love Thee; let the sober mind adore Thee; that when the deep darkness of the night shall have closed the day, faith may not know darkness, and the night may shine with faith. Suffer not the mind to sleep. May sin know sleep. Let faith refresh us chaste, and let it moderate the vapors of sleep. Let the depths of the heart, stripped of the slippery sense *of the flesh*, dream of Thee; nor, by the deceit of the envious foe, let terror disturb *thy* quiet *servants*. Let us implore Christ, and the Father, and the one Spirit of Christ and of the Father, O Trinity! powerful over all things, cherish those who pray *to Thee*.

IV

Let the choir of the new Jerusalem draw forth a new sweetness of honey, celebrating the paschal festival with sober joys. Here Christ, the unconquered lion, rising above the overwhelmed dragon, while he fills *the world* with his living voice, raises from death those who had finished *their time*. The wicked Tartarus gave back the prey which he had devoured; the bands free from captivity follow Jesus. He splendidly triumphs; preeminent in grandeur, He makes the country of the earth and that of the sky one republic. Let us, His suppliant soldiers, beseech our King by singing, that he may appoint us his fellow soldiers in his most glorious citadel. Through ages ignorant of limit, be there glory to the supreme Father, and honor to the Spirit, the Paraclete, along with the Son. Jesus, our redemption, our love and our longing! God, the Creator of all things! man unto the end of time! what clemency overcame Thee, that Thou shouldst carry our sins, suffering cruel death, that Thou mightest redeem us from death? Penetrating the barriers of Hell, redeeming Thy captives, victorious in a noble triumph, Thou sittest at the right hand of the Father. Let Thy very piety compel Thee to overcome our evils by sparing us, and salute with Thy countenance us enjoying our wish. Be Thou our joy, who art to be our reward: be our glory in Thee, ever through all ages.

V

O Christ! the sweet Ruler of all men, begotten from the mouth of the Eternal Father, kindly notice the prayers alike and the hymns of Thy suppliants.

Observe that Thy suppliant people resound with pure honor in Thy hall, O God, whose annual festivals return to be celebrated in their season. This house is known as solemnly dedicated to Thee, in which the people takes Thy blessed body, and drinks the blessed draught of Thy blood. Here the sacred waters wash out the inveterate sins, and take away offenses, and the race of the worshipers of Christ is created by the true chrism. Here health is brought to the sick, medicine to the weary, light to those deprived *of sight*, and all fear and all grief is driven away. Here the cruel plunder of the demon ceases, the obstinate monster becomes terrified, and leaving the bodies he had held, quickly flies into distant darkness. For in truth this place is called the hall of the Eternal King and the snowy gate of Heaven, which receives all the saints who seek their country; the gate which no whirlwind shakes, or wandering winds overturn, or rain-storms penetrate, or pitchy Tartarus, horrible with direful darkness, injures. We pray Thee, therefore, O God, that Thou mayest assent with serene countenance, guiding Thy servants, who, with the utmost love, celebrate the joys of Thy temple. Let no grievances of life torture us; let our days be joyful and our nights tranquil; let no one of us, when the world perishes, feel the fires of *Thy wrath*. May this day, on which Thou beholdest a hall consecrated to Thee, give everlasting joy to us; and flourish for a long space of time. Let glory proclaim the supreme Father, let glory *proclaim* the Son, and let us equally sing the Holy Spirit, through every age.

Selections from "On the Resurrection" and collected poems from
The Fathers, Historians, and Writers of the Church,
W.B. Kelly, Dublin, 1864

Chapter 27 • Prudentius: *Martyrdom of the Innocents*; *Martyrdom of St. Laurence*; *St. Vincent to Darian*; *Martyrdom of St. Hippolytus*

Aurelius Clemens Prudentius (b. ca. 348-?410) was born in Spain and became one of the outstanding Christian Latin poets of the era. The following excerpts are classic examples of how the Christians of the golden age of Catholicism made use of the verse form for the popularization of Christian teaching and practice. The poems are presented here in prose in order to emphasize their Christian content. St. Ambrose used the verse form and Commodian before him, and also Juvencus and Ausonius. The tradition was carried on by St. Thomas Aquinas, and more recently we have a similar use of poems by Cardinal Newman and Francis Thompson.

Martyrdom of the Innocents

The anxious tyrant hears that the Prince of Kings is at hand, who is to govern the nation of Israel and hold the palace of David. Frantic at the intelligence, he exclaims: My successor is upon me — we are driven out. Go, satellite! snatch thy sword — drench the cradles with blood — let every male infant perish — search the bosoms of the nurses, and let the infant dye the sword with blood between his mother's breasts. Therefore, the executioner, raging, transfixes with his naked sword the bodies just born, and searches out the new souls. Hail! ye flowers of the martyrs! whom the pursuer of Christ took off on the very threshold of life, as the whirlwind does the springing roses. Ye, the first victims of Christ, tender flock of immolated ones — ye play simple before the altar itself with your palm and your crowns. What profits so great an impiety? What does his crime avail Herod? Christ alone is taken away without hurt amid so many deaths; the offspring of the Virgin, alone untouched amid the torrents of blood of His own age, escaped the sword which was bereaving the young mothers. Thus of old Moses, the recoverer of his citizens, prefiguring Christ, escaped the foolish edicts of the wicked Pharaoh. But may our leader, having wounded the enemy, free from the darkness of death, us, who have been continually subdued to the command of error.

Martyrdom of St. Laurence

Rome, ancient parent of heathen temples, but now devoted to Christ, victorious under the leadership of Laurence, triumph *over* the barbarous rite. Thou hadst conquered proud kings: thou hadst held down nations with thy rein: thou now imposest the yoke of thy empire upon monstrous idols. This only glory was wanting to the distinction of the toga-wearing city, that it having conquered the barbarism of the nations, it should subdue the filthy Jupiter. Not by the turbulent strength of Cossus Camillus, or Caesar, but by the not bloodless battle of the martyr Laurence. After the continuous blaze had roasted his burned side, of his own accord he addresses the judge in a short discourse from the gridiron. Turn the part of my body already sufficiently long burned, and try what thy glowing Vulcan shall do. He says these things mocking, and then looks towards Heaven, and, pitying the city of Romulus, groans with compassion as he thus beseeches: O Christ, only Deity — O splendor, O virtue of the Father, O maker of the earth and sky, and author of those walls; who hast planted the scepter of Rome on the summit of human things, commanding that the world should obey the Quirinal toga and yield to her arms, in order that thou alone mightest subdue to thy laws, the manners, and observances, and languages, and dispositions of divers nations. Behold, the entire mortal race has gone under the sway of Remus. Dissonant rites speak and think the same things. This was pre-ordained, in order that the more readily the law of the Christian name might bind in one bond whatever land exists. Grant, O Christ, to thy Romans, that that state may be Christian, by which thou hast given, that there should be amongst the other states one mind in religion. Let all the members be united from every quarter into a combination; may the subject world become meek, and may its supreme head become meek. Let it perceive that the adjoining shores are uniting into one divine grace. Let Romulus become faithful, and Numa himself believe. The Trojan error still confounds the senate of the Catos. It penetrates in secret the fire-shrines, the exiled penates of the Phrygians. The senate worships the double-headed Janus and Sterculus. I am horrified to mention so many monsters of the fathers, and the rites of old Saturn. Wipe away, O Christ, this shame, send forth Thy Gabriel, that the erring Julian blindness may acknowledge the true God. And now we hold most faithful hostages of this hope, for here reign the two princes of the apostles. The one the caller of the Gentiles; the other possessing the first seat, opens the gates of eternity entrusted to him. Depart, adulterous Jupiter, defiled with the corruption of thy sister; leave Rome free, and fly from the people, now *the people* of Christ. Paul exterminates thee hence, the blood of Peter drives thee out. That very deed of Nero, which thou thyself didst arm, hurts thee.

St. Vincent to Darian

Here the judge, now more excited: Dost thou dare, he says, unfortunate man, to violate with harsh words this law of the gods and the emperors? Neither that sacred and public law to which the human race yields, nor, while thou fervently orderest, does the imminent danger move thee. For, receive this decree: either the altar is to be venerated by thee with incense and sod, or death is to be paid as the penalty in blood. He answered on the other hand: Come on, therefore, put forth whatever strength thou hast, I openly struggle against it. Receive what is our decision. There is Christ and God the Father. We are His servants and witnesses. Extort from us the faith, if thou canst. Torments, the dungeon, the iron hooks, and the metal plate hissing with flames, and the last of all penalties, death, is a sport to Christians. O your idle vanity, and the impotent decree of Caesar! You order divinities worthy of your own senses, to be worshiped. *Divinities* cut out by the hand of the smith, molten in molds, and by *aid* of bellows, which are destitute of voice or gait, motionless, blind, without tongue. To these are erected shrines, sumptuous with marble; to these the stricken necks of lowing oxen fall. There are there, present, spirits also, but they are the masters of your crimes and the diviners of your prosperity, wandering, powerless, sordid, who secretly compel you, incited to every impiety, to ravage the just with murders, and to assail the nation of the pious. They themselves know and feel that Christ prevails and lives, and that His kingdom, tremendous to the faithless, will even now be present. Those gods, who are also demons, cry out confessing when they are at length driven from the lurking places of *human* bodies. He, the profane judge, does not endure the martyr thundering these things: He exclaims, Stop ye his mouth, that the wicked man may not utter more.

Martyrdom of St. Hippolytus

The youths, round about in close array, repeated with clamor that he was the head of the Christ-worshiping races; that if the head were speedily extinguished, all the hearts of the multitude would freely be devoted to the Roman gods. They demand an unusual kind of death and newly-discovered punishments, *as an example*, at which example others may be terrified. He (*the judge*) sitting with a haughty neck: "What," he says, "is he called? They affirm that he is called Hippolytus. Therefore *let him* be Hippolytus — let him shake and excite yoked horses, and let him die torn asunder by wild horses." Scarcely *had he said* those things when the reins force together two animals ignorant how to submit their necks to the unaccustomed yoke; not stroked by the hand of a steady or quiet master, or previously subdued to bear the command of the horseman, but a wild herd lately taken from the wandering flock which savage fright drives in its untamed heart. And now the ties had united the resisting pair, and had connected their mouths with a discordant bond. Instead of a pole there is a rope which divides the backs of the two, and between them touches both the sides, and extending itself backwards a long way from the yoke behind the steps *of the horses*, is dragged along and passes the extremities of their feet. To the end of this, where upon the surface of the dust the beaten path follows the retreating paths of the horses, a noose fastens the legs of the man, and binds his feet in its tenacious knot, and ties them with a cable. After they arrayed with a sufficiently regulated preparation, the scourges, the bonds, and the wild animals, for the punishment of the martyr, they provoke them (the horses) with sudden threats and blows, and dig their sides with poisoned goads. The last saying of the venerable man *which was* heard is this: "Let those *horses* carry away my limbs; do thou, O Christ, carry away my soul." They break forth eagerly, and are borne on by blind terror, whither the noise and their tremor and their fury drive them. Their wildness kindles them, their impetus hurries them away, and the crashing noise urges them forward. Nor does their swift course feel the movable burden which they carry. They rush through the woods and through the rocks, nor does the bank of the river retard them, nor the torrent in their way restrain them. They level down the hedges, and break through all obstacles. They seek the low and broken ground, they leap over the high places. The ground rough with thorn-bearing roots tears off morsels cut bit by bit from the battered body of Hippolytus. A part lands upon the tops of the cliffs, a part sticks to the briars, the leaves are red with a part, the earth is damp with a part.

Selections from Prudentius are from
The Fathers, Historians, and Writers of the Church,
W.B. Kelly, Dublin, 1864

Chapter 28 • St. Hilary of Poitiers: *Dedication*; *On the Trinity*

Born of a noble pagan family, Hilary (ca. 315-ca. 367) studied Latin and Greek and classical philosophy. He was dissatisfied with the answers to the problems of human living proposed by the ancient philosophers and, in the tradition of Justin Martyr, turned to the Scriptures and Christian teaching. He became a bishop before 355, and was an ardent opponent of Arianism in the West, especially in Gaul. At the National Council of Paris in 361 he won most of the bishops to his position on the strength of the Nicene Creed. His main works are the twelve books *On the Trinity* and his hymns to celebrate the Redemption. He considered that the teaching on the divinity of Christ formed the cornerstone of the Church.

Dedication

We have obeyed thy admonitions, O prelate of Christ, having followed thy sweet commands, which, pious, thou gavest with thy mouth. Would *it be possible that I should* not sing the praises of so great a father, the gift and the work of God, as long as I should have a tongue, hoarsely croaking indeed, and worthy of no crowns, and an humble intellect, but still I intend to speak of exalted things.

It is always a worthy and just work to speak thanks to thee, O omnipotent Creator of the world, from whom as their principle all things derived their natal day, and the race of men and the wild herds *of the field*, and the thousand species of birds, and the hands which roam through the liquid fields, beheld the luminaries suddenly arise after the darkness through the dull firmament. All things are through thee, who createst the greatest things through thyself, nor *yet dost thou derive* thy origin from another; thou thyself an immortal spirit living throughout ages by ancient movement, wilt always be, because thou hast always been.

When old chaos covered all things, and there was neither beauty nor form in the abyss, thou, O God, wast acting within; even then arranging the springing walls of the world, and the various appearances of things and the souls that were to come into existence. And when, the mist of the night being overcome, he (*the world*) brought out his head, raising his sublime countenance, the darkness perceived it. Shortly afterwards, the Lord of *all* things dispersed the inert slumbers *of the elements*, and inactive matter, moved by the Divinity, became excited. And now the internal warmth cherishes it, and brings it into motion with gentle fire.

And, first of all, the free expanse of the heaven, embracing all *parts* of the world in its space, is suspended in a lofty orb, the heavy Earth descended with her inert weight to the bottom, and having fixed herself, grounded, she subsided into the sea. And in order that there might be a space of empty open region, where the soft air should nourish *all* things mortal, and through which so many gifts of the Father of things might issue, and when arisen might be borne through the void without any labor, the scattered waters are drawn together; by and by the watery plains are left within a certain limit, nor does the wave overpass her boundary. Then arises the kindly light, which, being ordered to be called day, bedewed the world with her soft luster, disclosing thy benefits and thy works, thy excellent gifts, which thou the Creator, with paternal kindness, wert preparing to establish, and in order that the expert life of man might become illustrious by ethereal arts, *that life* which rejoices to spend entire days *in work*, and tries its genius by the varied praise *of occupations*.

Black night follows the day, and thick darkness follows, which should bear slumber to wearied bodies and a like appearance and form to all things. For the day-*light* variously distinguishes the aspects of things, and the night being dispersed, gives to each thing its own color and animates the minds *of men* glowing to greater works, sharpening mortal breasts with various cares. Whereby the day is rather the form of life, and the night the image of death.

Then the Father establishing the poles and endowing them with light, distinguishes the stars and the constellations grouped with various figures. But the greater flight resides in the sun, whom, adorned with a bounteous gift, thou, O Creator, deemest worthy of full honor. He, fiery that he is, exalts his ray with lofty head, blushes with his broad face, and is borne along the walls of Heaven. Behold and wonder, a wondrous ornament; behold the new moon changes her course, collects *again* the fires which she loses, and quenching her horns, deprives her front of light; afterwards, however, she forms a circle with a complete orb. The nightly-shining luminary feeds the new born stars with light. Nor, however, is the machine which revolves in the eternal ether merely a picture of the sky, nor an arbitrary will — there exist a mind and reason beneath, and a suitable order for things. Hence instruction comes to the Earth, hence in fine counsel to all husbandmen; and those who wander over the deep seas, know the coming showers, and the fair dry weather; at what time the ploughman may take the oxen into the field, and the sailor may safely try the doubtful sea. The sky being furnished with fires, O best of Fathers, thou settest about adorning the earth, and dost endow with thy rich gift, the kingdoms of men and the dwellings of the herds and the resting place of birds. The fields lie level, the lofty swelling carries upward the hills, the valleys sink down, the flowering meadows bloom, the rock is hardened, the rich turf crumbles, the fountains break forth from whence all rivers have their origin. A thousand grasses of herbs arise in the fields. And now the crop shed the fruit from the tender ear, when as yet there was no yoke, nor any share of the plough, and no ox lowed in the furrowed fields. Behold also the vine full with the *juicy cluster*, as yet unexperienced of the pruning hook and ignorant of the hard iron, weaved its leafy shadows on the high hills. There arise the forms of various wild beasts, quadruped beings, also animals creeping upon the earth, and birds spring up, swift upon their painted wings through the clouds.

These things being completed, when the Creator sees that in the world, now rich, all things demand the care of a great king, who should govern the sea, the lands, and all things born, and who should look upon the high Heaven and should praise the great gifts of God, that those things should not be established in vain: then: Let us make man, Thou sayest. Tell us, O greatest One! concerning whom Thou now speakest. It is plain. Thy Son already now sits beside Thee on Thy holy throne, and looks upon the Earth, which he loves. But: Let us make man, Thou sayest, whose countenance shall be our image, and from my hands let him proceed into life. Then, O maker of things, Thou takest the soft part of the earth, and dost form man. Happy mortal, whose Father is the right hand of the Thunderer! oh! too happy, who derivest from Heaven both thy origin and thy form! If the noxious crimes of the Earth do not deceive thee, and flattering error do not overturn thee, thou wilt be a divinity, and returning to Heaven, wilt see the kingdoms which the Father discloses with His faithful mouth to the good. For, God bestowed of his own accord, many things upon thee at thy birth — first, a Heavenly face and countenance, resembling the Father, and a straight march of the feet, and an upright neck, lest there might be any delay to the eyes looking towards Heaven; then hands quick and ready, and the ministers of life; and a breast, the home of divine reason and the seat of lofty counsel, and *having* the honor of pouring forth the voice.

These things were granted to man alone, for the remaining *animals* are a dumb herd. It obtained belly, entrails, nerves, channels of veins, and blood, diffused throughout the body. But thou, O Omnipotent One! bounteous with peculiar munificence towards man, and by thy hands, and by the adorable favor of thy work, bestowing upon him a pledge from thy paternal piety, lest anything should be wanting to his divine countenance, *Thou* mixed up with his entire body, breathest into him the fire of the Spirit, and suppliest to him a rich portion of the divine mind. Then he is enabled to recollect things past, hence it is given to know present things, and it is allowed to the soul to see future things. Hence, we speak and sing God; hence also all the stars *revolve*, and the cultivation of the earth takes place, and the sea is moved; hence the arts, and the names of things, and modesty, and prudence, and justice; hence arise brave minds; hence proceeds honor, and the way which leads the virtuous to the thresholds of Heaven.

Therefore Thou settest over the lands, man, perfect with thy full endowment — *man*, to whom Thou delivered the reins of earthly things, that he may have and subdue all things to himself, and may live the perpetual lord of the Earth, thy servant, and may possess all things of the world, but may obey Thee alone.

After the first man did not fear to eat of the forbidden tree, and, deceived by wiles, gave himself to the serpent, he stands guilty and naked imploring a garment with downcast eyes, and he flies from the Lord and hides his face; his companion guilt follows him; a life subject to sin weakens his strength, the gift coming from Heaven; the fire which had been sent down from the sky gradually fails; the hearts of men, becoming torpid, stiffen with the cold of sin; then comes the care of food and of desire, the care of covering the body; and mortal concerns enter the sacred breast of man.

Hence arises the offspring of sin; thence springs a much worse generation, and a progeny still worse than the former follows, increasing unto crimes by steps — crimes which exasperate with goads the frantic hearts of men, and arm Thee, O Father, with various penalties. . . . Then first came unseasonable rain to descend from the clouds, to lie upon the unjust Earth; then first were thunder-bolts hurled from the sky, *previously* serene; then first did the horrid hail beat the vexed fields, and the broken air murmur with loud-sounding thunder. Nor, however, do those *evils* recall the wicked *from their crimes*. Impious fury besets the Earth, and rage is carried along with flowing rains. Wars are the delight *of men*, and slaughter also, and perjury, and fraud, and it gives delight to lie: it is their love to plunder, and to hide the theft. There is no faith amongst the nations — no regard for truth. The crime of the Earth is washed away by the deluge, and one man remains above the waters, the renewer of the race and of the people. The ark protects a few, preserving the seeds of the virtuous — a figure already shown of the laver to come.

After the swelling of the deluge ceased, the water subsided; the bird carried a leaf of the peaceful olive, and now, flying back with dry wings, it gave omens of peace.

Then arises a better race of people; then purer from the waters arises a race of men about to bring forth great descendants for the Earth. Thence came the heart of the priest devoted to piety; thence the boys prepared to sing amid the flames; thence the boy whom unfed lions did not touch. Then kings sang God, then the truth-speaking lips resplendent with the offspring of Heaven sound for the prophets upon the Earth. Although crime being vanquished, all things obeyed God, still even now a drop of poison sprinkled the ancient people, and there were traces of fraud which the good physician would wash away by better waters.

On the Trinity
Book I

When I was seeking an employment adequate to the powers of human life and righteous in itself, whether prompted by nature or suggested by the researches of the wise, whereby I might attain to some result worthy of that Divine gift of understanding which has been given us, many things occurred to me which in general esteem were thought to render life both useful and desirable.

I believe that men, prompted by nature herself, have raised themselves through teaching and practice to the virtues which we name patience and temperance and forbearance, under the conviction that right living means right action and right thought, and that Immortal God has not given life only to end in death; for none can believe that the Giver of good has bestowed the pleasant sense of life in order that it may be overcast by the gloomy fear of dying.

Some teachers brought forward large households of dubious deities, and under the persuasion that there is a sexual activity in divine beings narrated births and lineages from god to god. Others asserted that there were gods greater and less, of distinction proportionate to their power. Some denied the existence of any gods whatever, and confined their reverence to a nature which, in their opinion, owes its being to chance-led vibrations and collisions. On the other hand, many followed the common belief in asserting the existence of a

God, but proclaimed Him heedless and indifferent to the affairs of men. Again, some worshiped in the elements of earth and air the actual bodily and visible forms of created things; and, finally, some made their gods dwell within images of men or of beasts, tame, or wild, of birds or of snakes, and confined the Lord of the universe and Father of infinity within these narrow prisons of metal or stone or wood. These, I was sure, could be no exponents of truth, for though they were at one in the absurdity, the foulness, the impiety of their observances, they were at variance concerning the essential articles of their senseless belief.

While my mind was dwelling on these and on many like thoughts, I chanced upon the books which, according to the tradition of the Hebrew faith, were written by Moses and the prophets, and found in them words spoken by God the Creator testifying of Himself "I AM THAT I AM," and again HE THAT IS *hath sent me unto you.* I confess that I was amazed to find in them an indication concerning God so exact that it expressed in the terms best adapted to human understanding an unattainable insight into the mystery of the Divine nature. For no property of God which the mind can grasp is more characteristic of Him than existence, since existence, in the absolute sense, cannot be predicated of that which shall come to an end, or of that which has had a beginning, and He who now joins continuity of being with the possession of perfect felicity could not in the past, nor can in the future, be non-existent; for whatsoever is Divine can neither be originated nor destroyed. Wherefore, since God's eternity is inseparable from Himself, it was worthy of Him to reveal this one thing, that He is, as the assurance of His absolute eternity.

For such an indication of God's infinity the words "I AM THAT I AM'"were clearly adequate; but, in addition, we needed to apprehend the operation of His majesty and power. For while absolute existence is peculiar to Him Who, abiding eternally, had no beginning in a past however remote, we hear again an utterance worthy of Himself issuing from the eternal and Holy God, Who says, *Who holdeth the heaven in His palm and the earth in His hand, and again, The heaven is My throne and the earth is the footstool of My feet. What house will ye build Me or what shall be the place of My rest?*

I had come by reverent reflection on my own part to understanding this, but I found it confirmed by the words of the prophet, *Whither shall I go from Thy Spirit? Or Whither shall I flee from Thy face? If I ascend up into heaven, Thou art there; if I go down into hell, Thou art there also; if I have taken my wings before dawn and made my dwelling in the uttermost parts of the sea (Thou art there). For thither Thy hand shall guide me and Thy right hand shall hold me.* There is no space where God is not; space does not exist apart from Him. He is in heaven, in hell, beyond the seas; dwelling in all things and enveloping all. Thus He embraces, and is embraced by, the universe, confined to no part of it but pervading all.

Therefore, although my soul drew joy from the apprehension of this august and unfathomable Mind, because it could worship as its own Father and Creator so limitless an Infinity, yet with a still more eager desire it sought to know the true aspect of its infinite and eternal Lord, that it might be able to believe that that immeasurable Deity was appareled in splendor befitting the beauty of His wisdom. Then, while the devout soul was baffled and astray through its own feebleness, it caught from the prophet's voice this scale of comparison for God, admirably expressed, *By the greatness of His works and the beauty of the things that He hath made the Creator of worlds is rightly discerned.*

Yet my soul was weighed down with fear both for itself and for the body. It retained a firm conviction, and a devout loyalty to the true faith concerning God, but had come to harbor a deep anxiety concerning itself and the bodily dwelling which must, it thought, share its destruction. While in this state, in addition to its knowledge of the teaching of the Law and Prophets, it learned the truths taught by the Apostle in the Gospel; — *In the beginning was the Word, and the Word was with God, and the Word was God. The same was in the beginning with God. All things were made through Him, and without Him was not anything made. That which was made in Him is life, and the life was the light of men, and the light shineth in darkness, and the darkness apprehended it not. There was a man sent from God, whose name was John. He came for witness, that he might bear witness of the light. That was the true light, which lighteneth every man that cometh into this world. He was in the world, and the world was made through Him, and the world knew Him not. He came unto His own things, and they that were His own received Him not. But to as many as received Him He gave power to become sons of God, even to them that believe on His Name; which were born, not of blood, nor of the will of man, nor of the will of the flesh, but of God. And the Word became flesh and dwelt among us, and we beheld His glory, glory as of the Only-begotten from the Father, full of grace and truth.* Here the soul makes an advance beyond the attainment of its natural capacities, is taught more than it had dreamed concerning God. For it learns that its Creator is God of God; it hears that the Word is God and was with God in the beginning. It comes to understand that the

Light of the world was abiding in the world and that the world knew Him not; that He came to His own possession and that they that were His own received Him not; but that they who do receive Him by virtue of their faith advance to be sons of God, being born not of the embrace of the flesh nor of the conception of the blood nor of bodily desire, but of God; finally, it learns that the Word became flesh and dwelt among us, and that His glory was seen, which, as of the Only-begotten from the Father, is perfect through grace and truth.

Herein my soul, trembling and distressed, found a hope wider than it had imagined. First came its introduction to the knowledge of God the Father. Then it learnt that the eternity and infinity and beauty which, by the light of natural reason, it had attributed to its Creator belonged also to God the Only-begotten. It did not disperse its faith among a plurality of deities, for it heard that He is God of God; nor did it fall into the error of attributing a difference of nature to this God of God, for it learnt that He is full of grace and truth. Nor yet did my soul perceive anything contrary to reason in God of God, since He was revealed as having been in the beginning God with God. It saw that there are very few who attain to the knowledge of this saving faith, though its reward be great, for even His own received Him not, though they who receive Him are promoted to be sons of God by a birth, not of the flesh, but of faith. It learnt also that this sonship to God is not a compulsion but a possibility, for, while the Divine gift is offered to all, it is no heredity inevitably imprinted but a prize awarded to willing choice. And lest this very truth that whosoever will may become a son of God should stagger the weakness of our faith (for most we desire, but least expect, that which from its very greatness we find it hard to hope for), God the Word became flesh, that through His Incarnation our flesh might attain to union with God the Word. And lest we should think that this incarnate Word was some other than God the Word, or that His flesh was of a body different from ours, He dwelt among us that by His dwelling He might be known as the indwelling God, and, by His dwelling among us, known as God incarnate in no other flesh than our own, and moreover, though He had condescended to take our flesh, not destitute of His own attributes; for He, the Only-begotten of the Father, full of grace and truth, is fully possessed of His own attributes and truly endowed with ours.

This lesson in the Divine mysteries was gladly welcomed by my soul, now drawing near through the flesh to God, called to new birth through faith, entrusted with liberty and power to win the heavenly regeneration, conscious of the love of its Father and Creator, sure that He would not annihilate a creature whom He had summoned out of nothing into life. And it could estimate how high are these truths above the mental vision of man; for the reason which deals with the common objects of thought can conceive of nothing as existent beyond what it perceives within itself or can create out of itself. My soul measured the mighty workings of God, wrought on the scale of His eternal omnipotence, not by its own powers of perception but by a boundless faith; and therefore refused to disbelieve, because it could not understand, that God was in the beginning with God, and that the Word became flesh and dwelt among us, but bore in mind the truth that with the will to believe would come the power to understand.

For He took upon Him the flesh in which we have sinned that by wearing our flesh He might forgive sins; a flesh which He shares with us by wearing it, not by sinning in it. He blotted out through death the sentence of death, that by a new creation of our race in Himself He might sweep away the penalty appointed by the former Law. He let them nail Him to the cross that He might nail to the curse of the cross and abolish all the curses to which the world is condemned. He suffered as man to the utmost that He might put powers to shame. For Scripture had foretold that He Who is God should die; that the victory and triumph of them that trust in Him lay in the fact that He, Who is immortal and cannot be overcome by death, was to die that mortals might gain eternity. These deeds of God, wrought in a manner beyond our comprehension, cannot, I repeat, be understood by our natural faculties, for the work of the Infinite and Eternal can only be grasped by an infinite intelligence.

While I was thus engaged there came to light certain fallacies of rash and wicked men, hopeless for themselves and merciless towards others, who made their own feeble nature the measure of the might of God's nature. They claimed, not that they had ascended to an infinite knowledge of infinite things, but that they had reduced all knowledge, undefined before, within the scope of ordinary reason, and fixed the limits of the faith. Whereas the true work of religion is a service of obedience; and these were men heedless of their own weakness, reckless of Divine realities, who undertook to improve upon the teaching of God.

Not to touch upon the vain enquiries of other heretics — concerning whom however, when the course of my argument gives occasion, I will not be silent — there are those who tamper with the faith of the Gospel by denying, under the cloak of loyalty to the One God, the birth of God the Only-begotten. They assert that there was an extension of God into man, not a descent; that He, Who for the season that He took our flesh was Son of Man, had not been previously, nor was then, Son of God; that there was no Divine birth in His case, but an identity of Begetter and Begotten; and (to maintain what they consider a perfect loyalty to the unity of God) that there was an unbroken continuity in the Incarnation, the Father extending Himself into the Virgin, and Himself being born as His own Son. Others, on the contrary (heretics, because there is no salvation apart from Christ, Who in the beginning was God the Word with God), deny that He was born and declare that He was merely created. Birth, they hold, would confess Him to be true God, while creation proves His Godhead unreal; and though this explanation be a fraud against the faith in the unity of God, regarded as an accurate definition, yet they think it may pass muster as figurative language. They degrade, in name and in belief, His true birth to the level of a creation, to cut Him off from the Divine unity, that, as a creature called into being, He may not claim the fullness of the Godhead, which is not His by a true birth.

And first, I have so laid out the plan of the whole work as to consult the advantage of the reader by the logical order in which its books are arranged.

Thus, after the present first book, the second expounds the mystery of the Divine birth, that those who shall be baptized in the Name of the Father and of the Son and of the Holy Spirit may know the true Names, and not be perplexed about their sense but accurately informed as to fact and meaning, and so receive full assurance that in the words which are used they have the true Names, and that those Names involve the truth.

After this short and simple discourse concerning the Trinity, the third book makes further progress, sure though slow. Citing the greatest instances of His power, it brings within the range of faith's understanding that saying, in itself beyond our comprehension, *I in the Father and the Father in Me*, which Christ utters concerning Himself. Thus truth beyond the dull wit of man is the prize of faith equipped with reason and knowledge; for neither may we doubt God's Word concerning Himself, nor can we suppose that the devout reason is incapable of apprehending His might.

The fourth book starts with the doctrines of the heretics, and disowns complicity in the fallacies whereby they are traducing the faith of the Church.

The fifth book follows in reply the sequence of heretical assertion.

The sixth book reveals the full deceitfulness of this heretical teaching.

Next the seventh book, starting from the basis of a true faith now attained, delivers its verdict in the great debate. First, armed with its sound and incontrovertible proof of the impregnable faith, it takes part in the conflict raging between Sabellius and Hebion and these opponents of the true Godhead. It joins issue with Sabellius on his denial of the pre-existence of Christ, and with his assailants on their assertion that He is a creature. Sabellius overlooked the eternity of the Son, but believed that true God worked in a human body. Our present adversaries deny that He was born, assert that He was created, and fail to see in His deeds the works of very God. What both sides dispute, we believe. Sabellius denies that it was the Son who was working, and he is wrong; but he proves his case triumphantly when he alleges that the work done was that of true God. The Church shares his victory over those who deny that in Christ was very God. But when Sabellius denies that Christ existed before the worlds, his adversaries prove to conviction that Christ's activity is from everlasting, and we are on their side in this confutation of Sabellius, who recognizes true God, but not God the Son, in this activity. And our two previous adversaries join forces to refute Hebion, the second demonstrating the eternal existence of Christ, while the first proves that His work is that of very God. Thus the heretics overthrow one another, while the Church, as against Sabellius, against those who call Christ a creature, against Hebion, bears witness that the Lord Jesus Christ is very God of very God, born before the worlds and born in after times as man.

We have proved that His Name is an accurate description of Himself, that the title of Son is an evidence of birth, that in His birth He retained His Divine Nature, and with His nature His power, and that that power manifested itself in conscious and deliberate self-revelation. I have set down the Gospel proofs of each several point, shewing how His self-revelation displays His power, how His power reveals His nature, how His nature is His by birthright, and from His birth comes His title to the name of Son. Thus every whisper of blasphemy is silenced, for the Lord Jesus Christ Himself by the witness of His own mouth has taught us that He is, as His Name, His birth, His nature, His power declare, in the true sense of Deity, very God of very God.

While its two predecessors have been devoted to the confirmation of the faith in Christ as Son of God and true God, the eighth book is taken up with the proof of the unity of God, shewing that this unity is consistent with the birth of the Son, and that the birth involves no duality in the Godhead. First it exposes the sophistry with which these heretics have attempted to avoid, though they could not deny, the confession of the real existence of God, Father and Son; it demolishes their helpless and absurd plea that in such passages as, *And the multitude of them that believed were one soul and heart*, and again, *He that planteth and He that watereth are one*, and *Neither for these only do I pray, but for them also that shall believe on Me through their word, that they may all be one, even as Thou, Father, art in Me, and I in Thee, that they also may be in Us*, a unity of will and mind, not of Divinity, is expressed. From a consideration of the true sense of these texts we shew that they involve the reality of the Divine birth; and then, displaying the whole series of our Lord's self-revelations, we exhibit, in the language of Apostles and in the very words of the Holy Spirit, the whole and perfect mystery of the glory of God as Father and as Only-begotten Son. Because there is a Father we know that there is a Son; in that Son the Father is manifested to us, and hence our certainty that He is born the Only-begotten and that He is very God.

The ninth book, therefore, is employed in refuting the arguments by which the heretics attempt to invalidate the birth of God the Only-begotten; — heretics who ignore the mystery of the revelation hidden from the beginning of the world, and forget that the Gospel faith proclaims the union of God and man. For their denial that our Lord Jesus Christ is God, like unto God and equal with God as Son with Father, born of God and by right of His birth subsisting as very Spirit, they are accustomed to appeal to such words of our Lord as, *Why callest thou Me Good? None is good save One, even God*. They argue that by His report of the man who called Him good, and by His assertion of the goodness of God only; He excludes Himself from the goodness of that God Who alone is good and from that true Divinity which belongs only to One. With this text their blasphemous reasoning connects another, *And this is life eternal that they should know Thee the only true God, and Him Whom Thou didst send, Jesus Christ*. Here, they say, He confesses that the Father is the only true God, and that He Himself is neither true nor God, since this recognition of an only true God is limited to the Possessor of the attributes assigned. And they profess to be quite clear about His meaning in this passage, since He also says, *The Son can do nothing of Himself, but what He hath seen the Father doing*. The fact that He can only copy is said to be evidence of the limitation of His nature. There can be no comparison between Omnipotence and One whose action is dependent upon the previous activity of Another; reason itself draws an absolute line between power and the want of power. That line is so clear that He Himself has avowed concerning God the Father, *The Father is greater than I*. So frank a confession silences all demur; it is blasphemy and madness to assign the dignity and nature of God to One who disclaims them.

So utterly devoid is He of the qualities of true God that He actually bears witness concerning Himself, *But of that day and hour knoweth no one, neither the angels in heaven nor the Son, but God only*. A son who knows not his father's secret must, from his ignorance, be alien from the father who knows; a nature limited in knowledge cannot partake of that majesty and might which alone is exempt from the tyranny of ignorance.

We therefore expose the blasphemous misunderstanding at which they have arrived by distortion and perversion of the meaning of Christ's words. We account for those words by stating what manner of questions He was answering, at what times He was speaking, what partial knowledge He was designing to impart; we make the circumstances explain the words, and do not force the former into consistency with the latter. Thus each case of variance, that for instance between *The Father is greater than I*, and I and the Father are One, or between *None is good save One, even God*, and *He that hath seen Me hath seen the Father also*, or a difference so wide as that between *Father, all things that are Mine are Thine, and Thine are Mine*, and *That they may know Thee, the only true God,* or between *I in the Father and the Father in Me*, and *But of the day and hour knoweth no one, neither the angels in heaven nor the Son, but the Father only*, is explained by a discrimination between gradual revelation and full expression of His nature and power. Both are utterances of the same Speaker, and an exposition of the real force of each group will shew that Christ's true Godhead is no whit impaired because to form the mystery of the Gospel faith, the birth and Name of Christ were revealed gradually, and under conditions which He chose of occasion and time.

The purpose of the tenth book is one in harmony with the faith. For since, in the folly which passes with them for wisdom, the heretics have twisted some of the circumstances and utterances of the Passion into an insolent contradiction of the Divine nature and power of the Lord Jesus Christ, I am compelled to prove that this is a blasphemous misinterpretation, and that these things were put on record by the Lord Himself as evidences of His true and absolute majesty. In their parody of the faith they deceive themselves with words such as, *My soul is sorrowful even unto death*. He, they think, must be far removed from the blissful and passionless life of God, over Whose soul brooded this crushing fear of an impending woe, Who under the pressure of suffering even humbled Himself to pray, *Father, if it be possible, let this cup pass away from Me*, and assuredly bore the appearance of fearing to endure the trials from which He prayed for release; Whose whole nature was so overwhelmed by agony that in those moments on the Cross He cried, *My God, My God, why hast Thou forsaken Me?* forced by the bitterness of His pain to complain that He was forsaken: Who, destitute of the Father's help, gave up the ghost with the words, *Father, into Thy hands I commend My Spirit*. The fear, they say, which beset him at the moment of expiring made Him entrust His Spirit to the care of God the Father: the very hopelessness of His own condition forced Him to commit His Soul to the keeping of Another.

Their folly being as great as their blasphemy, they fail to mark that Christ's words, spoken under similar circumstances, are always consistent; they cleave to the letter and ignore the purpose of His words. There is the widest difference between *My soul is sorrowful even unto death*, and *Henceforth ye shall see the Son of Man sitting at the right hand of power*; so also between *Father, if it be possible, let this cup pass away from Me*, and *The cup which the Father hath given me, shall I not drink it?* and further between *My God, My God, why hast Thou forsaken Me*? and *Verily I say unto thee, To-day shalt thou be with Me in Paradise*, and between *Father, into your hands I commend My Spirit*, and *Father, forgive them, for they know not what they do;* and their narrow minds, unable to grasp the Divine meaning, plunge into blasphemy in the attempt at explanation. There is a broad distinction between anxiety and a mind at ease, between haste and the prayer for delay, between words of anguish and words of encouragement, between despair for self and confident entreaty for others; and the heretics display their impiety by ignoring the assertions of Deity and the Divine nature of Christ, which account for the one class of His words, while they concentrate their attention upon the deeds and words which refer only to His ministry on earth. I have therefore set out all the elements contained in the mystery of the Soul and Body of the Lord Jesus Christ; all have been sought out, none suppressed. Next, casting the calm light of reason upon the question, I have referred each of His sayings to the class to which its meaning attaches it, and so have shewn that He had also a confidence which never wavered, a will which never faltered, an assurance which never murmured, that, when He commended His own soul to the Father, in this was involved a prayer for the pardon of others. Thus a complete presentment of the teaching of the Gospel interprets and confirms all (and not some only) of the words of Christ.

And so — for not even the glory of the Resurrection has opened the eyes of these lost men and kept them within the manifest bound of the faith —

they have forged a weapon for their blasphemy out of a pretended reverence, and even perverted the revelation of a mystery into an insult to God. From the words, *I ascend unto My Father and your Father, to My God and your God*, they argue that since that Father is ours as much as His, and that God also ours and His, His own confession that He shares with us in that relation to the Father and to God excludes Him from true Divinity, and subordinates Him to God the Creator Whose creature and inferior He is, as we are, although He has received the adoption of a Son. Nay more, we must not suppose that He possesses any of the characters of the Divine nature, since the Apostle says, *But when He saith, all things are put in subjection, this is except Him Who did subject all things unto Him, for when all things shall have been subjected unto Him, then shall also He Himself be subjected to Him that did subject all things unto Him, that God may be all in all.* For, so they say, subjection is evidence of want of power in the subject and of its possession by the sovereign. The eleventh book is employed in a reverent discussion of this argument; it proves from these very words of the Apostle not only that subjection is no evidence of want of power in Christ but that it actually is a sign of His true Divinity as God the Son; that the fact that His Father and God is also our Father and God is an infinite advantage to us and no degradation to Him, since He Who has been born as Man and suffered all the afflictions of our flesh has gone up on high to our God and Father, to receive His glory as Man our Representative.

In this treatise we have followed the course which we know is pursued in every branch of education.

First came simple instruction for the untaught believer in the birth, the name, the Divinity, the true Divinity of Christ; since then we have quietly and steadily advanced till our readers can demolish every plea of the heretics; and now at last we have pitted them against the adversary in the present great and glorious conflict. The mind of men is powerless with the ordinary resources of unaided reason to grasp the idea of an eternal birth but they attain by study of things Divine to the apprehension of mysteries which lie beyond the range of common thought. They can explode that paradox concerning the Lord Jesus, which derives all its strength and semblance of cogency from a purblind pagan philosophy: the paradox which asserts, *There was a time when He was not, and He was not before He was born*, and *He was made out of nothing*, as though His birth were proof that He had previously been non-existent and at a given moment came into being, and God the Only-begotten could thus be subjected to the conception of time, as if the faith itself [by conferring the title of 'Son'] and the very nature of birth proved that there was a time when He was not. Accordingly they argue that He was born out of nothing, on the ground that birth implies the grant of being to that which previously had no being. We proclaim in answer, on the evidence of Apostles and Evangelists, that the Father is eternal and the Son eternal, and demonstrate that the Son is God of all with an absolute, not a limited, preexistence; that these bold assaults of their blasphemous logic — *He was born out of nothing*, and *He was not before He was born* — are powerless against Him; that His eternity is consistent with sonship, and His sonship with eternity; that there was in Him no unique exemption from birth but a birth from everlasting, for, while birth implies a Father, Divinity is inseparable from eternity.

Ignorance of prophetic diction and unskillfulness in interpreting Scripture has led them into a perversion of the point and meaning of the passage, *The Lord created Me for a beginning of His ways for His works*. They labor to establish from it that Christ is created, rather than born, as God, and hence partakes the nature of created beings, though He excel them in the manner of His creation, and has no glory of Divine birth but only the powers of a transcendent creature. We in reply, without importing any new considerations or preconceived opinions, will make this very passage of Wisdom display its own true meaning and object. We will show that the fact that He was created for the beginning of the ways of God and for His works, cannot be twisted into evidence concerning the Divine and eternal birth, because creation for these purposes and birth from everlasting are two entirely different things. Where birth is meant, there birth, and nothing but birth, is spoken of; where creation is mentioned, the cause of that creation is first named. There is a Wisdom born before all things, and again there is a wisdom created for particular purposes; the Wisdom which is from everlasting is one, the wisdom which has come into existence during the lapse of time is another.

Having thus concluded that we must reject the word 'creation' from our confession of faith in God the Only-begotten, we proceed to lay down the teachings of reason and of piety concerning the Holy Spirit, that the reader, whose convictions have been established by patient and earnest study of the preceding books, may be provided with a complete presentation of the faith. This end will be attained when the blasphemies of heretical teaching on this theme also have been swept away, and the mystery, pure and undefiled, of the Trinity which regenerates us has been fixed in terms of saving precision on the authority of Apostles and Evangelists. Men will no longer dare, on the strength of mere human reasoning, to rank among creatures that Divine Spirit, Whom we receive as the pledge of immortality and source of fellowship with the sinless nature of God.

I know, O Lord God Almighty, that I owe Thee, as the chief duty of my life, the devotion of all my words and thoughts to Thyself. The gift of speech which Thou hast bestowed can bring me no higher reward than the opportunity of service in preaching Thee and displaying Thee as Thou art, as Father and Father of God the Only-begotten, to the world in its blindness and the heretic in his rebellion. But this is the mere expression of my own desire; I must pray also for the gift of Thy help and compassion, that the breath of Thy Spirit may fill the sails of faith and confession which I have spread, and a favoring wind be sent to forward me on my voyage of instruction. We can trust the promise of Him Who said, *Ask, and it shall be given you, seek, and ye shall find, knock, and it shall be opened unto you*; and we in our want shall pray for the things we need. We shall bring an untiring energy to the study of Thy Prophets and Apostles, and we shall knock for entrance at every gate of hidden knowledge, but it is Thine to answer the prayer, to grant the thing we seek, to open the door on which we beat. Our minds are born with dull and clouded vision, our feeble intellect is penned within the barriers of an impassable ignorance concerning things Divine; but the study of Thy revelation elevates our soul to the comprehension of sacred truth, and submission to the faith is the path to a certainty beyond the reach of unassisted reason.

And therefore we look to Thy support for the first trembling steps of this undertaking, to Thy aid that it may gain strength and prosper. We look to Thee to give us the fellowship of that Spirit Who guided the Prophets and the Apostles, that we may take their words in the sense in which they spoke and assign its right shade of meaning to every utterance. For we shall speak of things which they preached in a mystery; of Thee, O God Eternal, Father of the Eternal and Only-begotten God, Who alone art without birth, and of the One Lord Jesus Christ, born of Thee from everlasting. We may not sever Him from Thee, or make Him one of a plurality of Gods, on any plea of difference of nature. We may not say that He is not begotten of Thee, because Thou art One. We must not fail to confess Him as true God, seeing that He is born of Thee, true God, His Father. Grant us, therefore, precision of language, soundness of argument, grace of style, loyalty to truth. Enable us to utter the things that we believe, that so we may confess, as Prophets and Apostles have taught us, Thee, One God our Father, and One Lord Jesus Christ, and put to silence the gainsaying of heretics, proclaiming Thee as God, yet not solitary, and Him as God, in no unreal sense.

Selections from "Dedication" are from
The Fathers, Historians, and Writers of the Church,
W.B. Kelly, Dublin, 1864
Selections from "On the Trinity" are from
A Select Library of Nicene and Post-Nicene Fathers of the Christian Church,
P. Schoff and H.Ware, editors,
Second Series, Volume IX, New York: Scribner's Sons, 1899

Chapter 29 • St. Jerome: Introduction to His Biography; *The Perpetual Virginity of Blessed Mary*; Letter to Magnus

Jerome (331/40-420) is famous as a Latin doctor of the Church, a brilliant theologian, translator, linguist, biographer, and Scripture scholar. He was another Renaissance man. He was educated in Rome in the Greek and Latin classics, philosophy, and rhetoric, and later studied at the thriving Catholic University at Trier. During his travels to the East, he was reluctantly ordained a priest at Antioch, studied biblical exegesis under Gregory of Nazianzus at Constantinople, and became acquainted with Gregory of Nyssa and other Greek theologians. He is well-known for his translation of the Scriptures into Latin, his Homilies, biographies of famous men, polemics against heresies, dialogues, and letters. He was a master of Christian Latin prose. For him the Pope of Rome and the faith of Rome constituted the supreme rule and standard of Catholic belief.

Introduction to His Biography

Those who are about to contend in a naval fight, previously, while in port and on a tranquil sea, turn their rudders, pull at the oars, prepare the grappling irons and hooks, and accustom the soldiery ranged along the decks to stand firmly upon an inclined step and slippery tread, in order that they may not fear in the real battle what they have learned in the sham battle. Thus, I who have long been silent, wish to be exercised at first in a small work, and, as it were, to wipe the dust from my tongue, in order that I may afterwards come to a more extensive history. For I have arranged (if indeed the Lord shall give me life, and my detractors shall cease from pursuing me, now at least that I fly and am hemmed in) to write, how and through whom, from the coming of the Savior up to our age, that is from *the days of* the apostles up to the days of our own time, the Church of Christ has arisen, and when grown up, has increased by persecutions, and been crowned by martyrdom; and how, after she reached the *period of* Christian Princes, she became greater in power and riches, but smaller in virtue.

Under the persecutors, Decius and Valerian, at the time when Cornelius at

Rome, and Cyprian in Carthage, suffered martyrdom with their happy blood, the cruel tempest ravaged many churches in Egypt and the Thebias. It was then the prayer of the Christian to be stricken with the sword for the name of Christ. But the crafty enemy, studying tortures slow to kill, desired to slay souls, not bodies; and Cyprian himself, who suffered under him, says: "to be killed was not allowed to those who wished to die." That the cruelty of this enemy may be known, we subjoin two examples, as an aid to memory.

He ordered a martyr persevering in the faith, and victorious amongst the racks and *heated* plates, to be smeared with honey, and to be placed, with his hands tied behind his back, under the hottest sun, in the hope that he might yield to the stings of flies, who had already overcome the kindled frying-pan.

He commanded another, blooming in his youthful years, to be led away into most delightful gardens, and there, amongst lilies and blushing roses, while a river wound its way beside him with a great murmur of its waters, and the wind just skimmed the leaves of the tree with its soft whisper, to be laid upon his back upon a bed made up of feathers, and lest he might throw himself off, to be left there bound with gentle ties of wreaths. Whither, when after all had withdrawn, a courtesan had come, she began to clasp his neck in her delicate embraces. The soldier of Christ knew not what he should do, nor where he should turn himself. Pleasure was overcoming him whom torments not vanquished. At length, inspired by Heaven, he spat into the face of her who was kissing him, his tongue which he had bitten off; and thus the greatness of his pain overcame the sense of passion.

The Perpetual Virginity of Blessed Mary
Against Helvidius

I was requested by certain of the brethren not long ago to reply to a pamphlet written by one Helvidius. I have deferred doing so, not because it is a difficult matter to maintain the truth and refute an ignorant boor who has scarce known the first glimmer of learning, but because I was afraid my reply might make him appear worth defeating. There was the further consideration that a turbulent fellow, the only individual in the world who thinks himself both priest and layman, one who, as has been said, thinks that eloquence consists in loquacity and considers speaking ill of anyone to be the witness of a good conscience, would begin to blaspheme worse than ever if opportunity of discussion were afforded him. He would stand as it were on a pedestal, and would publish his views far and wide. There was reason also to fear that when truth failed him he would assail his opponents with the weapon of abuse. But all these motives for silence, though just, have more justly ceased to influence me, because of the scandal caused to the brethren who were disgusted at his ravings.

I must call upon the Holy Spirit to express His meaning by my mouth and defend the virginity of the Blessed Mary. I must call upon the Lord Jesus to guard the sacred lodging of the womb in which He abode for ten months from all suspicion of sexual intercourse. And I must also entreat God the Father to show that the mother of His Son, who was a mother before she was a bride, continued a Virgin after her son was born. We have no desire to career over the fields of eloquence, we do not resort to the snares of the logicians or the thickets of Aristotle. We shall adduce the actual words of Scripture. Let him be refuted by the same proofs which he employed against us, so that he may see that it was possible for him to read what is written, and yet to be unable to discern the established conclusion of a sound faith.

His first statement was: "Matthew says, 'Now the birth of Jesus Christ was in this wise: When his mother Mary had been betrothed to Joseph, before they came together she was found with child of the Holy Spirit. And Joseph, her husband, being a righteous man, and not willing to make her a public example, was minded to put her away privately. But when he thought on these things, behold, an angel of the Lord appeared unto him in a dream, saying, Joseph, thou son of David, fear not to take unto thee Mary thy wife: for that which is conceived in her is of the Holy Spirit.' " Notice, he says, that the word used is BETROTHED, not INTRUSTED as you say, and of course the only reason why she was betrothed was that she might one day be married. And the Evangelist would not have said BEFORE THEY CAME TOGETHER if they were not to come together, for no one would use the phrase BEFORE HE DINED of a man who was not going to dine. Then, again, the angel calls her WIFE and speaks of her as UNITED to Joseph. We are next invited to listen to the declaration of Scripture: " 'And Joseph arose from his sleep, and did as the angel of the Lord commanded him, and took unto him his wife; and knew her not till she had brought forth her son.' "

There are things which, in your extreme ignorance, you had never read, and therefore you neglected the whole range of Scripture and employed your madness in outraging the Virgin. . . . You have set on fire the temple of the Lord's body, you have defiled the sanctuary of the Holy Spirit from which you are determined to make a team of four brethren and a heap of sisters come forth. In a word, joining in a chorus of the Jews you say, "Is not this the carpenter's son? is not his mother called Mary? and his brethren James, and Joseph and Simon, and Judas? and his sisters, are they not all with us? The word ALL would not be used if there were not a crowd of them." Pray tell me, who, before you appeared, was acquainted with this blasphemy? who thought the theory worth two-pence? You have gained your desire, and are become notorious by crime. I pass over faults of diction which abound in every book you write. I say not a word about your absurd introduction. Good heavens! I do not ask for eloquence, since, having none yourself, you applied for a supply of it to your brother Craterius. I do not ask for grace of style, I look for purity of soul: for with Christians it is the greatest of solecisms and of vices of style to introduce anything base either in word or action. I am come to the conclusion of my argument. I will deal with you as though I had as yet prevailed nothing; and you will find yourself on the horns of a dilemma. It is clear that our Lord's brethren bore the name in the same way that Joseph was called his father: "I and thy father sought thee sorrowing." It was His mother who said this, not the Jews. The Evangelist himself relates that His father and His mother were marvelling at the things which were spoken concerning Him, and there are similar passages which we have already quoted in which Joseph and Mary are called his parents. Seeing that you have been foolish enough to persuade yourself that the Greek manuscripts are corrupt, you will perhaps plead the diversity of readings. I therefore come to the Gospel of John, and there it is plainly written, "Philip findeth Nathanael, and saith unto him, We have found him of whom Moses in the law, and the prophets did write, Jesus of Nazareth, the son of Joseph." You will certainly find this in your manuscript. Now tell me, how is Jesus the son of Joseph when it is clear that He was begotten of the Holy Spirit? Was Joseph His true father? Dull as you are, you will not venture to say that. Was he His reputed father? If so, let the same rule be applied to them when they are called brethren, that you apply to Joseph when he is called father.

Now that I have cleared the rocks and shoals, I must spread sail and make all speed to reach his epilogue. Feeling himself to be a smatterer, he there produces Tertullian as a witness and quotes the words of Victorinus bishop of Petavium. Of Tertullian I say no more than that he did not belong to the Church. But as regards Victorinus, I assert what has already been proved from the Gospel — that he spoke of the brethren of the Lord not as being sons of Mary, but brethren in the sense I have explained, that is to say, brethren in point of kinship not by nature. We are, however, spending our strength on trifles, and, leaving the fountain of truth, are following the tiny streams of opinion. Might I not array against you the whole series of ancient writers? Ignatius, Polycarp, Irenaeus, Justin Martyr, and many other apostolic and eloquent men, who against Ebion, Theodotus of Byzantium, and Valentinus, held these same views, and wrote volumes replete with wisdom. If you had ever read what they wrote, you would be a wiser man. But I think it better to reply briefly to each point than to linger any longer and extend my book to an undue length.

I now direct the attack against the passage in which, wishing to show your cleverness, you institute a comparison between virginity and marriage. I could not forbear smiling, and I thought of the proverb, DID YOU EVER SEE A CAMEL DANCE? "Are virgins better," you ask, "than Abraham, Isaac, and Jacob, who were married men? Are the infants daily fashioned by the hands of God in the wombs of their mothers? And if so, are we bound to blush at the thought of Mary having a husband after she was delivered? If they find any disgrace in this, they ought not consistently even to believe that God was born of the Virgin by natural delivery. For according to them there is more dishonor in a virgin giving birth to God by the organs of generation, than in a virgin being joined to her own husband after she has been delivered." Add, if you like, Helvidius, the other humiliations of nature, the womb for nine months growing larger, the sickness, the delivery, the blood, the swaddling-clothes. Picture to yourself the infant in the enveloping membranes. Introduce into your picture the hard manger, the wailing of the infant, the circumcision on the eighth day, the time of purification, so that he may be proved to be unclean. We do not blush, we are not put to silence. The greater the humiliations He endured for me, the more I owe Him. And when you have given every detail, you will be able to produce nothing more shameful than the cross, which we confess, in which we believe, and by which we triumph over our enemies.

But as we do not deny what is written, so we do reject what is not written. We believe that God was born of the Virgin, because we read it. That Mary was married after she brought forth, we do not believe, because we do not read it. Nor do we say this to condemn marriage, for virginity itself is the fruit of marriage; but because when we are dealing with saints we must not judge rashly. If we adopt possibility as the standard of judgment, we might maintain that Joseph had several wives because Abraham had, and so had Jacob, and that the Lord's brethren were the issue of those wives, an invention which some hold with a rashness which springs from audacity not from piety. You say that

Mary did not continue a virgin: I claim still more, that Joseph himself on account of Mary was a virgin, so that from a virgin wedlock a virgin son was born. For if as a holy man he does not come under the imputation of fornication, and it is nowhere written that he had another wife, but was the guardian of Mary whom he was supposed to have to wife rather than her husband, the conclusion is that he who was thought worthy to be called father of the Lord, remained a virgin.

And now that I am about to institute a comparison between virginity and marriage, I beseech my readers not so suppose that in praising virginity I have in the least disparaged marriage, and separated the saints of the Old Testament from those of the New, that is to say, those who had wives and those who altogether refrained from the embraces of women; I rather think that in accordance with the difference in time and circumstance one rule applied to the former, another to us upon whom the ends of the world have come. So long as that law remained, "Be fruitful, and multiply and replenish the earth"; and "Cursed is the barren woman that beareth not seed in Israel," they all married and were given in marriage, left father and mother, and become one flesh. But once in tones of thunder the words were heard, "The time is shortened, that henceforth those that have wives may be as though they had none," cleaving to the Lord, we are made one spirit with Him. And why? Because "He that is unmarried is careful for the things of the Lord, how he may please the Lord; but he that is married is careful for the things of the world, how he may please his wife. And there is a difference also between the wife and the virgin. She that is unmarried is careful for the things of the Lord, that she may be holy both in body and in spirit: but she that is married is careful for the things of the world, how she may please her husband." Why do you cavil? Why do you resist? The vessel of election says this; he tells us that there is a difference between the wife and the virgin. Observe what the happiness of that state must be in which even the distinction of sex is lost. The virgin is no longer called a woman. "She that is unmarried is careful for the things of the Lord, that she may be holy both in body and in spirit." A virgin is defined as she that is holy in body and in spirit, for it is no good to have virgin flesh if a woman be married in mind.

"But she that is married is careful for the things of the world, how she may please her husband." Do you think there is no difference between one who spends her time in prayer and fasting, and one who must, at her husband's approach, make up her countenance, walk with mincing gait, and feign a shew of endearment? The virgin's aim is to appear less comely; she will wrong herself so as to hide her natural attractions. The married woman has the paint laid on before her mirror, and, to the insult of her Maker, strives to acquire something more than her natural beauty. Then come the prattling of infants, the noisy household, children watching for her word and waiting for her kiss, the reckoning up of expenses, the preparation to meet the outlay. On one side you will see a company of cooks, girded for the onslaught and attacking the meat; there you may hear the hum of a multitude of weavers. Meanwhile a message is delivered that the husband and his friends have arrived. The wife, like a swallow, flies all over the house. "She has to see to everything. Is the sofa smooth? Is the pavement swept? Are the flowers in the cups? Is dinner ready?" Tell me, pray, where amid all this is there room for the thought of God? Are these happy homes? Where there is the beating of drums, the noise and clatter of pipe and lute, the clanging of cymbals, can any fear of God be found? The parasite is snubbed and feels proud of the honor. Enter next the half-naked victims of the passions, a mark for every lustful eye. The unhappy wife must either take pleasure in them, and perish, or be displeased, and provoke her husband. Hence arises discord, the seedplot of divorce. Or suppose you find me a house where these things are unknown, which is a *rara avis* [rare bird] indeed: yet even there the very management of the household, the education of the children, the wants of the husband, the correction of the servants, cannot fail to call away the mind from the thought of God. "It had ceased to be with Sarah after the manner of women": so the Scripture says, and afterwards Abraham received the command, "In all that Sarah saith unto thee, hearken unto her voice." She who is not subject to the anxiety and pain of child-bearing and having passed the change of life has ceased to perform the functions of a woman, is freed from the curse of God: nor is her desire to her husband, but on the contrary her husband becomes subject to her, and the voice of the Lord commands him, "In all that Sarah saith unto thee, hearken unto her voice." Thus they begin to have time for prayer. For so long as the debt of marriage is paid, earnest prayer is neglected.

I do not deny that holy women are found both among widows and those who have husbands; but they are such as have ceased to be wives, or such as, even in the close bond of marriage, imitate virgin chastity. The Apostle, Christ speaking in him, briefly bore witness to this when he said, "She that is unmarried is careful for the things of the Lord, how she may please the Lord; but she that is married is careful for the things of the world, how she may please her husband." He leaves us the free exercise of our reason in the matter. He lays no necessity upon anyone nor leads anyone into a snare: he only persuades to that which is proper when he wishes all men to be as himself. He had not, it is true, a commandment from the Lord respecting virginity, for that grace surpasses the unassisted power of man, and it would have worn an air of immodesty to force men to fly in the face of nature, and to say in other words, I want you to be what the angels are. It is this angelic purity which secures to virginity its highest reward, and the Apostle might have seemed to despise a course of life which involves no guilt. Nevertheless in the immediate context he adds, "But I give my judgment, as one that hath obtained mercy of the Lord to be faithful. I think therefore that this is good by reason of the present distress, namely, that it is good for a man to be as he is." What is meant by *present distress*? "Woe unto them that are with child and to them that give suck in those days!" The reason why the wood grows up is that is may be cut down. The field is sown that it may be reaped. The world is already full, and the population is too large for the soil. Every day we are being cut down by war, snatched away by disease, swallowed up by shipwreck, although we go to law with one another about the fences of our property. It is only one addition to the general rule which is made by those who follow the Lamb, and who have not defiled their garments, for they have continued in their virgin state. Notice the meaning of *defiling*. I shall not venture to explain it, for fear Helvidius may be abusive. I agree with you, when you say, that some virgins are nothing but tavern women; I say still more that even adulteresses may be found among them, and, you will no doubt be still more surprised to hear, that some of the clergy are innkeepers and some monks unchaste. Who does not at once understand that a tavern woman cannot be a virgin, nor an adulterer a monk, nor a clergyman a tavern-keeper? Are we to blame virginity if its counterfeit is at fault? For my part, to pass over other persons and come to the virgin, I maintain that she who is engaged in huckstering, though for anything I know she may be a virgin in body, is no longer one in spirit.

I have become rhetorical and have disported myself a little like a platform orator. You compelled me, Helvidius; for brightly as the Gospel shines at the present day, you will have it that equal glory attaches to virginity and to the marriage state. And because I think that, finding the truth too strong for you, you will turn to disparaging my life and abusing my character (it is the way of weak women to talk tittle-tattle in corners when they have been put down by their masters), I shall anticipate you. I assure you that I shall regard your railing as a high distinction, since the same lips that assail me have disparaged Mary, and I, a servant of the Lord, am favored with the same barking eloquence as His mother.

LETTER LXX

To Magnus, An Orator of Rome

Jerome thanks Magnus, a Roman orator, for his services in bringing a young man named Sebesius to apologize to him for some fault that he had committed. He then replies to a criticism of Magnus on his fondness for making quotations from profane writers, a practice which he defends by the example of the fathers of the church and of the inspired penmen of scripture. He ends by hinting that the objection really comes not from Magnus himself but from Rufinus (here nicknamed Calpurnius Lanarius). The date of the letter is A.D. 397.

You ask me at the close of your letter why it is that sometimes in my writings I quote examples from secular literature and thus defile the whiteness of the church with the foulness of heathenism. I will now briefly answer your question. You would never have asked it, had not your mind been wholly taken up with Tully; you would never have asked it had you made it a practice instead of studying Volcatius to read the holy scriptures and the commentators upon them. For who is there who does not know that both in Moses and in the prophets there are passages cited from Gentile books and that Solomon proposed questions to the philosophers of Tyre and answered others put to him by them. In the commencement of the book of Proverbs he charges us to understand prudent maxims and shrewd adages, parables and obscure discourse, the words of the wise and their dark sayings; all of which belong by right to the sphere of the dialectician and the philosopher. The Apostle Paul also, in writing to Titus has used a line of the poet Epimenides: "the Cretians are always liars, evil beasts, slow bellies." Half of which line was afterwards adopted by Callimachus. It is not surprising that a literal rendering of the words into Latin should fail to preserve that meter seeing that Homer when translated into the same language is scarcely intelligible even in prose. In another epistle Paul quotes a line of Menander: "Evil communications corrupt good manners." And when he is arguing with the Athenians upon the Areopagus he calls Aratus as a witness citing from him the words "For we are also his offspring"; the close of a heroic verse. And as if this were not enough, that leader of the Christian army, that unvanquished pleader for the cause of Christ, skillfully turns a chance inscription into a proof of the faith. For he had learned from the true David to wrench the sword of the enemy out of his hand and with his own blade to cut off the head of the arrogant Goliath. He had read in Deuteronomy the command given by the voice of the Lord that when a captive woman had had her head shaved, her eyebrows and all her hair cut off, and her nails pared, she might then be taken to wife. Is it surprising that I too, admiring the fairness of her form and the grace of her eloquence, desire to make that secular wisdom which is my captive and my handmaid, a matron of the true Israel? Or that shaving off and cutting away all in her that is dead whether this be idolatry, pleasure, error, or lust, I take her to myself clean and pure and beget by her servants for the Lord of Sabaoth? My efforts promote the advantage of Christ's family, my so-called defilement with an alien increases the number of my fellow-servants. Hosea took a wife of whoredoms, Gomer the daughter of Diblaim, and this harlot bore him a son called Jezreel or the seed of God. Isaiah speaks of a sharp razor which shaves "the head of sinners and the hair of their feet"; and Ezekiel shaves his head as a type of that Jerusalem which has been an harlot, in sign that whatever in her is devoid of sense and life must be removed.

Cyprian, a man renowned both for his eloquence and for his martyr's death, was assailed — so Firmian tells me — for having used in his treatise against Demetrius passages from the Prophets and the Apostles which the latter declared to be fabricated and made up, instead of passages from the philosophers and poets whose authority he, as a heathen, could not well gainsay. Celsus and Porphyry have written against us and have been ably answered, the former by Origen, the latter by Methodius, Eusebius, and Apollinaris. Origen wrote a treatise in eight books, the work of Methodius extended to ten thousand lines, while Eusebius and Apollinaris composed twenty-five and thirty volumes respectively. Read these and you will find that compared with them I am a mere tyro in learning, and that, as my wits have long lain fallow, I can barely recall as in a dream what I have learned as a boy. The emperor Julian found time during his Parthian campaign to vomit forth seven books against Christ and, as so often happens in poetic legends, only wounded himself with his own sword. Were I to try to confute him with the doctrines of philosophers and stoics you would doubtless forbid me to strike a mad dog with the club of Hercules. It is true that he presently felt in battle the hand of our Nazarene or, as he used to call Him, the Galilean, and that a spear-thrust in the vitals paid him due recompense for his foul calumnies. To prove the antiquity of the Jewish people Josephus has written two books against Appio, a grammarian of Alexandria;

and in these he brings forward so many quotations from secular writers as to make me marvel how a Hebrew brought up from his childhood to read the sacred scripture could also have perused the whole library of the Greeks. Need I speak of Philo whom critics call the second or the Jewish Plato?

Let us now run through the list of our own writers. Did not Quadratus, a disciple of the apostles and bishop of the Athenian church, deliver to the Emperor Hadrian (on the occasion of his visit to the Eleusinian mysteries) a treatise in defense of our religion. And so great was the admiration caused in everyone by his eminent ability that it stilled a most severe persecution. The philosopher Aristides, a man of great eloquence, presented to the same Emperor an apology for the Christians composed of extracts from philosophic writers. His example was afterwards followed by Justin, another philosopher who delivered to Antoninus Pius and his sons and to the senate a treatise *against the Gentiles*, in which he defended the ignominy of the cross and preached the resurrection of Christ with all freedom. Need I speak of Melito, bishop of Sardis, of Apollinaris, chief-priest of the Church of Hierapolis, of Dionysius, bishop of the Corinthians, of Tatian, of Bardesanes, of Irenaeus, successor to the martyr Pothinus; all of whom have in many volumes explained the uprisings of the several heresies and tracked them back, each to the philosophic source from which it flows. Pantaenus, a philosopher of the Stoic school, was on account of his great reputation for learning sent by Demetrius, bishop of Alexandria, to India, to preach Christ to the Brahmans and philosophers there. Clement, a presbyter of Alexandria, in my judgment the most learned of men, wrote eight books of *Miscellanies* and as many of *Outline Sketches*, a treatise against the Gentiles, and three volumes called the *Pedagogue*. Is there any want of learning in these, or are they not rather drawn from the very heart of philosophy? Imitating his example Origen wrote ten books of *Miscellanies* in which he compares together the opinions held respectively by Christians and by philosophers, and confirms all the dogmas of our religion by quotations from Plato and Aristotle, from Numenius and Cornutus. Miltiades also wrote an excellent treatise against the Gentiles. Moreover Hippolytus and a Roman senator named Apollonius have each compiled apologetic works. The books of Julius Africanus who wrote a history of his own times are still extant, as also are those of Theodore who was afterwards called Gregory, a man endowed with apostolic miracles as well as with apostolic virtues. We still have the works of Dionysius, bishop of Alexandria, of Anatolius, chief priest of the church of Laodicea, of the presbyters Pamphilus, Pierius, Lucian, Malchion, of Eusebius, bishop of Caesarea, Eustathius of Antioch and Athanasius of Alexandria; of Eusebius of Emisa, of Triphyllius of Cyprus, of Asterius of Scythopolis, of the confessor Serapion, of Titus, bishop of Bostra; and the Cappadocians Basil, Gregory, and Amphilochius. All these writers so frequently interweave in their books the doctrines and maxims of the philosophers that you might easily be at a loss which to admire most, their secular erudition or their knowledge of the scriptures.

I will pass on to Latin writers. Can anything be more learned or more pointed than the style of Tertullian? His *Apology* and his books *Against the Gentiles* contain all the wisdom of the world. Minucius Felix, a pleader in the Roman courts, has ransacked all heathen literature to adorn the pages of his *Octavius* and of his treatise *Against the Astrologers* (unless indeed this latter is falsely ascribed to him). Arnobius has published seven books against the Gentiles, and his pupil Lactantius as many, besides two volumes, one *On Anger* and the other *On the Creative Activity of God*. If you read any of these you will find in them an epitome of Cicero's dialogues. The Martyr Victorinus though as a writer deficient in learning is not deficient in the wish to use what learning he has. Then there is Cyprian. With what terseness, with what knowledge of all history, with what splendid rhetoric and argument has he touched the theme that idols are no Gods! Hilary too, a confessor and bishop of my own day, has imitated Quintilian's twelve books both in number and in style, and has also shewn his ability as a writer in his short treatise against Dioscorus the physician. In the reign of Constantine the presbyter Juvencus set forth in verse the story of our Lord and Savior, and did not shrink from forcing into meter the majestic phrases of the Gospel. Of other writers dead and living I say nothing. Their aim and their ability are evident to all who read them.

You must not adopt the mistaken opinion, that while in dealing with the Gentiles one may appeal to their literature, in all other discussions one ought to ignore it; for almost all the books of all these writers — except those who like Epicurus are no scholars — are extremely full of erudition and philosophy. I incline indeed to fancy — the thought comes into my head as I dictate — that you yourself know quite well what has always been the practice of the learned in this matter. I believe that in putting this question to me you are only the mouthpiece of another who by reason of his love for the histories of Sallust might well be called Calpurnius Lanarius. Please beg of him not to envy eaters their teeth because he is toothless himself, and not to make light of the eyes of gazelles because he is himself a mole. Here as you see there is abundant material for discussing, but I have already filled the limits at my disposal.

Selections from "On the Resurrection" and collected poems from
The Fathers, Historians, and Writers of the Church,
W.B. Kelly, Dublin, 1864

Chapter 30 • St. Augustine: *Confessions*; *The Enchiridion*; *The City of God*

Considered by some as the greatest doctor and theologian of the Western Church, St. Augustine (354-430), through his writings, has had an influence on Christians and non-Christians of all ages. In a sense, every one of his writings is a classic of Catholicism and any selection of a representative sample of his works is difficult. The excerpt from *The Confessions* illustrates its importance in Christian mysticism. The *Enchiridion* (*Handbook* or *Manual*) is a very concise and precise explanation of the basic beliefs of Catholicism. His work on *The Trinity* is a classic summary of Catholic teaching on the subject. The *City of God* is a major work in the history of Christianity as well as the philosophy of history. The selections from the latter are indicative of Augustine's convictions on many basic problems.

Confessions

Chapter X

A conversation he had with his mother concerning the kingdom of heaven.

As the day now approached on which she was to depart this life (which day Thou knewst, we did not), it fell out — Thou, as I believe, by Thy secret ways arranging it — that she and I stood alone, leaning in a certain window, from which the garden of the house we occupied at Ostia could be seen; at which place, removed from the crowd, we were resting ourselves for the voyage, after the fatigues of a long journey. We then were conversing alone very pleasantly; and, "forgetting those things which are behind, and reaching forth unto those things which are before," we were seeking between ourselves in the presence of the Truth, which Thou art, of what nature the eternal life of the saints would be, which eye hath not seen, nor ear heard, neither hath entered into the heart of man. But yet we opened wide the mouth of our heart, after those supernal streams of Thy fountain, "the fountain of life," which is "with Thee"; that being sprinkled with it according to our capacity, we might in some measure weigh so high a mystery.

And when our conversation had arrived at that point, that the very highest pleasure of the carnal senses, and that in the very brightest material light, seemed by reason of the sweetness of that life, not only not worthy of comparison, but not even of mention, we, lifting ourselves with a more ardent affection towards "the Self-same," did gradually pass through all corporeal things, and even the heaven itself, whence sun, and moon, and stars shine upon the earth; yea, we soared higher yet by inward musing, and discoursing, and admiring Thy works; and we came to our own minds, and went beyond them, that we might advance as high as that region of unfailing plenty, where Thou feedest Israel for ever with the food of truth, and where life is that Wisdom by whom all these things are made, both which have been, and which are to come; and she is not made, but is as she hath been, and so shall ever be; yea, rather, to "have been," and "to be hereafter," are not in her, but only "to be," seeing she is eternal, for to "have been" and "to be hereafter" are not eternal. And while we were thus speaking, and straining after her, we slightly touched her with the whole effort of our heart; and we sighed, and there left bound "the first-fruits of the Spirit"; and returned to the noise of our own mouth, where the word uttered has both beginning and end. And what is like unto Thy Word, our Lord, who remaineth in Himself without becoming old, and "maketh all things new"?

We were saying, then, if to any man the tumult of the flesh were silenced — silenced the phantasies of earth, waters, and air — silenced, too, the poles; yea, the very soul be silenced to herself, and go beyond herself by not thinking of herself — silenced fancies and imaginary revelations, every tongue, and every sign, and whatsoever exists by passing away, since, if any could hearken, all these say, "We created not ourselves, but were created by Him who abideth for ever": If, having uttered this, they now should be silenced, having only quickened our ears to Him who created them, and He alone speak not by them, but by Himself, that we may hear His word, not by fleshly tongue, nor angelic voice, nor sound of thunder, nor the obscurity of a similitude, but might hear Him — Him whom in these we love — without these, like as we two now strained ourselves, and with rapid thought touched on that Eternal Wisdom which remaineth over all. If this could be sustained, and other visions of a far different kind be withdrawn, and this one ravish, and absorb, and envelop its beholder amid these inward joys, so that this life might be eternally like that one moment of knowledge which we now sighed after, were not this "Enter thou into the joy of Thy Lord"? And when shall that be? When we shall all rise again; but all shall not be changed.

26. Such things was I saying; and if not after this manner, and in these words, yet, Lord, Thou knowest, that in that day when we were talking thus, this world with all its delights grew contemptible to us, even while we spake. Then said my mother, "Son, for myself, I have no longer any pleasure in aught

in this life. What I want here further, and why I am here, I know not, now that my hopes in this world are satisfied. There was indeed one thing for which I wished to tarry a little in this life, and that was that I might see thee a Catholic Christian before I died. My God has exceeded this abundantly, so that I see thee despising all earthly felicity, made His servant — what do I here?"

The Enchiridion Addressed to Laurentius;
Being a Treatise on Faith, Hope, and Love
Argument

Laurentius having asked Augustine to furnish him with a handbook of Christian doctrine, containing in brief compass answers to several questions which he had proposed, Augustine shows him that these questions can be fully answered by any one who knows the proper objects of faith, hope, and love. He then proceeds, in the first part of the work (Chap. IX — CXIII), to expound the objects of faith, taking as his text the Apostles' Creed; and in the course of this exposition, besides refuting divers heresies, he throws out many observations on the conduct of life. The second part of the work (Chap. CXIV-CXVI) treats of the objects of hope, and consists of a very brief exposition of the several petitions in the Lord's prayer. The third and concluding part (Chap. CXVII-CXXII) treats of the objects of love, showing the pre-eminence of this grace in the gospel system, that it is the end of the commandment and the fulfilling of the law, and that God himself is love.

Chapter 2. — The Fear of God Is Man's True Wisdom

The true wisdom of man is piety. You find this in the book of holy Job. For we read there what wisdom itself has said to man: "Behold, the fear of the Lord [*pietas*], that is wisdom." If you ask further what is meant in that place by *pietas*, the Greek calls it more definitely θεοσέβεια, that is, the worship of God. The Greeks sometimes call piety εὐσέβεια, which signifies right worship, though this, of course, refers specially to the worship of God. But when we are defining in what man's true wisdom consists, the most convenient word to use is that which distinctly expresses the fear of God. And can you, who are anxious that I should treat of great matters in few words, wish for a briefer form of expression? Or perhaps you are anxious that this expression should itself be briefly explained, and that I should unfold in a short discourse the proper mode of worshipping God?

Chapter 3. — God Is to Be Worshipped through Faith, Hope, and Love

Now if I should answer, that God is to be worshipped with faith, hope, and love, you will at once say that this answer is too brief, and will ask me briefly to unfold the objects of each of these three graces, viz., what we are to believe, what we are to hope for, and what we are to love. And when I have done this, you will have an answer to all the questions you asked in your letter. If you have kept a copy of your letter, you can easily turn it up and read it over again: if you have not, you will have no difficulty in recalling it when I refresh your memory.

Chapter 4. — The Questions Propounded by Laurentius

You are anxious, you say, that I should write a sort of handbook for you, which you might always keep beside you, containing answers to the questions you put, viz.: what ought to be man's chief end in life; what he ought, in view of the various heresies, chiefly to avoid; to what extent religion is supported by reason; what there is in reason that lends no support to faith, when faith stands alone; what is the starting-point, what the goal, of religion; what is the sum of the whole body of doctrine; what is the sure and proper foundation of the Catholic faith. Now, undoubtedly, you will know the answers to all these questions, if you know thoroughly the proper objects of faith, hope, and love. For these must be the chief, nay, the exclusive objects of pursuit in religion. He who speaks against these is either a total stranger to the name of Christ, or is a heretic. These are to be defended by reason, which must have its starting-point either in the bodily senses or in the intuitions of the mind. And what we have neither had experience of through our bodily senses, nor have been able to reach through the intellect, must undoubtedly be believed on the testimony of those witnesses by whom the Scriptures, justly called divine, were written; and who by divine assistance were enabled, either through bodily sense or intellectual perception, to see or to foresee the things in question.

Chapter 5. — Brief Answers to These Questions

Moreover, when the mind has been imbued with the first elements of that faith which worketh by love, it endeavors by purity of life to attain unto sight, where the pure and perfect in heart know that unspeakable beauty, the full vision of which is supreme happiness. Here surely is an answer to your question as to what is the starting-point, and what the goal: we begin in faith, and are made perfect by sight. This also is the sum of the whole body of doctrine.

But the sure and proper foundation of the Catholic faith is Christ. "For other foundation," says the apostle, "can no man lay than that is laid, which is Jesus Christ." Nor are we to deny that this is the proper foundation of the Catholic faith, because it may be supposed that some heretics hold this in common with us. For if we carefully consider the things that pertain to Christ, we shall find that, among those heretics who call themselves Christians, Christ is present in name only: in deed and in truth He is not among them. But to show this would occupy us too long, for we should require to go over all the heresies which have existed, which do exist, or which could exist, under the Christian name, and to show that this is true in the case of each — a discussion which would occupy so many volumes as to be all but interminable.

Chapter 8. — The Distinction Between Faith and Hope, and the Mutual Dependence of Faith, Hope, and Love.

Again, can anything be hoped for which is not an object of faith? It is true that a thing which is not an object of hope may be believed. What true Christian, for example, does not believe in the punishment of the wicked? And yet such an one does not hope for it. And the man who believes that punishment to be hanging over himself, and who shrinks in horror from the prospect, is more properly said to fear than to hope. And these two states of mind the poet carefully distinguishes when he says: "Permit the fearful to have hope." Another poet, who is usually much superior to this one, makes a wrong use of the word, when he says: "If I have been able to hope for so great a grief as this." And some grammarians take this case as an example of impropriety of speech, saying, "He said *sperare* [to hope] instead of *timere* [to fear]." Accordingly, faith may have for its object evil as well as good; for both good and evil are believed, and the faith that believes them is not evil, but good. Faith, moreover, is concerned with the past, the present, and the future, all three. We believe, for example, that Christ died — an event in the past; we believe that He is sitting at the right hand of God — a state of things which is present; we believe that He will come to judge the quick and the dead — an event of the future. Again, faith applies both to one's own circumstances and those of others. Every one, for example, believes that his own existence had a beginning, and was not eternal, and he believes these same both of other men and other things. Many of our beliefs in regard to religious matter, again, have reference not merely to other men, but to angels also. But hope has for its object only what is good, only what is future, and only what affects the man who entertains the hope. For these reasons, then, faith must be distinguished from hope, not merely as a matter of verbal propriety, but because they are essentially different. The fact that we do not see either what we believe or what we hope for, is all that is common to faith and hope. In the Epistle to the Hebrews, for example, faith is defined (and eminent defenders of the Catholic faith have used the definition as a standard) "the evidence of things not seen." Although, should any one say that he believes, that is, has grounded his faith, not on words, nor on witnesses, nor on any reasoning whatever, but on the direct evidence of his own senses, he would not be guilty of such an impropriety of speech as to be justly liable to the criticism, "You saw, therefore you did not believe." And hence it does not follow that an object of faith is not an object of sight. But it is better that we should use the word "faith" as the Scriptures have taught us, applying it to those things which are not seen. Concerning hope, again, the apostle says: "Hope that is seen is not hope; for what a man seeth, why doth he yet hope for? But if we hope for that we see not, then do we with patience wait for it." When, then, we believe that good is about to come, this is nothing else but to hope for it. Now what shall I say of love? Without it, faith profits nothing; and in its absence, hope cannot exist. The Apostle James says: "The devils also believe, and tremble" — that is, they, having neither hope nor love, but believing that what we love and hope for is about to come, are in terror. And so the Apostle Paul approves and commends the "faith that worketh by love"; and this certainly cannot exist without hope. Wherefore there is no love without hope, no hope without love, and neither love nor hope without faith.

Chapter 9. — What We Are to Believe. In Regard to Nature It is Not Necessary For the Christian to Know More Than That the Goodness of the Creator Is the Cause of All Things

When, then, the question is asked what we are to believe in regard to religion, it is not necessary to probe into the nature of things, as was done by those whom the Greeks call *physici*; nor need we be in alarm lest the Christian should be ignorant of the force and number of the elements — the motion, and order, and eclipses of the heavenly bodies; the form of the heavens; the species and the natures of animals, plants, stones, fountains, rivers, mountains; about chronology and distances; the signs of coming storms; and a thousand other things which those philosophers either have found out, or think they have found out. For even these men themselves, endowed though they are with so much genius, burning with zeal, abounding in leisure, tracking some things by the aid of human conjecture, searching into others with the aids of history and experience, have not found out all things; and even their boasted discoveries are oftener mere guesses than certain knowledge. It is enough for the Christian to believe that the only cause of all created things, whether heavenly or earthly, whether visible or invisible, is the goodness of the Creator, the one true God; and that nothing exists but Himself that does not derive its existence from Him; and that He is the Trinity — to wit, the Father, and the Son begotten of the Father, and the Holy Spirit proceeding from the same Father, but one and the same Spirit of Father and Son.

Chapter 10. — The Supremely Good Creator Made All Things Good

By the Trinity, thus supremely and equally and unchangeably good, all things were created; and these are not supremely and equally and unchangeably good, but yet they are good, even taken separately. Taken as a whole, however, they are very good, because their *ensemble* constitutes the universe in all its wonderful order and beauty.

Chapter 11. — What Is Called Evil in the Universe Is But the Absence of Good

And in the universe, even that which is called evil, when it is regulated and put in its own place, only enhances our admiration of the good; for we enjoy and value the good more when we compare it with the evil. For the Almighty God, who, as even the heathen acknowledge, has supreme power over all things, being Himself supremely good, would never permit the existence of anything evil among His works, if He were not so omnipotent and good that He can bring good even out of evil. For what is that which we call evil but the absence of good? In the bodies of animals, disease and wounds mean nothing but the absence of health; for when a cure is effected, that does not mean that the evils which were present — namely, the diseases and wounds — go away from the body and dwell elsewhere: they altogether cease to exist; for the wound or disease is not a substance, but a defect in the fleshly substance — the flesh itself being a substance, and therefore something good, of which those evils — that is, privations of the good which we call health — are accidents. just in the same way, what are called vices in the soul are nothing but privations of natural good. And when they are cured, they are not transferred elsewhere: when they cease to exist in the healthy soul, they cannot exist anywhere else.

Chapter 12. —All Beings Were Made Good, But Not Being Made Perfectly Good, Are Liable to Corruption

All things that exist, therefore, seeing that the Creator of them all is supremely good, are themselves good. But because there are not, like their Creator, supremely and unchangeably good, their good may be diminished and increased. But for good to be diminished is an evil, although, however much it may be diminished, it is necessary, if the being is to continue, that some good should remain to constitute the being. For however small or of whatever kind the being may be, the good which makes it a being cannot be destroyed without destroying the being itself. An uncorrupted nature is justly held in esteem. But if, still further, it be incorruptible, it is undoubtedly considered of still higher value. When it is corrupted, however, its corruption is an evil, because it is deprived of some sort of good. For if it be deprived of no good, it receives no injury; but it does receive injury, therefore it is deprived of good. Therefore, so long as a being is in process of corruption, there is in it some good of which it is being deprived; and if a part of the being should remain which cannot be corrupted, this will certainly be an incorruptible being, and accordingly the process of corruption will result in the manifestation of this great good. But if it does not cease to be corrupted, neither can it cease to possess good of which corruption may deprive it. But if it should be thoroughly and completely consumed by corruption, there will then be no good left, because there will be no being. Wherefore corruption can consume the good only by consuming the being. Every being, therefore, is a good; a great good, if it can not be corrupted; a little good, if it can: but in any case, only the foolish or ignorant will deny that it is a good. And if it be wholly consumed by corruption, then the corruption itself must cease to exist, as there is no being left in which it can dwell.

Chapter 18. — It Is Never Allowable to Tell a Lie; But Lies Differ Very Much in Guilt, According to the Intention and the Subject

But here arises a very difficult and very intricate question, about which I once wrote a large book, finding it necessary to give it an answer. The question is this: whether at any time it can become the duty of a good man to tell a lie? For some go so far as to contend that there are occasions on which it is a good and pious work to commit perjury even, and to say what is false about matters that relate to the worship of God, and about the very nature of God Himself. To me, however, it seems certain that every lie is a sin, though it makes a great difference with what intention and on what subject one lies. For the sin of the man who tells a lie to help another is not so heinous as that of the man who tells a lie to injure another; and the man who by his lying puts a traveler on the wrong road, does not do so much harm as the man who by false or misleading representations distorts the whole course of a life. No one, of course, is to be condemned as a liar who says what is false, believing it to be true, because such an one does not consciously deceive, but rather is himself deceived. And, on the same principle, a man is not to be accused of lying, though he may sometimes be open to the charge of rashness, if through carelessness he takes up what is false and holds it as true; but on the other hand, the man who says what is true, believing it to be false, is, so far as his own consciousness is concerned, a liar. For in saying what he does not believe, he says what to his own conscience is false, even though it should in fact be true; nor is the man in any sense free from lying who with his mouth speaks the truth without knowing it, but in his heart wills to tell a lie. And, therefore, not looking at the matter spoken of, but solely at the intention of the speaker, the man who unwittingly says what is false, thinking all the time that it is true, is a better man than the one who unwittingly says what is true, but in his conscience intends to deceive. For the former does not think one thing and say another; but the latter, though his statements may be true in fact, has one thought in his heart and another on his lips: and that is the very essence of lying. But when we come to consider truth and falsehood in respect to the subjects spoken of, the point on which one deceives or is deceived becomes a matter of the utmost importance. For although, as far as a man's own conscience is concerned, it is a greater evil to deceive than to be deceived, nevertheless it is a far less evil to tell a lie in regard to matters that do not relate to religion, that to be led into error in regard to matters the knowledge and belief of which are essential to the right worship of God. To illustrate this by example: suppose that one man should say of some one who is dead that he is still alive, knowing this to be untrue; and that another man should, being deceived, believe that Christ shall at the end of some time (make the time as long as you please) die; would it not be incomparably better to lie like the former, than to be deceived like the latter? and would it not be a much less evil to lead some man into the former error, than to be led by any man into the latter?

Chapter 20. — Every Error Is Not a Sin

An Examination of the Opinion of the Academic Philosophers, that to Avoid Error We Should in All Cases Suspend Belief

I am not sure whether mistakes such as the following — when one forms a good opinion of a bad man, not knowing what sort of man he is; or when, instead of the ordinary perceptions through the bodily senses, other appearances of a similar kind present themselves, which we perceive in the spirit, but think we perceive in the body, or perceive in the body, but think we perceive in the spirit (such a mistake as the Apostle Peter made when the angel suddenly freed him from his chains and imprisonment, and he thought he saw a vision); or when, in the case of sensible objects themselves, we mistake rough for smooth, or bitter for sweet, or think that putrid matter has a good smell; or when we mistake the passing of a carriage for thunder; or mistake one man for another, the two being very much alike, as often happens in the case of twins (hence our great poet calls it "a mistake pleasing to parents") — whether these, and other mistakes of this kind, ought to be called sins. Nor do I now undertake to solve a very knotty question, which perplexed those very acute thinkers, the Academic philosophers: whether a wise man ought to give his assent to anything, seeing that he may fall into error by assenting to falsehood: for all things, as they assert, are either unknown or uncertain. Now I wrote three volumes shortly after my conversion, to remove out of my way the objections which lie, as it were, on the very threshold of faith. And assuredly it was necessary at the very outset to remove this utter despair of reaching truth, which seems to be strengthened by the arguments of these philosophers. Now in their eyes every error is regarded as a sin, and they think that error can only be avoided by entirely suspending belief. For they say that the man who assents to what is uncertain falls into error; and they strive by the most acute, but most audacious arguments, to show that, even though a man's opinion should by chance be true, yet that there is no uncertainty of its truth, owing to the impossibility of distinguishing truth from falsehood. But with us, "the just shall live by faith." Now, if assent be taken away, faith goes too; for without assent there can be no belief. And there are truths, whether we know them or not, which must be believed if we would attain to a happy life, that is, to eternal life. But I am not sure whether one ought to argue with men who not only do not know that there is an eternal life before them but do not know whether they are living at the present moment; nay, say that they do not know what it is impossible they can be ignorant of. For it is impossible that any one should be ignorant that he is alive, seeing that if he be not alive it is impossible for him to be ignorant for not knowledge merely, but ignorance too can be an attribute only of the living. But, forsooth, they think that by not acknowledging that they are alive they avoid error, when even their very error proves that they are alive, since one who is not alive cannot err. As, then, it is not only true, but certain, that we are alive, so there are many other things both true and certain; and God forbid that it should ever be called wisdom, and not the height of folly, to refuse assent to these.

Chapter 22.—A Lie Is Not Allowable, Even to Save Another From Injury

But every lie must be called a sin, because not only when a man knows the truth, but even when, as a man may be, he is mistaken and deceived, it is his duty to say what he thinks in his heart, whether it be true, or whether he only think it to be true. But every liar says the opposite of what he thinks in his heart, with purpose to deceive. Now it is evident that speech was given to man, not that men might therewith deceive one another, but that one man might make known his thoughts to another. To use speech, then, for the purpose of deception, and not for its appointed end, is a sin. Nor are we to suppose that there is any lie that is not a sin, because it is sometimes possible, by telling a lie, to do service to another. For it is possible to do this by theft also, as when we steal from a rich man who never feels the loss, to give to a poor man who is sensibly benefitted by what he gets. And the same can be said of adultery also, when, for instance, some woman appears likely to die of love unless we consent to her wishes, while if she lived she might purify herself by repentance; but yet no one will assert that on this account such an adultery is not a sin. And if we justly place so high a value upon chastity, what offense have we taken at truth, that, while no prospect of advantage to another will lead us to violate the former by adultery, we should be ready to violate the latter by lying? It cannot be denied that they have attained a very high standard of goodness who never lie except to save a man from injury; but in the case of men who have reached this standard, it is not the deceit, but their good intention, that is justly praised, and sometimes even rewarded. It is quite enough that the deception should be pardoned, without its being made an object of laudation, especially among the heirs of the new covenant, to whom it is said: "Let your communication be, Yea, yea; Nay, nay: for whatsoever is more than these cometh of evil." And it is on account of this evil, which never ceases to creep in while we retain this mortal vesture, that the co-heirs of Christ themselves say, "Forgive us our debts."

Chapter 23. — Summary of the Results of the Preceding Discussion

As it is right that we should know the causes of good and evil, so much of them at least as will suffice for the way that leads us to the kingdom, where there will be life without the shadow of death, truth without any alloy of error, and happiness unbroken by any sorrow, I have discussed these subjects with the brevity which my limited space demanded. And I think there cannot now be any doubt, that the only cause of any good that we enjoy is the goodness of God, and that the only cause of evil is the falling away from the unchangeable good of a being made good but changeable, first in the case of an angel, and afterwards in the case of man.

Chapter 24. — The Secondary Causes of Evil Are Ignorance and Lust

This is the first evil that befell the intelligent creation — that is, its first privation of good. Following upon this crept in, and now even in opposition to man's will, *ignorance* of duty, and *lust* after what is hurtful: and these brought in their train *error* and *suffering*, which, when they are felt to be imminent, produce that shrinking of the mind which is called *fear*. Further, when the mind attains the objects of its desire, however hurtful or empty they may be, error prevents it from perceiving their true nature, or its perceptions are overborne by a diseased appetite, and so it is puffed up with a *foolish joy*. From these fountains of evil, which spring out of defect rather than superfluity, flows every form of misery that besets a rational nature.

Chapter 26. — Through Adam's Sin His Whole Posterity Were Corrupted, and Were Born Under the Penalty of Death, Which He Had Incurred

Thence, after his sin he was driven into exile, and by his sin the whole race of which he was the root was corrupted in him, and thereby subjected to the penalty of death. And so it happened that all descended from him, and from the woman who had led him into sin, and was condemned at the same time with him — being the off-spring of carnal lust on which the same punishment of disobedience was visited — were tainted with the original sin, and were by it drawn through divers errors and sufferings into that last and endless punishment which they suffer in common with the fallen angels, their corrupter and masters, and the partakers of their doom. And thus "by one man sin entered into the world, and death by sin; and so death passed upon all men, for that all have sinned." By "the world" the apostle, of course, means in this place the whole human race.

Chapter 27. —The State of Misery to Which Adam's Sin Reduced Mankind, and the Restoration Effected Through the Mercy of God

Thus, then, matters stood. The whole mass of the human race was under condemnation, was lying steeped and wallowing in misery, and was being tossed from one form of evil to another, and having joined the faction of the fallen angels, was paying the well-merited penalty of that impious rebellion. For whatever the wicked freely do through blind and unbridled lust, and whatever they suffer against their will in the way of open punishment, this all evidently pertains to the just wrath of God. But the goodness of the Creator never fails either to supply life and vital power to the wicked angels (without which their existence would soon come to an end); or, in the case of mankind, who spring from a condemned and corrupt stock, to impart form and life to their seed, to fashion their members, and through the various seasons of their life, and in the different parts of the earth, to quicken their senses, and bestow upon them the nourishment they need. For He judged it better to bring good out of evil, than not permit any evil to exist. And if He had determined that in the case of men, as in the case of the fallen angels, there should be no restoration to happiness, would it not have been quite just, that the being who rebelled against God, who in the abuse of his freedom spurned and transgressed the command of his Creator when he could so easily have kept it, who defaced in himself the image of his Creator by stubbornly turning away from His light, who by an evil use of his free-will broke away from his wholesome bondage to the Creator's laws — would it not have been just that such a being should have been wholly and to all eternity deserted by God, and left to suffer the everlasting punishment he had so richly earned? Certainly so God would have done, had He been only just and not also merciful, and had He not designed that His unmerited mercy should shine forth the more brightly in contrast with the unworthiness of its objects.

Chapter 30. — Men Are Not Saved By Good Works, Nor By the Free Determinants of Their Own Will, But By the Grace of God Through Faith

But this part of the human race to which God has promised pardon and a share in His eternal kingdom, can they be restored through the merit of their own works? God forbid. For what good work can a lost man perform, except so far as he has been delivered from perdition? Can he do anything by the free determination of his own will? Again I say, God forbid. For it was by the evil use of his free-will that man destroyed both it and himself. For, as a man who kills himself must, of course, be alive when he kills himself, but after he has killed himself ceases to live, and cannot restore himself to life; so, when man by his own free-will sinned, then sin being victorious over him, the freedom of his will was lost. "For of whom a man is overcome, of the same is he brought in bondage." This is the judgment of the Apostle Peter. And as it is certainly true, what kind of liberty, I ask, can the bond-slave possess, except when it pleases him to sin? For he is freely in bondage who does with pleasure the will of his master. Accordingly, he who is the servant of sin is free to sin. And hence he will not be free to do right, until, being freed from sin, he shall begin to be the servant of righteousness. And this is true liberty, for he has pleasure in the righteous deed; and it is at the same time a holy bondage, for he is obedient to the will of God. But whence comes this liberty to do right to the man who is in bondage and sold under sin, except he be redeemed by Him who has said, "If the Son shall make you free, ye shall be free indeed?" And before this redemption is wrought in a man, when he is not yet free to do what is right, how can he talk of the freedom of his will and his good works, except he be inflated by that foolish pride of boasting which the apostle restrains when he says, "By grace are ye saved, through faith."

Chapter 31. — Faith Itself Is the Gift of God; and Good Works Will Not Be Wanting in Those Who Believe

And lest men should arrogate to themselves the merit of their own faith at least, not understanding that this too is the gift of God, this same apostle, who says in another place that he had "obtained mercy of the Lord to be faithful," here also adds: "and that not of yourselves; it is the gift of God; not of works, lest any man should boast." And lest it should be thought that good works will be wanting in those who believe, he adds further: "For we are His workmanship, created in Christ Jesus unto good works which God hath before ordained that we should walk in them." We shall be made truly free, then, when God fashions us, that is, forms and creates us anew, not as men — for He has done that already — but as good men, which His grace is now doing, that we may be a new creation in Christ Jesus, according as it is said: "Create in me a clean heart, O God." For God had already created his heart, so far as the physical structure of the human heart is concerned; but the psalmist prays for the renewal of the life which was still lingering in his heart.

Chapter 32. — The Freedom of the Will Is Also the Gift of God, for God Worketh in Us Both to Will and to Do

And further, should any one be inclined to boast, not indeed of his works, but of the freedom of his will, as if the first merit belonged to him, this very liberty of good action being given to him as a reward he had earned, let him listen to this same preacher of grace, when he says: "For it is God which worketh in you, both to will and to do of His own good pleasure," and in another place: "So, then, it is not of him that willeth, nor of him that runneth, but of God that showeth mercy." Now as, undoubtedly, if a man is of the age to use his reason, he cannot believe, hope, love, unless he will to do so, nor obtain the prize of the high calling of God unless he voluntarily run for it; in what sense is it "not of him that willeth, nor of him that runneth, but of God that showeth mercy," except that, as it is written, "the preparation of the heart is from the Lord?" Otherwise, if it is said, "It is not of him that willeth, nor of him that runneth, but of God that showeth mercy," because it is of both, that is, both of the will of man and of the mercy of God, so that we are to understand the saying, "It is not of him that willeth, nor of him that runneth, but of God that showeth mercy," as if it meant the will of man alone is not sufficient, if the mercy of God go not with it — then it will follow that the mercy of God alone is not sufficient, if the will of man go not with it; and therefore, if we may rightly say, "It is not of man that willeth, but of God that showeth mercy" because the will of man by itself is not enough, why may we not also rightly put it in the converse way: "It is not of God that showeth mercy, but of man that willeth," because the mercy of God by itself does not suffice? Surely, if no Christian will dare to say this, "It is not of God that showeth mercy, but of man that willeth," lest he should openly contradict the apostle, it follows that the true interpretation of the saying, "It is not of him that willeth, nor of him that runneth, but of God that showeth mercy," is that the whole work belongs to God, who both makes the will of man righteous, and thus prepares it for assistance, and assists it when it is prepared. For the man's righteousness of will precedes many of God's gifts, but not all; and it must itself be included among those which it does not precede. We read in Holy Scripture, both that God's mercy "shall meet me," and that His mercy "shall follow me." It goes before the unwilling to make him willing; it follows the willing to make his will effectual. Why are we taught to pray for our enemies, who are plainly unwilling to lead a holy life, unless that God may work willingness in them? And why are we ourselves taught to ask that we may receive; unless that He who has created in us the wish, may Himself satisfy the wish? We pray, then, for our enemies, that the mercy of God may prevent them, as it has prevented us: we pray for ourselves that His mercy may follow us.

Chapter 34. — The Ineffable Mystery of the Birth of Christ the Mediator Through the Virgin Mary

Now of this Mediator it would occupy too much space to say anything at all worthy of Him; and, indeed, to say what is worthy of Him is not in the power of man. For who will explain in consistent words this single statement, that "the Word was made flesh, and dwelt among us," so that we may believe on the only Son of God the Father Almighty, born of the Holy Ghost and the Virgin Mary? The meaning of the Word being made flesh, is not that the divine nature was changed into flesh, but that the divine nature assumed our flesh. And by "flesh" we are here to understand "man," the part being put for the whole, as when it is said: "By the deeds of the law shall no flesh be justified," that is, no man. For we must believe that no part was wanting in that human nature which He put on, save that it was a nature wholly free from every taint of sin — not such a nature as is conceived between the two sexes through carnal lust, which is born in sin, and whose guilt is washed away in regeneration; but such as it behoved a virgin to bring forth, when the mother's faith, not her lust, was the condition of conception. And if her virginity had been marred even in bringing Him forth, He would not have been born of a virgin; and it would be false (which God forbid) that He was born of the Virgin Mary, as is believed and declared by the whole Church, which, in imitation of His mother, daily brings forth members of His body, and yet remains a virgin. Read, if you please, my letter on the virginity of the holy Mary which I sent to that eminent man, whose name I mention with respect and affection, Volusianus.

Chapter 35. — Jesus Christ, Being the Only Son of God, Is at the Same Time Man

Wherefore Christ Jesus, the Son of God, is both God and man; God before all worlds; man in our world: God, because the Word of God (for "the Word was God"); and man, because in His one person the Word was joined with a body and a rational soul. Wherefore, so far as He is God, He and the Father are one; so far as He is man, the Father is greater than He. For when He was the only Son of God, not by grace, but by nature, that He might be also full of grace, He became the Son of man; and He Himself unites both natures in His own identity, and both natures constitute one Christ; because, "being in the form of God, He thought it not robbery to be," what He was by nature, "equal with God." But He made Himself of no reputation, and took upon Himself the form of a servant, not losing or lessening the form of God. And, accordingly, He was both made less and remained equal, being both in one, as has been said: but He was one of these as Word, and the other as man. As Word, He is equal with the Father; as man, less than the Father. One Son of God, and at the same time Son of man; one Son of man, and at the same time Son of God; not two Sons of God, God and man, but one Son of God: God without beginning; man with a beginning, our Lord Jesus Christ.

Chapter 36. — The Grace of God Is Clearly and Remarkably Displayed in Raising the Man Christ Jesus to the Dignity of the Son of God

Now here the grace of God is displayed with the greatest power and clearness. For what merit had the human nature in the man Christ earned, that it should in this unparalleled way be taken up into the unity of the person of the only Son of God? What goodness of will, what goodness of desire and intention, what good works, had gone before, which made this man worthy to become one person with God? Had He been a man previously to this, and had He earned this unprecedented reward, that He should be thought worthy to become God? Assuredly nay; from the very moment that He began to be man, He was nothing else than the Son of God, the only Son of God, the Word who was made flesh, and therefore He was God; so that just as each individual man unites in one person a body and a rational soul, so Christ in one person unites the Word and man. Now wherefore was this unheard — of glory conferred on human nature — a glory which, as there was no antecedent merit, was of course wholly of grace — except that here those who looked at the matter soberly and honestly might behold a clear manifestation of the power of God's free grace, and might understand that they are justified from their sins by the same grace which made the man Christ Jesus free from the possibility of sin? And so the angel, when he announced to Christ's mother the coming birth, saluted her thus: "Hail, thou that art full of grace", and shortly afterwards,

"Thou hast found grace with God." Now she was said to be full of grace, and to have found grace with God, because she was to be the mother of her Lord, nay, of the Lord of all flesh. But, speaking of Christ Himself, the evangelist John, after saying, "The Word was made flesh, and dwelt among us," adds, "and we beheld His glory, the glory as of the Only-begotten of the Father, full of grace and truth." When he says, "The Word was made flesh," this is "full of grace", when he says, "the glory of the only-begotten of the Father," this is "full of truth." For the Truth Himself, who was the Only-begotten of the Father, not by grace, but by nature, by grace took our humanity upon Him, and so united it with His own person that He Himself became also the Son of man.

Chapter 37. — The Same Grace Is Further Clearly Manifested in This That the Birth of Christ According to the Flesh Is of the Holy Ghost

For the same Jesus Christ who is the Only-begotten, that is, the only Son of God, our Lord, was born of the Holy Ghost and of the Virgin Mary. And we know that the Holy Spirit is the gift of God, the gift being Himself indeed equal to the Giver. And therefore the Holy Spirit also is God, not inferior to the Father and the Son. The fact, therefore, that the nativity of Christ in His human nature was by the Holy Spirit, is another clear manifestation of grace. For when the Virgin asked the angel how this which he had announced should be, seeing she knew not a man, the angel answered, "The Holy Ghost shall come upon thee, and the power of the Highest shall overshadow thee: therefore also that holy things which shall be born of thee shall be called the Son of God." And when Joseph was minded to put her away, suspecting her of adultery, as he knew she was not with child by himself, he was told by the angel, "Fear not to take unto thee Mary thy wife; for that which is conceived in her is of the Holy Ghost", that is, what thou suspectest to be begotten of another man is of the Holy Ghost.

Chapter 38. — Jesus Christ, According to the Flesh, Was Not Born of the Holy Spirit in Such a Sense That the Holy Spirit Is His Father

Nevertheless, are we on this account to say that the Holy Ghost is the father of the man Christ, and that as God the Father begat the Word, so God the Holy Spirit begat the man, and that these two natures constitute the one Christ; and that as the Word He is the Son of God the Father, and as man the Son of God the Holy Spirit, because the Holy Spirit as His father begat Him of the Virgin

Mary? Who will dare to say so? Nor is it necessary to show by reasoning how many other absurdities flow from this supposition, when it is itself so absurd that no believer's ears can bear to hear it. Hence, as we confess, "Our Lord Jesus Christ, who of God is God, and as man was born of the Holy Ghost and of the Virgin Mary, having both natures, the divine and the human, is the only Son of God the Father Almighty, from whom proceedeth the Holy Spirit." Now in what sense do we say that Christ was born of the Holy Spirit, if the Holy Spirit did not beget Him? Is it that He made Him, since our Lord Jesus Christ, though as God "all things were made by Him," yet as man was Himself made; as the apostle says, "who was made of the seed of David according to the flesh?" But as that created thing which the Virgin conceived and brought forth, though it was united only to the person of the Son, was made by the whole Trinity (for the works of the Trinity are not separable), why should the Holy Spirit alone be mentioned as having made it? Or is it that, when one of the Three is mentioned as the author of any work, the whole Trinity is to be understood as working? That is true, and can be proved by examples. But we need not dwell longer on this solution.

The City of God
Book One
Chapter 20. —That Christians Have No Authority for Committing Suicide in Any Circumstances Whatever

It is not without significance, that in no passage of the holy canonical books there can be found either divine precept or permission to take away our own life, whether for the sake of entering on the enjoyment of immortality, or of shunning, or ridding ourselves of anything whatever. Nay, the law, rightly interpreted, even prohibits suicide, where it says, "Thou shalt not kill." This is proved especially by the omission of the words "thy neighbor," which are inserted when false witness is forbidden: "Thou shalt not bear false witness against thy neighbor." Nor yet should any one on this account suppose he has not broken this commandment if he has borne false witness only against himself. For the love of our neighbor is regulated by the love of ourselves, as it is written, "Thou shalt love thy neighbor as thyself." If, then, he who makes false statements about himself is not less guilty of bearing false witness than if he had made them to the injury of his neighbor; although in the commandment prohibiting false witness only his neighbor is mentioned, and persons taking no pains to understand it might suppose that a man was allowed to be a false witness to his own hurt; how much greater reason have we to understand that a man may not kill himself, since in the commandment, "Thou shalt not kill," there is no limitation added nor any exception made in favor of any one, and least of all in favor of him on whom the command is laid?" Are we thus insanely to countenance the foolish error of the Manichaeans? Putting aside, then, these ravings, if when we say, Thou shalt not kill, we do not understand this of the plants, since they have no sensation, nor of the irrational animals that fly, swim, walk, or creep, since they are dissociated from us by their want of reason, and are therefore by the just appointment of the Creator subjected to us to kill or keep alive for our own uses, if so, then it remains that we understand that commandment simply of man. The commandment is, "Thou shalt not kill man," therefore neither another nor yourself, for he who kills himself still kills nothing else than man.

Chapter 21 — Of the Cases in Which We May Put Men to Death Without Incurring the Guilt of Murder

However, there are some exceptions made by the divine authority to its own law, that men may not be put to death. These exceptions are of two kinds, being justified either by a general law, or by a special commission granted for a time to some individual. And in this latter case, he to whom authority is delegated, and who is but the sword in the hand of him who uses it, is not himself responsible for the death he deals. And, accordingly, they who have waged war in obedience to the divine command, or in conformity with His laws, have represented in their persons the public justice or the wisdom of government, and in this capacity have put to death wicked men; such persons have by no means violated the commandment, "Thou shalt not kill." With the exception, then, of these two classes of cases, which are justified either by a just law that applies generally, or by a special intimation from God Himself, the fountain of all justice, whoever kills a man, either himself of another, is implicated in the guilt of murder. . . .

Book V

Chapter 9. — Concerning the Foreknowledge of God and the Free Will of Man To confess that God exists, and at the same time to deny that He has foreknowledge of future things, is the most manifest folly.

But, let these perplexing debatings and disputations of the philosophers go on as they may, we, in order that we may confess the most high and true God Himself, do confess His will, supreme power, and prescience. Neither let us be afraid lest, after all, we do not do by will that which we do by will, because He, whose foreknowledge is infallible, foreknew that we would do it. What is it, then, that Cicero feared in the prescience of future things? Doubtless it was this — that if all future things have been foreknown, they will happen in the order in which they have been foreknown; and if they come to pass in this order, there is a certain order of things foreknown by God; and if a certain order of things, then a certain order of causes, for nothing can happen which is not preceded by some efficient cause. But if there is a certain order of causes according to which everything happens which does happen, then by fate, says he, all things happen which do happen. But if this be so, then is there nothing in our own power, and there is no such thing as freedom of will; and if we grant that, says he, the whole economy of human life is subverted. In vain are laws enacted, in vain are reproaches, praises, chidings, exhortations had recourse to; and there is no justice whatever in the appointment of rewards for the good, and punishments for the wicked. And that consequences so disgraceful, and absurd, and pernicious to humanity may not follow, Cicero chooses to reject the foreknowledge of future things, and shuts up the religious mind to this alternative, to make choice between two things, either that something is in our own power, or that there is foreknowledge — both of which cannot be true; but if the one is affirmed, the other is thereby denied. He therefore, like a truly great and wise man, and one who consulted very much and very skillfully for the good of humanity, of those two chose the freedom of the will, to confirm which he denied the foreknowledge of future things; and thus, wishing to make men free, he makes them sacrilegious. . . .

Now, against the sacrilegious and impious darings of reason, we assert both that God knows all things before they come to pass, and that we do by our free will whatsoever we know and feel to be done by us only because we will it. But that all things come to pass by fate, we do not say; nay we affirm that nothing comes to pass by fate; for we demonstrate that the name of fate, as it is wont to be used by those who speak of fate, meaning thereby the position of the stars at the time of each one's conception or birth, is an unmeaning word, for astrology itself is a delusion. But an order of causes in which the highest efficiency is attributed to the will of God, we neither deny nor do we designate it by the name of fate, unless, perhaps, we may understand fate to mean that which is spoken, deriving it from *fari*, to speak; for we cannot deny that it is written in the sacred Scriptures. "God hath spoken once; these two things have if heard, that power belongeth unto God. Also unto Thee, O God, belongeth mercy: for Thou wilt render unto every man according to his works. . . ."

Chapter X

Wherefore, be it far from us, in order to maintain our freedom, to deny the prescience of Him by whose help we are or shall be free. Consequently, it is not in vain that laws are enacted, and that reproaches, exhortations, praises, and vituperations are had recourse to; for these also He foreknew, and they are of great avail, even as great as He foreknew that they would be of. Prayers, also, are of avail to procure those things which He foreknew that He would grant to those who offered them; and with justice have rewards been appointed for good deeds, and punishments for sins. For a man does not therefore sin because God foreknew that he would sin. Nay, it cannot be doubted but that it is the man himself who sins when he does sin, because He, whose foreknowledge is infallible, foreknew not that fate, or fortune, or something else would sin, but that the man himself would sin, who, if he wills not, sins not. But if he shall not will to sin, even this did God foreknow.

Book IX

Chapter 15. — Of the Man Christ Jesus, the Mediator Between God and Men

But if, as is much more probable and credible, it must needs be that all men, so long as they are mortal, are also miserable, we must seek an intermediate who is not only man, but also God, that, by the interposition of His blessed mortality, He may bring them out of their mortal misery to a blessed immortality. In this intermediate two things are requisite, that He become mortal, and that He do not continue mortal. He did become mortal, not rendering the divinity of the Word infirm, but assuming the infirmity of flesh. Neither did He continue mortal in the flesh, but raised it from the dead; I do not say that He is Mediator because He is the Word, for as the Word He is supremely blessed and supremely immortal, and therefore far from miserable mortals; but He is Mediator as He is man, for by His humanity He shows us that, in order to obtain that blessed and beatific good, we need not seek other mediators to lead us through the successive steps of this attainment, but that the blessed and beatific God, having Himself become a partaker of our humanity, has afforded us ready access to the participation of

His divinity. For in delivering us from our mortality and misery, He does not lead us to the immortal and blessed angels, so that we should become immortal and blessed by participating in which the angels themselves are blessed. Therefore, when He chose to be in the form of a servant, and lower than the angels, that He might be our Mediator, He remained higher than the angels, in the form of God — Himself at once the way of life on earth and life itself in heaven.

Book XI

Chapter 6 — That the World and Time Had Both One Beginning, and the One Did Not Anticipate the Other

For eternity and time are rightly distinguished by this, that time does not exist without some movement and transition, while in eternity there is no change, who does not see that there could have been no time had not some creature been made, which by some motion could give birth to change — the various parts of which motion and change, as they cannot be simultaneous, succeed one another — and thus, in these shorter or longer intervals of duration, time would begin? Since then, God, in whose eternity is no change at all, is the Creator and Ordainer of time, I do not see how He can be said to have created the world after spaces of time had elapsed, unless it be said that prior to the world there was some creature by whose movement time could pass. And if the sacred and infallible Scriptures say that in the beginning God created the heavens and the earth, in order that it may be understood that He had made nothing previously — for if He had made anything before the rest, this thing would rather be said to have been made "in the beginning" — then assuredly the world was made, not in time, but simultaneously with time. For that which is made in time is made both after and before some time — after that which is past, before that which is future. But none could then be past, for there was no creature by whose movements its duration could be measured. But simultaneously with time the world was made, if in the world's creation change and motion were created, as seems evident from the order of the first six or seven days. What kind of days these were it is extremely difficult, or perhaps impossible for us to conceive, and how much more to say!

Chapter 10 — Of the Simple and Unchangeable Trinity, Father, Son, and Holy Ghost, One God, in Whom Substance and Quality are Identical

There is, accordingly, a good which is alone simple, and therefore alone unchangeable, and this is God. By this Good have all others been created, but not simple, and therefore not unchangeable. "Created," I say — that is, made, not begotten. For that which is begotten of the simple Good is simple as itself, and the same as itself. These two we call the Father and the Son; and both together with the Holy Spirit are one God; and to this Spirit the epithet Holy is in Scripture, as it were, appropriated. And He is another than the Father and the Son, for He is neither the Father nor the Son. I say "another," not "another thing," because He is equally with them the simple Good, unchangeable and co-eternal. And this Trinity is one God; and none the less simple because a Trinity. For we do not say that the nature of the good is simple, because the Father alone possesses it, or the Son alone, or the Holy Ghost alone; nor do we say, with the Sabellian heretics, that it is only nominally a Trinity, and has no real distinction of persons; but we say it is simple, because it is what it has, with the exception of the relation of the persons to one another. For, in regard to this relation, it is true that the Father has a Son, and yet is not Himself the Son; and the Son has a Father, and is not Himself the Father. But, as regards Himself, irrespective of relation to the other, each is what He has; thus, He is in Himself living, for He has life, and is Himself the Life which He has.

It is for this reason, then, that the nature of the Trinity is called simple, because it has not anything which it can lose, and because it is not one thing and its contents another, as a cup and the liquor, or a body and its color, or the air and the light or heat of it, or a mind and its wisdom. For none of these is what it has: the cup is not liquor, nor the body color, nor the air light and heat, nor the mind wisdom. And hence they can be deprived of what they have, and can be turned or changed into other qualities and states, so that the cup may be emptied of the liquid of which it is full, the body be discolored, the air darken, the mind grow silly. The incorruptible body which is promised to the saints in the resurrection cannot, indeed, lose its quality of incorruption, but the bodily substance and the quality of incorruption are not the same thing. For the quality of incorruption resides entire in each several part, not greater in one and less in another; for no part is more incorruptible than another. The body, indeed, is itself greater in whole than in part; and one part of it is larger, another smaller, yet is not the larger more incorruptible than the smaller. The body, then, which is not in each of its parts a whole body, is one thing; incorruptibility, which is throughout complete, is another thing; — for every part of the incorruptible body, however unequal to the rest otherwise, is equally incorrupt. For the hand, *e.g.*, is not more incorrupt than the finger because it is larger than the finger; so, though finger and hand are unequal, their incorruptibility is equal. Thus, although incorruptibility is inseparable from an incorruptible body, yet the substance of the body is one thing, the quality of incorruption another. And therefore the body is not what it has. The soul itself, too, though it be always wise (as it will be eternally when it is redeemed), will be so by participating in the unchangeable wisdom, which it is not; for though the air be never robbed of the light that is shed abroad in it, it is not on that account the same thing as the light. I do not mean that the soul is air, as has been supposed by some who could not conceive a spiritual nature; but, with much dissimilarity, the two things have a kind of likeness, which makes it suitable to say that the immaterial soul is illumined with the immaterial light of the simple wisdom of God, as the material air is irradiated with material light, and that, as the air, when deprived of this light, grows dark, (for material darkness is nothing else than air wanting light,) so the soul, deprived of the light of wisdom, grows dark.

According to this, then, those things which are essentially and truly divine are called simple, because in them quality and substance are identical, and because they are divine, or wise, or blessed in themselves, and without extraneous supplement. In Holy Scripture, it is true, the Spirit of wisdom is called "manifold" because it contains many things in it; but what it contains it also is, and it being one is all these things. For neither are there many wisdoms, but one, in which are untold and infinite treasures of things intellectual, wherein are all invisible and unchangeable reasons of things visible and changeable which were created by it. For God made nothing unwittingly; not even a human workman can be said to do so. But if He knew all that He made, He made only those things which He had known. Whence flows a very striking but true conclusion, that this world could not be known to us unless it existed, but could not have existed unless it had been known to God.

Chapter 26. — Of the Image of the Supreme Trinity, Which We Find in Some Sort in Human Nature Even in Its Present State

And we indeed recognize in ourselves the image of God, that is, of the supreme Trinity, an image which, though it be not equal to God, or rather, though it be very far removed from Him — being neither co-eternal, nor, to say all in a word, consubstantial with Him — is yet nearer to Him in nature than any other of His works, and is destined to be yet restored, that it may bear a still closer resemblance. For we both are, and know that we are, and delight in our being, and our knowledge of it. Moreover, in these three things no true-seeming illusion disturbs us; for we do not come into contact with these by some bodily sense, as we perceive the things outside of us — colors, e.g., by seeing, sounds by hearing, smells by smelling, tastes by tasting, hard and soft objects by touching — of all which sensible objects it is the images resembling them, but not themselves which we perceive in the mind and hold in the memory, and which excite us to desire the objects. But, without any delusive representation of images or phantasms, I am most certain that I am, and that I know and delight in this. In respect of these truths, I am not at all afraid of the arguments of the Academicians, who say, What if you are deceived? For if I am deceived, I am. For he who is not, cannot be deceived; and if I am deceived, by this same token I am. And since I am if I am deceived, how am I deceived in believing that I am? for it is certain that I am if I am deceived. Since, therefore, I, the person deceived, should be, even if I were deceived, certainly I am not deceived in this knowledge that I am. And, consequently, neither am I deceived in knowing that I know. For, as I know that I am, so I know this also, that I know. And when I love these two things, I add to them a certain third thing, namely, my love, which is of equal moment. For neither am I deceived in this, that I love, since in those things which I love I am not deceived; though even if these were false, it would still be true that I *loved* false things. For how could I justly be blamed and prohibited from loving false things, if it were false that I loved them? But, since they are true and real, who doubts that when they are loved, the love of them is itself true and real? Further, as there is no one who does not wish to be happy, so there is no one who does not wish to be. For how can he be happy, if he is nothing?

Book V

Chapter 11. — Concerning the Universal Providence of God in the Laws of Which All Things Are Comprehended

Therefore God supreme and true, with His Word and Holy Spirit (which three are one), one God omnipotent, creator and maker of every soul and of every body; by whose gift all are happy who are happy through verity and not through vanity; who made man a rational animal consisting of soul and body, who, when he sinned, neither permitted him to go unpunished, nor left him without mercy; who has given to the good and to the evil, being in common with stones, vegetable life in common with trees, sensuous life in common with brutes, intellectual life in common with angels alone; from whom is every mode, every species, every order; from whom are measure, number, weight, from whom is every thing which has an existence in nature, of whatever kind it be, and of whatever value; from whom are the seeds of forms and the forms of seeds, and the motion of seeds and of forms; who gave also to flesh its origin, beauty, health, reproductive fecundity, disposition of members, and the salutary concord of its parts; who also to the irrational soul has given memory, sense, appetite, but to the rational soul, in addition to these, has given intelligence and will; who has not left, not to speak of heaven and earth, angels and men, but not even the entrails of the smallest and most contemptible animal, or the feather of a bird, or the little flower of a plant, or the leaf of a tree, without an harmony, and, as it were, a mutual peace among an its parts; — that God can never be believed to have left the kingdoms of men, their dominations and servitudes, outside of the laws of His providence.

Book XIX

Chapter 13 — Of the Universal Peace Which the Law of Nature Preserves Through All Disturbances, and By Which Every One Reaches His Desert in a Way Regulated By the Just Judge

The peace of the body then consists in the duly proportioned arrangement of its parts. The peace of the irrational soul is the harmonious repose of the appetites, and that of the rational soul the harmony of knowledge and action. The peace of body and soul is the well-ordered and harmonious life and health of the living creature. Peace between man and God is the well-ordered obedience of faith to eternal law. Peace between man and man is well-ordered concord. Domestic peace is the well-ordered concord between those of the family who rule and those who obey. Civil peace is a similar concord among the citizens. The peace of the celestial city is the perfectly ordered and harmonious enjoyment of God, and of one another in God. The peace of all things is the tranquility of order. Order is the distribution which allots things equal and unequal, each to its own place. . . .

And there is a nature in which evil does not or even cannot exist; but there cannot be a nature in which there is no good. Hence not even the nature of the devil himself is evil, in so far as it is nature, but it was made evil by being perverted. Thus he did not abide in the truth, but could not escape the judgment of the Truth; he did not abide in the tranquility of order, but did not therefore escape the power of the Ordainer. The good imparted by God to his nature did not screen him from the justice of God by which order was preserved in his punishment; neither did God punish the good which He had created, but the evil which the devil had committed. God did not take back all He had imparted to his nature, but something He took and something He left, that there might remain enough to be sensible of the loss of what was taken. And this very sensibility to pain is evidence of the good which has been taken away and the good which has been left. For, were nothing good left, there could be no pain on account of the good which had been lost. For he who sins is still worse if he rejoices in his loss of righteousness. But he who is in pain, if he derives no benefit from it, mourns at least the loss of health. . . .

Book XXII

Chapter 2. — Of the Eternal and Unchangeable Will of God

It is true that wicked men do many things contrary to God's will; but so great is His wisdom and power, that all things which seem adverse to His purpose do still tend towards those just and good ends and issues which He Himself has foreknown. And consequently, when God is said to change His will, as when, *e.g.*, He becomes angry with those to whom He was gentle, it is rather they than He who are changed, and they find Him changed in so far as their experience of suffering at His hand is new, as the sun is changed to injured eyes, and becomes as it were fierce from being mild, and hurtful from being delightful, though in itself it remains the same as it was. That also is called the will of God which He does in the heart of those who obey His commandments; and of this the apostle says, "For it is God that worketh in you both to will." As God's "righteousness" is used not only of the righteousness wherewith He Himself is righteous, but also of that which He produces in the man whom He justifies, so also that is called His law, which, though given by God, is rather the law of men. For certainly they were men to whom Jesus said, "It is written in your law," though in another place we read, "The law of his God is in his heart." According to this will which God works in men, He is said also to will what He Himself does not will, but causes His people to will; as He is said to know what He has caused those to know who were ignorant of it. For when the apostle says, "But now, after that ye have known God, or rather are known of God," we cannot suppose that God there for the first time knew those who were foreknown by Him before the foundation of the world; but He is said to have known them then, because then He caused them to know. According to this will, then, by which we say that God wills what He causes to be willed by others, from whom the future is hidden, He wills many things which He does not perform. . . .

But if we speak of that will of His which is eternal as His foreknowledge, certainly He has already done all things in heaven and on earth that He has willed — not only past and present things, but even things still future. But before the arrival of that time in which He has willed the occurrence of what He foreknew and arranged before all time, we say, It will happen when God wills. But if we are ignorant not only of the time in which it is to be, but even whether it shall be at all, we say, It will happen if God wills — not because God will then have a new will which He had not before, but because that event, which from eternity has been prepared in His unchangeable will, shall then come to pass.

Selections from "Confessions of St. Augustine" are from
A Select Library of the Nicene and Post-Nicene Fathers of the Christian Church,
Philip Schaff, D.D., LL.D., editor,
Volume I, Buffalo: The Christian Literature Company, 1886
Selections from "The Enchiridion" are from
St. Augustine, The Enchiridion on Faith, Hope and Love,
Henry Paolucci,
A Gateway Edition, Chicago: Henry Regnery Company, 1961
Selections from "The City of God" are from
Basic Writings of St. Augustine,
Whitney J. Oakes,
Volume Two, New York: Random House, 1948

Chapter 31 • St. Vincent of Lérins: *A Commonitory, Chapter XXIII*

As a young man, Vincent (d. ca. 450) was active in social, political, and military affairs. Later he became a monk at the monastery of St. Honorat near Cannes. His *Commonitories* were reminders that he wrote to himself in order to understand more clearly the teachings of the Church which were threatened and undermined at the time. His intention is "to describe what our ancestors have handed down and entrusted to us" (Chapter I). In order to remain secure in the integrity of faith, he was counseled to "fortify that faith . . . by the authority of the divine law . . . [and] by the tradition of the Catholic Church" (Chapter II). That tradition is summarily stated as involving what has been believed "everywhere, always, and by all" (Chapter III). The thirty-three chapters contain a simple presentation of the teachings of the Church and show a vast acquaintance with the Scriptures and writings of the orthodox, heretical, and schismatic authors. He fights against modernism and change while advocating progress in the development of the faith in such a way that he had a great appeal to Cardinal Newman when he was dealing with the same problem in his *Essay on the Development of Christian Doctrine*. The quoted chapter is very pertinent to some of the contemporary problems in the Church.

A Commonitory
Chapter XXIII

But, perhaps some one will say: Will there be endured, therefore, no progress of religion in the Church of Christ? Evidently such advancement must be had, and the very utmost advancement. For who is so envious of man and so odious to God, as to attempt to forbid that? but, nevertheless, it must be so, that it be a true progress, and not a change of faith, since it belongs to progress that each thing be enlarged into itself, but to change, that one thing be altered into another. Let, therefore, the understanding, the knowledge, the wisdom, as well of individuals as of all, as well of one man as of the entire Church, according to the degrees of ages and centuries, increase as it ought, and advance much and strenuously; but let it be all the while in its own kind, that is to say, in the same dogma, in the same sense, in the same opinion. Let the religion of the souls imitate the principle of the bodies, which, although in the course of years they develop and unfold their qualities, still remain the same as they were. There is a great difference between the bloom of boyhood and the maturity of old age. But they are the very same individuals who had been youths that become old men; and although the condition and habit of one and the same man be changed, nevertheless he is one and the same nature, one and the same person. As many as are the limbs of the infant, so many are the limbs of the man, and if there be any of those matters which are produced in periods of mature age, they were already implanted in the principle of the seed; so that nothing is afterwards produced in the old man which had not previously lain concealed in the boy. Whence it is not doubtful that this is the legitimate and right rule of advancing, this the admitted and most beautiful order of increase, if the proper period of the age discovers always those parts and forms in adults which the wisdom of the Creator had originally woven into it. Should the human form afterwards be altered into some appearance not of its own kind, it is assuredly necessary that something be added to the number of the limbs, or that something be withdrawn from them, so that either the whole body be lost, or becomes monstrous, or certainly is weakened. Thus also is it fitting that the dogma of the Christian religion follow those laws of progress — that is, that it be consolidated by years, that it be developed by time, that it be raised in height by age, but that it still remain incorrupt and untouched, and that it be full and perfect, with all the dimensions of its parts, and as it were with its own senses and members, so that it admit nothing farther of change, and sustain no loss of identity, no variation of definition.

For example, our ancestors anciently sowed in the crop of the Church the seeds of wheaten faith; it is very unjust and incongruous that we, their descendants, should gather, instead of the real truth of wheat, the substituted error of tares. But this rather is right and consistent, that the beginnings and the endings not differing from each other, we should reap from the increase of wheaten institution the fruit of wheaten dogma: so that, when anything be developed from the origin of those seeds, let it now also rejoice and be cultivated; nevertheless let nothing be changed from the character of the germ: although appearance, form, and distinction be added, let the nature, however, of each kind remain. For, far be it from us that rose-gardens of Catholic doctrine be changed into thistles and thorns. Forbid it, that in this spiritual paradise cockle and aconites come from the suckers of cinnamon and balsam. Whatever, therefore, in this Church of God, has been sown by the agricultural faith of the fathers, let this same be cultivated and respected by the industry of the sons; let the same flourish and ripen; let the same advance and be advanced. For it is lawful that those ancient dogmas of Heavenly philosophy be made accurate, and filed and polished by the course of time; but it is criminal that they be changed, criminal that they be lopped; criminal that they be mutilated. It is allowable for them to receive evidence, light, and distinctness, but they must retain their fullness, their integrity, their propriety. For, if once this license of impious fraud be admitted, I shudder to say how great a danger follows of cutting down and abolishing religion. For any part of a Catholic dogma being abandoned, another also, and likewise another, and then another and another, as if, according to custom and lawfully, will be abandoned. But then the parts *of the* dogma being repudiated one by one, what else follows at the end, but that the entire be repudiated in the same way? But also, on the other hand, if new *doctrine* begin to be mingled with old, foreign with native, and profane with sacred, it is inevitable that this custom must creep forward over the entire world, so that afterwards in the Church nothing will be left untouched, nothing unprofaned, nothing entire, nothing immaculate, but that in the same place henceforward will be the brothel of impious and disgraceful errors, where was before the sanctuary of chaste and incorrupt truth. But may the divine mercy avert this wickedness from the minds of His own children; let this rather be the madness of the impious. But the Church of Christ, the lawful and cautious guardian of the dogmas deposited with her, never changes anything in them, diminishes nothing, adds nothing, does not cut off what is necessary, does not lay on what is superfluous, does not lose what are hers, does not adopt what belong to strangers, but with all her industry aims at this one thing, that by faithfully and wisely handling ancient *doctrines*, if there be any of them unshapen and merely inchoate, she may make them accurate, and polish them; if there be any already expressed and declared, she may consolidate them; if there be any already confirmed and defined, she may guard them. In fine, what else did she ever labor *to accomplish* by the decrees of councils, than that what formerly was simply believed, should afterwards be more diligently believed; that what previously was laxly preached, should afterwards be more urgently preached; than that what had previously been cultivated with more freedom from apprehension, the same should afterwards be cultivated with more anxiety? This one thing I affirm, did the Catholic Church, when stirred up by the novelties of heretics, accomplish by the decrees of her councils, and nothing besides; unless that what she had originally received from the fathers by tradition only, that she should consign to her descendants by the handwriting of letters; by including a great sum of matters in a few letters, and for the most part, for sake of clearness of understanding, by marking with the distinction of a new title the not new meaning of faith.

Selections from "The Commonitory" are from
The Fathers, Historians, and Writers of the Church,
W.B. Kelly, Dublin, 1864

Chapter 32 • *The Confiteor*

The *Confiteor* is first heard of as the preparation for sacramental confession and as part of the preparation for Mass. In some form it was one of the private prayers said by the celebrant in the sacristy before he began Mass. In the tenth and eleventh centuries there are references to the fact that the priest recited such a prayer at the foot of the altar before Mass. Since the edition of Pius V (1566-1572), our present form is the only one used throughout the Roman Rite, except for some missals of religious orders.

Confiteor

I confess to Almighty God, to blessed Mary ever Virgin, to blessed Michael the Archangel, to blessed John the Baptist, the holy Apostles Peter and Paul, and all the saints, that I have sinned exceedingly in thought, word, and deed, through my fault, through my fault, through my most grievous fault. Therefore I beseech the blessed Mary ever Virgin, blessed Michael the Archangel, blessed John the Baptist, the holy Apostles, Peter and Paul, and all the saints, to pray to the Lord our God for me.

May the Almighty God have mercy on me, and forgive me my sins, and bring me to everlasting life. Amen.

May the Almighty and merciful Lord grant me pardon, absolution, and remission of all my sins. Amen.

The complete *Confiteor* can be found in many places, including
The New Baltimore Catechism,
No. 1, Official Revised Edition,
Benziger Brothers, 1941

Part V
Philosophical Perspectives and Basic Mysticism

Introduction

The writings here span the period from the latter half of the fifth century A.D. to the middle of the twelfth century. They deal with Christian mysticism, speculative theology in both the East and West, Western monasticism, and homiletics.

The influence of Dionysius the Pseudo-Areopagite on Western mysticism is obvious when one realizes how many knew of his writings and utilized them in dealing with the ascent of the soul to God and with the choice of names to express the ineffable nature of God.

This section also contains works that carry on the tradition of explaining the Trinity and Unity of God from philosophical perspectives. Boethius is known not only for his distinction of the various scientific approaches to knowledge that are found in his *De Trinitate*, but also for his development of many concepts, with their Latin definitions, for an understanding of basic Christian principles. His famous definition of a person as "an individual substance of a rational nature" can help to clarify contemporary confusion between the philosophico-theological understanding of a person and the modern psychological usage of the word "person" to refer to an acquired, variable characteristic or set of characteristics.

St. Benedict was instrumental in the perpetuation of classical learning when he established the monastery of Monte Cassino the same year that Justinian closed the schools of Athens. It is common knowledge that St. Thomas Aquinas spent his early ages as an oblate at this monastery. Benedict emphasized the value of learning for the development of Christianity, as did many of the people referred to in Part III of this collection.

St. John of Damascus made a great contribution by explaining the basic teachings of Catholicism to the Muslims, as did many Dominicans who were helped by St. Thomas Aquinas's treatise *On the Truth of the Catholic Faith*.

St. Bernard is well-known for his preaching for a Crusade and his differences with Abélard. His *Sermons* illustrate the depth of his mystical love of God.

Chapter 33 • Dionysius the Pseudo-Areopagite: *The Mystical Theology*; Letters

Very little is known about the fifth-century author of *The Mystical Theology, The Celestial Hierarchy, The Divine Names, The Ecclesiastical Hierarchy*, and various letters attributed to him. It has been generally agreed, at least after the time of Hilduin, abbot of the monastery of St. Denis in Paris, who was called to the Court School by Louis the Pious (c. 820) and translated these writings into Latin, that they were not the works of Dionysius the Areopagite. Hilduin had claimed them to be those of the Dionysius who had been converted by St. Paul in the Areopagus of Athens and who was the patron saint of the monastery of St. Denis. Internal evidence relative to the Neoplatonism of Proclus (c. 411-485) and references to people living at a later date, has convinced scholars that this person is not Dionysius the Areopagite. Some call him the Pseudo-Dionysius, but since his name could have been Dionysius, it may be better to designate him as Dionysius the Pseudo-Areopagite.

The works of this individual were instrumental in the popularization of the negative and positive theology of the Divine Names in the works of Maximus the Confessor (c. 580-662), John Scotus Eriugena (c. 810-c. 877), Bernard of Clairvaux (1090-1153), Richard of St. Victor (c. 1123-1173), St. Bonaventure (c. 1217-1274), St. Thomas Aquinas (1225-1274), St. Teresa of Ávila (1515-1582), St. John of the Cross (1542-1591), and others. There were also medieval Latin translations by John Scotus Eriugena, John the Saracen (twelfth century), and Robert Grosseteste (1175-1253).

John Duns Scotus (the Scot) is called Eriugena by some, but if Eriugena is a combined form of the old Irish word for Ireland (Eriu) and of part of the Greek word for born (gero), John may be claiming to be a Scot born in Ireland.

Mystical Theology

Chapter I

What the Divine Darkness Is

Most exalted Trinity, Divinity above all knowledge, whose goodness passes understanding, who dost guide Christians to divine wisdom; direct our way to the summit of thy mystical oracles, most incomprehensible, most lucid and most exalted, where the simple and pure and unchangeable mysteries of theology are revealed in the darkness, clearer than light, of that silence in which secret things are hidden; a darkness that shines brighter than light, that invisibly and intangibly illuminates with splendors of inconceivable beauty the soul that sees not. Let this be my prayer; but do thou, dear Timothy, diligently giving thyself to mystical contemplation, leave the senses, and the operations of the intellect, and all things sensible and intelligible, and things that are and things that are not, that thou mayest rise as may be lawful for thee, by ways above knowledge to union with Him who is above all knowledge and all being; that in freedom and abandonment for all, thou mayest be borne, through pure, entire and absolute abstraction of thyself from all things, into the supernatural radiance of the divine darkness.

But see that none of the uninitiated hear these things. I mean those who cleave to created things, and suppose not that anything exists after a supernatural manner, above nature; but imagine that by their own natural understanding they know Him who has made darkness His secret place. But if the principles of the divine mysteries are above the understanding of these, what is to be said of those yet more untaught, who call the absolute First Cause of all after the lowest things in nature, and say that He is in no way above the images which they fashion after various designs; of whom they should declare and affirm that in Him as the cause of all, is all that may be predicated positively of created things; while yet they might with more propriety deny these predicates to Him, as being far above all; holding that here denial is not contrary to affirmation, since He is infinitely above all notion of deprivation, and above all affirmation and negation.

Chapter II

How to Be United With, and to Give Praise to Him Who Is the Cause of All Things and Above All

We desire to abide in this most luminous darkness, and without sight or knowledge, to see that which is above sight or knowledge, by means of that very fact that we see not and know not. For this is truly to see and know, to praise Him who is above nature in a manner above nature, by the abstraction of all that is natural. It is needful, as I think, to make this abstraction in a manner precisely opposite to that in which we deal with the Divine attributes; for we add them together, beginning with the primary ones, and passing from them to the secondary, and so the last; but here we ascend from the last to the first, abstracting all, so as to unveil and know that which is beyond knowledge, and which in all things is hidden from our sight by that which can be known, and so to behold that supernatural darkness which is hidden by all such light as is in created things.

Chapter III

What Is Affirmed of God, and What Is Denied of Him

In our Outlines of Theology we have declared those matters which are properly the subject of Positive Theology; in what sense the holy divine nature is one, and in what sense three; what it is that is there called Paternity, and what Filiation; and what the doctrine of the Holy Spirit signifies; how from the uncreated and undivided good those blessed and perfect Lights have come forth, yet remained one with the divine nature, with each other, and in themselves, undivided by coeternal abiding in propagation; how Jesus though immaterial became material in the truth of human nature; and other things taken from Scripture we have expounded in the same place. Again in the *Book of Divine Names* (we have shown) how God is called Good, how Being, how Life and Wisdom and Virtue, with other names spiritually applied to Him. Then in the treatise of *Symbolical Theology* we saw what names have been transferred to Him from sensible things — what is meant by the divine forms and figures, limbs, instruments, localities, adornments, fury, anger and grief; drunkenness, oaths and curses, sleep and waking, with other modes of sacred and symbolical nomenclature. I think you will have understood why the last are more diffuse than the first; for the exposition of theological doctrine and the explanation of the divine names are necessarily shorter than the treatise on symbolism. Because in proportion as we ascend higher our speech is contracted to the limits of our view of the purely intelligible; and so now, when we enter that darkness which is above understanding, we pass not merely into brevity of speech, but even into absolute silence, and the negation of thought. Thus in the other treatise our subject took us from the highest to the lowest, and in the measure of this descent our treatment of it extended itself; whereas now we rise from beneath to that which is the highest, and accordingly our speech is restrained in proportion to the height of our ascent; but when our ascent is accomplished, speech will cease altogether, and be absorbed into the ineffable. But why, you will ask, do we add in the first and begin to abstract in the last? The reason is that we affirmed that which is above all affirmation by comparison with that which is most nearly related to it, and were therefore compelled to make a *hypothetical* affirmation; but when we abstract that which is above all abstraction, we must distinguish it also from those things which are most remote from it. Is not God more nearly life and goodness than air or a stone; must we not deny more fully that He is drunken or enraged, than that He can be spoken of or understood?

Chapter IV
That He Who Is the Supreme Cause of All Sensible Things Is Himself No Part of Those Things

SUMMARY. — The Creator is not a mere lifeless and unintelligible abstraction; yet He is wholly distinct from all forms of sensible existence.

Chapter V
That He Who Is the Supreme Cause of All Intelligible Things Is Himself No Part of Those Things

SUMMARY — The Creator is distinct from all merely intelligible forms of existence, being neither one of them nor all of them together.

Letter I
To Caius the Monk

Darkness is destroyed by light, especially by much light; ignorance is destroyed by knowledge, especially by much knowledge. You must understand this as implying not privation, but transcendence; and so you must say with absolute truth, that the ignorance which is of God is unknown by those who have the created light and the knowledge of created things, and that His transcendent darkness is obscured by any light, and itself obscures all knowledge. And if any one, seeing God, knows what he sees, it is by no means God that he so sees, but something created and knowable. For God abides above created intellect and existence and is known above all power of knowledge. Thus the knowledge of Him who is above all that can be known is for the most part ignorance.

Letter II

How can He who is beyond all things be also above the very principle of divinity and of goodness? By divinity and goodness must be understood the essence of the gift which makes us good and divine, or that unapproachable semblance of the supreme goodness and divinity whereby we also are made good and divine. For since this is the principle of deification and sanctification for those who are so deified and sanctified, then He who is the essential principle of all principles (and therefore the principle of divinity and goodness) is above that divinity and goodness by means of which we are made good and divine: moreover, since He is inimitable and incomprehensible, He is above imitation and comprehension as He is above those who imitate and partake of Him.

Letter V

To Dorotheus the Deacon

The divine darkness is the inaccessible light in which God is said to dwell. And since He is invisible by reason of the abundant outpouring of supernatural light, it follows that whosoever is counted worthy to know and see God, by the very fact that he neither sees nor knows Him, attains to that which is above sight and knowledge, and at the same time perceives that God is beyond all things both sensible and intelligible, saying with the Prophet, "Thy knowledge is become wonderful to me; it is high, and I cannot reach to it." In like manner, St. Paul, we are told, knew God, when he knew Him to be above all knowledge and understanding; wherefore he says that His ways are unsearchable and His judgments inscrutable, His gifts unspeakable, and His peace passing all understanding; as one who had found Him who is above all things, and whom he had perceived to be above knowledge, and separate from all things, being the Creator of all.

Selections from "The Mystical Theology" and letter are from
Mysticism: Its True Nature and Value,
with a translation of the "Mystical Theology" of Dionysius,
and of the Letters to Caius and Dorotheus
A.B. Sharpe, M .A.,
London: Sands and Company; St. Louis: B. Herder, 1910

Chapter 34 • Boethius: *On the Trinity*

Anicius Manlius Torquatus Severinus Boethius (ca. 475/80-525) is considered by some as one of the founders of the Middle Ages and the first scholastic. He received the best education available at Athens, and planned to make available to the Latin world the best of the ancient Greek philosophy in translation. Most people know him for his *Consolation of Philosophy*, written while he was in prison awaiting execution on a trumped-up charge of treason against Theodoric. He was a source of the logic of Aristotle for the later Middle Ages. The following work is a classic treatise in Christian Theology in which Boethius attempts to interpret the doctrine of the Trinity in accord with the philosophical teaching of Aristotle in the *Categories*. It is interesting to compare Boethius's treatment with other similar ones in this collection. A part of the commentary of St. Thomas Aquinas on this treatise received wide circulation in scholastic circles. Among the many works Boethius wrote, there is another theological treatise that contributed much to an understanding of the union of the divine and human natures in Christ. In his *On the Person and Two Natures in Christ,* he emphasizes that the word "persona" (person) does not refer to an acquired, variable, and accidental characteristic, as found in some contemporary writings in psychology, psychiatry, and sociology, but rather to the individual substance of an intellectual or rational nature. This understanding of person as identical with the individual human being is important for the conviction that a human embryo and/or human fetus is a human person in the substantial/essential order.

On the Trinity

Chapter One

The Catholic Teaching about the Trinity and Unity of God

The teaching of this faith about the unity of the Trinity is this: the Father is God, the Son is God, the Holy Spirit is God; hence Father, Son and Holy Spirit are one God and not three gods. The basis of this union is a lack of difference. For difference is employed by those who either add to or substract from the Trinity, like the Arians who divide it according to degrees of merit and reduce it to a plurality. For the principle of plurality is otherness and plurality cannot be understood except in terms of otherness.

The difference of three or any number of things can be reckoned either as generic, specific, or numerical; but a variety of accidents makes for a difference in number; for three men do not differ in genus or species but because of their accidents.

Chapter Two
The Divine Substance Is Form

Let us begin now and investigate each thing insofar as it can be understood and grasped. For, as it seems to have been well said, it is the task of an educated man to attempt to understand each thing in accordance with the way it is.

There are three parts of speculative science: 1) *natural*, which considers things in motion and not abstracted from matter; 2) *mathematical* which considers its object without motion and not abstracted because it considers the forms of bodies without matter and therefore without motion; yet these forms, since they are in matter, cannot be separated from it; 3) *theological*, without motion, abstract, and separable, for the substance of God lacks both matter and motion. Therefore we should consider natural things by reasoning, mathematicals by discipline, and theological matters by understanding. In the latter our attention should not be diverted to images in the imagination but rather consider that form itself which is truly form and not an image and which is being itself and that from which being comes. For all being is from form.

The divine substance is form without matter and so is one and is that which is. Other things are not that which they are for each one has its being from the beings of which it is constituted, i.e. from its parts; and it is this *and* this., i.e. its parts as conjoined, and not this or that singly. For example, earthy man is composed of soul and body, body *and* soul is, not body *or* soul. Hence that which is not from a part. What is not composed of this *and* this but only this, that really is that which is. And it is the most beautiful and the most powerful because it needs nothing. Wherefore this is truly one in which there is no number; nothing is in it other than that which is; nor can it be a subject for it is form and forms cannot be subjects.

Therefore there is no diversity in Him, no plurality as a result of diversity, no multitude because of accidents and for this reason no number.

Chapter Three
There Is No Number in the Divine Substance

Indeed, God is identical with God; He is not diverse either by accidents or by accidental differences found in a subject. But where there is not difference there is no plurality at all, therefore not a plurality of number; hence only unity.

If "God" is predicated three times as of Father, Son, and Holy Spirit, this triple predication does not designate many numerically. However this is implied by those who distinguish between them according to merit. It appears otherwise to Catholics when they set up a lack of difference and consider the form to be itself as form and to be nothing else than that which is. It is rightly a repetition of the same rather than an enumeration of the diverse when it is said, "The Father is God, the Son is God and the Holy Spirit is God and this trinity is one God," just as blade and brand is said to be one sword or "sun," "sun" indicate one sun.

Let this be for the time being sufficient to signify and demonstrate why every repetition of units does not indicate number and plurality. However when "Father," "Son," and "Holy Spirit" are spoken this does not indicate merely a verbal difference just as "blade" and "brand" are really but different words for the same thing. Father and Son and Holy Spirit are the same but they are not identical. Let us consider this for a while. When it is asked, "is the Father identical with the Son?", it is answered, "By no means." Again, "Is the one the same as the other?," the answer is negative. Therefore there is not between them a complete lack of difference. Thus number, which was explained above as due to a diversity of subjects, does apply. This will be considered briefly after we have treated of the way in which each thing is predicated of God.

Chapter Four

How God Is Classified According to the Categories

There are ten categories which are predicated universally of all things, i.e., substance, quality, quantity, relation, where, when, possession, position, action and passion. These are such as their subjects permit, for one of them is predicated as substance and the others are accidents. But when anyone attempts to use them as predicates of God they are changed completely. Relation cannot be predicated at all because substance in God is not truly substance but supersubstance. Likewise quality and the others which can be employed. Of these examples are provided to insure that they are understood. For when we say, "God" we seem to indicate a substance but one which is supersubstantial, just as when we say this: "He is just," just is a quality, but not an accidental one since it is substantial and supersubstantial. For God is not something different from justice but to be God is the same as to be just. Likewise when God is called great or greatest we seem to indicate quantity but the quantity which is the substance itself which we say is supersubstantial. It is the same to be God and to be great. Of His form it was shown before that He is form and truly one without any plurality. The categories are such that they indicate that things are as stated by the category applied. In other things they indicate division; in God conjunction and union in this fashion, for when we say that something, as God or man, is a substance, we predicate substance as if God or man is a substance. Yet there is a difference since a man is not entirely substance itself and so not substance. What he is involves things which are not man; but God is everything that He is; He is nothing but what He is and through this itself God is. Again we consider "just" as a quality as if it is the same as the subject of predication, i.e. if we say, "a just man" or "a just God" we say that the man himself or God is just. But there is a difference since man is one thing and just another, but God is the same as the just. Also man or God is called great as if man himself is great or God himself is great. But man alone is great whereas God is greatness itself. The rest of the categories are predicated neither of God nor of other things. For *where* can be predicated either of God or of man; of man, *as in the market place*, of God as *everywhere*. But in neither case is the predicate identical with the subject of predication. For man is not said to be in the market place in the same way as he is said to be white or long nor as it were circumscribed and determined by some property by which he can be designated in himself, but this category indicates only that the thing is related to other things. Of God it is not the same. For when He is said to be everywhere this does not mean He is in every place (actually He cannot be *in* a place in any way) but that every place is present to Him for occupation though He is not received in a place; and thus He is never said to be in a place since He is everywhere but not *in* a place.

When is predicated in the same way: it is said of a man that he came *yesterday*, of God that He is *always*. Here the predicate yesterday is not the same as the one said to have come but the predicate refers to him according to a temporal relationship. But when God is said to be always He is referred to as present to all past, present, and future time, which is said by some philosophers of the heavens and other immortal bodies. But it is not the same of God, for He is always, because the always of the present is in God. There is this difference between the present of our time, which is *now* and the divine present; our *now* by flowing makes time and sempiternity, whereas the divine now is permanent, not moving and unmoveable and it constitutes eternity. If you add "always" (*semper*) to "eternity" you get the continual, unceasing and perpetual flow of *now* which is called sempiternity.

Again to have or to do are considered in a similar fashion. We say of man that he runs or is clothed, of God that He rules possessing all things. Again nothing substantial is said in either case.

Likewise when I say "he runs or rules" or "he is now or always" there is a reference to action or time, if that divine always can be called time, but not to that by which something is, as the great is great by magnitude. Position and passion cannot be predicated of God nor can possession. Is it now clear what is the difference of the categories? Is it clear that some point out the things, as it were, whereas others refer to the circumstances, as it were? The former are truly predicated to reveal what a thing is: the latter do not refer to the being of the thing but rather relate to something somehow extrinsic. Those which designate anything to be something really are called predications; those which indicate something about subjects are called real accidents. Since God is not a subject the only real predication is designated as substance.

Chapter Five
How God Is in the Category of Relation

Let us speculate now about *relatives*. Everything said so far has been leading up to this discussion. The essence of relation does not consist in the fact that it is, but it consists rather in some sort of comparison; not always in reference to another but sometimes in regard to itself.

Wherefore if the Father and Son are said to be *relations* and they do not differ in any way than by *relation*, the *relation* does not make them different things because "relation" is not predicated of anything as if the *relation* were a real thing and so does not make that of which it is predicated an alterity of things; but rather, if it can be expressed at all, it indicates in what way that which can scarcely be understood is considered a variety of persons. For it is a supreme rule of truth that in incorporeal things diversity is due to differences and not to diverse locations. Nor can it be said that something happened to God so that He became Father, for He never began to be Father, because the production of the Son is substantial, though the predication of "Father" is relative. And if we recall all the prior statements concerning God we think of God the Son proceeding from God the Father and the Holy Spirit from both. These are incorporeal and thus do not differ locally. But since the Father is God, the Son is God and the Holy Spirit is God, and God has no differences by which He differs from God, He differs from none of them. But where differences are lacking there is no plurality; where there is no plurality there is unity. Nothing other than God could be generated from God and a repetition of units in numerable things does not constitute a plurality in every case. Hence the unity of the three is suitably established.

Chapter Six
How God in One and Three

But since no relation can refer to the same thing itself and since what is predicated absolutely lacks relation, the multitude of the Trinity is expressed by the predication of relation whereas the unity is due to a lack of difference of substance or of operation or of what is predicated absolutely. Thus the category of substance indicates the unity, relation indicates the Trinity and so only those things are spoken of each separately which are relative. For the Father is not the same as the Son nor are each the same as the Holy Spirit, yet Father and Son and Holy Spirit are the same God. They are the same as just, as good, as great, as everything that can be predicated absolutely.

Certainly we must understand that a relative predication is not always such that the predication involves different things, as in the case of servant relative to master, who are different things. For every equal is equal to the equal and like is like the like and the same is same with the same. The relation of Father to the Son and of each to the Holy Spirit is similar in the Trinity in that it is a relation of the same to the same. And if this cannot be found in all other things that is because of the difference that is known to exist in perishable things. We must accept whatever can be understood by the intellect itself and not be led astray by imagination. . . .

Selections from "On the Trinity" are from
Patrologiae cursus completus,
J-P. Migne,
Translated for this volume by Theodore E. James, Ph.D.,
Series Latina, Volume 64, Paris, 1844

Chapter 35 • St. Benedict: Rule of St. Benedict

There is no doubt but that this treatise is a classic of Catholicism in the area of religious discipline and ascetic practice. It represents the generally accepted mode of conduct for Christian monks of the West. St. Benedict (ca. 480-ca. 543) was born near Nursia in Italy about 480. He studied in Rome, and then decided to withdraw into solitude as a recluse. Though his establishment at Subiaco preceded it, the first truly Benedictine monastery was founded at Monte Cassino about 529. The chief rule of Western monasticism is a realistic, personal, and common-sense product of Benedict's experience as a monk, though he does admit that he is indebted to "The Rule of our holy father Basil." The Rule consists of a Prologue and seventy-three chapters dealing with all aspects of monastic life.

Rule of St. Benedict

Prologue

Listen, my son, to the counsel of the master and pay attention; willingly accept and advantageously fulfill the advice of a devoted father that you may return through the difficulty of obedience to him from whom you have withdrawn because of the idleness of a lack of obedience. First of all, whenever you begin a good work as him (Christ) with most insistent prayer that he bring it to perfection. . . . With our loins girded with faith and good works let us go forward in his way with the guidance of the Gospels in order that we may merit to see him who has called us to his kingdom. . . . We are going to set up a school for the Lord's service in which we hope there will be nothing that is too hard or difficult.

Chapter I

The Kinds of Monks

It is clear that there are four kinds of monks. The first is the Cenobites, that is those who abide in monasteries and serve under a rule and an abbot. The second are the Anchorites or Hermits who, not in the first fervor of religious life but after long periods of trial in a monastery, . . . go out well prepared for the battle to the solitary combat of the desert. The third kind is that of the hateful Sarabaites who have not been tested by any rule or experience and are as soft as lead. They still follow the standards of the world. . . . Their norm of conduct is their own good pleasure. . . . The fourth kind are called Gyrovagues who spend their whole lives traveling from monastery to monastery given up to their own desires and the enticements of gluttony. . . . Let us be concerned to set up a way of life for the Cenobites.

Chapter II
What the Abbot Should Be Like

An abbot who is worthy to rule over a monastery should remember his name and act accordingly. He is considered to hold the place of Christ in the community since he is given the name by the Apostle: "You have received the spirit of adoption of sons in which we cry out, Abba, Father." Thus the abbot ought not to teach or decide or order anything contrary to the law of God, God forbid, but his orders or teachings should be infused into the minds of his disciples like the leaven of divine justice. . . . Let him make no distinction of person in the monastery. He should not love one more than another unless he excels in good deeds and obedience. . . . He must accommodate himself to circumstances, using at one time severity and at another persuasive advice, showing now the rigor of a master and then again displaying the loving-kindness of a father. . . . Let him always remember that he has taken over the care of souls and will have to give an accounting of them.

Chapter III
Of Calling the Brethren to Council

As often as matters of importance have to be considered in the monastery let the abbot summon the whole community and let him put forward the question that has arisen. Then, after hearing the advice of the brethren let him weigh it over by himself and do what he shall judge most fitting. Now we have said that all should be summoned to take counsel for this reason that it is often to the younger that the Lord reveals what is best. But let the brethren give advice with all humility so as not to presume obstinately to defend their own opinions; rather let the matter depend on the abbot's judgment so that all should submit to whatever he decides as best. Yet just as it is right for disciples to obey their master, so it behooves him to order all things with prudence and justice. In all things let all follow the Rule as their master and let no one deviate from it without good reason. Let no one in the monastery follow his own desires, and let no one boldly presume to dispute with his abbot whether within or outside the monastery. . . . The abbot should do everything in the fear of the Lord and in observance of the Rule knowing that he will really have to give an account to God for all his decisions as to a most just judge. If it happens that matters of less moment have to be decided, let him avail himself of the advice of the seniors only. . . .

Chapter IV
The Instruments of Good Works

First of all love the Lord God with your whole heart, your whole soul and your whole strength. Then love your neighbor as yourself. Then do not kill; do not commit adultery; do not steal; do not covet; do not bear false witness; honor all men; do not do onto others what you do not wish to be done to you; deny yourself in order to follow Christ; chastise the body; do not seek an easy life; love fasting; help the poor; clothe the naked; visit the sick; bury the dead; assist the afflicted; comfort the sorrowing; avoid pagan conduct; prefer nothing to the love of Christ; do not give in to anger; do not keep a grudge; do not keep revenge in your heart; do not make a false peace; do not forsake charity; do not swear lest you perjure yourself; speak truth from the mouth and the heart; do not return evil for evil; wrong no one and bear the wrongs of others patiently; love your enemies; do not curse those who curse you but bless them; bear persecution for the sake of justice; do not be proud; don't be a wine-bibber; don't be a glutton; don't be a sleepyhead; don't be lazy; don't be a grumbler; don't be a detractor; trust in God; whatever good you see in yourself, attribute to God; know that evil is always done by you and blame yourself for it; fear the day of Judgment; abhor hell; desire eternal life with all spiritual longing; keep death daily before your eyes; be vigilant over all your actions; know that God sees you everywhere; when evil thoughts come, dash them on the rock of Christ and reveal them to your spiritual advisor; avoid evil and unbecoming talk, don't love loquacity; don't speak vain or frivolous words; don't love too much or excessive laughter; listen to holy reading with delight; apply yourself to frequent prayer; confess your sins daily with tears and sighs: amend your evil actions for the future; do not fulfill the desires of the flesh; despise Your own self-will; obey the commands of the abbot in all things even though, God forbid, he should act differently, keeping in mind the counsel of the Lord, "What they say, do ye; but what they do, do ye not"; do not desire to be considered holy before you really are but be it beforehand and then you may be more truly considered holy; keep the commandments of God every day; love chastity; hate no one; don't be jealous; don't give in to envy; do not love contention; avoid vainglory; respect the elderly; love the young; out of love for Christ pray for your enemies; make peace with your adversary before sundown; never despair of God's mercy. . . .

Chapter VI
Silence

. . . Because of the great value of silence permission to speak should be granted rarely. . . . As for buffoonery and vain and idle talk such is condemned. . . .

Chapter VII
Humility

The first grade of humility is to keep the fear of God always before you; let him be ever mindful of the commandments of God. . . . And watchful and guarding himself from sins and vices . . . let him remember that God is always watching him from heaven. . . . The second grade of humility is that a man love not his own will nor delight in satisfying his own desires but carry out . . . the will of God. The third grade of humility is for a man to submit himself to his superior in all obedience for the love of God. . . . The fourth grade of humility is that one should patiently bear all hard and contrary things done to him, even injuries, out of obedience. . . . The fifth grade of humility is to hide from the abbot no evil thoughts that bother you nor the sins committed in secret but confess them in all humility. . . . The sixth grade of humility is to be contented with the meanest and worst of everything. . . . The seventh grade of humility is not only to call himself lower and viler than all but to really believe himself to be. The eighth grade of humility is to do nothing but what is authorized by the common rule of the monastery or the example of his seniors. The ninth grade of humility is for a monk to refrain from speaking and keep silent unless a question be asked him. The tenth grade of humility is not to be easily moved and prompted to laughter. . . . The eleventh grade of humility is that when a monk speaks he do so gently and humbly and seriously and without laughter. . . . The twelfth grade of humility is that a monk should not only be humble in his heart but show it in all his behavior.

Chapter XXXIX
The Amount of Food

We consider it sufficient, on account of individual disabilities, that there be two cooked dishes for the daily meal . . . if any fruit or tender vegetables are available, let there be a third dish. Let one pound of bread suffice for a day. . . . Above all things avoid excess because nothing is so completely foreign to a Christian as excess. . . .

Chapter XLVIII
On Daily Manual Labor

Idleness is inimical to the soul, so the brethren should be occupied in manual labor at certain times and at others in spiritual reading. [There follow details about the work to be performed at various hours and at different seasons of the year.]

Chapter LIII
Reception of Guests

Let all guests be received as Christ. . . . Let suitable honor be shown to all but especially to pilgrims and members of the household of the faith. When a guest is announced let him be met by the prior or some of the brethren with every sign of charity and let them pray together and be united in peace. . . . The prior may break his fast for a guest unless it happens to be a special day of fast which cannot be broken; but the lifting of the fast does not apply to the brethren. . . . Let special care and concern be shown the poor and pilgrims because in them Christ is received most of all. . . .

Chapter LXIV
The Election of the Abbot

As regards the election of the abbot this rule must always be followed, namely that he is to be made abbot who is elected by the whole community, according to the fear of God, or even by a small part of the community provided it be done with a sounder counsel. Let him be chosen who is exemplary in merit of life and the knowledge of wisdom even if he should rank last in the order of the community. . . . Let the appointed abbot always be wary of what kind of burden he has accepted and to whom he must render an account of his stewardship; he should know that his duty is to be of help to the brethren rather than domineer them. He should be learned in the divine law . . . chaste, sober and merciful. . . . He should despise vices and love the brethren. Let him be prudent in correction and do nothing in excess . . . he should strive to be loved rather than feared. He should not be violent or vexed, too exacting or headstrong, jealous or too suspicious. . . . He should be provident and considerate in all his commands . . . discreet and temperate. . . . Above all let him safeguard the present Rule in all matters. . . .

Chapter LXV
The Prior of the Monastery

. . . Thus we have judged it expedient for the maintenance of peace and charity that the organization of the monastery be decided by the abbot himself. If it can be, let the whole business be carried on by deans as the abbot shall dispose. . . . If the needs of a place require it or if the community request it reasonably and with humility and the abbot consider it expedient, let the abbot himself with the advice of those who fear God, appoint as prior whomsoever he wishes. . . .

Chapter LXXIII
The Complete Observance of Righteousness Is Not Spelled Out in this Rule

We have written this Rule so that by observing it in monasteries we may show that we have attained in some measure both the uprightness of virtue and the beginning of the religious life. For him who would hasten to the perfection of the religious life there are, in addition, the teachings of the holy Fathers, the observation of which leads a man to the height of perfection. For what page or what utterance from the divine authority of the Old or New Testament is not a most correct norm of human life? Or what book of the holy Catholic Fathers does not resoundly proclaim how by a straight path we may reach our Creator? In addition, the Conferences of the Father and their Institutes and Lives and the Rule of our holy father Basil, what are they but instruments of virtue for good-living and obedient monks?

Selections from the "Rule of St. Benedict" were freely translated
by Theodore E. James expressly for this volume from
Sti. Benedicti: Regula Monachorum,
Cura D.P. Schmitz,
Belgium: J. Duculoti, 1946

Chapter 36 • St. Bede the Venerable: *The Passion of St. Alban and His Fellows Which Did Shed Their Blood for Christ's Sake; Homily: The Purification of the Blessed Virgin Mary*

Bede the Venerable (673-735) is honored for *The Ecclesiastical History of the English People*, but he is also considered to have been "the most skillful interpretor of the Scriptures" next to St. Gregory. The following selections are taken from both examples of his expertise.

Alban of Verulamium (d. ca. 304) was the first martyr of Britain, during the Diocletian persecution. Though a pagan, he gave shelter to a cleric, and, moved by the man's example, Alban was baptized. When the hiding place was discovered, Alban gave himself up in the cleric's place. He refused to deny his Christian faith, and was beheaded. A church and monastery were afterward erected at the spot, and the town of St. Albans grew up around it.

This account of the martyrdom is from *The Ecclesiastical History* by the Venerable Bede (673?-735), translated by Thomas Stapleton in 1565.

The Ecclesiastical History

Among others suffered Saint Alban: of whom Fortunatus priest in the book he wrote in the praise of virgins, speaking of the martyrs which from all coasts of the world came unto God, saith, *Albanum egregium faecunda Britannia profert*.

The fertile land of batfull Brittany
Bringeth forth Alban a martyr right worthy.

This Alban being yet but a pagan, when the cruel commandments of the wicked Princes were set forth against the Christians, received into his house one of the clergy which had fled from the persecutors: whom he perceiving both night and day to continue in praying and watching, being suddenly touched with the grace of God, began to follow the example of his faith and virtue, and by little and little instructed by his wholesome exhortations, forsaking his blind idolatry, became Christian with his whole heart. At length after the said person of the clergy had certain days tarried with him, it came to the ears of the Prince that this holy confessor of Christ (whose time was not yet come that God appointed for him to suffer martyrdom) lay hid in *Alban's* house. Whereupon he commanded his soldiers to search his house with all diligence. Whither when they were come, Saint Alban, appareled in his guest's and master's garments, offered himself to the soldiers, and so was brought bound unto the judge. It chanced that the judge the same time was doing sacrifice unto the devils before the altars. And when he had seen Alban, being all chafed with anger for that he feared not voluntarily to offer himself unto the soldiers and peril of death, for his guest, whom he had harbored, he commanded him to be brought before the idols of the devils, before whom he there stood. "And for so much," quoth he, "as thou hadst rather to convey away the rebel and traitor to our gods, than deliver him up unto the soldiers that he might sustain due punishment for his blasphemous despising of the gods, look what pains he should have suffered if he had been taken, the same shalt thou suffer, if thou refuse to practice the rites of our religion." But Saint Alban, which willfully had before discovered himself to the persecutors to be a Christian, little heeded the menaces of the Prince. But being thoroughly fenced with spiritual armor of grace, told him plainly to his face, that he would not obey his commandment. Then said the judge, "Of what house or stock art thou?" Alban answered: "What is that to thee of what house I am? but if thou be desirous to know of what religion I am, be it known unto thee that I am a Christian, and that I employ myself to Christian manners and exercises." Then the judge demanded him his name. "My parents," quoth he, "named me Alban: and I honor and worship the true and living God, which made all things of naught." Then the judge, being very wroth, said, "If thou wilt enjoy long life, come off, and do sacrifice unto the great god." Alban answered: "These sacrifices which you offer up unto the devils, neither help the offerers nor obtain them their desires, but rather purchase them for their reward eternal pains in hell fire." The judge, hearing this, being in a rage, commanded the holy confessor of God to be all beaten of the tormentors, thinking his constancy would relent at stripes, which refused to yield to words: but he showed himself not only patient, but also joyful in the middle of all his torments. The judge, when he saw he could be neither won with words, nor turned with torments from the religion of Christ's faith, commanded that he should be beheaded. In the way as he was led to his death, he came to a flood which, with a very swift course, ran betwixt him and the place where he should suffer. Now he saw a great company of all sexes, degrees, and ages going with him to the place of his execution, in so much that it seemed the judge was left alone at home without any to attend upon him. This company was so great, and the bridge they had to pass over so little, that it would be toward night ere they all could get over. Alban, longing much for his blessed death, and hasting to his martyrdom, coming to the river's side and making there his prayer with lifting up his eyes and heart to heaven, saw forthwith the bottom to have been dried up, and the water give place for him and the people to pass over dryshod as it were upon even ground. Which when among other the executioner which should have beheaded him did see, he made haste to meet him at the place appointed for his death, and there (not without the holy inspiration of God) he fell down flat before his feet, and casting from him the sword which he held in his hand ready drawn, desired rather that he might be executioned either for him or with him, rather than to do execution upon him. Whereupon this man being now made a fellow of that faith whereof before he was persecutor, and the sword lying in the ground before them, the other officers staggering and doubting all who might take it up and do the execution, the holy confessor of God with the people there assembled went unto a hill almost half a mile off from that place, beautifully garnished with divers herbs and flowers, nor rough or uneasy to climb, but smooth, plain and delectable, worthy and meet to be sanctified with the blood of the blessed martyr, unto the top whereof when he was ascended, he required of God to give him water: and straight there arose a spring of fair water before his feet whereby all might perceive that the river before was by this means dried. For he which left no water in the river would not have required it in the top of the mountain, but that it was so expedient, for the glory of God in his holy martyr. For behold, the river, having obeyed the martyr, and served his devotion, leaving behind a testimony of duty and obedience, returned to its nature again. Here therefore this most valiant martyr, being beheaded, received the crown of life which God promiseth to them that love him. But he which there took upon him to do that wicked execution had short joy of his naughty deed: for his eyes fell upon the ground with the head of the holy martyr. There also was beheaded the soldier which, being called of God, refused to strike the holy confessor of God: of whom it is open and plain, that though he was not christened in the fount, yet he was baptized in the bath of his own blood and so made worthy to enter into the kingdom of heaven. Now the judge, seeing so many strange and heavenly miracles wrought by this holy martyr, gave commandment that the persecution should cease, beginning to honor in the saints of God the constant and patient suffering of death, by the which he thought at first to bring them from the devotion of their faith. Saint Alban suffered his martyrdom the 22nd day of June, nigh unto the city of Verulamium. Whereafter the Christian Church being quietly calmed and settled again, there was a temple builded of a marvellous rich work, and worthy for such a martyrdom. In the which place truly even unto this day are sick persons cured, and many miracles wrought. There suffered also about that time Aaron and Julius, town dwellers of the city of the Legions, and many other both men and women in sundry places, which after divers fell and cruel torments sustained in all parts of their bodies, by perfect victory achieved by patience, yielded their souls unto the joys of heaven.

Homily 15, Concerning the Purification of the Blessed Virgin Mary

I will see you again:

These words of the Lord apply to all the faithful, who strive amid the team and pain of this present life to reach eternal joy. With good reason they lament and weep with sorrow in this present life, for they are not yet able to see him whom they love. They know that, as long as they are in this mortal body, wanderers from their true country they must be, and from their own people. They doubt not that it is through hard work and struggle that they must reach their crown. Their sorrow shall be turned into joy when, once the contest of this life is ended, they receive the reward of eternal life of which the Psalmist sings: They that sow in tears shall reap in joy.

But while the faithful weep the world rejoices; for rightly it is only in this present life that the worldlings will have any joy at all, those who place no hope in the joys of another life or who are without hope that they can attain them. This can be understood especially of the persecutors of the Christian faith; for having tormented and slain the martyrs, they rejoiced that they had conquered. But not for long, because while the martyrs were crowned in secret, these others suffered eternal punishment both for their unbelief and for their murders. To these it was said by the mouth of the prophets: Behold my servants shall rejoice, while you shall be confounded. Behold my servants shall praise for joyfulness of heart, and you shall cry for sorrow of heart, and shall howl for grief of spirit (Isaias 65.14).

She remembers no more, he says, the anguish, for joy that a man is born into the world. As the woman rejoices because a man-child is born into the world, so the Church is filled with exultation at the birth of the Christian peoples into life eternal; because of whose birth she now grieves and is in labor, as a woman who gives birth in this present life. Nor should it seem strange to anyone that he is said to be born who leaves this present life. For just as he is said to be born who comes forth from his mother's womb into the light, so also may he truly be said to be born who is delivered of the bonds of the flesh and lifted up to life eternal. For this reason it is the custom of the Church to call those days on which the death of the martyrs and saints of the Church is commemorated their birth or *Natalitia*.

When he says I will see you again and your heart shall rejoice, he meant: I will see you; I will snatch you from the jaws of your enemies; I will crown you as victors; I will prove to you that I was ever with you as you fought, like a witness. For when would he not see his own in the midst of their trials, since he has promised that he will be with them always, even to the end of the world? When the faithful died in the midst of their tortures their adversaries thought that they were without aid, saying; Where is their God. One such as these, surrounded with torments, may well cry out: Behold, O Lord, my afflictions; because the enemy is exalted (Lam. I. 9), which means to say: Since the enemy who torments me raises his hand against the lowly ones of thine in pride, sustain us by thy help, O Triumphant Creator; prove to us that thou hast seen our struggles when our enemies are driven off and defeated, and that those struggles are pleasing to thee. . . .

If then, brethren, we are afflicted by salutary sufferings . . . if with due sorrow we weep for our own sins and for the miseries of our neighbors, the Lord will see us again, that is, he will show himself to us in the future who once deigned to see us and bestow on us the knowledge of his faith. He will see us that he may crown us who once saw us that he might call us. He will see us and our heart will rejoice, and our joy no man shall take from us; for this is the sole reward of those who suffer for God's sake, to rejoice for ever in his sight (Patrologia Latina 94 Bk. II, *Hom*. 5).

Selections from St. Bede are from
A Treasury of Christianity,
Anne Fremantle, editor,
New York: Viking Press, 1953

Chapter 37 • St. John of Damascus: *On the Orthodox Faith*

The Syrian theologian John Damascenus (ca. 675/700-ca. 749/754) was educated at the court of the Caliph in Damascus. He had the opportunity to become a court official as successor to his father, but preferred to enter the monastery of St. Sabas in Palestine after ordination to the priesthood. Most of his work was of a literary nature, trying to uphold orthodoxy against the attacks of the time. His work is said to have served as a model for the *Book of the Sentences* of Peter of Lombard in the twelfth century. St. Thomas Aquinas quotes this work on many occasions. John is especially famous for his exposition of Catholic teaching, presenting it in a manner that made it intelligible to the Muslims in the eighth century.

Exposition of the Orthodox Faith
Chapter III
Proof that there is a God

That there is a God, then, is no matter of doubt to those who receive the Holy Scriptures, the Old Testament, I mean, and the New; nor indeed to most of the Greeks. For, as we said, the knowledge of the existence of God is implanted in us by nature. But the wickedness of the Evil One has prevailed so mightily against man's nature as even to drive some into denying the existence of God, that most foolish and woefulest pit of destruction (whose folly David, revealer of the Divine meaning, exposed when he said, "The fool said in his heart, there is no God").

All things, that exist, are either created or uncreated. If, then, things are created, it follows that they are also wholly mutable. For things, whose existence originated in change, must also be subject to change, whether it be that they perish or that they become other than they are by act of will. But if things are uncreated they must in all consistency be also wholly immutable of quality and of movement in space. Things then that are mutable are also wholly created. But things that are created must be the work of some maker, and the maker cannot have been created. For if he had been created, he also must surely have been created by some one, and so on till we arrive at something uncreated. The Creator, then, being uncreated, is also wholly immutable. And what could this be other than Deity?

And even the very continuity of the creation, and its preservation and government, teach us that there does exist a Deity, who supports and maintains and preserves and ever provides for this universe. For how could opposite natures, such as fire and water, air and earth, have combined with each other so as to form one complete world, and continue to abide in indissoluble union, were there not some omnipotent power which bound them together and always is preserving them from dissolution?

What is it that gave order to things of heaven and things of earth, and all those things that move in the air and in the water, or rather to what was in existence before these, viz., to heaven and earth and air and the elements of fire and water? What was it that mingled and distributed these? What was it that set these in motion and keeps them in their unceasing and unhindered course? Was it not the Artificer of these things, and He Who hath implanted in everything the law whereby the universe is carried on and directed? Who then is the Artificer of these things? Is it not He Who created them and brought them into existence? For we shall not attribute such a power to the spontaneous. For, supposing their coming into existence was due to the spontaneous; what of the power that put all in order? And let us grant this, if you please. What of that which has preserved and kept them in harmony with the original laws of their existence? Clearly it is something quite distinct from the spontaneous. And what could this be other than Diety?

Chapter IV

Concerning the Nature of Deity: That It Is Incomprehensible

It is plain, then, that there is a God. But what He is in His essence and nature is absolutely incomprehensible and unknowable. For it is evident that He is incorporeal.

But even this gives no true idea of His essence, to say that He is unbegotten, and without beginning, changeless and imperishable, and possessed of such other qualities as we are wont to ascribe to God and His environment. For these do not indicate what He is, but what He is not. But when we would explain what the essence of anything is, we must not speak only negatively. In the case of God, however, it is impossible to explain what He is in His essence, and it befits us the rather to hold discourse about His absolute separation from all things. For He does not belong to the class of existing things: not that He has no existence, but that He is above all existing things, nay even above existence itself. For if all forms of knowledge have to do with what exists, assuredly that which is above knowledge must certainly be also above essence: and, conversely, that which is above essence will also be above knowledge.

Chapter V

Proof that God is one and not many

We have, then, adequately demonstrated that there is a God, and that His essence is incomprehensible.

The Deity is perfect, and without blemish in goodness, and wisdom, and power, without beginning, without end, everlasting, uncircumscribed, and in short, perfect in all things. Should we say, then, that there are many Gods, we must recognize difference among the many. For if there is no difference among them, they are one rather than many. But if there is difference among them, what becomes of the perfectness? For that which comes short of perfection, whether it be in goodness, or power, or wisdom, or time, or place, could not be God. But it is this very identity in all respects that shews that the Deity is one and not many.

Again, if there are many Gods, how can one maintain that God is uncircumscribed? For where the one would be, the other could not be.

Further, how could the world be governed by many and saved from dissolution and destruction, while strife is seen to rage between the rulers? For difference introduces strife. And if any one should say that each rules over a part, what of that which established this order and gave to each his particular realm? For this would the rather be God. Therefore, God is one, perfect, uncircumscribed, maker of the universe, and its preserver and governor, exceeding and preceding all perfection.

Moreover, it is a natural necessity that duality should originate in unity.

Chapter VI

Concerning the Word and the Son of God: A Reasoned Proof

So then this one and only God is not Wordless. And possessing the Word, He will have it not as without a subsistence, nor as having had a beginning, nor as destined to cease to be. For there never was a time when God was not Word: but He ever possesses His own Word, begotten of Himself.

Chapter VII

Concerning the Holy Spirit

Just as, when we heard of the Word of God, we considered it to be not without subsistence, nor the product of learning, nor the mere utterance of voice, nor as passing into the air and perishing, but as being essentially subsisting, endowed with free volition, and energy, and omnipotence: so also, when we have learnt about the Spirit of God, we contemplate it as the companion of the Word and the revealer of His energy, and not as mere breath without subsistence.

For to conceive of the Spirit that dwells in God as after the likeness of our own spirit, would be to drag down the greatness of the divine nature to the lowest depths of degradation. But we must contemplate it as an essential power, existing in its own proper and peculiar subsistence, proceeding from the Father and resting in the Word, and shewing forth the Word, neither capable of disjunction from God in Whom it exists, and the Word Whose companion it is, nor poured forth to vanish into nothingness, but being in subsistence in the likeness of the Word, endowed with life, free volition, independent movement, energy, ever willing that which is good, and having power to keep pace with the will in all its decrees, having no beginning and no end. For never was the Father at any time lacking the Word, nor the Word in the spirit.

Chapter VIII
Concerning the Holy Trinity

We believe, then, in One God, one beginning, having no beginning, uncreated, unbegotten, imperishable and immortal, everlasting, infinite, uncircumscribed, boundless, or infinite power, simple, uncompound, incorporeal, without flux, passionless, unchangeable, unalterable, unseen, the fountain of goodness and justice, the light of the mind, inaccessible; a power known by no measure, measurable only by His own will alone (for all things that He wills He can), creator of all created things, seen or unseen, of all the maintainer and preserver, for all the provider, master and lord and king over all, with an endless and immortal kingdom; having no contrary, filling all, by nothing encompassed, but rather Himself the encompasser and maintainer and original possessor of the universe, occupying all essences intact and extending beyond all things, and being separate from all essence as being super-essential and above all things and absolute God, absolute goodness, and absolute fullness: determining all sovereignties and rank, being placed above all sovereignty and rank, above essence and life and word and thought: being Himself very light and goodness and life and essence, inasmuch as He does not derive His being from another, that is to say, of those things that exist: but being Himself the fountain of being to all that is, of life to the living, of reason to those that have reason; to all the cause of all good: perceiving all things even before the have become: one essence, one divinity, one power, one will, one energy, one beginning, one authority, one dominion, one sovereignty, made known in three perfect subsistences and adored with one adoration, believed in and ministered to by all rational creation, united without confusion and divided without separation (which indeed transcends thought). (We believe) in Father and Son and Holy Spirit where into also we have been baptized.

(We believe) in one Father, the beginning, and cause of all: begotten of no one: without cause or generation, alone subsisting: creator of all: but Father of one only by nature. His Only-begotten Son and our Lord and God and Savior Jesus Christ, and Producer of the most Holy Spirit. And in one Son of God, the Only-begotten, our Lord, Jesus Christ: begotten of the Father, before all the ages: Light of Light, true God of true God: begotten, not made, consubstantial with the Father, through Whom all things are made: and when we say He was before all the ages we shew that His birth is without time or beginning: for the Son of God was not brought into being out of nothing, He that is the effulgence of the glory, the impress of the Father's subsistence, the living wisdom and power, the Word possessing interior subsistence, the essential and perfect and living image of the unseen God. But always He was with the Father and in Him, everlastingly and without beginning begotten of Him. For there never was a time when the Father was and the Son was not, but always the Father and always the Son, Who was begotten of Him, existed together. For He could not have received the name Father apart from the Son: for if He were without the Son, He could not be the Father: and if He thereafter had the Son, thereafter He became the Father, not having been the Father prior to this, and He was changed from that which was not the Father and became the Father. This is the worst form of blasphemy. For we may not speak of God as destitute of nature generative power: and generative power means, the power of producing from one's self, that is to say, from one's own proper essence, that which is like in nature to one's self.

Likewise we believe also in one Holy Spirit, the Lord and Giver of Life: Who proceedeth from the Father and resteth in the Son: the object of equal adoration and glorification with the Father and Son, since He is coessential and co-eternal: the Spirit of God, direct, authoritative, the fountain of wisdom, and life, and holiness: God existing and addressed along with Father and Son:

uncreated, full, creative, all-ruling, all-effecting, all-powerful, of infinite power, Lord of all creation and not under any lord; deifying, not deified: filling, not filled: shared in, not sharing in: sanctifying, not sanctified: the intercessor, receiving the supplications of all: in all things like to the Father and Son: proceeding from the Father and communicated through the Son, and participated in by all creation, through Himself creating, and investing with essence and sanctifying, and maintaining the universe: having subsistence, existing in its own proper and peculiar subsistence, inseparable and indivisible from Father and Son, and possessing all the qualities that the Father and Son possess, save that of not being begotten or born.

For the Father is without cause and unborn: rather He is Himself the beginning and cause of the existence of all things in a definite and natural manner. But the Son is derived from the Father after the manner of generation, and the Holy Spirit likewise is derived from the Father, yet not after the manner of generation, but after that of procession.

For in these *hypostatic* or personal properties alone do the three holy subsistences differ from each other, being indivisibly divided not by essence but by the distinguishing mark of their proper and peculiar subsistence.

Chapter XXX
Concerning Prescience and Predetermination

We ought to understand that while God knows all things beforehand, yet He does not predetermine all things. For He knows beforehand those things that are in our power, but He does not predetermine them. For it is not His will that there should be wickedness nor does He choose to compel virtue. So that predetermination is the work of the divine command based on foreknowledge. But on the other hand God predetermines those things which are not within our power in accordance with His prescience. For already God in His prescience has pre-judged all things in accordance with His goodness and justice.

Bear in mind, too, that virtue is a gift from God implanted in our nature, and that He Himself is the source and cause of all good, and without His cooperation and help we cannot will or do any good thing. But we have it in our power either to abide in virtue and follow God, Who calls us into ways of virtue, or to stray from paths of virtue, which is to dwell in wickedness, and to follow the devil who summons but cannot compel us. For wickedness is nothing else than the withdrawal of goodness, just as darkness is nothing else than the withdrawal of light. While then we abide in the natural state we abide in virtue, but when we deviate from the natural state, that is from virtue, we come into an unnatural state and dwell in wickedness.

Selections from "On the Orthodox Faith" are from
An Exact Exposition of the Orthodox Faith,
From A Select Library of Nicene and Post-Nicene Fathers of the Christian Church,
Second Series, Volume IX,
P. Schaff and H. Wace, editors,
New York: Chas. Scribner's Sons, 1899

Chapter 38 • St. Bernard of Clairvaux: Sermons

Bernard of Clairvaux (ca. 1090-1153) was one of the most influential men of his time in the ecclesiastical-political sphere as well as in the mystical. At an early age, he entered the Cistercian monastery at what is now called Citeaux, and in about 1115 founded the monastery of Clairvaux, where he remained as abbot for the rest of his life. However, he was not a recluse. Through his Sermons, Letters, and Treatises, which totaled over 800 items, he exerted a profound influence on the people in every category of the lay, religious, and secular life. His altercation with Abélard is well-known. He preached the Second Crusade, was advisor of popes and princes, and traveled widely in the interest of peace. His mysticism had roots in John Scotus Erigena, Dionysius the Pseudo-Areopagite, and St. Paul, and he is said to have influenced the establishment of the *devotio moderna* found in the *Imitation of Christ*. The Sermons quoted are typical of this aspect of Catholicism.

First Sermon

No one who, even to the extent of the name, is faithful, doubts that the eternal happiness of the Heavenly country, after which our pilgrimage sighs, and, on the other hand, that the punishments of Hell prepared for the wicked, exceed not only all sense of the human body, but all understanding of the heart. And would that this faith lived in all, and that desire on the one side and fear on the other should follow belief as should be proper. For what reason is there why we do not desire to avoid such misery (*as that of Hell*), and to reach such glory (*as that of Heaven*), even through the midst of swords, or, if it were necessary, half burned, unless that our faith is insensible and dead? To this is added for the completion of our misfortune, for the obstruction of our salvation, for the occasion of our perdition, that in the weighing of both ends, our feeling does not accord with our judgment, but in the consideration of the ways, we do not sufficiently hold even the very judgment of truth. Nor is it wonderful if our desire be moved by no delight of virtues, when it is torpid even regarding that eternal blessedness: or if he do not fear the bitterness of sin, who does not dread even the very eternal punishments prepared for the Devil and his angels? Unless *it be* what happens in other matters, that we are accustomed to desire more vehemently the pleasing things, and to dread more vehemently the hurtful things, the experience of which is nearer to us, even though they be far less than things more remote.

This I cannot sufficiently wonder at, *namely*, why our faith, which seems so certain in things future, stumbles in things present. It is thus, ye foolish sons of Adam, that not judging nor discerning what is true, while you have promises both of this life which now is, and of the future life, in that which you are at once to experience, you show yourselves querulous, incredulous, and unfaithful; that it evidently appears to happen, that the faith of a future promise is left to you only for a finishing stroke of your damnation. The very same, indeed, is to be considered regarding the threat. For, does not the very same God, who asserts that a kingdom is prepared for the elect, and fire for the reprobate, utter with the same mouth and with the same truth, that whosoever do not approach to Him, labor and are burthened, but that those who approach, will not fail according to the trepidation of human smallness of soul, but will be refreshed by Him? He who promises a kingdom ineffably delightful, the same testifies that His yoke is sweet and His burthen light. He who promises eternal blessedness in one country, again promises also present rest and refection upon our journey. In fine, the prophet speaks, saying: "Neither eye hath seen, nor ear hath heard, nor hath it entered into the heart of man, what God hath prepared for those who love Him." And we all readily believe it. The Lord Himself of the prophet speaks: "Come to me, all you that labor and are burthened, and I will refresh you: take my yoke upon you, and you shall find rest for your souls, for my yoke is sweet and my burthen light." And how many turn away the ear of the heart! for, perhaps, they do not venture to turn away the ears of the body. What kind of incredulity is this — nay, what insanity! As if either wisdom could be deceived, or truth could deceive. As if charity be either unwilling to give what if offers, or omnipotence is not able to pay what it promises.

For, what man is there so given to pleasure and luxury, who would not desire sobriety and chastity, if he were certain that they would be more agreeable to him? Who is there so ambitious who would not be content with all lowliness and poverty, if he knew that charity (as is the fact) which does not seek her own profit, is more amiable than all dignities? Who is there so avaricious who would not altogether despise riches if he believed that poverty were more pleasant? But now, Christ cries out in vain concerning the lightness of His burthen; without reason He affirms that His yoke is sweet: since by those also who are ranked by the name of Christians, the burthen of the Devil and the yoke of the flesh and of this world is considered more delightful. But whence has Thou such inconsiderateness as is laid to Thy charge by those, O Lord my God? Why has Thou promised so publicly what Thou art so easily detected in not fulfilling? Thou dost assert that Thy spirit is sweet beyond honey and honeycomb; and behold they have found to be sweeter the flesh of hunting, the flesh (O shame!) of a harlot, and the vanity of the world. Woe to the miserable men! they judge *ex parte*, and they despise as bitter Thy hidden manna which they have not tasted. Surely they who have experienced both, they know that God is true, but that every man is a liar. Their testimony, therefore, ought to be too faithworthy; but, together with Thy promises, the experience of Thy friends also, is laughed at and contemned. For the carnal man does not perceive those things which are of the Spirit of God, but they appear folly to him. Nor is it wonderful, that he who does not believe a God who promises, should not believe a man who has experienced *the truth of the promises*. Therefore, we are considered insane who affirm that the cross of the Lord is sweet, who magnify the delight of poverty, who extol the glory of humility, who utter forth the delights of poverty, who extol the glory of humility, who utter forth the delights of chastity. The prophet also is considered insane along with us, who says that he has been delighted in the testimonies of the Lord as in all riches.

Ye who are wise in your own eyes, prefer to the divine testimonies, not all riches, but a few which you may beg, however you can, so that our faith never has a testimony. Let it be with you in secret, in privacy, where not even your Father who is in Heaven may see it, but may say: "I know you not." You firmly believe that God is just, true — a rewarder, omnipotent, supremely good, eternal. Show yourselves deaf adders, lest at any time you may hear the voice of Him who hastens and who says: "Show me thy faith without works." How much does it cost you to believe? But do not enter upon the way of the testimonies, since it is difficult, rough, and impossible wherein to walk. Miserable and unhappy men, who have not found the way of the dwelling of the city. And, therefore, do you walk upon a pathless course and not in the way. For the end of the ways which appear to you good, which you judge to be delightful (for neither have they anything of true delight), sinks into the depth of Hell. Then shall there be weeping and gnashing of teeth. Awake, therefore, ye drunkards, and weep, lest perpetual weeping overtake you not expecting it. For when you will have said peace and security, then will a sudden ruin come upon you as upon one having a child in the womb, and you shall not escape, manifestly according to your desert, who now knowingly lose the time of flying, and fly from the means of escaping.

"Pray", says the Lord, "that your flight be not in the winter, nor on the Sabbath." Fly while it is yet the acceptable time, and the pleasing way is shown to you. Fly during the six days which it is allowed to work. Fly in the six testimonies of these qualities which we have touched above; of justice, of truth, of reward, of omnipotence, of supreme goodness, of eternity, lest perhaps you may so much give as you endure unwillingly the testimony of the seventh, namely, of the testimony of the divine wrath. Offspring of vipers, who has taught you to fly from the wrath to come? It is in the way of death in which you run — the way of perdition whose end sinks into the depth of Hell. Still, however, there is hope, because the end of the way, that is of life, has not yet come. Hasten to anticipate the good, lest being suddenly surprised, there you lie. Come, my children, hear me; I will show you the way of salvation, the way of the testimonies of God, in which delight ye as in all riches.

It remains that thou study perseverance. For this is the consummation of the way, and has the testimony of eternity. For the perseverance of our life is the image of the divine eternity; so that as He is, we may be in this world, imitating according to the measure of our possibility His unchangeableness. Since to this effect the wise man says: "The fool changeth as the moon, the wise man remaineth as the sun." This is, therefore, the way, most dearly beloved: walk in it, since by ascending from virtue to virtue the God of Gods is seen in Zion. To the glory of whose vision may He Himself bear us, the Lord of riches and King of glory, who is the way, the truth, and the life, Christ Jesus, our Lord.

Second Sermon

Very frequently thinking upon the ardor of the desire of the fathers sighing after the presence of Christ in the flesh, I am touched with compunction, and confounded within myself, and now I scarcely restrain my tears, so much am I ashamed of the lukewarmness and torpor of these miserable times. For, to which of us does the actual exhibition of this grace infuse so much joy, as the promise enkindled desire in the ancient saints? For, behold, how many will rejoice in this nativity of His which is about to be celebrated; but would that they rejoice at the nativity and not at vanity. Therefore, this expression breathes from their burning desire, and the feelings of their pious expectation: "Let him kiss me with the kiss of his mouth." Truly, whoever was then able to be spiritual, felt in spirit how great was the grace diffused upon his lips. Wherefore, speaking in the desire of his soul, he said, "Let him kiss me with the kiss of his mouth"; truly desirous in all ways, not to be cheated of the participation of so much sweetness.

For every perfect one said: Why bring me the oratorical [*word-sowing*] lips of the prophets? Let Himself rather, who is beautiful in shape beyond the sons of man, kiss me with the kiss of His mouth. I no longer hear Moses, for he has become for me of a hesitating tongue: the lips of Isaiah are unclean; Jeremiah knows not how to speak, because he is a boy, and the prophets are all tongueless. Let Him speak, of whom they speak — let Him speak. Let Him kiss me with the kiss of His mouth. Let Him not speak to me in them or through them, since water is dark in the clouds of the air; but let Himself kiss me with the kiss of His mouth, whose gracious presence and the admirable streams of whose doctrine may they be in me a fountain of water leaping forth into life everlasting. Is not a more plentiful grace infused into us from Him, whom the Father hath anointed with the oil of gladness beyond His fellows? If, however, he deign to kiss me with the kiss of His mouth, whose living and active speech is indeed a kiss to me, not indeed the union of the lips, which sometimes belies the peace of the soul; but, manifestly the infusion of joys, the revelations of secrets, the wonderful, and in some degree undistinguishable, mingling of the light from above and of the illuminated mind. Since he who adheres to God is one spirit. With reason, therefore, I do not admit dreams and visions, I wish not for figures and riddles, I even contemn the angelic forms. Since my Jesus far excels those in His form and in His heart, I do not, therefore, ask any other angel or man, but I ask Himself to kiss me with the kiss of His mouth, nor do I presume that I am to be kissed by His mouth (for this belongs to the peculiar happiness and singular prerogative of the man taken up *into Heaven*), but humble, I ask that He may kiss me with the kiss of His mouth, which is the common lot of many who can say, "And we all have received from His fullness."

Attend. — Let the Word taking flesh be the kiss which kisses: let the thing kissed be the flesh which is taken; but the kiss, that which is formed from the kisses, and from that which is kissed. Namely the person made up from both, the mediator of God and man, the man Christ Jesus. For this reason, therefore, none of the saints presumed to say "Let him kiss me with his mouth," but merely with the kiss of his mouth, preserving this prerogative to him, on whom in a singular degree and once for all the mouth of the word was impressed, when the plentitude of the entire Divinity bestowed itself upon him corporally. Happy kiss, and wonderful for its stupendous condescension; in which it is not mouth that is pressed to mouth, but God is united to man; and there, indeed, the contact of the lips signifies the embrace of the souls, but here the confederation of natures reconciles things human with things divine, reducing to peace the things which are on Earth and those which are in Heaven. For this kiss, therefore, each saint of the ancient times sighed, because they felt beforehand that pleasure and exultation were amassed therein, and that all the treasures of wisdom and knowledge were hidden in Him, and because they themselves desired to receive from His fullness.

I feel that what is said pleases you: but learn now another meaning of the words. It did not escape the saints, even before the coming of the Savior, that God was thinking thoughts of peace towards the race of mortals. For neither would He make a word upon Earth which He would not reveal to His prophets. His Word, however, was hidden from many. For faith, at that time was scarce upon Earth, and a very slender hope in many of those who awaited the redemption of Israel. But those who had foreknowledge of it; they also, preached, that the Christ would come in the flesh, and with Him peace. Whence one of them: "And there will be peace," he says, "in our Earth when He shall come." Nay, they preached with every confidence as they had heard from above, that through Him men would recover the grace of God. That which was fulfilled in his own time John the precursor of the Lord knew, and related, saying: the grace and the truth of our Lord Jesus Christ has been accomplished: and that this is the truth, the whole Christian people now experiences.

O root of Jesse, Thou who standest for a sign of the nations, how many kings and prophets wished to see Thee, and have not seen Thee! Happy, however, from amongst all, thou, O Simeon, whose old age was in plenteous mercy! For he exulted that he might see the sign of his desire, and he saw it and was glad, and having received the kiss of peace, is dismissed in peace: first, however, pronouncing openly that Jesus was born for a sign which should be contradicted. It was altogether so. Contradiction was offered to the sign of peace which had arisen, but it was by those who hated peace. For, to men of good will, it was peace: to men of ill will, a root of scandal and a stone of stumbling. Herod, in fine, was disturbed, and all Jerusalem with him, since *the Savior* came to His own, and His own received Him not. Happy were those shepherds, in their night watch, who were held worthy of the sight of this sign. Then it hid itself from the wise and the prudent, and revealed itself to little ones. And

Herod wished to see it, but because he was not of good will, he did not deserve to see it, since it was a sign of peace, given only to men of good will. But to Herod, and those like him, was given only the sign of Jonas the Prophet. Moreover, to the shepherds: "and this," says the angel, "shall be a sign to you"; to you who are humble; to you who are obedient; to you who are not highminded; to you who are watching and meditating upon the law of God day and night. "This," he says, "shall be to you a sign." What *shall* be a sign? What the angels promised, what the people sought for, what the prophets foretold; this, the Lord has done now, and has shown to you: in which the unbelieving may receive faith, the cowardly may receive hope, the perfect may receive security. A sign of what thing? A sign of forgiveness, of grace, of peace, of which there will be no end. This, therefore, is the sign. "You shall find the infant wrapped in swaddling clothes, and laid in a manger." God, however, is in Him, "reconciling the world to Himself." He will die on account of your sin, and will rise for your justification, that being justified through faith you may have peace with God. This sign of peace, the Prophet formerly placed before King Achaz to be sought from the Lord his God, whether in Heaven above, or in the Earth below. But the impious king refused, unhappy man, not believing that in this sign the lowest were to be united with the highest in peace, inasmuch as the places below the Earth being saluted by the Lord descending to them, themselves also receive the sign of peace in the holy days: and the Heavenly spirits partake the same in eternal sweetness nothing the less, when He has returned to the Heavens.

My sermon must be brought to a close: but in order that I may draw together in a short summary what has been argued therein, it appears that this holy kiss was necessarily given to the world for two reasons — first, that it might make itself believed by the weak, and might satisfy the desire of the just; then that the kiss was nothing else than the mediator of God and man, the man Jesus Christ, who with the Father and the Holy Spirit, liveth and reigneth God, world without end. Amen.

Selections from "Sermons" are from
The Fathers, Historians, and Writers of the Church,
W.B. Kelly, Dublin, 1864

Part VI
Devotional Classics

Introduction

These writings appeared from the twelfth to the sixteenth centuries. They can be classified as treatises that are devotional, philosophical, theological, poetic, propaedeutic, and mystical.

The Little Flowers of St. Francis is especially devotional in its recounting of the miraculous activities in the life of St. Francis, and of the value of the simple imitation of the saint's reliance on the complete love of Jesus.

In the works of St. Bonaventure and St. Thomas Aquinas, we meet a devotional and philosophico-theological view of the Christian way of life, what is believed and understood, and how one mounts by degrees to a union with God. Each of these saints and doctors of the Catholic Church shows that the affective response to the knowledge of God will be an overflow of mystical delight. It has been said that Dante's *Divine Comedy* is a poetic Gothic cathedral that illustrates, along with the journey of the soul to God and complete happiness, some of the ideas of Bonaventure and Thomas.

Francis Thompson, the famous English poet, portrayed St. Ignatius of Loyola as "true, fresh, brilliant," possessing a great insight into human nature and eternal values. Ignatius had a charisma that appealed to great men, and was able to communicate with charisma to others and thereby unite them under the banner of Christ the King. His *Spiritual Exercises* have influenced many to rise from the purgative way through the contemplative way to the unitive way of love of Jesus.

The writings of St. Teresa of Ávila and St. John of the Cross appropriately close this section. Each of the writers presented here would agree that all philosophical, theological, and devotional activity, all asceticism, all contemplative prayer should lead the individual soul to mystical union with God.

Chapter 39 • St. Francis of Assisi: *The Little Flowers of St. Francis;* Rule of the Friars Minor

The "Fioretti" is a series of anecdotes and devotional stories concerning the life and activities of St. Francis of Assisi (ca. 1181-1226) and his closest companions. The excerpt reproduced here is concerned mainly with various aspects of the stigmata which St. Francis received two years before his death, an event recalled by St. Bonaventure in his *Journey of the Mind to God*. The "Fioretti" is characterized by a simple devotion to and childlike love for the popular manifestations of total commitment to Christ.

The original rule of St. Francis was made up of a few precepts and counsels taken from the Gospels. The rapid and widespread expansion of the Order founded by St. Francis made it necessary to draw up a more detailed set of regulations. Yet the form quoted here is still more simple and less detailed than the previous one of the Benedictines.

Of the Most Holy Stigmata of St. Francis

Of the Fourth Consideration of the Most Holy Stigmata

As touching the fourth consideration, it must be known that, after the true love of Christ had perfectly transformed St. Francis into the true image of Christ crucified; having finished the fast of forty days in honor of St. Michael the Archangel upon the holy mountain of Alvernia; after the festival of St. Michael, the angelical man, St. Francis, descended from the mountain with Friar Leo and with a devout farmer, upon whose ass he sat, because by reason of the wounds in his feet he could not well go afoot. Now, when St. Francis had come down from the mountain, the fame of his sanctity was already noised abroad throughout the land; for it had been reported by the shepherds how they had seen the mountain of Alvernia all ablaze, and that this was the token of some great miracle which God had wrought upon St. Francis; wherefore, when the people of the district heard that he was passing, they all flocked to see him, both men and women, small and great, and all of them with much devotion and desire sought to touch him and to kiss his hands; and not being able to resist the devotion of the people, albeit he had bandaged the palms of his hands, nevertheless, the better to hide the most holy stigmata, he bandaged them yet more and covered them with his sleeves, and only gave them his fingers to kiss. But albeit he endeavored to conceal and to hide the mystery of the most holy stigmata, to avoid every occasion of worldly glory, it pleased God for His own glory to show forth many miracles by virtue of the said most holy stigmata, and singularly in that journey from Vernia to Santa Maria degli Angeli, and very many thereafter in divers parts of the world, both during his life and after his glorious death; to the end that their occult and marvelous virtue, and the extreme charity and mercy of Christ, towards him to whom He had so marvelously given them, might be manifested to the world by clear and evident miracles; whereof we will set forth some in this place. Thus, when St. Francis was drawing nigh unto a village which was upon the borders of the country of Arezzo, a woman came before him, weeping sore and holding her child in her arms; the which child was eight years old and had been dropsical for four years; and his belly was so terribly swollen that, when he stood upright, he could not see his feet; and this woman laid that son of hers before him, and besought him to pray God for him; and St. Francis first betook himself to prayer and then, when he had prayed, laid his holy hands upon the belly of the child; and anon, all the swelling disappeared, and he was made perfectly whole, and he gave him back to his mother, who received him with very great joy, and led him home, thanking God and St. Francis; and she willingly showed her son that was healed to all those of the district who came to her house to see him.

Now, as hath been said above, albeit St. Francis, as much as in him lay, strove to hide the most holy Stigmata, and, from the time when he received them, always went with his hands bandaged and with stockings on his feet, yet, for all that he could do, he could not prevent many of the friars from seeing and touching them in divers manners, and particularly the wound in his side, the which he endeavored with special diligence to hide. Thus, a friar, who waited on him, induced him, by a pious fraud, to take off his habit, that the dust might be shaken out of it; and, since he removed it in his presence, that friar saw clearly the wound in his side; and, swiftly putting his hand upon his breast, he touched it with three fingers and thus learned its extent and size; and in like manner his Vicar saw it at that time.

The highest pontiff, Pope Alexander [IV], while preaching to the people in the presence of all the cardinals (among whom was the holy Friar Buonaventura, who was a cardinal) said and affirmed that he had seen with his own eyes the most holy Stigmata of St. Francis, when he was yet alive.

At the death of St. Francis, not only did the Madonna Jacopa and her sons together with all her company see and kiss his glorious and holy Stigmata, but also many citizens of Assisi; among whom was a knight of wide renown and a great man, who was named Messer Jerome, the which doubted much thereof and was incredulous concerning them, even as was St. Thomas concerning those of Christ, and to certify himself and others, in the presence of all the friars and the lay folk, he boldly moved the nails in the hands and feet, and touched the wound in the side before them all. Whereby he was thereafter a constant witness of that verity, swearing upon the Book that so it was, and so he had seen and touched. St. Clare, likewise, beheld and kissed the glorious and sacred Stigmata of St. Francis, together with her nuns, which were present at his burying.

The glorious confessor of Christ, St. Francis, passed from this life in the year of our Lord 1226, on the fourth day of October, on Saturday, and was buried on Sunday. That year was the twentieth year of his conversion, to wit when he began to do penance, and was the second year after the imprinting of the most holy Stigmata; and it was in the forty-fifth year from his birth.

Thereafter was St. Francis canonized in 1228, by Pope Gregory IX, who came in person to Assisi to canonize him. And this sufficeth touching the fourth consideration.

The Rule of the Friars Minor

Chapter I

In the Name of the Lord Here Begins the Life of the Friars Minor

This is the rule and life of the friars minor, namely to observe the holy Gospel of our Lord Jesus Christ by living in obedience, without private property and in chastity. Brother Francis promises obedience and reverence to our lord Pope Honorius [III] and his canonically elected successors and to the Roman Church. And the other friars are required to obey brother Francis and his successors.

Chapter II

Of Those Who Wish to Embrace This Life and How They Should Be Received

If any should desire to embrace this life and be associated with our friars they should be sent to their provincial ministers to whom alone and not to any others is granted the right to accept friars. But the ministers should examine them carefully concerning the Catholic faith and the sacraments of the Church. And if they believe in all these matters and wish to acknowledge them faithfully and observe them firmly to the letter . . . they shall be told about the word of the holy gospel that they should go and sell everything they have and strive to give it to the poor.

Afterwards let them be given the garments of probation, namely two tunics without cowls and a cincture and drawers and a cape reaching down to the belt, unless something else may seem at some time more appropriate to these same ministers in the sight of God. After they have completed a year of probation let them be received to obedience promising to observe this life and Rule always.

Chapter III
On the Divine Office and Fasting and How the Friars Ought to Travel in the World

Chapter IV
That the Friars Should Not Receive Money

I strongly advise all the friars not to receive coins or money in any way either directly or through an intermediary. However the ministers and guardians alone shall take care through spiritual friends of the needs of the infirm and for the clothing of the other friars according to the locale and the seasons and the frigid regions, as they see fit. With this exception, as was said, they should not accept coins or money.

Chapter V
The Manner of Working

Let those friars work faithfully and devotedly, as God has given them the strength, so that inimical idleness of the soul may be avoided and they may not extinguish the spirit of holy prayer and devotion to which all other temporal matters should be subservient.

Chapter VI
That the Friars Should Appropriate Nothing for Themselves and Concerning Begging and the Infirm

Chap VIII
On the Election of the Minister General of this Brotherhood and on the Chapter at Pentecost

Chapter IX
About Preachers

The friars should not preach in the diocese of any bishop if they have been forbidden to do so. And no friar should dare to preach at all to the people unless he has been examined and approved by the minister general of this brotherhood and the office of preaching has been granted to him by the minister general. I, also, advise and exhort those friars that, in their preaching, their eloquence be balanced and pure, of utility and edification for the people because of the information it contains concerning vices and virtues, punishment and glory, along with a brevity of speech, because "a short word has the Lord made upon the earth."

Chapter X
On Fraternal Admonition and Correction

But I advise and exhort in the Lord Jesus Christ that the friars avoid all pride, vainglory, envy, avarice, care and worldly solicitude, detraction and murmuring. They should not undertake the teaching of the liberal arts to the unlearned but they should concern themselves with the desire above all things to have the spirit of the Lord and its holy operation, to pray always to him with a pure heart and to have humility, patience in persecution and in infirmity and to love those who persecute and revile and contradict us because the Lord says, "Love your enemies . . . and pray for those that persecute and calumniate you. Blessed are they that suffer persecution for justice's sake for theirs is the kingdom of heaven. But he that shall persevere unto the end, he shall be saved."

Chapter XII
Of Those Going Among the Saracens and Other Infidels

Any brothers who should desire under divine inspiration to go among the Saracens and other infidels should request permission to do so from their provincial ministers. But the ministers should grant this permission to none unless they seem to be suited for this mission.

In virtue of obedience I charge the ministers that they request from our lord the Pope that one of the cardinals of the holy Roman Church be assigned as the governor, protector, and corrector of this brotherhood so that always subordinated and prostrated at the feet of the same holy Church, stable in the Catholic faith, we may observe poverty and humility and the holy Gospel of our Lord Jesus Christ as we have firmly promised.

(This Rule was approved by Pope Honorius III in 1223.)

Selections from "The Little Flowers" are from
The Little Flowers of St. Francis of Assisi,
translated by W. Heywood, London: Methuen, 1906
Selections from "The Rule of the Friars" were
translated freely for this volume by Theodore E. James,
from *Liber Vitae Seu Regulae S. Francisi Expositio*,
P.K. Kazenberger, O.F.M.,
Romae: Pontificium Athenaeum Antonianum, 1948

Chapter 40 • St. Bonaventure: *Journey of the Mind to God*

Born as Giovanni di Fidanza near Viterbo in 1221, St. Bonaventure (1221-1274) entered the Franciscan Order, studied at Paris under Alexander of Hales, and taught there until 1255. He was elected general of his order in 1257 and became cardinal bishop of Albano in 1273. Bonaventure's title of *Doctor Seraphicus* gives some idea of the basis for his classical influence on his contemporaries and future generations. His mystical works bring the influence of Dionysius the Pseudo-Areopagite, Bernard of Clairvaux, and Hugh of St. Victor to full blossom. One of the greatest works by Bonaventure is the *Journey of the Mind to God.*

Introduction

At the beginning I call upon the first beginning from whom all illuminations descend as from *the Father of Lights, from whom is every best gift and every perfect gift* (James 1.17), namely the eternal Father. I call upon Him through his Son, our Lord Jesus Christ, that by the intercession of the most blessed Virgin Mary, mother of the same God and our Lord Jesus Christ, and of blessed Francis, our leader and father, He illumine the eyes of our mind *so that we direct our steps in the way of that peace which surpasses all understandings* (Eph. 1.17; Luc. 1.79; Phil. 4.7; John 14.27). Our Lord Jesus Christ proclaimed and bestowed that peace. Our father Saint Francis reiterated the same message, proclaiming peace at the beginning and end of every sermon, wishing peace to everyone in every greeting, sighing for ecstatic peace in every act of contemplation as a citizen of that Jerusalem of which that man of peace spoke, *who was peaceable with those who hated peace*; pray for the things that are for the peace of Jerusalem (Ps. 119.7; 121.6). For he knew that the throne of Solomon would only endure in peace since it was written: His place is in peace and his abode in Zion. (Ps. 75.3)

Because I would seek this peace with an eager spirit, following the example of the most blessed father Francis, I, a sinner, who have succeeded him, though all unworthy, as the seventh Minister General of the Brothers after the passing of our most blessed father, it happened by the Divine Will that about the 33rd year after the death of the Saint I went aside to Mount Alverno as to a quiet place with a desire to seek that peace. And being there a while and considering in mind certain ways of leading the mind to God, among other things there came to mind that miracle which in the aforesaid place happened to blessed Francis himself, namely the vision of the winged Seraph (Is. 6.2) in the form of the Crucified. While considering this it was immediately obvious to me that that vision signified the contemplative ecstasy of our father and the way by which he reached it.

By those six wings (of the Seraph) can be understood the six supports of illuminations by which the soul is disposed, as it were, by stages or steps to approach peace through the elevations of Christian wisdom. However, the only way is through the most ardent love of the Crucified who so transformed Paul, *caught up to the third heaven* (2. Cor. 12.2), into Christ that he could say, *with Christ I am nailed to the cross*, and *I live, now not I but Christ lives in me* (Gal. 2.19-20). Christ also so took over the mind of Francis that the spirit was made manifest in the flesh; actually he bore the most sacred stigmata of the passion in his body for two years before his death. Therefore the images of the six seraphic wings symbolize the six gradual illuminations which begin with creatures and lead to God, to whose presence no one enters directly except through the Crucified. For *he who enters into the sheepfold not by the door, but climbs in another way, the same is a thief and a robber* (John 10.1). *If anyone enter through this door, he shall go in and out and shall find* pastures (*ib.* 9-10). For the same reason John says in the *Apocalypse: Blessed are they that wash their robes in the blood of the Lamb that they may have a right to the tree of life and may enter in by the gates into the city* (Apol. 22.14). This is to say, as it were, that one cannot enter the heavenly Jerusalem through contemplation unless he enter by the blood of the Lamb as by a door. No one is disposed in any way to divine contemplation, which leads to mental elevations, unless with Daniel he be *a man of desires* (Dan. 9.23). However desires are enkindled in us in a two-fold way, namely through the insistence of prayer, which makes one roar *with the groaning of the heart*,(Ps. 37.9) and through the flash of vision by which the mind is turned most directly and most intensely to the rays of light.

Therefore, first of all, I invite the reader to groan in prayer with the help of Jesus crucified by whose blood we are cleansed from the stains of our vices lest by chance he believe that it is sufficient that there be reading without unction, speculation without devotion, investigation without admiration, circumspection without exultation, industry without piety, knowledge without charity, understanding without humility, study without divine grace, an image without divinely inspired wisdom. Therefore I propose suitable speculations to those prepared by divine grace, to the humble and pious, to the sorrowful and devout, to those anointed with the *oil of divine gladness* (Ps. 44.8), to the lovers of divine wisdom and to those inflamed with its desire, to those desiring to dedicate themselves to the praise, love and even delight to God, implying that the image offered by the exterior world is of little or no value unless the image of our mind be cleaned and polished. Therefore bestir yourself, O man of God, to heed the gnawing goad of your conscience before you lift up your eyes to the rays of wisdom shining in its image, lest by chance you fall from the vision itself of those rays into a deeper ditch of darkness.

I have made up my mind to divide the treatise into seven chapters prefixing titles to each to facilitate an understanding of what is said in them. Hence I request that you consider the intention of the writer rather than the performance, the sense of the words rather than their unpolished forms, the truth rather than elegance of expression, the stirring up of desire rather than the education of the intellect. To accomplish this the development of these considerations should not be run through in a routine way but should be carefully meditated upon.

The Speculation of a Mendicant in a Solitary Place

Chapter 1

The Stages of the Ascent to God and the Contemplation of Him through His Traces in the Universe

Blessed is the man whose help is from Thee: in his heart he has disposed to ascend by steps in the vale of tears, in the place which he has set (Ps. 86.6-7). Since beatitude is nothing but the enjoyment of the highest good and the highest good is above us, no one can be made happy unless he mounts beyond himself by an ascent of heart rather than by that of the body. But we cannot be raised above ourselves unless we be assisted by a higher power raising us up. For it makes no difference how well the interior stages are arranged if the divine help does not accompany them. However, the divine help will assist those who ask for it humbly and devoutly; and this is to sigh for it in this *vale of tears*, namely to seek it through fervent prayer. Thus prayer is the mother and beginning of the elevating action. So Dionysius in his book *On Mystical Theology*, wishing to instruct us in mental ecstasy, makes prayer the first condition. Hence let us pray and say to the Lord our God, *conduct me O Lord, in*

Thy way and I will walk in Thy truth; let my heart rejoice that it may fear Thy name.(Ps. 85.11).

Praying in this way we are illumined by the knowledge of the stages of the ascent to God. For since the totality of things, according to the state of our condition, is a ladder of ascent to God and in things some are a trace, others an image, some corporeal, others spiritual, some temporal, others everlasting and likewise some outside us, others within us, in order that we reach the contemplation of the First Principle, which is most spiritual and eternal and above us, it is fitting that we pass through the vestige which is corporeal and temporal and outside us; and this is to be led in the way of God. We should then enter into our mind which is an everlasting image of God, spiritual and within us; and this is to enter into the truth of God. We should finally ascend to what is eternal, most spiritual and above us gazing on the First Principle; and this is to rejoice in the knowledge of God and in the reverence of his majesty. This, therefore, is *the three days' journey into the wilderness* (Exodus 3.18); this is the three-fold illumination of one day and the first is like evening, the second like morning, and the third like noon; this concerns the three-fold existence of things, namely, in matter, in the intelligence and in the divine art according to which it is said, *let it be made, he made it* and *it was made* (Gen. 1.3). This also concerns the three-fold substance in Christ who is our corporeal, spiritual and divine ladder.

According to this three-fold procedure our mind has three main aspects: one is concerned with external corporeal things and thus is called animality or sensuality; another looks within into itself and thus is called spirit; the third looks above and thus is said to be mind. We should dispose ourselves for the knowledge of God by all these ways so that we love Him *with our whole mind, our whole heart and our whole soul* (Mark 12.30). In this consists the perfect fulfillment of the Law and along with it Christian wisdom.

However, since each of the aforesaid modes is twofold, according as it is fitting to consider God as *alpha* and *omega* or insofar as it is a question of seeing God in each of these modes as *through* an image and *in* an image, or because each one of these considerations is joined to the other or may be considered in its purity, it is necessary that these three principal stages be increased to six so that, just as God perfected the universe in six days and rested on the seventh so the human mind is led most orderly to the rest of contemplation by six successive stages of illumination. As a symbol of this the throne of Solomon is reached by six steps (I Kings 10.19); the Seraphs whom Isaias saw had six wings (Is. 6.2); after six days *the Lord called Moses from the midst of the cloud* (Ex. 24.16) and Christ after six days, according to Matthew (Matt. 17.1-2), *led his disciples up into the mountains and was transfigured before them.*

Hence in proportion to the six stages of ascent to God there are six stages of the powers of the soul by which we ascend from the depths to the heights, from the externals to the internals and from temporals we rise to the eternals, namely *sense, imagination, reason, intellect, intelligence and the peak of the mind* or the spark of synderesis. We have these grades of powers which were implanted in us by Nature, deformed by sin, reformed by grace and to be purified by justice, exercised by knowledge and perfected by wisdom.

For according to the original plan of nature man was created capable of the repose of contemplation and so *God placed him in a paradise of delights* (Gen. 2.15). But turning away from the true light to the changeable good he was bent down through his own fault, and his whole race through the original sin which infects the human nature in a two-fold manner; *ignorance* infects the mind and *concupiscence* the flesh. Hence man sits in darkness blinded and fallen and he does not see the light of heaven unless grace helps him with righteousness against concupiscence and knowledge succors him with wisdom against ignorance. All this is done by Jesus Christ *who of God is made unto us wisdom and justice and sanctification and redemption* (I Cor. 1.30). Since he is the *power* of God and the wisdom of God, the incarnate Word *full of grace and truth*, he has made *grace* and *truth,* has infused the grace of charity, which, since it is of a pure heart and good conscience and unfeigned faith, rectifies the whole soul according to its aforementioned triple aspect. He has taught the knowledge of truth according to the triple mode of theology, namely symbolic, literal and mystical, so that through the symbolic we use sensibles rightly, through the literal we use intelligibles rightly and through the mystical we are caught up to supermental heights.

It is necessary that anyone wishing to mount up to God should avoid sin which deforms nature and exercise the aforementioned natural powers with reforming grace through prayer; he must in conversation strive for purifying justice; in meditation he must strive for the illumination of knowledge; in contemplation he must strive for the wisdom that perfects. Hence just as no one reaches wisdom except through grace, righteousness and knowledge, so no one reaches contemplation except by a penetrating meditation, holy conversation and devout prayer. Just as therefore grace is the basis both of the rectitude of the will and of the illumination of a perceptive reason, so we should first pray, then we must live well and thirdly, we must strive for the manifestations of truth and ascend gradually until we reach *the lofty mountain where the God of gods is seen in Zion* (Ps. 83.8).

The supreme power and wisdom and benevolence of the Creator shines forth in created things just as the bodily sense announces it in a three-fold way to the interior sense. For the senses of the body assist the intellect when it investigates rationally or believes faithfully or contemplates intellectually.

One who contemplates considers the actual existence of things; one who believes considers the habitual course of things and one who reasons considers the potential preeminence of things.

Selections from "Journey of the Mind to God" were translated by
Theodore E. James, Ph.D.,
from *Sancti Bonaventurae ex Ordine Minorum S.R.E. Cardinalis Episcopi Albanensis Eximii Ecclesiae Doctoris Operum T.F. Lugduni*, 1668

Chapter 41 • St. Thomas Aquinas: Hymns; Sermon; *On the Truth of the Catholic Faith; Summa Theologiae; Commentary on the 'Divine Names' of Dionysius*

St. Thomas (1225-1274) was born in Rocca Secca in the county of Aquino about seventy-eight miles from Rome. At an early age he was sent to the Benedictine monastery of Monte Cassino as an oblate, and learned the fundamentals of the Christian life there. He attended the University of Naples, and joined the Dominicans in 1244. He studied at Paris under Albert the Great (1245-1248), and went with him to Cologne for further study (1248-1252). He became a master of theology and taught theology in Paris and at the Papal Court at Anagni, Orvieto, Rome, and Viterbo. His influence in every area of Catholic doctrine, life, and worship is extraordinary. Many are well-informed about the depth and breadth of his influence in speculative theology and philosophy, but not too many of our contemporaries are now aware of his reputation in the area of Christian poetry and affective mysticism. The following excerpts attempt to bring out these aspects, as well as some of his important philosophical and theological contributions to classical Catholicism.

Hymn

Feast of Corpus Christi[1]

Of the glorious Body telling,
O my tongue, Its mystery sing;
And the Blood, all price excelling,
Which for this world's ransoming
In a noble womb once dwelling
He shed forth, the Gentiles' King.

Given for us, for us descending
Of a Virgin to proceed,
Man with man in converse blending
Scattered He the Gospel seed:
Till His sojourn drew to ending
Which He closed in wondrous deed.

At the Last Great Supper seated,
Circled by His brethren's band,
All the Law required, completed,
In the Feast its statutes planned,
To the twelve Himself He meted
For their Food, with His own Hand.

Word made Flesh, by word He maketh
Very bread His Flesh to be;
Man for wine Christ's Blood partaketh;
And if senses fail to see,
Faith alone the true heart waketh
To behold the Mystery.

Therefore, we, before It bending,
This great Sacrament adore;
Types and shadows have their ending
In the new rite evermore;
Faith, our outward sense amending,
Maketh good defects before.

Honor, laud, and praise addressing
To the Father and the Son.
Might ascribe we, virtue, blessing,
And eternal benison;
Holy Ghost, from Both progressing.
Equal laud to Thee be done. Amen.

Hymn

Let old things pass away;
Let all be fresh and bright;
And welcome we with hearts renewed
This Feast of new delight.

Upon this hallowed eve,
Christ with his brethren ate,
Obedient to the olden Law,

The Pasch before Him set.
Which done — Himself entire,
The True Incarnate God,
Alike on each, alike on all,
His sacred Hands bestowed.

He gave His Flesh; He gave
His Precious Blood; and said,
"Receive and drink ye all of This
For your salvation shed."

Thus did the Lord appoint
This sacrifice sublime,
And made His Priests the ministers
Through all the bounds of time.

Farewell to types! henceforth
We feed on Angels' Food;
The slave — O, wonder! — eats the Flesh
Of his Incarnate God!

O Blessed Three in One!
Visit our hearts, we pray,
And lead us on through Thine own paths
To Thy eternal day. Amen.

Fourth Lesson

The lesson is taken from the sermons of St. Thomas of Aquin.

The immeasurable benefits, which the goodness of God hath bestowed on Christian people, have conferred on them also a dignity beyond all price. "For what nation is there so great, who hath gods so nigh unto them, as the Lord, our God, is" unto us? The Only-begotten Son of God, being pleased to make us "partakers of the Divine nature," took our nature upon Him being Himself made Man that He might make men gods. And all, as much of ours as He took, He applied to our salvation. On the Altar of the Cross He offered up His Body to God the Father as a sacrifice for our reconciliation; He shed His Blood as the price whereby He redeemeth us from wretchedness and bondage, and the washing whereby He cleanseth us from all sin. And for a noble and abiding memorial of that so great work of His goodness, He hath left unto His faithful ones the Same His very Body for Meat, and the Same His very Blood for Drink, to be fed upon under the appearance of bread and wine.

Hymn

The Word of God proceeding forth,
Yet leaving not the Father's side,
And going to His work on earth,
Had reached at length life's eventide.

By a disciple to be given
To rivals for His Blood athirst;
Himself, the very Bread of Heaven,
He gave to His disciples first.

He gave Himself in either kind;
His precious Flesh; His Precious Blood;
Of flesh and blood is man combined,
And He of man would be the Food.

In Birth, man's Fellow-man was He;
His Meat, while sitting at the Board;
He died, his Ransomer to be:
He reigns, to be his Great Reward.

O Saving Victim, slain to bless!
Who openest heaven's bright gates to all;
The attacks of many a foe oppress;
Give strength in strife, and help in fall.

To God, the Three in One, ascend
All thanks and praise for evermore;
He grant the life that shall not end,
Upon the heavenly country's shore.
Amen.

On the Truth of the Catholic Faith[2]
BOOK ONE
Introduction
What Is the Function of a Wise Man

The usual practice, which Aristotle (Topics 2.1.102a3Ø) thinks should be followed in naming things, has generally led to the designation of men as wise who order things correctly and govern them well. Whence among other things which men consider applicable to a wise man Aristotle (Meta. 1.2.982a18) mentions that "it belongs to him to put things in order." But of all things to be governed and ordered to a goal the principle of governing and ordering must be taken from the goal. For then each thing is best disposed when it is suitably ordered to its goal. For the goal of each thing is its good. Whence we observe in the arts that one definite thing is the controlling factor and principle, as it were, if it functions as a goal. Just as the medical art directs the art of the pharmacists and orders it because health, about which medicine is concerned, is the goal of all the medicine prepared by the pharmacists' art. A similar thing appears in the art of sailing in relation to the art of shipbuilding and in the military art as regards the equestrian art and all implements of war.

The arts which control others are called architectonic or master arts and those who are proficient in them are designated as wise. But these artists treat of particular goals of certain things. And, since they are not concerned with the universal goal of all things they are merely designated as wise in this or that area. But the name of wise man absolutely is reserved to him alone who is concerned about the goal of the whole universe which is also its source. Thus, as the Philosopher says (*loc. cit.*) it is the function of a wise man to be concerned about the highest causes.

The last goal of each thing is the one intended by its first author or mover. But the first author and mover of the universe is an intellect, as we shall prove later. Therefore the last goal of the universe should be the good of an intellect and this is truth. Therefore truth must be the last goal of the whole universe and the chief function of wisdom is to consider this goal.

So divine wisdom clothed in flesh asserted that He came into this world to make evident the truth as He says, "For this was I born and for this came I into the world: that I should give testimony to the truth" (John 18.37). The Philosopher also considers that first philosophy is the knowledge of truth, not just of any kind but of that truth which is the source of all truth, namely that which pertains to the first principle of the being of everything. Thus its truth is the principle of all truth since the relation of things as regards truth is the same as their relation in being.

However it is the same to pursue one of a pair of contraries as to draw away from the other, just as medicine leads to health so it excludes sickness. Whence just as it is the role of a wise man to contemplate especially the truth of the first principle and disseminate truth concerning the others, so it must fight against the contrary falsity.

Thus it is appropriate that the two-fold function of a wise man be declared by Wisdom itself in the proposed words: to meditate on the divine truth which is the truth itself and to publish it abroad, as is indicated by the words, "my mouth shall meditate truth"; to fight against the error opposed to truth, as is signified by, "and my lips shall hate wickedness." By these words the falsity opposed to the divine truth is designated and this is contrary to that religion which is called piety. Hence it is given the name of impiety.

Summa Theologiae[3]

The Priesthood of Christ

ARTICLE 1

Is It Suitable That Christ Should Be a Priest?

I reply that the proper office of a priest is to be a mediator between God and the people insofar as he conveys divine things to the people. Whence a priest is said to be a giver of sacred things according to Malachia 2.7, "they shall seek the law from his mouth," i.e. from the priest's mouth. Or, again, he is said to be a priest insofar as he offers the prayers of the people to God and in some way makes satisfaction to God for their sins, as the Apostle says, "For every high priest taken from among men is ordained for men in the things that appertain to God, that he may offer up gifts and sacrifices for sins" (Heb. 5.1). This is especially suitable as regards Christ. For through Him are gifts conferred on men, according to Peter (II Peter 1.4) saying "Through whom (namely Christ) He hath given us most great and precious promises that by these you may be made partakers of the divine nature." He also re-united the human race to God, according to that saying (Colos. 1. 19-20), "In Him (Christ) it hath well pleased the Father that all fullness should dwell and through Him to reconcile all things unto Himself." Hence it is most suitable for Christ to be a priest.

ARTICLE 2

Was Christ Both Priest and Victim?

I reply that, as Augustine says in *The City of God,* Book 10, c. 5, "Every visible sacrifice is a sacrament, *i.e.*, a sacred sign, of an invisible sacrifice." However an invisible sacrifice is one in which a man offers his spirit to God, according to the Psalm (50.19), "a sacrifice to God is an afflicted spirit." And so every thing which is offered to God may be called a sacrifice if it carries a man's spirit to God. Thus man needs sacrifice for three reasons: for the remission of sin, because of which man is turned from God and so the Apostle says (Heb. 5.1), "that the offering of gifts and sacrifices for sins is the duty of a priest"; secondly that man may be kept in the state of grace and always clinging to God, in whom peace and salvation are found. Whence even in the Old law a peace-victim was immolated for the salvation of the offerors, as is found in Leviticus 3; thirdly in order that the spirit of man be united perfectly with God which will be the case especially in glory. Hence even in the Old Law was offered a holocaust, *i.e.*, a totally consumed victim, as is said in Leviticus 1. All these have come to us through the humanity of Christ. For, in the first place, our sins have been rubbed out, according to Rom. 4.25, "He was delivered up for our sins"; secondly, we have received through Him the grace which saves us, as is said in Heb. 5.9, "He became to all that obey Him the cause of eternal salvation"; thirdly, through Him we have acquired the perfection of glory (Heb. 10.19), "We have a confidence in the entering into the Holies," *i.e.*, in the heavenly glory. Thus Christ Himself as man was not only a priest but also a perfect victim, being at the same time a victim for sin, and a perfect victim and a holocaust.

ARTICLE 3

Is Expiation of Sins the Effect of the Priesthood of Christ?

I reply that two things are required for the perfect cleansing of sins, just as there are two aspects of sin, *i.e.*, stain of sin and the debt of punishment. The stain of sin is washed away by grace by which the heart of the sinner is turned back to God; the debt of punishment is totally removed because man makes satisfaction to God. The priesthood of Christ accomplishes both of these. For in virtue of its grace is given to us by which our hearts are converted to God, according to the saying in Rom. 3.24-25, "Being justified freely by His grace through the redemption that is in Christ Jesus whom God hath proposed to be a propitiation through faith in His blood." He also satisfied for us completely insofar as he bore our infirmities and carried our sorrows (Is. 53.4). Whence it is clear that the priesthood of Christ has the full power of expiating sins.

The Existence of God[4]

Regarding the question whether God exists

I reply by saying that it can be proved in five ways that God exists

The first and more evident way is taken from an aspect of motion. For it is certain and evident to sense that in this world some things are moved (in motion). But everything which is moved (in motion) is moved by another; for nothing is moved (in motion) except insofar as it is in potency to that to which it is moved; on the other hand, some thing moves (is a mover) insofar as it is in act; for to move (as a mover) is nothing else but to educe something from potency to act. However, something cannot be reduced from potency to act except by some being already in act: just as what is actually hot, as fire, makes the wood, which is hot in potency, to be actually hot, and in this way moves and alters it. However, it is not possible that the same thing be at the same time in act and potency according to the same thing, but only according to diverse things; for what is actually hot, cannot be at the same time potentially hot, but it is at the same time potentially cold. Therefore it is impossible that something be a mover and moved in the same respect and in the same way, or that it move itself. Therefore what is moved (in motion) must be moved by another. Therefore if that by which it is moved, is moved, it is necessary that it itself be moved by another, and that by another. In this matter one cannot proceed to infinity because then there would be no first moved and so no other mover, because secondary movers cannot move except through that which is moved by the first mover, just as a stick does not move (is not in motion) except through this that it is moved by the hand. Therefore it is necessary to have recourse to some first mover which is not moved by any other; and this all understand to be God.

[The unmoved mover, since it is unmoved, is not in potency; since it is a mover, it is in act. A being in act without any potency is pure act in the order of existence or existence itself. This is God.]

The second way is from the notion of efficient cause. In regard to sensible things themselves, we find there is an order of efficient causes. There is no case known, neither is it, indeed, possible, in which a thing is found to be the efficient cause of itself; for if so it would be prior to itself, which is impossible. Now in efficient causes it is not possible to go on to infinity, because in all efficient causes following in order, the first is the cause of the intermediate cause, and the intermediate is the cause of the ultimate cause, whether the intermediate cause be several or only one. Now to take away the cause is to take away the effect. Therefore, if there be no first cause among efficient causes, there will be no ultimate, nor any intermediate cause. But if in efficient causes it is possible to go on to infinity, there will be no first efficient cause, neither will there be an ultimate effect, nor any intermediate efficient causes; all of which is plainly false. Therefore, it is necessary to admit a first efficient cause, to which everyone gives the name of God.

The third way is derived from the possible and the necessary and is this: we really find in things some which are possible to be and not to be, since they are found to be generated and corrupted, and thus are possible to be and not to be. However, it is impossible for all such things to always exist, because what is thus possible not to be at some time is not. Therefore if all things are possible not to be, at some time nothing would be in the number of things. But if this is true, even now nothing would be, because what is not does not begin to be except by means of something which is. If therefore, nothing was in existence, it would be impossible that something should begin to be; and, thus, even now nothing would be, which is clearly false. Therefore all beings are not possible beings, but there must be something necessary in the number of things. However, every necessary being either has the cause of its necessity from another or not. But it is not possible that there be a procession to infinity in regards to necessary beings which have a cause of their necessity, just as was the case regarding efficient causes as was proved in this article. Therefore it is necessary to posit something which is necessary in itself, not having a cause of its necessity from another, but which is the cause of necessary existence for the others; all call this God.

The fourth way is derived from the grades found in things. For there is found in things something more and less good, and true, and noble, and such of others of the same kind. But more and less are spoken about different things according as they approach differently something which is the greatest, just as the hotter is what approaches closer to what is hottest. Therefore there is something which is truest and best and most noble, and consequently greatest in being. For whatever are truest are greatest in being, as it says in 2 *Metaphysics* (text 4). However what is called the greatest in some class is the cause of all things which are members of that class; just as fire, which is the greatest in heat, is the cause of all hot things, as is said in the same book. Therefore there is something which is the cause of existence, and goodness, and perfections of any kind. This being we call God.

The fifth way is derived from the ordering of things. For example, we notice that some things lacking knowledge, namely natural bodies, act for a goal. This is evident from the fact that they operate always or more frequently in the same manner in order to strive for what is best. Whence it is evident that they reach the goal by design rather than by chance. But those things lacking knowledge do not tend toward a goal unless directed by someone with knowledge and intelligence, just as an arrow is directed by the archer. Therefore there is something intelligent by whom all natural beings are ordered to a goal. This being we call God.

Commentary on the 'Divine Names' of Dionysius[5]
How God May be Known

"We should investigate now how we acquire knowledge about God since He is neither understood nor sensed nor is He anything existing among all existing things. Can we say this truthfully seeing that we know him not from his nature? For this is unknown and it exceeds all understanding and reason and vision. But by means of the arrangement of all things, which is proposed by Him and involves certain images and similitudes of his divine exemplars, we ascend by the way of denial, transcendence, and the affirmation of the cause of all to that which is above all things as well as we can in accord with a life ordered by virtue. Wherefore God is known in all things and outside all things; He is known through cognition and through ignorance; of Him we have understanding and discourse and knowledge and touch and sense and opinion and phantasy and a name and all the others. Yet He is not understood nor talked about nor named and He is not anything among existing things nor is He known in any of those existing and He is all things in all and nothing in any and He is known in all and known to no one from anything. For we assert this of God rightly and He is praised from all existing things according to the proportion they bear to Him as their cause. Again there is that most divine knowledge of God which is known through ignorance according as a union is established above the mind when the mind withdraws from all else and then puts itself aside and is united with the supersplendent rays; then and there it is illumined by the unscrutable depths of wisdom. This wisdom is to be known indeed from all things, and have said. For it is, according to the Scriptures, the efficient cause of all ruling all things and the cause of the indissoluble harmony and order of all things linking the ends of the first things with the beginnings of the subsequent things and achieving beautifully one union and harmony of all."

Thus we should inquire how "we know God." For after Dionysius has shown how God knows, here he shows how God is known. In this matter he does three things: first, he presents a doubt, secondly, he solves it, there where he says, "can we say this truthfully since we know Him not from his nature?"; thirdly, he deduces a conclusion where he says, "wherefore God is known in all things and outside all things."

Therefore he says first that since it was said that God knows all things through His essence, which is above the intellect and sense and above all existing things, it remains to inquire how we can know God since He is not understood but is above all intelligibles, nor sensed because above all sensibles, nor is He anything in the number of existing things but above all existing things. And yet all our knowledge is by means of intellect or sense and we only know existing things.

Then when he says, "can we say this truthfully since we know God not from His nature?", he solves the proposed doubt because the question is put in such a way that it infers the solution under questioning. Therefore this is the solution: that we know God not by His nature as if we were seeing His essence itself, for His essence is unknown to the creature and exceeds not only sense but also all human reason and also every angelic mind as far as it concerns the natural power of reason and vision. Whence we can know his essence only as a result of a gift of grace. Therefore we do not know God by seeing His essence but we know Him from the order of the whole universe. For the totality of creatures itself is proposed to us by God in order that we know God through them insofar as the ordered universe has certain images and imperfect similitudes of divine things which are compared to the former as exemplary principles or models.

Thus from the order of the universe as by "a certain way and order we ascend" to God "who is above all" by our intellect and in accord with our "strength." We do this in three ways: firstly, indeed and principally, "by denying all of Him," insofar as we do not judge any of those things which we perceive in the order of creatures to be God or to be compatible with God; secondly, by transcendence, for we do not remove from God the perfections of creatures such as life, wisdom and the rest, because of some defect in God but because He exceeds every perfection of a creature; thus we remove wisdom from Him because He exceeds all wisdom; thirdly, as regards the causality of all things when we consider that whatever is in creatures proceeds from God as its cause. Hence our knowledge is directly contrary to God's knowledge, for God knows creatures through His own nature, but we know God through creatures.

Whether the Object of Faith Can Be Something Seen[6]

I reply that faith involves an assent of the intellect to what is believed. However the intellect assents to anything in one of two ways: in one way because it is moved to it by the object itself which is either known through itself, as is evident in regard to first principles which are understood, or through something else known, as is clear as regards conclusions of which there is scientific knowledge; in another way the intellect assents to something not because it is sufficiently moved by the object itself but because of a certain choice by which it inclines freely to one side rather than to another. If this occurs with doubt and fear as regards the other side there will be opinion. But if it occurs with certitude and without such fear there will be faith. However those things are said to be seen which themselves move our intellect or sense to a knowledge of themselves. Whence it is clear that neither faith nor opinion can be of those things which can be seen of themselves either by intellect or sense. . . .

Whether It Is Necessary for Salvation That We Believe Something Which Is Above Our Natural Reason[7]

I reply that in all properly ordered natures it is found that two things concur for the perfection of a lower nature; one which is in accord with its own proper motion, the other which is in accord with the motion of a higher nature. . . . It is only the created rational nature which has an immediate order to God because other creatures do not attain to anything universal but only to something particular and they participate in the divine goodness either by just existing, as do inanimates, or also by living and by knowing singulars, as do plants and animals. But the rational nature, insofar as it knows the universal notion of good and being, has an immediate order to the universal principle of being.

Hence the perfection of the rational creature not only consists in what is compatible to it according to its own nature but also in that which is given to it by a certain supernatural participation in the divine goodness. Whence it was said above in 1.2.q.3.a.8 that the final happiness of man consists in a certain supernatural vision of God; man cannot acquire this vision except he learn about it from God the teacher, according to John 6.45, "Everyone that hath heard of the Father and hath learned cometh to me." Man becomes a participant in this discipline not instantaneously but successively according to the mode of his nature. Every such learner must believe in order to reach perfect knowledge, just as, also, the Philosopher says in Book I of *The Sophistical Refutations*, c.2, "that the learner must believe."

Hence in order for man to reach the perfect vision of happiness there is prerequired that he believe in God as a pupil believes in the master teaching him.

Whether Charity Is Friendship[8]

I reply that according to the Philosopher in 8 *Ethics* c.2 and 3, not just any love involves the notion of friendship but only the love of benevolence when, namely, we love someone and will him good. However if we do not will good to what is loved but want it for ourselves, as we are said to love wine or a horse or something of that kind, it is not a love of friendship, but of a certain concupiscence. For it is ridiculous to say that someone has a friendship with wine or a horse. But neither does benevolence suffice for the essence of friendship but there is also required a certain mutual love because a friend is friendly to a friend. Such a mutual benevolence is based on some kind of communication.

Therefore since there is some kind of communication of man with God according as he communicates his beatitude to us, it is fitting that some friendship be based on this communication. Of this communication there is mention in I Cor. 1.9, "God is faithful, by whom you are called unto the fellowship of His Son." And the love based on this communication is charity. Whence it is clear that charity is a certain friendship of man and God.

Notes

1. *The Roman Breviary*, translated by John the Marquess of Bude. Vol. III, Edinburgh and London: Wm. Blackwood & Sons, 1908.
2. Translated from the Latin for this volume by Theodore E. James, Ph.D.
3. Translated by Theodore E. James, Ph.D. from the *Summa Theologiae* III, q. 22, a. 1-3.
4. Sancti Thomae Aquinatis, *Summae Theologiae Prima Pars*, Quaestio II De Deo, Articulus III Utrum Deus sit. Translated from the Pecci edition, Paris, 1889, by Theodore E. James, Ph.D.
5. *In Librum Beati Dionysii De Divinis Nominibus Commentaria*, C. 7 Lect. 4. *Sancti Thomae Aquinatis Opera Omnia*, t. XV, New York: Musurgia Publishers, 1950. Translated for this volume by Theodore E. James, Ph.D.

6. *S. Theol.* 2.2.q.1.a.4. Translated by Theodore E. James, Ph.D.
7. *Summa Theologiae* 2.2.q.2.a.3. Translated from the Latin by Theodore E. James, Ph.D.
8. *S. Theol.* 2.2.q.23.a.1. Translated by Theodore E. James, Ph.D.

Chapter 42 • Dante Alighieri: *Divine Comedy: Paradise*

Without a doubt the greatest of the Italian poets, Dante Alighieri (1265-1321) was born in Florence and spent a large part of his life in active service to this municipality. His reputation as a poet rests mainly on the *Divina Commedia*, a lengthy epic poem about the poet's journey through hell and purgatory to the final bliss of heaven. The poem is an allegorical picture of certain fundamental teachings of Christianity. The excerpt reproduced here is an appropriate conception of the final happiness achieved by the blessed in heaven.

Canto XXXI

In fashion, as a snow white rose, lay then
Before my view the saintly multitude,
Which in His own blood Christ espoused. Meanwhile,
That other host, that soar aloft to gaze
And celebrate His glory, whom they love,
Hovered around; and, like a troop of bees,
Amid the vernal sweets alighting now,
Now clustering, where their fragrant labor glows,
Flew downward to the mighty flower, or rose
From the redundant petals, streaming back
Unto the steadfast dwelling of their joy,
Faces had they of flame, and wings of gold:
The rest was whiter than the driven snow;
And, as they flitted down into the flower,
From range to range, fanning their plumy loins,
Whisper'd the peace and ardor, which they won
From that soft winnowing. Shadow none, the vast
Interposition of such numerous flight
Cast, from above, upon the flower, or view
Obstructed aught. For, through the universe,
Wherever merited, celestial light
Glides freely, and no obstacle prevents.
All there, who reign in safety and in bliss,

Ages long past or new, on one sole mark
Their love and vision fix'd. O trinal beam
Of individual star, that charm'st them thus!
Vouchsafe one glance to gild our storm below.
 If the grim brood, from Arctic shores that roam'd,
(Where Helice for ever, as she wheels,
Sparkles a mother's fondness on her son.)
Stood in mute wonder 'mid the works of Rome,
When to their view the Lateran arose
In greatness more than earthly; I, who then
From human to divine had past, from time
Unto eternity, and out of Florence
To justice and to truth, how might I chuse
But marvel too? 'Twixt gladness and amaze,
In sooth no will had I to utter aught,
Or hear. And, as a pilgrim, when he rests
Within the temple of his vow, looks round
In breathless awe, and hopes some time to tell
Of all its goodly state; e'en so mine eyes
Coursed up and down along the living light,
Now low, and now aloft, and now around,
Visiting every step. Looks I beheld,
Where charity in soft persuasion sat;
Smiles from within, and radiance from above;
And, in each gesture, grace and honor high.
 So roved my ken, and in its general form
All Paradise survey'd: when round I turn'd
With purpose of my lady to inquire
Once more of things, that held my thought suspense.
But answer found from other than I ween'd;
For, Beatrice, when I thought to see,
I saw instead a senior, at my side,
Robed, as the rest, in glory. Joy benign
Glow'd in his eye, and o'er his cheek diffused,
With gestures such as spake a father's love.
And "Whither is she vanish'd?" straight I ask'd.
 "By Beatrice summon'd," he replied,

"I come to aid thy wish. Looking aloft
To the third circle from the highest, there
Behold her on the throne, wherein her merit
Hath placed her." Answering not, mine eyes I raised,
And saw her, where aloof she sat, her brow
A wreath reflecting of eternal beams.
Not from the center of the sea so far
Unto the region of the highest thunder,
As was my ken from hers; and yet the form
Came through that medium down, unmix'd and pure.
"O Lady! thou in whom my hopes have rest;
Who, for my safety, hast not scorn'd, in Hell
To leave the traces of thy footsteps mark'd;
For all mine eyes have seen, I to thy power
And goodness, virtue owe and grace. Of slave
Thou hast to freedom brought me: and no means,
For my deliverance apt, has left untried.
Thy liberal bounty still toward me keep:
That, when my spirit, which thou madest whole,
Is loosen'd from this body, it may find
Favor with thee." So I my suit preferr'd:
And she, so distant, as appear'd, look'd down,
And smiled; then toward the eternal fountain turn'd
And thus the senior, holy and revered:
"That thou at length mayst happily conclude
Thy voyage, (to which end I was despatch'd,
By supplication moved and holy love,)
Let thy upsoaring vision range, at large,
This garden through: for so, by ray divine
Kindled, thy ken a higher flight shall mount;
And from Heaven's Queen, whom fervent I adore
All gracious aid befriend us; for that I
am her own faithful Bernard." Like a wight,
Who haply from Croatia wends to see
Our Veronica, and, the while 'tis shown,
Hangs over it with never-sated gaze,
And, all that he hath heard revolving, saith

Unto himself in thought: "And didst Thou look
E'en thus, O Jesus, my true Lord and God?
And was this semblance Thine?" So gazed I then
Adoring; for the charity of him,
Who musing, in this world that peace enjoy'd,
Stood livelily before me. "Child of grace!"
Thus he began: "Thou shalt not knowledge gain
Of this glad being, if thine eyes are held
Still in this depth below. But search around
The circles, to the furthest, till thou spy
Seated in state, the Queen that of this realm
Is sovran." Straight mine eyes I raised; and bright,
As, at the birth of morn, the eastern clime
Above the horizon, where the sun declines;
So to mine eyes, that upward, as from vale
To mountain sped, at the extreme bound, a part
Excell'd in luster all the front opposed.
And as the glow burns ruddiest o'er the wave,
That waits the ascending team, which Phaeton
Ill knew to guide, and on each part the light
Diminish'd fades, intensest in the midst;
So burn'd the peaceful oriflame, and slack'd
On every side the living flame decay'd.
And in that midst their sporative pennons waved
Thousands of Angels; in resplendence each
Distinct, and quaint adornment. At their glee
And carol, smiled the Lovely One of Heaven,
That joy was in the eyes of all the blest.
Had I a tongue in eloquence as rich,
As is the coloring in fancy's loom,
'Twere all too poor to utter the least part
Of that enchantment. When he saw mine eyes
Intent on her, that charm'd him; Bernard gazed
With so exceeding fondness, as infused
Ardor into my breast, unfelt before.

Canto XXXII

ARGUMENT. — St. Bernard shows him, on their several thrones, the other blessed souls, of both the Old and New Testament, explains to him that their places are assigned them by grace, and not according to merit; and, lastly, tells him that if he would obtain power to descry what remained of the heavenly vision, he must unite with him in supplication to Mary.

Freely the sage, though wrapt in musings high,
Assumed the teacher's part, and mild began:
"The wound, that Mary closed, she open'd first,
Who sits so beautiful at Mary's feet.
The third in order, underneath her, lo!
Rachel with Beatrice: Sarah next;
Judith; Rebecca; and the gleaner-maid,
Meek ancestress of him, who sang the songs
Of sore repentance in his sorrowful mood.
All, as I name them, down from leaf to leaf,
Are, in gradation, throned on the rose.
And from the seventh step, successively,
Adown the breathing tresses of the flower,
Still doth the file of Hebrew dames proceed.
For these are a partition wall, whereby
The sacred stairs are sever'd, as the faith
In Christ divides them. On this part, where blooms
Each leaf in full maturity, are set
Such as in Christ, or e'er He came, believed.
On the other, where an intersected space
Yet shows the semicircle void, abide
All they, who look'd to Christ already come
And as our Lady on her glorious stool,
And they who on their stools beneath her sit,
This way distinction make; e'en so on his,
The mighty Baptist that way marks the line
(He who endured the desert, and the pains
Of martyrdom, and, for two years, of Hell,
Yet still continued holy), and beneath,
Augustin; Francis; Benedict; and the rest,

Thus far from round to round. So Heaven's decree
Forecasts, this garden equally to fill,
With faith in either view, past or to come.
Learn too, that downward from the step, which cleaves,
Midway, the twain compartments, none there are
Who place obtain for merit of their own,
But have through others' merit been advanced,
On set conditions; spirits all released,
Ere for themselves they had the power to chuse.
And, if thou mark and listen to them well,
Their childish looks and voice declare as much.
"Here, silent as thou art, I know thy doubt;
And gladly will I loose the knot, wherein
Thy subtil thoughts have bound thee. From this realm
Excluded, chance no entrance here may find;
No more than hunger, thirst, or sorrow can.
A law immutable hath stablish'd all;
Nor is there aught thou seest, that doth not fit,
Exactly, as the finger to the ring.
It is not, therefore, without cause, that these
O'erspeedy comers to immortal life,
Are different in their shares of excellence.
Our Sovran Lord, that settleth this estate
In love and in delight so absolute,
That wish can dare no further, every soul,
Created in His joyous sight to dwell,
With grace, at pleasure, variously endows.
And for a proof the effect may well suffice.
And 'tis moreover most expressly mark'd
In holy Scripture, where the twins are said
To have struggled in the womb. Therefore, as grace
Inweaves the coronet, so every brow
Weareth its proper hue of orient light.
And merely in respect to his prime gift,
Not in reward of meritorious deed,
Hath each his several degree assign'd.
In early times with their own innocence

More was not wanting, than the parents' faith,
To save them: those first ages past, behoved
That circumcision in the males should imp
The flight of innocent wings; but since the day
Of grace hath come, without baptismal rites
In Christ accomplished, innocence herself
Must linger yet below. Now raise thy view
Unto the visage most resembling Christ:
For, in her splendor only, shalt thou win
The power to look on Him." Forthwith I saw
Such floods of gladness on her visage shower'd,
From holy spirits, winging that profound;
That, whatsoever I had yet beheld,
Had not so much suspended me with wonder,
Or shown me such similitude of God.
And he, who had to her descended, once,
On earth, now hail'd in Heaven; and on poised wing,
"Ave, Maria, Gratia, Plena," sang:
To whose sweet anthem all the blissful court,
From all parts answering, rang: that holier joy
Brooded the deep serene. "Father revered!
Who deign'st, for me, to quit the pleasant place
Wherein thou sittest, by eternal lot;
Say, who that Angel is, that with such glee
Beholds our Queen, and so enamor'd glows
Of her high beauty, that all fire he seems."
So I again restored to the lore
Of my wise teacher, he, whom Mary's charms
Embellish'd, as the sun the morning star,
Who thus in answer spoke: "In him are summ'd,
Whate'er of buxomness and free delight
May be in spirit, or in Angel, met:
And so beseems: for that he bare the palm
Down unto Mary, when the Son of God
Vouchsafed to clothe Him in terrestrial weeds.
Now let thine eyes wait heedful on my words;
And note thou of this just and pious realm

The chiefest nobles. Those, highest in bliss,
The twain, on each hand next our Empress throned,
Are as it were two roots unto this rose:
He to the left, the parent, whose rash taste
Proves bitter to his seed; and, on the right,
That ancient father of the holy Church,
Into whose keeping Christ did give the keys
Of this sweet flower; near whom behold the seer,
That, ere he died, saw all the grievous times
Of the fair bride, who with the lance and nails
Was won. And near unto the other, rests
The leader, under whom, on manna, fed
The ungrateful nation, fickle and perverse.
On the other part, facing to Peter, lo!
Where Anna sits, so well content to look
On her loved daughter, that with moveless eye
She chants the loud hosanna: while, opposed
To the first father of your mortal kind,
Is Lucia, at whose hest thy lady sped,
When on the edge of ruin closed thine eye.
"But (for the vision hasteneth to an end)
Here break we off, as the good workman doth,
That shapes the cloak according to the cloth;
And to the Primal Love our ken shall rise;
That thou mayst penetrate the brightness, far
As sight can bear thee. Yet, alas! in sooth
Beating thy pennons, thinking to advance,
Thou backward fall'st. Grace then must first be gain'd;
Her grace, whose might can help thee. Thou in prayer
Seek her: and, with affection, whilst I sue,
Attend, and yield me all thy heart." He said;
And thus the saintly orison began.

Canto XXXIII

ARGUMENT. — St. Bernard supplicates the Virgin Mary that Dante may have grace given him to contemplate the brightness of the Divine Majesty, which is accordingly granted; and Dante then himself prays to God for ability to show forth some part of the celestial glory in his writings. Lastly, he is admitted to a glimpse of the great mystery, the Trinity and the Union of Man with God.

"O Virgin Mother, daughter of thy Son!
Created beings all in lowliness
Surpassing, as in height above them all;
Term by the eternal counsel pre-ordain'd;
Ennobler of thy nature, so advanced
In thee, that its great Maker did not scorn,
To make Himself his own creation,
For in thy womb rekindling shone the love
Reveal'd, whose genial influence makes now
This flower to germin in eternal peace;
Here thou to us, of charity and love,
Art, as the noon-day torch; and art, beneath,
To mortal men, of hopes a living spring.
So mighty art thou, Lady, and so great,
That he, who grace desireth, and comes not
To thee for aidance, fain would have desire
Fly without wings. Not only him, who asks,
Thy bounty succors; but doth freely oft
Forerun the asking. Whatso'er may be
Of excellence in creature, pity mild,
Relenting mercy, large munificence,
Are all combined in thee. Here kneeleth one,
Who of all spirits hath review'd the state,
From the world's lowest gap unto this height.
Suppliant to thee he kneels, imploring grace
For virtue yet more high, to lift his ken
Toward the Bliss Supreme. And I, who ne'er
Coveted sight, more fondly, for myself,
Than now for him, my prayers to thee prefer,
(And pray they be not scant,) that thou wouldst
Each cloud of his mortality away, drive
Through thine own prayers, that on the sovran joy
Unveil'd he gaze. This yet, I pray thee, Queen,

Who canst do what thou wilt; that in him thou
Wouldst, after all he hath beheld, preserve
Affection sound, and human passions quell.
Lo! where, with Beatrice, many a saint
Stretch their clasp'd hands, in furtherance of my suit."
The eyes, that Heaven with love and awe regards,
Fix'd on the suitor, witness'd, how benign
She looks on pious prayers: then fasten'd they
On the everlasting fight, wherein no eye
Of creature, as may well be thought, so far
Can travel inward. I, meanwhile, who drew
Near to the limit, where all wishes end,
The ardor of my wish (for so behoved)
Ended within me. Beckoning smiled the sage,
That I should look aloft: but, ere he bade,
Already of myself aloft I look'd;
For visual strength, refining more and more,
Bare me into the ray authentical
Of sovran light. Thenceforward, what I saw,
Was not for words to speak, nor memory's self
To stand against such outrage on her skill.
As one, who from a dream awaken'd, straight,
All he hath seen forgets; yet still retains
Impression of the feeling in his dream;
E'en such am I: for all the vision dies,
As 'twere, away; and yet the sense of sweet,
That sprang from it, still trickles in my heart.
Thus in the sun-thaw is the snow unseal'd;
Thus in the winds on flitting leaves was lost
The Sibyl's sentence. O eternal beam!
(Whose height what reach of mortal thought may soar?)
Yield me again some little particle
Of what Thou then appearedst; give my tongue
Power, but to leave one sparkle of Thy glory,
Unto the race to come, that shall not lose
Thy triumph wholly, if Thou waken aught
Of memory in me, and endure to hear

The record sound in this unequal strain.
 Such keenness from the living ray I met,
That, if mine eyes had turn'd away, methinks,
I had been lost; but, so emboldened, on
I pass'd, as I remember, till my view
Hover'd the brink of dread infinitude.
 O grace, unenvying of Thy boon! that gavest
Boldness to fix so earnestly my ken
On the everlasting splendor, that I look'd,
While sight was unconsumed, and, in that depth,
Saw in one volume clasp'd of love, whate'er
The universe unfolds; all properties
Of substance and of accident, beheld,
Compounded, yet one individual light
The whole. And of such bond methinks I saw
The universal form; for that whene'er
I do but speak of it, my soul dilates
Beyond her proper self; and, till I speak,
One moment seems a longer lethargy,
Than five-and-twenty ages had appear'd
To that emprize, that first made Neptune wonder
At Argo's shadow darkening on his flood.
 With fixed heed, suspense and motionless,
Wondering I gazed; and admiration still
Was kindled as I gazed. It may not be,
That one, who looks upon that light, can turn
To other object, willingly, his view.
For all the good, that will may covet, there
Is summ'd; and all, elsewhere defective found,
Complete. My tongue shall utter now, no more
E'en what remembrance keeps, than could the babe's
That yet is moisten'd at his mother's breast.
Not that the semblance of the living light
Was changed, (that ever as at first remain'd,)
But that my vision quickening, in that sole
Appearance, still new miracles descried,
And toil'd me with the change. In that abyss

Of radiance, dear and lofty, seem'd, methought,
Three orbs of triple hue, clipt in one bound.
And, from another, one reflected seem'd,
As rainbow is from rainbow: and the third
Seem'd fire, breathed equally from both. O speech!
How feeble and how faint art thou, to give
Conception birth. Yet this to what I saw
Is less than little. O eternal Light!
Sole in Thyself that dwell'st; and of Thyself
Sole understood, past, present, or to come;
Thou smiledst, on that circling, which in Thee
Seem'd as reflected splendor, while I mused;
For I therein, methought, in its own hue
Beheld our image painted: steadfastly
I therefore pored upon the view. As one,
Who versed in geometric lore, would fain
Measure the circle; and, though pondering long
And deeply, that beginning, which he needs,
Finds not: e'en such was I, intent to scan
The novel wonder, and trace out the form,
How to the circle fitted, and therein
How placed; but the flight was not for my wing;
Had not a flash darted athwart my mind,
And, in the spleen, unfolded what it sought.
Here vigor fail'd the towering fantasy:
But yet the will roll'd onward, like a wheel
In even motion, by the Love impell'd,
That moves the sun in Heaven and all the stars.

Selection from
The Divine Comedy of Dante Alighieri, Paradise,
Translated by Henry F. Cary,
New York: The Collier Press, 1909

Chapter 43 • St. Catherine of Siena: *A Treatise of Prayer*

St. Catherine (1347-1380) was born in Siena, the youngest of twenty-five children. Her mystical experiences began at age six. She entered the Third Order of St. Dominic in 1364 and soon after a circle of followers formed around her. She was influential in the Crusade against the Turks, and she played a major role in persuading the Pope to return from Avignon to Rome. In 1375, she received the stigmata. Her chief work, the *Dialogues*, and a collection of letters reveal her brilliance. The *Dialogues* were dictated to her followers, as Catherine was illiterate, like most women of her time. She was declared a Doctor of the Church in 1970.

Dialogues

A Treatise of Prayer

Of the means which the soul takes to arrive at pure and generous love; and here begins the Treatise of Prayer

"When the soul has passed through the doctrine of Christ crucified, with true love of virtue and hatred of vice, and has arrived at the house of self-knowledge and entered therein, she remains, with her door barred, in watching and constant prayer, separated entirely from the consolations of the world. Why does she thus shut herself in? She does so from fear, knowing her own imperfections, and also from the desire, which she has, of arriving at pure and generous love. And because she sees and knows well that in no other way can she arrive thereat, she waits, with a lively faith for My arrival, through increase of grace in her. How is a lively faith to be recognized? By perseverance in virtue, and by the fact that the soul never turns back for anything, whatever it be, nor rises from holy prayer, for any reason except (note well) for obedience or charity's sake. For no other reason ought she to leave off prayer, for, during the time ordained for prayer, the Devil is wont to arrive in the soul, causing much more conflict and trouble than when the soul is not occupied in prayer. This he does in order that holy prayer may become tedious to the soul, tempting her often with these words: '*This prayer avails thee nothing, for thou needest attend to nothing except thy vocal prayers.*' He acts thus in order that, becoming wearied and confused in mind, she may abandon the exercise of prayer, which is a weapon with which the soul can defend herself from every adversary, if grasped with the hand of love, by the arm of free choice in the light of the Holy Faith."

Here, touching something concerning the Sacrament of the Body of Christ, the complete doctrine is given; and how the soul proceeds from vocal to mental prayer, and a vision is related which this devout soul once received.

"Know, dearest daughter, how, by humble, continual, and faithful prayer, the soul acquires, with time and perseverance, every virtue. Wherefore should she persevere and never abandon prayer, either through the illusion of the Devil or her own fragility, that is to say, either on account of any thought or movement coming from her own body, or of the words of any creature. The Devil often places himself upon the tongues of creatures, causing them to chatter nonsensically, with the purpose of preventing the prayer of the soul. All of this she should pass by, by means of the virtue of perseverance. Oh, how sweet and pleasant to that soul and to Me is holy prayer, made in the house of knowledge of self and of Me, opening the eye of the intellect to the light of faith, and the affections to the abundance of My charity, which was made visible to you, through My visible only-begotten Son, who showed it to you with His blood! Which Blood inebriates the soul and clothes her with the fire of divine charity, giving her the food of the Sacrament [which is placed in the tavern of the mystical body of the Holy Church] that is to say, the food of the Body and Blood of My Son, wholly God and wholly man, administered to you by the hand of My vicar, who holds the key of the Blood. This is that tavern, which I mentioned to thee, standing on the Bridge, to provide food and comfort for the travellers and the pilgrims, who pass by the way of the doctrine of My Truth, lest they should faint through weakness. This food strengthens little or much, according to the desire of the recipient, whether he receives sacramentally or virtually. He receives sacramentally when he actually communicates with the Blessed Sacrament. He receives virtually when he communicates, both by desire of communion, and by contemplation of the Blood of Christ crucified, communicating, as it were, sacramentally, with the affection of love, which is to be tasted in the Blood which, as the soul sees, was shed through love. On seeing this the soul becomes inebriated, and blazes with holy desire and satisfies herself, becoming full of love for Me and for her neighbour. Where can this be acquired? In the house of self-knowledge with holy prayer, where imperfections are lost, even as Peter and the disciples, while they remained in watching and prayer, lost their imperfection and acquired perfection. By what means is this acquired? By perseverance seasoned with the most holy faith.

"But do not think that the soul receives such ardour and nourishment from prayer, if she pray only vocally, as do many souls whose prayers are rather words than love. Such as these give heed to nothing except to completing Psalms and saying many paternosters. And when they have once completed their appointed tale, they do not appear to think of anything further, but seem to place devout attention and love in merely vocal recitation, which the soul is not required to do, for, in doing only this, she bears but little fruit, which pleases Me but little. But if thou askest Me, whether the soul should abandon vocal prayer, since it does not seem to all that they are called to mental prayer, I should reply "*No.*" The soul should advance by degrees, and I know well that, just as the soul is at first imperfect and afterwards perfect, so also is it with her prayer. She should nevertheless continue in vocal prayer, while she is yet imperfect, so as not to fall into idleness. But she should not say her vocal prayers without joining them to mental prayer, that is to say, that while she is reciting, she should endeavour to elevate her mind in My love, with the consideration of her own defects and of the Blood of My only-begotten Son, wherein she finds the breadth of My charity and the remission of her sins. And this she should do, so that self-knowledge and the consideration of her own defects should make her recognize My goodness in herself and continue her exercises with true humility. I do not wish defects to be considered in particular, but in general, so that the mind may not be contaminated by the remembrance of particular and hideous sins. But, as I said, I do not wish the soul to consider her sins, either in general or in particular, without also remembering the Blood and the broadness of My mercy, for fear that otherwise she should be brought to confusion. And together with confusion would come the Devil, who has caused it, under colour of contrition and displeasure of sin, and so she would arrive at eternal damnation, not only on account of her confusion, but also through the despair which would come to her, because she did not seize the arm of My mercy. This is one of the subtle devices with which the Devil deludes My servants, and, in order to escape from his deceit, and to be pleasing to Me, you must enlarge your hearts and affections in My boundless mercy, with true humility. Thou knowest that the pride of the Devil cannot resist the humble mind, nor can any confusion of spirit be greater than the broadness of My good mercy, if the soul will only truly hope therein. Wherefore it was, if thou remember rightly, that, once, when the Devil wished to overthrow thee, by confusion, wishing to prove to thee that thy life had been deluded, and that thou hadst not followed My will, thou didst that which was thy duty, which My goodness (which is never withheld from him who will receive it) gave thee strength to do, that is thou didst rise, humbly trusting in My mercy, and saying: *'I confess to my Creator that my life has indeed been passed in darkness, but I will hide myself in the Wounds of Christ crucified, and bathe myself in His Blood and so shall my iniquities be consumed, and with desire will I rejoice in my Creator.'* Thou rememberest that then the Devil fled, and, turning round to the opposite side, he endeavoured to inflate thee with pride, saying: *'Thou art perfect and pleasing to God, and there is no more need for thee to afflict thyself or to lament thy sins.'* And once more I gave thee the light to see thy true path, namely, humiliation of *thyself, and thou didst answer the Devil with these words: 'Wretch that I am, John the Baptist never sinned and was sanctified in his mother's womb. And I have committed so many sins, and have hardly begun to know them with grief and true contrition, seeing who God is, who is ofended by me, and who I am, who offend Him.'* Then the Devil, not being able to resist thy humble hope in My goodness, said to thee: *'Cursed that thou art, for I can find no way to take thee. If I put thee down through confusion, thou risest to Heaven on the wings of mercy, and if I raise thee on high, thou humblest thyself down to Hell, and when I go into Hell thou persecutest me, so that I will return to thee no more, because thou strikest me with the stick of charity.'* The soul, therefore, should season the knowledge of herself with the knowledge of My goodness, and then vocal prayer will be of use to the soul who makes it, and pleasing to Me, and she will arrive, from the vocal imperfect prayer, exercised with perseverance, at perfect mental prayer; but if she simply aims at completing her tale, and, for vocal abandons mental prayer, she will never arrive at it. Sometimes the soul will be so ignorant that, having resolved to say so many prayers vocally, and I, visiting her mind sometimes in one way, and sometimes in another, in a flash of self-knowledge or of contrition for sin, sometimes in the broadness of My charity, and sometimes by placing before her mind, in diverse ways, according to My pleasure and the desire of the soul, the presence of My Truth, she (the soul), in order to complete her tale, will abandon My visitation, that she feels, as it were, by conscience, rather than abandon that which she had begun. She should not do so, for, in so doing, she yields to a deception of the Devil. The moment she feels her mind disposed by My visitation, in the many ways I have told thee, she should abandon vocal prayer; then, My visitation past, if there be time, she can resume the vocal prayers which she had resolved to say, but if she has not time to complete them, she ought not on that account to be troubled or suffer annoyance and confusion of mind; of course provided that it were not the Divine office which clerics and religious are bound and obliged to say under penalty of offending Me, for, they must, until death, say their office. But if they, at the hour appointed for saying it, should feel their minds drawn and raised by desire, they should so arrange as to say it before or after My visitation, so that the debt of rendering the office be not omitted. But, in any other case, vocal prayer should be immediately abandoned for the said cause. Vocal prayer, made in the way that I have told thee, will enable the soul to arrive at perfection, and therefore she should not abandon it, but use it in the way that I have told thee.

"And so, with exercise in perseverance, she will taste prayer in truth, and the food of the Blood of My only-begotten Son, and therefore I told thee that some communicated virtually with the Body and Blood of Christ, although not sacramentally; that is, they communicate in the affection of charity, which they taste by means of holy prayer, little or much, according to the affection with which they pray. They who proceed with little prudence and without method, taste little, and they who proceed with much, taste much. For the more the soul tries to loosen her affection from herself, and fasten it in Me with the light of the intellect, the more she knows; and the more she knows, the more she loves, and, loving much, she tastes much. Thou seest then, that perfect prayer is not attained to through many words, but through affection of desire, the soul raising herself to Me, with knowledge of herself and of My mercy, seasoned the one with the other. Thus she will exercise together mental and vocal prayer, for, even as the active and contemplative life is one, so are they. Although vocal or mental prayer can be understood in many and diverse ways, for I have told thee that a holy desire is a continual prayer, in this sense that a good and holy will disposes itself with desire to the occasion actually appointed for prayer in addition to the continual prayer of holy desire, wherefore vocal prayer will be made at the appointed time by the soul who remains firm in a habitual holy will, and will sometimes be continued beyond the appointed time, according as charity commands for the salvation of the neighbour, if the soul see him to be in need, and also her own necessities according to the state in which I have placed her. Each one, according to his condition, ought to exert himself for the salvation of souls, for this exercise lies at the root of a holy will, and whatever he may contribute, by words or deeds, towards the salvation of his neighbour, is virtually a prayer, although it does not replace a prayer which one should make oneself at the appointed season, as My glorious standard-bearer Paul said, in the words, *'He who ceases not to work ceases not to pray.'* It was for this reason that I told thee that prayer was made in many ways, that is, that actual prayer may be united with mental prayer if made with the affection of charity, which charity is itself continual prayer. I have now told thee how mental prayer is reached by exercise and perseverance, and by leaving vocal prayer for mental when I visit the soul. I have also spoken to thee of common prayer, that is, of vocal prayer in general, made outside of ordained times, and of the prayers of good-will, and how every exercise, whether performed, in oneself or in one's neighbour, with good-will, is prayer. The enclosed soul should therefore spur herself on with prayer, and when she has arrived at friendly and filial love she does so. Unless the soul keep to this path, she will always remain tepid and imperfect, and will only love Me and her neighbour in proportion to the pleasure which she finds in My service."

Selections from "A Treatise of Prayer" are from
The Dialogue of the Seraphic Virgin Catherine of Siena,
Algar Thorold,
Westminster, Maryland: The Newman Press, 1950

Chapter 44 • *The Imitation of Christ*

This work has probably been *the* best seller, after the Bible, of all Catholic books. Written in the fifteenth century, it is strictly devotional and openly hostile to any form of speculation or scholastic discussion. It has been traditionally ascribed to Thomas à Kempis, though more recent scholarship makes it originally the work of Gerard Groote. Irrespective of the identity of the author, the contents present the particular attitude of the beliefs and practices of the Brothers of the Common Life in the early fifteenth century in the Netherlands. It shows us how a devout Catholic can cultivate a deep, mystical devotion to Christ, the Sacraments, and the Christian way of life.

The First Book

Admonitions, Useful for a Spiritual Life

Chapter I

Of the Imitation of Christ, and Contempt of All the Vanities of the World.

"He that followeth Me shall not walk in darkness," saith the Lord. These are the words of Christ, by which we are admonished, how we ought to imitate His life and manners, if we will be truly enlightened, and be delivered from all blindness of heart.

Let therefore our chiefest endeavor be, to meditate upon the life of JESUS CHRIST.

The doctrine of Christ exceedeth all the doctrines of holy men; and he that hath the Spirit, will find therein the hidden manna.

But it falleth out, that many who often hear the Gospel of Christ, are yet but little affected, because they have not the Spirit of Christ.

But whosoever would fully and feelingly understand the words of Christ, must endeavor to conform his life wholly to the life of Christ.

What will it avail thee to dispute profoundly of the Trinity, if thou be void of humility, and art thereby displeasing to the Trinity?

Surely high words do not make a man holy and just; but a virtuous life maketh him dear to God.

I had rather feel compunction, than understand the definition thereof.

If thou didst know the whole Bible by heart, and the sayings of all the philosophers, what would all that profit thee without the love of God, and without His grace?

Vanity of vanities; all is vanity, except to love God, and to serve Him only.

This is the highest wisdom, by contempt of the world to tend towards the kingdom of Heaven.

Vanity therefore it is, to seek after perishing riches, and to trust in them.

It is also vanity to hunt after honors, and to climb to high degree.

It is vanity to follow the desires of the flesh, and to labor for that for which thou just afterwards suffer more grievous punishment.

Vanity it is, to wish to live long, and to be careless to live well.

It is vanity to mind only this present life, and not to foresee those things which are to come.

It is vanity to set thy love on that which speedily passeth away, and not to hasten thither where everlasting joy abideth.

Call often to mind that proverb, "The eye is not satisfied with seeing, nor the ear filled with hearing."

Endeavor therefore to withdraw thy heart from the love of visible things, and to turn thyself to the invisible.

For they that follow their sensuality, do stain their own consciences, and lose the favor of God.

Chapter II
Of the Humble Conceit of Ourselves

All men naturally desire to know; but what availeth knowledge without the fear of God?

Surely, an humble husbandman that serveth God, is better than a proud philosopher that, neglecting himself, labors to understand the course of the heavens.

Whoso knows himself well, grows more mean in his own conceit, and delighteth not in the praises of men.

If I understood all things in the world, and were not in charity, what would that help me in the sight of God, who will judge me according to my deeds?

Cease from an inordinate desire of knowing, for therein is much distraction and deceit.

The learned are well pleased to seem so to others, and to be accounted wise.

There be many things, which to know doth little or nothing profit the soul:

And he is very unwise, that is intent upon other things than those that may avail him for his salvation.

Many words do not satisfy the soul; but a good life comforteth the mind, and a pure conscience giveth great assurance in the sight of God.

How much the more thou knowest, and how much the better thou understandest, so much the more grievously shalt thou therefore be judged, unless thy life be also more holy.

Be not therefore exalted in thine own mind for any art or science which thou knowest, but rather let the knowledge given thee, make thee more humble and cautious.

If thou thinkest that thou understandest and knowest much, know also that there be many things more which thou knowest not.

Affect not to be overwise, but rather acknowledge thine own ignorance.

Why wilt thou prefer thyself before others, since there be many more learned, and more skillful in the Scripture than thou art?

If thou wilt know or learn anything profitably, desire to be unknown, and to be little esteemed by man.

The highest and most profitable reading is the true knowledge and consideration of ourselves.

It is great wisdom and perfection to esteem nothing of ourselves, and to think always well and highly of others.

If thou shouldst see another openly sin, or commit some heinous offense, yet oughtest thou not to esteem the better of thyself; for thou knowest not how long thou shalt be able to remain in good estate.

We are all frail, but thou oughtest to esteem none more frail than thyself.

Chapter III
Of the Doctrine of Truth

Happy is he whom truth by itself doth teach, not by figures and words that pass away; but as it is in itself.

Our own opinion and our own sense do often deceive us, and they discern but little.

What availeth it to cavil and dispute much about dark and hidden things; whereas for being ignorant of them we shall not be so much as reproved at the Day of Judgment?

It is a great folly to neglect the things that are profitable and necessary, and give our minds to that which is curious and hurtful: we have eyes and see not.

And what have we to do with *genus* and *species*, the dry notions of logicians?

He to whom the Eternal Word speaketh, is delivered from a world of unnecessary conceptions.

From that one Word are all things, and all speak that One; and this is the Beginning, which also speaketh unto us.

No man without that Word understandeth or judgeth rightly.

He to whom all things are one, he who reduceth all things to one, and seeth all things in one, may enjoy a quiet mind, and remain peaceable in God.

O God, who art the truth, make me one with Thee in everlasting charity.

It is tedious to me often to read and hear many things: In Thee is all that I would have and can desire.

Let all doctors hold their peace; let all creatures be silent in Thy sight; speak Thou alone unto me.

The more a man is united within himself, and becometh inwardly simple and pure, so much the more and higher things doth he understand without labor; for that he receiveth intellectual light from above.

A pure, sincere, and stable spirit is not distracted, though it be employed in many works; for that it works all to the honor of God, and inwardly being still and quiet, seeks not itself in anything it doth.

Who hinders and troubles thee more than the unmortified affections of thine own heart?

A good and godly man disposeth within himself beforehand those things which he is outwardly to act;

Neither do they draw him according to the desires of an inordinate inclination, but he ordereth them according to the prescript of right reason.

Who hath a harder combat than he that laboreth to overcome himself?

This ought to be our endeavor, to conquer ourselves, and daily to wax stronger and to make a further growth in holiness.

All perfection in this life hath some imperfection mixed with it; and no knowledge of ours is without some darkness.

A humble knowledge of thyself is a surer way to God than a deep search after learning;

Yet learning is not to be blamed, nor the mere knowledge of anything whatsoever to be disliked, it being good in itself, and ordained by God; but a good conscience and a virtuous life is always to be preferred before it.

But because many endeavor rather to get knowledge than to live well, therefore they are often deceived, and reap either none, or very slender profit of their labors.

Oh, if men bestowed as much labor in the rooting out of vices, and planting of virtues, as they do in moving of questions, neither would there so much hurt be done, nor so great scandal be given in the world, nor so much looseness be practiced in Religious Houses.

Truly, at the Day of Judgment we shall not be examined what we have read, but what we have done; not how well we have spoken, but how religiously we have lived.

Tell me now, where are all those Doctors and Masters, with whom thou wast well acquainted, whilst they lived and flourished in learning?

Now others possess their livings and perhaps do scarce ever think of them. In their lifetime they seemed something, but now they are not spoken of.

Oh, how quickly doth the glory of the world pass away! Oh, that their life had been answerable to their learning! then had their study and reading been to good purpose.

How many perish by reason of vain learning in this world, who take little care of the serving of God; and because they rather choose to be great than humble, therefore they become vain in their imaginations.

He is truly great, that is great in charity.

He is truly great, that is little in himself, and that maketh no account of any height of honor.

He is truly wise, that accounteth all earthly things as dung, that he may gain Christ.

And he is truly learned, that doeth the will of God, and forsaketh his own will.

The Second Book

Admonitions Tending to Things Internal

Chapter I

Of the Inward Life

"The Kingdom of God is within you," saith the Lord. Turn thee with thy whole heart unto the Lord, and forsake this wretched world, and thy soul shall find rest.

Learn to despise outward things, and to give thyself to things inward, and thou shalt perceive the Kingdom of God to come in thee.

"For the Kingdom of God is peace and joy in the Holy Ghost," which is not given to the unholy.

Christ will come unto thee, and show thee His consolation, if thou prepare for Him a worthy mansion within thee.

All His glory and beauty is from within, and there He delighteth Himself.

The inward man He often visiteth; and hath with him sweet discourses, pleasant solace, much peace, familiarity exceeding wonderful.

O faithful soul, make ready thy heart for this Bridegroom, that He may vouchsafe to come unto thee, and dwell within thee.

For thus saith He, "If any love Me, he will keep My words, and We will come unto him, and will make our abode with him."

Give therefore admittance unto Christ, and deny entrance to all others.

When thou hast Christ thou art rich, and hast enough. He will be thy faithful and provident helper in all things, so as thou shalt not need to trust in men.

For men soon change, and quickly fail; but Christ remaineth for ever, and standeth by us firmly unto the end.

There is no great trust to be put in a frail and mortal man, even though he be profitable and dear unto us: neither ought we to be much grieved if sometimes he cross and contradict us.

They that to-day take thy part, to-morrow may be against thee; and often do they turn right round like the wind.

Put all thy trust in God, let Him be thy fear, and thy love: He shall answer for thee, and will do in all things what is best for thee.

Thou hast not here an abiding city; and wheresoever thou be, thou art a stranger and pilgrim: neither shalt thou ever have rest, unless thou be most inwardly united unto Christ.

Why dost thou here gaze about, since this is not the place of thy rest? In Heaven ought to be thy home, and all earthly things are to be looked upon as it were by the way.

All things are passing away, and thou together with them.

Beware thou cleave not unto them, lest thou be caught and so perish. Let thy thought be on the Most High, and thy prayer for mercy directed unto Christ without ceasing.

If thou canst not contemplate high and heavenly things, rest thyself in the passion of Christ, and dwell willingly in His sacred wounds.

For if thou fly devoutly unto the wounds and precious marks of the Lord Jesus, thou shalt feel great comfort in tribulation: neither wilt thou much care for the slights of men, and wilt easily bear words of detraction.

Christ was also in the world, despised of men, and in greatest necessity, forsaken by His acquaintance and friends, in the midst of slanders.

Christ was willing to suffer and be despised; and darest thou complain of any man?

Christ had adversaries and backbiters; and dost thou wish to have all men thy friends and benefactors?

Whence shall thy patience attain her crown, if no adversity befall thee?

If thou art willing to suffer no adversity, how wilt thou be the friend of Christ?

Suffer with Christ, and for Christ, if thou desire to reign with Christ.

If thou hadst but once perfectly entered into the secrets of the Lord Jesus, and tasted a little of His ardent love, then wouldst thou not regard thine own convenience, or inconvenience, but rather wouldst rejoice at slanders, if they should be cast upon thee; for the love of Jesus maketh a man despise himself.

A lover of Jesus and of the Truth, and a true inward Christian, and one free from inordinate affections, can freely turn himself unto God, and lift himself above himself in spirit, and with joy remain at rest.

He that judgeth of all things as they are, and not as they are said or esteemed to be, is truly wise, and taught of God rather than of men.

He that can live inwardly, and make small reckoning of things without, neither requireth places nor expecteth times, for performing of religious exercises.

A spiritual man quickly recollecteth himself, because he never poureth out himself wholly to outward things.

He is not hindered by outward labor, or business which may be necessary for the time: but as things fall out, so he accommodates himself to them.

He that is well ordered and disposed within himself, cares not for the strange and perverse behavior of men.

A man is hindered and distracted, in proportion as he draweth external matters unto himself.

If it were well with thee, and thou wert well purified from sin, all things would fall out to thee for good, and to thy advancement in holiness.

But many things displease, and often trouble thee; because thou art not yet perfectly dead unto thyself, nor separated from all earthly things.

Nothing so defileth and entangleth the heart of man, as the impure love to creatures.

If thou refuse outward comfort, thou will be able to contemplate the things of Heaven, and often to receive internal joy.

Chapter IV

Of a Pure Mind, and Simple Intention

By two wings, a man is lifted up from things earthly, namely, by Simplicity and Purity.

Simplicity ought to be in our intention, Purity in our affection. Simplicity doth tend towards God; Purity doth apprehend and, as it were, taste Him.

No good action will hinder thee, if thou be inwardly free from inordinate affection.

If thou intend and seek nothing else but the will of God and the good of thy neighbor, thou shalt thoroughly enjoy inward liberty.

If thy heart were sincere and upright, then every creature would be unto thee a looking-glass of life, and a book of holy doctrine.

There is no creature so small and mean, that it doth not show the goodness of God.

If thou wert inwardly good and pure then wouldst thou be able to see and understand all things well without impediment.

A pure heart penetrateth Heaven and hell.

Such as every one is inwardly, so he judgeth outwardly.

If there be joy in the world, surely a man of pure heart possesseth it.

And if there be anywhere tribulation and affliction, an evil conscience best knows it.

The Third Book

Of Inward Consolation

Chapter I

Of Christ's Speaking Inwardly to the Faithful Soul

"I Will hearken what the Lord God speaketh in me."

Blessed is the soul which heareth the Lord speaking within her, and receiveth from His mouth the word of consolation.

Blessed are the ears that gladly receive the pulses of the Divine whisper, and give no heed to the many whisperings of this world.

Blessed indeed are those ears which listen not after the voice which is sounding without, but for the Truth teaching inwardly.

Blessed are the eyes which are shut to outward things, but intent on things eternal.

Blessed are they that enter far into things internal, and endeavor to prepare themselves more and more, by daily exercises, for the receiving of heavenly secrets.

Blessed are they who are glad to have time to spare for God, and shake off all worldly hindrances.

Let go all transitory things, and seek those that be everlasting.

What are all temporal things but seducing snares? and what can all creatures avail thee, if thou be forsaken by the Creator?

Bid farewell therefore to all things else, and labor to please thy Creator, and to be faithful unto Him, that so thou mayest be able to attain unto true blessedness.

Chapter III
That the Words of God Are to Be Heard With Humility, and that Many Weigh Them Not

My son, hear My words, words of greatest sweetness, surpassing all the knowledge of the philosophers and wise men of this world.

"My words are Spirit and Life," and not to be weighed by the understanding of man.

They are not to be drawn forth for vain approbation, but to be heard in silence, and to be received with all humility and great affection.

And I said, Blessed is the man whom Thou shalt instruct, O Lord, and shalt teach out of Thy law, that Thou mayest give him rest from the evil days, and that he be not desolate upon earth.

For a small income, a long journey is undertaken; for everlasting life, many will scarce once lift a foot from the ground.

The most pitiful reward is sought after; for a single piece of money sometimes there is shameful contention; for a vain matter and slight promise men fear not to toil day and night.

But, alas! for an unchangeable good, for inestimable reward, for the highest honor, and glory without end, they grudge even the least fatigue.

Chapter IV
That We Ought to Live in Truth and Humility Before God

My son, walk thou before Me in truth, and ever seek Me in simplicity of thy heart.

He that walketh before Me in truth, shall be defended from evil attacks, and the Truth shall set him free from seducers, and from the slanders of unjust men.

If the Truth shall have made thee free, thou shalt be free indeed, and shalt not care for the vain words of men.

O Lord, it is true. According as Thou sayest, so, I beseech Thee, let it be with me; let Thy Truth teach me, guard me, and preserve me safe to the end.

Let it set me free from all evil affection and inordinate love; and I shall walk with Thee in great liberty of heart.

I will teach thee (saith the Truth) those things which are right and pleasing in My sight.

Reflect on thy sins with great displeasure and grief; and never esteem thyself to be anything, because of any good works.

In truth thou art a sinner; thou art subject to and encumbered with many passions. Of thyself thou always tendest to nothing; speedily art thou cast down, speedily overcome, speedily disordered, speedily dissolved.

Thou hast nothing whereof thou canst glory, but many things for which thou oughtest to account thyself vile; for thou art much weaker than thou art able to comprehend.

And therefore let nothing seem much unto thee whatsoever thou doest.

Let nothing seem great, nothing precious and wonderful, nothing worthy of estimation, nothing high, nothing truly commendable and to be desired, but that alone which is eternal.

Let the eternal Truth be above all things pleasing to thee. Let thy own extreme unworthiness be always displeasing to thee.

Fear nothing, blame nothing, flee nothing, so much as thy vices and sins; which ought to be more unpleasing to thee than any losses whatsoever of things earthly.

Some walk not sincerely in My sight, but, led by a certain curiosity and pride, wish to know My secrets, and to understand the high things of God, neglecting themselves and their own salvation.

These oftentimes, when I resist them, for their pride and curiosity do fall into great temptations and sins.

Fear thou the judgments of God, and dread the wrath of the Almighty. Do not, however, discuss the works of the Most High, but search diligently thine own iniquities, in how great things thou hast offended, and how many good things thou hast neglected.

Some carry their devotion only in books, some in pictures; some in outward signs and figures.

Some have Me often in their mouths, but little in their hearts.

Others there are who, being illuminated in their understandings, and purged in their affection, do always aspire after things eternal, are unwilling to hear of the things of this world, and do serve the necessities of nature with grief; and these perceive what the Spirit of Truth speaketh in them.

For He teacheth them to despise earthly, and to love heavenly things; to neglect the world, and to desire Heaven all the day and night.

Chapter V

Of the Wonderful Effect of Divine Love

I will always bless and glorify Thee, with Thy only-begotten Son, and the Holy Ghost, the Comforter, for ever and ever.

Ah, Lord God, Thou Holy Lover of my soul, when Thou comest into my heart, all that is within me shall rejoice.

Thou art my Glory and the Exultation of my heart: Thou art my Hope and Refuge in the day of my trouble.

But because I am as yet weak in love, and imperfect in virtue, I have need to be strengthened and comforted by Thee; visit me therefore often, and instruct me with all holy discipline.

Set me free from evil passions, and heal my heart of all inordinate affections; that being inwardly cured and thoroughly cleansed, I may be made fit to love, courageous to suffer, steady to persevere.

Love is a great thing, yea, a great and thorough good; by itself it makes everything that is heavy, light; and it bears evenly all that is uneven.

For it carries a burden which is no burden, and makes everything that is bitter, sweet and tasteful.

The noble love of Jesus impels a man to do great things, and stirs him up to be always longing for what is more perfect.

Love desires to be aloft, and will not be kept back by anything low and mean.

Love desires to be free.

Chapter XLVIII

Of the Day of Eternity, and This Life's Straitnesses

O Most blessed mansion of the City which is above! O most clear day of eternity, which night obscureth not, but the highest Truth ever enlighteneth! O day ever joyful, ever secure, and never changing into a contrary state!

O that that day might once appear, and that all these temporal things were at an end!

To the Saints indeed it shineth glowing with uninterrupted brightness, but to those who are pilgrims on the earth, it appeareth only afar off, and as through a glass.

The Citizens of Heaven do know how joyful that day is, but the banished children of Eve bewail the bitterness and tediousness of this.

The days of this life are few and evil, full of sorrows and straitnesses.

Here a man is defiled with many sins, ensnared with many passions, held fast by many fears, wracked with many cares, distracted with many curiosities, entangled with many vanities, compassed about with many errors, worn away with many labors, burdened with temptations, enervated by pleasures, tormented with want.

O when shall these evils be at an end? when shall I be delivered from the miserable bondage of my sins? when shall I be mindful, O Lord, of Thee alone? when shall I fully rejoice in Thee?

When shall I enjoy true liberty without all impediments whatsoever, without all trouble of mind and body?

When shall I have solid peace, peace secure and undisturbed, peace within and peace without, peace every way assured?

O merciful Jesus, when shall I stand to behold Thee? when shall I contemplate the glory of Thy Kingdom? when wilt Thou be unto me all in all?

O when shall I be with Thee in Thy Kingdom, which Thou hast prepared for Thy beloved ones from all eternity?

I am left, a poor and banished man, in the land of mine enemies, where there are daily wars and very great calamities.

Comfort my banishment, assuage my sorrow; for my whole desire sigheth after Thee.

Chapter VIII

Of the Oblation of Christ on the Cross, and of Resignation of Ourselves

The Voice of the Beloved.

As I of Mine own will did offer up Myself unto God the Father for thy sins, My hands stretched out on the cross, and My body stripped and laid bare, so that nothing remained in Me that was not wholly turned into a sacrifice for the appeasing of the divine Majesty:

In like manner oughtest thou also to offer thyself willingly unto Me every day in the Holy Communion, as a pure and sacred oblation, with all thy strength and affections, and to the utmost reach of thy inward faculties.

What do I require of thee more, than that thou study to resign thyself entirely unto Me?

Whatsoever thou givest besides thyself, is of no value in My sight, for I seek not thy gifts but thee.

As it would not suffice thee to have all things whatsoever, besides Me; so neither can it please Me, whatsoever thou givest, if thou offer not thyself.

Offer up thyself unto Me, and give thyself wholly for God, and thy offering shall be accepted.

Behold, I offered up Myself wholly unto My Father for thee; I give also My whole Body and Blood for thy food, that I might be wholly thine, and that thou mightest continue Mine to the end.

But if thou stand upon thyself, and dost not offer thyself up freely unto My will, the oblation is not complete, neither will there be entire union between us.

Therefore a free offering up of thyself into the hands of God ought to go before all thine actions, if thou desire to obtain liberty and grace.

For this is the cause why so few become illuminated and inwardly free, because they cannot endure wholly to deny themselves.

My sentence standeth sure, Unless a man forsake all, he cannot be My disciple. If thou therefore desire to be My disciple, offer up thyself unto Me with thy whole affections.

Selections from
The Imitation of Christ,
Thomas á Kempis,
London and Glasgow: Collins' Clear Type Press

Chapter 45 • St. Ignatius of Loyola: *The Spiritual Exercises*

Ignatius (1491-1556) was born of noble parents in the castle of Loyola near Azpeitia, Guipuzcoa, Spain. While recuperating from a serious wound incurred in battle during his service in the army, Ignatius was converted from a dissolute life to one of total commitment to Jesus. Though he studied at many colleges in Spain and, later, at Paris, he is not famous for any great scholastic achievement. His strength lay in the area of spiritual direction. The *Spiritual Exercises* reproduced here are a classic presentation of the journey of the soul to God along the ways that have been canonized by the traditional usage of mystics of all ages. They are a very successful instrument utilized by many spiritual directors, as well as by the members of the Society of Jesus, which he founded in 1534 and which received papal approval in 1540.

The Spiritual Exercises of St. Ignatius

Under the name of Spiritual Exercises is understood every method of examination of conscience, of meditation, of contemplation, of vocal and mental prayer, and of other spiritual operations, as shall be afterwards declared: the term of spiritual exercises is applied to any method of preparing and disposing the soul to free itself from all inordinate affections, and after it has freed itself from them, to seek and find the will of God concerning the ordering of life for the salvation of one's soul.

As in all the Spiritual Exercises that follow we make use of acts of the understanding when reasoning, and of acts of the will when exciting the affections, we are to take notice that in the acts of the will, when we are conversing vocally or mentally with God our Lord or with His Saints greater reverence is required on our part than when we make use of the understanding in reasoning.

First Principle and Foundation

Man was created to praise, reverence, and serve God our Lord, and by this means to save his soul; and the other things on the face of the earth were created for man's sake, and in order to aid him in the prosecution of the end for which he was created. Whence it follows, that man must make use of them in so far as they help him to attain his end, and in the same way he ought to withdraw himself from them in so far as they hinder him from it. It is therefore necessary that we should make ourselves indifferent to all created things, in so far as it is left to the liberty of our free will to do so, and is not forbidden; in such sort that we do not for our part wish for health rather than sickness, for wealth rather than poverty, for honor rather than dishonor, for a long life rather than a short one; and so in all other things, desiring and choosing only those which most lead us to the end for which we were created.

First Week

The First Exercise

The First Exercise is a meditation by means of the three powers of the soul. It contains in itself, after a preparatory prayer and two preludes, three principal points and a colloquy.

The preparatory prayer is to ask our Lord for grace that all my intentions, actions, and operations may be ordained purely to the service and praise of His Divine Majesty.

The first prelude is a composition of place, seeing the spot.

The second prelude is to ask of God our Lord that which I wish and desire.

The first point will be to apply the memory to the first sin, which was that of the angels;

I say, to bring to memory the sin of the angels, how they were created in grace, yet being unwilling to help themselves by the means of their liberty in the work of paying reverence and obedience to their Creator and Lord, falling into pride, they were changed from grace to malice, and hurled from Heaven to Hell; and then in turn to reason more in particular with the understanding, and thus in turn to move still more the affections by means of the will.

The second point will be to do the same, *i.e.*, to apply the three powers to the sin of Adam and Eve; bringing before the memory how for that sin they were condemned to so long a season of penance, and how much corruption came upon the human race, so many men being put on the way to Hell.

The third point will be to do in like manner also in regard to the third sin, *i.e.*, the particular sin of some one person who for one mortal sin has gone to Hell; and many others without number have been condemned for fewer sins than I have committed.

Colloquy. Imagining Christ our Lord before us and placed on the Cross, to make a colloquy with Him, asking Him how, being our Creator, He has condescended to become Man, and in place of eternal life has debased Himself to temporal death, thus to die for my sins. Again, to look at myself, asking myself what I have done for Christ, what I am doing for Christ, what I ought to do for Christ; and then seeing Him in this state and thus fixed to the Cross, to give expression to what shall present itself to my mind.

The Second Exercise

The Second Exercise is a meditation upon sins; it contains, after the preparatory prayer and the two preludes, five points and a colloquy.

Let the preparatory prayer be the same.

The first prelude will be the same composition of place.

The second is to ask for what I desire; it will be here to beg great and intense grief and tears on account of my sins.

The first point is the series of sins, that is to say, to recall to memory all the sins of my life, looking at them from year to year or from period to period.

The second point is to weigh the sins, considering the deformity and the malice that every mortal sin committed contains in itself, even supposing that it were not forbidden.

The third point is to consider who I am.

The fourth point is to consider who God is, against Whom I have sinned, looking at His attributes, comparing them with their contraries in myself: His wisdom with my ignorance, His omnipotence with my weakness, His justice with my iniquity, His goodness with my malice.

The fifth point is an exclamation of wonder.

The whole to conclude with a colloquy of mercy, reasoning and giving thanks to God our Lord, for having given me life till now, and proposing through His grace to amend henceforward.

The Third Exercise

The Third Exercise is a repetition of the first and second Exercise: making three colloquies.

The first colloquy to our Lady, in order that she may obtain for me grace from her Son and Lord for three things; the first, that I may feel an interior knowledge of my sins, and an abhorrence of them; the second, that I may feel the deordination of my actions, in order that, abhorring it, I may amend and regulate myself; the third, to beg for a knowledge of the world, in order that, abhorring it, I may put away from myself worldly and vain things; and after this an *Ave Maria*.

The second colloquy will be to do the same to the Son, in order that He may obtain for me from the Father the same grace; and with this the *Anima Christi*.

The third colloquy will be to do the same to the Father, that the same eternal Lord may grant it to me; and with this a *Pater noster*.

The Kingdom of Christ

The Call of the Temporal King Helps to Contemplate the Life of the Eternal King.

Let the preparatory prayer be as usual.

The first prelude is a composition of place, seeing the spot. It will be here to see with the eyes of the imagination the synagogues, towns, and villages, through which Christ our Lord preached.

The second prelude will be to ask for the grace which I desire. It will be here to ask the grace from our Lord, that I may not be deaf to His call, but prompt and diligent to accomplish His most holy will.

The first point is to place before my eyes a human king, elected by the hand of God our Lord, whom all princes and all Christians reverence and obey.

The second is to consider how this king speaks to all his subjects, saying: "My will is to reduce to subjection all the lands of the infidels: wherefore, whoever desires to come with me must be contented to eat what I eat, to drink and be clothed as I, etc.; and likewise he must labor as I do during the day, and watch during the night, etc., in order that afterwards he may have part with me in the victory, as he has had in the toils."

The third is to consider what good subjects ought to answer to a king so liberal and so kind; and consequently if any one did not welcome the request of such a king, how we would deserve to be censured by all the world, and deemed a slothful knight.

The second part of this Exercise consists in applying the above example of the temporal king to Christ our Lord, in conformity with the three aforesaid points.

And as regards the first point, if we consider the temporal king's summons to his subjects, how much more worthy of consideration is it to see Christ our Lord, the Eternal King, and in front of Him the whole entire world, all of whom and each in particular He calls, and says: "My will is to conquer the whole world, and all My enemies, and thus to enter into the glory of My Father. Whoever, therefore, desires to come with Me must labor with Me, in order that following Me in suffering, he may likewise follow Me in glory."

The second point is to consider that all who enjoy the use of judgment and reason will offer their whole selves for labor.

The third point is that those who wish to show greater affection, and to signalize themselves in every kind of service of their Eternal King and Universal Lord, not only will offer their persons to toils, but also by going against their own sensuality, and their love of the flesh and of the world, will make offers of greater worth and moment, saying:

Eternal Lord of all things, I make my oblation with Thy favor and help, in presence of Thine infinite goodness, and in presence of Thy glorious Mother, and of all the saints of the heavenly court, protesting that I wish and desire, and that it is my deliberate determination (provided only it be to Thy greater service and praise), to imitate Thee in bearing all kinds of insult and contumely, and all kinds of poverty, as well actual poverty as poverty of spirit, if only Thy Divine Majesty be pleased to choose and receive me to this life and state.

This Exercise will be made twice in the day, namely, in the morning on rising, and one hour before dinner or supper.

During the second week, and also henceforward, it helps much to read occasionally out of the *Imitation of Christ*, or the Gospels, or the *Lives of the Saints*.

Second Week

The First Day and the First Contemplation

The first day and the first contemplation is upon the Incarnation. It contains the preparatory prayer, three preludes, and three points, and a colloquy.

The usual preparatory prayer.

The first prelude is to call to mind how the three Divine Persons beheld all the surface of the terrestrial globe, covered with men. And how, seeing all men descending into Hell, They determined, in Their eternity, that the Second Person should become Man to save the human race, and thus, when the fullness of time had come, They sent the Angel St. Gabriel to our Lady.

The second prelude will be to behold in particular the house and chamber of our Lady in the town of Nazareth in the province of Galilee.

The third is to ask for what I want: it will here be to ask for an interior knowledge of our Lord, Who for me has become Man, that I may love Him and follow Him more.

At the end a colloquy is to be made, thinking what I ought to say to the Three Divine Persons, or to the Eternal Word Incarnate, or to His Mother and our Lady, making petition according to what each feels in himself, in order to follow and imitate better our Lord, thus newly become incarnate, and then say a *Pater noster*.

The Second Contemplation
The second contemplation is on the nativity

The first prelude is the history. It will be here to think how our Lady, already with child, left Nazareth, together with St. Joseph, and a servant girl, in order to go to Bethlehem to pay the tribute which Caesar imposed on these countries.

The first point is to see the persons: that is to say, to see our Lady, and St. Joseph, and the serving-maid, also the Infant Jesus, after His birth, accounting myself a poor and unworthy servant, looking at and contemplating them and tending them in their necessities as though I were present there, with all possible homage and reverence; and after that to reflect inwardly in order to derive some profit.

The Second Day

Take for the first and second contemplation the Presentation in the temple, and the Flight into Egypt as a place of exile; and two repetitions will be made of those two contemplations, and the application of the five senses to them, in the same way as was done on the preceding day.

The Third Day

Consider how the Child Jesus was obedient to His parents at Nazareth, and how they afterwards found Him in the Temple.

Introductory Remarks to Considering States of Life

Having already considered the example which Christ our Lord has given us for the first state, which consists in the observance of the Commandments, while He was obedient to His parents; and likewise the example He has given us for the second, which consists in evangelical perfection, when He remained in the Temple, leaving His adopted father, and his natural Mother, to be entirely free to apply Himself to the service of His Divine Father; let us at the same time that we contemplate His life, begin to investigate and to ask in what kind of life or state His Divine Majesty is pleased to make use of us.

And thus by way of some introduction to it, in the first Exercise that follows we will consider the intention of Christ our Lord, and on the other side that of the enemy of our human nature, and the manner in which we ought to dispose ourselves in order to arrive at perfection in whatever state or kind of life God shall give us to elect.

Fourth Day

The meditation on Two Standards, the one of Christ, the chief Leader and our Lord; the other of Lucifer, the mortal enemy of our human nature.

The usual preparatory prayer.

The first prelude is the history: it will be here, how Christ calls and desires all under His banner: Lucifer on the contrary under his.

The second prelude is a composition of place, seeing the spot: it will be here to see a vast plain of all the region round Jerusalem, where the Leader of all the good is Christ our Lord: and to imagine another plain in the country of Babylon, where the chief of the enemy is Lucifer.

The third prelude is to ask for what I want: it will be here to ask for knowledge of the deceits of the wicked chieftain, and for help to guard against them, and for knowledge of the true life which our chief and true Leader points out, and for grace to imitate Him.

The first point is to imagine the chieftain of all the enemy as seated in the great plain of Babylon, and as it were on a lofty throne of fire and smoke, in aspect horrible and fearful.

The second point is to consider how he summons together innumerable devils, how he disperses them, some to one city, some to another, and so on throughout the whole world, omitting not any provinces, places, or states of life or any persons in particular.

The third point is to consider the address which he makes, and how he warns them to lay snares and chains; telling them how they are first to tempt men to covet riches (as he is wont to do in most cases), so that they more easily come to the vain honor of the world, and then to unbounded pride; so that the first step is riches, the second honor, the third pride; and from these three steps he leads them to all other vices.

In the same way, on the other hand, we are to consider the sovereign and true Leader, Christ our Lord.

The first point is to consider how Christ our Lord, in aspect fair and beautiful, takes His station in a great plain of the country of Jerusalem on a lowly spot.

The second point is to consider how the Lord of the whole world chooses out so many persons, Apostles, disciples, etc., and sends them throughout the whole world diffusing His sacred doctrine through all states and conditions of persons.

The third point is to consider the address which Christ our Lord makes to all His servants and friends, whom He sends on this expedition, recommending to them that they seek to help all, by guiding them first to the highest degree of poverty of spirit, and even to actual poverty, if His Divine Majesty be pleased and should choose to elect them to it; leading them, secondly, to a desire of reproaches and contempt, because from these two humility results. So that there are three steps: first, poverty opposed to riches; secondly, reproaches and contempt opposed to worldly honor; thirdly, humility opposed to pride; and from these three steps let them conduct them to all other virtues.

I will make a colloquy to our Lady to obtain for me grace from her Son and Lord that I may be received under His standard.

I will ask the same from the Son, that He obtain for me this grace from the Father;

I will ask the same from the Father, that He grant me this grace; then say a *Pater noster*.

The Three Classes

On the same fourth day will be made the meditation on the Three Classes of Men, in order to embrace that which is best.

The first prelude is the history, which is concerning three classes of men, each of which has acquired ten thousand ducats, not purely and as they ought through the love of God; and all desire to save their souls, and to find in peace God our Savior, ridding themselves of the burden and impediment to this end which they find in their affection to the money acquired.

The second prelude will be to see myself standing before God our Lord and all His saints, for the purpose of obtaining a desire and knowledge of that which is more pleasing to His Divine Goodness.

The third prelude is to beg the grace to choose that which is most for the glory of His Divine Majesty, and for the salvation of my soul.

The first class would like to shake off the affection which they have for the money acquired, so as to find in peace God our Lord, and so as to know how to save their souls; but they take no means even up to the hour of death.

The second class desire to shake off the affection, but in such a way as to remain in possession of what they have gained, so as to result in bringing God to what they desire; and they do not determine to leave the money in order to go to God, even although this would be the better state for them.

The third class wish to shake off the affection in such way as to have no desire to retain the money, or not, so that they desire only to wish for it or not according as God our Lord shall give them to wish it, and according as it shall seem to them for the greater service and praise of His Divine Majesty; so that the desire of being able the better to serve God our Lord is what moves them to take or leave the money.

It is to be noted, that when we feel any affection or repugnance to actual poverty, when we are not indifferent to poverty or riches, it will help much to the rooting out of such a disordered affection, in our colloquies, even though it be against the flesh, to ask Christ our Lord to chose us to a state of actual poverty, protesting that we desire, petition, and ask for that only which may be to the service and praise of His Divine Goodness.

The Fifth Day

A contemplation on the departure of Christ our Lord from Nazareth to the River Jordan, and how He was baptized.

The Sixth Day

How Christ our Lord went from the River Jordan to the desert, including what happened there; keeping the same form in everything as on the fifth day.

The Seventh Day

How St. Andrew and the others followed Christ our Lord.

The Eighth Day

The Sermon on the Mount on the Eight Beatitudes.

The Ninth Day

How Christ our Lord appeared to His disciples walking on the waters.

The Tenth Day

How our Lord preached in the Temple.

The Eleventh Day

On the raising up of Lazarus.

The Twelfth Day

On the events of Palm Sunday.

The Three Degrees of Humility

The first degree of humility is necessary for eternal salvation; it is, that I so submit and humble myself, so far as I can, as in all things to obey the law of God our Lord, in such wise that even though men should make me lord of all created things in this world, for the sake of my own temporal life I would not enter into deliberation about breaking a commandment, whether Divine or human, which bound me under mortal sin.

The second degree is more perfect humility than the first; it consists in finding myself in such a state as not to desire nor be more disposed towards riches than towards poverty, towards honor than dishonor, towards the desire of a long life than a short life, provided only equal service be rendered to God our Lord, and the prospect of the salvation of my soul be equal; and, it consists likewise in never entering into deliberation about committing a venial sin, neither for the sake of all created things, nor even if on that account men should deprive me of life.

The third degree is the most perfect humility; when, the first and second degree being included, and supposing equal praise and glory to redound to the Divine Majesty, the better to imitate Christ our Lord, and to become actually more like to Him, I desire and choose rather poverty with Christ poor, than riches; contempt with Christ condemned, than honors; and when I desire to be esteemed as useless and foolish for Christ's sake, Who was first held to be such, than to be accounted wise and prudent in this world.

And thus it will be very profitable for him who desires to obtain this third degree of humility, to make the above-mentioned triple colloquy of the Classes, imploring our Lord to be pleased to elect him to this third degree of greater and more perfect humility, in order the better to imitate and serve Him, if it be for the equal or greater service and praise of His Divine Majesty.

Third Week

The First Contemplation

The first contemplation is how Christ our Lord proceeded from Bethany to Jerusalem, including the Last Supper. Call to mind how Christ our Lord sent from Bethany two disciples to Jerusalem to prepare the supper, and how afterwards He Himself went thither with the other disciples, and how, after having eaten the Paschal Lamb, and after having supped, He washed their feet and gave to His disciples His most holy Body and precious Blood, and made them a discourse, after Judas had gone to sell his Lord.

Ask for that which I want: here it will be to feel grief, affliction, and confusion, because for my sins our Lord is going to His Passion.

Consider what Christ our Lord suffers, or wishes to suffer in His Humanity, according to the portion of His Passion which is being contemplated.

Consider how the Divinity hides itself, that is to say, how it could destroy its enemies, and does not, and how it allows the most holy Humanity to suffer so cruelly.

The Second Contemplation

The second contemplation will comprise the events from the Supper to the Garden inclusively.

It will be here how Christ our Lord descended with His eleven disciples from Mount Zion, where He made the Supper, to the valley of Josaphat, leaving eight of them in one part of the valley, and the other three in a place in the Garden, and betaking Himself to prayer, how He sweated as it were drops of blood, and after He had three times prayed to the Father and aroused His three disciples, and after His enemies had fallen down at the sound of His voice, how Judas gave Him the kiss of peace, and how St. Peter cut off the ear of Malchus, which Christ restored to its place; and how, having been apprehended as a malefactor, they drag Him down the valley and up the slope to the house of Annas.

Ask for that which I want: the peculiar grace to be demanded in the Passion is sorrow with Christ in sorrow, anguish with Christ in anguish, tears and interior pain for the pain Christ has suffered for me.

The Second Day

The contemplation will be on the events from the Garden to the house of Annas inclusively, and in the morning on the events from the house of Annas to the house of Caiaphas inclusively, and afterwards the two repetitions and the application of the senses, according to what has been said.

The Third Day

On the events from the house of Caiaphas to Pilate inclusively, and Pilate to Herod inclusively.

The Fourth Day

On the events from Herod to Pilate, making contemplation on one half of the mysteries at the house of Pilate; and then taking the remaining mysteries in that house.

The Fifth Day

On the events from the house of Pilate till Christ was laid on the Cross; and His elevation on the Cross till His Death.

The Sixth Day

From the taking down from the Cross to the Burial, exclusively; and on the events from the Burial, inclusively, to our Lady's arrival at her house, after the Burial of her Son.

The Seventh Day

A contemplation of all the Passion will be made, the exercitant will consider as frequently as he can during all the day, how the Sacred Body of Christ our Lord remained detached and separated from the soul, and will call to mind when and how It was buried; pondering also on the solitude of our Lady in such great grief and affliction of spirit, and then on the other hand on that of the disciples.

Fourth Week

The First Contemplation

How Christ our Lord Appeared to Our Lady

How after Christ had expired on the Cross, and His Body remained separated from the soul and united to the Divinity, His blessed Soul, likewise united to the Divinity, descended to Limbo, whence releasing the souls of the just, and coming to the sepulcher, and rising again, He appeared in Body and Soul to His blessed Mother.

Ask for that which I want: it will be here to ask for grace to be intensely glad and to rejoice in such great glory and joy of Christ our Lord.

Consider how the Divinity which in the Passion seemed to hide itself, now appears in the most holy Resurrection and most miraculously shows itself by its most true and holy effects.

Contemplation for Obtaining Love

Two things are to be noticed here:

The first is, that love ought to show itself in deeds rather than words.

The second is, that love consists in mutual interchange on either side, that is to say, in the lover sharing what he has with the beloved, and on the other hand, in the beloved sharing with the lover, so that if the one love knowledge, honor, riches, he shares it with him who has them not, and thus the one share all with the other.

See myself standing before God our Lord and His angels and saints who are interceding for me.

It will be here to ask for an interior knowledge of the great benefits I have received, that thoroughly grateful for the favors received, I may in everything love and serve His Divine Majesty.

The first point is to call to mind the benefits received in my creation redemption, and the particular favors bestowed on me, dwelling with great affection on how much God has done for me, and how much He has given me of His possessions, and how, after all that, He desires to give me Himself in so far as He can according to His Divine ordinance; and then I will inwardly reflect what I ought on my side, with great reason and justice, to offer and give to His Divine Majesty, that is to say, all my possessions and myself with them, saying, as one who makes an offering, with great affection:

"Take, O Lord, and receive all my liberty, my memory, my understanding, and all my will, all that I have and possess. Thou hast given it to me; to Thee, O Lord, I restore it: this is Thine, dispose of it according to all Thy will. Give me Thy love and Thy grace, for this is enough for me."

Rules For Thinking with the Church

In Order to Know Rightly What We Ought to Hold in the Church Militant, The Following Rules Are to Be Observed

I. Laying aside all private judgment, we ought to keep our minds prepared and ready to obey in all things the true Spouse of Christ our Lord, which is our Holy Mother, the Hierarchical Church.

II. The second is to praise confession made to a priest, and the reception of the most Blessed Sacrament, once a year, and what is better once a month, and still better every eight days, always with the requisite and fitting dispositions.

III. The third is to praise the frequent hearing of Mass, also hymns, psalms, and long prayers, both in and out of the Church, and likewise the hours ordained at fixed times for the Divine Office, for prayers of any kind, and for the canonical hours.

IV. The fourth is to praise greatly religious orders, and a life of virginity and continency, and not to praise the married state as much as any of these.

V. The fifth is to praise the vows of religion of Obedience, Poverty, and Chastity.

VI. The sixth is to praise the relics of saints, showing veneration to the relics, and praying to the saints, and to praise likewise the Stations, pilgrimages, indulgences, jubilees, Bulls of the *Cruciata*, candles lighted in churches.

VII. The seventh is to praise the precepts with regard to fasts and abstinences, as those of Lent, Ember days, Vigils, Fridays, and Saturdays; likewise not only interior but exterior penances.

VIII. To praise the construction and the ornaments of churches; and also the veneration of images, according to what they represent.

IX. Finally to praise all the precepts of the Church, keeping our minds ready to seek reasons to defend, never to impugn them.

X. We ought to be very ready to approve and praise the constitutions, recommendations, and habits of life of our Superiors.

XI. The eleventh is to praise positive and scholastic theology; for as it is rather the object of the positive doctors, as St. Jerome, St. Augustine, St. Gregory, etc., to stir up the affections to the love and service of God our Lord in all things; so it is rather the object of the scholastic doctors, as St. Thomas, St. Bonaventure, and the Master of the Sentences, etc., to define and explain more exactly, in conformity with the wants of our times, what is necessary for salvation, the better to attack and to expose all errors and fallacies; because the scholastic doctors being of later date can avail themselves not only of the right understanding of the Holy Scriptures, and of the writings of the Holy positive doctors, but being themselves illuminated and enlightened by the Divine Power, profit by the Councils, Canons, and Constitutions of our Holy Mother the Church.

XII. We ought to guard against making comparisons between the living and the blessed who have passed away, for no slight error is committed in this, as for example, in saying: He knows more than St. Augustine; He is as great or greater than St. Francis; He is another St. Paul in holiness and virtue, etc.

XIII. To make sure every way, we ought always to hold that we believe what the Hierarchical Church pronounces it so; believing that between Christ our Lord the Bridegroom and the Church His Bride there is one and the same Spirit, which governs and directs us to the salvation of our souls; and that our Holy Mother the Church is guided and ruled by the same Spirit and Lord that gave the Ten Commandments.

XIV. Although it is very true that no one can be saved without being predestined, and without having faith and grace, we must be very careful in our manner of speaking and treating of all on this subject.

XV. We ought not habitually to speak much of Predestination; but if sometimes mention be made of it in any way, we must so speak that the common people may not fall into error, as happens sometimes when they say: It is already fixed whether I am to be saved or damned, and there cannot be any other result whether I do good or ill: and, becoming slothful in consequence, they neglect works conducive to their salvation, and to the spiritual profit of their souls.

XVI. In the same way it is to be noticed that we must take heed lest by speaking much with great earnestness on Faith, without distinction or explanation, occasion be given to the people to become slothful and sluggish in good works, whether it be before or after that faith is formed in charity.

XVII. In like manner we ought not to speak or to insist on the doctrine of Grace so strongly, as to give rise to that poisonous teaching that robs us of our free-will. Therefore, we may treat of Faith and Grace, as far as we may with the help of God, for the greater praise of His Divine Majesty; but we must, especially in these dangerous times of ours, avoid handling the subject in such a manner that works or free-will receive any detriment, or come to be accounted for nothing.

XVIII. Although it is above all things praiseworthy to greatly serve God our Lord out of pure love, yet we ought greatly to praise the fear of His Divine Majesty, because not only is filial fear a pious and most holy thing, but even servile fear, when one cannot rise to anything better, and more useful, is of great help to him to escape from mortal sin; and, after he has escaped from it, he easily attains to filial fear, which is altogether acceptable and pleasing to God our Lord, because it is inseparable from Divine love.

The End.

Translated from the original Spanish by M. Sullivan, New York, 1881

Chapter 46 • The Council of Trent: Canons and Decrees

The Council of Trent (1545-1563) was an ecumenical council held in response to the Protestant Reformation. It defined Catholic doctrine in a way that made the split with the Protestants irrevocable. It declared, in contrast to the Protestant reliance on Scripture alone, that Scripture and Tradition were to be received with "equal reverence." The Latin Vulgate text of Scripture was declared the authentic version upon which Catholic teaching was to be based.

a. *On Scripture and Tradition.*

Session IV, 8 April 1546.

Concilium Tridentinum, Diariorum, etc. Nova Collectio

(Freiburg, 1901-), v. 91. Denzinger, 783.

The Holy, Oecumenical and General Synod of Trent . . . having this aim always before its eyes, that errors may be removed and the purity of the Gospel be preserved in the Church, which was before promised through the prophets in the Holy Scriptures and which our Lord Jesus Christ the Son of God first published by his own mouth and then commanded to be preached through his Apostles to every creature as a source of all saving truth and of discipline of conduct; and perceiving that this truth and this discipline are contained in written books and in unwritten traditions, which were received by the Apostles from the lips of Christ himself, or, by the same Apostles, at the dictation of the Holy Spirit, and were handed on and have come down to us; following the example of the orthodox Fathers, this Synod receives and venerates, with equal pious affection and reverence, all the books both of the New and the Old Testaments, since one God is the author of both, together with the said Traditions, as well those pertaining to faith as those pertaining to morals, as having been given either from the lips of Christ or by the dictation of the Holy Spirit and preserved by unbroken succession in the Catholic Church. . . .

b. *On Original Sin.*

Session V, 17 June 1546.

C. Tr. v. 238 sqq. Denzinger, 788 sqq.

1. If any one does not confess that the first man Adam, when he had transgressed the command of God in Paradise, straightway lost that holiness and

righteousness in which he had been established, and through the offence of this disobedience incurred the wrath and indignation of God, and therefore incurred death, which God had before threatened to him, and, with death, captivity under the power of him who thereafter had the power of death, namely the devil, and that the whole of Adam, through the offence of that disobedience, was changed for the worse in respect of body and soul: let him be anathema.

2. If any one asserts that the disobedience of Adam injured only himself and not his offspring . . . or that . . . only death and the pains of the body were transferred to the whole human race, and not the sin also, which is the death of the soul: let him be anathema [Rom. 5:12].

3. If any one asserts that the sin of Adam — which in origin is one and which has been transmitted to all mankind by propagation, not through imitation, and is in every man and belongs to him — can be removed either by man's natural powers or by any other remedy than the merit of the one mediator our Lord Jesus Christ. . . .

4. If any one denies that infants who have just issued from their mother's womb are to be baptized, even if born of baptized parents, or says that they are indeed baptized for the remission of sins but that they are not infected with any original sin from Adam such as would need expiation by the layer of regeneration for the attainment of eternal life; whence it follows that in regard to them the formula of baptism for remission of sins is to be understood not in its true but in a false sense. . . .

c. *On Justification.*

Session VI, January 1547.

C. Tr. v. 797 sqq. Denzinger, 811 sqq.

Canons on Justification.

[The following propositions, among others, were anathematized.]

1. That man can be justified before God by his own works, which are done either in the strength of human nature or through the teaching of the law, apart from the divine grace through Jesus Christ.

2. That this grace is given through Jesus Christ solely to the end that a man may be able more easily to live justly and to earn eternal life, as if he could, though with great difficulty, do both these through his free will, without grace.

3. That without the prevenient inspiration of the Holy Spirit and his aid a man can believe, hope and love, or can repent, as he should, so that on him the grace of justification may be conferred.

4. That the free will of man, moved and aroused by God, does not co-operate at all by responding to the awakening call of God, so as to dispose and prepare itself for the acquisition of the grace ofjustification, nor can it refuse that grace, if it so will, but it does nothing at all, like some inanimate thing, and is completely passive.

5. That man's free will has been wholly lost and destroyed after Adam's sin.

6. That it is not in the power of man to make his ways evil, but that evil works as well as good are wrought by God, not just by way of permission but even by his own personal activity; so that the betrayal of Judas is no less his work than the calling of Paul.

7. That all works before justification, for whatever reason they were done, are in truth sins and deserve the hatred of God, or that the more strongly a man strives to dispose himself to receive Grace, the more grievously he sins.

9. That the impious is justified by faith alone — if this means that nothing else is required by way of cooperation in the acquisition of the grace of justification, and that it is in no way necessary for a man to be prepared and disposed by the motion of his own will.

15. That a man reborn and justified is bound by faith to believe that he is assuredly in the number of the predestinate.

23. That a man once justified can no more sin, nor can he lose the grace, and so he that falls into sin was never truly justified; or that it is possible altogether to avoid all sins, even venial sins. . . .

24. That justification once received is not preserved and even increased in the sight of God through good works; but that these same works are only fruits and signs of justification, not causes of its increase.

d. *On the Eucharist.*

Session XIII, October 1551.

C. Tr. v. 996. Denzinger, 874 sqq.

Chapter 4. *On Transubstantiation.*

Since Christ our Redeemer said that that which he offered under the appearance of bread was truly his body, it has therefore always been held in the Church of God, and this holy Synod now declares anew, that through consecration of the bread and wine there comes about a conversion of the whole substance of the bread into the substance of the body of Christ our Lord, and of the whole substance of the wine into the substance of his blood. And this conversion is by the Holy Catholic Church conveniently and properly called transubstantiation.

Chapter 5. *On the worship and veneration of the Holy Eucharist.*

And so no place is left for doubting that all Christ's faithful should in their veneration display towards this most Holy Sacrament the full worship of adoration *[latriae cultum]* which is due to the true God, in accordance with the custom always received in the Catholic Church. For it is not the less to be adored because it was instituted by Christ the Lord that it might be taken and eaten.

Canons on the Holy Eucharist.

Mansi, xxxiii. 84 C sq. Denzinger, 883 sqq.

3. On the Eucharist. If any one denies that in the venerable sacrament of the Eucharist the whole Christ is contained under each species and in each separate part of each species: let him be anathema.

9. If any one denies that each and all of Christ's faithful, of either sex, having come to years of discretion, is bound to communicate at least once a year in Eastertide, in accordance with the precept of Holy Mother Church: let him be anathema.

e. *On Penance.*

Session XIV, November 1551.

Canons on the Sacrament of Penance.

Mansi, xxxiii. 99 C sqq. Denzinger, 911 sqq.

[The following propositions, among others, are anathematized.]

1. That penance is not truly and properly a sacrament in the Catholic Church, instituted for the faithful by Christ our Lord, for their reconciliation to God whenever they fall into sin after baptism.

2. That baptism itself is the sacrament of penance (as if there were not two distinct sacraments) and that therefore it is not right to call penance the "second plank after shipwreck.

3. That the words of our Lord and Saviour, 'Whosesoever sins', etc. [John XX. 22], are not to be understood of the power of remitting or retaining sins in the sacrament of penance, as the Catholic Church has always, from the first, understood them: but . . . that they refer to the authority to preach the Gospel.

4. That for entire and perfect remission of sins three acts are not required in

a penitent, to be as it were the matter of the sacrament, namely contrition, confession and satisfaction.

6. That sacramental confession was neither instituted by divine authority, nor is it necessary to salvation by divine authority; or that the method of private confession to a priest alone, a method always observed from the first down to this day by the Catholic Church, is alien from the institution and command of Christ, and is a human invention.

f. *On the Most Holy Sacrifice of the Mass.*

Session XXII, September 1562.

C. Tr. viii. 699 sq. Denzinger, 938 sqq.

Chapter 2. And since in this divine Sacrifice which is performed in the Mass, that same Christ is contained in a bloodless sacrifice who on the altar of the cross once offered himself with the shedding of his blood: the holy Synod teaches that this sacrifice is truly propitiatory, and through it it comes about that if with true hearts and right faith, with fear and reverence, with contrition and penitence, we approach God we "attain mercy and find grace and help in time of need" [Hebrews iv. 16]. For God, propitiated by the oblation of this sacrifice, granting us grace and the gift of penitence, remits our faults and even our enormous sins. For there is one and the same victim, now offering through the ministry of the priesthood, who then offered himself on the cross; the only difference is in the method of the offering. The fruits of this (the bloody) oblation are perceived most fully through this bloodless oblation; so far is it from taking any honour from the former. Wherefore it is rightly offered, in accordance with the tradition of the Apostles, not only for the sins, penances, satisfactions and other necessities of the faithful living, but also for the dead in Christ, whose purification is not yet accomplished.

g. *On Purgatory and Invocation of Saints.*

Session XXV, December 1563.

C. Tr. ix. 1077 sq. Denzinger, 983 sq.

Since the Catholic Church, taught by the Holy Spirit from the sacred writings and the ancient traditions of the Fathers, has taught, in holy Councils and lately in this oecumenical Synod, that there is a purgatory and that souls there detained are helped by the intercessions of the faithful, but most of all by the acceptable sacrifice of the altar, this sacred Synod instructs bishops to take earnest care that the sound doctrine concerning purgatory handed down by the holy Fathers and sacred Councils be by Christ's faithful believed, held, taught and everywhere preached. But among the unlettered folk let the more difficult and subtler questions, which do not tend to edification [1 Tim. i. 4] and from which no increase of piety is wont to arise, be excluded from public preaching. And let them not permit any public handling of matters uncertain or those which labour under an appearance of falsehood. And let them prohibit, as scandals and sources of offence to the faithful, things which pander to curiosity and superstition or which savour of base lucre.

The holy Synod enjoins on all bishops and others on whom is laid the duty and charge of teaching, that they diligently instruct the faithful, in accordance with the use of the Catholic and Apostolic Church (received from the earliest age of the Christian religion), the consensus of the holy Fathers and the decrees of the Sacred Councils, firstly-concerning the intercession of saints, the invocation of saints, the honour due to relics, and the lawful use of images; teaching them that the Saints who reign with Christ offer their prayers to God on behalf of men, that it is good and useful to invoke them in supplication and to have recourse to their prayers, their help and their succour for the obtaining of benefits from God through his Son, Jesus Christ our Lord, who is our only Saviour and Redeemer. . . .

h. *On Indulgences.*

Session XXV.

C. Tr. ix. 1105. Denzinger, 989.

Since the power of conferring indulgences has been granted to the Church by Christ, and since the Church has made use of this divinely given power even from the earliest times, the holy Synod teaches and enjoins that the use of indulgences, which is greatly salutary for Christian people and has been approved by the authority of sacred Councils, is to be retained in the Church. . . .

III. The Tridentine Profession of Faith, 1564

From the Bull of Pius IV, *Injunctum nobis*, November 1564:

Mansi, xxxiii. 220 B sqq. Denzinger, 994 sqq.

[Issued to be recited publicly by all bishops and beneficed clergy. It is the symbol imposed to this day on all converts to Roman Catholicism.]

I, *N*, with steadfast faith believe and profess each and all the things contained in the Symbol of faith which the holy Roman Church uses, namely "I believe in One God, etc. [The Nicene Creed]."

I most firmly acknowledge and embrace the Apostolical and ecclesiastical traditions and other observances and constitutions of the same Church. I acknowledge the sacred Scripture according to that sense which Holy Mother Church has held and holds, to whom it belongs to decide upon the true sense and interpretation of the holy Scriptures, nor will I ever receive and interpret the Scripture except according to the unanimous consent of the Fathers.

I profess also that there are seven sacraments. . . . I embrace and receive each and all of the definitions and declarations of the sacred Council of Trent on Original Sin and Justification.

I profess likewise that true God is offered in the Mass, a proper and propitiatory sacrifice for the living and the dead, and that in the most Holy Eucharist there are truly, really and substantially the body and blood, together with the soul and divinity of Our Lord Jesus Christ, and that a conversion is made of the whole substance of bread into his body and of the whole substance of wine into his blood, which conversion the Catholic Church calls transubstantiation. I also confess that the whole and entire Christ and the true sacrament is taken under the one species alone.

I hold unswervingly that there is a purgatory and that the souls there detained are helped by the intercessions of the faithful; likewise also that the Saints who reign with Christ are to be venerated and invoked; that they offer prayers to God for us and that their relics are to be venerated. I firmly assert that the images of Christ and of the ever-Virgin Mother of God, as also those of other Saints, are to be kept and retained, and that due honour and veneration is to be accorded them; and I affirm that the power of indulgences has been left by Christ in the Church, and that their use is very salutary for Christian people.

I recognize the Holy Catholic and Apostolic Roman Church as the mother and mistress of all churches; and I vow and swear true obedience to the Roman Pontiff, the successor of blessed Peter, the chief of the Apostles and the representative [*vicarius*] of Jesus Christ.

I accept and profess, without doubting, the traditions, definitions and declarations of the sacred Canons and Oecumenical Councils and especially those of the holy Council of Trent; and at the same time I condemn, reject and anathematize all things contrary thereto, and all heresies condemned, rejected and anathematized by the Church. This true Catholic Faith (without which no one can be in a state of salvation), which at this time I of my own will profess and truly hold, I, *N*, vow and swear, God helping me, most constantly to keep and confess entire and undefiled to my life's last breath, and that I will endeavour, as far as in me shall lie, that it be held, taught and preached by my subordinates or by those who shall be placed under my care: so help me God and these Holy Gospels of God.

Selections are taken from
Documents of the Christian Church,
Selected and Edited by Henry Bettenson, Second Edition,
London: Oxford University Press, 1963

Chapter 47 • St. Teresa of Ávila: *Autobiography*; *The Interior Castle*

St. Teresa (1515-1582) is regarded by many as one of the greatest mystics of the Catholic Church. Her writings reveal an intense simplicity and complete dedication to the love of Jesus. They were so expressive of the ardor of her inner life that they inflamed many who read them with a desire to imitate her in her embrace of the contemplative life. Strange as it may seem, her contemplative ardor did not prevent her from being extremely active in a practical way: she founded many communities of nuns who tried to follow her in her inspired work. In fact it was her contemplative life that supplied her with the rationale and support for her practical activity. Her *Autobiography* is a classical example of deep personal love of God mingled with humor and common sense. The Reformed Carmelite Order was approved by Pope Gregory XIII in 1580. Pope Gregory XV canonized her in 1622 along with Ignatius Loyola, Francis Xavier, Isidore, and Philip Neri.

Teresa was a person of great natural gifts, lively humor, sound judgment, and deep spiritual insight. In this work she explains, in a spiritual way, how the human soul, by cooperating with the grace of God, can make a successful journey from sin to the rapture of Divine Union. The Interior Castle is illustrated metaphorically as involving seven mansions as abodes of the soul at different stages of the journey. "In my Father's house there are many mansions" (John 14:2). Teresa was the first woman to be honored by the title Doctor of the Church, conferred in 1970 by Paul VI.

Autobiography

Chapter VIII

When I was in the midst of the pleasures of the world, the remembrance of what I owed to God made me sad, and when I was praying to God my worldly affections disturbed me. This is so painful a struggle that I know not how I could have borne it for a month, let alone for so many years. Nevertheless, I can trace distinctly the great mercy of our Lord to me, while thus immersed in the world, in that I had still the courage to pray. I say courage, because I know of nothing in the whole world which requires greater courage than plotting treason against the King, knowing that He knows it, and yet never withdrawing from His presence; for, granting that we are always in the presence of God, yet it seems to me that those who pray are in His presence in a very different sense; for they, as it were, see that He is looking upon them, while others may be for days together without even once recollecting that God sees them.

When I was ill, I was well with God. I contrived that those about me should be so, too, and I made supplications to our Lord for this grace, and spoke frequently of Him. Thus, with the exception of that year of which I have been speaking, during eight and twenty years of prayer, I spent more than eighteen in that strife and contention which arose out of my attempts to reconcile God and the world. As to the other years, of which I have now to speak, in them the grounds of the warfare, though it was not slight, were changed; but inasmuch as I was — at least, I think so — serving God, and aware of the vanity of the world, all has been pleasant, as I shall show hereafter.

The reason, then, of my telling this at so great a length is that, as I have just said, the mercy of God and my ingratitude, on the one hand, may become known; and, on the other, that men may understand how great is the good which God works in a soul when He gives it a disposition to pray in earnest, though it may not be so well prepared as it ought to be. If that soul perseveres in spite of sins, temptations, and relapses, brought about in a thousand ways by Satan, our Lord will bring it at last — I am certain of it — to the harbor of salvation, as He has brought me myself, for so it seems to me now. May His Majesty grant I may never go back and be lost! He who gives himself to prayer is in possession of a great blessing, of which many saintly and good men have written — I am speaking of mental prayer — glory be to God for it! and, if they had not done so, I am not proud enough, though I have but little humility, to presume to discuss it.

I may speak of that which I know by experience; and so, I say, let him never cease from prayer who has once begun it, be his life ever so wicked; for prayer is the way to amend it, and without prayer such amendment will be much more difficult. Let him not be tempted by Satan, as I was, to give it up, on the pretense of humility; let him rather believe that His words are true Who says that, if we truly repent, and resolve never to offend Him, He will take us into His favor again, give us the graces He gave us before, and occasionally even greater, if our repentance deserve it. And as to him who has not begun to pray, I implore him by the love of our Lord not to deprive himself of so great a good.

O infinite Goodness of my God! I seem to see Thee and myself in this relation to one another. O Joy of the angels! when I consider it, I wish I could wholly die of love! How true it is that Thou endurest those who will not endure Thee! Oh, how good a friend art Thou, O my Lord! how Thou comfortest and endurest, and also waitest for them to make themselves like unto Thee, and yet, in the meanwhile, art Thyself so patient of the state they are in! Thou takest into account the occasions during which they seek Thee, and for a moment of penitence forgettest their offenses against Thyself.

I do not understand what there can be to make them afraid who are afraid to begin mental prayer, nor do I know what it is they dread. The devil does well to bring this fear upon us, that he may really hurt us; if, by putting me in fear, he can make me cease from thinking of my offenses against God, of the great debt I owe Him, of the existence of heaven and hell, and of the great sorrows and trials He underwent for me. That was all my prayer, and had been, when I was in this dangerous state, and it was on those subjects I dwelt whenever I could; and very often, for some years, I was more occupied with the wish to see the end of the time I had appointed for myself to spend in prayer, and in watching the hour-glass, than with other thoughts that were good. If a sharp penance had been laid upon me, I know of none that I would not very often have willingly undertaken, rather than prepare myself for prayer by self-recollection. And certainly the violence with which Satan assailed me was so irresistible, or my evil habits were so strong, that I did not betake myself to prayer; and the sadness I felt on entering the oratory was so great, that it required all the courage I had to force myself in. They say of me that my courage is not slight, and it is known that God has given me a courage beyond that of a woman; but I have made a bad use of it. In the end our Lord came to my help; and then, when I had done this violence to myself, I found greater peace and joy than I sometimes had when I had a desire to pray.

I used to pray to our Lord for help, but, as it now seems to me, I must have committed the fault of not putting my whole trust in His Majesty, and of not thoroughly distrusting myself. I sought for help, took great pains; but it must be that I did not understand how all is of little profit if we do not root out all confidence in ourselves, and place it wholly in God. I wished to live, but I saw dearly that I was not living, but rather wrestling with the shadow of death; there was no one to give me life, and I was not able to take it. He Who could have given it me had good reasons for not coming to my aid, seeing that He had brought me back to Himself so many times, and I as often had left Him.

Chapter IX

My soul was now grown weary; and the miserable habits it had contracted would not suffer it to rest, though it was desirous of doing so. It came to pass one day, when I went into the oratory, that I saw a statue which they had put by there, and which had been procured for a certain feast observed in the house. It was a representation of Christ most grievously wounded; and so devotional, that the very sight of it, when I saw it, moved me — so well did it show forth that which He suffered for us. So keenly did I feel the evil return I had made for those wounds, that I thought my heart was breaking. I threw myself on the ground beside it, my tears flowing plenteously, and implored Him to strengthen me once for all, so that I might never offend Him any more.

For many years, nearly every night before I fell asleep, when I recommended myself to God, that I might sleep in peace, I used always to think a little of the mystery of the prayer in the Garden — yea, even before I was a nun, because I had been told that many indulgences were to be gained thereby. For my part, I believe that my soul gained very much in this way, because I began to practice prayer without knowing what it was; and, now that it had become my constant habit, I was saved from omitting it, as I was from omitting to bless myself with the sign of the cross before I slept.

It was a help to me also to look on fields, water, and flowers. In them I saw traces of the Creator — I mean, that the sight of these things was a book unto me; it roused me, made me recollected, and reminded me of my ingratitude and of my sins. My understanding was so dull that I could never represent in the imagination either heavenly or high things in any form whatever, until our Lord placed them before me in another way.

I was so little able to put things before me by the help of my understanding, that, unless I saw a thing with my eyes, my imagination was of no use whatever. I could not do as others do, who can put matters before themselves so as to become thereby recollected. I was able to think of Christ only as man. But so it was; and I never could form any image of Him to myself, though I read much of His beauty, and looked at pictures of Him. I was like one who is blind, or in the dark, who, though speaking to a person present, and feeling his presence, because he knows for certain that he is present — I mean, that he understands him to be present, and believes it — yet does not see him. It was thus with me when I used to think of our Lord. This is why I was so fond of images. Wretched are they who, through their own fault, have lost this blessing; it is clear enough that they do not love our Lord — for if they loved Him, they would rejoice at the sight of His picture, just as men find pleasure when they see the portrait of one they love.

At this time, the *Confessions* of St. Augustine were given me. Our Lord seems to have so ordained it, for I did not seek them myself, neither had I ever seen them before. I had a very great devotion to St. Augustine, because the monastery in which I lived when I was yet in the world was of his Order; and also because he had been a sinner — for I used to find great comfort in those Saints whom, after they had sinned, our Lord converted to Himself. I thought they would help me, and that, as our Lord had forgiven them, so also He would forgive me. One thing, however, there was that troubled me — I have spoken of it before — our Lord had called them but once, and they never relapsed; while my relapses were now so many. This it was that vexed me. But calling to mind the love that He bore me, I took courage again. Of His mercy I never doubted once, but I did very often of myself.

When I began to read the *Confessions*, I thought I saw myself there described, and began to recommend myself greatly to this glorious Saint. When I came to his conversion, and read how he heard that voice in the garden, it seemed to me nothing less than that our Lord had uttered it for me: I felt so in my heart. I remained for some time lost in tears, in great inward affliction and distress. 0 my God, what a soul has to suffer because it has lost the liberty it had of being mistress over itself! And what torments it has to endure! I wonder now how I could live in torments so great: God be praised Who gave me life, so that I might escape from so fatal a death! I believe that my soul obtained great strength from His Divine Majesty, and that He must have heard my cry, and had compassion upon so many tears.

Chapter X

I used to have at times, as I have said, though it used to pass quickly away — certain commencements of that which I am going now to describe. When I formed those pictures within myself of throwing myself at the feet of Christ, as I said before, and sometimes even when I was reading, a feeling of the presence of God would come over me unexpectedly, so that I could in no wise doubt either that He was within me, or that I was wholly absorbed in Him. It was not by way of vision; I believe it was what is called mystical theology. The soul is suspended in such a way that it seems to be utterly beside itself. The will loves; the memory, so it seems to me, is as it were lost; and the understanding, so I think, makes no reflections — yet is not lost: as I have just said, it is not at work, but it stands as if amazed at the greatness of the things that it understands; for God wills it to understand that it understands nothing whatever of that which His Majesty places before it.

The comparison which now presents itself seems to me to be good. These joys in prayer are like what those of heaven must be. As the vision of the saints, which is measured by their merits here, reaches no further than our Lord wills, and as the blessed see how little merit they had, every one of them is satisfied with the place assigned him: there being the very greatest difference between one joy and another in heaven, and much greater than between one spiritual joy and another on earth — which is, however, very great. And in truth, in the beginning, a soul in which God works this grace thinks that now it has scarcely anything more to desire, and counts itself abundantly rewarded for all the service it has rendered Him. And there is reason for this: for one of those tears — which, as I have just said, are almost in our own power, though without God nothing can be done — cannot, in my opinion, be purchased with all the labors of the world, because of the great gain it brings us. And what greater gain can we have than some testimony of our having pleased God? Let him, then, who shall have attained to this, give praise unto God — acknowledge himself to be one of His greatest debtors; because it seems to be His will to take him into His house, having chosen him for His kingdom, if he does not turn back.

If, then, it is lawful, and so meritorious, always to remember that we have our being from God, that He has created us out of nothing, that He preserves us, and also to remember all the benefits of His death and Passion, which He suffered long before He made us, for every one of us now alive — why should it not be lawful for me to discern, confess, and consider often that I was once accustomed to speak of vanities, and that now our Lord has given me the grace to speak only of Himself?

Here, then, is a precious pearl, which, when we remember that it is given us, and that we have it in possession, powerfully invites us to love. All this is the fruit of prayer founded on humility. What, then, will it be when we shall find ourselves in possession of other pearls of greater price, such as contempt of the world and of self, which some servants of God have already received? It is clear that such souls must consider themselves greater debtors — under greater obligations to serve Him: we must acknowledge that we have nothing of ourselves, and confess the munificence of our Lord, Who, on a soul so wretched and poor, and so utterly undeserving, as mine is — for whom the first of these pearls was enough, and more than enough — would bestow greater riches than I could desire.

Blessed be God for all, and may His infinite Majesty make use of me! Our

Lord knoweth well that I have no other end in this than that He may be praised and magnified a little, when men shall see that on a dunghill so foul and rank He has made a garden of flowers so sweet. May it please His Majesty that I may not by my own fault root them out, and become again what I was before. And I entreat your reverence, for the love of our Lord, to beg this of Him for me, seeing that you have a dearer knowledge of what I am than you have allowed me to give of myself here.

The Interior Castle (1577)
The Seventh Mansion
Chapter IV

It will be well, Sisters, to tell you what end the Lord has in view in granting so many favours in this world. Though by their efforts, you must have understood, if you have reflected on the matter, I wish to speak again about it here, for let no-one think that is merely for the delectation of these souls; that would be a serious mistake.

His Majesty can do us no greater favour than that of giving us a life which will be an imitation of that lived by his well-beloved Son. I am therefore convinced that these favours are intended to fortify our weakness, as I have already said several times, so that we may be able to imitate him in suffering much. We have always seen that those who were nearest to Christ our Lord were those who have the most severe trials.

If his Majesty displayed his love for us by such terrible sacrifices and torments, how can you wish to please him by words along? Do you know what it means to be truly spiritual? It is to make ourselves the slaves of God, to belong to him, to be stamped with his brand, which is that of the +, and as those who have already given him their liberty, he can sell us as slaves to the whole world, as he was. In this he would not only do you no injury, but no small favor, and if you are not prepared for this, have no fear that you have made such progress, for the foundation of this entire spiritual building is humility. If this be not perfectly sincere, even for your own sakes, the Lord will not wish to raise the edifice to any height, lest it collapse utterly.

Therefore, Sisters, in order to lay good foundations, strive to be the least of all, and the slave of all, considering how and by what means you can please and serve your Sisters, for acting thus, you will do more for yourselves than for them, laying stones so firmly, that your Castle will not fall down. I repeat, that for this it is necessary not to rely on prayer and contemplation alone, for if you do not acquire virtues, and exercise yourselves in them, you will always remain dwarfs, and please God that you only cease to grow, but you know very well, that he who is not growing is dwindling, and I hold it is impossible to love to be content to be at a standstill.

To conclude, my Sisters, do not let us build towers without foundations, for the Lord does not consider so much the greatness of our deeds, as the love with which they are performed, and when we do all that we can, his Majesty will make it possible for us to do more and more. May we not tire, then, but during this short life, and perhaps it will be shorter for some of us than we think, let us offer to the Lord, interiorly and exteriorly, whatever we are able, so that his Majesty may unite it with that which he offered to his Father for us on the Cross, that it may have the value which our good-will has merited for it, however insignificant our works may be.

May it please his Majesty, Sisters, and my daughters, that we may all arrive where we may praise him for ever, and that he will give me the grace to perform somewhat of all that I have said, by the merits of his Son, who liveth and reigneth for ever and ever. Amen.

But I assure you that I am filled with confusion, and therefore, I beg you the same Lord, not to forget this poor, miserable woman in your prayers.

Selections from the "Autobiography" are taken from the
Autobiography of St. Teresa,
Edited by Benedict Williamson,
London: Burns, Oates and Washbourne, 1910
Selections from "The Interior Castle" are taken from
The Interior Castle,
St. Teresa of Jesus,
Westminster, Maryland: The Newman Bookshop, 1945

Chapter 48 • St. John of the Cross: *Spiritual Canticle*

The *Spiritual Canticle* of John of the Cross (1542-1591) is another classic in the tradition of mysticism in the Catholic Church. John has been successful in the combination of certain points of scholastic theology with the affective awareness of mystical theology. His *Dark Night of the Soul* and *The Ascent of Mount Carmel* are classic expressions of his total dedication to Divine Love. The poems, a happy blend of ecstatic love and lyric beauty, helped to gain John of the Cross the reputation of Spain's finest lyric poet.

Spiritual Canticle
Prologue

Forasmuch as these stanzas appear to be written with a certain degree of fervor of love for God, Whose wisdom and love are so vast that, as is said in the Book of Wisdom, they reach from one end to another, and the soul which is informed and moved by Him has to some extent this same abundance and impetus in its words, I do not now think of expounding all the breadth and plenteousness imbued in them by the fertile spirit of love, for it would be ignorance to think that sayings of love understood mystically, such as those of the present stanzas, can be fairly explained by words of any kind. For the Spirit of the Lord, Who helps our infirmity, as Saint Paul says, dwells in us and makes intercession for us, with groanings unutterable, pleading for that which we cannot well understand or comprehend, so as to express it ourselves. For who can write down that which He reveals to loving souls wherein He dwells? And who can set forth in words that which He makes them to feel? And lastly, who can express that which He makes them to desire? Of a surety, none; nay, indeed, not the very souls through whom He passes. It is for this reason that, by means of figures, comparisons and similitudes, they allow something of that which they feel to overflow and utter secret mysteries from the abundance of the Spirit, rather than explain these things rationally. These similitudes, if they be not read with the simplicity of the spirit of love and understanding embodied in them, appear to be nonsense rather than the expression of reason, as may be seen in the divine Songs of Solomon and in other books of Divine Scripture, where, since the Holy Spirit cannot express the abundance of His meaning in common and vulgar terms, He utters mysteries in strange figures and similitudes. Whence it follows that no words of holy doctors, albeit they have said much and may yet say more, can ever expound these things fully, neither could they be expounded in words of any kind. That which is expounded of them, therefore, is ordinarily the least part of that which they contain.

Since these Stanzas, then, have been composed under the influence of a love which comes from abounding mystical understanding, they cannot be fairly expounded, nor shall I attempt so to expound them, but only to throw upon them some light of a general kind. And this I think to be best, for the sayings of love are better left in their fullness, so that everyone may pluck advantage from them according to his manner and to the measure of his spirit, than abbreviated in a sense to which not every taste can accommodate itself. And thus, although they are expounded after a certain manner, there is no reason why anyone should be bound to this exposition. For mystical wisdom (which comes through love, whereof the present Stanzas treat) needs not to be understood distinctly in order to produce love and affection in the soul; it is like to faith, whereby we love God without understanding Him.

I shall therefore be very brief, although I shall be unable to refrain from extending myself in certain places where the matter requires it, and where occasion offers to expound and treat certain points and effects of prayer, for since there are many such in the Stanzas I cannot refrain from treating of some. But I shall leave aside the commonest of them and note briefly the most extraordinary, which come to pass in those that, by the favor of God, have left behind the beginners' state. And this for two reasons: the one, that there are so many things written for beginners; the other, that I speak herein with your Reverence by your command, and to your Reverence Our Lord has granted the favor of drawing you forth from these beginnings and leading you farther onward into the bosom of His Divine love. Thus I trust that, although I write here of certain points of scholastic theology concerning the interior commerce of the soul with its God, it will not be in vain to have talked somewhat after the manner of pure spirit; for though your Reverence may lack the practice of scholastic theology, wherein are comprehended Divine verities, you lack not that of mystical theology, which is attained through love, and wherein these verities are not only known but also experienced.

And to the end that all I say (which I desire to submit to better judgment, and entirely so to that of Holy Mother Church) may be the better received, I think not to affirm aught that is mine, trusting to my own experience, or to that of other spiritual persons of which I have known, or to that which I have heard from them (although I purpose to make use of both) unless it be confirmed and expounded by authorities from Divine Scripture, at the least in those things which appear to be the most difficult of comprehension. 'And first I shall set down all the Stanzas together, and then in order shall set down each one separately with intent to expound it, whereof I shall expound each line, setting it down at the beginning of its exposition.

Songs Between the Soul and the Spouse Bride

1. Whither hast thou hidden thyself, And hast left me,
O Beloved, to my sighing?
Thou didst flee like the hart, having wounded me:
I went out after thee, calling, and thou wert gone.
2. Shepherds, ye that go Yonder, through the sheepcotes, to the hill,
If perchance ye see him that I most love, Tell ye
him that I languish, suffer and die.
3. Seeking my loves, I will go o'er yonder mountains and banks;
I will neither pluck the flowers nor fear the wild beasts;
I will pass by the mighty and cross the frontiers.

Questions to the Creatures

4. O woods and thickets, Planted by the hand of the Beloved!
O meadow of verdure, enamelled with flowers, Say if he has passed by you.

Answer of the Creatures

5. Scattering a thousand graces, He passed through these groves in haste,
And, looking upon them as he went, Left them, by
his glance alone, clothed with beauty.

Bride

6. Ah, who will be able to heal me! Surrender thou
thyself now completely.
From to-day do thou send me now no other messenger,
For they cannot tell me what I wish.
7. And all those that serve Relate to me a thousand graces of thee,

And all wound me the more And something that
they are stammering leaves me dying.
8. But how, O life, dost thou persevere, Since thou
livest not where thou livest,
And since the arrows make thee to die which thou
receivest From the conceptions of the Beloved
which thou formest within thee?
9. Since thou has wounded this heart, Wherefore didst thou not heal it?
And wherefore, having robbed me of it, hast thou
left it thus And takest not the prey that thou hast spoiled?
10. Quench thou my griefs, Since none suffices to remove them.
And let mine eyes behold thee, Since thou art their
light and for thee alone I wish to have them.
11. O crystalline fount, If on that thy silvered surface
Thou wouldst of a sudden form the eyes desired
Which I bear outlined in my inmost parts!
12. Withdraw them, Beloved, for I fly away.

The Spouse

Return thou, dove,
For the wounded hart appears on the hill At the air of
thy flight, and takes refreshment.

Bride

13. My Beloved, the mountains, The solitary, wooded valleys.
The strange islands, the sonorous rivers, The whisper
of the amorous breezes,
14. The tranquil night, At the time of the rising of the dawn,
The silent music, the sounding solitude, The supper
that recreates and enkindles love.
15. Our flowery bed, Encompassed with dens of lions,
Hung with purple and builded in peace,
Crowned with a thousand shields of gold.
16. In the track of thy footprint The young girls run along by the way.
At the touch of a spark, at the spiced wine, Flows
forth the Divine balsam.
17. In the inner cellar, of my Beloved have I drunk,

And, when I went forth over all this meadow,

Then knew I naught And lost the flock which I followed aforetime.

18. There he gave me his breast; There he taught me a science most delectable;

And I gave myself to him indeed, reserving nothing;

There I promised him to be his bride.

19. My soul has employed itself And all my possessions in his service:

Now I guard no flock nor have I now other office,

For now my exercise is in loving alone.

20. If, then, on the common land, From henceforth I

am neither seen nor found.

You will say that I am lost; That, wandering love-stricken, I lost my way and was found.

21. With flowers and emeralds Gathered in the cool mornings

We will make the garlands flowering in thy love

And interwoven with one hair from my head.

22. By that hair alone Which thou regardest fluttering on my neck,

Beholding it upon my neck, thou wert captivated,

And wert wounded by one of mine eyes.

23. When thou didst look on me, Thine eyes imprinted upon me thy grace;

For this cause didst thou love me greatly, Whereby

mine eyes deserved to adore that which they saw in thee.

24. Despise me not, For, if thou didst find me swarthy,

Now canst thou indeed look upon me, Since thou

didst look upon me and leave in me grace and beauty.

25. Catch us the foxes, For our vineyard is now in flower,

While we make a bunch of roses, And let none appear upon the hill.

26. Stay thee, dead north wind. Come, south wind, that awakenest love;

Breathe through my garden and let its odors flow,

And the Beloved shall pasture among the flowers.

Spouse

27. The Bride has entered Into the pleasant garden of her desire,

And at her pleasure rests, Her neck reclining on the

gentle arms of the Beloved.

28. Beneath the apple-tree, There wert thou betrothed to me;

There did I give thee my hand And thou wert redeemed where thy mother had been corrupted.

29. Birds of swift wing, Lions, harts, leaping does,
Mountains, valleys, banks, waters, breezes, heats,
And terrors that keep watch by night,
30. By the pleasant lyres And by the sirens' song, I conjure you,
Cease your wrath and touch not the wall, That
the Bride may sleep more securely.

Bride

31. O nymphs of Judaea, While mid the flowers and
rose-trees the amber sends forth perfume,
Dwell in the outskirts And desire not to touch our thresholds.
32. Hide thyself, dearest one, And look with thy face
upon the mountains,
And desire not to speak, But look upon her companion
who travels mid strange islands.

Spouse

33. The little white dove Has returned to the ark with the bough,
And now the turtle-dove Has found the mate of her
desire on the green banks.
34. In solitude she lived And in solitude now has built her nest,
And in solitude her dear one alone guides her, Who
likewise in solitude was wounded by love.

Bride

35. Let us rejoice, Beloved, And let us go to see ourselves in thy beauty,
To the mountain or the hill where flows the pure water;
Let us enter farther into the thicket.
36. And then we shall go forth To the lofty caverns of the
rock which are well hidden,
And there shall we enter And taste the new wine of the
pomegranates.
37. There wouldst thou show me That which my soul desired,
And there at once, my life, wouldst thou give me
That which thou gavest me the other day.
38. The breathing of the air, The song of the sweet philomel,
The grove and its beauty in the serene night, With

a flame that consumes and gives no pain.

39. For none saw it, Neither did Aminadab appear,

And there was a rest from the siege, And the cavalry came down at the sight of the waters.

Selections from the translated *Spiritual Canticle,*
by E. Allison Peers,
in Doubleday Image Book by special arrangement with the Newman Press, 1961
Reprinted with permission of Paulist-Newman Press

Part VII
Practice of Basic Catholic Teachings

Introduction

In the excerpts from St. Francis de Sales' *Introduction to a Devout Life*, from *The Hound of Heaven* of Francis Thompson, from *The Dream of Gerontius* of Cardinal Newman, and from *The Faith of our Fathers* by Cardinal Gibbons are emphasized the ways in which a Catholic can put into practice the basic beliefs that have been stressed in the previous readings.

Excerpts from modern and contemporary papal pronouncements concerning a workable social order, as found in Pope Leo XIII's *Rerum Novarum* and Pope Pius XI's *On Social Reconstruction*, present ideas of value for us today.

The Encyclical of Pope St. Pius X is a masterpiece that points the finger at the fundamental attitude or mentality of the Modernists — as does Cardinal Newman — shown by their adoption of beliefs and conduct that have been repeatedly criticized and condemned by those who accept the traditional beliefs defended by the Catholic Magisterium. The Modernists, in their belief that modern science is the absolute norm of reality and truth and that people individually and collectively determine the norms of morality, are merely repeating what is found in the teachings of those condemned long ago.

Today this attitude may go by the name of secular humanism and even religious humanism. Whatever the name for it, be it materialism or communism, pro-choice attitudes, liberalism, naturalism, me-ism, hedonism, the Way, or "whatever," it is the same song that is not found in the New Testament, is contrary to the teachings of the Apostles, is outlawed by the Magisterium of the Catholic Church, and dissents from the materials presented in this collection.

"Glory be to the Father, Son, and Holy Spirit, as it was in the beginning is now and forever."

Chapter 49 • St. Francis de Sales: *Introduction to a Devout Life*

One of the outstanding religious leaders of the Counter-Reformation, Francis de Sales (1567-1622) was originally trained for law, but decided to enter the priesthood instead. As a priest he was spurred on by the love of Jesus to attempt to heal the breach between Catholics and Protestants. His preaching won him much success in his endeavors, and he was made co-adjutor bishop of Geneva in 1599 and bishop in 1602. He was active in setting up schools in his diocese, and was especially devoted to the welfare of the poor. The *Introduction to a Devout Life* is widely read and presents a cross section of the then current teaching on the theoretical and practical aspects of Catholicism.

In addition to the author's Dedicatory Prayer and Notice to the Reader, the *Introduction to a Devout Life* covers 252 pages, comprising 5 parts and 119 chapters. The excerpts attempt to present the most important parts of this work.

Introduction to a Devout Life

Part First

Containing instructions and exercises for conducting the soul from her first desire till she be brought to a full resolution to embrace a devout life.

Chapter I

The Description of True Devotion.

True devotion, Philothea, presupposes, not a partial, but a thorough love of God. For inasmuch as divine love adorns the soul, it is called grace, making us pleasing to the Divine Majesty, inasmuch as it gives us the strength to do good, it is called charity; but when it is arrived at that degree of perfection by which it not only makes us do well, but also work diligently, frequently, and readily, then it is called devotion.

Good people, who have not as yet attained to devotion, fly towards God by their good works, but rarely, slowly and heavily; but devout souls ascend to Him by more frequent, prompt, and lofty flights. In short, devotion is nothing else but that spiritual agility and vivacity by which charity works in us, or we work by her, with alacrity and affection; and as it is the business of charity to make us observe all God's commandments, generally and without exception, so it is the part of devotion to make us observe them more fully and with diligence. Wherefore he who observes not all the commandments of God cannot be esteemed either good or devout; since to be good he must be possessed of charity; and to be devout, besides charity, he must show a cheerfulness and alacrity in the performance of charitable actions.

As devotion, then, consists in a certain excellent degree of charity, it makes us not only active and diligent in the observance of God's commandments, but it also excites us to the performance of every good work with an affectionate alacrity, though it be not of precepts, but only of counsel.

The Holy Spirit, by the mouths of all the saints, and our Savior by his own, assure us that a devout life is a life of all others the most sweet, happy, and amiable.

The world beholds devout people to fast, pray, suffer injuries, serve the sick, and give alms to the poor; it sees them watch over themselves, restrain their anger, stifle their passions, deprive themselves of sensual pleasures, and perform other actions in themselves painful and rigorous; but the world discerns not the inward cordial devotion which renders all these actions agreeable, sweet, and easy.

Although they make use of the world and worldly things, yet they use them in a most pure and moderate manner, not taking more of them than is necessary for their condition. Such are devout persons.

As in the creation, God commanded the plants to bring forth their fruits, each one according to its kind, so he commands all Christians, who are the living plants of his Church, to bring forth the fruits of devotion, each according to his quality and vocation. Devotion ought, then, to be not only differently exercised by the gentleman, the tradesman, the servant, the prince, the widow, the maid, and the married woman, but its practice should be also adapted to the strength, the employments, and obligations of each one in particular.

The soul that aspires to the honor of being spouse to the Son of God must divest herself of the old man, and clothe herself with the new, by forsaking sin, and removing every obstacle which may prevent her union with God.

The exercise of purifying the soul neither can nor ought to end but with our life; let us not then be disturbed at the sight of our imperfections, for perfection consists in fighting against them; and how can we fight against them without seeing them, or overcome them without encountering them? Our victory consists not in being insensible to them, but in refusing them our consent; now to be displeased with them, is not to consent to them. It is absolutely necessary for the exercise of our humility that we should sometimes meet with wounds in this spiritual warfare; but then we are never overcome, unless we either lose our life or our courage. Now, imperfections or venial sins cannot deprive us of our spiritual life, which is not lost, but by mortal sin. It then only remains that we lose not our courage.

If you desire to undertake a devout life, you must not only cease to sin, but also cleanse your heart from all affections to sin; for, besides the danger of a relapse, these wretched affections will so perpetually weaken and depress your spirits, that they will render you incapable of practicing good works with alacrity and diligence, in which, nevertheless, consists the very essence of devotion.

Chapter IX
The First Meditation.—On Our Creation
Preparation

1. Place yourself in the presence of God. 2. Beseech him to inspire you.

Considerations.

Consider that so many years ago you were not yet in the world, and that your being was a mere nothing.

God has drawn you out of this nothing, to make you what you now are, merely out of his own pure goodness, having no need of you whatever.

Consider the being that God has given you; it is the greatest in this visible world, capable of eternal life, and of being perfectly united to his Divine Majesty.

God has not placed you in this world because he had need of you, for you are altogether unprofitable to him, but only to exercise his goodness in you, by giving you his grace and glory. To this end he has given you an understanding, to know him; a memory, to be mindful of him; a will, to love him; an imagination to represent his benefits to yourself: eyes to behold his wonderful works; a tongue, to praise him; and so of the other faculties.

1. Give thanks to God. Bless thy God, O my soul! and let all that is within me praise his holy name; for his goodness has drawn me forth, and his mercy has created me out of nothing. 2. Offer. O my God! I offer to thee the being thou has given me; from my heart I dedicate and consecrate it to thee. 3. Pray. O God! strengthen me in these affections and resolutions. O holy Virgin Mary! recommend them to the mercy of thy Son, with all those for whom I ought to pray.

Consider the gifts of the mind. How many are there in the world stupid, frantic, or mad, and why are not you of this number? Because God has favored you. How many are there who have been brought up rudely, and in gross ignorance? and you, by God's providence, have received a good and liberal education.

Consider the spiritual graces. You are a child of the Catholic Church; God has taught you to know him, even from your childhood. How often has he given you his sacraments? How many internal illuminations and reprehensions for your amendment? How frequently has he pardoned your faults? How often has he delivered you from those dangers of eternal perdition to which you were exposed? And were not all these years past given you as so many favorable opportunities of working out your salvation? Consider a little, by descending to particulars, how sweet and gracious God has been to you.

Chapter XIII
The Fifth Meditation—On Death

Consider the uncertainty of the day of your death. O my soul! thou shalt one day depart out of this body! but when shall the time be? Shall it be in winter or in summer? In the city or in the country? By day or by night? Shall it be suddenly or after due preparation? By sickness or by accident? Shalt thou have leisure to make thy confession? Shalt thou be assisted by thy spiritual father? Alas! of all this we know nothing; one thing only is certain; we shall die, and sooner than we imagine.

Consider that then the world shall end for you, for it shall last no longer to you; it shall be reversed before your eyes; for then the pleasures, the vanities, the worldly joys, and vain affections, of your life shall seem like empty shadows and airy clouds. Ah, wretch! for what toys and deceitful vanities have I offended my God? You shall then see that, for a mere nothing, you have forsaken him. On the other hand, devotion and good works will then seem to you sweet and delightful. Oh, why did I not follow this lovely and pleasant path? Then the sins which before seemed very small will appear as large as mountains, and your devotion very small.

Consider the long and languishing farewell which your soul shall then give to this poor world. She shall then bid adieu to riches, vanities, and vain company; to pleasures, pastimes, friends, and neighbors; to kindred, children, husband, and wife; in a word, to every creature; and finally to her own body, which she shall leave pale, ghastly, hideous, and loathsome.

Consider with what precipitancy they will carry off this body to bury it under the earth; after which the world will think no more of you than you have thought of others. "The peace of God be with him," shall they say, and that is all. O death! how void art thou of regard or pity!

Consider how the soul, being departed from the body, takes her flight to the right hand or to the left. Alas! whither shall yours go? What way shall it take? No other than that which it began here in this world.

Chapter XIV
The Sixth Meditation — On Judgment

After the time God has prescribed for the duration of this world; after many dreadful signs and presages, which shall cause men to wither away through fear and apprehension; a fire, raging like a torrent, shall burn and reduce to ashes the whole face of the earth; nothing that exists shall escape its fury.

After this deluge of flames and of thunderbolts, all men shall rise from their graves, excepting such as are already risen, and at the voice of the angel they shall appear in the valley of Josaphat. But, alas! with what difference! for some shall arise with glorious and resplendent bodies; others in bodies most hideous and frightful.

Consider the majesty with which the Sovereign Judge will appear, surrounded by all the angels and saints. Before him shall be borne his cross, shining more brilliantly than the sun; a standard of mercy to the good, and of rigor to the wicked.

This Sovereign Judge, by his awful command, which shall be suddenly executed, shall separate the good from the bad, placing the one at his right hand, and the other at his left. O everlasting separation, after which these two companies shall never more meet together!

This separation being made, and the book of conscience opened, all men shall clearly see the malice of the wicked, and their contempt of divine grace; and, on the other hand, the penitence of the good, and the effect of the grace which they have received; for nothing shall be hidden. O good God! what confusion will this be to the one, and what consolation to the other!

Consider the last sentence of the wicked: "Depart from me, ye cursed, into everlasting fire, which was prepared for the devil and his angels." Ponder well these awful words. "Depart from me." A sentence of eternal banishment against those miserable wretches, excluding them from his presence for all eternity. He calls them cursed. O my soul, what a curse! A general curse, including all manner of evils! — a general curse, which comprises all time and eternity! He adds, "into everlasting fire!" Behold, O my heart! this vast eternity. O eternal eternity of pains, how dreadful art thou!

Consider the contrary sentence of the good. "Come," saith the Judge. O the sweet word of salvation, by which God draws us to himself, and receives us into the bosom of his goodness! "Ye blessed of my Father." O dear blessing, which comprises all blessings! "Possess the kingdom prepared for you from the foundation of the world." O good God! what an excess of bounty! for this kingdom shall never have an end.

Detest your sins, which alone can condemn on that dreadful day.

Ah! I will judge myself now that I may not be judged then! I will examine my conscience, and condemn myself; I will accuse myself, and amend my life that the eternal Judge may not condemn me on that dreadful day. I will, therefore, confess my sins, and receive all necessary advice.

Chapter XVI

The Eighth Meditation — On Paradise

Consider the glory, the beauty, and the multitude of the inhabitants of this happy country; millions of millions of angels, of cherubim and seraphim; choirs of apostles, prophets, martyrs, confessors, virgins, and holy women; the multitude is innumerable. O how glorious is this company! The least of them is more beautiful to behold than the whole world; what a sight then will it be to behold them all! But, O my God! how happy are they! They sing incessantly harmonious songs of eternal love! They always enjoy a state of felicity.

There are some people who are naturally of a light, others of a morose temper; some of an obstinate disposition, others inclined to indignation; some prone to anger, others to love; in short, there are few in whom we may not observe some of these imperfections. Now, although they are peculiar and natural to each of us, yet by care and a contrary affection, we may not only correct and moderate them, but even altogether free ourselves from them; and I tell you, it is necessary that you should do so. For as there is no nature, though never so good, which may not be perverted to evil by vicious habits, so there is no disposition, though never so perverse, that may not, by the grace of God and our own industry, be brought under and overcome.

But, above all, I recommend to you mental prayer, or the prayer of the heart, and particularly that which has for its object the life and passion of our Lord. By making him the frequent subject of your meditation, your whole soul will be replenished with him; you will imbibe his spirit, and frame all your actions according to the model of his. As he is the light of the world, it is then in him, by him, and for him, that we ought to acquire luster, and be enlightened.

The recitation of the Beads or Rosary, is a most profitable way of praying, provided you know how to say them properly; to this end, procure one of those little books which teach the manner of reciting them.

After the act of the imagination follows meditation, or the act of the understanding, which consists in making reflections and considerations, in order to raise up our affections to God and heavenly things. Hence meditation must not be confounded with study or other thoughts or reflections which have not the love of God or our spiritual welfare for their object; but something else, as, for example, to acquire learning and knowledge, to write or dispute.

Last of all, we must conclude our meditation by forming three acts, which must be done with the utmost humility. The first is to return thanks to God for the good affections and resolutions with which he has inspired us, and for his goodness and mercy, which we have discovered in the mystery of the meditation. The second is to offer our affections and resolutions to his goodness and mercy, in union with the death, the blood, and the virtues of his Divine Son. The third is to conjure God to communicate to us the graces and virtues of his Son, and to bless our affections and resolutions, that we may faithfully reduce them to practice. We then pray for the Church, our pastors, friends, and others, imploring for that end the intercession of the Blessed Virgin, and of the angels and saints; and, lastly, as I have already observed, we conclude by saying *Our Father*, and *Hail Mary*, and *Glory be to the Holy Spirit*.

Hitherto I have said nothing of the most holy, sacred, and august sacrament and sacrifice of the Mass; the center of the Christian religion, the heart of devotion, and the soul of piety; a mystery so ineffable as to comprise within itself the abyss of divine charity; a mystery in which God communicates himself really to us, and in a special manner replenishes our souls with spiritual graces and favors.

Endeavor, therefore, to assist at Mass every day, that you may jointly, with the priest, offer up the holy sacrifice of your Redeemer, to God his Father, for yourself and the whole Church.

Our Savior has left the holy sacrament of penance and confession to his Church, that in it we might cleanse ourselves from all our iniquities, as often as we should be defiled by them.

Confess yourself humbly and devoutly once every week, and always, if possible, before you communicate, although your conscience should not reproach you with the guilt of mortal sin, for by confession you not only receive absolution from the venial sins you confess, but likewise strength to avoid them, light to discern them well, and grace to repair all the damage you may have sustained by them. You will also practice the virtues of humility, obedience, sincerity.

To the end that we should live forever, our Savior has instituted the most venerable sacrament of the Eucharist, which contains really his flesh and his blood. Whoever, therefore, frequently eateth of this food, with devotion, so effectually confirmeth the health of his soul that it is almost impossible he should be poisoned by any kind of evil affection; for we cannot be nourished with this flesh of life, and at the same time live with the affections of death.

The truly patient man neither complains himself nor desires to be pitied by others; he speaks of his sufferings with truth and sincerity, without murmuring, complaining, or aggravating the matter. He patiently receives condolence, unless he is pitied for an evil which he does not suffer, for then he modestly declares that he does not suffer on that account, and thus he continues peaceable betwixt truth and patience, acknowledging, but not complaining of the evil.

In the sickness offer up all your griefs and pains as a sacrifice to our Lord, and beseech him to unite them with the torments he suffered for you. Obey your physician, take your medicines, food, and other remedies, for the love of God, remembering the gall he took for your sake:

Consider frequently Christ Jesus crucified, naked, blasphemed, slandered, forsaken, and overwhelmed with all sorts of troubles, sorrows, and labors; and remember that all your sufferings, either in quality or quantity, are not comparable to his, and that you can never suffer anything for him equal to that which he has endured for you.

Live Jesus! to whom, with the Father and Holy Spirit, be all honor and glory, now and throughout the endless ages of eternity—Amen.

Selections from "Introduction to a Devout Life" are from
St. Francis of Sales,
From the French of St. Francis de Sales,
Ratisbon, Rome, New York, and Cincinnati: Frederick Pustet and Company

Chapter 50 • St. Louis de Montfort: *True Devotion to the Blessed Virgin*

Renowned for his preaching, which converted many, St. Louis de Montfort (1673-1716) was born in Montfort, France. He studied at the Jesuit college in Rennes and was ordained in 1700. While working as a chaplain in a hospital, he began a group that grew into the Daughters of Divine Wisdom, whose rule he wrote. St. Louis was made a missionary apostolic by Clement XI. His *True Devotion to the Blessed Virgin* was published shortly before his becoming a Dominican tertiary. In 1715 he organized a group of priests as Missionaries of the Company of Mary (the Montfort Fathers). He was canonized in 1947 by Pope Pius XII.

Particular and Interior Practices For Those Who Seek Perfection

In addition to the exterior devotional practices we have just listed — which must not be omitted through negligence or contempt, but cultivated as faithfully as the state of life and condition of each person allows — here are some very sanctifying interior practices for those whom the Holy Ghost has called to a high perfection.

These practices can be summarized in four phrases: to do all our actions *through Mary, with Mary, in Mary*, and *for Mary*, in order to do them more perfectly through Jesus, with Jesus, in Jesus and for Jesus.

1 — *Through Mary*

We must do our action through Mary: that is, we must obey the Blessed Virgin in all things, and be led in all things by her spirit, which spirit is the Holy Spirit of God. Those who are led by the Spirit of God are the children of God: *Qui Spiritu Dei aguntur, ii sunt filii Dei* (*Rom.* 8, 14). Those who are led by the Spirit of Mary are children of Mary, and therefore children of God, as we have shown; and among those who claim to worship the Blessed Virgin, those only are true and faithful worshipers who are led by her spirit. I have said that the Spirit of Mary is the Spirit of God, because Mary was never led by her own spirit, but always by the Spirit of God, Who has taken such intimate possession of her that He has become her own spirit.

Hence it is that Saint Ambrose says: *Sit in singulis anima Mariae, ut magnificet Dominum: sit in singulis spiritus Mariae, ut exultet in Deo. . .*"

"Let the soul of Mary be in each person, that he may magnify the Lord: let the spirit of Mary be in each person, that he may rejoice in God." Happy indeed is the soul which, after the example of the good Jesuit Brother, Rodriguez, is wholly possessed and ruled by the Spirit of Mary, which is a spirit sweet and strong, zealous and prudent, humble and brave, pure and profound!

If he is to be led by the spirit of Mary, a person must: (1) renounce his own spirit, his own counsels and desires, before performing any action — for example, before saying his prayers, celebrating or hearing Mass, receiving Holy Communion; because if we were to follow the dark counsels of our own spirit, and the darkness of our own will and mode of acting, however good they might seem to us, we would be placing an obstacle to the spirit of Mary: (2) he must yield himself to the spirit of Mary, so as to be directed and led in whatever way pleases her. He must deliver himself into her virginal hands, as an instrument in the hands of a craftsman, and as a lute in the hands of a virtuoso. He must abandon himself to Mary, like a stone that is cast into the sea — which he can do in an instant and quite simply, by a mere glance of the mind, a slight movement of the will, or a few words such as: *I renounce myself, I give myself to you, my dear Mother*. And even though a person may experience no emotional fervour in this act of spiritual union, it is none-the-less real for all that — just as real as it would be (which God forbid) were we to give ourselves to Satan, and with a similar lack of emotion in doing so; (3) from time to time, he must renew the same act of offering and of union, during and after the performance of the action. The more frequently he does this, the more will he be sanctified, and the sooner will he attain to union with Jesus Christ — a union which invariably and necessarily follows union with Mary, since the spirit of Mary is the spirit of Jesus.

2 — With Mary

We must carry out our actions with Mary: that is, in all that we do we must look to Mary as the flawless model of every virtue and of perfection. The Holy Ghost has given us, in her, the visible image of perfection in a mere creature, so that we may imitate her according to our spiritual capacity. In everything that we undertake, therefore, we must consider how Mary performed such an action, or how she would perform it were she now in our place. For this purpose, we should study and ponder the great virtues which Mary practiced during her life on earth, and especially: (1) her lively Faith, which led her to believe unhesitatingly the message of the Angel; a Faith which she kept undimmed to the very foot of the Cross; (2) her profound humility, which caused her to hide herself, to remain silent, to submit herself in all things, and to take the lowest place; (3) her divine purity, which never has had nor ever shall have its equal under God. These we must ponder, and all her other virtues as well. Let me repeat that Mary is the great and unique mould of God, designed to create living images of God at little cost and in but a short time; and that a person who has discovered this mould, and who loses himself in it, is quickly transformed in Jesus Christ, of whom this mould is the true reproduction.

3 — In Mary

We must perform our actions *in Mary*. To understand this, we must first grasp several truths.

In the first place, we must appreciate that the Blessed Virgin is the true earthly paradise of the New Adam, and that the original earthly paradise was only her symbol. In this earthly paradise, therefore, there are mysterious and wonderful riches, beauties, rarities and delights, which the New Adam, Jesus Christ, has left there. It is in this paradise that He found His delight during nine months, and wherein He effected His wonders, lavishing His riches with the munificence of a God. This holy place is composed solely of an immaculate and virginal soil, from which has been formed and nourished, by the operation of the Holy Ghost, the New Adam without spot or stain. It is this earthly paradise of Mary which truly contains the tree of life whose Fruit was the Fruit of Life — Jesus Christ; and the tree of the knowledge of good and evil, which has given light to the world. In this divine place, there are trees planted by the hand of God and bedewed with His divine unction, which have borne and which daily bear fruits agreeable to the taste of God. There are flower-beds beautified with richly coloured and varied flowers of the virtues, whose scent is wafted even among the Angels. In this blessed place, there are green fields of hope, impregnable towers of strength, enchanting houses of trust. The Holy Spirit alone can make us realize the truth hidden under the metaphors drawn from material things. We find in this blessed Eden, an air of perfect purity, a shadowless sun of the Divinity, a radiant and nightless day of Christ's holy Humanity, an ardent and undying furnace of charity which seizes upon all the iron cast into it and transmutes that iron to gold. Here, too, we find a river of humility which wells up out of the ground, and which, dividing into four branches, waters all this enchanted place — these four branches being the four cardinal virtues.

Through the Fathers of the Church, the Holy Ghost also calls Mary the Eastern Gate by which the great High-priest, Jesus Christ, enters into the world and goes forth from it; He has come the first time into the world by her, and it is also by her that He will return at His second coming. Be it noted also that Mary is called the Sanctuary of the Divinity; the Resting-place of the Most Blessed Trinity; the Throne of God; the City of God; the Temple of God; the World of God. All these different appellations and praises are very justly hers, in relation to the different wonders which the Most High God has accomplished in Mary.

What richness! What glory! What joy! What happiness it is to be able to enter and dwell in Mary — in whom God has set up the throne of His supreme glory! But it is difficult for sinners like us to have the permission, the ability and the light to enter into so great and so holy a place, which is protected — not, as was the first Eden, by one of the Cherubim — but by the Holy Ghost Himself who has taken complete possession of Mary and who says of her: *Hortus conclusus soror mea sponsa, hortus conclusus, fons signatus* ["A closed-in garden, my sister, my bride, a closed-in garden, a sealed fountain."] (*Cant*. 4, 12). Mary is enclosed; Mary is sealed. The miserable children of Adam and Eve, driven from the earthly paradise, can enter the second earthly paradise only by a special grace of the Holy Ghost — a grace which they must merit. When, by our fidelity, we have obtained this signal grace, we must remain in the beautiful interior of Mary. We must remain there with joy; we must rest peacefully there; we must rely on Mary with confidence; we must hide ourselves trustfully in her and lose ourselves unreservedly — in order that, in her virginal womb: (1) we may be nourished with the milk of her grace and of her maternal compassion; (2) we may be set free from troubles, fears and scruples; (3) we may be shielded from all our enemies, from the world, the devil and sin — which can never find a place in Mary. Hence it is that she says: *Qui operantur in me, non peccabunt*. . . "They that work in me shall not sin" *(Eccli*. 24, 30): in other words, those who dwell in spirit in the Blessed Virgin, shall not be guilty of grievous sin; (4) we may be formed in Jesus Christ and Jesus Christ in us; because, say the Fathers, Mary's womb is the House of the divine Mysteries, where Jesus Christ and all His elect have been formed: *Homo et homo natus est in ea* ["One and all were born in her."] (*Psalm* 86 [87], 5).

4 — *For Mary*

Finally, we must do all our actions *for Mary*. Since we have given ourselves over entirely to her service, it is but fitting that we should do everything for her, as her domestics, her servants and her slaves. Not, of course, that we take her as the final end of our services, for Jesus Christ alone is that; but we look to her as our proximate end, our mysterious intercessor, and our easy way to Jesus Christ. Hence, like good servants and slaves, we must not remain idle, but, with her protecting assistance, we must undertake and carry out great things for this august Queen. We must defend her prerogatives when they are questioned; we must uphold her glory when it is attacked; we must draw as many as we can to her service and to this true and solid devotion; we must speak out boldly against those who outrage her Son by making an abuse of her devotion, and at the same time we must labour to establish this true way of honouring her. But in reward for these little services, we must expect nothing from her except the glory of belonging to so loving a Princess, and the happiness of being united through her, with Jesus, her Son, by a bond that neither time nor eternity will break.

Glory be to Jesus in Mary!

Glory be to Mary in Jesus!

Glory be to God alone!

Appendix

Act of Consecration to Jesus Christ, the Incarnate Wisdom, by the Hands of Mary

O Eternal and Incarnate Wisdom! O most amiable and adorable Jesus, true God and true Man, only Son of the Eternal Father, and of Mary, ever Virgin! I adore You profoundly in Your eternal dwelling in the bosom and magnificence of Your Father; and in Your dwelling, at the time of Your Incarnation, in the virginal bosom of Mary.

I thank You for having emptied Yourself, taking the form of a slave, in order to rescue me from cruel slavery to Satan. I praise and glorify You for having deigned to submit Yourself in all things to Mary, Your Holy Mother, in order to make me, through Her, Your faithful slave. But, alas! in my ungratefulness and infidelity, I have not kept the promises which I made so solemnly at my Baptism. I have not fulfilled my obligations; I do not deserve to be called Your child or Your slave; and since there is nothing in me which does not merit Your repulse and Your anger, I no longer dare to come by myself into the presence of Your Most holy and august Majesty. Hence it is that I have recourse to the intercession of Your Blessed Mother, whom You have given to me as my Mediatrix with Your Divine Majesty; and it is through her that I hope to obtain from You contrition and the pardon of my sins, together with the gift of Wisdom and the grace to preserve it.

Hail, therefore, O Immaculate Mary, living Tabernacle of the Divinity, wherein the hidden Wisdom of the Eternal God deigns to accept the adoration of Angels and of men! Hail, Queen of Heaven and of earth, to whose empire all is subject which is less than God Himself! Hail, sure Refuge of sinners, whose mercy is refused to no man! Grant that I may obtain my wish of possessing the Divine Wisdom; and in return, deign to accept the promises and the offerings which, out of the depths of my lowliness, I make to you.

I, (N.N.). . ., an unfaithful sinner, today renew and ratify the promises of my Baptism, and I place this renewal in your hands. I renounce forever Satan, with his works and pomps; and I give myself entirely to Jesus Christ, the Incarnate Wisdom, that I may walk in His footsteps all my life, carrying my cross. And in order that I may be more faithful to Him than I have hitherto been, I choose you today, O Mary, in the presence of the whole Court of Heaven, to be my Mother and my Mistress. I give and consecrate to you, as your slave, my body and my soul; my interior and exterior possessions; and even the value of my good actions — past, present and to come. I give you the full and entire right to dispose of me and all that I have, without the least reservation, in accordance with your good pleasure, and to the greatest glory of God, both in time and in eternity.

Receive, O gracious Virgin, this little offering of my slavery, in honour of the manner in which the Eternal Wisdom deigned to subject Himself to you as your Child, and in union with this subjection. Receive it also as a tribute of homage to the power which both your Divine Son and you possess over this little worm and miserable sinner; and as an act of thanksgiving for the privileges which the Blessed Trinity has bestowed upon you. I protest that I desire henceforth to be really and sincerely your slave, seeking your honour and obedient to you in all things.

O Mother most admirable, present me to your dear Son as His eternal slave, so that, having redeemed me through you, He may also receive me through you! O Mother of Mercy, obtain for me the grace to receive the true Wisdom of God, and to that end deign to number me among those whom you love, whom you teach, whom you lead, whom you nourish and protect as your children and your slaves. O Virgin most faithful, make me in all things so perfect a disciple, imitator and slave of the Incarnate Wisdom, Jesus Christ, your Son, that, by your intercession and example, I may attain to the fullness of His age on earth and of His glory in Heaven. Amen.

Qui potest capere, capiat ["You who can, grasp."].

Quis sapiens, et intelliget haec? ["Who knows and understands this?]

Selections taken from
True Devotion to the Blessed Virgin,
St. Louis-Marie de Montfort,
translated from the French by Malachy Gerard Carroll,
New York: Society of St. Paul, 1962

Chapter 51 • Pope Benedict XIV: *Peregrinantes*; *Cum Religiosi*

Benedict XIV was born of a noble Bolognese family in 1675 and named Prospero Lorenzo Lamberfini. He studied at the Collegium Clemintinum in Rome, concentrating on law and theology, though he also studied the Fathers of the Church. He was creeded a cardinal by Benedict XIII in 1728. He was named pope in 1740 and wrote many encyclicals to apply the doctrine of the Church to the problems of his age. He was referred to as "a scholar pope."

Peregrinantes

Encyclical of Pope Benedict XIV Proclaiming a Holy Year for 1750

May 5, 1749

To all the faithful of Christ, Greetings and Apostolic Benediction.

That we are pilgrims from the Lord and seekers after our future homeland, that we all have sinned and have frequently abandoned the way of God's commandants and like foolish sheep have wandered astray, is well established. If we should say that we have not sinned, we deceive ourselves. Our conscience bears witness to our many transgressions, which cause us to fear death and the approaching judgment of God. If we should say that we have not sinned, we make God a liar. But of course His judgments are true and just, and we must endure His scourges because we have sinned against Him, have acted unjustly, and have committed iniquity. For this reason He does not cease to punish and castigate us so that we may return to Him before Judgment Day.

Care for Sinners

The Church continually looks after its members so that it may recall sinners to the path of salvation and obtain pardon for their sins. The Church offers mercy to the guilty; but few listen to the salutary warnings of the Church. Many are entangled with evil affections or bound by the cares and pleasures of life. They fly from the spirit of penitence and the discipline of improving their character; they despise God's goodness, patience, and forbearance. The Church generously offers indulgences at all times, but some neglect them ruinously and others make no effort to acquire them properly and desire them. Meanwhile our days are running out, and we shall be poured out like water on the earth. But when the just Judge has appeared, we may learn too late that our hard and impenitent hearts have stored up wrath for us and that whatever we have not done penance for remains to be punished by the divine Judge.

Holy Year

2. Therefore, Our predecessors chose certain times during the course of the centuries to remind all the faithful of the approaching end of the world, and to instill in them a greater zeal for correcting their sins, thus obtaining the salvation of their souls. This was done of old each hundredth year. Later, considering the length of a generation, they decided to enact a holy year every twenty-five years. In this way, almost everyone — at least once in his lifetime — could experience these general means for obtaining propitiation and indulgence. The Church would also prescribe an appropriate list of penitential exercises. This holy year, a year of renovation, penance, reconciliation, and grace, will begin on the next winter solstice. We beseech all who answer to the name of Catholic to observe it.

3. The kingdom of heaven is at hand; heed Our preaching and do penance. Little children, it is the last hour; return to the Lord and be reconciled with God. The world and its concupiscences will pass; but eternal life is promised only to those who have done the will of God. What is the will of God but your salvation? To fulfill this will, the Church calls you. She devotes the entire coming year to public exercises of religion and piety; she desires that all her children who have been nourished with the milk of Catholic doctrine, may merit the mercy and grace of God, both for themselves individually as well as for the whole brotherhood. She opens the doors of the churches and her charitable heart to the arriving multitudes. To all who ask sincerely, she promises forgiveness.

4. One can have an unshakeable confidence in this promise for a number of reasons. First of all is the supreme power of binding and loosing, given by the Redeemer to Peter and his successors, and Peter's inestimable merits. The treasury of satisfaction, composed of the merits, sufferings, and virtues of Christ, His Virgin Mother, and all the saints and entrusted to Us for dispensation also inspires confidence. The blood of the Apostles and martyrs of old, poured out on the earth like water to build up the Church, cries to the Lord for

pardon and peace for the faithful. In addition, Church discipline has been conformed both to the rigor of the ecclesiastical rule by assigning works of penance and to the spirit of Christian clemency by granting indulgences. Finally, the holiness of the proposed goal, the profit of the Christian people, and the example of those who have gone before us in the faith provide still more reasons for confidence in this promise.

5. Therefore, what time and the custom of Our predecessors recommend, We shall accomplish. We proclaim and promulgate a great and universal Jubilee in this Our City for next year, 1750. It is to begin with the first vespers of the vigil of the Nativity and is to continue for the entire year. It will glorify God Himself, exalt the Catholic Church, and sanctify all the Christian people.

Requirements for the Indulgence

6. During this year We Mercifully grant complete indulgence, remission, and pardon of all their sins to all the faithful of Christ, both men and women, who are truly penitent and who fulfill the following spiritual exercises. They must have confessed and communed. If they are residents of Rome or of Vatican City they must have piously visited the basilicas of the Blessed Peter and Paul, of St. John Lateran, and of St. Mary Major at least once a day for thirty successive or interrupted days. These days may be computed by the natural rhythm of the sun or by the ecclesiastical rhythm of the daily divine service. In the latter case a day is to be counted from first vespers of one day until the end of twilight of the following day. If they are pilgrims or foreigners, they must visit these churches for at least fifteen such days. Both Romans and non-Romans must have piously prayed for the exaltation of the Holy Church, for the extermination of heresies, for concord among Catholic princes, and for the salvation and tranquility of the Christian people.

Some Unable to Fulfill all Conditions

7. Some who set out to fulfill these requirements may be physically unable to complete their visitations to the churches. If they are truly penitent, have confessed, and received holy communion, We want them to share in the indulgence and remission mentioned above just as if they had actually fulfilled all the conditions.

8. Rouse your enthusiasm at the announcement of so great a gift offered you. Undertake the task that can save your souls with great eagerness and

fervor. Let not the comforts of home hold you back; let not the labor of the journey frighten you. Weigh the spiritual gift by the standards of the Christian faith and do not permit the eagerness of worldly men for earthly treasure to surpass the desire of the faithful for heavenly treasures.

The New Rome

9. The great reward of your journey will be spiritual renewal. What can delight a Christian more than to behold the glory of the cross of Christ where it shines supreme on earth and to see with one's own eyes the monuments of victory by which our faith has conquered the world? It will even be possible to see the summit of the ages bowed in reverence to religion. This one-time Babylon no longer extends the threats of arms and war for the destruction of nations and the subjugation of kingdoms. Rather, it recommends proper discipline for the education and salvation of the peoples. Once the memory of old superstitions had been buried in oblivion, sincere worship of the true God and the majesty of sacred rites shone everywhere like a jewel. When the shrines of false deities had been overtuned by true religion, then churches were consecrated to the supreme God. In addition, the impious games and mad spectacles of the circus were obliterated from the minds of men; the cemeteries of the martyrs were visited; the monuments of tyrants were overthrown; tombs of the Apostles were built by the emperors themselves; the precious ornaments of Roman pride were transformed into places of worship; and the more eminent shrines to the provincial gods were converted from pagan temples into Christian churches. Finally, the sight of the countless multitudes converging on the City this year from everywhere will fill your heart with joy. When each one recognizes so many other Catholics of different nations and languages and rejoices with them all in brotherly love in the presence of their common Mother, the Roman Church, he will perceive the dew of heavenly benedictions, as if it descends from the top of Hermon near at hand and is poured out on him and on the inhabitants of the Holy City.

Those Who Have Left the Church

10. Our great hope is that those who long ago, deceived by lies of the devil, left the Church might now return to the unity of the Catholic faith. Do they not hear her voice calling them most lovingly to her embrace? Do they not understand that when they left the faith they began to direct their course by human conventions and they handed themselves over to be taught by

others who willfully led them astray with various foreign doctrines? But alas! How many there are among them who are not ignorant of these things! And indeed they do not deny that the foundations of each individual sect are weak and, if shaken a little, collapse easily. But what is more to be deplored is their evil lack of interest in the things of God. Because of this they despise the light of truth and the voice of their conscience. As enemies both of the Catholic Church and of their own souls, they refuse to understand what they ought to do. Nor do they wish to examine the straightaway of the Lord which is the only way back to the portals of salvation. May they at least be awakened by the example of your faith and devotion to consider that they will have no excuse on the Judgment Day if they continue to spurn the reasons which have been offered to them for recognizing the truth. May your obvious agreement in the worship of God, in the discipline of Christian life, and in reverence toward the Pope, spiritual Father of every Catholic, all serve as an incentive for emulation and an occasion for shame among those who have left the Church. Our whole desire is that the earth be filled with the knowledge of the Lord, the honor of God, and the purity of the Christian faith, and that holiness of character flourish and increase among all nations. We ask this as though drawing up a line of battle. We hope to obtain this through the intercession of your prayers. The most clement Lord says that He is moved by your intercessions. At the same time We shall pray for peace for the Catholic Church, for the happiness of Christian princes, and the safety of all the faithful.

Wage a New Kind of War

11. But you, Venerable Brothers, leaders of the Catholic religion, Patricians, Primates, Archbishops, and Bishops who serve as ambassadors among the Christian people, call a meeting, gather the people, announce to them the holy year. Endeavor to see that our plan is effective, both for the glory of God and the benefit of the whole Church. God has granted His people peace after the calamities of a long war; may this gift which God gave for the temporal tranquility of His people lead also to the improvement and, finally, to the eternal salvation of this same people. A new kind of war against the enemies of our salvation must now be waged. The license of thinking and acting must be curbed. The luxury and the pride of life must be restrained and cupidity for gain must be kept in check. All impurity must be purged and all enmity eliminated. All hatreds must be abolished.

12. To action, therefore, you priests, ministers of God. Sound the trumpets and declare a spiritual war against the enemies of the cross of Christ. Strengthen the languid hands of your soldiers and straighten their bent knees. In the first place, make straight the path for those who have decided to come to this citadel of religion, this impregnable stronghold. Let them hear from you that they are not called here for leisurely roaming nor to view strange sights; but they are summoned to carry arms in a Christian militia and to undertake the labors of fighting and war. What are the arms that Satan fears if not the vigils of the pious, their prayers, fastings, almsgivings, their works of Christian humility and of mercy? By these the tyrannical domination of human cupidity is overcome, and the kingdom of love is strengthened and extended.

13. While going forth into this pious war, it is fitting that those protected by the cross of Christ and those gathered together in the armor of God advance so that no occasion of doing harm is given to the attacking enemy. Let these peaceful, harmonious, modest, and religious soldiers proceed on their journey. While they ask the guidance, mercy, and assistance of God (whose banner they profess to follow), may His discipline prove them worthy so that they may deserve to obtain the promised crown of victory. But you, Venerable Brothers, while you strive to inspire them with these goals, bear in mind that the office of exhortation and persuasion is easy. Example, however, is stronger than words; it is more effective to teach by doing than by talking. Therefore, let the splendor of your holy actions shine before them, so that seeing your good works they may conform their lives and habits to the standard of yours. Do not forget hospitality, service, and sharing. While the Church shows a more abundant mildness for the spiritual needs of the faithful, let the temporal necessities of the poor also be relieved with greater mercy.

Advice to Secular Leaders

14. Our most dear sons in Christ, the Emperor elect, the kings, and all Catholic princes, have received blessing upon blessing from Him by whom kings rule. We beg that they may be ardently inflamed with pious zeal to promote the glory of God. Above all, may they aid the zeal and vigilance of Our Venerable Brothers, the bishops and higher leaders, and order their magistrates and ministers to help them, so that the license of evildoers may be restrained and the zeal of the good supported by kingly aid and favor. Especially let them show generosity toward pilgrims. Let them see to it that they travel safely

without being harrassed by wicked men. Rather, let them be received lovingly in hospitals, homes, and public inns and, after being refreshed with food and necessities, let them proceed happily on their journey returning with joy to their fatherland. In this way kings and princes may incline God favorably toward themselves, so that they may live long and happily on earth. Then in the end, they may be received into the eternal tabernacles by these same poor people toward whom they showed mercy and in whom Christ is fed and nourished.

15. Now in order that the knowledge of this letter may more easily reach all the faithful, We desire that copies of it, printed and signed by a public notary and marked with the seal of an ecclesiastical dignitary, have the same authority which the present letter would have if shown and displayed.

16. No one may weaken or oppose this document of Our indiction, promulgation, concession, exhortation, petition, and will. But if any one does presume to do so, may he know that he will incur the indignation of the omnipotent God and of His apostles, Peter and Paul.

Given in Rome, at St. Mary Major, in the year of the Incarnation of our Lord 1749, May 5, the ninth year of our Pontificate.

English translation: Bernard A. Hausmann, S.J.

Cum Religiosi

Encyclical of Pope Benedict XIV on Catechesis
June 26, 1754

To the Patriarchs, Archbishops, and Bishops of Italy.

Venerable Brothers, We give you Greeting and the Apostolic Blessing.

Removal of Impediments to Marriage

Religious men, devoted to the improvement of divine worship, have informed Us that it would be best to appoint special ministers in Our patriarchal basilicas, St. John Lateran, St. Peter's on the Vatican, and St. Mary Major's; their purpose would be to instruct those sent to these basilicas by the Apostolic Chancery to perform there the required servile works. These works are required before they are granted the object of their journey to Rome, which is the removal of an impediment to marriage. The aim of this instruction is to enable these people to be duly and beneficially cleansed by the Sacrament of Penance and to partake of the Sacrament of the Altar in a worthy manner. The Chancery demands that they receive both of these sacraments in addition to making the sacred pilgrimage to the seven churches and to ascending the holy stairway.

We have issued timely orders on this subject before, as may be seen from Our encyclical letter of last January 16th to the Cardinals who are archpriests of the said basilicas. We have subsequently been reliably informed of the great zeal shown in this important work by some of the canons and other clergy of the said basilicas; they constantly and eagerly press on with the careful carrying out of Our commands. Because of these reports, We have experienced a specially deep joy, and with all Our heart, have rendered due thanks to the Most High God Who is the source of all good things.

Many Ignorant of the Mysteries of the Faith

We could not rejoice, however, when it was subsequently reported to Us that in the course of religious instruction preparatory to Confession and Holy Communion, it was very often found that these people were ignorant of the mysteries of the faith, even of those matters which must be known by *necessity of means;* consequently, they were ineligible to partake of the Sacraments. Although the ministers mentioned continue unceasing instruction to eradicate this great evil, yet this evil greatly distresses the people requesting and waiting for their dispensation. For oppressed by poverty and begging for their food with their own hands, they wish to leave the city as quickly as possible, to return to their homelands and marry; this is the purpose of their journey, and they are undeterred by the discomforts of public and heavy penance.

Bishops Not at Fault

2. At the start of Our pontificate, We wrote an encyclical letter to increase the zeal of Our Venerable Brothers to ensure that in every diocese the elements and precepts of Christian doctrine be explained and learned. We have read both the old and new reports of their diocesan synods; We know they are filled with instructions and exhortations, and that they include everything helpful for transmitting Christian doctrine. Therefore We heartily assert Our conviction that in this matter none of the bishops can be found lacking in the Apostolic office entrusted to him; the fact that some members of their dioceses are ignorant is not due to their fault or negligence. It must clearly be attributed either to the obstinacy of their subjects who, despite the commands of their superiors, have avoided instruction in their Christian doctrine; they have, in fact, seldom if ever gathered to hear the word of God explained in preaching. Or it could be attributed to the slowness of some for learning what is taught. Or, perhaps it is

because that although they learned the elements of Christian teaching in their earliest years, when they were older, they ceased learning and building upon the foundation of their youth. Because of this, they are gradually reduced to a state like that of people who were not taught in their early years or who never received instruction in Christian doctrine. Although these setbacks have continued in spite of every measure taken by Our Venerable Brothers, We must nonetheless stir up their zeal again by this encyclical letter. And they are obligated anew to take every step and care possible in this matter on which the eternal salvation of the souls entrusted to them depends.

Work of St. Charles Borromeo

3. Each one of you, Venerable Brothers, has thoroughly understood the measures taken by St. Charles Borromeo, both in his own large diocese of Milan and in the entire province of which he was Metropolitan. He took these measures in order to establish a fruitful method of transmitting Christian doctrine, and he labored greatly in order to strongly sustain this religious education. And when he observed that his toil had not borne the fruit he desired, he did not despair, but instead increased his cares and concerns as is seen in the fifth synod of Milan: "We have hitherto shown great care in looking after the instruction of individual Christians in the fundamental doctrines in the Christian faith; but since we realize that we have profited little so far, we are led by the importance of the matter to make these additional decisions." For it was enough for that holy prelate to see that the need still existed, and thus to address himself to the work a second time; in this endeavor, he added cares to cares and minimized the many measures he had employed up till then. In like manner, it was enough for the Assyrian king to be informed that the nations did not know the commands of God: "and it was announced to the king of the Assyrians, and said: the nation which you transferred and sent to dwell in the cities of Samaria do not know the laws of God's land." He at once sent a priest to teach those nations the commands of God: "And the King of the Assyrians gave commands, saying: bring there one of the priests which you led off as prisoners and let him go and dwell with them and teach them the laws of God's land" (4 [2] Kings 17).

Teach the Fundamentals of the Faith

4. Therefore with the example of St. Charles Borromeo before Us, We encourage you and implore you by the mercy of Jesus Christ not to despair in

this important work of handing on the fundamentals of the Christian faith, even if hitherto you have devoted all your zeal and care to it. See to it that every minister performs carefully the measures laid down by the holy Council of Trent and by the statutes of your synods: that on fixed days school-masters and mistresses should teach Christian doctrine; that confessors should perform this part of their duty whenever anyone stands at their tribunal who does not know what he must by *necessity of means* know to be saved; that priests should also provide this instruction before uniting spouses in marriage; that fathers of families and lords of houses should be gravely advised of the duty imposed on them of being themselves instructed and of seeing to the instruction in the commandments of Christian doctrine of their sons and of the members of their household; that the practice of reciting aloud properly-composed acts of Faith, Hope and Charity by the priest and people before or after the parish mass should be preserved in the dioceses in which it is customary and be carefully introduced where it is not. Parish priests should not avoid their duty of at least on feast days, explaining the Gospel to the people from the altar when there is no sermon. In addition, they are obliged to teach them the chief mysteries of our holy religion, the commandments of God and the Church, and everything which is necessary for their worthy partaking of the Sacraments. Preachers should also follow this path, recalling the salutary advice that they should join instruction to exhortation whenever their hearers stand in need of both. Finally, the best method for instructing ignorant men in Christian doctrine is indicated by St. Augustine who says *(de Cath. Rud.*, 10) that the most fruitful procedure is to ask questions in a friendly fashion after the explanation; from this questioning one can learn whether each one understood what he heard or whether the explanation needs repeating. In order that the learner grasp the matter, "we must ascertain by questioning whether the one being catechised has understood, and in accordance with his response, we must either explain more clearly and fully or not dwell further on what is known to them, etc. But if a man is very slow, he must be mercifully helped and the most necessary doctrines especially should be briefly imparted to him." We are assured that you yourselves will pursue many more paths than We point out to you in this encyclical letter. In the meantime, Venerable Brothers, We lovingly impart to you and to the flock entrusted to your care Our Apostolic Blessing.

Given at Castelgandolfo on the 26th of June 1754 in the fourteenth year of Our Pontificate.

▩ POPE BENEDICT XIV ▩

Selections taken from
The Papal Encyclicals 1740-1878,
Claudia Carlen, I.H.M.,
A Consortium Book, McGratt Publishing Company, 1981

Chapter 52 • St. Paul of the Cross (1694-1775): *In the Heart of God*

Paul Francis Danei was born on January 3, 1694. At about the age of twenty-six he had a vision of Our Lady in a black habit with the name of Jesus and a cross in white on the front and was told by her to found a religious order devoted to preaching the passion of Christ. The Passionists were approved by Pope Clement XIV in 1769. Paul was canonized on October 19, 1867.

In the Heart of God

Be faithful to God's Will.
Allow God to take root in you.
Through Christ may your whole life be a hymn of praise.
Watch and pray.

The truth of God's love was shown on the cross of his beloved son, Jesus.

And the way to grow in our relationship with God in times of physical or mental stress is to strengthen ourselves by doing the things that God desires.

It is a sign of great holiness when one is resigned in everything to the will of God.

Everything that God wills is for our good.

He knows how to console us when we least expect it. (II, 589)

If anyone hurts you, look on him as someone of great value and, with the eyes of one who loves, see him as the person chosen by God to clothe you in holiness and in the patience, silence and meekness of Jesus Christ.

If you can learn to see God's will as a source of strength, taking every difficulty you go through as something which comes not just from circumstances but from the loving hand of God your creator, you will soon be speeding along the short road to holiness. (I, 574)

The troubles we have in life, if we see them as part of God's loving plan and accept them as being what he wants for us, will actually help us to grow in knowledge and love of him.

Even when things are at their worst, keep your peace of heart and accept whatever God sends you as being for your good.

God is your guide, your father, your teacher, your husband.

In everything that happens the best thing you can do is abandon yourself to his will. (I, 209)

The easiest way to keep your peace of heart is to accept everything as coming directly from the hands of the God who loves you. If you do this, any pain or persecution, anything which is difficult to accept will be transformed into a source of joy, happiness and peace.

May your prayer each day be: "Thy will be done on earth as it is in heaven." (I, 717-718)

Silence and recollection are two very effective ways of bringing ourselves before the Lord and entering into the sanctuary of his love.

"When peaceful silence lay over all, and night had run the half of her swift course, down from the heavens leapt your all-powerful word". Wis. 18:14-15.

When a person comes to terms with his feelings, when he lives in God and walks by the light of faith, he has attained that stillness of the night which God is waiting for.

It is then that the Word of God comes to birth in him in a way which is entirely of the spirit, entirely of God.

Remain within your deepest self, in the interior kingdom of your spirit. I, 558.

Remember that your soul is a temple of the living God. "The kingdom of God is within you." (I, 655)

Night and day let your aim be to remain in simplicity and gentleness, calmness and serenity, and in freedom from created things, so that you will find your joy in the Lord Jesus.

Love silence and solitude, even when in the midst of a crowd or when caught up in your work.

Physical solitude is a good thing, provided that it is backed up by prayer and a holy life, but far better than this is solitude of the heart, which is the interior desert in which your spirit can become totally immersed in God, and can hear and savour the words of eternal life. (III, 745)

With great purity of intention, aim in everything to do what pleases God.

Always remain faithful to God and genuinely accept whatever he wishes.

In this way you prepare yourself to receive the gift of interior peace.

You are becoming true and constant in worshipping the most high in spirit and in truth.

Live more and more by faith, hope and love.

From time to time remind yourself of your lowliness of heart and renew your dedication to the Lord; visit him frequently in the Eucharist and unite yourself with him in spirit; in this way you will keep the fire of love burning on the altar of your heart.

Interior peace is found by praying the life and Passion of the Lord.

This is the door through which we go into the desert of our heart. It is the surest way.

Once there, worship your God "in spirit and in truth."

Remain there, admitting your own need and your utter helplessness. It is then that you will receive everything from the Lord.

"If you utter what is precious, and not what is worthless, you shall be as my own mouth." Jer. 15:19.

Jeremiah wishes to say that we must separate that which comes to us from God, which is precious, from that which comes solely from ourselves, which is worthless.

All we have to do is this: we must know how to give to God that which is his and to hold firm to what is ours: the truth of our own nothingness.

In this way we will learn the wisdom of the saints. (I, 558)

Everything is contained in the Passion of Jesus.

Do your best to stay hidden in the wounds of Jesus. In this way you will become rich in everything that is good and filled with God's true light, so that you will be able to fly to perfect holiness.

God wishes you to attain this peace of heart, because he hides one of his great treasures within himself.

If you remain constant in meditation, he will give you this marvellous gift, the greatest gift of all, because in him is to be found all that is good and it is he who brings to completion everything you do.

Temple of the living God, ask the Lord to lead your spirit into that sheepfold which is your heavenly father's heart.

No one can enter it except through Jesus Christ our Lord, God and Saviour.

The sheep who wish to enter this sheepfold must become like the shepherd who is "gentle and humble of heart."

Lose yourself totally in God; love; be still.

Rest in the heart of God, in a silence of faith and love.

Be reborn every moment to a new life of love in the word of God, Jesus Christ. (I, 526)

In naked faith and without images, clothe yourself always in the sufferings of Jesus.

It is love which unites and which makes our own the sufferings of the one we love. It is through love that you will make the sufferings of Jesus your own.

Don't be surprised if you cannot explain what God is doing for you. If you could explain, it would not be the work of God.

Receive what God gives you, love wholeheartedly, and that is enough.

Close the door to what is merely created.

Nourish yourself on love. Like a little child, remain in the truth of your own nothingness, and accept whatever God gives you.

I warn you: don't give in to "spiritual curiosity". Often in this loving rest we want to try to find out what God is actually doing.

That's a temptation. So what we should do is allow ourselves to be led in all simplicity and forget about our usual way of learning or knowing things. We should stop thinking about our own happiness so as to desire nothing else but what God wants and what pleases him.

God is purifying you like gold in a fire.

How does he do it?

He purifies you with the fire of physical pain or mental anguish, with things that give rise to feelings of bitterness.

He makes you live a dying life, a life rich in everything that is good, without you understanding how he does so.

Be thankful to God, give glory and honour to him alone.

And rest in the knowledge of your own nothingness, naked, poor in spirit, detached from all created things, allowing your nothingness to disappear in the unlimited all, who is God.

In the deepest part of your being, your pains and worries are lost from sight.

At the surface level you can do nothing except feel the pain you are going through, but on a deeper level you must try to be joyful because of what is God's desire, accepting this pain which goes on outside your "interior castle" as coming from him, and from absolutely no one else. Remain in this interior desert of your heart no matter what you are doing.

When you find that you have been drawn away by some distraction, come back promptly but gently, allowing your faith to give you a little boost, and go on resting in God with a lover's attentiveness, yet without straining your mind, forcing yourself or fussing about it.

III

Love your brother in God.

Love God in your brother.

Share with others:

Be with them in the sufferings, their joys, their hopes.

May your favourite brothers

be those who are poor.

May all creation bring you

to love God.

Let us love the saints in God, let us love our brother in God, let us love God in our brother. (I, 327)

See your brother in the side of Jesus Christ and then you will love him with a pure and holy love.

Always remember the great commandment of love which Jesus gave to his disciples before going to his death: "I give you a new commandment: love one another as I have loved you."

What marvellous words!

When we truly love it is a clear sign that we are true disciples of the one who, out of love for us, was crucified.

Love can take many hearts and make them one, uniting them in the love of God: it makes them open, friendly, peaceful, one in mind and heart; it makes them capable of learning the will of God. (IV, 257)

Show the same kindness to everyone, and live detached from all created things. (III, 332)

See the good that is in others, always looking on them with great kindness, as God does; at the same time, do not gloss over your own wickedness or hard-heartedness. (I, 309)

Take notice of what you yourself are doing, not what others are doing, except when what they do can be an encouragement to you. (IV, 28)

Be as simple as a child: always see the best in everyone and, with good intention, excuse the one who hurts you, seeing whatever harm he does as the result of some temptation. (I, 309)

What destroys community is judging other people's actions while losing sight of one's own. (IV, 227)

To maintain and increase charity, choose to think the best about everyone. (IV, 209)

What a joy you give to God and what merit you yourself gain when you stop yourself from saying anything unwise, cutting or hurtful! (II, 65)

Love the enemies of God.

Learn how to share your sufferings and to help one another in your need. (II, 323)

Serve others willingly: be kind to everyone, since God is preparing a great treasure for you. (I, 490)

Be pleasant and obliging to one another. Offer service to one another. Comfort one another. (I, 57)

It is a great gift from the Lord to be able to love wholeheartedly those whom we find unattractive, seeing them as the noble instruments which God uses to help us grow in holiness. (II, 296)

As to dislikes, dispel them gently by showing warmth for people; make an interior act of charity at the same time, but do it calmly. (I, 107)

True charity removes all resentments and helps us to make progress by not being preoccupied with ourselves. (II, 65)

The spirit of a true servant of the Most High is shown by always practicing a discrete austerity oneself, while at the same time being totally loving and gentle with others. (I, 650)

Show kindness to the poor.

Visit them, comfort them, console them.

The friends of the poor are God's most beloved friends.

Read the forehead of a poor man and you will find written there the name of Jesus Christ.

Have courage, poor of Jesus Christ, since paradise is yours! How unfortunate are the rich, since their riches, if they refuse to share them, will only torment them more and more in Hell!

It would not be just for us to be exempt from the scourge which afflicts the world.

We should be the first to share the unhappiness of others, to take upon ourselves the sorrows of others, and to unite ourselves with all the suffering peoples of the world.

Let all creation help you to praise God.

Give yourself the rest you need. When you are walking alone, listen to the sermon preached to you by the flowers, the trees, the shrubs, the sky, the sun and the whole world. Notice how they preach to you a sermon full of love, of praise of God, and how they invite you to proclaim the greatness of the one who has given them being. (I, 418)

IV

Walk in humility, simplicity and peace before your God.

God loves those who become like little children; it is to them that he reveals his wonders. (I, 308)

The humble of heart are the delight of God. (II, 467)

You will have become a perfect imitator of the Lord who "made himself nothing" (Phil. 2, 7) when you are humble enough to be willing to be "despised by men and rejected by the people" (Ps. 21 [22], 7), just as he was, when you are simple enough and childlike enough to be quite content to be the last of all, not thought of as anyone exceptional, when the thing that is least on your mind is your reputation or what others think of you.

To do good and to know that nothing we do on our own is good is a sign of no small humility.

From humility of heart is born serenity, gentleness in our dealings with others, interior peace, and indeed everything that is good.

Whoever knows himself in depth and knows God is truly humble of heart. (I, 541)

You must come to realize more and more how totally dependent you are: you can do nothing, you know nothing, you have nothing. "Without me you can do nothing" says Christ (Jn. 15.5), and the sooner you realise how helpless you are, the more able you will be to let God make you a great saint. (III, 69)

Everything is summed up in this: know how to give to God that which is God's and to keep for ourselves that which is our own, namely, our true nothingness. Whoever knows this has learned the wisdom of the saints. (I, 558)

God can do nothing with those who want to make something of themselves. "If anyone thinks he is something when he is nothing, he deceives himself" (Gal. 6, 3) says the apostle whose name I bear so unworthily. (II, 491)

Whoever wishes to find the true all, which is God, must sink down into his own nothingness. (I, 471)

God, by essence, is he who is: "I am who I am." Ex. 3, 14.

We, on the other hand, are they who are not; for no matter how much we search into the depths of our being, the only thing we discover there is our own nothingness; and he who sins has an even greater need of God, because sin is utter nothingness, far greater than the nothingness in man.

Out of nothing God created everything that is, both visible and invisible. But out of sin God's power cannot fashion anything, because sin is a horrible nothingness which sets itself up against the one who is infinitely perfect, against infinite being itself.

So great is the infinite goodness of God that he can bring good even out of evil itself. By justifying the sinner he shows that he is all-powerful, more so than if he were to create a thousand worlds more vaste and beautiful than our own, because when he justifies the sinner he lifts him out of a pit in much deeper than that of his nothingness; he lifts him out of his sinfulness. (I, 471-472)

Allow your nothingness to disappear in the joy of the Lord. There is nothing which pleases God more than when we admit that without him we are nothing. This upsets the evil one and makes him run away. (I, 50)

There is no more effective way of preparing ourselves for battle and putting on the armour of God than to acknowledge our own need and our emptiness before God, believing firmly that we cannot be victorious unless God is on our side; from this we can see that a man must throw his own nothingness into the all which is God and, with confidence, fight bravely, being certain that he will win the victory. (I, 282)

Sink down in your own nothingness "passivo modo," naked, poor, acknowledging that everything good comes from God: "O God, from you all good things come."

What we have to offer is our nothingness and emptiness.

John the Baptist, a very humble man, said "I am not" (Jn. 1, 20). Yet "among those born of women there has risen no one greater than he" (Mt. 11, 11).

Allow yourself to be moved by the fragrance of God which captivates our hearts. May all your efforts bring you to the realisation that, of yourself, you are nothing and that the one who is all is God.

Whoever discovers the truth of his own nothingness has found the way we must go if we want to meet God. What he has found is of great importance because our heavenly Father reveals himself to those who are humble of heart. (II, 260)

He who knows his own nothingness and remains in it knows the truth. I, 488.

Anyone who can admit to his own nothingness with honesty and sincerity is like a tree planted beside flowing waters which can bring forth fruit at the proper time. (III, 289)

God, by essence, is truth itself. When he sees, someone who lives in the knowledge of his own nothingness and remains always in the truth, not in falsehood, he draws that person by love into the depths of his own self, and with his life-giving grace he refreshes him continually.

So it is that that man becomes like a tree which is able to bring forth fruit not simply in the spring, summer and autumn of consolations but even in the winter of desolation; for even in times of mental anguish or physical pain he can bring forth fruit through charity, obedience and all sorts of good works.

He who reduces himself to dust and ashes will be raised up by the Holy Spirit.

The greatest will be he who makes himself the least. He it is who will be able to gain easy access to the "wine cellar," the royal chamber from which we can pass into that hidden sanctuary where the soul can speak heart to heart with the God who loves him.

Let us always be sure to remain in our own territory, within the frontiers of our nothingness and sinfulness. When we do so, God will be more inclined to lead us out of it into his own land, and to draw us into the immensity of his infinite being.

Convinced of your own nothingness and stripped of everything, throw yourself with complete trust into the abyss of all that is good and allow the infinite goodness of God to accomplish its divine work within you; in other words, allow God's goodness to light up your life, to transform it by love, and to make it a divine life, a life which is holy.

In this way you will live, but the life which is within you and the life that you lead will be the very life of God, who is goodness itself.

God can work these wonders with those who accept their own nothingness and become like little children, giving to him with humility and love the glory that is his.

Let us remain in nothingness and not raise ourselves up until God himself raises us up.

When God wishes to raise someone up, he does so with gentle force; I tell you it is gentle, yet it is so strong that the soul is unable to resist.

So remain in the presence of God in pure faith, in knowledge and meditation of your own nothingness, of your sins and your weakness; as far as possible, however, your soul must be left free to follow the living breath of the Holy Spirit.

If there are times when you are able to remain calm when surrounded by suffering and misunderstanding, don't make too much of this, since the devil could use it to make you conceited.

It is better not to overrate your own judgment or impressions; instead, have reverence for God and do not trust solely in yourself, having no other aim in mind but to do the will of God.

The world is full of snares and only the truly humble escape them. (I, 541)

Do not put your trust in yourself, even if your prayer seems to be having good effects.

Do not act as judge of your own situation, but put no trust in yourself and worship the Father of light in spirit and in truth. (I, 542)

It is written: "Happy the man who trusts not simply in himself."

If you do anything wrong, don't get upset. Instead, open yourself up to the warmth of God's love, admitting your need of him and genuinely turning back to him, with humble, strong and whole-hearted repentance. Then, having regained your peace, go on with the rest of your life!

The God who became a man and willingly suffered terrible pains out of love for us is always at your side.

He is nearer to you than your skin is to your flesh, nearer to you than you are to yourself.

Faith tells us that your soul is the temple of the living God, that God lives in you; enter into yourself, then, and worship him in spirit and in truth.

"The true worshippers of the Father worship him in spirit and in truth." (III, 359)

The just man lives by faith.

You are the temple of the living God.

Visit this interior temple, and see if its lamps are burning: by this I mean the lamps of faith, hope and charity.

Genuine prayer is made in spirit and in truth. Our prayer is worthwhile not when it is accompanied by pleasant feelings, but when it is made in spirit and in truth.

When the Lord adds "and in truth", he means that we should remain in the pure and simple awareness of our own nothingness without stealing from God the glory which is his.

Do not cling to the gifts you have received, so that you will be able to cling to the one who gave them.

Abandon yourself into the hands of God, like a ship with neither oars nor sails, letting go of yourself totally.

He who makes himself dust and ashes, he it is that the Holy Spirit will raise up and then plunge into the abyss of infinite love, which is a consuming fire.

In this fire allow all your imperfections to be burnt away.

In this way you will be reborn to a new life, a life which is completely divine, completely holy, a life which is all love.

You will undergo this divine birth through the Word of God who is Jesus our Lord.

May Jesus bring you to be reborn to a life of love; if you remain faithful, this birth both spiritual and divine will take place within the interior temple of your spirit not just today but every day.

Remember that this work which God does within you takes place in the innermost part of your spirit, that part which no creature, neither angelic nor human, can touch, since it is God alone who lives in this hidden place which is the essence, the interior, the sanctuary of your soul.

Recollection is the internal desert in which God speaks to you the words of eternal life.

The more this interior recollection takes place in faith, without consoling feelings, the more pure and noble it is.

Remain in the interior kingdom of your truest self.

"The kingdom of God is within you."

Renew your belief in this frequently.

When you study, when you work, when you eat, when you lie down, when you rise, lift up your heart to God with love.

The true servant of God is the person who walks in company with Jesus Christ.

His interior peace is always with him, no matter where he goes.

It is a great asset.

It does not change what you have to do; but whatever you do, you put more into it and do it better, because you are doing it out of love.

You will be able to do the same work as everyone else, while speaking with God at the same time; keep your serenity, follow God's will in doing whatever you have to do today.

In this way, you will be praying all the time.

In this recollection of heart worship God in spirit and in truth, placing yourself in your nothingness; in this way you will receive everything from the Lord.

Remain hidden in God: "Your life is hidden with Christ in God."

True peace has God's love as its source. I, 768.

It is a gift of the Holy Spirit; it makes us grow in love. (IV, 227)

Be joyful in the Lord because you have peace of heart. How great is the joy which makes us children of God. "Blessed are the peacemakers, for they shall be called sons of God."

The fear of the Lord which is a gift of the Holy Spirit is not an upsetting thing.

On the contrary, it brings us peace. (II, 458)

The sort of fear which upsets us should be avoided like the plague, but the true fear of the children of God, which keeps us alert lest we should do anything which is repugnant to him or should fail to serve him wholeheartedly, this sort of fear brings us happiness.

For it does not rob us of our peace of heart but rather makes it increase. (I, 177)

Even if your whole world is turned upside down, don't lose your peace of heart. (III, 396)

Nothing, except sin, can separate you from God.

Aim at keeping your peace of heart, because the enemy fishes in troubled waters. (III, 399)

No difficulties will be able to upset you if you carry the Lord within you.

Try to maintain your peace, no matter what happens, even in the midst of storms, by keeping your heart set on the things that are above. (II, 705)

Adore and love the will of the Lord. (III, 591)

Take everything that happens as coming from the hands of God, who loves you; in this way every trial will become a ounce of peace and joy since God is not a burden, but rather comfort, joy and cheerfulness. (III, 407; 1, 717)

Chase all gloominess from your heart and, even if you do something wrong, don't get upset, since that would do you even more harm than your wrongdoing. Instead, humble yourself gently, ask God's pardon, decide that you'll do better in future and joyfully continue on your way.

Hope . . . even when surrounded by unhappiness.

The source of your joy is the eternal happiness of God.

Selections taken from
In the Heart of God: The Spiritual Teaching of Saint Paul of the Cross,
Printed by John S. Burns and Sons, Glasgow, n.d.

Chapter 53 • St. Alphonsus Liguori: *The Glories of Mary*

Alphonsus Liguori was born in Naples in 1696 and died near there in 1787. He was canonized in 1839 and named a Doctor of the Church in 1871. He systematized moral theology as part of his pastoral activities. The fact that he championed the Immaculate Conception of the Blessed Mary is clarified in the presented excerpts. God the Father would certainly want His Daughter to be conceived immaculately, as did the Son want His Mother to be so conceived, and the Holy Spirit want for His Spouse.

Conclusion

I wish to conclude this discourse, which I have prolonged beyond the limits of the others, because our Congregation has this Blessed Virgin Mary, precisely under the title of her Immaculate Conception, for its principal Patroness. I say that I wish to conclude by giving in as few words as possible the reasons which make me feel certain, and which, in my opinion, ought to convince every one of truth of so pious a belief, and which is so glorious for the divine Mother, that is, that she was free from original sin.

There are many Doctors who maintain that Mary was exempted from contracting even the debt of sin: for instance, Cardinal Galatino,[1] Cardinal Cusano,[2] De Ponte,[3] Salazar,[4] Catharinus,[5] Novarino,[6] Viva,[7] De Lugo,[8] Egidio,[9] Denis the Carthusian,[10] and others. And this opinion is also probable; for if it is true that the wills of all men were included in that of Adam, as being the head of all, and this opinion is maintained as probable by Gonet,[11] Habert,[12] and others, founded on the doctrine of St. Paul, contained in the fifth chapter to the Romans.[13]

If this opinion, I say, is probable, it is also probable that Mary did not contract the debt of sin; for whilst God distinguished her from the common of men by so many graces, it ought to be piously believed that he did not include her will in that of Adam.

This opinion is only probable, and I adhere to it as being more glorious for my sovereign Lady. But I consider the opinion that Mary did not contract the sin of Adam as certain; and it is considered so, and even as proximately definable as an article of faith (as they express it), by Cardinal Everard, Duval,[14]

Raynauld,[15] Lossada, [16] Viva,[17] and many others. I omit, however, the revelations which confirm this belief, particularly those of St. Bridget, which were approved of by Cardinal Turrecremata, and by four Sovereign Pontiffs, and which are found in various parts of the sixth book of her Revelations.[18]

But on no account can I omit the opinions of the holy Fathers on this subject, whereby to show their unanimity in conceding this privilege to the divine Mother.

St. Ambrose says, "Receive me not from Sarah, but from Mary; that it may be an uncorrupted Virgin, a Virgin free by grace from every stain of sin."[19]

Origen speaking of Mary, asserts that "she was not infected by the venomous breath of the serpent."[20]

St. Ephrem, that "she was immaculate, and remote from all stain of sin."[21]

An ancient writer, in a sermon, found among the works of St. Augustine, on the words "Hail, full of grace," says, "By these words the angel shows that she was altogether (remark the word 'altogether') excluded form the wrath of the first sentence, and restored to the full grace of blessing."[22]

The author of an old work, called the Breviary of St. Jerome, affirms that "that cloud was never in darkness, but always in light."[23]

St. Cyprian, or whoever may be the author of the work on the 77th [78th] Psalm, says, "Nor did justice endure that that vessel of election should be open to common injuries; for being far exalted above others, she partook of their nature, not of their sin."[24]

St. Amphilochius, that "He who formed the first Virgin without deformity, also made the second one without spot or sin."[25]

St. Sophronius, that "the Virgin is therefore called immaculate, for in nothing was she corrupt."[26]

St. Ildephonsus argues, that "it is evident that she was free from original sin."[27]

St. John Damascene says, that the serpent never had any access to this paradise."[28]

St. Peter Damian, that "the flesh of the Virgin, taken from Adam, did not admit of the stain of Adam."[29]

St. Bruno affirms, "that Mary is that uncorrupted earth which God blessed, and was therefore free from all contagion of sin."[30]

St. Bonaventure, "that our Sovereign Lady was full of preventing grace for her sanctification; that is, preservative grace against the corruption of original sin."[31]

St. Bernardine of Siena argues, that "it is not to be believed that he, the Son of God, would be born of a Virgin, and take her flesh, were she in the slightest degree stained with original sin."[32]

St. Laurence Justinian affirms, "that she was prevented in blessings from her very conception."[33]

The Blessed Raymond Jordano, on the words, *Thou hast found grace,* says, "thou hast found a singular grace, O most sweet Virgin, that of preservation from original sin."[34] And many other Doctors speak in the same sense.

But, finally, there are two arguments that conclusively prove the truth of this pious belief.

The first of these is the universal concurrence of the faithful. Father Egidius, of the Presentation,[35] assures us that all the religious Orders follow this opinion; and a modern author tells us that though there are ninety-two writers of the order of St. Dominic against it, nevertheless there are a hundred and thirty-six in favor of it, even in that religious body. But that which above all should persuade us that our pious belief is in accordance with the general sentiment of Catholics, is that we are assured of it it in the celebrated bull of Alexander VII, *Sollicitudo omnium ecclesiarum,* published in 1661, in which he says, "This devotion and homage towards the Mother of God was again increased and propagated, . . . so that the universities having adopted this opinion" (that is, the pious one) "already nearly all Catholics have embraced it."[36] And in fact this opinion is defended in the universities of the Sorbonne, Álcala, Salamanca, Coimbra, Cologne, Mentz, Naples, and many others, in which all who take their degrees are obliged to swear that they will defend the doctrine of Mary's Immaculate Conception. The learned Petavius mainly rests his proofs of the truth of this doctrine on the argument taken from the general sentiment of the faithful.[37] An argument, writes the most learned bishop Julius Torni, which cannot do otherwise than convince; for, in fact, if nothing else does, the general consent of the faithful makes us certain of the sanctification of Mary in her mother's womb, and of her Assumption, in body and soul, into heaven. Why, then, should not the same general feeling and belief, on the part of the faithful, also make us certain of her Immaculate Conception?

The second reason, and which is stronger than the first, that convinces us that Mary was exempt from original sin, is the celebration of her Immaculate Conception commanded by the universal Church. And on this subject I see, on the one hand, that the Church celebrates the first moment in which her soul was created and infused into her body: for this was declared by Alexander VII, in the above-named bull, in which he says that the Church gives the same worship to Mary in her Conception, which is given to her by those who hold the pious belief that she was conceived without original sin. On the other hand, I hold it as certain, that the Church cannot celebrate anything which is not holy, according to the doctrine of the holy Pope St. Leo,[38] find that of the Sovereign Pontiff St. Eusebius: "In the Apostolic See the Catholic religion was always preserved spotless."[39] All theologians, with St. Augustine,[40] St. Bernard,[41] and St. Thomas, agree on this point; and the latter, to prove that Mary was sanctified before her birth, makes use of this very argument: "The Church celebrates the nativity of the Blessed Virgin; but a feast is celebrated only for a saint: therefore the Blessed Virgin was sanctified in her mother's womb."[42] But if it is certain, as the angelic Doctor says, that Mary was sanctified in her mother's womb, because it is only on that supposition that the Church can celebrate her nativity, why are we not to consider it as equally certain that Mary was preserved from original sin from the first moment of her conception, knowing as we do that it is in this sense that the Church herself celebrates the feast?

Finally, in confirmation of this great privilege of Mary, we may be allowed to add the well-known innumerable and prodigious graces that our Lord is daily pleased to dispense throughout the kingdom of Naples, by means of the pictures of her Immaculate Conception.*

*These effects of the divine mercy have shone forth in a no less wonderful manner in France and elsewhere, especially in 1832 and during the following years, by means of the miraculous medal of which every one has heard. Since the time when St. Alphonsus wrote this discourse and the dissertations that one may read on the same subject in his other works (Theol. mor. 1. 7, c. 2. — Opera dogm. sess. 5), the devotion to "Mary conceived without sin" continued to grow throughout the Catholic world, being sustained and favored more and more by the Holy See, and by the signal marks of her heavenly protection. Finally, yielding to the multiplied solicitations of the Bishops, of the clergy, of the religious Orders, of the reigning sovereigns, and of the laity, Pope Pius IX, during the Pontifical Mass celebrated in the Basilica of the Vatican, December 8, 1854, in the presence of the bishops assembled from all parts of the world, solemnly pronounced the decree by which he defined as an article of faith, that the Blessed Virgin Mary had been protected and preserved from every stain of original sin from the first instant of her conception, in accordance with the text the Bull published the following day: Definimus doctrinam, qua tenet

Beatissimam Virginem Mariam in primo instanti sua conceptionis fuisse, singulari omnipotentia Dei gratia et privilegio, intuitu meritorum Christi Jesu, Salvatoris humani generis, ab omni originalis culpæ labe preservatam immunem, esse a Deo revelatam, atque idcirco ab omnibus fidelibus firmiter constanterque credendam. This glorious event was hailed at Rome, as well as by the whole world, with extraordinary demonstrations of joy and gratitude. What pleasure, what delight must it have given in heaven to our saint, who during his life here below labored with so much zeal to bring about such a declaration, and who protested with an oath, as we see in the prayer that concludes this discourse, that he was ready to shed his blood in so beautiful a cause! — ED.

Selections are taken from
The Glories of Mary by St. Alphonsus De Liguori, Doctor of the Church,
Edited by Reverend Eugene Grimm,
Brooklyn: Redemptorist Fathers, 1931

Notes:

1. De Arc. *l. 7,* passim.
2. Excit. *l. 8,* Sicut lil.
3. In Cant. *l. 2.* exh. *19.*
4. Pro Imm. Conc. *c. 7.*
5. De Pecc. orig. *c.* ult.
6. Umbra Virg. exc. *18.*
7. *P. 8, d. I, q. 2, a. 2.*
8. De Inc. *d. 7, s. 3, 4.*
9. De Imm. Conc. *l. 2, q. 4, a. 5.*
10. De Dign. M. *l. I, a. 13.*
11. Clyp. *p. 2, tr. 5, d. 7, a. 2.*
12. Tr. de Vit. et Pecc. *c. 7, § I.*
13. Rom. *5, 2.*
14. De Pecc. *q.* ult. *a. 7.*
15. Piet. Lugd. erga V. Imm. *n. 20.*
16. Disc. Thomist de Imm. Conc.
17. *P. 8, d. I, q. 2, a. 2.*
18. Rev. *l. 6, c. 12, 49. 55.*
19. *"Suspice me non ex Sara, sed ex Maria ut incorrupta sit Virgo, sed Virgo per gratiam ab omni integra labe peccati."* —In Ps. *cxviii, s. 22.*
20. *"Nec serpentis venenosis afflatibus infecta est."* —In Div. hom. *I.*

21. *"Immaculata et ab omni peccati labe alienissima."* —Orat. ad Deip.

22. *"Ave 'gratia plena!' Quibus verbis ostendit ex integro iram exclusam primae sententiae, et plenam benedictionis gratiam restitutam."* —Serm. 123, E. B. app.

23. *Nubes illa non fuit in tenebris, sed semper in luce."* —Brev. In Ps. 77.

24. *"Nec sustinebat justitia ut illud Vas electionis communibus lassaretur injuriis; quoniam, plurimum a caeteris differens, natura communicabat, non culpa."* —De Chr. Op. De Nat.

25. *"Qui antiquam illam virgine-n sine probro condidit, ipse et secundam sine nota et crimine fabricatus est."* —In S. Deip. el Sim.

26. *"Virginem ideo dici immaculatam, quia in nullo corrupta est."* —In Conc. (Ecum. 6, act. II.)

27. *"Constat eam ab omni originaali peccato fuisse immunem."* —Cont. Disp. de Virginit. M.

28. *"Ad hunc paradisum serpens aditum non habuit."* —In Dorm. Deip. or. 2.

29. *"Caro Virgins, ex Adam assumpta, maculas Adae non admisit."* —In Assumpt.

30. *Haec est incorrupta terra illa cui benedixit Dominus, ab omni proterea peccati contagione libera."* — In Ps.. *ci.*

31. *"Domina nostra fuit plena gratia praeveniente in sua sanctificatione, gratia scilicet preservativa contra foeditatem originalis culpae."* —De B. V. *s. 2.*

32. *"Non est credendum, quod ipse Filius Dei voluerit nasci ex virgine, et sumere ejus carnem, quae esset maculata ex aliquo peccato originali."* —Quadr. *s. 49, p. I.*

33. *"Ab ipsa sui conceptione, in benedictionibus est praeventa."* —In Annunt.

34. *" 'Invenisti gratiam;' invenisti, O dulcissima Virgo! gratian coelestem; quia fuit in te ab originis labe praeservatio."* —Cont. de V.M. *c. 6.*

35. De Imm. Conc. *1. 3. q. 6, a. 3.*

36. *"Aucta rursus et propagata fuit pietas haec et cultus erga Deiparam. . . . ita ut, accedentibus plerisque celebrioribus academiis ad hanc sententiam, jam fere omnes Catholici eam amplectantur."*

37. De *Inc. 1. 14, c. 2.*

38. Ep. decret. *4, c. 2.*

39. *"In Sede Apostolica, extra maculam semper et Catholica servata religio."* —Decr. causa *24, q. I, c. I. c.* In sede.

40. *S. 310, 314,* Ed. B.

41. *Epist. 174.*

42. *"Ecclesia celebrat Nativitatem Beatae Virginis; non autem celebratur festum in Ecclesia, nisi pro aliquo Sancto: ergo Beata Virgo fuit in utero sanctificata." P. 3, q. 27, a. I.*

Chapter 54 • John Henry Cardinal Newman: *Apologia Pro Vita Sua; The Dream of Gerontius*

John Henry Newman (1801-1890) was one of the outstanding figures of English letters and religious controversy in England during the nineteenth century. Born in London, he studied at Trinity College, Oxford, and received a fellowship at Oriel College, where he tutored after his ordination in the Church of England. He was deeply religious and became actively involved in many controversies with his colleagues over the practical living of the Christian life. His contention that the Thirty-nine Articles were consistent with Catholicism led to serious opposition from Anglicans. He went into seclusion for more than a year in order to resolve his own spiritual conflicts. In 1845 he became a Catholic, went to Rome, and was ordained as a Catholic priest. Some consider that *the Apologia Pro Vita Sua* is his greatest work, "a masterpiece of religious autobiography." The *Dream of Gerontius* is one of his best and most widely read poems. Newman is also known for his *Idea of a University; Development of Christian Doctrine, Grammar of Assent* and two volumes of *Sermons and Discourses.*

Apologia Pro Vita Sua

I was brought up from a child to take great delight in reading the Bible; but I had no formed religious convictions till I was fifteen. Of course I had perfect knowledge of my catechism. . . .

Starting then with the being of a God which is as certain to me as the certainty of my own existence, though when I try to put the grounds of that certainty into logical shape, I find it difficult in doing so in mood and figure to my satisfaction, I look out of myself into the world of men, and there I see a sight which fills me with unspeakable distress. The world seems simply to give the lie to that great truth, of which my whole being is so full; and the effect upon me, is, in consequence, as a matter of necessity, as confusing as if it denied that I am in existence myself. If I looked into a mirror, and did not see my face, I should have the sort of feeling which actually comes upon me, when I look into this living busy world, and see no reflection of its Creator. This is, to me, one of the great difficulties of this absolute primary truth, to which I referred just now. Were it not for this voice, speaking so clearly in my conscience and my heart, I should be an atheist, or a pantheist, or a polytheist when I looked into the world. I am speaking for myself only; and I am far from denying the real force of the arguments in proof of a God, drawn from the general facts of human society, but these do not warm me or enlighten me; they do not take away the winter of my desolation, or make the buds unfold and the leaves grow within me, and my moral being rejoice. The sight of the world is nothing else than the prophets scroll, full of "lamentations, and mourning, and woe. . ."

What shall be said to this heart-piercing, reason-bewildering fact? I can only answer, that either there is no Creator, or this living society of men is in a true sense discarded from His presence. And so I argue about the world; — *if* there be a God, *since* there is a God, the human race is implicated in some terrible aboriginal calamity. It is out of joint with the purposes of its Creator. This is a fact, a fact as true as the fact of its existence; and thus the doctrine of what is theologically called original sin becomes to me almost as certain as that the world exists, and as the existence of God.

And now, supposing it were the blessed and living will of the Creator to interfere in this anarchical condition of things, what are we to suppose would be the methods which might be necessarily or naturally involved in His object of mercy? Since the world is in so abnormal a state, surely it would be no surprise to me, if the interposition were of necessity equally extraordinary — or what is called miraculous. But that subject does not directly come into the scope of my present remarks. Miracles, as evidence, involve an argument; and of course I am thinking of some means which does not immediately run into argument. I am rather asking what must be the face-to-face antagonist, by which to withstand and baffle the fierce energy of passion and the all-corroding, all-dissolving scepticism of the intellect in religious inquiries? I have no intention at all to deny, that truth is the real object of our reason, and that, if it does not attain to truth, either the premise or the process is in fault; but I am not speaking of right reason, but of reason as it acts in fact and concretely in fallen man. I know that even the unaided reason, when correctly exercised, leads to a belief in God, in the immortality of the soul, and in a future retribution; but I am considering it actually and historically; and in this point of view, I do not think I am wrong in saying that [the] tendency is towards a simple unbelief in matters of religion. No truth, however sacred, can stand against it, in the long run; and hence it is that in the pagan world, when our Lord came, the last traces of the religious knowledge of former times were all but disappearing from those portions of the world in which the intellect had been active and had had a career.

And in these latter days, in like manner, outside the Catholic Church things are tending, with far greater rapidity than in that old time from the circumstance of the age, to atheism in one shape or other. What a scene, what a prospect, does the whole of Europe present at this day! and not only Europe, but every government and every civilization through the world, which is under the influence of the European mind! Especially, for it most concerns us, how sorrowful, in the view of religion, even taken in its most elementary, most attenuated form, is the spectacle presented to us by the educated intellect of England, France, and Germany! Lovers of their country and of their race, religious men, external to the Catholic Church, have attempted various expedients to arrest fierce willful human nature in its onward course, and to bring it into subjection. The necessity of some form of religion for the interests of humanity has been generally acknowledged: but where was the concrete representative of things invisible, which would have the force and toughness necessary to be a breakwater against the deluge? Three centuries ago the establishment of religion, material, legal, and social, was generally adopted as the best expedient for the purpose, in those countries which separated from the Catholic Church; and for a long time it was successful; but now the crevices of those establishments are admitting the enemy. Thirty years ago, education was relied upon: ten years ago there was a hope that wars would cease for ever, under the influence of commercial enterprise and the reign of the useful and fine arts; but will any one venture to say that there is anything anywhere on this earth, which will afford a fulcrum for us, whereby to keep the earth from moving onwards?

The judgment, which experience passes on establishments or education, as a means of maintaining religious truth in this anarchical world, must be extended even to Scripture, though Scripture be divine. Experience proves surely that the Bible does not answer a purpose, for which it was never intended. It may be accidentally the means of the conversion of individuals, but a book, after all, cannot make a stand against the wild living intellect of man, and in this day it begins to testify, as regards its own structure and contents, to the power of that universal solvent, which is so successfully acting upon religious establishments.

Supposing then it to be the Will of the Creator to interfere in human affairs, and to make provisions for retaining in the world a knowledge of Himself, so definite and distinct as to be proof against the energy of human scepticism, in such a case — I am far from saying that there was no other way — but there is nothing to surprise the mind, if He should think fit to introduce a power into the world, invested with the prerogative of infallibility in religious matters. Such a provision would be a direct, immediate, active, and prompt means of withstanding the difficulty; it would be an instrument suited to the need; and when I find that this is the very claim of the Catholic Church, not only do I feel no difficulty in admitting the idea, but there is a fitness in it, which recommends it to my mind. And thus I am brought to speak of the Church's infallibility, as a provision, adapted by the mercy of the Creator, to preserve religion in the world, and to restrain that freedom of thought, which of course in itself is one of the greatest of our natural gifts, and to rescue it from its own suicidal excesses. And let it be observed that, neither here nor in what follows, shall I have occasion to speak directly on the revealed body of truths, but only as they bear upon the defense of natural religion. I say, that a power, possessed of infallibility in religious teaching, is happily adapted to be a working instrument, for smiting hard and throwing back the immense energy of the aggressive intellect: — and in saying this, as in the other things that I have to say, it must still be recollected that I am all along bearing in mind my main purpose, which is a defense of myself.

I am defending myself here from a plausible charge brought against Catholics, as will be seen better as I proceed. The charge is this: — that I, as a Catholic, not only make profession to hold doctrines which I cannot possibly believe in my heart, but that I also believe in the existence of a power on earth, which at its own will imposes upon men any new set of *credenda*, when it pleases, by a claim to infallibility; in consequence, that my own thoughts are not my own property; that I cannot tell that to-morrow I may not have to give up what I hold to-day, and that the necessary effect of such a condition of mind must be a degrading bondage, or a bitter inward rebellion relieving itself in secret infidelity, or the necessity of ignoring the whole subject of religion in a sort of disgust, and of mechanically saying everything that the Church says, and leaving to others the defense of it. As then I have above spoken of the relation of my mind towards the Catholic Creed, so now I shall speak of the attitude which it takes up in the view of the Church's infallibility.

And first, the initial doctrine of the infallible teacher must be an emphatic protest against the existing state of mankind. Man had rebelled against his Maker. It was this that caused the divine interposition; and the first act of the divinely accredited messenger must be to proclaim it. The Church must denounce rebellion as of all possible evils the greatest. She must have no terms with it; if she would be true to her Master, she must ban and anathematize it.

This is the meaning of a statement which has furnished matter for one of those special accusations to which I am at present replying: I have, however, no fault at all to confess in regard to it; I have nothing to withdraw, and in consequence I here deliberately repeat it. I said, "The Catholic Church holds it better for the sun and moon to drop from heaven, for the earth to fail, and for all the many millions on it to die of starvation in extremest agony, as far as temporal affliction goes, than that one soul, I will not say, should be lost, but should commit one single venial sin, should tell one willful untruth, or should steal one poor farthing without excuse." I think the principle here enunciated to be the mere preamble in the formal credentials of the Catholic Church, as an Act of Parliament might begin with a "*Whereas*." It is because of the intensity of the evil which has possession of mankind, that a suitable antagonist has been provided against it; and the initial act of that divinely commissioned power is of course to deliver her challenge and to defy the enemy. Such a preamble then gives a meaning to her position in the world, and an interpretation to her whole course of teaching and action.

In like manner she has ever put forth, with most energetic distinctness, those other great elementary truths, which either are an explanation of her mission or give a character to her work. She does not teach that human nature is irreclaimable, else wherefore should she be sent? not that it is to be shattered and reversed, but to be extricated, purified, and restored; not that it is a mere mass of evil, but that it has the promise of great things, and even now has a virtue and a praise proper to itself. But in the next place she knows and she preaches that such a restoration, as she aims at effecting in it, must be brought about, not simply through any outward provision of preaching and teaching, even though it be her own, but from a certain inward spiritual power or grace imparted directly from above, and which is in her keeping. She has it in charge to rescue human nature from its misery, but not simply by raising it upon its own level, but by lifting it up to a higher level than its own. She recognizes in it real moral excellence though degraded, but she cannot see it free from earth except by exalting it towards heaven. It was for this end that a renovating grace was put into her hands, and therefore from the nature of the gift, as well as from the reasonableness of the case, she goes on, as a further point, to insist, that all true conversion must begin with the first springs of thought, and to teach that each individual man must be in his own person one whole and perfect temple of God, while he is also one of the living stones which build up a visible religious community. And thus the distinctions between nature and grace, and between outward and inward religion, become two further articles in what I have called the preamble of her divine commission.

Such truths as these she vigorously reiterates, and pertinaciously inflicts upon mankind; as to such she observes no half-measures, no economical reserve, no delicacy or prudence. "Ye must be born again," is the simple, direct form of words which she uses after her Divine Master; "your whole nature must be re-born, your passions, and your affections, and your aims, and your conscience, and your will, must all be bathed in a new element, and reconsecrated to your Maker, and, the last not the least, your intellect." It was for repeating these points of her teaching in my own way, that certain passages of one of my volumes have been brought into the general accusation which has been made against my religious opinions. The writer has said that I was demented if I believed, and unprincipled if I did not believe, in my statement that a lazy, ragged, filthy, story-telling beggar-woman, if chaste, sober, cheerful, and religious, had a prospect of heaven, which was absolutely closed to an accomplished statesman, or lawyer, or noble, be he ever so just, upright, generous, honorable, and conscientious, unless he had also some portion of the divine Christian grace; yet I should have thought myself defended from criticism by the words which our Lord used to the chief priests, "The publicans and harlots go into the kingdom of God before you." And I was subjected again to the same alternative of amputations, for having ventured to say that consent to an unchaste wish was indefinitely more heinous than any lie viewed apart from its causes, its motives, and its consequences; though a lie, viewed under the limitation of these conditions, is a random utterance, an almost outward act, not directly from the heart, however disgraceful it may be, whereas we have the express words of our Lord to the doctrine that "whoso looketh on a woman to lust after her, hath committed adultery with her already in his heart." On the strength of these texts I have surely as much right to believe in these doctrines as to believe in the doctrine of original sin, or that there is a supernatural revelation, or that a Divine Person suffered, or that punishment is eternal.

Passing now from what I have called the preamble of that grant of power, with which the Church is invested, to that power itself, infallibility, I make two brief remarks: on the one hand, I am not here determining anything about the essential seat of that power, because that is a question doctrinal, not historical and practical; nor, on the other hand, am I extending the direct subject-matter, over which that power has jurisdiction, beyond religious opinion: — and now as to the power itself.

This power, viewed in its fullness, is as tremendous as the giant evil which has called for it. It claims, when brought into exercise in the legitimate manner, for otherwise of course it is but dormant, to have for itself a sure guidance into the very meaning of every portion of the divine message in detail, which was committed by our Lord to His apostles. It claims to know its own limits, and to decide what it can determine absolutely and what it cannot. It claims, moreover, to have a hold upon statements not directly religious, so far as this, to determine whether they indirectly relate to religion, and, according to its own definitive judgment, to pronounce whether or not, in a particular case, they are consistent with revealed truth. It claims to decide magisterially, whether infallibly or not, that such and such statements are or are not prejudicial to the apostolic *depositum* of faith, in their spirit or in their consequences, and to allow them, or condemn and forbid them, accordingly. It claims to impose silence at will on any matters, or controversies, of doctrine, which on its own *ipse dixit* it pronounces to be dangerous, or inexpedient, or inopportune. It claims that whatever may be the judgment of Catholics upon such acts, these acts should be received by them with those outward marks of reverence, submission, and loyalty, which Englishmen, for instance, pay to the presence of their sovereign, without public criticism on them, as being in their matter inexpedient, or in their manner violent or harsh. And lastly, it claims to have the right of inflicting spiritual punishment, of cutting off from the ordinary channels of the divine life, and of simply excommunicating, those who refuse to submit themselves to its formal declarations. Such is the infallibility lodged in the Catholic Church, viewed in the concrete, as clothed and surrounded by the appendages of its high sovereignty: it is, to repeat what I said above, a supereminent prodigious power sent upon earth to encounter and master a giant evil.

The Dream of Gerontius

I

Gerontius

Jesu, Maria — I am near to death,
And Thou art calling me; I know it now.
Not by the token of this faltering breath,
This chill at heart, this dampness on my brow,
(Jesu, have mercy! Mary, pray for me!)
'Tis this new feeling, never felt before,

(Be with me, Lord in my extremity!)
That I am going, that I am no more.
'Tis this strange innermost abandonment,
(Lover of souls! great God! I look to Thee,)
This emptying out of each constituent
And natural force, by which I come to be.
Pray for me, O my friends; a visitant
Is knocking his dire summons at my door,
The like of whom, to scare me and to daunt,
Has never, never come to me before;
'Tis death — O loving friends, your prayers! — 'tis he!. . .
As though my very being had given way,
As though I was no more a substance now,
And could fall back on nought to be my stay,
(Help, loving Lord! Thou my sole Refuge, Thou,)
And turn no whither, but must needs decay
And drop from out the universal frame
Into that shapeless, scopeless, blank abyss,
That utter nothingness, of which I came:
This is it that has come to pass in me;
Oh horror! this is it, my dearest, this;
So pray for me, my friends, who have not strength to pray.

Gerontius

Rouse thee, my fainting soul, and play the man;
And through such waning span
Of life and thought as still has to be trod,
Prepare to meet thy God.
And while the storm of that bewilderment
Is for a season spent,
And, ere afresh the ruin on me fall,
Use well the interval.

Gerontius

Firmly I believe and truly
God is three, and God is One;
And I next acknowledge duly

Manhood taken by the Son.
And I trust and hope most fully
In that Manhood crucified;
And each thought and deed unruly
Do to death, as He has died.
Simply to His grace and wholly
Light and life and strength belong,
And I love, supremely, solely,
Him the holy, Him the strong.
And I hold in veneration,
For the love of Him alone,
Holy Church, as His creation,
And hear teachings, as His own.
And I take with joy whatever
Now besets me, pain or fear,
And with a strong will I sever
All the ties which bind me here.
Adoration aye be given,
With and through the angelic host,
To the God of earth and heaven
Father, Son, and Holy Ghost.

Selections from the "Apologia Pro Vita Sua" are from
Apologia Pro Vita Sua,
John Henry Newman,
New York: Longmans, Green & Co., n.d.

Chapter 55 • Francis Thompson: *The Hound of Heaven*

Francis Thompson (1859-1907) was originally educated for the priesthood, but left the seminary before ordination and studied medicine. After eight years he gave up his studies and went to London, where he led a rather depraved life and suffered intensely from poverty, ill-health, and drug addiction. He was rehabilitated by Wilfred and Alice Meynell, who recognized his great ability as a poet. The "Hound of Heaven," considered by some as his best poem, is a classic account of the futile attempt of a soul to escape the love of God.

The Hound of Heaven

I fled Him, down the nights and down the days;
I fled Him, down the arches of the years;
I fled Him, down the labyrinthine ways
Of my own mind; and in the midst of tears
I hid from Him, and under running laughter.
Up vistaed hopes I sped;
And shot, precipitated,
Adown Titanic glooms of chasmed fears,
From those strong Feet that followed, followed after.
But unhurrying chase,
And unperturbed pace,
Deliberate speed, majestic instancy,
They beat — and a Voice beat
More instant than the Feet —
"All things betray thee, who betrayest Me."
I pleaded, outlaw-wise,
By many a hearted casement, curtained red,
Trellised with intertwining charities;
(For, though I knew His love Who followed,
Yet was I sore adread
Lest, having HIm, I must have naught beside.)
But, if one little casement parted wide,
The gust of His approach would clash it to:

Fear wist not to evade, as Love wist to pursue.
Across the margent of the world I fled,
And troubled the gold gateways of the stars,
Smiting for shelter on their clanged bars;
Fretted to dulcet jars
And silvern chatter the pale ports o' the moon.
I said to Dawn: Be sudden — to Eve: Be soon;
With thy young skiey blossoms heap me over
From this tremendous Lover —
Float thy vague veil about me, lest He see!
I tempted all His servitors, but to find
My own betrayal in their constancy,
In faith to Him their fickleness to me,
Their traitorous trueness, and their loyal deceit.
To all swift things for swiftness did I sue;
Clung to the whistling mane of every wind.
But whether they swept, smoothly fleet,
The long savannahs of the blue,
Or whether, Thunder-driven,
They clanged his chariot 'thwart a heaven,
Plashy with flying lightnings round the spurn o' their feet: —
Fear wist not to evade as Love wist to pursue.
Still with unhurrying chase,
And unperturbed pace,
Deliberate speed, majestic instancy,
Came on the following Feet,
And a Voice above their beat —
"Naught shelters thee, who wilt not shelter Me."

I sought no more that after which I strayed
In face or man or maid;
But still within the little children's eyes
Seems something, something that replies,
They at least are for me, surely for me!
I turned me to them very wistfully:
But just as their young eyes grew sudden fair
With dawning answers there,

Their angel plucked them from me by the hair.
"Come then, ye other children, Nature's — share
With me" (said I) "your delicate fellowship;
Let me greet you lip to lip,
Let me twine with you caresses,
Wantoning
With our Lady-Mother's vagrant tresses,
Banqueting
With her in her wind-walled palace,
Underneath her azured dais,
Quaffing, as your taintless way is,
From a chalice
Lucent-weeping out of the dayspring."
So it was done:
I in their delicate fellowship was one —
Drew the bolt of Nature's secrecies.
I knew all the swift importings
On the willful face of skies;
I knew how the clouds arise
Spurned of the wild sea-snortings;
All that's born or dies
Rose and drooped with; made them shapers
Of mine own moods, or wailful or divine;
With them joyed and was bereaven.
I was heavy with the even,
When she lit her glimmering tapers
Round the day's dead sanctities.
I laughed in the morning's eyes.
I triumphed and I saddened with all weather,
Heaven and I wept together,
And its sweet tears were salt with mortal mine;
Against the red throb of its sunset-heart
I laid my own to beat,
And share commingling heat;
But not by that, by that, was eased my human smart,
In vain my tears were wet on Heaven's grey cheek.
For ah! we know not what each other says,

These things and I; in sound I speak —
Their sound is but their stir, they speak by silences.
Nature, poor stepdame, cannot slake my drouth;
Let her, if she would owe me,
Drop yon blue bosom-veil of sky, and show me
The breasts o' her tenderness:
Never did any milk of hers once bless
My thirsting mouth.
Nigh and nigh draws the chase.
With unperturbed pace,
Deliberate speed, majestic instancy;
And past those noised Feet
A voice comes yet more fleet —
"Lo! naught content thee, who content'st not Me."
Naked I wait Thy love's uplifted stroke!
My harness piece by piece Thou hast hewn from me,
And smitten me to my knee;
I am defenseless utterly.
I slept, methinks, and woke,
And, slowly gazing, find me stripped in sleep.
In the rash lustihead of my young powers,
I shook the pillaring hours
And pulled my life upon me; grimed with smears,
I stand amid the dust o' the mounded years —
My mangled youth lies dead beneath the heap.
My days have cracked and gone up smoke,
Have puffed and burst as sun-starts on a stream.
Yea, faileth now even dream
The dreamer, and the lute the lutanist;
Even the linked fantasies, in whose blossomy twist
I swung the earth a trinket at my wrist,
Are yielding; cords of all too weak account
For earth with heavy griefs so overplussed.
Ah! is Thy love indeed
A weed, albeit an amaranthine weed,
Suffering no flowers except its own to mount?
Ah! must —

Designer infinite!—
Ah! must Thou char the wood ere Thou canst limn with it?
My freshness spent its wavering shower i' the dust;
And now my heart is as a broken fount,
Wherein tear-drippings stagnate, spilt down ever
From the dank thoughts that shiver
Upon the sighful branches of my mind.
Such is; what is to be?
The pulp so bitter, how shall taste the rind?
I dimly guess what Time in mists confounds;
Yet ever and anon a trumpet sounds
From the dim battlements of Eternity;
Those shaken mists a space unsettle, then
Round the half-glimpsed turrets slowly wash again.
But not ere him who summoneth
I first have seen, enwound
With glooming robes purpureal, cypress-crowned;
His name I know, and what his trumpet saith.
Whether man's heart or life it be which yields
Thee harvest, must Thy harvest-fields
Be dunged with rotten death?
Now of that long pursuit
Comes on at hand the bruit;
That Voice is round me like a bursting sea;
"And is thy earth so marred,
Shattered in shard on shard?
Lo, all things fly thee, for thou fliest Me!
Strange, piteous, futile thing!
Wherefore should any set thee love apart?
Seeing none but I makes much of naught" (He said),
"And human love needs human meriting:
How hast thou merited—
Of all man's dotted clay the dingiest clot?
Alack, thou knowest not
How little worthy of any love thou art!
Whom wilt thou find to love ignoble thee,
Save Me, save only Me?

All which I took from thee I did but take,
Not for thy harms,
But just that thou might'st seek it in My arms.
All which thy child's mistake
Fancies as lost, I have stored for thee at home:
Rise, clasp My hand, and come!"
Halts by me that footfall:
Is my gloom, after all,
Shade of His hand, outstretched caressingly?
"Ah, fondest, blindest, weakest,
I am He Whom thou seekest!
Thou dravest love from thee, who dravest Me."

From the
Complete Poetical Works of Francis Thompson,
New York: Boni and Liveright, n.d.

Chapter 56 • Pope Leo XIII: *Aeterni Patris; Rerum Novarum*

Giocchino Vicenzo Pecci (b. 1810, pope 1878-1903) was born in the Papal States in Italy in 1810. After studying at the Jesuit college in Viterbo (1818-1824) he went to the Roman College (1824-1832). He was ordained as a priest in 1837, and entered the diplomatic service of the Papal States. After serving as a delegate (provincial governor) to Benevenuto in 1838, he went to Perugia, and in 1843 was apostolic nuncio to Brussels, being named Archbishop a little later. While bishop of Perugia (1846) he was very interested in the religious and intellectual improvement of the clergy under his care, opposed rationalism and secular liberalism, and advocated the study of the works of St. Thomas Aquinas in Catholic seminaries. This interest saw fruition in the encyclical *Aeterni Patris* presented here.

During his life he learned much about the economic, political, and social activities and needs of the working man. His approach in this area was somewhat of an inductive procedure based on his actual experiences rather than a purely theoretical or speculative analysis. The encyclical *Rerum Novarum* is an expression of his convictions about the evils of socialism and the importance of private property for the personal well-being of the working man. To do away with private property, to transfer ownership, management, and financial results of private property to the State would be an unjust situation for the working man and would deprive him of his basic dignity and rights as a person. It is said that his approach may have been influenced by Cardinal Gibbons.

His encyclical *Providentissimus Deus* in 1893 explains in detail how Catholics should interpret the Bible.

It is said of Leo XIII that he was "a man gifted with superior intelligence, energetic temperament, a keen awareness of his personal worth, and a discriminating sense for public relations."

The content of the encyclical *Aeterni Patris* is presented almost completely because it ties in well with some of the preceding contents of this collection, especially those from the Scriptures, the Fathers and Doctors of the Church both of the East and the West, and the Scholastics — in particular St. Thomas Aquinas.

Aeterni Patris

Encyclical of Pope Leo XIII
On the Restoration of Christian Philosophy
August 4, 1879

The only-begotten Son of the Eternal Father, who came on earth to bring salvation and the light of divine wisdom to men, conferred a great and wonderful blessing on the world when, about to ascend again into heaven, He commanded the Apostles to go and teach all nations and left the Church which He had founded to be the common and supreme teacher of the peoples. And the Church built upon the promises of its own divine Author, whose charity it imitated, so faithfully followed out His commands that its constant aim and chief wish was this: to teach religion and contend forever against errors. To this end assuredly have tended the incessant labors of individual bishops; to this end also the published laws and decrees of councils, and especially the constant watchfulness of the Roman Pontiffs, to whom, as successors of the blessed Peter in the primacy of the Apostles, belongs the right and office of teaching and confirming their brethren in the faith. Since, then, according to the warning of the apostle, the minds of Christ's faithful are apt to be deceived and the integrity of the faith to be corrupted among men by philosophy and vain deceit, the supreme pastors of the Church have always thought it their duty to advance, by every means in their power, science truly so called, and at the same time to provide with special care that all studies should accord with the Catholic faith, especially philosophy, on which a right interpretation of the other sciences in great part depends. . . .

Therefore, Divine Providence itself requires that, in calling back the people to the paths of faith and salvation, advantage should be taken of human science also — an approved and wise practice which history testifies was observed by the most illustrious Fathers of the Church. They, indeed, were wont neither to belittle nor undervalue the part that reason had to play, as is summed up by the great Augustine when he attributes to this science "that by which the most wholesome faith is begotten . . . is nourished, defended, and made strong."

In the first place, philosophy, if rightly made use of by the wise, in a certain way tends to smooth and fortify the road to true faith, and to prepare the souls of its disciples for the fit reception of revelation; for which reason it is well called by ancient writers sometimes a steppingstone to the Christian faith, sometimes the prelude and help of Christianity, sometimes the Gospel teacher. And, assuredly, the God of all goodness, in all that pertains to divine things, has not only manifested by the light of faith those truths which human intelligence could not attain of itself, but others, not altogether unattainable by reason, that by the help of divine authority they may be made known to all at once and without any admixture of error. Hence it is that certain truths which were either divinely proposed for belief, or were bound by the closest chains to the doctrine of faith, were discovered by pagan sages with nothing but their natural reason to guide them, were demonstrated and proved by becoming arguments. For, as the Apostle says, the invisible things of Him, from the creation of the world, are clearly seen, being understood by the things that are made: His eternal power also and divinity; and the Gentiles who have not the Law show, nevertheless, the work of the Law written in their hearts. But it is the most fitting to turn these truths, which have been discovered by the pagan sages even, to the use and purposes of revealed doctrine, in order to show that both human wisdom and the very testimony of our adversaries serve to support the Christian faith — a method which is not of recent introduction, but of established use, and has often been adopted by the holy Fathers of the Church.

Both Gregory of Nazianzus and Gregory of Nyssa praise and commend a mode of disputation in Basil the Great; while Jerome especially commends it in Quadratus, a disciple of the Apostles, in Aristides, Justin, Irenaeus, and very many others.

But if natural reason first sowed this rich field of doctrine before it was rendered fruitful by the power of Christ, it must assuredly become more prolific after the grace of the Savior has renewed and added to the native faculties of the human mind. And who does not see that a plain and easy road is opened up to faith by such a method of philosophic study?

In the first place, then, this great and noble fruit is gathered from human reason, that it demonstrates that God is; for the greatness of the beauty and of the creature the Creator of them may be seen so as to be known thereby. Again, it shows God to excel in the height of all perfections, especially in infinite wisdom before which nothing lies hidden, and in absolute justice which no depraved affection could possibly shake; and that God, therefore, is not only true but truth itself, which can neither deceive nor be deceived. Whence it clearly follows that human reason finds the fullest faith and authority united in the word of God. In like manner, reason declares that the doctrine of the Gospel has even from its very beginning been made manifest by certain wonderful signs, the established proofs, as it were, of unshaken truth; and that all, therefore, who set faith in the Gospel do not believe rashly as though following cunningly devised fables, but, by a most reasonable consent, subject their intelligence and judgment to an authority which is divine. And of no less importance is it that reason most clearly sets forth that the Church instituted by Christ (as laid down in the Vatican Council), on account of its wonderful spread, its marvelous sanctity, and its inexhaustible fecundity in all places, as well as of its Catholic unity and unshaken stability, is in itself a great and perpetual motive of belief and an irrefragable testimony of its own divine mission.

Its solid foundations having been thus laid, a perpetual and varied service is further required of philosophy, in order that sacred theology may receive and assume the nature, form, and genius of a true science. For in this, the most noble of studies, it is of the greatest necessity to bind together, as it were, in one body the many and various parts of the heavenly doctrines, that, each being allotted to its own proper place and derived from its own proper principles, the whole may join together in a complete union; in order, in fine, that all and each part may be strengthened by its own and the others' invincible arguments. Nor is that more accurate or fuller knowledge of the things that are believed, and somewhat more lucid understanding, as far as it can go, of the very mysteries of faith which Augustine and the other fathers commended and strove to reach, and which the Vatican Council itself declared to be most fruitful, to be passed over in silence or belittled. Those will certainly more fully and more easily attain that knowledge and understanding who to integrity of life and love of faith join a mind rounded and finished by philosophic studies, as the same Vatican Council teaches that the knowledge of such sacred dogmas ought to be sought as well from analogy of the things that are naturally known as from the connection of those mysteries one with another and with the final end of man.

Lastly, the duty of religiously defending the truths divinely delivered, and of resisting those who dare oppose them, pertains to philosophic pursuits. Wherefore, it is the glory of philosophy to be esteemed as the bulwark of faith and the strong defense of religion. As Clement of Alexandria testifies, the doctrine of the Savior is indeed perfect in itself and wanteth naught, since it is the power and wisdom of God. And the assistance of the Greek philosophy maketh not the truth more powerful; but, inasmuch as it weakens the contrary arguments of the sophists and repels the veiled attacks against the truth, it has been fitly called the hedge and fence of the vine. For, as the enemies of the Catholic name, when about to attack religion, are in the habit of borrowing their weapons from the arguments of philosophers, so the defenders of sacred science draw many arguments from the store of philosophy which may serve to uphold revealed dogmas. Nor is the triumph of the Christian faith a small one in using human reason to repel powerfully and speedily the attacks of its adversaries by the hostile arms which human reason itself supplied. This species of religious strife St. Jerome, writing to Magnus, notices as having been adopted by the Apostle of the Gentiles himself, Paul, the leader of the Christian army and the invincible orator, battling for the cause of Christ, skillfully turns even a chance inscription into an argument for the faith.

Moreover, the Church herself not only urges, but even commands, Christian teachers to seek help from philosophy. For, the fifth Lateran Council advises teachers of philosophy to pay close attention to the exposition of fallacious arguments; since, as Augustine testifies, "if reason is turned against the authority of sacred Scripture, no matter how specious it may see, it errs in the likeness of truth; for true it cannot be."

But in order that philosophy may be found equal to the gathering of those precious fruits which we have indicated, it behooves it above all things never to turn aside from that path which the Fathers have entered upon from a venerable antiquity, and which the Vatican Council solemnly and authoritatively approved. As it is evident that very many truths of the supernatural order which are far beyond the reach of the keenest intellect must be accepted, human reason, conscious of its own infirmity, dare not affect to itself too great powers, nor deny those truths, nor measure them by its own standard, nor interpret them at will; but receive them, rather, with a full and humble faith, and esteem it the highest honor to be allowed to wait upon heavenly doctrines like a handmaid and attendant, and by God's goodness attain to them in any way whatsoever. But in the case of such doctrines as the human intelligence may perceive, it is equally just that philosophy should make use of its own method, principles, and arguments — not, indeed, in such fashion as to seem rashly to withdraw from the divine authority. But, since it is established that those things which become known by revelation have the force of certain truth, and that those things which war against faith war equally against right reason, the Catholic philosopher will know that he violates at once faith and the laws of reason if he accepts any conclusion which he understands to be opposed to revealed doctrine.

Those, therefore, who to the study of philosophy unite obedience to the Christian faith, are philosophizing in the best possible way; for the splendor of the divine truths, received into the mind, helps the understanding, and not only detracts in nowise from its dignity, but adds greatly to its nobility, keenness, and stability. For surely that is a worthy and most useful exercise of reason when men give their minds to disproving those things which are repugnant to faith and proving the things which conform to faith. In the first case they cut the ground from under the feet of error and expose the viciousness of the arguments on which error rests; while in the second case they make themselves masters of weighty reasons for the sound demonstration of truth and the satisfactory instruction of any reasonable person. Whoever denies that such study and practice tend to add to the resources and expand the faculties of the mind must necessarily and absurdly hold that the mind gains nothing from discriminating between the true and the false. Justly, therefore, does the Vatican Council commemorate in these words the great benefits which faith has conferred upon reason: *Faith frees and saves reason from error, and endows it with manifold knowledge*. A wise man, therefore, would not accuse faith and look upon it as opposed to reason and natural truths, but would rather offer heartfelt thanks to God, and sincerely rejoice that, in the density of ignorance and in the flood-tide of error, holy faith, like a friendly star, shines down upon his path and points out to him the fair gate of truth beyond all danger of wandering.

If, venerable brethren, you open the history of philosophy, you will find as We have just said proved by experience. The philosophers of old who lacked the gift of faith, yet were esteemed so wise, fell into many appalling errors while, on the other hand, the early Fathers and Doctors of the Church, who well understood that, according to the divine plan, the restorer of human science is Christ, who is the power and the wisdom of God, and in whom are hid all the treasures of wisdom and knowledge, took up and investigated the books of the ancient philosophers, and compared their teachings with the doctrines of revelation, and, carefully sifting them, they cherished what was true and wise in them and amended or rejected all else. For, as the all-seeing God against the cruelty of tyrants raised up mighty martyrs to the defense of the Church, men prodigal of their great lives, in like manner to false philosophers and heretics He opposed men of great wisdom, to defend, even by the aid of human reason, the treasure of revealed truths. Thus, from the very first stages of the Church, the Catholic doctrine has encountered a multitude of most bitter adversaries, who, deriding the Christian dogmas and institutions, maintained that there were many gods, that the material world never had a beginning or cause, and that the course of events was one of blind and fatal necessity, not regulated by the will of Divine Providence.

But the learned men whom We call apologists speedily encountered these teachers of foolish doctrine and, under the guidance of faith, found arguments in human wisdom also to prove that one God, who stands preeminent in every kind of perfection, is to be worshiped; that all things were created from nothing by His omnipotent power; that by His wisdom they flourish and serve each their own special purposes. Among these St. Justin Martyr claims the chief place.

Quadratus, also, and Aristides, Hermias, and Athenagoras stood nobly forth in that time. Nor did Irenaeus, the invincible martyr and Bishop of Lyons, win less glory in the same cause when, forcibly refuting the perverse opinions of the Orientals, the works of the Gnostics, scattered broadcast over the territories of the Roman Empire, he explained (according to Jerome) the origin of each heresy and in what philosophic source it took its rise. But who knows not the disputations of Clement of Alexandria, which the same Jerome thus honorably commemorates: "What is there in them that is not learned, and what that is not of the very heart of philosophy?" He himself, indeed, with marvelous versatility treated of many things of the greatest utility for preparing a history of philosophy, for the exercise of the dialectic art, and for showing the agreement between reason and faith. . . . Arnobius, also, in his works against the pagans, and Lactantius in the divine *Institutions* especially, with equal eloquence and strength strenuously strive to move men to accept the dogmas and precepts of Catholic wisdom, not by philosophic juggling, after the fashion of the Academicians, but vanquishing them partly by their own arms, and partly by arguments drawn from the mutual contentions of the philosophers. But the writings on the human soul, the divine attributes, and other questions of mighty moment which the great Athanasius and Chrysostom, the prince of orators, have left behind them are, by common consent, so supremely excellent that it seems scarcely anything could be added to their subtlety and fullness. And, not to cover too wide a range, we add to the number of the great men of whom mention has been made the names of Basil the Great and of the two Gregories, who, on going forth from Athens, that home of all learning, thoroughly equipped with all the harness of philosophy, turned the wealth of knowledge which each had gathered up in a course of zealous study to the work of refuting heretics and preparing Christians.

But Augustine would seem to have wrested the palm from all. Of a most powerful genius and thoroughly saturated with sacred and profane learning, with the loftiest faith and with equal knowledge, he combated most vigorously all the errors of his age. What topic of philosophy did he not investigate? What region of it did he not diligently explore, either in expounding the loftiest mysteries of the faith to the faithful, or defending them against the full onslaught of adversaries, or again when, in demolishing the fables of the Academicians or the Manichaeans, he laid the safe foundations and sure structure of human science, or followed up the reason, origin, and causes of the evils that afflict man? How subtly he reasoned on the angels, the soul, the human mind, the will and free choice, on religion and the life of the blessed, on time and eternity, and even on the very nature of changeable bodies. Afterwards, in the East, John Damascene, treading in the footsteps of Basil and of Gregory Nazianzen, and in the West, Boethius and Anselm following the doctrines of Augustine, added largely to the patrimony of philosophy.

Later on, the doctors of the middle ages, who are called Scholastics, addressed themselves to a great work — that of diligently collecting, and sifting,and storing up, as it were, in one place, for the use and convenience of posterity the rich and fertile harvests of Christian learning scattered abroad in the voluminous works of the holy Fathers. And with regard, venerable brethren, to the origin, drift, and excellence of this scholastic learning, it may be well here to speak more fully in the words of one of the wisest of Our predecessors, Sixtus V: "By the divine favor of Him who alone gives the spirit of science, and wisdom, and understanding, and who through all ages, as there may be need, enriches His Church with new blessings and strengthens it with new safeguards, there was founded by Our fathers, men of eminent wisdom, the Scholastic theology, which two glorious doctors in particular, the angelic St. Thomas and the seraphic St. Bonaventure, illustrious teachers of this faculty, . . . with surpassing genius, by unwearied diligence, and at the cost of long labors and vigils, set in order and beautified, and when skillfully arranged and clearly explained in a variety of ways, handed down to posterity. . . .

Although these words seem to bear reference solely to Scholastic theology, nevertheless they may plainly be accepted as equally true of philosophy and its praises. For, the noble endowments which make the Scholastic theology so formidable to the enemies of truth — to wit, as the same Pontiff adds, "that ready and close coherence of cause and effect, that order and array as of a disciplined army in battle, those clear definitions and distinctions, that strength of argument and those keen discussions, by which light is distinguished from darkness, the true from the false, expose and strip naked, as it were, the falsehoods of heretics wrapped around by a cloud of subterfuges and fallacies" —

those noble and admirable endowments, We say, are only to be found in a right use of that philosophy which the Scholastic teachers have been accustomed carefully and prudently to make use of even in theological disputations. Moreover, since it is the proper and special office of the Scholastic theologians to bind together by the fastest chain human and divine science, surely the theology in which they excelled would not have gained such honor and commendation among men if they had made use of a lame and imperfect or vain philosophy.

Among the Scholastic Doctors, the chief and master of all towers Thomas Aquinas, who, as Cajetan observes, because "he most venerated the ancient doctors of the Church, in a certain way seems to have inherited the intellect of all." The doctrines of those illustrious men, like the scattered members of a body, Thomas collected together and cemented, distributed in wonderful order, and so increased with important additions that he is rightly and deservedly esteemed the special bulwark and glory of the Catholic faith. With his spirit at once humble and swift, his memory ready and tenacious, his life spotless throughout, a lover of truth for its own sake, richly endowed with human and divine science, like the sun he heated the world with the warmth of his virtues and filled it with the splendor of his teaching. Philosophy has no part which he did not touch finely at once and thoroughly; on the laws of reasoning, on God and incorporeal substances, on man and other sensible things, on human actions and their principles, he reasoned in such a manner that in him there is wanting neither a full array of questions, nor an apt disposal of the various parts, nor the best method of proceeding, nor soundness of principles or strength of argument, nor dearness of elegance of style, nor a facility for explaining what is abstruse.

Moreover, the Angelic Doctor pushed his philosophic inquiry into the reasons and principles of things, which because they are most comprehensive and contain in their bosom, so to say, the seeds of almost infinite truths, were to be unfolded in good time by later masters and with a goodly yield. Arid as he also used this philosophic method in the refutation of error, he won this title to distinction for himself: that, single-handed, he victoriously combated the errors of former times, and supplied invincible arms to put those to rout which might in after-times spring up. Again, clearly distinguishing, as is fitting, reason from faith, while happily associating the one with the other, he both preserved the rights and had regard for the dignity of each; so much so, indeed what reason, borne on the wings of Thomas to its human height, can scarcely rise higher, while faith could scarcely expect more or stronger aids from reason than those which she has already obtained through Thomas.

For these reasons most learned men, in former ages especially, of the highest repute in theology and philosophy, after mastering with infinite pains the immortal works of Thomas, gave themselves up not so much to be instructed in his angelic wisdom as to be nourished upon it. It is known that nearly all the founders and lawgivers of the religious orders commanded their members to study and religiously adhere to the teachings of St. Thomas, fearful lest any of them should swerve even in the slightest degree from the footsteps of so great a man. To say nothing of the family of St. Dominic, which rightly claims this great teacher for its own glory, the statutes of the Benedictines, the Carmelites, the Augustinians, the Society of Jesus, and many others all testify that they are bound by this law.

And, here, how pleasantly one's thoughts fly back to those celebrated schools and universities which flourished of old in Europe — to Paris, Salamanca, Álcala, to Douay, Toulouse, and Louvain, to Padua and Bologna, to Naples and Coimbra, and to many another! All know how the fame of these seats of learning grew with their years, and that their judgment, often asked in matters of grave moment, held great weight everywhere. And we know how in those great homes of human wisdom, as in his own kingdom, Thomas reigned supreme; and that the minds of all, of teachers as well as of taught, rested in wonderful harmony under the shield and authority of the Angelic Doctor.

But, furthermore, Our predecessors in the Roman pontificate have celebrated the wisdom of Thomas Aquinas by exceptional tributes of praise and the most ample testimonials. Clement VI in the bull *In Ordine*; Nicholas V in his brief to the friars of the Order of Preachers, 1451; Benedict XIII in the bull *Prestiosus*, and others bear witness that the universal Church borrows luster from his admirable teaching; while St. Pius V declares in the bull *Mirabilis* that heresies, confounded and convicted by the same teaching, were dissipated, and the whole world daily freed from fatal errors; others, such as Clement XIII in the bull *Verbo Dei*, affirm that most fruitful blessings have spread abroad from his writings over the whole Church, and that he is worthy of the honor which is bestowed on the greatest Doctors of the Church, on Gregory and Ambrose, Augustine and Jerome; while others have not hesitated to propose St. Thomas for the exemplar and master of the universities and great centers of learning whom they may follow with unfaltering feet. On which point the words of Blessed Urban V to the University of Toulouse are worthy of recall: "It is our will, which We hereby enjoin upon you, that ye follow the teaching of Blessed Thomas as the true and Catholic doctrine and that ye labor with all your force to profit by the same." Innocent XII followed the example of Urban in the case of the University of Louvain in the letter in the form of a brief addressed to that university on February 6, 1694, and Benedict XIV in the letter in the form of a brief addressed on August 26, 1752, to the Dionysius College in Granada; while to these judgments of great Pontiffs on Thomas Aquinas comes the crowning testimony of Innocent VI: "His teaching above that of other, the canonical writings alone excepted, enjoys such a precision of language, an order of matters, a truth of conclusions, that those who hold to it are never found swerving from the path of truth, and he who dare assail it will always be suspected of error."

The ecumenical councils, also, where blossoms the flower of all earthly wisdom, have always been careful to hold Thomas Aquinas in singular honor. In the Councils of Lyons, Vienna, Florence, and the Vatican one might almost say that Thomas took part and presided over the deliberations and decrees of the Fathers, contending against the errors of the Greeks, of heretics and rationalists, with invincible force and with the happiest results. But the chief and special glory of Thomas, one which he has shared with none of the Catholic Doctors, is that the Fathers of Trent made it part of the order of conclave to lay upon the altar, together with sacred Scripture and the decrees of the supreme Pontiffs, the *Summa* of Thomas Aquinas, whence to seek counsel, reason, and inspiration.

A last triumph was reserved for this incomparable man — namely, to compel the homage, praise, and admiration of even the very enemies of the Catholic name. For it has come to light that there were not lacking among the leaders of heretical sects some who openly declared that, if the teaching of Thomas Aquinas were only taken away, they could easily battle with all Catholic teachers, gain the victory, and abolish the Church. A vain hope, indeed, but no vain testimony.

Therefore, venerable brethren, as often as We contemplate the good, the force, and the singular advantages to be derived from his philosophic discipline which Our Fathers so dearly loved. We think it hazardous that its special honor should not always and everywhere remain, especially when it is established that daily experience, and the judgment of the greatest men, and to crown all, the voice of the Church, have favored the Scholastic philosophy. Moreover, to the old teaching a novel system of philosophy has succeeded here and there, in which We fail to perceive those desirable and wholesome fruits which the Church and civil society itself would prefer. For it pleased the struggling innovators of the sixteenth century to philosophize without any respect for faith, the power of inventing in accordance with his own pleasure and bent being asked and given in turn by each one. Hence, it was natural that systems of philosophy multiplied beyond measure, and conclusions differing and clashing one with another arose about those matters even which are the most important in human knowledge. From a mass of conclusions men often come to wavering and doubt; and who knows not how easily the mind slips from doubt to error? But, as men are apt to follow the lead given them, this new pursuit seems to have caught the souls of certain Catholic philosophers, who, throwing aside the patrimony of ancient wisdom, chose rather to build up a new edifice than to strengthen and complete the old by aid of the new — ill-advisedly, in sooth, and not without detriment to the sciences. For, a multiform system of this kind, which depends on the authority and choice of any professor, has a foundation open to change, and consequently gives us a philosophy not firm, and stable, and robust like that of old, but tottering and feeble. And if, perchance, it sometimes finds itself scarcely equal to sustain the shock of its foes, it should recognize that the cause and the blame lie in itself. In saying this We have no intention of discountenancing the learned and able men who bring their industry and erudition, and, what is more, the wealth of new discoveries, to the service of philosophy; for, of course, We understand that this tends to the development of learning. But one should be very careful lest all or his chief labor be exhausted in these pursuits and in mere erudition. And the same thing is true of sacred theology, which, indeed, may be assisted and illustrated by all kinds of erudition, though it is absolutely necessary to approach it in the grave manner of the Scholastics, in order that, the forces of revelation and reason being united in it, it may continue to be "the invincible bulwark of the faith."

With wise forethought, therefore, not a few of the advocates of philosophic studies, when turning their minds recently to the practical reform of philosophy, aimed and aim at restoring the renowned teaching of Thomas Aquinas and winning it back to its ancient beauty.

Many of those who, with mind alienated from the faith, hate Catholic institutions, claim reason as their sole mistress and guide. Now, We think that, apart from the supernatural help of God, nothing is better calculated to heal those minds and to bring them, into favor with the Catholic faith than the solid doctrine of the Fathers and the Scholastics, who so clearly and forcibly demonstrate the firm foundations of the faith, its divine origin, its certain truth, the arguments that sustain it, the benefits it has conferred on the human race, and its perfect accord with reason, in a manner to satisfy completely minds open to persuasion, however unwilling and repugnant.

For, the teachings of Thomas on the true meaning of liberty, which at this time is running into license, on the divine origin of all authority, on laws and their force, on the paternal and just rule of princes, on obedience to the higher powers, on mutual charity one toward another — on all of these and kindred subjects — have very great and invincible force to overturn those principles of the new order which are well known to be dangerous to the peaceful order of things and to public safety. In short, all studies ought to find hope of advancement and promise of assistance in this restoration of philosophic discipline which We have proposed. The arts were wont to draw from philosophy, as from a wise mistress, sound judgment and right method, and from it, also, their spirit, as from the common fount of life. When philosophy stood stainless in honor and wise in judgment, then, as facts and constant experience showed, the liberal arts flourished as never before or since; but, neglected and almost blotted out, they lay prone, since philosophy began to lean to error and join hands with folly. Nor will the physical sciences themselves, which are now in such great repute, and by the renown of so many inventions draw such universal admiration to themselves, suffer detriment, but find very great assistance in the restoration of the ancient philosophy. For, the investigation of facts and the contemplation of nature is not alone sufficient for their profitable exercise and advance; but, when facts have been established, it is necessary to rise and apply ourselves to the study of the nature of corporeal things, to inquire into the laws which govern them and the principles whence their order and varied unity and mutual attraction in diversity arise. To such investigations it is wonderful what force and light and aid the Scholastic philosophy, if judiciously taught, would bring.

And here it is well to note that our philosophy can only by the grossest injustice be accused of being opposed to the advance and development of natural science. For, when the Scholastics, following the opinion of the holy Fathers, always held in anthropology that the human intelligence is only led to the knowledge of things without body and matter by things sensible, they well understood that nothing was of greater use to the philosopher than diligently to search into the mysteries of nature and to be earnest and constant in the study of physical things. And this they confirmed by their own example; for St. Thomas, Blessed Albertus Magnus, and other leaders of-the Scholastics were never so wholly rapt in the study of philosophy as not to give large attention to the knowledge of natural things; and, indeed, the number of their sayings and writings on these subjects, which recent professors approve of and admit to harmonize with truth, is by no means small. Moreover, in this very age many illustrious professors of the physical sciences openly testify that between certain and accepted conclusions of modern physics and the philosophic principles of the schools there is no conflict worthy of the name.

While, therefore, We hold that every word of wisdom, every useful thing by whomsoever discovered or planned, ought to be received with a willing and grateful mind, We exhort you, venerable brethren, in all earnestness to restore the golden wisdom of St. Thomas, and to spread it far and wide for the defense and beauty of the Catholic faith, for the good of society, and for the advantage of all the sciences. The wisdom of St. Thomas, We say; for if anything is taken up with too great subtlety by the Scholastic doctors, or too carelessly stated — if there be anything that ill agrees with the discoveries of a later age, or, in a word, is improbable in whatever way — it does not enter Our mind to propose that for imitation to Our age. Let carefully selected teachers endeavor to implant the doctrine of Thomas Aquinas in the minds of students, and set forth clearly his solidity and excellence over others. Let the universities already founded or to be founded by you illustrate and defend this doctrine, and use it for the refutation of prevailing errors. But, lest the false for the true or the corrupt for the pure be drunk in, be ye watchful that the doctrine of Thomas be drawn from his own fountains, or at least from those rivulets which, derived from the very fount, have thus far flowed, according to the established agreement of learned men, pure and clear; be careful to guard the minds of youth from those which are said to flow thence, but in reality are gathered from strange and unwholesome streams.

But well do We know that vain will be Our efforts unless, venerable brethren, He helps Our common cause who, in the words of divine Scripture, is called the God of all knowledge; by which we are also admonished that "every best gift and every perfect gift is from above, coming down from the Father of lights," and again: "If any of you want wisdom, let him ask of God, who giveth to all men abundantly, and upbraideth not: and it shall be given him."

Therefore in this also let us follow the example of the Angelic Doctor, who never gave himself to reading or writing without first begging the blessing of God, who modestly confessed that whatever he knew he had acquired not so much by his own study and labor as by the divine gift; and therefore let us all, in humble and united prayer, beseech God to send forth the spirit of knowledge and of understanding to the children of the Church and open their senses for the understanding of wisdom. And that we may receive fuller fruits of the divine goodness, offer up to God the most efficacious patronage of the Blessed Virgin Mary, who is called the seat of wisdom; having at the same time as advocates St. Joseph, the most chaste spouse of the Virgin, and Peter and Paul, the chiefs of the Apostles, whose truth renewed the earth which had fallen under the impure blight of error, filling it with the light of heavenly wisdom.

In fine, relying on the divine assistance and confiding in your pastoral zeal, most lovingly We bestow on all of you, venerable brethren, on all the clergy and the flocks committed to your charge, the apostolic benediction as a pledge of heavenly gifts and a token of Our special esteem.

Given at St. Peter's, in Rome, the fourth day of August, 1879, the second year of our pontificate.

Rerum Novarum
Encyclical of Pope Leo XIII
On the Relations of Capitol and Labor
May 15, 1891

That the spirit of revolutionary change, which has long been disturbing the nations of the world, should have passed beyond the sphere of politics and made its influence felt in the cognate sphere of practical economics is not surprising. The elements of the conflict now raging are unmistakable: in the vast expansion of industrial pursuits and the marvelous discoveries of science; in the changed relations between masters and workmen; in the enormous fortunes of some few individuals, and the utter poverty of the masses; in the increased self-reliance and closer mutual combination of the working classes; as also, finally, in the prevailing moral degeneracy. The momentous gravity of the state of things now obtaining fills every mind with painful apprehension; wise men are discussing it; practical men are proposing schemes; popular meetings, legislatures, and rulers of nations are all busied with it — and actually there is no question which has taken a deeper hold on the public mind. . . .

Socialists and Private Property

To remedy these wrongs the Socialists, working on the poor man's envy of the rich, are striving to do away with private property, and contend that individual possessions should become the common property of all, to be administered by the State or by municipal bodies. They hold that by thus transferring property from private individuals to the community, the present mischievous state of things will be set to rights, inasmuch as each citizen will then get his fair share of whatever there is to enjoy. But their contentions are so clearly powerless to end the controversy that were they carried into effect the workingman himself would be among the first to suffer. They are, moreover, emphatically unjust, because they would rob the lawful possessor, bring State action into a sphere not within its competence, and create utter confusion in the community.

It is surely undeniable that, when a man engages in remunerative labor, the impelling reason and motive of this work is to obtain property, and thereafter to hold it as his very own. If one man hires out to another his strength or skill, he does so for the purpose of receiving in return what is necessary for sustenance and education; he therefore expressly intends to acquire a right full and real, not only to the remuneration, but also to the disposal of such remuneration, just as he pleases. Thus, if he lives sparingly, saves money, and, for greater security, invests his savings in land, the land, in such case, is only his wages under another form; and, consequently, a workingman's little estate thus purchased should be as completely at his full disposal as are the wages he receives for his labor. But it is precisely in such power of disposal that ownership consists, whether the property consist of land or chattels. Socialists, therefore, by endeavoring to transfer the possessions of individuals to the community, strike at the interests of every wage earner, for they deprive him of the liberty of disposing of his wages, and thus of all hopes and possibility of increasing his stock and of bettering his condition in life. . . .

Man's Natural Right and His Social and Domestic Duties

The rights here spoken of, belonging to each individual man, are seen in a much stronger light if they are considered in relation to man's social and domestic obligations.

In choosing a state of life, it is indisputable that all are at full liberty either to follow the counsel of Jesus Christ as to virginity, or to enter into the bonds of marriage. No human law can abolish the natural and primitive right of marriage, or in any way limit the chief and principle purpose of marraige, ordained by God's authority from the beginning: *Increase and multiply*. Thus we have the Family; the "society" of a man's own household; a society limited indeed in numbers, but a true "society," anterior to every kind of State or nation, with rights and duties of its own, totally independent of the commonwealth.

That right of property, therefore, which has been proved to belong naturally to individual persons, must also belong to a man in his capacity of head of a family; nay, such a person must possess this right so much the more clearly in proportion as his position multiplies his duties. For it is a most sacred law of nature that a father must provide food and all necessaries for those whom he has begotten; and, similarly, nature dictates that a man's children, who carry on, as it were, and continue his own personality, should be provided by him with all that is needful to enable them honorably to keep themselves from want and misery in the uncertainties of this mortal life. Now, in no other way can a father effect this except by the ownership of profitable property, which he can transmit to his children by inheritance. A family, no less than a State, is, as we have said, a true society, governed by a power within itself, that is to say, by the father. Wherefore, provided the limits be not transgressed which are prescribed by the very purposes for which it exists, the Family has, at least, equal rights with the State in the choice and pursuits of those things which are needful to its preservation and its just liberty. . . .

Our first and most fundamental principle, therefore, when we undertake to alleviate the condition of the masses, must be the inviolability of private property. This laid down, We go on to show where we must find the remedy that we seek.

The Church Alone Can Solve the Social Problems

We approach the subject with confidence, and in the exercise of the rights which belong to Us. For no practical solution of this question will ever be found without the assistance of Religion and of the Church. It is We who are the chief guardian of Religion, and the chief dispenser of what belongs to the Church, and we must not by silence neglect the duty which lies upon Us. Doubtless this most serious question demands the attention and the efforts of others besides Ourselves — of the rulers of States, of employers of labor, of the wealthy, and of the working population themselves for whom We plead, but We affirm without hesitation that all the strivings of men will be vain if they leave out the Church. . . .

The Christian Interdependence of Capital and Labor

The great mistake that is made in the matter now under consideration, is to possess oneself of the ideal that class is naturally hostile to class; that rich and poor are intended by nature to live at war with one another. So irrational and so false is this view, that the exact contrary is the truth. Just as the symmetry of the human body is the result of the disposition of the members of the body, so in a State it is ordained by nature that these two classes should exist in harmony and agreement, and should, as it were, fit into one another, so as to maintain the equilibrium of the body politic. Each requires the other; capital cannot do without labor, nor labor without capital. Mutual agreement results in pleasantness and good order; perpetual conflict necessarily produces confusion and outrage. Now, in preventing such strife as this, and in making it impossible, the efficacy of Christianity is marvelous and manifold. First of all, there is nothing more powerful than Religion (of which the Church is the interpreter and guardian) in drawing rich and poor together, by reminding each class of its duties to the other, and especially of the duties of justice. Thus Religion teaches the laboring man and the workman to carry out honestly and well all equitable agreements freely made, never to injure capital, nor to outrage the person of an employer; never to employ violence in representing his own cause, nor to engage in riot and disorder, and to have nothing to do with men of evil principles, who work upon the people with artful promises, and raise foolish hopes which usually end in disaster and in repentance when too late. Religion teaches the rich man and the employer that their work-people are not their slaves; that they must respect in every man his dignity as a man and as a Christian; that labor is nothing to be ashamed of, if we listen to right reason and to Christian philosophy, but is an honorable employment, enabling a man to sustain his life in an upright and creditable way; and that it is shameful and inhuman to treat men like chattels to make money by, or to look upon them merely as so much muscle or physical power. Thus, again, Religion teaches that, as among the workmen's concerns are Religion herself, and things spiritual and mental, the employer is bound to see that he has time for the duties of piety; that he be not exposed to corrupting influences and dangerous occasions; and that he be not led away to neglect his home and family or to squander his wages. Then, again, the employer must never tax his work-people beyond their strength, nor employ them in work unsuited to their sex or age. His great and principal obligation is to give to everyone that which is just. . . .

The State's Share in the Relief of Poverty

It cannot, however, be doubted that to attain the purpose of which We treat, not only the Church, but all human means must conspire. All who are concerned in the matter must be of one mind and must act together. It is in this, as in the Providence which governs the world; results do not happen save where all the causes cooperate.

Let us now, therefore, inquire what part the State should play in the work of remedy and relief.

By the State We here understand, not the particular form of government which prevails in this or that nation, but the State as rightly understood; that is to say, any government conformable in its institutions to right reason and natural law, and to those dictates of the Divine wisdom which We have expounded in the Encyclical on the Christian Constitution of the State. The first duty, therefore, of the rulers of the State should be to make sure that the laws and institutions, the general character and administration of the commonwealth, shall be such as to produce of themselves public well-being and private prosperity. This is the proper office of wise statesmanship and the work of the heads of the State. Now a State chiefly prospers and flourishes by morality, by well-regulated family life, by respect for religion and justice, by the moderation and equal distribution of public burdens, by the progress of the arts and of trade, by the abundant yield of the land — by everything which makes the citizens better and happier. Here, then, it is in the power of a ruler to benefit every order of the State, and amongst the rest to promote in the highest degree the interests of the poor; and this by virtue of his office, and without being exposed to any suspicion of undue interference — for it is the province of the commonwealth to consult for the common good. And the more that is done for the working population by the general laws of the country, the less need will there be to seek for particular means to relieve them.

Whenever the general interests or any particular class suffers, or is threatened with, evils which can in no other way be met, the public authority must step in to meet them. Now, among the interests of the public, as of private individuals, are these: that peace and good order should be maintained; that family life should be carried on in accordance with God's laws and those of nature; that Religion should be reverenced and obeyed; that a high standard of morality should prevail in public and private life; that the sanctity of justice should be respected, and, that no one should injure another with impunity; that the members of the commonwealth should grow up to man's estate strong and robust, and capable, if need be, of guarding and defending their country. If by a strike, or other combination of workmen, there should be imminent danger of disturbance to the public peace; or if circumstances were such that among the laboring population the ties of family life were relaxed; if Religion were found to suffer through the workmen not having time and opportunity to practice it; if in workshops and factories there were danger to morals through the mixing of the sexes or from any occasion of evil; or if employers laid burdens upon the workmen which were unjust, or degraded them with conditions that were repugnant to their dignity as human beings; finally, if health were endangered by excessive labor, or by work unsuited to sex or age — in these cases there can be no question that, within certain limits, it would be right to call in the help and authority of the law. The limits be determined by the nature of the occasion which calls of the law's interference — the principles being this, that the law must not undertake more, nor go further, than is required for the remedy of the evil or the removal of the danger. . . .

Save the Laborers from the Cruelty of Speculators in Labor

If we turn now to things exterior and corporeal, the first concern of all is to save the poor workers from the cruelty of grasping speculators, who use human beings as mere instruments for making money. It is neither justice nor humanity so to grind men down with excessive labor as to stupefy their minds and wear out their bodies. Man's powers like his general nature, are limited, and beyond these limits he cannot go. His strength is devoted and increased by use and exercise, but only on condition of due intermission and proper rest. Daily labor, therefore, must be so regulated that it may not be protracted during longer hours than strength admits. How many and how long the intervals of rest should be, will depend upon the nature of the work, on circumstances of time and place, and on the health and strength of the workman. Those who labor in mines and quarries, and in work within the bowels of the earth, should have shorter hours in proportion, as their labor is more severe and more trying to health. Then, again, the season of the years must be taken into account; for not infrequently a kind of labor is easy at one time which at another is intolerable or very difficult. Finally, work which is suitable for a strong man cannot reasonably be required from a woman or a child. . . .

Multiply Workingmen's Associations

In the last place — employers and workmen may themselves effect much in the matter of which We treat, by means of those institutions and organizations which afford opportune assistance to those in need, and which draw the two orders more closely together. Among these may be enumerated: Societies for mutual help; various foundations established by private persons for providing for the workman, and for his widow or his orphans, in sudden calamity, in sickness, and in the events of death; and what are called "patronages," or institutions for the care of boys and girls, for young people, and also for those of more mature age.

The most important of all are Workmen's Associations; for these virtually include all the rest. History attests what excellent results were effected by the Artificer's Guilds of a former day. They were the means not only of many advantages to the workmen, but in no small degree of the advancement of art, as numerous monuments remain to prove. Such associations should be adapted to the requirements of the age in which we live — an age of greater instruction, of different customs, and of more numerous requirements in daily life. It is gratifying to know that there are actually in existence not a few Societies of this nature, consisting either of workmen alone, or of workmen and employers together; but it were greatly to be desired that they should multiply and become more effective. . . .

The Advantages of Lawful Combination

And here we are reminded of the Confraternities, Societies, and Religious Orders which have arisen by the Church's authority and the piety of the Christian people. The annals of every nation down to our own times testify to what they have done for the human race. It is indisputable on ground of reason alone, that such associations, being perfectly blameless in their objects, have the sanction of the law of nature. On their religious side, they rightly claim to be responsible to the Church alone. The administrators of the State, therefore, have no rights over them, nor can they claim any share in their management; on the contrary, it is the State's duty to respect and cherish them, and, if necessary, to defend them from attack. It is notorious that a very different course has been followed, more especially in our own times. In many places the State has laid violent hands on these communities, and committed manifold injustices against them; it has placed them under the civil law, taken away their rights as corporate bodies, and robbed them of their property. In such property the Church had her rights, each member of the body had his or her rights, and there were also the rights of those who had founded or endowed them for a definite purpose, and of those for whose benefits and assistance they existed. Wherefore, We cannot refrain from complaining of such spoliation as unjust and fraught with evil results; and with the more reason because, at the very time when the law proclaims that association is free to all, We see that Catholic societies, however peaceable and useful, are hindered in every way, whilst the utmost freedom is given to men whose objects are at once hurtful to Religion and dangerous to the State.

Associations of every kind, and especially those of working men, are now far more common than formerly. In regard to many of these there is no need at present to inquire whence they spring, what are their objects or what mean they use. But there is a good deal of evidence which goes to prove that many of these societies are in the hands of invisible leaders, and are managed on principles far from compatible with Christianity and the public well-being; and that they do their best to get into their hands the whole field of labor and to force workmen either to join them or to starve. Under these circumstances the Christian workmen must do one of two things; either join associations in which their religion will be exposed to peril, or form associations among themselves — unite their forces and courageously shake off the yoke of unjust and intolerable oppression. No one who does not wish to expose man's chief good to extreme danger will hesitate to say that the second alternative must by all means be adopted. . . .

As far as regards the Church, its assistance will never be wanting, be the time or the occasion what it may; and it will intervene with greater effect in proportion as its liberty of action is the more unfettered; let this be carefully noted by those whose office it is to provide for the public welfare. Every minister of holy Religion must throw into the conflict all the energy of his mind, and all the strength of his endurance; with your authority, Venerable Brethren, and by your example, they must never cease to urge upon all men of every class, upon the high as well as the lowly, the Gospel doctrines of Christian life; by every means in their power they must strive for the good of the people; and above all they must earnestly cherish in themselves, and try to arouse in others, Charity, the mistress and queen of virtues. For the happy results we all long for must be chiefly brought about by the plenteous outpouring of Charity; of that true Christian Charity which is the fulfilling of the whole Gospel law, which is always ready to sacrifice itself for other's sake, and which is man's surest antidote against worldly pride and immoderate love of self, that Charity whose office is described and whose God-like features are drawn by the Apostle St. Paul in these words: *Charity is patient, is kind, . . . seeketh not her own, . . . suffereth all things, . . . endureth all things.*

On each of you, Venerable Brethren, and on your Clergy and people, as an earnest of God's mercy and a mark of our affection, We lovingly in the Lord bestow the Apostolic Benediction.

Given at St. Peter's in Rome, the fifteenth day of May, 1891, the fourteenth year of our Pontificate.

The complete text of the Encyclical Letter is in
The American Catholic Review for July, 1891

Chapter 57 • St. Thérèse of Lisieux: *Love of God*

St. Thérère of Lisieux (1873-1897), in her work entitled *Love of God*, gives us a perfect example of her conviction that love of God is generous, thoughtful, tender, and encourages the entire spiritual immolation of self.

Love of God

Once we realize that God is merciful Love, we go to Him with confidence. In its turn, "confidence leads to love."[1] Now, love is the soul of the Way of Spiritual Childhood, just as it is the foundation and guiding principle of the spiritual life and is the only means by which the soul can rise to full perfection. For without love, we will not have either the fidelity or the generosity that are required to bring our efforts to a successful end.

Carmel has always affirmed the primacy of love, especially through those two outstanding witnesses, St. Teresa of Ávila and St. John of the Cross. It was only natural, then, that St. Thérèse of Lisieux should have imbibed the spirit of her Order. She had particularly admired St. John of the Cross, the Father of the Carmelite Reform, whose works were always at her elbow. There she had read that "love alone can repay love" and that "it is all important that we fill our lives with acts of love, in order that our soul may be quickly consumed and arrive with short delay at the vision of God."[2]

Such thoughts must inevitably have had a motivating influence on a soul as loving as hers, for from her tenderest years Thérèse had thirsted for the contemplation of God. In fact, as soon as she became acquainted with these passages, she began to repeat them to herself in order to stimulate her love.

Nevertheless, it would be wrong to attribute Thérèse's love to those sources alone, for she had also a deep appreciation of the Gospels. In them she saw God manifesting Himself as essential Love; she saw clearly that "God is love" (I John 4:16).[3] There also she learned the extent of God's love for us and concluded that His love is a merciful love that delights in stooping down to our miseries in order to deliver us from them. God, thus, bends down to our nothingness, to transform it into a fiery love for Himself.[4] Having gained this insight, Thérèse, like St. John, devoted herself wholeheartedly to the task of making her life a complete act of love. At a later date she wrote that God had chosen her particularly in order that she might glorify His infinite mercy.[5]

This faith in God's merciful Love is truly the root principle of the entire Thérèsian spirituality. From it springs its fundamental characteristics. It developed in the soul of Thérèse that ardent love which animated her throughout life. It inspired her with the noble desire of offering herself as a victim to merciful Love, in order to receive torrents of that divine love — which so many reject — and to love God *WITH HIS OWN LOVE.*

Strongly characteristic of childhood, love is the feeling that predominates one's early years. The child loves its parents tenderly and gives expression to his affection in many charming ways. This was an additional reason for giving love a prominent place in the Way of Spiritual Childhood.

In numerous texts Thérèse brings out the important role of love: "I understand so very well that it is only through love that we can render ourselves pleasing to the good Lord, that love is the one thing I long for. The science of love is the only science I desire."[6] She told her cousin Marie Guérin: "I know of no other means to reach perfection than by love. To love: how perfectly our hearts are made for this! Sometimes I look for another word to use, but, in this land of exile, no other word so well expresses the vibrations of our soul. Hence, we must keep to that one word: love."[7] "Regarding self," she told her sister Leonie, "I find it very easy to practice perfection, for I realize that we have merely to take Jesus by His Heart."[8] Finally, she declared to Celine: "Merit does not consist in doing or giving much. It consists in loving much."[9]

Love was both the driving force and objective of all her actions. Just as she looked at all the attributes of God through the prism of His merciful love, so did she endeavor to do everything out of love and for love, "to give pleasure to the good Lord," to "Jesus,"[10] to "give Him joy, that He might be loved."[11] "How easy it is to please Jesus, to ravish His Heart," she wrote to Celine. "We have merely to love Him, while, at the same time, forgetting ourselves."[12] And to Leonie: "If you wish to be a saint, it is easy . . . aim only at pleasing Jesus, at uniting yourself intimately with Him."[13]

Although every virtue has its own proper motive, Thérèse motivated all her virtuous acts by love. She affirmed that she had learned this method from Jesus Himself: "Directors make people advance in perfection by performing a great number of acts of virtue, and they are right. But my Director, who is Jesus Himself, teaches me to do everything through love."[14]

She knew, of course, that saints ordinarily work for the glory of God but, she said, "I am a little soul and I labor solely for His pleasure. I would be happy to suffer the greatest pains, were it only to make Him smile even once."[15]

She put all the energy she possessed in the service of love, as is evident from her own words in the poem *A Lily Among Thorns:*

"When my youthful heart was afire
with the flame we call love,
You came and claimed it for Yourself.
And You alone, O Jesus, could satisfy my soul,
For boundless was my need of loving You."[16]

The keen obligation St. Thérèse felt of giving Jesus all her love was intensely sharpened because He had not only preserved her from any grievous sin, but even from any fully voluntary fault. As she said, He had remitted all her faults in advance. In that preservation from faults she saw the proof of God's unique love for her, of Jesus' desire "that she should love Him unto folly."[17]

For her part, seeing that God is so little loved even by those who have consecrated themselves to Him, and "knowing that Jesus is thirsting more than ever for love," she desired to make up for it, to make compensation to God for the ingratitude of men, to make her life one great act of love, to love Jesus "more than He had ever been loved before."[18]

In reality, her life was a continual act of love: "While growing up," (she is speaking about the time when she was about five years old) "I loved the good Lord more and more. I often gave my heart to Him. I did my best to please Jesus in all my actions and was very careful never to offend Him."[19]

The perfection of her smallest actions, her love of suffering, her ardent zeal for souls, as well as her profound recollection which kept her united to Christ in all circumstances, mark the extent of her love. This, usually, was not a mere sensible feeling, though sometimes, under the influence of an emotion, she had transports of love which she was unable to control. She had had experiences of this kind even before her entrance into Carmel in 1887.[20] She was similarly favored on several occasions after becoming a Carmelite.

While finishing the manuscript written for Mother Mary Gonzaga, she was seized with one of these transports of love, and it was this which inspired her to write one of the most beautiful pages we possess: "You know, O my God," she exclaims, "that I have never desired to love anyone but You, and that I seek no other glory. Your love went before me in my childhood. It has grown with me and now, it is an abyss of which I cannot sound the depth. Love attracts love. Mine leaps towards You. I would like to fill the abyss which attracts it, but, alas! it is not even a drop of dew lost in the ocean! In order to love You as You love me, I must borrow your own love. . . . O my Jesus, it seems to me that You could not fill any soul with more love than you have given to me. . . . No, here below, I cannot conceive a greater immensity of love than that which it has pleased You to bestow gratuitously on me without any merit on my part."[21]

On another occasion, while walking in the garden supported by Mother Agnes, she stopped to look at a small white hen which covered her chicks with her wings, her eyes filled with tears and Mother Agnes said to her: "You are crying!" — "I cannot answer you at this moment," she replied, "I am too greatly moved."

Having returned to the infirmary she explained: "I wept because I remembered that the good Lord used that comparison in the Gospel to make us believe in His love. That is the way He has acted towards me throughout my life. He has hidden me entirely under His wings. A moment ago I was unable to control myself. My heart was overflowing with gratitude and love. It is a good thing that the good Lord hides Himself from my sight and only rarely and, as it were, through bars,[22] shows me the effects of His mercy."[23]

How well those words reveal her intense love!

She said that her loving desires were for her "the greatest of martyrdoms." It was in order to satisfy that desire of love that she wanted to keep her eyes always fixed on the divine Word, her "Eagle whom she adored," and to remain under the fascination of His gaze. She begged Him to dive down on His prey and carry it off to the Furnace of love, to plunge her into that Furnace for all eternity.[24] She added, however, that she did not see very well what more she would have after her death than what she already bad. "I know," she said, "that I shall see the good Lord, but as far as being with Him, I already am totally with Him here on earth."[25] Hence, she declared that if she were not to attain some day to those higher regions of love to which her soul aspired, she would, nevertheless, have tasted more sweetness here below in her martyrdom and folly, than she would enjoy amidst the delights of her heavenly Fatherland.[26]

Thérèse's love for God and our Lord had all the qualities which a human soul could hope for. She loved with a love that was most exclusive and complete. It was most disinterested, generous, tender and delicate.

1. Thérèse's Exclusive Love

First of all, it is certain that no other love ever touched her heart, and that Jesus possessed it entirely. She was still very young when she felt a great desire of never loving anyone but the good Lord, to find no joy except in Him.[27] Jesus was "her first, her only friend, the one and only one whom she loved; He was her All."[28]

"Jesus," she sang, "You alone can satiate my heart.

There's nothing here below that can beguile me.

You are my only love."[29]

This singleness of her love for Christ was chiefly the fruit of her first Communion, and it continued to grow even stronger as time went on. "When Jesus shall have transported me to the blessed shore of Carmel," she wrote a few days before her entrance, "I will give myself entirely to Him, for I want to live for Him alone."[30]

However, when she had entered the cloister, her heart, thirsting for affection, felt very lonely and friendless. Instinctively, she turned to her Mother Prioress (Mother Marie de Gonzaga), but, sensing the danger that she might become too much attached to her Superior, she immediately repressed her feeling, for she knew that Jesus wanted her for Himself alone: "He knows well that if He gave me but a shadow of happiness, I would attach myself to it with all the energy and all the powers of my heart."

During her retreat before receiving the habit, she reaffirmed her resolution: "Since I cannot find any creature that satisfies my heart. I want to give everything to Jesus. I will not give even one atom of my love to creatures."[31]

On the day of her profession, in order that that disposition might be the soul of her holocaust, she placed over her heart the following prayer: "O Jesus! May I never seek nor find anyone but You alone! May creatures mean nothing to me and may I mean nothing to them, but may You, Jesus, be everything!"[32]

She was wont afterwards to renew this resolution to love Christ only with a vehement fervor that revealed how strongly and completely it bound her to Him. "Let us not leave anything in our heart except Jesus," she wrote to Celine.[33] And to Mother Agnes: "You know the One whom I love and whom alone I want to please." "Jesus alone; no one but Him. The grain of sand is so small. If it wished to put anyone beside Him in its heart, there would be no room for Jesus."[34]

2. Thérèse's Disinterested Love

The most perfect selflessness marked Thérèse's love for God, for she loved Him solely for what He is in Himself: Perfection and Infinite Charity. This divine Charity suffused her soul with love of gratitude for all God has done for us in preparing us for eternal happiness with Himself by giving His only begotten Son to become one of us.[35] She loved Jesus for Himself and for His excessive love which made Him sacrifice Himself unto death for sinners. Never did she love in order to receive. She never even thought of serving God "in order to merit heaven or obtain graces." "I do not want to give," she said, "in order to receive. I am not a self-seeker. It is God that I love and not myself."[36]

This does not mean that she was indifferent to the acquisition of merits. To Mother Agnes who had asked her, "Do you want to acquire merits?" she answered: "Yes, but not for myself; for souls, for the needs of the Church."[37]

Neither does it mean that she was not interested in eternal beatitude. She wished to reach the degree of glory which God had destined for her.[38] From her infancy she had longed for that happiness, and the desire had constantly increased. Her letters express this on every page. It was this hope which, to a great extent, sustained her in her sufferings, especially during the cruel trial of her father's illness.[39] Despite these facts, she did not labor and suffer in view of reward. "My dear Celine," she wrote, "you understand that it is not to win a crown or to gain merit for myself; it is to give pleasure to Jesus;" for "it is not glory, even heavenly glory that my heart seeks. . . . My glory will be the splendor reflected on me from the brow of my mother the Church. What I seek is love. I want nothing else but to love You, O Jesus."[40]

In this connection, she confessed that it was with a certain repugnance that she sang at Sext on Sundays, in a faulty Latin translation, the words in which the Psalmist declares that He fulfills the divine law in view of recompense (*propter retributionem*). While singing these words, Thérèse protested interiorly: "O my Jesus, You know well that it is not for the reward that I serve You, but solely because I love You and in order to save souls."[41]

Nevertheless, the thought of eternal happiness prompted her to love even more: "Reflecting that eternal reward has no proportion to our small sacrifices in this life," she wrote, "I wanted to love Jesus passionately . . . give Him a thousand marks of love, as long as I was able to do so."[42]

She had the same disinterestedness regarding the favors or consolations which God ordinarily grants to souls that serve Him generously: "Jesus does not want us to serve Him for His gifts; it is He Himself who must be our reward."[43] "I do not desire sensible affection, a love that I feel, but only a love that is felt by Jesus. Oh! to love Him and cause Him to be loved!"[44] She even said that she was happy not to be consoled, and commended others to be detached from such favors, so that they might be attached to Jesus alone.

With keen psychological insight she recognized that self-love often insinuates itself into sensible affection, especially when it is accompanied bv consolations. "You do not feel your love for your Spouse," she writes to Celine. "You would like to have your heart be a flame that rises towards Him without a trace of smoke. . . . But notice that the smoke that surrounds you is intended only for you. It has for its purpose to hide from your eyes your love for Jesus. The flame is seen by Him alone. In this way, He has it all for Himself, for when He lets us catch a glimpse of it, self-love soon comes along like an evil wind that extinguishes everything."[45] This thought Thérèse summarized thus: "Our love for Jesus is truly great when we do not feel its sweetness. It then becomes a martyrdom. . . .[46] When, on the contrary, we begin to seek ourselves, true love dies away.[47] Unfortunately, many serve Jesus when He consoles them, but few are willing to keep Him company when He is asleep."[48]

She went so far in her desire to love God for Himself alone that she would have been glad to have God remain unaware of her good actions: "I love Him so much that I would like to give Him pleasure without His knowing that it is I. When He knows that I am giving Him pleasure and sees it, He is, as it were, obliged to return love for it. I would not like to give Him that much trouble."[49]

She knew, of course, that such a thing is impossible, but this was her way of expressing the distinterestedness of her love.

3. Thérèse's Generous Love

As can easily be deduced from her selflessness, Thérèse's love is also marked by a very great generosity. Very early in life, almost as it were by instinct, she had understood that love is proved by deeds and is nourished by sacrifice. Hence, she was always careful never to refuse anything to Jesus, but to give without stint, never neglecting anything that could please Him. "We do not bargain when we love."[50] "Jesus," she writes, "teaches me not to refuse Him anything and to be pleased when He gives me an opportunity for proving to Him that I love Him. This I do peacefully, with complete abandonment."[51]

However, such are we that we are not always equally well-disposed. Especially is this true when our Lord seems to deprive us of His presence and to leave us to ourselves. "Life is often burdensome," she confessed to Celine.

"What a bitterness, but also what sweetness! Yes, life is painful. It is hard to begin a day of labor. . . . If only we could feel Jesus! We would do everything for Him . . . but no! He seems to be miles away. We are alone with ourselves. Oh, what annoying company we are to ourselves when Jesus is not present . . . but . . . He is not far away. He is right there, quite near and looking at us. Indeed, He is there begging us to offer Him our sorrow . . . He hides, but we feel that He is present."[52] Hence, "the grain of sand determines to set to work without joy or courage or energy. This good-will, then, eases and energizes His undertaking. He wants to labor through love."[53]

Elsewhere she says: "What great grace is ours when, in the morning, we seem to be filled with lassitude and to lack both courage and strength to practice virtue! Then is the ideal moment to put the axe to the root of the tree, though our effort may lag for a few moments and we may neglect to gather our treasures. This is the critical moment, for we may be tempted to give up everything. However, we can repair everything and even gain in grace through an act of love, though it be unaccompanied by any sensible feeling. Jesus smiles. He helps us without appearing to do so and the tears He sheds over the wicked are wiped away by our poor, feeble efforts, by our small gift of love. Love can accomplish all things. Things that are 'most impossible' become easy where love is at work."[54]

She herself proved the truth of these words. She gave to God all He asked. "To love," she wrote, "means giving everything and giving ourselves."[55] "I love Him so much that I am always satisfied with anything He sends me." "I love all that He does."[56] Hence, at the end of her life, she was able to testify in her favor that since the age of three she had never refused anything to God.[57]

Jesus repeatedly proclaimed that men prove their love for Him by fulfilling the divine will. That is why believing souls try to conform to that rule. For them to live in union with God's will is to live in God, Thérèse lived such a life; she loved to say that "her only desire, her only joy on earth, was to do God's will."

"Perfection," she also declared, "consists in doing the will of God, in being what He wants us to be." She proved this admirably during her religious life. If, in every state of life, we must recognize God's will in the orders of our lawful superiors, this is even more true of religious life where everything is regulated by obedience and tends by means of it to lead us to perfection.

Thérèse had understood this. On the day of her profession, she asked God the grace of fulfilling her promises to perfection. It was her intention to live the Carmelite life as it had been planned by her Mother, St. Teresa of Ávila. In this she saw an infallible means of living "in truth." This, to her, was the straight way that leads to God.

"How great and numerous the anxieties from which we free ourselves," she said, "when we take the vow of obedience! How happy are simple religious! Their only compass is the will of their superiors; hence, they are always certain of being on the right path. They need not fear to be mistaken even when it seems certain that the superiors are mistaken. But when we stop looking at that infallible compass, when we leave the path pointed out to us, under the pretext of doing the will of God, and because He does not seem to enlighten properly those who, nevertheless, represent Him, we immediately get lost in arid roads where the waters of grace are soon dried up."[58]

Even when we are treated with severity, we must see in it a permission of God. "I know well, my mother, that you deal with me as with a soul that is weak, as with a spoiled child. Hence, I have no difficulty in bearing the burden of obedience, but, it seems to me, from what I feel in the depths of my heart, that I would not change my conduct and that my love for you would not weaken if you preferred to handle me with severity, for I would still see that it is the will of Jesus that you should act thus for the greater good of my soul."[59]

She instilled her novices with the same love of obedience to the rule: "Even if all were to fail in the observance of the rule," she said, "that would not be a reason for justifying ourselves," and, repeating the words of her holy Mother, St. Teresa, she added that "everyone should act as if the perfection of the Order depended on her personal conduct."

Religious life, considered in itself, usually gives no opportunity for anything but ordinary actions; hence, Thérèse had no opportunity of undertaking work of any importance. Moreover, she considered herself to be "but a very small soul which can offer only very small things to God."[60]

But very small things can have very great value; for the latter depends on the love with which they are done: "Our Lord considers not so much the greatness of our actions nor the difficulty that accompanies them. He has no need of our works but craves only our love."[61]

And so a soul that desires to correspond to the love of God, endeavors to mark all her actions, even the most indifferent, with that divine stamp, and it is this that gives them their inestimable value.

Thérèse applied herself to the observance of the Rule with all the care which works done for God deserve, and with all the love of which she was capable. Obedience guided her at every moment and her fidelity was absolute.

Mother Agnes testified at the Apostolic Process that she did not remember having ever seen her sister disobey even once, not even in the smallest matters.[62] Sister Marie of the Trinity, likewise, affirmed: "I lived always with her and, yet, I never saw her commit the smallest imperfection. I always saw her behave in the way that she believed to be the more perfect. As Thérèse corrected me when I committed a fault, I would have liked to find some imperfection in her in order to be able to excuse myself, but I never did."[63]

One of her novices confessed that she avoided Thérèse because she found her too perfect. Others have affirmed that they never heard her take part in useless conversation or waste a minute of her time. They never noticed in her one moment of bad humor, nor "a lack of charity." On no occasion did they find her "being in the least unfaithful to the smallest point of the Rule."[64] Not only did she obey the orders of her Superiors, but she did what she guessed were their wishes, and an advice, once given to her, remained in force, as far as she herself was concerned, until the end of her life.[65]

"When I wanted to recall the text of one of our rules," a novice declared, "I had merely to watch the way Sister Thérèse acted."[66]

She had even acquired the habit of obeying each one of her sisters.[67] She was most punctual. As soon as the bell sounded, she interrupted the conversation or stopped writing, leaving a word unfinished. One day, seeing her older sister continue to write down some important counsel after the bell had sounded, she said: "It is much better to lose that and to perform an act of regularity. If only we knew the value of regularity!"[68]

We can now understand why, a short time before her death, Thérèse was able to say that, if she had to live her life over again, she would act as she had done. How many of us will be able to make such a declaration at that supreme moment?

All work that is undertaken for God should be done with special care and attention. Unfortunately, that does not always happen, even in religious life. Thérèse had more than one occasion to observe this and she deplored the fact that "many perform their actions in a careless or nonchalant way; few fulfill their duties as perfectly as possible."

Religious life, however, implies more than regular observances. It is often seasoned with renunciations and sacrifices. Thérèse learned this from her own experience but she accepted everything in a spirit of perfect submission to the divine will: "Allow Jesus to take and give whatever He wills," she said, "perfection consists in doing His will."[69] It even happens that God, judging a soul to be capable of showing Him a greater love, sends her trials which give her an opportunity for such love. "The greatest honor He can do to a soul is not to give her much, but to ask much from her."[70]

It was thus that God acted towards Thérèse. He tried her severely in both body and soul, and, during the last months of her life especially, she suffered a true martyrdom.

We might expect that being exhausted by illness and hovering between life and death, she would have felt a great longing for heaven and exulted at the thought that she was soon to possess God, who had been the object of all her desires; but she showed nothing of the kind.

In her, the very strongest aspirations were subordinated to the divine will. The desire of pleasing God was so deeply anchored in Thérèse's soul that she no longer desired anything for herself. "The only thing that satisfies me," she said, "is doing the will of God. . . . What pleases me most is what God loves and what He chooses for me."[71]

She did not ask that prayers should be offered to give her relief in her sufferings: "I have asked the good Lord not to hear the prayers which would put an obstacle in the way of His designs in my regard."[72]

She did not prefer to die rather than to live; or, if at times she expressed some satisfaction because she felt death was near, it was only because God was calling her. "I am glad to die," she wrote, "not because I shall be freed from suffering here below; on the contrary, suffering is the only thing which seems desirable to me in this valley of tears. But I am glad to die because I know well that such is the will of God."[73] And a little later: "The thought of heavenly bliss gives me no joy. . . . It is only the thought of accomplishing God's will which constitutes all my joy."[74] The latter consideration was completed, as she expresses it elsewhere, by the hope of loving God as much as she had desired it, and "of causing Him to be loved by a multitude of souls."[75]

4. Her Love Was Tender and Thoughtful

Finally, Thérèse's love was tender and thoughtful. It was this delicacy that made her hide her sufferings, for fear that God would see them and suffer on their account.[76] This, of course, is pious exaggeration, for Thérèse knew that God does not change and that He is unable to experience pain. But those sentiments express in a childlike way the extreme sensitivity of her soul.

The same delicacy prevented her from invoking God directly to obtain temporal graces from Him. She did not want Him, as she expressed it naively, "to experience the regret of having to refuse those that were not in conformity with His will."[77] She transmitted such petitions through the hands of the Blessed Virgin; for since Mary knows God's designs, she would present to Him only those prayers that were agreeable to Him.

It has been said that her love was a filial love, the love of a child for his Father in heaven. It is certain that Thérèse loved God in a filial manner. She had towards God, considered as a father, that confident love "which has no fears, which goes to sleep and forgets itself as it lies on the Heart of its God, like a child in its father's arms."[78] "She loved God, as a child loves his father," said Sister Genevieve, "and used the most unexpected ways to express her affection."[79]

She also loved Jesus in a very particular way. As soon as we begin to read her writings, we notice that it is above all Jesus that she desired to please. The part which Jesus had in her love was such that, according to her sisters' testimony, her interior life was "centered in Jesus."[80]

She dealt with Him with that familiarity which seems natural to those who remember that our God has "loved us to excess." She herself told us that she loved to "take hold of Jesus through His Heart," and to "caress Him."

"To You alone, O Jesus, I must cling;
And running to Your arms, dear Lord,
There let me hide;
Loving with childlike tenderness."

On several occasions she urged her correspondents to act likewise.[81] If any one had objected that such conduct showed a lack of respect and exaggerated sentimentalism, Thérèse would, no doubt, have answered that a most tender love and even familiarity are quite compatible with the greatest reverence. For Jesus called us brothers and friends.

He surrounds us with loving care; He even anticipates the desires of those who are totally devoted to Him. Hence, He allows us to approach Him in a familiar, intimate way. God has revealed Himself as Love; "God is Charity." Jesus, by His example, has revealed that one loves truly only when one pushes love to its extreme consequences, "because of the excessive charity with which He loved us." Hence, we cannot claim that we love God unless we love Him to that same degree and give ourselves entirely to Him. Thérèse's message, which is entirely based on love, reminds us of this truth in an admirable manner. Her life was a living illustration of it. We owe an immense debt of love to God, for "He has loved us first" and from all eternity "in perpetual charity." We are debtors towards Jesus Christ because of His life and His death. To so much love we should have responded by an unwavering fidelity. May we, henceforth, apply ourselves to the task of rendering to God love for love!

Love is, at the same time, the root principle, the food and the end of all spiritual life. Without it we cannot forget ourselves nor give ourselves to God. Without it, we will lack fidelity and generosity. This is what Thérèse meant when, on the eve of her death, she told Sister Genevieve: "It is love alone that counts."

Notes

1. Letter addressed to Sr. Genevieve, Sept. 17, 1896.
2. *The Living Flame*, Str. I. 15, 6. She had written that motto at the bottom of her coat of arms. *The Story of a Soul*, 313; Manuscript addressed to Mother Agnes, Chapters 1-8 of *The Story of a Soul*, f. 86.
3. I John, IV, 16.
4. *The Story of a Soul*, I, 5; Manuscript addressed to Mother Agnes: Chapters 1-8 of *The Story of a Soul*, f. 2 v.; *The Story of a Soul*, XI. 217; Manuscript addressed to Sr. Marie du S. Coeur: Chapter 11 of *The Story of a Soul*, f. 3 v.
5. *The Story of a Soul*, VIII, 147; Manuscript addressed to Mother Agnes: Chapters 1-8 of *The Story of a Soul*, f. 83 v.
6. *The Story of a Soul*, XI, 208; Manuscript addressed to Sr. Marie du S. Coeur: Chapter 11 of *The Story of a Soul*, f. 1.
7. Letter addressed to Marie Guerin, July, 1890.
8. Leonie, July 12. 1896.
9. Celine, July 6, 1893.
10. This expression is repeated sixteen times in her writings. *Etudes et Documents*, 6th Year, p. 22.
11. *Esprit*, pp. 9-12.
12. Celine, July 6, 1893.
13. Letter addressed to Sr. Leonie, July 17, 1897.
14. Letter addressed to Celine, July 6, 1893.
15. *Novissima Verba*, July 16.
16. Poem: *Un lys au milieu des épines*.
17. *The Story of a Soul*, IV. 65; Manuscript addressed to Mother Agnes: Chapters 1-8 of *A Story of a Soul*, f. 39.
18. *The Story of a Soul*, XI, 210; M.B., f. 1 v.; *Novissima Verba*, August 7; *The Eternal Canticle*; Letter addressed to Mother Agnes., Jan. 8, 1889.
19. *The Story of a Soul*, II, 26; IV. 70; V, 87; Manuscript addressed to Mother Agnes: Chapters 1-8 of *The Story of a Soul*, f. 15 v.; 44 v.; f. 52 v.
20. *The Story of a Soul*, V, 87; Manuscript addressed to Mother Agnes: Chapters 1-8 of *The Story of a Soul*, f. 52.

21. *The Story of a Soul*, X, 201; Manuscript addressed to Mother Marie de Gonzague: Chapters 9 and 10 of *The Story of a Soul*, f. 35.
22. *Canticle of Canticles*, II, 9.
23. *Novissima Verba*, June 7.
24. S.M., du S.C., Sept. 14, 1896.
25. *The Story of a Soul*, XII, 226; *Novissima Verba*, May 15.
26. *The Story of a Soul*, XI, 219; Manuscript addressed to Sr. Marie du S. Coeur: Chapter 11 of *The Story of a Soul*, f. 4.
27. *The Story of a Soul*, IV, 62; Manuscript addressed to Mother Agnes: Chapters 1-8 of *The Story of a Soul*, f. 36 v.
28. Letter addressed to Celine, Dec. 31, 1889; Letter addressed to Sr. Genevieve., Sept. 14, 1896; *The Story of a Soul*, XI, 219; M.B., f. 4 v.
29. Poem: *Jésus seul*.
30. Letter addressed to Mother Agnes, March, 1888.
31. Letter addressed to Mother Agnes, Jan. 7-8, 1889.
32. *The Story of a Soul*, VIII, 134; Manuscript addressed to Mother Agnes: Chapers 1-8 of *The Story of a Soul*, f. 76 bis.
33. Letter addressed to Celine, April 26, 1889.
34. Letter addressed to Mother Agnes, Sept. 1890; May, 1889.
35. Act of Offering.
36. Apostolic Process, August 1890: Letter addressed to Mother Agnes.
37. *Novissima Verba*, August 18.
38. Act of Offering.
39. Letter addressed to Mother Agnes, March, 1888; May, 1890; Letter addressed to Celine, July 14, 1889; August 19, 1894.
40. Letter addressed to Celine, July 18, 1893; *The Story of a Soul*, XI, 218; Manuscript addressed to Sr. Marie du S. Coeur: Chapter 11 of *The Story of a Soul*, f. 4; Diocesan Process, There., S., Aug.; Apostolic Process, deposition of Sr. Marie de la Trinité.
41. *Conseils et Souvenirs dans H.A.* (as found in *The Story of a Soul*), 289.
42. *The Story of a Soul*, V, 79; Manuscript addressed to Mother Agnes: Chapters 1-8 of *The Story of a Soul*, f. 47 v.
43. Letter addressed to Celine, August, 1893.
44. Letter addressed to Mother Agnes, August, 1890.
45. Letter addressed to Celine, May, 1890; Jan., 1889.
46. Letter addressed to Celine, July 14, 1889.
47. *Souvenirs inédits*; *Esprit de Sainte Thérèse de l'Enfant-Jésus* 39.
48. Letter addressed to Celine, July 7, 1894.
49. *Conseils et Souvenirs dans H.A.* (as found in *The Story of a Soul*), 296. Thought of St. John of the Cross.
50. Letter addressed to Mother Agnes, Oct. 8, 1887; Letter addressed to Celine, April 26, 1889; Poem: *Vivre d' amour.*
51. Letter addressed to Celine, July 6, 1893.
52. Letter addressed to Celine, July 23, 1888.
53. Letter addressed to Celine, Feb. 28, 1889.
54. Letter addressed to Celine, Oct., 1889.
55. Poem: *Pourquoi je t' aime o Marie*.

56. *Novissima Verba*, July 6; *The Story of a Soul*, XII, 237.
57. *Conseils et Souvenirs dans H.A.* (as found in *The Story of a Soul*), 266.
58. *The Story of a Soul*, I, 15; Manuscript addressed to Mother Agnes: Chapters 1-8 of *The Story of a Soul*, f. 2 v.; Deposition of Sr. Genevieve; Deposition of Mother Agnes, Jan. 8, 1889; Letter addressed to Sr. Leonie, April 28, 1895; Letter addressed to Abbé Belliere, July 18, 1897.
59. *The Story of a Soul*, IX, 164; Manuscript addressed to Mother Marie de Gonzague: Chapter 9 and 10 of *The Story of a Soul*, f. 11.
60. *The Story of a Soul*, X. 196; Manuscript addressed to Mother Marie de Gonzague: Chapter 9 and 10 of *The Story of a Soul*, f. 39.
61. *The Story of a Soul*, XI 210; Manuscript addressed to Sr. Marie du S. Coeur: Chapter 11 of *TheStory of a Soul*, f. 1 v.; Letter addressed to Celine, Oct. 20, 1888.
62. Apostolic Process, August 1890: Letter addressed to Mother Agnes; Letter addressed to Sr. Genevieve. *Circulaire nécrologique*.
63. André Noche, S.J., in: *La Petite Sainte de Max. Vandermeersch devant la critigue et devant les textes. Editions St. Paul, 1950*, 421.
64. André Noche, S.J., in: *La Petite Sainte de Max. Vandermeersch devant la critigue et devant les textes. Editions St. Paul, 1950*, 421.
65. André Noche, S.J., in: *La Petite Sainte de Max. Vandermeersch devant la critigue et devant les textes. Editions St. Paul, 1950*, 513; Apostolic Process, August 1890: Letter addressed to Mother Agnes, Deposition of Sr. Genevieve.
66. Deposition of Sr. Marie de La Trinité.
67. Deposition of Sr. Genevieve.
68. Petitot, O.P.: *Sainte Thérèse of Lisieux. Une renaissance spirituelle. Editions de la Revue des Jeunes. Paris. Desclée*, 43-44.
69. Letter addressed to Celine, July 6, 1893.
70. Letter addressed to Abbé Belliere, Dec. 26, 1896.
71. *Novissima Verba*, August 30-Sept. 4.
72. *Novissima Verba*, August 10.
73. Letter addressed to Abbe Belliere, June 9, 1897.
74. Letter addressed to Abbe Belliere, July 18, 1897.
75. Letter addressed to Father Rouland, July 14, 1897.
76. *Conseils et Souvenirs dans H.A.* (as found in *The Story of a Soul*), 296.
77. *Esprit de Sainte Thérèse de l'Enfant-Jésus*, 47.
78. *La mélodie de Sainte Cécile*.
79. Laveille: *Sainte Thérèse de l'Enfant-Jésus*, 253.
80. Doc. Lis.
81. Letter addressed to Sr. Leonie, July 12, 1896; Letter addressed to Abbe Belliere, July 18, 1897; *The Story of a Soul*, XII. 246;
C.S., 289; Poem: *Jésus seul*.

Selections from the
Complete Spiritual Doctrine of St. Thérèse of Lisieux,
Reverend Francios Jamart, O.C.D.,
translated by Reverend Walter Van De Putte, C.S.Sp.,
St. Paul Publications, 1961

Chapter 58 • Pope St. Pius X: *Errors of the Modernists; On the Doctrines of the Modernists*

Giuseppe Sarto, who reigned as Supreme Pontiff from 1903 to 1914 and was canonized in 1954, continued many of the projects and convictions of his predecessor, Leo XIII, regarding the Christian social order and the great value of the philosophy of Thomas Aquinas. He considered the latter to be a solid bulwark against the attacks of Modernism, which was judged to involve "the insidious maneuvers of a type of new science" aimed at the destruction of the traditional beliefs of Catholicism. The encyclical *Pascendi Gregis* of 1907 emphasizes the heresies contained in Modernism and how they oppose the classical dogmas of the Church. The Oath against modernism is found in the *motu proprio Sacrorum Antistitum* (1910), stressing, among other things, five pivotal points relative to Modernism:

1. God can be known and proved to exist by natural reason;

2. The external signs of revelation, especially miracles and prophecies, are signs giving certainty and are adapted to all men and times, including the present;

3. The Church was founded by Christ on earth;

4. There is a deposit of faith, and the assertion that dogmas change from one sense to another one different from that held by the Church is heretical;

5. Faith is not a blind sense welling up from the depths of the subconscious under the impulse of the heart and of a will trained to morality, but a real assent of the intellect to truth when hearing it from an external source.

Syllabus Condemning the Errors of the Modernists
Lamentabili Sane
July 3, 1907

With truly lamentable results, our age, casting aside all restraint in its search for the ultimate causes of things, frequently pursues novelties so ardently that it rejects the legacy of the human race. Thus it falls into very serious errors, which are even more serious when they concern sacred authority, the interpretation of Sacred Scripture, and the principal mysteries of Faith. The fact that many Catholic writers also go beyond the limits determined by the Fathers and the Church herself is extremely regrettable. In the name of higher knowledge and historical research (they say), they are looking for the progress of dogmas which is, in reality, nothing but the corruption of dogmas.

These errors are being daily spread among the faithful. Lest they captivate the faithful's minds and corrupt the purity of their faith, His Holiness, Pius X, by Divine Providence, Pope, has decided that the chief errors should be noted and condemned by the Office of this Holy Roman and Universal Inquisition.

Therefore, after a very diligent investigation and consultation with the Reverend Consultors, the Most Eminent and Reverend Lord Cardinals, the General Inquisitors in matters of faith and morals have judged the following propositions to be condemned and proscribed. In fact, by this general decree, they are condemned and proscribed.

1. The ecclesiastical law which prescribes that books concerning the Divine Scriptures are subject to previous examination does not apply to critical scholars and students of scientified exegesis of the Old and New Testament.

2. The Church's interpretation of the Sacred Books is by no means to be rejected; nevertheless, it is subject to the more accurate judgments and correction of the exegetes.

3. From the ecclesiastical judgments and censures passed against free and more scientific exegesis, one can conclude that the Faith the Church proposes contradicts history and that Catholic teaching cannot really be reconciled with the true origins of the Christian religion.

4. Even by dogmatic definitions the Church's magisterium cannot determine the genuine sense of the Sacred Scriptures.

5. Since the deposit of faith contains only revealed truths, the Church has no rights to pass judgments on the assertions of the human sciences.

6. The "Church learning" and the "Church teaching" collaborate in such a way in defining truths that it only remains for the "Church teaching" to sanction the opinions of the "Church learning."

7. In proscribing errors, the Church cannot demand any internal assent from the faithful by which the judgments she issues are to be embraced.

8. They are free from all blame who treat lightly the condemnations passed by the Sacred Congregation of the Index or by the Roman Congregations.

9. They display excessive simplicity or ignorance who believe that God is really the author of the Sacred Scriptures.

10. The inspiration of the books of the Old Testament consists in this: The Israelite writers handed down religious doctrines under a peculiar aspect which was either little or not at all known to the Gentiles.

11. Divine inspiration does not extend to all of Sacred Scriptures so that it renders its parts, each and every one, free from every error.

12. If he wishes to apply himself usefully to Biblical studies, the exegete must first put aside all preconceived opinions about the supernatural origin of Sacred Scripture and interpret it the same as any other merely human document.

13. The Evangelists themselves, as well as the Christians of the second and third generations, artificially arranged the evangelical parables. In such a way they explained the scanty fruit of the preaching of Christ among the Jews.

14. In many narrations the Evangelists recorded, not so much things that are true, as things which, even though false, they judged to be more profitable for their readers.

15. Until the time the canon was defined and constituted, the Gospels were increased by additions and corrections. Therefore there remained in them only a faint and uncertain trace of the doctrine of Christ.

16. The narrations of John are not properly history, but a mystical contemplation of the Gospel. The discourses contained in his Gospel are theological meditations, lacking historical truth concerning the mystery of salvation.

17. The fourth Gospel exaggerated miracles not only in order that the extraordinary might stand out but also in order that it might become more suitable for showing forth the work and glory of the Word Incarnate.

18. John claims for himself the quality of witness concerning Christ. In reality, however, he is only a distinguished witness of the Christian life, or of the life of Christ in the Church at the close of the first century.

19. Heterodox exegetes have expressed the true sense of the Scriptures more faithfully than Catholic exegetes.

20. Revelation could be nothing else than the consciousness man acquired of his revelation to God.

21. Revelation, constituting the object of the Catholic faith, was not completed with the Apostles.

22. The dogmas the Church holds out as revealed are not truths which have fallen from heaven. They are an interpretation of religious facts which the human mind has acquired by laboring effort.

23. Opposition may, and actually does, exist between the facts narrated in Sacred Scripture and the Church's dogmas which rest on them. Thus the critic may reject as false facts the Church holds as most certain.

24. The exegete who constructs premises from which it follows that dog-

mas are historically false or doubtful is not to be reproved as long as he does not directly deny the dogmas themselves.

25. The assent of faith ultimately rests on a mass of probabilities.

26. The dogmas of the Faith are to be held only according to their practical sense; that is to say, as preceptive norms of conduct and not as norms of believing.

27. The divinity of Jesus Christ is not proved from the Gospels. It is a dogma which the Christian conscience has derived from the notion of the Messias.

28. While He was exercising His ministry, Jesus did not speak with the object of teaching He was the Messias, nor did His miracles tend to prove it.

29. It is permissible to grant that the Christ of history is far inferior to the Christ Who is the object of faith.

30. In all the evangelical texts the name "Son of God" is equivalent only to that of "Messias." It does not in the least way signify that Christ is the true and natural Son of God.

31. The doctrine concerning Christ taught by Paul, John, and the Councils of Nicaea, Ephesus, and Chalcedon is not that which Jesus taught but that which the Christian conscience conceived concerning Jesus.

32. It is impossible to reconcile the natural sense of the Gospel texts with the sense taught by our theologians concerning the conscience and the infallible knowledge of Jesus Christ.

33. Everyone who is not led by preconceived opinions can readily see that either Jesus professed an error concerning the immediate Messianic coming or the greater part of His doctrine as contained in the Gospels is destitute of authenticity.

34. The critics can ascribe to Christ a knowledge without limits only on a hypothesis which cannot be historically conceived and which is repugnant to the moral sense. That hypothesis is that Christ as man possessed the knowledge of God and yet was unwilling to communicate the knowledge of a great many things to His disciples and posterity.

35. Christ did not always possess the consciousness of His Messianic dignity.

36. The Resurrection of the Savior is not properly a fact of the historical order. It is a fact of merely the supernatural order (neither demonstrated nor demonstrable) which the Christian conscience gradually derived from other facts.

37. In the beginning, faith in the Resurrection of Christ was not so much in the fact itself of the Resurrection as in the immortal life of Christ with God.

38. The doctrine of the expiatory death of Christ is Pauline and not evangelical.

39. The opinions concerning the origin of the Sacraments which the Fathers of Trent held and which certainly influenced their dogmatic canons are very different from those which now rightly exist among historians who examine Christianity.

40. The Sacraments had their origin in the fact that the Apostles and their successors, swayed and moved by circumstances and events, interpreted some idea and intention of Christ.

41. The Sacraments are intended merely to recall to man's mind the ever beneficent presence of the Creator.

42. The Christian community imposed the necessity of Baptism, adopted it as a necessary rite, and added to it the obligation of the Christian profession.

43. The practice of administering Baptism to infants was a disciplinary evolution, which became one of the causes why the Sacrament was divided into two, namely, Baptism and Penance.

44. There is nothing to prove that the rite of the Sacrament of Confirmation was employed by the Apostles. The formal distinction of the two Sacraments of Baptism and Confirmation does not pertain to the history of primitive Christianity.

45. Not everything which Paul narrates concerning the institution of the Eucharist (I Cor. 11:23-25) is to be taken historically.

46. In the primitive Church the concept of the Christian sinner reconciled by the authority of the Church did not exist. Only very slowly did the Church accustom herself to this concept. As a matter of fact, even after Penance was recognized as an institution of the Church, it was not called a Sacrament since it would be held as a disgraceful Sacrament.

47. The words of the Lord, "Receive the Holy Spirit; whose sins you shall forgive, they are forgiven them and whose sins you shall retain, they are retained" (John 20:22-23), in no way refer to the Sacrament of Penance, in spite of what it pleased the Fathers of Trent to say.

48. In his Epistle (Ch. 5:14-15) James did not intend to promulgate a Sacrament of Christ but only commend a pious custom. If in this custom he happens to distinguish a means of grace, it is not in that rigorous manner in which it was taken by the theologians who laid down the notion and number of the Sacraments.

49. When the Christian supper gradually assumed the nature of a liturgical

action those who customarily presided over the supper acquired the sacerdotal character.

50. The elders who fulfilled the office of watching over the gatherings of the faithful were instituted by the Apostles as priests or bishops to provide for the necessary ordering of the increasing communities and not properly for the perpetuation of the Apostolic mission and power.

51. It is impossible that Matrimony could have become a Sacrament of the new law until later in the Church since it was necessary that a full theological explication of the doctrine of grace and the Sacraments should first take place before Matrimony should be held as a Sacrament.

52. It was far from the mind of Christ to found a Church as a society which would continue on earth for a long course of centuries. On the contrary, in the mind of Christ the kingdom of heaven together with the end of the world was about to come immediately.

53. The organic constitution of the Church is not immutable. Like human society, Christian society is subject to a perpetual evolution.

54. Dogmas, Sacraments and hierarchy, both their notion and reality, are only interpretations and evolutions of the Christian intelligence which have increased and perfected by an external series of additions the little germ latent in the Gospel.

55. Simon Peter never even suspected that Christ entrusted the primacy in the Church to him.

56. The Roman Church became the head of all the churches, not through the ordinance of Divine Providence, but merely through political conditions.

57. The Church has shown that she is hostile to the progress of the natural and theological sciences.

58. Truth is no more immutable than man himself, since it evolved with him, in him, and through him.

59. Christ did not teach a determined body of doctrine applicable to all times and all men, but rather inaugurated a religious movement adapted or to be adapted to different times and places.

60. Christian Doctrine was originally Judaic. Through successive evolutions it became first Pauline, then Joannine, finally Hellenic and universal.

61. It may be said without paradox that there is no chapter of Scripture, from the first of Genesis to the last of the Apocalypse, which contains a doctrine absolutely identical with that which the Church teaches on the same mat-

ter. For the same reason, therefore, no chapter of Scripture has the same sense for the critic and the theologian.

62. The chief articles of the Apostles' Creed did not have the same sense for the Christians of the first ages as they have for the Christians of our time.

63. The Church shows that she is incapable of effectively maintaining evangelical ethics since she obstinately clings to immutable doctrines which cannot be reconciled with modern progress.

64. Scientific progress demands that the concepts of Christian doctrine concerning God, creation, revelation, the Person of the Incarnate Word, and Redemption be re-adjusted.

65. Modern Catholicism can be reconciled with true science only if it is transformed into a non-dogmatic Christianity; that is to say, into a broad and liberal Protestantism.

The following Thursday, the fourth day of the same month and year, all these matters were accurately reported to our Most Holy Lord, Pope Pius X. His Holiness approved and confirmed the decree of the Most Eminent Fathers and ordered that each and every one of the above-listed propositions be held by all as condemned and proscribed.

Peter Palombelli,
Notary of the Holy Roman and Universal Inquisition

Pascendi Gregis
On the Doctrines of the Modernists
Venerable Brethren, Health and
The Apostolic Blessing:

Duty of the Apostolic See

One of the primary obligations assigned by Christ to the office divinely committed to Us of feeding the Lord's flock is that of guarding with the greatest vigilance the deposit of the faith delivered to the saints, rejecting the profane novelties of words and the gainsaying of knowledge falsely so called. There has never been a time when this watchfulness of the supreme pastor was not necessary to the Catholic body, for owing to the efforts of the enemy of the human race, there have never been lacking "men speaking perverse things," "vain talkers and seducers," "erring and driving into error." It must, however, be confessed that these latter days have witnessed a notable increase in the number of the enemies of the Cross of Christ, who, by arts entirely new and full of deceit, are striving to destroy the vital energy of the Church, and, as far as in them lies, utterly to subvert the very Kingdom of Christ. Wherefore We may no longer keep silence, lest We should seem to fail in Our most sacred duty, and lest the kindness that, in the hope of wiser counsels, We have hitherto shown them, should be set down to lack of diligence in the discharge of Our office.

Necessity of Immediate Action

That We should act without delay in this matter is made imperative especially by the fact that the partisans of error are to be sought not only among the Church's open enemies; but, what is to be most dreaded and deplored, in her very bosom, and are the more mischievous the less they keep in the open. We allude, Venerable Brethren, to many who belong to the Catholic laity, and, what is much more sad, to the ranks of the priesthood itself, who, animated by a false zeal for the Church, lacking the solid safeguards of philosophy and theology, nay more, thoroughly imbued with the poisonous doctrines taught by the enemies of the Church, and lost to all sense of modesty, put themselves forward as reformers of the Church; and, forming more boldly into line of attack, assail all that is most sacred in the work of Christ, not sparing even the Person of the Divine Redeemer, Whom, with sacrilegious audacity, they degrade to the condition of a simple and ordinary man.

Finally, there is the fact which is all but fatal to the hope of cure that their very doctrines have given such a bent to their minds, that they disdain all authority and brook no restraint; and relying upon a false conscience, they attempt to ascribe to a love of truth that which is in reality the result of pride and obstinacy.

The Modernist Personality

To proceed in an orderly manner in this somewhat abstruse subject, it must first of all be noted that the Modernist sustains and includes within himself a manifold personality; he is a philosopher, a believer, a theologian, an historian, a critic, an apologist, a reformer. These roles must be clearly distinguished one from another by all who would accurately understand their system and thoroughly grasp the principles and the outcome of their doctrines.

Agnosticism

We begin, then, with the philosopher. Modernists place the foundation of religious philosophy in that doctrine which is commonly called *Agnosticism*. According to this teaching human reason is confined entirely within the field of phenomena, that is to say, to things that appear, and in the manner in which they appear: it has neither the right nor the power to overstep these limits. Hence it is incapable of lifting itself up to God, and of recognizing His existence, even by means of visible things. From this it is inferred that God can never be the direct object of science, and that, as regards history, He must not be considered as an historical subject. Given these premises, everyone will at once perceive what becomes of *Natural Theology*, of the *motives of credibility*, of *external revelation*. The Modernists simply sweep them entirely aside; they include them in *Intellectualism*, which they denounce as a system which is ridiculous and long since defunct. Nor does the fact that the Church has formally condemned these portentous errors exercise the slightest restraint upon them. Yet the Vatican Council has defined, "If anyone says that the one true God, our Creator and Lord, cannot be known with certainty by the natural light of human reason by means of the things that are made, let him be anathema"; and also, "If anyone says that it is not possible or not expedient that man be taught, through the medium of divine revelation, about God and the worship to be paid Him, let him be anathema"; and finally, "If anyone says that divine revelation cannot be made credible by external signs, and that therefore men should be drawn to the faith only by their personal internal experience or by private inspiration, let him be anathema" (*De Fide*, can. 3). It may be asked, in what way do the Modernists contrive to make the transition from *Agnosticism*, which is a state of pure nescience, to scientific and historic *Atheism*, which is a doctrine of positive denial; and consequently, by what legitimate process of reasoning; they proceed from the fact of ignorance as to whether God has in fact intervened in the history of the human race or not, to explain this history, leaving God out altogether, as if He really had not intervened. Let him answer who can. Yet it is a fixed and established principle among them that both science and history must be atheistic: and within their boundaries there is room for nothing but *phenomena*; God and all that is divine are utterly excluded.

We shall soon see clearly what, as a consequence of this most absurd teaching, must be held touching the most sacred Person of Christ, and the mysteries of His life and death, and of His Resurrection and Ascension into Heaven.

Vital Immanence

However, this *Agnosticism* is only the negative part of the system of the Modernists: the positive part consists in what they call *vital immanence*. Thus they advance from one to the other. Religion, whether natural or supernatural, must, like every other fact, admit of some explanation. But when natural theology has been destroyed, and the road to revelation closed by the rejection of the arguments of credibility, and all external revelation absolutely denied, it is clear that this explanation will be sought in vain outside of man himself. It must, therefore, be looked for in man; and since religion is a form of life, the explanation must certainly be found in the life of man. In this way is formulated the principle of *religious immanence*. Moreover, the first actuation, so to speak, of every vital phenomenon and religion, as noted above, belongs to this category — is due to a certain need or impulsion; but speaking more particularly of life, it has its origin in a movement of the heart, which movement is called a *sense*. Therefore, as God is the object of religion, we must conclude that faith, which is the basis and foundation of all religion, must consist in a certain interior sense, originating in a need of the divine. This need of the divine, which is experienced only in special and favorable circumstances, cannot of itself appertain to the domain of consciousness, but is first latent beneath consciousness, or, to borrow a term from modern philosophy, in the subconsciousness, where also its root lies hidden and undetected.

Therefore, in virtue of the first canon deduced from agnosticism, whatever there is in His history suggestive of the divine, must be rejected. Then, according to the second canon, the historical Person of Christ was transfigured by faith; therefore everything that raises it above historical conditions must be removed. Lastly, the third canon, which lays down that the Person of Christ has been *disfigured* by faith, requires that everything should be excluded, deeds and words and all else, that is not in strict keeping with His character, condition, and education, and with the place and time in which He lived. A method of reasoning which is passing strange, but in it we have the Modernist criticism.

So far, Venerable Brethren, there has been no mention of the intellect. It also, according to the teaching of the Modernists, has its part in the act of faith. In that sense of which We have frequently spoken, since *sense* is not knowledge, they say God, indeed, presents Himself to man, but in a manner so confused and indistinct that He can hardly be perceived by the believer. It is therefore necessary that a certain light should be cast upon this sense so that God may clearly stand out in relief and be set apart from it. This is the task of the intellect, whose office it is to reflect and to analyze; and by means of it, man first transforms into mental pictures the vital phenomena which arise within him, and then expresses them in words. Hence the common saying of Modernists: that the religious man must think his faith.

The operation of the mind in this work is a double one: first, by a natural and spontaneous act it expresses its concept in a simple, popular statement; then, on reflection and deeper consideration, or, as they say, *by elaborating its thought*, it expresses the idea in *secondary* propositions, which are derived from the first, but are more precise and distinct. These *secondary* propositions, if they finally receive the approval of the supreme Magisterium of the Church, constitute *dogma*.

The Modernist as Believer: Individual Experience and Religious Certitude

Thus far, Venerable Brethren, We have considered the Modernist as a Philosopher. Now if we proceed to consider him as a believer, and seek to know how the believer, according to Modernism, is marked off from the Philosopher, it must be observed that, although the Philosopher recognizes *the reality of the divine* as the object of faith, still this *reality* is not to be found by him but in the heart of the believer, as an object of feeling and affirmation, and therefore confined within the sphere of phenomena; but the question as to whether in itself it exists outside that feeling and affirmation is one which the Philosopher passes over and neglects. For the Modernist believer, on the contrary, it is an established and certain fact that the *reality* of the divine does really exist in itself and quite independently of the person who believes in it. If you ask on what foundation this assertion of the believer rests, he answers: In the personal *experience* of the individual.

In *the religious sense* one must recognize a kind of intuition of the heart which puts man in immediate contact with the reality of God and infuses such a persuasion of God's existence and His action both within and without man as far to exceed any scientific conviction. They assert, therefore, the existence of a real experience, and one of a kind that surpasses all rational experience.

Tradition, as understood by the Modernists, is a communication with others of an *original experience*, through preaching by means of the intellectual formula. To this formula, in addition to its *representative* value, they attribute a species of *suggestive* efficacy which acts firstly in the believer by stimulating the *religious sense*, should it happen to have grown sluggish, and by renewing the *experience* once acquired, and secondly, in those who do not yet believe by awakening in them for the first *time the religious sense* and producing the experience. Hence should it be further asked whether Christ has wrought real miracles, and made real prophecies, whether He rose truly from the dead and ascended into Heaven, the answer of agnostic science will be in the negative and the answer of faith in the affirmative — yet there will not be, on that account, any conflict between them. For it will be denied by the philosopher as a philosopher speaking to philosophers and considering Christ only in His *historical reality*; and it will be affirmed by the believer as a believer speaking to believers and considering the life of Christ as lived again by the faith and in the faith.

Hence we have the Modernist axiom that the religious evolution ought to be brought into accord with the moral and intellectual, or as one whom they regard as their leader has expressed it, ought to be subject to it. Finally, man does not suffer a dualism to exist in himself, and the believer therefore feels within him an impelling need so to harmonize faith with science that it may never oppose the general conception which science sets forth concerning the universe.

So, too, when they treat of philosophy, history, and criticism, are wont to display a manifold contempt for Catholic doctrines, for the Holy Fathers, for the Ecumenical Councils, for the ecclesiastical Magisterium; and should they be taken to task for this, they complain that they are being deprived of their liberty. Lastly, maintaining the theory that faith must be subject to science, they continuously and openly rebuke the Church on the ground that she resolutely refuses to submit and accommodate her dogmas to the opinions of philosophy; while they, on their side, having for this purpose blotted out the old theology, endeavor to introduce a new theology which shall support the aberrations of philosophers.

The Church

A wider field for comment is opened when we come to what the Modernist school has imagined to be the nature of the Church. They begin with the supposition that the Church has its birth in a double need; first, the need of the individual believer to communicate his faith to others, especially if he has had some original and special experience, and secondly, when the faith has become common to many, the need of the *collectivity* to form itself into a society and to guard, promote, and propagate the common good. What, then, is the Church?

It is the product of the *collective conscience*, that is to say of the association of individual consciences which by virtue of the principle of *vital permanence*, depend all on one first believer, who for Catholics is Christ. Now every society needs a directing authority to guide its members towards the common end, to foster prudently the elements of cohesion, which in a religious society are doctrine and worship. Hence the triple authority in the Catholic Church, *disciplinary, dogmatic, liturgical*. The nature of this authority is to be gathered from its origin, and its rights and duties from its nature.

It is for the ecclesiastical authority, therefore, to adopt a democratic form, unless it wishes to provoke and foment an intestine conflict in the consciences of mankind. The penalty of refusal is disaster. For it is madness to think that the sentiment of liberty, as it now obtains, can recede. Were it forcibly pent up and held in bonds, the more terrible would be its outburst, sweeping away at once both Church and religion. Such is the situation in the minds of the Modernists, and their one great anxiety is, in consequence, to find a way of conciliation between the authority of the Church and the liberty of the believers.

The State must be separated from the Church, and the Catholic from the Citizen. Every Catholic, from the fact that he is also a citizen, has the right and the duty to work for the common good in the way he thinks best, without troubling himself about the authority of the Church, without paying any heed to its wishes, its counsels, its orders — nay, even in spite of its rebukes. For the Church to trace out and prescribe for the citizen any line of action, on any pretext whatsoever, is to be guilty of an abuse of authority, against which one is bound to protest with all one's might.

But it is not enough for the Modernist school that the State should be separated from the Church. For as faith is to be subordinated to science as far as phenomenal elements are concerned, so too in temporal matters the Church must be subject to the State.

Their general direction for the Church is as follows: that the ecclesiastical authority, since its end is entirely spiritual, should strip itself of that external pomp which adorns it in the eyes of the public. In this, they forget that while religion is for the soul, it is not exclusively for the soul, and that the honor paid to authority is reflected back on Christ who instituted it.

To conclude this whole question of faith and its various branches, we have still to consider, Venerable Brethren, what the Modernists have to say about the development of the one and the other. First of all they lay down the general principle that in a living religion everything is subject to change, and must in fact be changed. In this way they pass to what is practically their principal doctrine, namely, *evolution*. To the laws of evolution everything is subject under penalty of death — dogma, Church, worship, the Books we revere as sacred, even faith itself. The enunciation of this principle will not be a matter of surprise to anyone who bears in mind what the Modernists have had to say about each of these subjects.

Hence, by those who study more closely the ideas of the Modernists, evolution is descibed as a resultant from the conflict of two forces, one of them tending towards progress, the other towards conservation. The conserving force exists in the Church and is found in tradition; tradition is represented by religious authority, and this both by right and in fact. For by right it is in the very nature of authority to protect tradition, and, in fact, since authority, raised as it is above the contingencies of life, feels hardly, or not at all, the spurs of progress. The progressive force, on the contrary, which responds to the inner needs, lies in the individual consciences and works in them — especially in such of them as are in more close and intimate contact with life. The individual consciences, or some of them, act on the collective conscience, which brings pressure to bear on the depositaries of authority to make terms and to keep to them.

With all this in mind, one understands how it is that the Modernists express astonishment when they are reprimanded or punished. What is imputed to them as a fault they regard as a sacred duty. They understand the needs of consciences better than anyone else, since they come into closer touch with them than does the ecclesiastical authority. Nay, they embody them, so to speak, in themselves. Hence, for them to speak and to write publicly is a bounden duty. Let authority rebuke them if it pleases — they have their own conscience on their side and an intimate experience which tells them with certainty that what they deserve is not blame but praise.

It is thus, Venerable Brethren, that for the Modernists, whether as authors or propagandists, there is to be nothing stable, nothing immutable in the Church.

On the subject of revelation and dogma in particular, the doctrine of the Modernists offers nothing new. We find it condemned in the Syllabus of Pius IX, where it is enunciated in these terms: "Divine revelation is imperfect, and therefore subject to continual and indefinite progress, corresponding with the progress of human reason"; and condemned still more solemnly in the Vatican Council: "The doctrine of the faith which God has revealed has not been proposed to human intelligences to be perfected by them as if it were a philosophical system, but as a divine deposit entrusted to the Spouse of Christ to be faithfully guarded and infallibly interpreted. Hence also that sense of the sacred dogmas is to be perpetually retained which our Holy Mother the Church has once declared, nor is this sense ever to be abandoned on plea or pretext of a more profound comprehension of the truth." Nor is the development of our knowledge, even concerning the faith, barred by this pronouncement; on the contrary, it is supported and maintained. For the same Council continues: "Let intelligence and sciences and wisdom, therefore, increase and progress abundantly and vigorously in individuals and in the mass, in the believer and in the whole Church, throughout the ages and the centuries — but only in its own kind, that is, according to the same dogma, the same sense, the same acceptation."

Thus, when treating of Christ, the historian must set aside all that surpasses man in his natural condition, according to what psychology tells us of him, or according to what we gather from the place and period of his existence. Thus, they will not allow that Christ ever uttered those things which do not seem to be within the capacity of the multitudes that listened to Him. Hence they delete from His *real* history and transfer to faith all the allegories found in His discourses. We may peradventure enquire on what principle they make these divisions? Their reply is that they argue from the character of the man, from his condition of life, from his education, from the complexus of the circumstances under which the facts took place, in short, if We understand them aright, on a principle which in the last analysis is merely *subjective*. Their method is to put themselves into the position and person of Christ, and then to attribute to Him what they would have done under like circumstances. In this way, absolutely *a priori* and acting on philosophical principles which they hold but which they profess to ignore, they proclaim that Christ, according to what they call His *real* history, was not God and never did anything divine, and that as man He did and said only what they, judging from the time in which He lived, consider that He ought to have said or done. Thus, as we have already said, we have a twofold Christ: a real Christ, and a Christ, the one of faith, who never really existed; a Christ who has lived at a given time and in a given place, and a Christ who has never lived outside the pious meditations of the believer — the Christ for instance, whom we find in the Gospel of St. John, which, according to them, is mere meditation from beginning to end.

And now with Our eyes fixed upon the whole system, no one will be surprised that We should define it to be the synthesis of all heresies. Undoubtedly, were anyone to attempt the task of collecting together all the errors that have been broached against the faith and to concentrate into one the sap and substance of them all, he could not succeed in doing so better than the Modernists have done. Nay, they have gone farther than this, for, as We have already intimated, their system means the destruction not of the Catholic religion alone, but of all religion. Hence the rationalists are not wanting in their applause, and the most frank and sincere amongst them congratulate themselves in having found in the Modernists the most valuable of all allies.

In the first place, with regard to studies, We will and strictly ordain that scholastic philosophy be made the basis of the sacred sciences. And let it be clearly understood above all things that when We prescribe scholastic philosophy We understand chiefly that which the Angelic Doctor has bequeathed to us, and We, therefore, declare that all the ordinances of Our Predecessor on this subject continue fully in force, and, as far as may be necessary, We do decree anew, and confirm, and order that they shall be strictly observed by all. In seminaries where they have been neglected it will be for the Bishops to exact and require their observance in the future; and let this apply also to the Superiors of religious orders. Further, We admonish Professors to bear well in mind that they cannot set aside St. Thomas, especially in metaphysical questions, without grave disadvantage.

On this philosophical foundation the theological edifice is to be carefully raised. Promote the study of theology, Venerable Brethren, by all means in your power, so that your clerics on leaving the seminaries may carry with them a deep admiration and love of it, and always find in it a source of delight.

We will add that We deem worthy of praise those with full respect for tradition, the Fathers, and the ecclesiastical magisterium, endeavor, with well balanced judgment, and guided by Catholic principles (which is not always the case), to illustrate positive theology by throwing upon it the light of true history. It is certainly necessary that positive theology should be held in greater appreciation than it has been in the past, but this must be done without detriment to scholastic theology; and those are to be disapproved as Modernists who exalt positive theology in such a way as to seem to despise the scholastic.

With regard to secular studies, let it suffice to recall here what Our Predecessor has admirably said: *Apply yourselves energetically to the study of natural sciences: in which department the things that have been so brilliantly discovered, and so usefully applied, to the admiration of the present age, will be the object of praise and commendation to those who come after us* (Leo XIII. Afloc., March 7, 1880). But this is to be done without interfering with sacred studies, as Our same Predecessor prescribed in these most weighty words: *If you carefully search for the cause of those errors you will find that it lies in the fact that in these days when the natural sciences absorb so much study, the more severe and lofty studies have been proportionately neglected — some of them have almost passed into oblivion, some of them are pursued in a half-hearted or superficial way, and, sad to say, now that the splendor of the former estate is dimmed, they have been disfigured by perverse doctrines and monstrous errors. (Loc. cit.)* We ordain, therefore, that the study of natural sciences in the seminaries be carried out according to the law.

All these prescriptions, both Our own and those of Our Predecessor are to be kept in view whenever there is question of choosing directors and professors for seminaries and Catholic Universities. Anyone who in any way is found to be tainted with Modernism is to be excluded without compunction from these offices, whether of government or of teaching, and those who already occupy them are to be removed. The same policy is to be adopted towards those who openly or secretly lend countenance to Modernism either by extolling the Modernists and excusing their culpable conduct, or by carping at scholasticism, and the Fathers, and the Magisterium of the Church, or by refusing obedience to ecclesiastical authority in any of its depositories; and towards those who show a love of a novelty in history, archaeology, biblical exegesis; and finally towards those who neglect the sacred sciences or appear to prefer to them the secular. In all this question of studies, Venerable Brethren, you cannot be too watchful or too constant, but most of all in the choice of professors, for as a rule the students are modelled after the pattern of their masters. Strong in the consciousness of your duty, act always in this matter with prudence and with vigor.

Equal diligence and severity are to be used in examining and selecting candidates for Holy Orders.

Episcopal Vigilance Over Publications

It is also the duty of the Bishops to prevent writings in Modernists, or whatever savors of Modernism or promotes it, from being read when they have been published, and to hinder their publication when they are not.

Censorship

It is not enough to hinder the reading and the sale of bad books — it is also necessary to prevent them from being published. Hence, let the Bishops use the utmost strictness in granting permission to print.

Conclusion

This, Venerable Brethren, is what We have thought it Our duty to write to you for the salvation of all who believe. The adversaries of the Church will doubtlessly abuse what We have said to refurbish the old calumny by which We are traduced as the enemy of science and of the progress of humanity. As a fresh answer to such accusations, which the history of the Christian religion refutes by never-failing evidence, it is Our intention to establish by every means in our power a special Institute in which, through the co-operation of those Catholics who are most eminent for their learning, the advance of science and every other department of knowledge may be promoted under the guidance and teaching of Catholic truth, God grant that We may happily realize Our design with the assistance of all those who bear a sincere love for the Church of Christ.

Given at St. Peter's, Rome, on the eighth day of September, one thousand nine hundred and seven, the fifth year of our Pontificate.

Pius X, Pope

Chapter 59 • James Cardinal Gibbons: *The Faith of Our Fathers*

Cardinal Gibbons (1834-1921) was an extraordinary example of an American Catholic prelate dedicated to ecumenism in the difficult late nineteenth and early twentieth centuries. These were crucial times for Catholicism in America, and Cardinal Gibbons was one of the members of the Catholic hierarchy who succeeded well in his dual commitment to American democracy and Catholicism — in fact, he considered American democracy as a special opportunity for the Church.

He was born in Baltimore, studied at St. Charles College, was ordained in 1861, and became in succession vicar apostolic of North Carolina in 1868, bishop of Richmond in 1872, coadjutor and finally successor to the archbishop of Baltimore in 1877, and a cardinal in 1886.

He was very influential in establishing the Catholic University of America in Washington, D.C.

The Faith of Our Fathers
Introduction

My Dear Reader: — Perhaps this is the first time in your life that you have handled a book in which the doctrines of the Catholic Church are expounded by one of her own sons.

I do not wonder that the Church is hated by those who learn what she is from her enemies. It is natural for an honest man to loathe an institution whose history he believes to be marked by bloodshed, crime, and fraud.

Had I been educated as they were, and surrounded by an atmosphere hostile to the Church, perhaps I should be unfortunate enough to be breathing vengeance against her to-day, instead of consecrating my life to her defense.

It is not of their hostility that I complain, but because the judgment they have formed of her is based upon the reckless assertions of her enemies, and not upon those of impartial witnesses.

Remember that nothing is so essential as the salvation of your immortal soul, "for what doth it profit a man, if he gain the whole world, and lose his own soul?"

May God give you light to see the truth, and, having seen it, may He give you courage and strength to follow it!

Chapter I

The Blessed Trinity, the Incarnation, Etc.

The Catholic Church teaches that there is but one God, who is infinite in knowledge, in power, in goodness, and in every other perfection; who created all things by His omnipotence, and governs them by His Providence.

In this one God there are three distinct Persons — the Father, the Son, and the Holy Spirit, who are perfectly equal to each other.

We believe that Jesus Christ, the Second Person of the Blessed Trinity, is perfect God and perfect Man. "He is God of the substance of the Father, begotten before time; and He is Man of the substance of His Mother, born in time." Out of love for us, and in order to rescue us from the miseries entailed upon us by the disobedience of our first parents, the Divine Word descended from heaven, and became Man in the womb of the Virgin Mary, by the operation of the Holy Spirit. He was born on Christmas day, in a stable at Bethlehem.

After having led a life of obscurity for about thirty years, chiefly at Nazareth, He commenced His public career. He associated with Him a number of men who are named Apostles, whom He instructed in the doctrines of the religion which He established.

For three years, He went about doing good, giving sight to the blind, hearing to the deaf, healing all kinds of diseases, raising the dead to life, and preaching throughout Judea the new Gospel of peace.

On Good Friday He was crucified on Mount Calvary, and thus purchased for us redemption by His death. Hence Jesus exclusively bears the title of *Savior* and *Redeemer*.

We are commanded, by Jesus, suffering and dying for us, to imitate Him by the crucifixion of our flesh, and by acts of daily mortification. "If any one," He says, "will come after Me, let him deny himself, and take up his cross daily and follow Me."

The Cross is held in the highest reverence by Catholics, because it was the instrument of our Savior's crucifixion.

We do not, of course, attach any intrinsic virtue to the Cross; this would be sinful and idolatrous. Our veneration is referred to Him who died upon it.

It is also a very ancient and pious practice for the faithful to make on their person the sign of the Cross, saying at the same time: "In the name of the Father, and of the Son, and of the Holy Spirit."

By the sign of the cross we make a profession of our faith in the Trinity and the Incarnation, and perform a most salutary act of religion.

We believe that on Easter Sunday Jesus Christ manifested His divine power by raising Himself to life, and that having spent forty days on earth, after His resurrection, instructing His disciples, He ascended to heaven from the Mount of Olives.

On the Feast of Pentecost, or Whitsunday, ten days after His Ascension, our Savior sent, as He had promised, His Holy Spirit to His disciples, while they were assembled together in prayer. The Holy Spirit purified their hearts from sin, and imparted to them a full knowledge of those doctrines of salvation which they were instructed to preach. On the same Feast of Pentecost the Apostles commenced their sublime mission, from which day, accordingly, we date the active life of the Catholic Church.

Our Redeemer gave the most ample authority to the Apostles to teach in His name; commanding them to "preach the Gospel to every creature."

He was pleased to stamp upon His Church certain shining marks, by which every sincere inquirer could easily recognize her as His only Spouse. The principal marks or characteristics of the true Church are her Unity, Sanctity, Catholocity, and Apostolicity, to which may be added the Infallibility of her teaching and the Perpetuity of her existence.

Chapter II
The Unity of the Church

By unity is meant that the members of the true Church must be united in the belief of the same doctrines of revelation, and in the acknowledgement of the authority of the same pastors. Heresy and schism are opposed to Christian unity. By heresy, a man rejects one or more articles of the Christian faith. By schism, he spurns the authority of his spiritual superiors. That our Savior requires this unity of faith and government in His members, is evident from various passages of Holy Writ.

Unity of government is not less essential to the Church of Christ than unity of doctrine. Our divine Savior never speaks of His Churches, but of His *Church.* He does not say: "Upon this rock I will build my Churches," but, "Upon this rock I will build my Church," from which words we must conclude, that it never was His intention to establish or to sanction various conflicting denominations, but one corporate body, with all the members united under one visible Head; for as the Church is a visible body, it must have a visible head.

In fact, our common sense alone, apart from revelation, is sufficient to convince us that God could not be the author of various opposing systems of religion. God is essentially one. He is Truth itself. How could the God of truth affirm, for instance, to one body of Christians that there are three Persons in God, and to another that there is only one Person in God? How could He say to one individual that Jesus Christ is God, and to another that He is only man, How can He tell me that the punishments of the wicked are eternal, and tell another that they are not eternal? One of these contradictory statements must be false. "God is not the God of dissension, but of peace."

The same admirable unity that exists in matters of faith, is also established in the government of the Church. All the members of the vast body of Catholic Christians are as intimately united to one visible Chief as the members of the human body are joined to the head. The faithful of each Parish are subject to their immediate Pastor. Each Pastor is subordinate to his Bishop, and each Bishop of Christendom acknowledges the jurisdiction of the Bishop of Rome, the successor of St. Peter, and Head of the Catholic Church.

But it may be asked, is not this unity of faith impaired by those doctrinal definitions which the Church has promulgated from time to time? We answer: No new dogma, unknown to the Apostles, not contained in the primitive Christian revelation, can be admitted. For the Apostles received the whole deposit of God's word, according to the promise of our Lord: "When He shall come, the Spirit of truth, He shall teach you all truth." And so the Church proposes the doctrines of faith, such as they came from the lips of Christ, and as the Holy Spirit taught them to the Apostles at the birth of the Christian law — doctrines which know neither variation nor decay.

Hence, whenever it has been defined that any point of doctrine pertained to the Catholic faith, it was always understood that this was equivalent to the declaration that the doctrine in question had been revealed to the Apostles, and had come down to us from them, either by Scripture or tradition. And as the acts of all the Council, and the history of every definition of faith evidently show, it was never contended that *a new revelation* had been made, but every inquiry was directed to this one point — whether the doctrine in question was contained in the Sacred Scriptures or in the Apostolic traditions.

A revealed truth frequently has a very extensive scope, and is directed against error under its many changing forms. Nor is it necessary that those who receive this revelation in the first instance, should be explicitly acquainted with its full import, or cognizant of all its hearings.

So, too, in the beginning, many truths might have been proposed somewhat *obscurely* or *less clearly*; they might have been *less urgently insisted upon*, because there was no heresy, no contrary teaching to render a more explicit declaration necessary. Now, a doctrine which is *implicitly, less clearly, not so earnestly* proposed, may be overlooked, misunderstood, called in question; consequently, it may happen that some articles are now universally believed in the Church, in regard to which doubts and controversies existed in former ages, even within the bosom of the Church. "Those who err in belief do but serve to bring out more clearly the soundness of those who believe rightly. For there are many things which *lay hidden in the Scriptures*, and when heretics were cut off, they vexed the Church of God with disputes; then the hidden things were *brought to light*, and the will of God was made known."

This kind of *progress in faith* we can and do admit; but the truth is not changed thereby. As Albertus Magnus says: "It would be more correct to style this the progress of the believer in the faith, than of the faith in the believer."

The Church of Christ is a faithful and ever watchful guardian of the dogmas which have been committed to her charge. In this sacred deposit she changes nothing, she takes nothing from it, she adds nothing to it."

Chapter VII
Infallible Authority of the Church

The Church has authority from God to teach regarding faith and morals; and in her teaching she is preserved from error by the special guidance of the Holy Spirit.

The prerogative of infallibility is clearly deduced from the attributes of the Church already mentioned. The Church is One, Holy, Catholic, and Apostolic. Preaching the same creed everywhere, and at all times; teaching holiness and truth, she is, of course, essentially unerring in her doctrine.

That the Church was infallible in the Apostolic age, is denied by no Christian. We never question the truth of the Apostles' declarations; they were, in fact, the only authority in the Church for the first century. The new Testament was not completed till the close of the first century. There is no just ground for denying to the Apostolic teachers of the nineteenth century in which we live, a prerogative clearly possessed by those of the first, especially as the divine Word nowhere intimates that this unerring guidance was to die with the Apostles.

It will not suffice to tell me: "We have an infallible Scripture as a substitute for an infallible apostolate of the first century," for an infallible book is of no use to me without an infallible interpreter.

We have positive evidence from Scripture that the Church cannot err in her teachings. Our blessed Lord, in constituting St. Peter Prince of His Apostles, says to him: "Thou are Peter, and upon this rock I will build My Church, and the gates of hell shall not prevail against it."

Jesus sends forth the Apostles with plenipotentiary powers to preach the Gospel. "As the Father," He says, "hath sent Me, I also send you." "Going therefore, teach all nations, teaching them to observe all things whatsoever I have commanded you." "Preach the Gospel to every creature." "Ye shall be witnesses unto Me in Jerusalem, and in all Judea, and Samaria, and even to the uttermost part of the earth."

This commission evidently applies not to the Apostles only, but also to their successors, to the end of time, since it was utterly impossible for the Apostles personally to preach to the whole world.

From these passages, we see, on the one hand, that the Apostles and their successors have received full powers to announce the Gospel; and on the other, that their hearers are obliged to listen with docility, and to obey not merely by an external compliance, but also by an internal assent of the intellect.

Chapter VIII
The Church and the Bible

The Church, as we have just seen, is the only divinely constituted teacher of Revelation.

Now, the Scripture is the great depository of the Word of God. Therefore, the Church is the divinely appointed Custodian and Interpreter of the Bible. For her office of infallible Guide were superfluous, if each individual could interpret the Bible for himself.

No nation ever had a greater veneration for the Bible than the Jewish people. And yet the Jews never dreamed of settling their religious controversies by a private appeal to the Word of God.

Whenever any religious dispute arose among the people, it was decided by the High Priest and the Sanhedrin, which was a council consisting of seventy-two civil and ecclesiastical judges. The sentence of the High Priest and of his associate judges was to be obeyed under penalty of death.

"But he that will . . . refuse to obey the commandment of the priest, that man shall die, and thou shalt take away the evil from Israel."

Does our Savior reverse this state of things when He comes on earth? Does He tell the Jews to be their own guides in the study of the Scriptures? By no means; but He commands them to obey their constituted teachers, no matter how disedifying might be their private lives. "Then said Jesus to the multitudes and to His disciples: The Scribes and Pharisees sit upon the chair of Moses. All things therefore whatsoever they shall say to you, observe and do."

Of the twelve Apostles, the seventy-two disciples, and early followers of our Lord, only eight have left us any of their sacred writings. And the Gospels and Epistles were addressed to particular persons or particular churches. They were written on the occasion of some emergency, just as Bishops issue Pastoral letters, to correct abuses which may spring up in the Church, or to lay down some rules of conduct for the faithful. The Apostles are never reported to have circulated a single volume of the Holy Scripture, but "they going forth, preached everywhere, the Lord cooperating with them."

We often hear the shibboleth: "The Bible, and the Bible only must be your guide." Why then do you go to the useless expense of building fine churches, and Sabbath-schools? What is the use of your preaching sermons and catechizing the young, if the Bible at home is a sufficient guide for your people?

The Catholic Church, in the plenitude of her authority, in the third Council of Carthage (A.D. 397), separated the chaff from the wheat, and declared what Books were Canonical, and what were apocryphal. Even to this day, the Christian sects do not agree among themselves as to what books are to be accepted as genuine.

But even when you are assured that the Bible contains the Word of God, and nothing but the Word of God, how do you know that the translation is faithful? The Books of Scripture were originally written in Hebrew and Greek, and you have only the translation. Before you are certain that the translation is faithful, you must study the Hebrew and Greek languages, and then compare the translation with the original. How few are capable of this gigantic undertaking!

But after having ascertained to your satisfaction that the translation is faithful, still the Scriptures can never serve as a complete Rule of Faith, and a complete guide to heaven, independently of an authorized, living interpreter.

A competent guide, such as our Lord intended for us, must have three characteristics. It must be within the reach of every one; it must be clear and intelligible; it must be able to satisfy us on all questions relating to faith and morals.

1st. A complete guide of salvation must be within the reach of every inquirer after truth; for, God "wishes all men to be saved, and to come to the knowledge of the truth"; and therefore he must have placed within the reach of every one the means of arriving at the truth. Now, it is clear that the Scriptures could not at any period have been accessible to every one.

They could not have been accessible *to the primitive Christians*, because they were not all written for a long time after the establishment of Christianity.

It was not till the close of the fourth century that the Church framed her Canon of Scripture, and declared the Bible, as we now possess it, to be the genuine word of God. And this was the golden age of Christianity! The most perfect Christians lived and died and went to heaven before the most important parts of the Scriptures were written. And what would have become of them if the Bible alone had been their guide?

The art of printing was not invented till the fifteenth century (1440). How utterly impossible it was to supply every one with a copy of the Scriptures *from the fourth to the fifteenth century!* During that long period, Bibles had to be copied with the pen. There were but a few hundred of them in the Christian world, and these were in the hands of the clergy and the learned.

It was well for Luther that he did not come into the world until a century after the immortal discovery of Guttenberg. A hundred years earlier, his idea of directing two hundred and fifty millions of men to read the Bible would have been received with shouts of laughter, and would inevitably have caused his removal from the pulpit of Wittenberg to a hospital for the insane.

But even if the Bible were at all times accessible to every one, how many millions exist in every age and country, not excepting our own age of boasted enlightenment, who are not accessible to the Bible, because they are incapable of reading the Word of God! Hence, the doctrine of private interpretation would render many men's salvation not only difficult, but impossible.

2d. A competent religious guide must be clear and intelligible to all, so that every one may full understand the true meaning of the instructions it contains. Is the Bible a book intelligible to all?

The Fathers of the Church, though many of them spent their whole lives in the study of the Scriptures, are unanimous in pronouncing the Bible a book full of knotty difficulties. And yet we find in our days pedants, with a mere smattering of biblical knowledge, who see no obscurity at all in the Word of God, and who presume to expound it from Genesis to Revelation. "Fools rush in where angels fear to tread."

Does not the conduct of the Reformers conclusively show the utter folly of interpreting the Scriptures by private judgment? As soon as they rejected the oracle of the Church, and set up their own private judgment as the highest standard of authority, they could hardly agree among themselves on the meaning of a single important text.

3d. A rule of faith, or a competent guide to heaven, must be able to instruct in all the truths necessary for salvation. Now the Scriptures alone do not contain all the truths which a Christian is bound to believe, nor do they explicitly enjoin all the duties which he is obliged to practice.

We must, therefore, conclude that the Scriptures *alone* cannot be a sufficient guide and rule of faith, because they cannot, at any time, be within the reach of every inquirer; because they are not of themselves clear and intelligible even in matters of the highest importance, and because they do not contain all the truths necessary for salvation.

God forbid that any of my readers should be tempted to conclude from what I have said that the Catholic Church is opposed to the reading of the Scriptures, or that she is the enemy of the Bible.

For fifteen centuries, the Church was the sole guardian and depository of the Bible; and if she really feared that sacred Book, who was to prevent her, during that long period, from tearing it in shreds and scattering it to the winds?

Printing was invented in the fifteenth century, and almost a hundred years later came the Reformation. It is often triumphantly said, and I suppose there are some who, even at the present day, are ignorant enough to believe the assertion, that the first edition of the Bible ever published after the invention of printing, was the edition of Martin Luther. The fact is, that before Luther put his pen to paper, no fewer than fifty-six editions of the Scriptures had appeared on the continent of Europe, not to speak of those printed in Great Britain. Of those editions, twenty-one were published in German, one in Spanish, four in French, twenty-one in Italian, five in Flemish, and four in Bohemian.

These facts ought, I think, to convince every candid mind that the Church, far from being opposed to the reading of the Scriptures, does all she can to encourage their perusal.

Chapter XI
Infallibility of the Popes

1st. The infallibility of the Popes does not signify that they are inspired.

2d. Infallibility does not mean that the Pope is impeccable, or specially exempt from liability to sin. The Popes have been, indeed, with few exceptions, men of virtuous lives. Many of them are honored as martyrs. Seventy-nine out of the two hundred and fifty-nine that sat on the chair of Peter, are invoked upon our altars as saints eminent for their holiness.

The avowed enemies of the Church charge only five or six Popes with immorality. Thus, even admitting the truth of the accusations brought against them, we have forty-three virtuous to one bad Pope, while there was a Judas Iscariot among the twelve Apostles.

3d. Bear in mind, also, that divine assistance is guaranteed to the Pope, not in his capacity as private teacher, but only in his official capacity, when he judges of faith and morals as Head of the Church.

4th. Finally, the inerrability of the Popes, being restricted to questions of faith and morals, does not extend to the natural sciences, such as astronomy or geology, unless where error is presented under the false name of science, and arrays itself against revealed truth. Nor does it regard purely political questions, such as the form of government a nation ought to adopt, or for what candidates we ought to vote.

What, then, is the real doctrine of Infallibility? It simply means that the Pope, as successor of St. Peter, Prince of the Apostles, by virtue of the promises of Jesus Christ, is preserved from error of judgment when he promulgates to the Church a decision on faith or morals.

Chapter XIV
Is It Lawful to Honor the Blessed Virgin Mary as a Saint, to Invoke Her as an Intercessor, and to Imitate Her as a Model?

Is It Lawful to Honor Her?

Now, if the land of Judea is looked upon as hallowed ground, because Jesus dwelt there; if the Apostles were considered as models of holiness, because they were the chosen companions and pupils of our Lord in His latter years, how peerless must have been the sanctity of Mary, who gave Him birth, whose breast was His pillow, who nursed and clothed Him, etc.

Now of all who have participated in the ministry of the Redemption, there is none who filled any position so exalted, so sacred, as is the incommunicable office of Mother of Jesus; and there is no one consequently that *needed* so high a degree of holiness as she did.

When we call the Blessed Virgin the Mother of God, we assert our belief in two things: 1st. That her Son, Jesus Christ, is true man, else she were not a *mother*. 2d. That He is true God, else she were not the *Mother of God*. In other words, we affirm that the Second Person of the Blessed Trinity the Word of God, who in His divine nature is from all eternity begotten of the Father, consubstantial with Him, was in the fullness of time again begotten, by being born of the Virgin, thus taking to Himself, from her maternal womb, a human nature of the same substance with hers.

The Church teaches us that she was always a Virgin, a Virgin before her espousals, during her married life, and after her spouse's death. "The Angel Gabriel was sent from God . . . to a Virgin espoused to a man whose name was Joseph, . . . and the Virgin's name was Mary."

That she remained a Virgin till after the birth of Jesus is expressly stated in the Gospel. It is not less certain that she continued in the same state during the remainder of her days; for in the Apostles' and the Nicene Creed, she is called a Virgin, and that epithet cannot be restricted to the time of our Savior's birth. It must be referred to her whole life, inasmuch as both creeds were compiled long after she had passed away.

The dogma of the Immaculate Conception is thus expressed by the Church: "We define that the Blessed Virgin Mary in the first moment of her conception, by the singular grace and privilege of Almighty God, in virtue of the merits of Jesus Christ, the Savior of the human race, was preserved free from every stain of original sin."

This immunity of Mary from original sin is exclusively due to the merits of Christ, as the Church expressly declares. She needed a Redeemer as well as the rest of the human race, and therefore was "redeemed, but in a more sublime manner."

Although the Immaculate Conception was not formulated into a dogma of faith till 1854, it is at least implied in Holy Scripture. It is in strict harmony with the place which Mary holds in the economy of Redemption, and has virtually received the pious assent of the faithful from the earliest days of the Church.

Chapter XV
Sacred Images

The doctrine of the Catholic Church regarding use of sacred images, is clearly and fully expressed by the General Council of Trent in the following words: "The images of Christ, and of His Virgin Mother, and of other Saints, are to be had and retained, especially in churches; and a due honor and veneration is to be given to them: not that any divinity or virtue is believed to be in them, for which they are to be honored, or that any prayer is to be made to them, or that any confidence is to be placed in them, as was formerly done by the heathens, who placed their hopes in idols; but because the honor which is given them is referred to the originals which they represent, so that by the images which we kiss, and before which we uncover our heads or kneel, we adore Christ, and venerate His saints, whose likeness they represent."

Is not our country flooded with obscene pictures and immodest representations, which corrupt our youth? If the agenda of Satan employ means so vile for their bad end; if they are cunning enough to pour through the senses, into the hearts of the unwary, the insidious poison of sin, by placing before them lascivious portraits; in God's name, why should not we sanctify the souls of our children by means of pious emblems? Why should not we make the eye the instrument of edification, as the enemy makes it the organ of destruction? Shall the pen of the artist, the pencil [brush] of the painter, and the chisel of the sculptor be prostituted to the basest purposes? God forbid! The arts were intended to be the handmaids of religion.

Chapter XVI
Purgatory and Prayers for the Dead

The Catholic Church teaches that, besides a place of eternal torments for the wicked and of everlasting rest for the righteous, there exists in the next life a middle state of temporary punishment, allotted for those who have died in venial sin, or who have not satisfied the justice of God for sins already forgiven. She also teaches us that, although the souls consigned to this intermediate state, commonly called purgatory, cannot help themselves, they may be aided by the suffrages of the faithful on earth. The existence of purgatory naturally implies the correlative dogma — the utility of praying for the dead.

Chapter XVII
Civil and Religious Liberty

A man enjoys *religious* liberty when he possesses the free right of worshipping God according to the dictates of a right conscience, and of practicing a form of religion most in accordance with his duties to God. Every act infringing on his freedom of conscience is justly styled religious intolerance. This religious liberty is the true right of every man, because it corresponds with a most certain duty which God has put upon him.

A man enjoys *civil* liberty when he is exempt from the arbitrary will of others, and when he is governed by equitable laws established for the general welfare of society. So long as, in common with his fellow-citizens, he observes the laws of the state, any exceptional restraint imposed upon him, in the exercise of his rights as a citizen, is so far an infringement on his civil liberty.

I here assert the proposition that the Catholic Church has always been the zealous promoter of religious and civil liberty, and that whenever any encroachments on these sacred rights of man were perpetrated by professing members of the Catholic faith, these wrongs, far from being sanctioned by the Church, were committed in palpable violation of her authority.

Conversion and coercion are two terms that can never be reconciled. It has ever been a cardinal maxim, inculcated by sovereign Pontiffs and other Prelates, that no violence or undue influence should be exercised by Christian princes or missionaries in their efforts to convert souls to the faith of Jesus Christ.

The Church is, indeed, intolerant in this sense, that she can never confound truth with error; nor can she admit that any man is conscientiously free to reject the truth when its claims are convincingly brought home to the mind.

The Church has not only respected the conscience of the people in embracing the religion of their choice, but she has also defended their *civil* rights and liberties against the encroachments of temporal sovereigns.

The conflict between Church and State has never died out, because the Church has felt it to be her duty, in every age, to raise her voice against the despotic and arbitrary measures of princes.

Chapter XIX

Grace—The Sacraments—Original Sin—Baptism—Its Necessity—Its Effects—Manner of Baptizing

The grace of God is that supernatural assistance which He imparts to us, through the merits of Jesus Christ, for our salvation. It is called *supernatural*, because no one by his own natural ability can acquire it.

The grace of God is obtained chiefly by prayer and the Sacraments.

A Sacrament is a visible sign instituted by Christ, by which grace is conveyed to our souls. Three things are necessary to constitute a Sacrament, viz.: a visible sign, invisible grace, and the institution by our Lord Jesus Christ.

Thus, in the Sacrament of Baptism, there is the outward sign, which consists in the pouring of water, and in the formula of words which are then pronounced; the interior grace or sanctification which is imparted to the soul: "Be baptized, . . . and you shall receive the gift of the Holy Spirit" and the ordinance of Jesus Christ, who said: "Teach all nations, baptizing them in the name of the Father, and of the Son, and of the Holy Spirit."

Our Savior instituted seven Sacraments, namely, Baptism, Confirmation, Eucharist, Penance, Extreme Unction, Orders, and Matrimony, which I shall explain separately.

According to the teachings of Holy Writ, man was created in a state of innocence and holiness, and after having spent on this earth his allotted term of years, he was destined, without tasting death, to be translated to the perpetual society of God in heaven. But in consequence of his disobedience, he fell from his high estate of righteousness; his soul was defiled by sin; he became subject to death and to various ills of body and soul, and forfeited his heavenly inheritance.

Adam's transgression was not confined to himself, but was transmitted, with its long train of dire consequences, to all his posterity. It is called *original* sin because it is derived from our original progenitor.

God, in passing sentence of condemnation on Adam, consoled him by the promise of a Redeemer to come. "I will put enmities," saith the Lord, "between thee and the woman, and thy seed and her seed; she shall crush thy head." Jesus, the seed of Mary, is the chosen one who was destined to crush the head of the infernal serpent. And "when the fullness of time was come, God sent His Son, made of a woman, . . . that He might redeem them that were under the law, that we might receive the adoption of sons."

Jesus Christ, our Redeemer, came to wash away the defilement from our souls, and to restore us to that divine friendship which we had lost by the sin of Adam.

Now He tells us in His Gospel that Baptism is the essential means established for washing away the stain of original sin, and the door by which we find admittance into His Church.

Chapter XX
The Sacrament of Confirmation

Confirmation is a Sacrament in which, through the imposition of the Bishop's hands, unction, and prayer, baptized persons receive the Holy Spirit, that they may steadfastly profess their faith and lead upright lives.

This Sacrament is called *Confirmation*, because it confirms or strengthens the soul by divine grace. Sometimes it is named *the laying on of hands*, because the Bishop imposes his hands on those whom he confirms. It is also known by the name of Chrism, because the forehead of the person confirmed is anointed with chrism in the form of a cross.

Frequent mention is made of this Sacrament in the Holy Scripture. In the Acts, it is written that "When the Apostles who were in Jerusalem had heard that Samaria had received the word of God, they sent unto them Peter and John, who, when they were come, prayed for them that they might receive the Holy Spirit; for He was not yet come upon any of them, but they were only baptized in the name of the Lord Jesus. Then they laid their hands on them, and they received the Holy Spirit."

Chapter XXI
The Holy Eucharist

Among the various dogmas of the Catholic Church, there is none which rests on stronger Scriptural authority than the doctrine of the Real Presence of Jesus Christ in the Holy Eucharist. So copious, indeed, and so clear are the passages of the New Testament which treat of this subject, that I am at a loss to determine which to select, and find it difficult to compress them all within the compass of this short chapter.

I shall select three classes of arguments from the New Testament which satisfactorily demonstrate the Real Presence of Christ in the Blessed Sacrament. The first of these texts speaks of the promise of the Eucharist; the second of its institution; and the third of its use among the faithful.

To begin with the words of the promise. While Jesus was once preaching near the coast of the Sea of Galilee, He was followed, as usual, by an immense multitude of persons, who were attracted to Him by the miracles which He wrought, and the words of salvation which He spoke. Seeing that the people had no food, He multiplied five loaves and two fishes to such an extent as to supply the wants of five thousand men, besides women and children.

Our Lord considered the present a favorable occasion for speaking of the Sacrament of His body and blood, which was to be distributed, not to a few thousands, but to millions of souls; not in one place, but everywhere; not at one time, but for all days, to the end of the world, "I am," He says to His hearers, "the bread of life. . . . I am the living bread which came down from heaven. If any man eat of this bread, he shall live forever; and the bread which

I will give, is My flesh for the life of the world. The Jews, therefore, disputed among themselves, saying: How can this man give us His flesh to eat? Then Jesus said to them: Amen, amen, I say to you: Unless ye eat the flesh of the Son of man, and drink His blood, ye shall not have life in you. He that eateth My flesh and drinketh My blood, hath everlasting life, and I will raise him up on the last day. For My flesh is meat indeed, and My blood is drink indeed."

The best and the most reliable interpreters of our Savior's words are certainly the multitude, and the disciples who were listening to Him. They all understood the import of His language precisely as it is explained by the Catholic Church. They believed that our Lord spoke literally of His body and blood.

Even His disciples gave expression to their doubt in this milder form: "This saying is hard, and who can hear it?" So much were they shocked at our Savior's promise, that "after this many of His disciples went back, and walked no more with Him."

But in the present instance, does our Savior alter His language when He finds His words taken in the literal sense? Does He tell His hearers that He has spoken figuratively? Does He soften the tone of his expressions? Far from weakening the force of His words, He repeats what He said before, and in language more emphatic: "Amen, amen, I say unto you, Unless ye eat the flesh of the Son of Man, and drink His blood, ye shall not have life in you."

When our Savior beheld the Jews and many of His disciples abandoning Him, turning to the chosen twelve, He said feelingly to them: "Will ye also go away?" And Simon Peter answered Him: "Lord, to whom shall we go? Thou hast the words of eternal life."

So far, I have dwelt on the words of the Promise. I shall now proceed to the words of the Institution, which are given in almost the same expressions by St. Matthew, St. Mark, and St. Luke. In the Gospel according to St. Matthew, we read the following narrative: "And while they were at supper, Jesus took bread, and blessed and broke, and gave to His disciples, and said: Take ye and eat. This is My body. And taking the chalice, He gave thanks, and gave to them, saying: Drink ye all of this; for this is My blood of the New Testament, which shall be shed for many unto remission of sins."

The Fathers of the Church, without an exception, re-echo the language of the Apostle of the Gentiles, by proclaiming the Real Presence of our Lord in the Eucharist. I have counted the names of sixty-three Fathers and eminent ecclesiastical writers flourishing between the first and the sixth century, all of whom proclaim the Real Presence — some by explaining the mystery, others by thanking God for this inestimable gift, and others by exhorting the faithful to its worthy reception.

But why multiply authorities? At the present day, every Christian communion throughout the world, with the sole exception of Protestants, proclaims its belief in the Real Presence of Christ in the Sacrament.

The sacrifice of the Mass is the consecration of the bread and wine into the body and blood of Christ, and the oblation of this body and blood to God, by the ministry of the priest, for a perpetual memorial of Christ's sacrifice on the cross. The Sacrifice of the Mass is identical with that of the cross, both having the same victim and High Priest — Jesus Christ.

The only difference consists in the manner of the oblation. Christ was offered up on the cross in a bloody manner, and in the Mass He is offered up in an unbloody manner.

Chapter XXVI
The Sacrament of Penance

The whole history of Jesus Christ is marked by mercy and compassion for suffering humanity. From the moment of His incarnation till the hour of His death, every thought and word and act of His divine life was directed toward the alleviation of the ills and miseries of fallen man.

But while Jesus occupied Himself in bringing relief to corporal infirmities, *the principal object of His mission was to release the soul from the bonds of sin*. The very name of Jesus indicates this important truth: "Thou shalt call His name Jesus," says the angel, "for He shall save His people from their sins."

As the Church was established by Jesus Christ to perpetuate the work which he had begun, it follows that the reconciliation of sinners to God was to be the principal office of the Church.

His plan, therefore, must have been to appoint ministers of reconciliation to act in His name. It has always, indeed, been the practice of Almighty God, both in the Old and New Law, to empower human agents to execute His merciful designs.

But have we Gospel authority to show that our Savior did confer on the Apostles and their successors the power to forgive sins?

In the Gospel of St. Matthew, our Savior thus addresses Peter: "Thou art Peter, and on this rock I will build My Church. . . . And I will give to thee the key of the kingdom of heaven, and whatsoever thou shalt bind on earth shall be bound also in heaven, and whatsoever thou shalt loose on earth shall be loosed also in heaven."

In the Gospel of St. John we have a still more striking declaration of the absolving power given by our Savior to His Apostles.

Jesus, after His resurrection, thus addresses His disciples: "Peace be to you. As the Father hath sent Me, I also send you. . . . Receive ye the Holy Spirit; whose sins ye shall forgive, they are forgiven them, and whose sins ye shall retain, they are retained."

It follows, that the power of forgiving sins, on the part of God's minister, involves the obligation of confessing them on the part of the sinner. The priest is not empowered to give absolution to every one indiscriminately. But how will he judge of the disposition of the sinner, unless he knows his sins? and how will the priest know his sins, unless they are confessed? All the Fathers of the Church, from the first to the last, insist upon the necessity of Sacramental Confession as a divine institution.

Chapter XXVIII
Extreme Unction

Extreme Unction is a Sacrament in which the sick, by the anointing with holy oil and the prayers of the priests, receive spiritual succor, and even corporeal strength when such is conducive to their salvation. This unction is called *Extreme*, because it is usually the last of the holy unctions administered by the Church.

The Apostle St. James clearly refers to this Sacrament, and points out its efficacy in the following words: "Is any man sick among you; let him bring in the priests of the Church, and let them pray over him, anointing him with oil in the name of the Lord, and the prayer of faith shall save the sick man; and the Lord shall raise him up; and if he be in sins, they shall be forgiven him."

Chapter XXIX
The Priesthood

The exalted dignity of the Priest is derived not from the personal merits for which he may be conspicuous, but from the sublime functions which he is charged to perform. To the carnal eye, the Priest looks like other men, but to the eye of faith, he is exalted above the angels, because he exercises powers not given even to angels.

The Priest is the *ambassador of God*, appointed to vindicate His honor and to proclaim His glory. If it is esteemed a great privilege for a citizen of the United States to represent our country in any of the courts of Europe, how much greater is the prerogative to represent the court of heaven among the nations of the earth!" As the Father hath sent Me," says our Lord to His Apostles, "I also send you." "Going, therefore, teach ye all nations, . . . teaching them to observe all things whatsoever I have commanded you. And, behold, I am with you all day, even to the consummation of the world."

Not only does Jesus empower the priests to preach in His name, but he commands to listen and obey.

"He that heareth you, heareth Me; and he that despiseth you, despiseth Me; and he that despiseth Me, despiseth Him that sent Me."

To sum up the titles of a Catholic Priest:

He is a *king*, reigning not over unwilling subjects, but over the hearts and affections of his people.

He is a *shepherd*, because he leads his flock into the delicious pastures of the Sacraments, and shelters them from the wolves that lie in wait for their souls.

He is a *father*, because he breaks the bread of life to his spiritual children, whom he has begotten in Christ Jesus through the Gospel.

He is a *judge*, whose office it is to pass sentence of pardon on self-accusing criminals.

He is a *physician*, because he heals their souls from the loathsome distempers of sin.

If the Priest should be eminent for his learning, he should be still more conspicuous for his virtues, for he is expected to preach more by example than by precept.

Chapter XXXI
Matrimony

Matrimony is not only a natural contract between husband and wife, but it has been elevated for Christians, by Jesus Christ, to the dignity of a Sacrament: "Husbands," says the Apostle, "love your wives, as Christ also loved the Church and delivered Himself up for it, . . . so also ought men to love their wives as their own bodies. . . . For this cause shall a man leave his father and mother, and shall adhere to his wife, and they shall be one flesh. This is a great sacrament: but I speak in Christ and in the Church."

In these words the Apostle declares that the union of Christ with His Church is the type or model of the bond subsisting between man and wife. Now the union between Christ and His Church is supernatural and sealed by divine grace. Hence, also, is the fellowship of a Christian husband and wife cemented by the grace of God. The wedded couple are bound to love one another during their whole lives, as Christ has loved His Church, and to discharge the virtues proper to the married state. In order to fulfill these duties, special graces of our Savior are required.

The Gospel forbids a man to have more than one wife, and a wife to have more than one husband. "Have you not read," says our Savior, "that He who made man in the beginning, made them male and female? And He said, for this cause shall man leave father and mother, and shall cleave unto *his wife, and they too shall be in one flesh.*

What therefore God hath joined together, let no man put asunder. And I say to you, that whosoever shall put away his wife, except it be for fornication, and shall marry another, committeth adultery: and he that shall marry her that is put away, committeth adultery." Our Savior here emphatically declares that the nuptial bond is ratified by God Himself, and hence that no man, nor any legislation framed by men, can validly dissolve the contract.

There are some who regard the Catholic Church as too severe in proclaiming the absolute indissolubility of marriage. But it should be borne in mind, that it is not the Church, but the divine Founder of the Christian religion, that has given us the law. She merely enforces its observance.

Selections from
The Faith of Our Fathers,
James Cardinal Gibbons,
John Murphy Company, 1905

Chapter 60 • Pope Pius XI: *Casti Connubii; Quadragesimo Anno*

Achille Ratti (as pope, 1922-1939) was born in Desio near Milan in 1857. He studied in Milan and at the Gregorian University in Rome, and was ordained in 1879. Because of his proficiency in philosophy and palaeography, he gained the attention of Pope Leo XIII, and was later named chief librarian of the Ambrosian Library in Milan. Pope Pius X called him to Rome to become vice prefect of the Vatican Library. He was nuncio to Poland in 1919, and was named an archbishop by Pope Benedict XV, who made him a cardinal. He was elected the 260th Pope on February 6, 1922, and took the name of Pius XI. All during his pontificate he was concerned with the economic, political, social, educational, familial, and individual activities of all people. He was a staunch opponent of Fascism, National Socialism, Communism, and every form of political, social, and economic theory which deprived people of any of their personal rights. His program for social and economic reform was presented *in Quadragesimo Anno* (*On Social Reconstruction*), a classic of Catholic teaching. His encyclical *Casti Connubii*, *On Christian Marriage,* is an excellent Catholic exhortation to uphold and preserve the classic teaching of the Church on marriage and the family, as found in the Gospels, the teaching of St. Paul, and the homilies of John Chrysostom, to mention but a few. In *Quadragesimo Anno* he incorporates the contents of the *Rerum Novarum* of Leo XIII and subsequent Christian social and economic reform. He also refers to the teaching of his predecessor Leo XIII as a source of his teachings.

Casti Connubii
On Christian Marriage

How great is the dignity of chaste wedlock, Venerable Brethren, may be judged best from this, that Christ Our Lord, Son of the Eternal Father, having assumed the nature of fallen man, with His loving desire of compassing the redemption of our race, not only ordained it in an especial manner as the principle and foundation of domestic society and therefore of all human intercourse, but also raised it to the rank of a truly "great" Sacrament of the New Law, restored it to the original purity of its Divine institution, and accordingly entrusted all its discipline and care to His Spouse the Church.

In order, however, that amongst men of every nation and every age the desired fruits may be obtained from this renewal of matrimony, it is necessary first of all that men's minds be illuminated with the true doctrine of Christ regarding it; and secondly, that Christian spouses, the weakness of their wills strengthened by the internal grace of God, shape all their ways of thinking and of acting in conformity with that pure law of Christ as to obtain true peace and happiness for themselves and for their families.

I. Nature and Dignity of Christian Marriage

And to begin with that same Encyclical, which is wholly concerned in vindicating the divine institution of matrimony, its sacramental dignity and its perpetual stability, let it be repeated as an immutable and inviolable fundamental doctrine that matrimony was not instituted or restored by man but by God; not by man were the laws made to strengthen and confirm and elevate it but by God, the Author of nature, and by Christ Our Lord by Whom nature was redeemed, and hence these laws cannot be subject to any human decrees or to any contrary pact even of the spouses themselves. This is the doctrine of Holy Scripture; this is the constant tradition of the Universal Church; this the solemn definition of the sacred Council of Trent, which declares and establishes from the words of Holy Writ itself that God is the Author of the perpetual stability of the marriage bond, its unity and its firmness.

Yet although matrimony is of its very nature of divine institution, the human will, too, enters into it and performs a most noble part. For each individual marriage, inasmuch as it is a conjugal union of a particular man and woman, arises only from the free consent of each of the spouses; and this free act of the will, by which each party hands over and accepts those rights proper to the state of marriage, is so necessary to constitute true marriage that it cannot be supplied by any human power.

This freedom, however, regards only the fact whether the contracting parties really wish to enter upon matrimony or to marry this particular person; but the nature of matrimony is entirely independent of the free will of man, so that if one has once contracted matrimony he is thereby subject to its Divinely made laws and its essential properties. For the Angelic Doctor, writing on conjugal fidelity and on offspring, says: "These things are so contained in matrimony by the very marriage pact that if anything to the contrary were expressed in the consent which makes the marriage, it would not be a true marriage."

Spiritual Union

By matrimony, therefore, the souls of the contracting parties are joined and knit together more immediately and intimately than are their bodies, and that not by any passing affection of sense or spirit, but by a deliberate and firm act of the will; and from this union of souls by God's decree, a sacred and inviolable bond arises. Hence the nature of this contract, which is proper and peculiar to it alone, makes it entirely different both from the union of animals entered into by the blind instinct of nature alone in which neither reason nor free will plays a part, and also from the unions of men which are far removed from all true and honorable unions of wills and enjoy none of the rights of family life.

From this it is clear that legitimately constituted authority has the right and therefore the duty to restrict, to prevent, and to punish those base unions which are opposed to reason and to nature; but since it is a matter which flows from human nature itself, no less certain is the teaching of Our predecessor, Leo XIII, of happy memory.

II. Blessings and Benefits of Matrimony

Now when We come to explain, Venerable Brethren, what are the blessings that God has attached to true matrimony, and how great they are, there occur to Us the words of that illustrious Doctor of the Church whom We commemorated recently in Our Encyclical *Ad salutem* on the occasion of the fifteenth centenary of his death. "These," says St. Augustine, "all are the blessings of matrimony on account of which matrimony itself is a blessing; offspring, conjugal faith and the sacrament." And how under these three heads is contained a splendid summary of the whole doctrine of Christian marriage, the holy Doctor himself expressly declares when he said: "By conjugal faith it is provided that there should be no carnal intercourse outside the marriage bond with another man or woman; with regard to offspring, that children should be begotten of love, tenderly cared for and educated in a religious atmosphere; finally, in its sacramental aspect that the marriage bond should not be broken and that a husband or wife, if separated, should not be joined to another even for the sake of offspring. This we regard as the law of marriage by which the fruitfulness of nature is adorned and the evil of incontinence is restrained.

Thus amongst the blessings of marriage, the child holds the first place. And indeed the Creator of the human race Himself, Who in His goodness wished to use men as His helpers in the propagation of life, taught this when, instituting marriage in Paradise, He said to our first parents, and through them to all future spouses: "Increase and multiply, and fill the earth." As St. Augustine admirably deduces from the words of the holy Apostle Saint Paul to Timothy when he says: "The Apostle himself is therefore a witness that marriage is for the sake of generation: 'I wish,' he says, 'young girls to marry.' And, as if some one said to him, 'Why?,' he immediately adds: 'To bear children, to be mothers of families.' "

How great a boon of God this is, and how great a blessing of matrimony is clear from a consideration of man's dignity and of his sublime end. For man surpasses all other visible creatures by the superiority of his rational nature alone. Besides, God wishes men to be born not only that they should live and fill the earth, but much more that they may be worshippers of God, that they may know Him and love Him and finally enjoy Him forever in heaven; and this end, since man is raised by God in a marvelous way to the supernatural order, surpasses all that eye hath seen, and ear heard, and all that hath entered into the heart of man. From which it is easily seen how great a gift of divine goodness and how remarkable a fruit of marriage are children born by the omnipotent power of God through the cooperation of those bound in wedlock.

But Christian parents must also understand that they are destined not only to propagate and preserve the human race on earth, indeed not only to educate any kind of worshippers of the true God, but children who are to become members of the Church of Christ, to raise up fellow-citizens of the Saints, and members of God's household, that the worshippers of God and Our Savior may daily increase.

The blessing of offspring, however, is not completed by the mere begetting of them, but something else must be added, namely, the proper education of the offspring.

Since, however, We have spoken fully elsewhere on the Christian education of youth, let us sum it all up by quoting once more the words of St. Augustine: "In 'the offspring' it is provided that they should be begotten lovingly and educated religiously," and this is also expressed succinctly in the Code of Canon Law: "The primary end of marriage is the procreating and the education of children."

The second blessing of matrimony which We said was mentioned by St. Augustine, is the blessing of conjugal honor which consists in the mutual fidelity of the spouses in fulfilling the marriage contract, "so that what belongs to one of the parties by reason of this contract sanctioned by Divine law, may not be denied to him or permitted to any third person, nor may there be conceded to one of the parties that which, being contrary to the rights and laws of God and entirely opposed to matrimonial faith, can never be conceded."

Nay, that mutual familiar intercourse between the spouses themselves, if the blessing of conjugal faith is to shine with becoming splendor, must be distinguished by chastity in such wise that husband and wife must conform themselves in all things to the law of God and nature, and endeavor always to follow the will of the most wise and holy Creator with the greatest reverence toward the work of God.

The love, then, of which we are speaking is not that based on the passing lust of the moment nor does it consist in pleasing words only, but in the deep attachment of the heart which is expressed in action, since love is proved by deeds.

Domestic society being confirmed therefore by this bond of love, it is necessary that there should flourish in it "order of love," as St. Augustine calls it. This order includes both primacy of the husband with regard to the wife and children, and the ready subjection of the wife and her willing obedience which the Apostle commends in these words: "Let women be subject to their husbands as to the Lord, because the husband is the head of the wife, as Christ is the head of the Church."

This subjection, however, does not deny or take away the liberty which fully belongs to the woman both in view of her dignity as a human person, and in view of her most noble office as wife and mother and companion; nor does it bid her obey her husband's every request even if not in harmony with right reason or with the dignity due a wife; nor, in fine, does it imply that the wife should be put on a level with those persons who in law are called minors, to whom it is not customary to allow free exercise of their rights, on account of their lack of mature judgment, or of their ignorance of human affairs. But it forbids that exaggerated license which cares not for the good of the family; it forbids that in this body which is the family, the heart be separated from the head to the great detriment of the whole body and the proximate danger of ruin. For if the man is the head, the woman is the heart, and as he occupies the chief place in ruling, so she may and ought to claim for herself the chief place in love.

Again, this subjection of wife to husband in its degree and manner may vary according to the different conditions of persons, place and time; in fact, if the husband neglect his duty, it falls to the wife to take his place in directing the family. But the structure of the family and its fundamental law established and confirmed by God, must always and everywhere be maintained intact.

These, then, are the elements which compose the blessing of conjugal faith:

unity, chastity, charity, honorable noble obedience, which are at the same time an enumeration of the benefits which are bestowed on husband and wife in their married state, benefits by which the peace, the dignity and the happiness of matrimony are securely preserved and fostered. Wherefore it is not surprising that this conjugal faith has always been counted amongst the most priceless and special blessings of matrimony.

Indissolubility

But this accumulation of benefits is completed and, as it were, crowned by that blessing of Christian marriage which in the words of St. Augustine we have called the sacrament, by which is denoted both the indissolubility of the bond and the raising and hallowing of the contract by Christ Himself, whereby He made it an efficacious sign of grace.

In the first place Christ Himself lays stress on the indissolubility and firmness of the marriage bond when He says: "What God hath joined together let no man put asunder," and: "Everyone that putteth away his wife and marrieth another committeth adultery, and he that marrieth her that is put away from her husband committeth adultery."

And St. Augustine clearly places what he calls the blessing of matrimony in this indissolubility when he says: "In the sacrament it is provided that the marriage bond should not be broken, and that a husband or wife, if separated, should not be joined to another even for the sake of offspring."

And this inviolable stability, although not in the same perfect measure in every case, belongs to every true marriage, for the word of the Lord: "What God hath joined together let no man put asunder," must of necessity include all true marriages without exception, since it was spoken of the marriage of our first parents, the prototype of every future marriage.

Benefits of Indissolubility

Indeed, how many and how important are the benefits which flow from the indissolubility of matrimony cannot escape anyone who gives even a brief consideration either to the good of the married parties and the offspring or to the welfare of human society. First of all, both husband and wife possess a positive guarantee of the endurance of this stability which that generous yielding of their persons and the intimate fellowship of their hearts by their nature strongly require, since true love never falls away. Besides, a strong bulwark is set up in defense of a loyal chastity against incitements to infidelity, should any be encountered either from within or from without; any anxious fear lest in adversity or old age the other spouse would prove unfaithful is precluded and in its place there reigns a calm sense of security.

Moreover, the dignity of both man and wife is maintained and the mutual aid is most satisfactorily assured, while through the indissoluble bond, always enduring, the spouses are warned continuously that not for the sake of perishable things nor that they might serve their passions, but that they might procure one for the other high and lasting good have they entered into the nuptial partnership, to be dissolved only by death. For the training and education of children, which must extend over a period of many years, it is splendidly adapted, since the grave and long enduring burdens of this office are best borne by the united efforts of the parents. Nor do lesser benefits accrue to human society as a whole, for experience has taught that unassailable stability in matrimony is a fruitful source of virtuous life and of habits of integrity. Where this order of things obtains, the happiness and well-being of the nation are safeguarded. As the families and individuals are, so also is the State, for it is made up of them even as a body is of its members. Hence those who vigorously uphold the inviolable stability of matrimony make a real contribution both to the individual welfare of husband, wife and offspring, as well as to the general welfare of mankind (Eph. 5, 32).

Adultery Always Wrong

It follows, therefore, that they are destroying mutual fidelity, who think that the ideas and morality of our present time concerning a certain harmful and false friendship with a third party can be countenanced, and who teach that greater freedom of feeling and action in such external relations should be allowed to man and wife, particularly as many (so they consider) are possessed of an inborn sexual tendency, which cannot be satisfied within the narrow limits of monogamous marriage. That rigid attitude which condemns all sensual affections and actions with a third party they imagine to be narrowing of mind and heart, something obsolete, or an abject form of jealousy, and as a result they look upon whatever penal laws are passed by the State for the preserving of conjugal faith as void or to be abolished. Such unworthy and idle opinions are condemned by that noble instinct which is found in every chaste husband and wife, and that even by the light of the testimony of nature alone, a testimony that is sanctioned and confirmed by the command of God, "Thou shalt not commit adultery," and the words of Christ, "Whosoever shall look on a woman to lust after her hath already committed adultery with her in his heart." The force of this Divine precept can never be weakened by a merely human custom, bad example or pretext of human progress.

Secularized Marriage

We have so far, Venerable Brethren, shown the excellency of the first two blessings of Christian wedlock which the modern disturbers of society are attacking. And now considering that the third blessing, which is that of the "Sacrament," far surpasses the other two, we should not be surprised to find that this, because of its outstanding excellence, is much more sharply attacked by the same people. They put forward in the first place that matrimony belongs entirely to the profane and purely civil sphere, that it is not to be committed to the religious society, the Church of Christ, but to civil society alone. They then add that the marriage contract is to be freed from any indissoluble bond, and that separation and divorce are not only to be tolerated but sanctioned by the law; from which it follows finally that, robbed of all its holiness, matrimony should be enumerated amongst the secular and civil institutions. The first point is contained in their contention that the civil act itself should stand for the marriage contract (civil matrimony). Moreover, they want it to be no cause for reproach that marriages be contracted by Catholics with non-Catholics without any reference to religion or recourse to the ecclesiastical authorities. The second point, which is but a consequence of the first, is to be found in their excuse for complete divorce and in their praise and encouragement of those civil laws which favor loosening the bond itself.

As the salient features of the religious character of all marriage, and particularly of the sacramental marriage of Christians, have been treated at length and supported by weighty arguments in the Encyclical Letter of Leo XIII, a letter which We have frequently recalled to mind and expressly made Our own, We refer you to it, repeating here only a few points.

Even by the light of reason alone and particularly if the ancient records of history are investigated, if the unwavering popular conscience be interrogated and the manners and institutions of all races examined, it is sufficiently obvious that there is a certain sacredness and religious character attaching even to the purely natural union of man and woman, "not something added by chance but innate, not imposed by men but involved in the nature of things," since it has "God for its Author and has been even from the beginning a foreshadowing of the Incarnation of the Word of God." This sacredness of marriage which is intimately connected with religion and all that is holy, arises from the Divine origin we have just mentioned, from its purpose which is the begetting and educating of children of God and the binding of man and wife to God through Christian love and mutual support, and finally, it arises from the very nature of wedlock, whose institution is to be sought for in the far-seeing Providence of God, whereby it is the means of transmitting life, thus making the parents the ministers as it were of the Divine omnipotence. To this must be added that new element of dignity which comes from the Sacrament by which the Christian marriage is so ennobled and raised to such a level that it appeared to the Apostle as "a great Sacrament," "honorable in every way."

All Divorce Forbidden

Others, taking a step further, simply state that marriage, being a private contract, is, like other private contracts, to be left to the consent and good pleasure of both parties, and so can be dissolved for any reason whatsoever. Opposed to all these reckless opinions, Venerable Brethren, stands the unalterable law of God, fully confirmed by Christ, a law that can never be deprived of its force by the decrees of men, the ideas of a people or the will of any legislator. "What God hath joined together, let no man put asunder." And if any man, acting contrary to this law, shall have put asunder, his action is null and void, and the consequence remains, as Christ Himself has explicitly confirmed: "Everyone that putteth away his wife and marrieth another, committeth adultery: and he that marrieth her that is put away from her husband committeth adultery." Moreover these words refer to every kind of marriage, even that which is natural and legitimate only. For, as has already been observed, that indissolubility by which the loosening of the bond is once and for all removed from the whim of the parties and from every secular power, is a property of every true marriage.

Let that solemn pronouncement of the Council of Trent be recalled to mind in which, under the stigma of anathema, it condemned these errors:

If anyone should say that on account of heresy or the hardships of cohabitation or a deliberate abuse of one party by the other, the marriage tie may be loosened, let him be anathema.

And again:

If anyone should say that the Church errs in having taught or in teaching that according to the teaching of the Gospel and the Apostles, the bond of marriage cannot be loosed because of the sin of adultery of either party, or that neither party, even though one be innocent, having given no cause for the sin of adultery, can contract another marriage during the lifetime of the other and that he commits adultery who marries another after putting away his adulterous wife, and likewise that she commits adultery who puts away her husband and marries another: let him be anathema.

If, therefore, the Church has not erred and does not err in teaching this, and consequently it is certain that the bond of marriage cannot be loosed even on account of the sin of adultery, it is evident that all the other weaker excuses that can be and are usually brought forward are of no value whatsoever, and the objections brought against the firmness of the marriage bond are easily answered. For, in certain circumstances, imperfect separation of the parties is allowed, the bond not being severed.

May the Father, "of whom all paternity in heaven and earth is named," who strengthens the weak and gives courage to the pusillanimous and faint-hearted; may Christ Our Lord and Redeemer, "the Institutor and Perfector of the holy Sacraments," who desired marriage to be and made it the mystical image of His own ineffable union with the Church; may the Holy Ghost, the God of love, Light of minds and Strength of wills, grant that all may perceive what We by this letter have expounded concerning the holy Sacrament of Matrimony, the wonderful law and will of God respecting it, the errors and impending dangers, and the remedies with which they can be counteracted. May all admit it with a ready win, and by the grace of God put it into practice, so that fruitfulness dedicated to God will flourish again vigorously in Christian wedlock. That God, the Author of all graces, from whom comes every willing and accomplishing, may bring this about, and deign to give it bountifully according to the greatness of His liberality and omnipotence, We most humbly pour forth Our earnest prayer at the throne of His grace; and as a token of the abundant blessing of the same Omnipotent God, we most lovingly grant to you, Venerable Brethren, and to the clergy and people committed to your zealous vigilance, the Apostolic Benediction.

Given at Rome, in Saint Peter's, this thirty-first day of December, of the year 1930, the ninth of Our Pontificate.

Quadragesimo Anno
On Social Reconstruction
II. The Church's Authority in Social and Economic Matters
A. Right and Duty of the Church to Speak

41. But before proceeding to discuss these problems, We lay down the principle long since clearly established by Leo XIII, that it is Our right and

Our duty to deal authoritatively with social and economic problems. It is not, of course, the function of the Church to lead men to transient and perishable happiness only, but to that which is eternal. Indeed the Church believes "that it would be wrong for her to interfere without just cause in such earthly concerns," but she never can relinquish her God-given task of interposing her authority, not indeed in technical matters, for which she has neither the suitable equipment nor the mission, but in all those that have a bearing on moral conduct. *For the deposit of truth entrusted to Us by God, and Our weighty office of propagating, interpreting and urging in season and out of season the entire moral law, demand that both social and economic questions be brought within Our supreme jurisdiction, in so far as they refer to moral issues.*

42. For, though economic science and moral discipline are guided each by its own principles in its own sphere, it is false that the two orders are so distinct and alien to each other that the former in no way depends on the latter. The so-called laws of economics, derived from the nature of earthly goods and from the qualities of human body and soul, determine what aims are unattainable or attainable in economic matters and what means are therefore necessary. On the other hand, reason itself clearly deduces from the individual and social nature of things and of men, what is the end of object of the whole economic order assigned by God the Creator.

43. *For it is the moral law alone which commands us to seek in all our conduct our supreme and final end, and to strive directly in our specific actions for those ends which nature, or rather the Author of Nature, has established for them, duly subordinating particular aims to our last end.* If this law be faithfully obeyed, the result will be that specific economic aims, whether of society as a body or of individuals, will find their proper place within the universal order of ends, and as a consequence we shall be led by progressive stages to the final end of all, God Himself, our highest and lasting good.

B. The Right of Property

44. Descending now to details, We commence with ownership, or the right of property. You are aware, Venerable Brethren and beloved children, how strenuously Our predecessor of happy memory defended the right of property against the teachings of the Socialists of his time, showing that the abolition of private ownership would not prove to be beneficial, but grievously harmful to the working classes. Yet, since there are some who falsely and unjustly accuse the Supreme Pontiff and the Church of upholding, both then and now, the wealthier

class against the propertyless, insecure workers, and since controversy has arisen among Catholics as to the true sense of Pope Leo's teaching, We thought it well to defend from calumny the Leonine doctrine in this matter, which is the Catholic doctrine, and to safeguard it against false interpretations.

Its Individual and Social Character

45. First, let it be made clear beyond all doubt that neither Leo XIII nor those theologians who have taught under the guidance and direction of the Church have ever denied or called in question *the twofold aspect of ownership, which is individual or social according as it regards individuals or concerns the common good*. Their unanimous contention has always been that the right to own private property has been given to man by nature, or rather by the Creator Himself, not only in order that individuals may be able to provide for their own needs and those of their families, but also that, by means of it, the goods which the Creator has destined for the human race may truly serve this purpose. Now, these ends cannot be secured unless some definite and stable order is maintained.

46. A double danger must therefore be carefully avoided. On the one hand, if the social and public aspect of ownership be denied or minimized one falls into individualism, as it is called; on the other hand, the rejection or diminution of its private and individual character necessarily leads to some form of collectivism, or something approaching it. To disregard these dangers would be to rush headlong into the quicksands of that moral, juridical, and social modernism which We condemned in the encyclical letter issued at the beginning of Our pontificate. Let this be noted particularly by those seekers after novelties who launch against the Church the odious calumny that she allowed a pagan concept of ownership to creep into the teachings of her theologians and who maintain that another concept must be substituted, which in their astounding ignorance they call Christian.

Obligations Inherent in Ownership

47. That We may keep within bounds the controversies which have arisen concerning ownership and the duties attaching to it, We reassert in the first place the fundamental principle laid down by Leo XIII, that *the right of property must be distinguished from its use* (R.N., 19). It belongs to what is called commutative justice faithfully to respect the possessions of others and not to encroach on the rights of another by exceeding one's

own rights of ownership. The putting of one's own possessions to proper use, however, does not fall under this form of justice, but under certain other virtues, and therefore it is "a duty which is not enforced by human laws" (R.N., 19). Hence it is false to contend that the right of ownership and its proper use are bounded by the same limits; and it is even less true that the very misuse or even the nonuse of ownership destroys or forfeits the right to it.

48. Most helpful, therefore, and worthy of all praise are the efforts of those who, in a spirit of harmony and with due regard for the traditions of the Church, seek to, determine the precise nature of these duties and to define the limitations imposed by the requirements of social life upon the right of ownership itself or upon its use. On the contrary, it is a grievous error so to weaken the individual character of ownership as actually to destroy it.

The Right and Duty of the State

49. It follows from the twofold character of ownership, which We have termed individual and social, that men must take into account in this matter not only their own advantage but also the common good. *To define in detail these duties, when the need occurs and when the natural law does not do so, is the function of government. Provided that the natural and divine law be observed, the public authority, in view of the true necessity of the common good, may specify more accurately what is licit and what is illicit for property owners in the use of their possessions.* Moreover, Leo XIII had wisely taught that "the limits of private possession have been left to be fixed by man's own industry and by the laws of individual peoples" (R.N., 7).

History proves that ownership, like other elements of social life, is not absolutely rigid, and this doctrine We ourselves have given utterance to on a previous occasion in the following terms: "How varied are the forms which property has assumed. First, the primitive form used among rude and savage peoples, which still exists in certain localities even in our day; then, that of the patriarchal age; later various tyrannical types (We use the word in its classical meaning); finally the feudal and monarchic systems down to the varieties of more recent times" (Allocution to the Convention of Italian Catholic Action, May 16, 1926).

It is plain, however, that the state may not discharge this duty in an arbitrary manner. Man's natural right of privately possessing and transmitting property by inheritance must be kept intact and cannot be taken away by the state, for "man is older than the state" (R.N, 6), and "the domestic household is anterior both in idea and in fact to the gathering of men into a commonwealth" (R.N., 10). Hence the prudent Pontiff had already declared it unlawful for the state to exhaust the means of individuals by crushing taxes and tributes: "The right to possess private property is from nature, not from man; and the state has only the right to regulate its use in the interest of the public good, but by no means to abolish it altogether" (R.N., 35).

However, when civil authority adjusts ownership to meet the needs of the public good, it acts not as an enemy but as the friend of private owners; for thus it effectively prevents the possession of private property, intended by nature's Author in His wisdom for the support of human life, from creating intolerable evils and so rushing to its own destruction. It does not, therefore, abolish but protects private ownership, and far from weakening the right of private property, it gives it new strength.

Obligations with Respect to Superfluous Income

50. At the same time a man's superfluous income is not left entirely to his own discretion. We speak of that portion of his income which he does not need in order to live as becomes his station. On the contrary, the grave obligations of almsgiving, beneficence and liberality which rest upon the wealthy are constantly insisted upon in telling words by Holy Scripture and the Fathers of the Church.

51. However, according to the teaching of the Angelic Doctor, the investment of a large income in such a manner that favorable opportunities for employment may abound (on the supposition that the labor employed produces results which are really useful) is to be considered an act of real liberality particularly appropriate to the needs of our time (*Summa Theologiae*, 2-2. q. 134).

Titles of Acquiring Ownership

52. *The original acquisition of property takes place by first occupation and by labor, or, as it is called, specification.* This is the universal teaching of tradition and the doctrine of Our predecessor, Leo, despite unreasonable assertions to the contrary, nor is wrong done to any man by the occupation of unclaimed goods which belong to nobody. *The only form of labor, however, which gives the workingman a title to its fruits is that which a man exercises as his own master, and by which property acquires some new form or increment.*

C. Property ("Capital") and Labor

53. Altogether different is the labor one man hires out to another, and which is expended on another's property. To it apply especially the words of Leo XIII: "It is only by the labor of the workingman that states grow rich" (R.N., 27). Is it not indeed apparent that *the huge possessions which constitute human wealth are begotten by and flow from the hands of the working man*, toiling either unaided or with the assistance of tools and machinery which wonderfully intensify his efficiency?

Universal experience teaches us that no nation has ever yet risen from want and poverty to a better and loftier station without the unremitting toil of all its citizens, both those who direct work and those who follow orders. *But it is no less self-evident that these ceaseless labors would have remained ineffective, indeed could never have been attempted, had not God, the Creator of all things, in His goodness bestowed in the first instance the wealth and resources of nature*, its treasures and its powers. For what else is work but the application of one's forces of mind and body on, or by means of, these gifts of nature?

Now, the natural law, or rather, God's will manifested by it, demands that right order be observed in the application of natural resources to human need; and this order consists in everything having its proper owner. Hence it follows that unless man apply his labor to his own property, an association must be formed between his toil and his neighbor's property, for each is helpless without the other. This was what Leo XIII had in mind when he wrote: "Capital cannot do without labor, nor labor without capital" (R.N., 15). It is therefore entirely false to ascribe the results of their combined efforts to either party alone; and *it is flagrantly unjust that either should deny the efficacy of the other and claim the entire product.*

Unjust Claims of "Capital"

54. Property, in the sense of capital, however, was long able to appropriate to itself excessive advantages. It claimed all the products and profits, and left to the laborer the barest minimum necessary to repair his strength. For *by an inexorable economic law, it was held, all accumulation of capital falls to the share of the wealthy, while by the same law the workingman must remain perpetually in indigence or reduced to the minimum needed for existence*. It is true that the actual state of things was not always and everywhere as deplorable as the liberalistic tenets of the so-called Manchester School might lead us to conclude; but it cannot be denied that the steady drift of economic and social

institutions was in this direction. These false opinions and specious axioms were vehemently attacked, as was to be expected, and that not merely by those whom such principles deprived of their innate right to better their condition.

Unjust Claims of Labor

55. The cause of the harassed workingman was espoused by the "intellectuals," as they are called, who set up in opposition to this fictious law another equally false moral principle: that all products and profits, excepting those required to repair and replace invested capital, belong by every right to the workingman. This error, more subtle than that of the Socialists who hold that all means of production should be transferred to the state — or, as they term it, "socialized" — is for that reason more dangerous and apt to deceive the unwary. It is an alluring poison, consumed with avidity by many not deceived by open socialism.

Norm of Just Distribution

56. To prevent erroneous doctrines of this kind from blocking the path of justice and peace, the advocates of these opinions should have hearkened to the wise words of Our predecessor: "The earth, however divided among private owners, ceases not thereby to minister to the needs of all" (R.N., 7). This teaching We Ourselves reaffirmed above when we wrote that the division of goods which is effected by private ownership is ordained by nature itself and has for its purpose that created things may minister to man's needs in orderly and stable fashion. These principles must be constantly borne in mind if we would not wander from the path of truth.

57. Now, not every kind of distribution of wealth and property among men is such that it can at all, and still less can adequately, attain the end intended by God. *Wealth, therefore, which is constantly being augmented by social and economic progress, must be so distributed amongst the various individuals and classes of society that the common good of all, of which Leo XIII spoke, is thereby promoted. In other words, the good of the whole community must be safeguarded. By these principles of social justice one class is forbidden to exclude the other from a share in the profits.* This sacred law is violated by a wealthy class who, as it were, carefree in their possessions, deem it a just state of things that they should receive everything and the laborer nothing. It is violated also by a propertyless wage-earning class who demand for themselves all the fruits of production, as being the product of their hands. Such men, vehemently incensed against the violation of

justice by capitalists, go too far in wrongly vindicating the one right of which they are conscious. They attack and seek to abolish all forms of ownership and all income not obtained by labor, whatever be their nature or whatever function these represent in human society, for the sole reason that they are not acquired by toil. In this connection it must be noted that the appeal made by some to the words of the apostle: "If any man will not work, neither let him eat" (2 Thess. 3:10), is as inept as it is unfounded. The apostle is here passing judgment on those who refuse to work though they could and ought to do so; he admonishes us to use diligently our time and our powers of body and mind, and not to become burdensome to others as long as we are able to provide for ourselves. In no sense does he teach that labor is the sole title to a living or to an income (*ibid.*, 8-10).

58. *Each one, then, must receive his due share, and the distribution of created goods must be brought into conformity with the demands of the common good, that is, of social justice. For every sincere observer is conscious that the vast differences between the few who hold masive wealth and the many who live in destitution constitute a grave evil in modern society.*

D. Improving the Lot of Non-Owning Workers

59. This is the aim which Our predecessor urged as the necessary object of our efforts: the uplifting of propertyless, insecure working people. It calls for more emphatic assertion and more insistent repetition on the present occasion because these salutary injunctions of the Pontiff have not infrequently been forgotten, deliberately ignored or deemed impracticable, though they were both feasible and imperative. They have lost none of their force or wisdom for our own age, even though the horrible "pauperism" of the days of Leo XIII is less prevalent today. The condition of the workingman has indeed been improved and rendered more equitable, particularly in the larger and more civilized states, where the laboring class can no longer be said to be universally in misery and want. But after modern machinery and modern industry had progressed with astonishing speed and taken possession of many newly colonized countries no less than of the ancient civilizations of the Far East, the number of the dispossessed laboring masses, whose groans mount to heaven from these lands, increased beyond all measures.

Moreover, there is the immense army of hired rural laborers, whose condition is depressed in the extreme and who have no hope of ever obtaining "a share in the land" (R.N., 35). These, too, unless proper and efficacious remedies be applied, will remain perpetually sunk in the proletarian condition.

60. It is true that there is a formal difference between paupers and propertyless, insecure workers. *Nevertheless, the immense number of propertyless wage earners on the one hand, and the enormous wealth of the fortunate few on the other, are an unanswerable argument that the earthly goods so abundantly produced in this age of industrialism are far from rightly distributed and equitably shared among the various classes of men.*

Remedies

a. Economic Life Must Be Informed by Christian Principles

136. For this pitiable ruin of souls, which, if it continues, will frustrate all efforts to reform society, there can be no other remedy than a frank and sincere return to the teachings of the gospel. Men must observe anew the precepts of Him who alone has the words of eternal life (John 6:70), words which, even though heaven and earth be changed, shall not pass away (Matt. 24:35).

All those versed in social matters urgently demand a reasonable arrangement of economic life which will introduce sound and true order. But this order, which We ourselves desire and make every effort to promote, will be quite faulty and imperfect unless man's activities harmoniously unite to imitate and, as far as is humanly possible, attain the marvelous unity of the divine plan. *This is the perfect order which the Church preaches with intense earnestness, and which right reason demands: which places God as the first and supreme end of all created activity, and regards all created goods as mere instruments under God, to be used only in so far as they help toward the attainment of our supreme end.*

Nor is it to be imagined that remunerative occupations are thereby belittled or deemed less consonant with human dignity. On the contrary, we are taught to recognize and reverence in them the manifest will of God the Creator, who placed man upon earth to work it and use it in various ways in order to supply his needs. *Those who are engaged in production are not forbidden to increase their fortunes in a lawful and just manner: indeed it is just that he who renders service to society and develops its wealth should himself have his proportionate share of the increased riches the community enjoys, provided always that he respects the laws of God and the rights of his neighbor, and uses his property in accord with faith and right reason.* If these principles be observed by all, everywhere and at all times, not merely the production and acquisition of good, but also the use of wealth, now so often inordinate, will within a short time be brought back again to the standards of equity and just distribution.

Mere sordid selfishness, which is the disgrace and the great crime of the present age, will be opposed in very deed by the kindly and forcible law of Christian moderation, whereby man is commanded to seek first the Kingdom of God and His justice, confiding in God's liberality and definite promise that temporal goods, also, in so far as he needs them, will be added unto him (Matt. 6:33).

b. The Function of Charity

137. Now, in effecting this reform, charity, "which is the bond of perfection" (Col. 3:14), must play a leading part. How completely deceived are those rash reformers who, zealous only for commutative justice, proudly disdain the help of charity! Assuredly charity cannot take the place of justice officially due and unfairly withheld. But even though a state of things be pictured in which every man receives at last all that is his due, a wide field will nevertheless remain open for charity. For justice alone, even though faithfully observed, can remove indeed the cause of social strife, but can never bring about a union of hearts and minds. Yet this union, binding men together, is the main principle of stability in all institutions, no matter how perfect they may seem, which aim at establishing social peace and promoting mutual aid. In its absence, as repeated experience proves, the wisest regulations come to nothing. Then only will it be possible to unite all in harmonious striving for the common good, when all sections of society have the intimate conviction that they are members of one great family and children of the same heavenly Father and, further, that they are "one body in Christ and everyone members one of another" (Rom. 12:5), so that "if one member suffer anything, all members suffer it" (1 Cor. 12:26). Then the rich and others in power will change their former neglect of their poorer brethren into solicitous and effective love, will listen with kindly feeling to their just complaints, and will readily forgive them the faults and mistakes they possibly make. Workingmen, too, will lay aside all feelings of hatred or envy, which the instigators of social strife exploit so skillfully. Not only will they cease to feel discontent at the position assigned them by divine providence in human society; they will become proud of it, well aware that they are working usefully and honorably for the common good, according to each one's task and function, and are following closely in the footsteps of Him who, being in the form of God, chose to become a carpenter among men, and to be known as the Son of the Carpenter.

An Arduous Task

138. Because of this new diffusion throughout the world of the gospel spirit, which is a spirit of Christian moderation and of universal charity, We confidently look forward to that complete and much desired renewal of human society, and to "the Peace of Christ in the Kingdom of Christ," to which We firmly resolved at the very beginning of Our pontificate to devote all Our care and all Our pastoral solicitude. You, Venerable Brethren, who by ordinance of the Holy Spirit rule with Us the Church of God, are laboring strenuously and with admirable zeal in all parts of the world, inclusive of missions among pagans, toward this same end of capital importance and necessity today. Receive your well-deserved meed of praise, and with you all those, of the clergy and laity, whom We rejoice to see daily taking part in this great work and affording valuable help. These are Our beloved sons devoted to Catholic Action, who with extraordinary zeal aid Us in the solution of social problems, in so far as the Church in virtue of her divine institution has the right and the duty to concern herself with them. With repeated insistence We exhort all these in the Lord to spare no labor and be overcome by no difficulty, but to become daily more courageous and valiant (Deut. 31:7).

The task We propose to them is indeed difficult, for well We know that many are the obstacles to be overcome on either side, whether among the higher classes of society or the lower. Still, let them not lose heart. To face stern combats is the part of a Christian: and to endure severe labor is the lot of those who, as good soldiers of Christ (2 Tim. 2:4), follow closely in His footsteps.

139. Relying, therefore solely on the omnipotent assistance of Him who "will have all men to be saved" (I Tim. 2:4), let us devote all our energies to helping those unhappy souls who are turned away from God; let us withdraw them from the temporal cares in which they are too much involved, and teach them to aspire with confidence to things that are eternal. At times, indeed, this will be easier to accomplish than appears at first sight; for if in the depths of even the most abandoned hearts there lurk, like sparks beneath the ashes, spiritual forces of unexpected strength — a clear testimony of a "naturally Christian soul" — how much more then must these abide in the hearts of the many who, largely through ignorance and unfavorable surroundings, have wandered into error!

140. For the rest, the ranks of the workingmen themselves provide glad signs of coming social reconstruction. To the great job of Our heart We discern among them the massed cohort of young workers who listen readily to the call

of divine grace and strive with splendid zeal to win their fellows to Christ. No less praise is due to those leaders of workingmen's organizations who, sacrificing their own interests and anxious only for the good of their companions, strive with prudence to promote their just demands and bring them into harmony with the prosperity of the entire craft; and who allow no obstacles or misgivings to deter them from this noble task. Further, many young men destined soon by reason of their talents or their wealth to hold distinguished places in the foremost ranks of society are studying social problems with growing earnestness. These youths encourage the fairest hopes that they will dedicate themselves to social reconstruction.

The Course to Follow

141. Present circumstances, therefore, Venerable Brethren and beloved children, indicate clearly the course to be followed. Nowadays, as more than once in the history of the Church, we are confronted with a world which in large measure has almost fallen back into paganism. In order to bring back to Christ these whole classes of men who have denied Him, we must gather and train from amongst their very ranks auxiliary soldiers of the Church, men who know well their mentality and their aspirations, and who with kindly fraternal charity will be able to win their hearts. *Undoubtedly the first and immediate apostles of the workingmen must themselves be workingmen, while the apostles of the industrial and commercial world should themselves be employers and merchants.*

142. It is your chief duty, Venerable Brethren, and that of your clergy, to seek diligently, to select prudently and train fittingly these lay apostles, among workingmen and among employers.

No easy task is here imposed upon the clergy, wherefore *all candidates for the sacred priesthood must be adequately prepared to meet it by intense study of social matters*. It is particularly necessary, however, that they whom you specially select and devote to this work show themselves endowed with a keen sense of justice, ready to oppose with real, manly constancy unjust claims and unjust actions; that they avoid every extreme with consummate prudence and discretion; above all, that they be thoroughly imbued with the charity of Christ, which alone has power to incline men's hearts and will firmly and gently to the laws of equity and justice. This course, already productive of success in the past, we must follow now with alacrity.

143. Further, We earnestly exhort in the Lord the beloved sons who are

chosen for this task to devote themselves wholeheartedly to the formation of the men entrusted to them. In the execution of this most priestly and apostolic work, *let them make opportune use of the powerful resources of Christian training, by instructing youth, by founding Christian associations, by forming study circles on Christian lines.*

Above all, let them hold in high esteem and employ with diligence for the benefit of their disciples the Spiritual Exercises, a most precious means of personal and of social reform, as We said in Our encyclical *Mens Nostra. These Exercises We declared in express terms* to be most useful for the laity in general and *especially for workingmen*, and We warmly recommended them; for in that school of the spirit not only are excellent Christians formed, but real apostles of every state of life are trained and enkindled with the fire of the Heart of Christ. From that school they will go forth, as the Apostles from the cenacle in Jerusalem, strong in faith, unconquerable in steadfastness under trials, aflame with zeal, eager only for the spread in every way of the Kingdom of Christ.

144. And, in truth, the world has nowadays sore need of valiant soldiers of Christ, who strain every thew and sinew to preserve the human family from the dire havoc which would befall it were the teachings of the gospel to be flouted, and a social order permitted to prevail which spurns no less the laws of nature than those of God. For herself, the Church of Christ, built upon the solid rock, has nothing to fear, for she knows that the gates of hell shall not prevail against her (Matt. 16:18); and the experience of centuries has taught her that storms, even the most violent, pass, leaving her stronger and triumphantly victorious. But her maternal bosom cannot but be stirred at the thought of the countless ills which tempests of this the kind occasion to so many thousands; at the thought, above all, of immense spiritual evils which ensue, entailing the eternal ruin of so many souls redeemed by the blood of Christ.

145. No stone, then, must be left unturned to avert these grave misfortunes from human society. Toward this one aim must tend all our effort and endeavor, supported by assiduous and fervent prayers to God. For, with the assistance of divine grace, the destiny of the human family lies in our hands.

146. Let us not Permit, Venerable Brethlen and beloved children, the children of this world to seem wiser in their generation than we who by God's goodness are children of light (Luke 16:8). We see these men select and train with utmost shrewdness resolute disciples, who spread their false doctrines more widely every day among men of every station and of every clime. And

when it becomes a question for attacking more vehemently the Church of Christ, we see them lay aside their internal quarrels, line up harmoniously into a single battleline, and strive with united forces toward this common aim.

Close Union and Cooperation are Urged

147. No one indeed is unaware of the many and splendid works in the social and economic field, as well as in education and religion, laboriously set in motion with indefatigable zeal by Catholics. But this admirable and self-sacrificing activity not infrequently loses some of its effectiveness by being directed into too many different channels. *Let, then, all men of good will*, who under the pastors of the Church wish to fight this good and peaceful fight of Christ, stand united; let all, under the leadership and instruction of the Church, strive to play their part — each according to his talents, powers and station — in the Christian renewal of human society which Leo XIII inaugurated in his immortal encyclical *Rerum Novarum*. Let them seek, not themselves and the things that are their own, but the things that are Jesus Christ's (Phil. 2:21). Let them not urge their own ideas with undue persistence, but be ready to abandon them, however admirable, should the greater common good seem to require it; that in all and above all Christ may reign and rule, to whom be honor and glory and power forever and ever (Apoc. 5:13).

148. That this happy result may be attained, Venerable Brethren and beloved children, We impart to you all, members of the great Catholic family entrusted to Our care, *but with special affection of Our heart to artisans and other workingmen engaged in manual labor, by divine providence committed to Us in a particular manner, and to Christian employers and managers*, with paternal affection, the Apostolic benediction.

149. Given at Rome, at Saint Peter's, the fifteenth day of May, in the year 1931, the tenth year of Our pontificate.

Pius XI, Pope

Chapter 61 • G. K. Chesterton: *The Romance of Orthodoxy*; *The Marvel*; *Luther's Bonfire*; *A Christmas Carol*

Gilbert K. Ghesterton (1874-1936) is considered a voluminous writer in many fields. He was converted from Anglicanism to Roman Catholicism in 1922. Among his many works, *Orthodoxy* is an example of how he thought about philosophy and religion; "The Marvel" is an excerpt from *The Everlasting Man*; *Luther's Bonfire* may refer to the story that the Reformer publicly burned the *Summa* and other works of Thomas Aquinas; and *A Christmas Carol* is an example of his poetic ability applied to the birth of Jesus.

The Romance of Orthodoxy

Christian doctrine detected the oddities of life. It not only discovered the law, but it foresaw the exceptions. Those underrate Christianity who say that it discovered mercy; any one might discover mercy. In fact every one did. But to discover a plan for being merciful and also severe — *that* was to anticipate a strange need of human nature. For no one wants to be forgiven for a big sin as if it were a little one. . . . This was the big fact about Christian ethics; the discovery of the new balance. Paganism had been like a pillar of marble, upright because proportioned with symmetry. Christianity was like a huge and ragged and romantic rock, which, though it sways on its pedestal at a touch, yet, because its exaggerated excrescences exactly balance each other, is enthroned there for a thousand years. In a Gothic cathedral the columns were all different, but they were all necessary. Every support seemed an accidental and fantastic support; every buttress was a flying buttress. So in Christendom apparent accidents balanced.

Becket wore a hair shirt under his gold and crimson, and there is much to be said for the combination; for Becket got the benefit of the hair shirt while the people in the street got the benefit of the crimson and gold. It is at least better than the manner of the modern millionaire, who has the black and the drab outwardly for others, and the gold next his heart. But the balance was not always in one man's body as in Becket's; the balance was often distributed over the whole body of Christendom. Because a man prayed and fasted on the

Northern snows, flowers could be flung at his festival in the Southern cities; and because fanatics drank water on the sands of Syria, men could still drink cider in the orchards of England. This is what makes Christendom at once so much more perplexing and so much more interesting than the Pagan empire; just as Amiens Cathedral is not better but more interesting than the Parthenon. If any one wants a modern proof of all this, let him consider the curious fact that, under Christianity, Europe (while remaining a unity) has broken up into individual nations. Patriotism is a perfect example of this deliberate balancing of one emphasis against another emphasis. . . .

It is exactly this which explains what is so inexplicable to all the modern critics of the history of Christianity. I mean the monstrous wars about small points of theology, the earthquakes of emotion about a gesture or a word. It was only a matter of an inch; but an inch is everything when you are balancing. The Church could not afford to swerve a hair's breadth on some things if she was to continue her great and daring experiment of the irregular equilibrium. Once let one idea become less powerful and some other idea would become too powerful. It was no flock of sheep the Christian shepherd was leading, but a herd of bulls and tigers, of terrible ideals and devouring doctrines, each one of them strong enough to turn to a false religion and lay waste the world. Remember that the Church went in specifically for dangerous ideas; she was a lion-tamer. The idea of birth through a Holy Spirit, of the death of a divine being, of the forgiveness of sins, or the fulfilment of prophecies, are ideas which, any one can see, need but a touch to turn them into something blasphemous or ferocious. The smallest link was let drop by the artificers of the Mediterranean, and the lion of ancestral pessimism burst his chain in the forgotten forests of the north. Of these theological equalizations I have to speak afterwards. Here it is enough to notice that if some small mistake were made in doctrine, huge blunders might be made in human happiness. A sentence phrased wrong about the nature of symbolism would have broken all the best statues in Europe. A slip in the definitions might stop all the dances; might wither all the Christmas trees or break all the Easter eggs. Doctrines had to be defined within strict limits, even in order that man might enjoy general human liberties. The Church had to be careful, if only that the world might be careless.

This is the thrilling romance of Orthodoxy. People have fallen into a foolish habit of speaking of orthodoxy as something heavy, humdrum and safe. There never was anything so perilous or so exciting as orthodoxy. It was sanity: and to be sane is more dramatic than to be mad. It was the equilibrium of a man behind madly rushing horses, seeming to stoop this way and sway that, yet in every attitude having the grace of statuary and the accuracy of arithmetic. The Church in its early days went fierce and fast with any warhorse; yet it is utterly unhistoric to say that she merely went mad along one idea, like a vulgar fanaticism. She swerved to left and right, so as exactly to avoid enormous obstacles. She left on one hand the huge bulk of Arianism, buttressed by all the worldly powers to make Christianity too worldly. The next instant she was swerving to avoid an orientalism, which would have made it too unworldly. The orthodox Church never took the tame course or accepted the conventions; the orthodox Church was never respectable. It would have been easier to have accepted the earthly power of the Arians. It would have been easy, in the Calvinistic seventeenth century, to fall into the bottomless pit of predestination. It is easy to be a madman: it is easy to be a heretic. It is always easy to let the age have its head; the difficult thing is to keep one's own. It is always easy to be a modernist; as it is easy to be a snob. To have fallen into any of those open traps of error and exaggeration which fashion after fashion and sect after sect set along the historic path of Christendom — that would indeed have been simple. It is always simple to fall; there are an infinity of angles at which one falls, only one at which one stands. To have fallen into any one of the fads from Gnosticism to Christian Science would indeed have been obvious and tame. But to have avoided them all has been one whirling adventure; and in my vision the heavenly chariot flies thundering through the ages, the dull heresies sprawling and prostrate, the wild truth reeling but erect.

The Marvel

There are people who say they wish Christianity to remain as a spirit. They mean, very literally, that they wish it to remain as a ghost. But it is not going to remain as a ghost. What follows this process of apparent death is not the lingering of the shade; it is the resurrection of the body. These people are quite prepared to shed pious and reverential tears over the Sepulchre of the Son of Man; what they are not prepared for is the Son of God walking once more upon the hills of morning. These people, and indeed most people, were indeed by this time quite accustomed to the idea that the old Christian candlelight would fade into the light of common day. To many of them it did quite honestly appear like that pale yellow flame of a candle when it is left burning in daylight. It was all the more unexpected, and therefore all the more unmistakable, that the seven-branched candle-stick suddenly towered to heaven like a miraculous tree and flamed until the sun turned pale. But other ages have seen the day conquer the candlelight and then the candlelight conquer the day. Again and again, before our time, men have grown content with a diluted doctrine. And again and again there has followed on that dilution, coming as out of the darkness in a crimson cataract, the strength of the red original wine. And we only say once more today as has been said many times by our fathers: "Long years and centuries ago our fathers or the founders of our people drank, as they dreamed, of the blood of God. Long years and centuries have passed since the strength of that giant vintage has been anything but a legend of the age of giants. Centuries ago already is the dark time of the second fermentation, when the wine of Catholicism turned into the vinegar of Calvinism. Long since that bitter drink has been itself diluted; rinsed out and washed away by the waters of oblivion and the wave of the world. Never did we think to taste again even that bitter tang of sincerity and the spirit, still less the richer and the sweeter strength of the purple vineyards in our dreams of the age of gold. Day by day and year by year we have lowered our hopes and lessened our convictions; we have grown more and more used to seeing those vats and vineyards overwhelmed in the water-floods and the last savour and suggestion of that special element fading like a stain of purple upon a sea of grey. We have grown used to dilution, to dissolution, to a watering down that went on for ever. But Thou hast kept the good wine until now."

This is the final fact, and it is the most extraordinary of all. The Faith has not only often died but it has often died of old age. It has not only been often killed but it has often died a natural death; in the sense of coming to a natural and necessary end. It is obvious that it has survived the most savage and the most universal persecutions from the shock of the Diocletian fury to the shock of the French Revolution. But it has a more strange and even a more weird tenacity; it has survived not only war but peace. It has not only died often but degenerated often and decayed often; it has survived its own weakness and even its own surrender. We need not repeat what is so obvious about the beauty of the end of Christ in its wedding of youth and death. But this is almost as if Christ had lived to the last possible span, had been a white-haired sage of a hundred and died of natural decay, and then had risen again rejuvenated, with trumpets and the rending of the sky. It was said truly enough that human Christianity in its recurrent weakness was sometimes too much wedded to the powers of the world; but if it was wedded it has very often been widowed. It is a strangely immortal sort of widow. An enemy may have said at one moment that it was but an aspect of the power of the Caesars; and it sounds as strange today as to call it an aspect of the Pharaohs. An enemy might say that it was the official faith of feudalism; and it sounds as convincing now as to say that it was bound to perish with the ancient Roman villa. All these things did indeed run their course to its normal end; and there seemed no course for the religion but to end with them. It ended and it began again.

"Heaven and earth shall pass away, but my words shall not pass away." The civilization of antiquity was the whole world, and men no more dreamed of its ending than of the ending of daylight. They could not imagine another order unless it were in another world. The civilization of the world has passed away and those words have not passed away. In the long night of the Dark Ages feudalism was so familiar a thing that no man could imagine himself without a lord; and religion was so woven into that network that no man would have believed they could be torn asunder. Feudalism itself was torn to rags and rotted away in the popular life of the true Middle Ages; and the first and freshest power in that new freedom was the old religion. Feudalism had passed away, and the words did not pass away. The whole medieval order, in many ways so complete and almost cosmic a home for man, wore out gradually in its turn; and here at least it was thought that the words would die. They went forth across the radiant abyss of the Renaissance and in fifty years were using all its light and learning for new religious foundations, new apologetics, new saints. It was supposed to have been withered up at last in the dry light of the Age of Reason; it was supposed to have disappeared ultimately in the earthquake of the Age of Revolution. Science explained it away; and it was still there. History disinterred it in the past; and it appeared suddenly in the future. Today it stands once more in our path; and even as we watch it, it grows.

If our social relations and records retain their continuity, if men really learn to apply reason to the accumulating facts of so crushing a story, it would seem that sooner or later even its enemies will learn from their incessant and interminable disappointments not to look for anything so simple as its death. They may continue to war with it, but it will be as they war with nature; as they war with the landscape, as they war with the skies. 'Heaven and earth shall pass away, but my words shall not pass away.' They will watch for it to stumble; they will watch for it to err; they will no longer watch for it to end. Insensibly, even unconsciously, they will in their own silent anticipations fulfil the relative terms of that astounding prophecy: they will forget to watch for the mere extinction of what has so often been vainly extinguished; and will learn instinctively to look first for the coming of the comet or the freezing of the star.

From *The Everlasting Man*

Luther's Bonfire

We must be just to those huge human figures who are in fact the hinges of history. However strong, and rightly strong, be our own controversial conviction, it must never mislead us into thinking that something trivial has transformed the world. So it is with that great Augustinian monk, who avenged all the ascetic Augustinians of the Middle Ages; and whose broad and burly figure has been big enough to block out for four centuries the distant human mountain of Aquinas. It is not, as the moderns delight to say, a question of theology. The Protestant theology of Martin Luther was a thing that no modern Protestant would be seen dead in a field with; or if the phrase be too flippant, would be specially anxious to touch with a barge-pole. That Protesiantism was pessimism; it was nothing but bare insistence on the hopelessness of all human virtue, as an attempt to escape hell. That Lutheranism is now quite unreal; more modern phases of Lutheranism are rather more unreal; but Luther was not unreal. He was one of those great elemental barbarians, to whom it is indeed given to change the world. To compare those two figures bulking so big in history, in any philosophical sense, would of course be futile and even unfair. On a great map like the mind of Aquinas, the mind of Luther would be almost invisible. But it is not altogether untrue to say, as so many journalists have said without caring whether it was true or untrue, that Luther opened an epoch; and began the modern world.

He was the first man who ever consciously used his consciousness; or what was later called his Personality. He had as a fact a rather strong personality. Aquinas had an even stronger personality; he had a massive and magnetic presence; he had an intellect that could act like a huge system of artillery spread over the whole world; he had that instantaneous presence of mind in debate, which alone really deserves the name of wit. But it never occurred to him to use anything except his wits in defence of a truth distinct from himself. It never occurred to Aquinas to use Aquinas as a weapon. There is not a trace of his ever using his personal advantages, of birth or body or brain or breeding, in debate with anybody. In short, he belonged to an age of intellectual unconsciousness, to an age of intellectual innocence, which was very intellectual. Now Luther did begin the modern mood of depending on things not merely intellectual. It is not a question of praise or blame; it matters little whether we say that he was a strong personality, or that he was a bit of a big bully. When he quoted a Scripture text, inserting a word that is not in Scripture, he was content to shout back at all hecklers: 'Tell them that Dr. Martin Luther will have it so!' That is what we now call Personality. A little later it was called Psychology. After that it was called Advertisement or Salesmanship. But we are not arguing about advantages or disadvantages. It is due to this great Augustinian pessimist to say, not only that he did triumph at last over the Angel of the Schools, but that he did in a very real sense make the modern world. He destroyed Reason; and substituted Suggestion.

It is said that the great Reformer publicly burned the *Summa Theologica* and the works of Aquinas; and with the bonfire of such books this book may well come to an end. They say it is very difficult to burn a book; and it must have been exceedingly difficult to burn such a mountain of books as the Dominican had contributed to the controversies of Christendom. Anyhow, there is something lurid and apocalyptic about the idea of such destruction, when we consider the compact complexity of all that encyclopaedic survey of social and moral and theoretical things. All the close-packed definitions that excluded so many errors and extremes; all the broad and balanced judgments upon the clash of loyalties or the choice of evils; all the liberal speculations upon the limits of government and the proper conditions of justice; all the distinctions between the use and abuse of private property; all the rules and exceptions about the great evil of war; all the allowances for human weakness and all the provisions for human health: all this mass of medieval humanism shrivelled and curled up in smoke before the eyes of its enemy; and that great passionate peasant rejoiced darkly; because the day of the Intellect was over. Sentence by sentence it burned, and syllogism by syllogism; and the golden maxims turned to golden flames in that last and dying glory of all that had once been the great wisdom of the Greeks. One great central Synthesis of history, that was to have linked the ancient with the modern world, went up in smoke and, for half the world, was forgotten like a vapour.

For a time it seemed that the destruction was final. It is still expressed in the amazing fact that (in the North) modern men can still write histories of philosophy in which philosophy stops with the last little sophists of Greece and Rome, and is never heard of again until the appearance of such a third-rate philosopher as Francis Bacon. And yet this small book, which will probably do nothing else, or have very little other value, will be at least a testimony to the fact that the tide has turned once more. It is four hundred years after; and this book, I hope (and I am happy to say I believe), will probably be lost and forgotten in the flood of better books about St. Thomas Aquinas, which are at this moment pouring from every printing-press in Europe, and even in England and America. Compared with such books, it is obviously a very slight and amateurish production. But it is not likely to be burned; and if it were, it would not leave even a noticeable gap in the pouring mass of new and magnificent work, which is now daily dedicated to the *philosophia perennis*; to the Everlasting Philosophy.

From *St. Thomas Aquinas*.

A Christmas Carol

The Christ-child lay on Mary's lap,
His hair was like a light.
(O weary, weary were the world,
But here is all aright.)
The Christ-child lay on Mary's breast,
His hair was like a star.
(O stern and cunning are the kings,
But here the true hearts are.)
The Christ-child lay on Mary's heart,
His hair was like a fire.
(O weary, weary is the world,
But here the world's desire.)
The Christ-child stood at Mary's knee,
His hair was like a crown,
And all the flowers looked up at Him,
And all the stars looked down.

(1899)

Selections from
G.K. Chesterton: An Anthology,
Selected with an Introduction by D.B. Wyndham Lewis,
Oxford University Press, 1957

Chapter 62 • Pope Pius XII: *Mystici Corporis; Divino Afflante Spiritu*

In 1876 Eugenio Pacelli (pope, 1939-1958) was born in Rome, where he received most of his education, was ordained, and trained for the papal diplomatic service. In 1912 he was named Undersecretary of State, and in 1917, as bishop, he became nuncio to Bavaria. Named cardinal in 1929, and Secretary of State later, he was tireless in his travels and activities, negotiating peaceful relations with peoples and governments all over the world. On the third ballot he was elected pope on March 2, 1939, and took the name of Pius XII. Following in the footsteps of his predecessors he spoke out boldly against every attempt of states to lessen or destroy the rights of individuals and the family. The first encyclical reproduced here is a classic example of Catholic teaching on the nature of the Church that had been presented by St. Paul and elaborated by the fathers and doctors of the Church, especially by St. Augustine and St. Thomas Aquinas. The second is to encourage modern Scripture scholarship.

Mystici Corporis
The Mystical Body of Christ

Venerable Brothers: Health and Apostolic Benediction.

We first learned of the Mystical Body of Christ, which is the Church, from the lips of the Redeemer Himself.

And a first observation to be made is that the society established by the Redeemer of the human race is not unlike its Divine Founder, Who was persecuted, calumniated and tortured by those very men whom He had undertaken to save.

The more men are withdrawn from the vanities of this world and from an inordinate love of temporal things, certainly the more likely it is that they will perceive the light of heavenly mysteries. But the vanity and emptiness of earthly riches are more manifest today than perhaps at any other period, when kingdoms and States are crumbling, when huge piles of goods and all kinds of wealth are sunk in the measureless depths of the sea, and cities, towns and fertile fields are strewn with massive ruins and defiled with the blood of brothers. The chief reason for Our present exposition of this sublime doctrine is our solicitude for the souls entrusted to us.

Add to this, that recent documents on Catholic Action, by drawing closer the bonds of union between Christians and between them and the ecclesiastical hierarchy and especially the Roman Pontiff, have undoubtedly helped not a little to place this truth in its proper light. Nevertheless, while We can derive legitimate joy from all this, We must confess that grave errors in regard to this doctrine are being spread among those outside the true Church, and that among the faithful, too, inaccurate or thoroughly false ideas are entering which turn minds aside from the straight path of truth.

For while there still survives a false *rationalism*, which ridicules anything that transcends and defies the power of human genius, and which is accompanied by a cognate error, *popular naturalism* they call it, which sees and wants to see in the Church nothing but a juridical and social union; there is, on the other hand, a false *mysticism* creeping in, which, in its attempt to eliminate the immovable frontier that separates creatures from their Creator, garbles the Sacred Scriptures.

PART I

The Mystical Body of Christ — His One, True Church

When one reflects on this doctrine, one recalls immediately the words of the Apostle: "Where sin abounded, grace did more abound." All know that the Father of the whole human race was constituted by God in a state so exalted that He was to hand on to His posterity, together with earthly existence, the heavenly life of Divine grace. But after the unhappy fall of Adam, the universal progeny of mankind, infected by a hereditary stain, lost their sharing of the Divine Nature, and we were all children of wrath. But God, all merciful, "so loved the world as to give His only-begotten Son" and the Word of the Eternal Father, through this same Divine love, assumed human nature from the race of Adam — but an innocent and spotless nature it was — so that He, as a new Adam, might be the source whence the grace of the Holy Spirit should flow unto all the children of the first parent. Through the sin of the first man they had been excluded from adoption into the children of God; through the Word Incarnate, made brothers according to the flesh of the only-begotten Son of God, they would receive the power to become the sons of God. It was possible for Him personally, immediately to impart these graces to men; but He wished to do so only through a visible Church that would be formed by the union of men, and thus through that Church every man would perform a work of collaboration with Him in dispensing the graces of Redemption. The Word of

God willed to make use of our nature, when in excruciating agony He would redeem mankind; in much the same way throughout the centuries He makes use of the Church that the work begun might endure.

If we would define and describe this true Church of Jesus Christ — which is the One, Holy, Catholic, Apostolic, Roman Church — we shall find no expression more noble, more sublime or more Divine than the phrase which calls it "the Mystical Body of Jesus Christ." This title is derived from and is, as it were, the fair flower of the repeated teaching of Sacred Scripture and the Holy Fathers.

A) "The Body" — is the Church

That the Church is a body is frequently asserted in Sacred Scripture. "Christ," says the Apostle, "is the Head of the Body of the Church." If the Church is a body, it must be an unbroken unity according to those words of Paul: "Though many, we are one body in Christ." But it is not enough that the Body of the Church be an unbroken unity; it must also be something definite and perceptible to the senses, as Our predecessor of happy memory, Leo XIII, in his Encyclical *Satis cognitum* asserts: "The Church is visible because she is a Body." Hence they err in a matter of Divine truth, who imagine the Church to be invisible, intangible, a something merely "pneumatological," as they say, by which many Christian communities, though they differ from each other in their profession of faith, are united by a bond that eludes the senses.

But a body calls also for a multiplicity of members, which are linked together in such a way as to help one another. So in the Church the individual members do not live for themselves alone, but also help their fellows, and all work in mutual collaboration for their common comfort and for the more perfect building up of the whole Body.

Again, as in nature a body is not formed by any haphazard grouping of members but must be constituted of organs, that is, members that have not the same function and are arranged in due order; so for this reason above all the Church is called a body, that it is constituted by the coalescence of structurally united parts, and that it has a variety of members reciprocally dependent. It is thus the Apostle describes the Church when he writes: "As in one body we have many members, but all the members have not the same office: so we being many are one body in Christ, and everyone members one of another."

One must not think, however, that this ordered or "organic" structure of the Body of the Church contains only hierarchical elements and with them is complete; or, as an opposite opinion holds, that it is composed only of those who enjoy charismatic gifts, — though members gifted with miraculous powers will never be lacking in the Church. That those who exercise sacred power in this Body are its first and chief members, must be maintained uncompromisingly. It is through them, commissioned by the Divine Redeemer Himself, that Christ's apostolate as teacher, king, priest, is to endure.

At the same time, when the Fathers of the Church sing the praises of this Mystical Body of Christ with its ministries, its variety of ranks, its offices, its conditions, its order, its duties, they are thinking not only of those who have received sacred orders, but of all those, too, who, following the evangelical counsels, pass their lives either actively among men or in the silence of the cloister, or who aim at combining the active and contemplative life according to their Institute. They were thinking of those who, though living in the world, consecrate themselves wholeheartedly to spiritual or corporal works of mercy; as well as those who live in the state of holy matrimony.

Sacraments in the Body-Life

Now we see how the human body is given its own means to provide for its own life, health and growth and for the same of all its members. Similarly the Savior of mankind, out of His infinite goodness, has provided in a marvelous way for His Mystical Body, endowing it with the Sacraments; so that by so many consecutive, graduated graces, as it were, its members should be supported from the cradle to life's last breath, and that the social needs of the Church might also be generously provided for.

As all know, through the waters of Baptism those who are born into this world, being dead in sin, are not only born again and made members of the Church, but, being stamped with a spiritual seal, they become capable and fit to receive the other sacraments. By the chrism of Confirmation, the faithful are given added strength to protect and defend the Church, their Mother, and the faith she has given them. In the Sacrament of Penance a saving medicine is offered to the Church's members who have fallen into sin, not only to provide for their own health, but to remove from other members of the Mystical Body all danger of contagion, or rather to affirm them the tonic of virtuous example.

Nor is that enough; for in the Holy Eucharist the faithful are nourished and grow strong at the same table, and in a Divine, ineffable way are brought into union with each other and with the Divine Head of the whole Body. Finally, like a devoted mother, the Church is at the bedside of those who are sick unto death; and if it be not always God's will that by the sacred anointing of the sick she restore health to this mortal body, yet she does minister supernatural medicine for wounded souls, and sends new citizens on to Heaven to enjoy forever the happiness of God — new advocates assigned to her.

For the social needs of the Church, Christ has provided in a particular way by two sacraments which He instituted. Through Matrimony, when the contracting parties are ministers of grace to each other, provision is made for the external and properly regulated increase of Christian society and, what is of greater importance, for the correct religious education of the offspring, without which this Mystical Body would be in grave danger. Through Holy Orders, men are set aside and consecrated to God, to offer in sacrifice the Eucharistic Victim, to feed the flock of the faithful with the Bread of Angels and the food of doctrine, to guide them in the way of God's commandments and counsels, to strengthen them with all the other supernatural helps.

Here it is pertinent to remark that, just as at the beginning of time God gave man's body the most extraordinary power to subject all creatures to himself and to increase and multiply and fill the earth, so at the beginning of the Christian era He gave the Church those means that were needed to overcome dangers without number and to fill not only the whole world but the realm of heaven as well.

Who Are Members of the Body

Only those are really to be included as members of the Church who have been baptized and profess the true faith and who have not unhappily withdrawn from Body-unity or for grave faults been excluded by legitimate authority. "For in one Spirit," says the Apostle, "were we all baptized into one Body, whether Jews or Gentiles, whether bond or free." As, therefore, in the true Christian community there is only one Body, one Spirit, one Lord and one Baptism, so there can be only one Faith. And so if a man refuse to hear the Church, let him be considered — so the Lord commands — as a heathen and a publican. It follows that those who are divided in faith or government cannot be living in one Body such as this, and cannot be living the life of its one Divine Spirit.

Sinful Members

One must not imagine that the Body of the Church, just because it bears the name of Christ, is made up during the days of its earthly pilgrimage only of members conspicuous for their holiness, or consists only of the group of those whom God has predestined to eternal happiness. It is the Savior's infinite mercy that allows place in His Mystical Body here for those whom He did not exclude from the banquet of old. For not every sin, however grave and enormous it be, is such as to sever a man automatically from the Body of the Church, as does schism or heresy or apostasy. Men may lose charity and Divine grace through sin and so become incapable of supernatural merit, and yet not be deprived of all life, if they hold on to faith and Christian hope, and illumined from above they are spurred on by the strong promptings of the Holy Spirit to salutary fear and by God are moved to prayer and penance for their sins.

Let everyone then abhor sin, which defiles the members of our Redeemer; but if anyone unhappily falls and his obstinacy has not made him unworthy of communion with the faithful, let him be received with all affection and let eager charity see in him a weak member of Jesus Christ. For, as the Bishop of Hippo remarks, it is better "to be cured within the Church's community than to be cut off from its body as incurable members." "No reason to despair of the health of whatever is still part of the body; once it has been cut off, it can be neither cured nor healed."

B) "Of Christ" — The Redeemer's Role

In the course of the present study, Venerable Brothers, we have thus far seen that the Church has been so constituted that it may be likened to a body. We must now explain clearly and precisely why it is to be called not merely a body, but the Body of Jesus Christ. This follows from the fact that Our Lord is the Founder, the Head, the Support and the Savior of this Mystical Body.

For while fulfilling His office as preacher, He chose Apostles, sending them as He had been sent by the Father, namely as teachers, rulers, instruments of holiness in the assembly of the believers; He appointed their chief and His Vicar on Earth; He made known to them all things whatsoever He had heard from His Father; He also established Baptism by which those who should believe would be incorporated in the Body of the Church; and finally, when He came to the close of His life, at the Last Supper, He instituted the wonderful Sacrifice and Sacrament of the Eucharist.

The New Covenant

And first of all, by the death of Our Redeemer, the New Testament took the place of the Old Law which had been abolished; then the Law of Christ together with its mysteries, laws, institutions and sacred rites was ratified for the whole world in the blood of Jesus Christ. For, while our Divine Savior was preaching in a restricted area — He was not sent but to the sheep that were lost of the house of Israel — the Law and the Gospel were together in force; but on the gibbet of His death Jesus made void the Law with its decrees, fastened the handwriting of the Old Testament to the Cross, establishing the New Testament in His blood, shed for the whole human race. "To such an extent, then says Saint Leo the Great, speaking of the Cross of Our Lord, "was there effected a transfer from the Law to the Gospel, from the Synagogue to the Church, from many sacrifices to one Victim, that, as Our Lord expired, that mystical veil which shut off the innermost part of the temple and its sacred secret from the main temple was rent violently from top to bottom."

On the Cross, then, the Old Law died, soon to be buried and to be a bearer of death, in order to give way to the New Testament, of which Christ had chosen the Apostles as qualified ministers; and it is by the power of the Cross that Our Savior, although He had been constituted the Head of the whole human family in the womb of the Blessed Virgin, exercises fully the office itself of Head in His Church. "For it was through His triumph on the Cross," according to the teaching of the Angelic and Common Doctor, "that He won power and dominion over the gentiles," by that same victory He increased that immense treasury of graces, which, as He reigns in glory in Heaven, He lavishes continuously on His mortal members. It was by His blood shed on the Cross that God's anger was removed, and that all the heavenly gifts, especially the spiritual graces of the New and Eternal Testament, could then flow from the fountains of our Savior for the salvation of men, of the faithful first of all. It was on the tree of the Cross, finally, that He entered into possession of His Church, that is, all the members of His Mystical Body; for they would not have been united to this Mystical Body through the waters of Baptism except by the salutary virtue of the Cross, by which they had been already brought under the complete sway of Christ.

But if Our Savior, by His death became, in the full and complete sense of the word, the Head of the Church, it was likewise through His blood that the Church was endowed with that fullest communication of the Holy Spirit, through which, from the time when the Son of Man was lifted up and glorified on the gibbet by His sufferings, she is divinely illumined. For then, as Augustine notes, with the rending of the veil of the temple it happened that the dew of the Paraclete's gifts, which heretofore had descended only on the fleece, that is on the people of Israel, fell copiously and abundantly (while the fleece remained dry and deserted) on the whole earth, that is, on the Catholic Church, which is confined by no boundaries of race or territory.

Just as, at the first moment of the Incarnation, the Son of the Eternal Father adorned with the fullness of the Holy Spirit the human nature which was substantially united to Him, that it might be a fitting instrument of the Divinity of the sanguinary task of the Redemption, so at the hour of His precious death He wished that His Church should be enriched with the abundant gifts of the Paraclete, in order that, in dispensing the Divine fruits of the Redemption, it might be for the Incarnate Word a powerful instrument that would certainly never fail. For the juridical mission of the Church, and the power to teach, govern and administer the Sacraments derive their supernatural efficacy and force for the building up of the Body of Christ from the fact that Jesus Christ, hanging on the Cross, opened up to His Church the fountain of Divine graces, which protect it from ever teaching men false doctrine, and enable it to rule them for their soul's salvation through supernatural enlightened Pastors and to bestow on them abundant heavenly graces.

That this Mystical Body which is the Church should be called Christ's, is proved, in the second place, from the fact that He must be universally acknowledged as its actual head. "He," as St. Paul says, "is the Head of the Body, the Church." He is the Head from whom the whole body, perfectly organized, "groweth and maketh increase unto the edifying of itself."

You are aware, Venerable Brothers, of the brilliant language used by the masters of Scholastic Theology, and chiefly by the Angelic and Common Doctor, when treating this question; and you know that the reasons advanced by Aquinas are a faithful reflection of the mind and writings of the Holy Fathers, who after all merely repeated and commented on the inspired word of Sacred Scripture.

However, for the good of all we wish to touch this point briefly. And, first of all, it is clear that the Son of God and of the Blessed Virgin is to be called the Head of the Church for His singular pre-eminence.

Because Christ is so exalted, He alone by every right rules and governs the Church; and herein is yet another reason why He must be likened to a head.

But our Divine Savior governs and guides His community also directly and personally. For it is He who reigns within the minds and hearts of men and bends and subjects to His purpose their will even when rebellious. "The heart of the King is in the hand of the Lord; whithersoever he will, he shall turn it."

By this interior guidance the "Shepherd and Bishop of our souls" not only watches over individuals, but exercises His providence over the universal Church as well, whether by enlightening and giving courage to the Church's rulers for the loyal and effective performance of their respective duties, or by singling out from the body of the Church — especially when times are grave — men and women of conspicuous holiness, who may point the way for the rest of Christendom to the perfecting of His Mystical Body.

Besides, from Heaven Christ never ceases to look down with extraordinary love on His unspotted Spouse so sorely tried in her earthly exile; and when He sees her in danger, either Himself or through the ministry of His Angels, or through her whom we hail the Help of Christians, and other heavenly advocates, takes her out of the tempestuous sea, and in calm and tranquil waters comforts her with the peace "which surpasseth all understanding."

Visibly, Through His Vicar the Pope

But we must not think that He rules only in a hidden or extraordinary way. On the contrary, our Divine Redeemer also governs His Mystical Body in a visible way and ordinarily through His Vicar on earth. You know, Venerable Brothers, that after He had ruled the "little flock" Himself during His mortal pilgrimage, when about to leave this world and return to the Father, Christ Our Lord entrusted to the chief of the Apostles the visible government of the entire community He had founded. He was all wise; and how could He leave without a visible head the body of the Church He had founded as a human society?

Nor against this may one argue, that the primacy of jurisdiction established in the Church gives such a Mystical Body two heads. For Peter in virtue of his Primacy is only Christ's Vicar; so that there is only one chief Head of this Body, namely Christ. He never ceases personally to guide the Church by an unseen hand, though at the same time He rules it externally, visibly through him who is His representative on earth. After His glorious Ascension into Heaven, this Church rested not on Him alone, but on Peter, too, its visible foundation stone. That Christ and His Vicar constitute one only Head is the solemn teaching of Our predecessor of immortal memory, Boniface VIII, in the Apostolic Letter *Unam Sanctam*; and his successors have never ceased to repeat the same.

They, therefore, walk the path of dangerous error who believe that they can accept Christ as the Head of the Church, while they reject genuine loyalty to His Vicar on earth. They have taken away the visible head, broken the visible bonds of unity, and they leave the Mystical Body of the Redeemer in such obscurity and so maimed, that those who are seeking the haven of eternal salvation cannot see it and cannot find it.

But "if the Word emptied Himself, taking the form of a slave," it was that He might make His brothers in the flesh partakers of the Divine Nature, in this earthly exile through sanctifying grace, in Heaven through the joys of eternal bliss. The reason why the only begotten Son of the Eternal Father wished to be a Son of Man, was that we might be made conformed to the image of the Son of God and be renewed according to the image of Him who created us. Let those, then, who glory in the name of Christian all look to our Divine Savior as the most exalted and most perfect exemplar of all virtues; but then let them also, by careful avoidance of sin and assiduous practice of virtue, bear witness by their conduct to His teaching and His life, so that when God appears they may be like unto Him and see Him as He is.

The whole Body of the Church, no less than the individual members, should bear resemblance to Christ. Such is His will. And we see that realized when following in the footsteps of her Founder she teaches, she governs and offers the Divine Sacrifice. Embracing the evangelical counsels she reflects the Redeemer's poverty, obedience and virginal purity. Enriched with institutes of many different kinds as with so many precious jewels, she points out Christ deep in prayer on the mountain, or preaching to the people or healing the sick and wounded and bringing sinners back to the path of virtue, or in a word doing good to everyone. What wonder then if, while she walks this earth, she be persecuted like Christ, hounded and weighed down with sorrows.

Christ must be acknowledged Head of the Church for this reason too, that, as supernatural gifts have found their supreme fullness and perfection in Him, it is from this fullness that His mystical Body receives. It is an observation made by a number of Fathers, that as the Head of our mortal body is the seat of all the senses, while the other parts of our organism have only the sense of touch, so all the powers that are found in Christian society, all the gifts, all the extraordinary graces, all attain their utmost perfection in the Head, Christ. "In Him it hath well pleased the Father that all fullness should dwell." He is gifted with those supernatural powers that accompany the hypostatic union. Is not the Holy Spirit dwelling in Him with a fullness of grace, than which no greater can be imagined? To Him has been given "power over all flesh"; "all the treasures of wisdom and knowledge are in Him" abundantly. The knowledge which is called "vision," He possesses with such clarity and comprehensiveness that it surpasses similar celestial knowledge found in all the saints of Heaven. So full of grace and truth is He, that of His inexhaustible fullness we have all received.

These words of the disciple, whom Jesus loved, lead us to the last reason why Christ our Lord should be declared in a very particular way Head of His Mystical Body. In us the nerves reach from the head to all parts of the body and give them the power to feel and move; in like manner our Savior communicates power to His Church so that the things of God are understood more clearly and more eagerly desired by the faithful. From Him shines into the Body of the Church whatever light illumines supernaturally the minds of those who believe, from Him every grace to make them holy, as He is holy.

Holiness begins from Christ; by Christ it is effected. For no act conducive to salvation can be performed unless it proceeds from Him as its supernatural cause.

If we examine closely this Divine principle of life and power given by Christ, in so far as it constitutes the very source of every gift and created grace, we easily see that it is nothing else than the Holy Spirit, the Paraclete who proceeds from the Father and the Son, and who is called in a special way the "Spirit of Christ" or the "Spirit of the Son."

Support of His Mystical Body, there is no reason why We should explain it further; but rather let us all, giving perpetual thanks to God, meditate on it with a humble and attentive mind. For what Our Lord, hanging on the Cross, began, He does not cease to continue always and uninterruptedly amid the joys of Heaven: "Our Head," says St. Augustine, "intercedes for us: some members He is receiving, others He is chastising, others cleansing, others consoling, others creating, others calling, others recalling, others correcting, others renewing." But to us it has been granted to collaborate with Christ in this work of salvation, "from one and through one saved and saving."

Mystical—Why So Named

And now, Venerable Brothers, We come to that part of Our explanation, in which We desire to make clear that the Body of Christ, which is the Church, should be called mystical. This word, used by many early writers, has the sanction of numerous Pontifical documents. There are several reasons why it should be used; for by it we may distinguish the Body of the Church, which is a society whose Head and Ruler is Christ, from His physical Body, which born of the Virgin Mother of God now sits at the right hand of the Father and rests hidden under the Eucharistic veil; as well as from any ordinary body in the natural order, whether physical or moral. This latter distinction is of greater importance in view of modern errors.

In a natural body the principle of unity so unites the parts that each lacks its own individual subsistence; on the contrary in the Mystical Body that mutual union, though intrinsic, links the members by a bond which leaves to each intact his own personality. Besides, if we examine the relation existing between the several members and between the members and the head, in every physical, living body, all the different members are ultimately destined to the good of the whole alone; while every moral association of men, if we look to its ultimate usefulness, is in the end directed to the advancement of all and of every single member. For they are persons. And so — to return to our theme — as the Son of the Eternal Father came down from Heaven for the salvation of us all, He likewise established the Body of the Church and enriched it with the Divine Spirit to assure immortal souls attaining their happiness, according to the words of the Apostle: "All things are yours; but you are Christ's; and Christ is God's." For the Church exists both for the good of the faithful, and to give glory to God and Jesus Christ whom He sent.

But if we compare a Mystical Body to a moral body, here again we must notice that the difference between them is not slight, rather it is very considerable and very important. In the moral body, the principle of union is nothing more than the common end, and the common cooperation of all under authority for the attainment of that end; whereas in the Mystical Body, of which We are speaking, this collaboration is supplemented by a distinct internal principle, which exists effectively in the whole and in each of its parts, and whose excellence is such, that of itself it is vastly superior to whatever bonds of union may be found in a physical or moral body. This is something, as We said above, not of the natural but of the supernatural order. Essentially it is something infinite, uncreated: the Spirit of God, Who, as the Angelic Doctor says, "numerically one and the same, fills and unifies the whole Church."

Superior to Human Societies

Hence, this word in its correct signification gives us to understand that the Church, a perfect society of its kind, is not made up of merely moral and juridical elements and principles. It is far superior to all other human societies; it surpasses them as grace surpasses nature, as things immortal are above all those that perish. Such human societies, and in the first place Civil Society, are by no means to be despised or belittled. But the Church in its entirety is not found within this natural order, any more than the whole of man is encompassed within the organism of our mortal body.

Through the Eucharistic Sacrifice Christ our Lord wished to give special evidence to the Faithful of our union among ourselves and with our Divine Head, marvelous as it is and beyond all praise. For here the sacred ministers act in the person not only of Our Savior but of the whole Mystical Body and of everyone of the Faithful. In this act of sacrifice through the hands of the priest, whose word alone has brought the Immaculate Lamb to be present on the altar, the Faithful themselves with one desire and one prayer offer It to the Eternal Father — the most acceptable victim of praise and propitiation for the Church's universal needs.

The Sacrament of the Eucharist is itself a striking image of the Church's unity, if we consider how in the bread to be consecrated many grains go to form one substance; and in it the very Author of supernatural grace is given to us, so that through Him we may receive the Spirit of charity, in which we are bidden to live now not our life but the life of Christ, and in all the members of His social Body to love the Redeemer Himself.

Venerable Brothers, in explaining this mystery that surrounds the hidden union of us all with Christ, We have thus far as Teacher of the universal Church illumined the mind with the light of truth. Our pastoral office now demands that We add a stimulus for the heart to love this Mystical Body with a burning love that will enkindle not only thoughts and words but also deeds.

That such a love, solidly grounded and undivided, may abide and increase in our souls, we must accustom ourselves to see Christ in the Church. It is Christ who lives in the Church, who teaches, governs and sanctifies through her. It is Christ, too, who manifests Himself differently in different members of His society. Once the Faithful try to live in this spirit of conscious faith, they will not only pay due honor and reverence to the superior members of this Mystical Body, especially those who according to Christ's mandate will have to render an account of our souls, but they will take to their hearts those members who are the object of Our Savior's special love: the weak, the mean, the wounded and the sick, who are in need of natural or supernatural assistance; children whose innocence is so easily exposed to danger these days and whose little hearts are as wax to be molded; and finally the poor, in helping whom we touch, as it were, through His supreme mercy the very person of Jesus Christ.

Venerable Brothers, may the Virgin Mother of God grant the prayers of

Our paternal heart — and they are yours too — and obtain for all a true love of the Church. Her sinless soul was filled with the Divine Spirit of Jesus Christ more than all other created souls; and "In the name of the whole human race," she gave her consent for a "spiritual marriage between the Son of God and human nature." Within her virginal womb Christ Our Lord already bore the exalted title of Head of the Church; in a marvelous birth she brought Him forth as source of all supernatural life, and presented Him, new born, as Prophet, King and Priest to those who were the first come of Jews and Gentiles to adore Him. Her only Son, yielding to a mother's prayer in "Cana of Galilee," performed the miracle by which "His disciples believed in Him." Free from all sin, original and personal, always most intimately United with her Son, as another Eve she offered Him on Golgotha to the Eternal Father for all the children of Adam sin-stained by his fall, and her mother's rights and mother's love were included in the holocaust. Thus she who corporally was the mother of our Head, through the added title of pain and glory became spiritually the mother of all His members. She it was who through her powerful prayers obtained the grace that the Spirit of our Divine Redeemer, already given to the Church on the Cross, should be bestowed through miraculous gifts on the newly founded Hierarchy on Pentecost. Bearing with courage and confidence the tremendous burden of her sorrows and desolation, truly the Queen of Martyrs, she more than all the faithful "filled up those things that are wanting of the sufferings of Christ . . . for His Body, which is the Church"; and she continued to show for the Mystical Body of Christ, born from the pierced Heart of the Savior, the same mother's care and ardent love with which she clasped the Infant Jesus to her warm and nourishing breast.

Invocation of Mary

May she, then, most holy mother of all Christ's members, to whose Immaculate Heart We have trustingly consecrated all men, her body and soul refulgent with the glory of Heaven where she reigns with her Son — may she never cease to beg from Him that a continuous, copious flow of graces may pass from its glorious Head into all the members of the Mystical Body. May she throw about the Church today, as in times gone by, the mantle of her protection and obtain from God that now at last the Church and all mankind may enjoy more peaceful days.

With full confidence in this hope, from an overflowing heart, We impart to you all, Venerable Brothers, and to the flocks confided to your care, as a promise of heavenly graces and a token of Our special affection the Apostolic Benediction.

Given at Rome, at St. Peter's, June 29, the Feast of the Holy Apostles Peter and Paul, 1943, the fifth of Our Pontificate.

Divino Afflante Spiritu
On the Reading of Sacred Scripture
Introduction

Inspired by the Divine Spirit, the Sacred Writers composed those books, which God, in His paternal charity towards the human race, deigned to bestow on them in order "to teach, to reprove, to correct, to instruct in justice: that the man of God may be perfect, furnished to every good work." (2 Tim. 3, 16f.) This heaven-sent treasure the Holy Church considers as the most precious source of doctrine on faith and morals. No wonder therefore that, as she received it intact from the hands of the Apostles, so she kept it with all care, defended it from every false and perverse interpretation and used it diligently as an instrument for securing the eternal salvation of souls, as almost countless documents in every age strikingly bear witness.

Solicitude of Sovereign Pontiffs

Our Predecessors, when the opportunity occurred, recommended the study or preaching or in fine the pious reading and meditation of the Sacred Scriptures. Pius X most heartily commended the society of St. Jerome, which strives to promote among the faithful — and to facilitate with all its power — the truly praiseworthy custom of reading and meditating on the holy Gospels . . . proclaiming it "a most useful undertaking, as well as most suited to the times". . . . And Benedict XV . . . exhorted "all the children of the Church, especially clerics, to reverence the Holy Scripture, to read it piously and meditate it constantly"; he reminded them "that in these pages is to be sought that food, by which the spiritual life is nourished unto perfection," and "that the chief use of Scripture pertains to the holy and fruitful exercise of the ministry of preaching."

Fruits of Manifold Initiative

We firmly hope that in the future reverence for, as well as the use and knowledge of, the Sacred Scriptures will everywhere more and more increase for the good of souls, provided the method of biblical studies laid down by Leo XIII, explained more clearly and perfectly by his Successors, and by Us confirmed and amplified — which indeed is the only safe way and proved by experience — be more firmly, eagerly and faithfully accepted by all, regardless of the difficulties which, as in all human affairs, so in this most excellent work will never be wanting.

Use of Scripture in Instruction of Faithful

Whosoever considers the immense labors undertaken by Catholic exegetes during well nigh two thousand years, so that the word of God, imparted to men through the Sacred Letters, might daily be more deeply and fully understood and more intensely loved, will easily be convinced that it is the serious duty of the faithful, and especially of priests, to make free and holy use of this treasure, accumulated throughout so many centuries by the greatest intellects. For the Sacred Books were not given by God to men to satisfy their curiosity or to provide them with material for study and research, but, as the Apostle observes, in order that these Divine Oracles might "instruct us to salvation, by the faith which is in Christ Jesus" and "that the man of God may be perfect, furnished to every good work." (2 Tim. 3, 15. 17.)

Let priests therefore, who are bound by their office to procure the eternal salvation of the faithful, after they have themselves by diligent study purused the sacred pages and made them their own by prayer and meditations, assiduously distribute the heavenly treasure's of the Divine word by sermons, homilies and exhortations; let them confirm the Christian doctrine by sentences from the Sacred Books and illustrate it by outstanding examples from sacred history and in particular from the Gospel of Christ Our Lord; and — avoiding with the greatest care those purely arbitrary and far-fetched adaptations, which are not a use, but rather an abuse of the Divine word — let them set forth all this with such eloquence, lucidity and clearness that the faithful may not only be moved and inflamed to reform their lives, but may also conceive in their hearts the greatest veneration for the Sacred Scripture.

The same veneration the Bishops should endeavor daily to increase and perfect among the faithful committed to their care, encouraging all those initiatives by which men, filled with apostolic zeal, laudably strive to excite and foster among Catholics a greater knowledge of and love for the Sacred Books. Let them favor therefore and lend help to those pious associations whose aim it is to spread copies of the Sacred Letters, especially of the Gospels, among the faithful, and to procure by every means that in Christian families the same be read with piety and devotion; let them efficaciously recommend by word and example, whenever the liturgical laws permit, the Sacred Scriptures translated, with the approval of the Ecclesiastical authority, into modern languages; let them themselves give public conference or dissertations on biblical subjects, or see that they are given by other public orators well versed in the matter.

Let the ministers of the Sanctuary support in every way possible and diffuse in fitting manner among all classes of the faithful the periodicals which so laudably and with such heartening results are published from time to time in various parts of the world, whether to treat and expose in a scientific manner biblical questions, or to adapt the fruits of these investigations to the sacred ministry, or to benefit the faithful. Let the ministers of the Sanctuary be convinced that all this, and whatsoever else an apostolic zeal and a sincere love of the Divine word they find suitable to this high purpose, will be an efficacious help to the cure of souls.

The Value of the Divine Word

If these things which We have said, Venerable Brethren and beloved sons, are necessary in every age, much more urgently are they needed in our sorrowful times, when almost all peoples and nations are plunged in a sea of calamities. . . . Who can heal these mortal wounds of the human family if not He, to Whom the Prince of the Apostles, full of confidence and love, addresses these words: "Lord, to whom shall we go? Thou hast the words of eternal life." (John 6, 69.)

To this Our most merciful Redeemer we must therefore bring all back by every means in our power: for He is the Divine consoler of the afflicted; He it is Who teaches all, whether they be invested with public authority or are bound in duty to obey and submit, true honesty, absolute justice and generous charity; it is He in fine, and He alone, Who can be the firm foundation and support of peace and tranquility: "For other foundation no man can lay, but that which is laid: which is Christ Jesus." (I Cor. 3, 11.) This the author of salvation, Christ, will men more fully know, more ardently love and more faithfully imitate in proportion as they are more assiduously urged to know and meditate the Sacred Letters, especially the New Testament, for, as St. Jerome, the Doctor of Stridon says: "To ignore the Scripture is to ignore Christ"; and again: "If there is anything in this life which sustains a wise man and induces him to maintain his serenity amidst the tribulations and adversities of the world, it is in the first place, I consider, the meditation and knowledge of the Scriptures."

There those who are wearied and oppressed by adversities and afflictions will find true consolation and Divine strength to suffer and bear with patience; there — that is in the Holy Gospels — Christ, the highest and greatest example of justice, charity and mercy, is present to all; and to the lacerated and trembling human race are laid open the fountains of that Divine grace without which both peoples and their rulers can never arrive at, never establish, peace in the state and unity of heart; there in fine will all learn Christ, 'Who is the head of all principality and power' (Col. 2, 10) and 'Who of God is made unto us wisdom and justice and sanctification and redemption.' (1 Cor. 1, 30.)

Exhortation to All Those Who Cultivate Biblical Studies

Having expounded and recommended those things which are required for the adaptation of Scripture studies to the necessities of the day, it remains, Venerable Brethren and beloved sons, that to biblical scholars who are devoted sons of the Church and follow faithfully her teaching and direction, We address with paternal affection, not only Our congratulations that they have been chosen and called to so sublime an office, but also Our encouragement to continue with every renewed vigor, with all zeal and care, the work so happily begun. Sublime office, We say; for what is more sublime than to scrutinize, explain, propose to the faithful and defend from unbelievers the very word of God, communicated to men under the inspiration of the Holy Ghost?

With this spiritual food the mind of the interpreter is fed and nourished "to commemoration of faith, the consolation of hope, the exhortation of charity." (*Contra Faustum*, St. Augustine.) "To live amidst these things, to mediate these things, to know nothing else, to seek nothing else, does it not seem to you already here below a foretaste of the heavenly kingdom?" (*Epistle* 53, 10 of St. Jerome.) Let also the minds of the faithful be nourished with this same food, that they may draw from thence the knowledge and love of God and the progress in perfection and the happiness of their own individual souls. Let, then, the interpreters of the Divine Oracles devote themselves to this holy practice with all their heart. "Let them pray, that they may understand" (*De Doctrina Christ.*, St. Augustine); let them labor to penetrate ever more deeply into the secrets of the Sacred Pages; let them teach and preach, in order to open to others also the treasures of the word of God.

Selections from
The Papal Encyclicals,
Claudia Carlen, I.H.M.,
A Consortium Book, McGrath Publishing Company, 1981

Chapter 63 • Pope John XXIII: *Pacem in Terris*

Angelo Giuseppe Roncalli (pope, 1958-1963), the successor of Pius XII, was born in Sotto il Monte near Bergamo, Italy, in 1881. Educated at Bergamo and Rome, after receiving the doctorate in theology, he was ordained in 1904. While serving as secretary to the Archbishop of Bergamo for more than nine years, he gained experience in many forms of Catholic action and became familiar with the problems of the working people. At the same time he was a teacher of apologetics, ecclesiastical history, and patrology in the diocesan seminary. He served in World War I as a medical corpsman and later as chaplain. Raised to the rank of archbishop in 1925 he was sent as a diplomatic representative of the Vatican to Bulgaria. He also served as apostolic delegate to Turkey and Greece, and became nuncio to France in 1944. While active in Turkey he introduced the Turkish language in the Divine Worship c. 1939. He was made a cardinal priest in 1953 and became the patriarch of Venice. He was elected Pope as John XXIII on October 28, 1958.

The high point of his pontificate is considered by some to have been the summoning of the Second Vatican Council in order to achieve renewal in the total life of the Catholic Church. Unfortunately, Pope John did not live to see the completion of the work of Vatican II, the purpose of which was to increase the Catholic Faith in the members of the Church, renew the morals of Christians, adapt ecclesiastical discipline to the needs and modes of the times, and emphasize the Catholic principles of ecumenism. Yet he influenced the contents of the final actions of the Council, as is evident when one compares *Mater et Magistra* and *Pacem in Terris* with the decrees of that Council. *Mater et Magistra* follows in the tradition of *Rerum Novarum* of Leo XIII and *Quadragesimo Anno* of Pius XI by applying some of their principles to the changing social conditions.

The diary of John XXIII, *Journey of a Soul*, is said to present a "profound interior life and unwavering trust in the Divine Providence."

Pacem in Terris

> Peace on earth, which all men of every era have most eagerly yearned for, can be firmly established only if the order laid down by God be dutifully observed.
>
> The progress of learning and the inventions of technology clearly show that, both in living things and in the forces of nature, an astonishing order reigns, and they also bear witness to the greatness of man, who can understand

that order and create suitable instruments to harness those forces of nature and use them to his benefit.

But the progress of science and the inventions of technology show above all the infinite greatness of God, Who created the universe and man himself. He created all things out of nothing, pouring into them the abundance of His wisdom and goodness. God also created man in His own *image and likeness*, endowed him with intelligence and freedom, and made him lord of creation.

Order in Human Beings

How strongly does the turmoil of individual men and peoples contrast with the perfect order of the universe! It is as if the relationships which bind them together could be controlled only by force.

But the Creator of the world has imprinted in man's heart an order which his conscience reveals to him and enjoins him to obey: *This shows that the obligations of the law are written in their hearts; their conscience utters its own testimony*. And how could it be otherwise? For whatever God has made shows forth His infinite wisdom, and it is manifested more clearly in the things which have greater perfection.

But fickleness of opinion often produces this error, that many think that the relationships between men and States can be governed by the same laws as the forces and irrational elements of the universe, whereas the laws governing them are of quite a different kind and are to be sought elsewhere, namely, where the Father of all things wrote them, that is, in the nature of man.

By these laws men are most admirably taught, first of all how they should conduct their mutual dealings among themselves, then how the relationships between the citizens and the public authorities of each State should be regulated, then how States should deal with one another, and finally how, on the one hand individual men and States, and on the other hand the community of all peoples, should act towards each other, the establishment of such a community being urgently demanded today by the requirements of universal common good.

Every man is a person with rights and duties. . . .

Indeed, precisely because he is a person he has rights and obligations flowing directly and simultaneously from his very nature. And as these rights and obligations are universal and inviolable so they cannot in any way be surrendered.

Rights

The right to life and a worthy standard of living. . .
Rights pertaining to moral and cultural values

By the natural law every human being has the right to respect for his person, to his good reputation; the right to freedom in searching for truth and in expressing and communicating his opinions, and in pursuit of art, within the limits laid down by the moral order and the common good; and he has the right to be informed truthfully about public events.

The natural law also gives man the right to share in the benefits of culture, and therefore the right to a basic education and to technical and professional training in keeping with the stage of educational development in the country to which he belongs. Every effort should be made to ensure that persons be enabled, on the basis of merit, to go on to higher studies, so that, as far as possible, they may occupy posts and take on responsibilities in human society in accordance with their natural gifts and the skills they have acquired.

The right to worship God according to one's conscience. . . .

The right to choose freely one's state of life. . . .

Economic rights

If we turn our attention to the economic sphere it is clear that man has a right by the natural law not only to an opportunity to work, but also to go about his work without coercion.

To these rights is certainly joined the right to demand working conditions in which physical health is not endangered, morals are safeguarded, and young people's normal development is not impaired. Women have the right to working conditions in accordance with their requirements and their duties as wives and mothers.

From the dignity of the human person, there also arises the right to carry on economic activities according to the degree of responsibility of which one is capable. Furthermore — and this must be specially emphasized — the worker has a right to a wage determined according to criterions of justice, and sufficient, therefore, in proportion to the available resources, to give the worker and his family a standard of living in keeping with the dignity of the human person.

The right to private property, even of productive goods, also derives from the nature of man. This right, as We have elsewhere declared, *is an effective means for safeguarding the dignity of the human person and for the exercise of responsibility in all fields; it strengthens and gives serenity to family life, thereby increasing the peace and prosperity of the state.*

However, it is opportune to point out that there is a social duty essentially inherent in the right of private property.

Political rights

The dignity of the human person involves the right to take an active part in public affairs and to contribute one's part to the common good of the citizens.

The human person is also entitled to a juridical protection of his rights, a protection that should be efficacious, impartial and inspired by the true norms of justice. . . .

Duties

Rights and duties necessarily linked in the one person

The natural rights with which We have been dealing are, however, inseparably connected, in the very person who is their subject, with just as many respective duties; and rights as well as duties find their source, their sustenance and their inviolability in the natural law which grants or enjoins them.

Therefore, to cite a few examples, the right of every man to life is correlative with the duty to preserve it; his right to a decent standard of living with the duty of living it becomingly; and his right to investigate the truth freely, with the duty of seeking it ever more completely and profoundly.

Reciprocity of rights and duties between persons

Once this is admitted, it also follows that in human society to one man's right there corresponds a duty in all other persons: the duty, namely, of acknowledging and respecting the right in question.

Mutual collaboration

Since men are social by nature they are meant to live with others and to work for one another's welfare. A well-ordered human society requires that men recognize and observe their mutual rights and duties. It also demands that each contribute generously to the establishment of a civic order in which rights and duties are more sincerely and effectively acknowledged and fulfilled.

An attitude of responsibility

The dignity of the human person also requires that every man enjoy the right to act freely and responsibly. For this reason, therefore, in social relations man should exercise his rights, fulfill his obligations and, in the countless forms of collaboration with others, act chiefly on his own responsibility and initiative. This is to be done in such a way that each one acts on his own decision, of set purpose and from a consciousness of his obligation, without being moved by force or pressure brought to bear on him externally. For any human society that is established on relations of force must be regarded as inhuman, inasmuch as the personality of its members is repressed or restricted, when in fact they should be provided with appropriate incentives and means for developing and perfecting themselves.

Social life in truth, justice, charity and freedom

A civic society is to be considered well-ordered, beneficial and in keeping with human dignity if it is grounded on truth.

This will be accomplished when each one duly recognizes both his rights and his obligations towards others. Furthermore, human society will be such as We have just described it, if the citizens, guided by justice, apply themselves seriously to respecting the rights of others and discharging their own duties; if they are moved by such fervor of charity as to make their own the needs of others and share with others their own goods; if, finally, they work for a closer fellowship in the world of spiritual values. Yet this is not sufficient; for human society is bound together by freedom, that is to say, in ways and means in keeping with the dignity of its citizens, who accept the responsibility of their actions, precisely because they are by nature rational beings.

God and the moral order

The order which prevails in society is by nature moral. Grounded as it is in truth, it must function according to the norms of justice, it should be inspired and perfected by mutual love, and finally it should be brought to an ever more refined and human balance in freedom.

Now an order of this kind, whose principles are universal, absolute and unchangeable, has its ultimate source in the one true God, Who is personal and transcends human nature. Inasmuch as God is the first Truth and the highest Good, He alone is that deepest source from which human society can draw its vitality, if that society is to be well ordered, beneficial, and in keeping with human dignity.

Characteristics of the present day

Our age has three distinctive characteristics.

First of all, the working classes have gradually gained ground in economic and public affairs. They began by claiming their rights in the socio-economic sphere: they extended their action then to claims on the political level, and finally applied themselves to the acquisition of the benefits of a more refined culture. They insist that they be always regarded as men with a share in every sector of human society: in the social and economic sphere, in the fields of learning and culture, and in public life.

Secondly, it is obvious to everyone that women are now taking a part in public life. This is happening more rapidly perhaps in nations of Christian civilization, and, more slowly but broadly, among peoples who have inherited other traditions or cultures. Since women are becoming ever more conscious of their human dignity, they will not tolerate being treated as mere material instruments, but demand rights befitting a human person both in domestic and in public life.

Finally, in the modern world human society has taken on an entirely new appearance in the field of social and political life. For since all nations have either achieved or are on the way to achieving independence, there will soon no longer exist a world divided into nations that rule others and nations that are subject to others.

On the contrary, the conviction that all men are equal by reason of their natural dignity has been generally accepted. Hence racial discrimination can in no way be justified, at least doctrinally or in theory. And this is of fundamental importance and significance for the formation of human society according to those principles which We have outlined above. For, if a man becomes conscious of his rights, he must become equally aware of his duties. Thus he who possesses certain rights has likewise the duty to claim those rights as marks of his dignity, while all others have the obligation to acknowledge those rights and respect them.

When the relations of human society are expressed in terms of rights and duties, men become conscious of spiritual values, understand the meaning and significance of truth, justice, charity and freedom, and become deeply aware that they belong to this world of values. Moreover, when moved by such concerns, they are brought to a better knowledge of the true God Who is personal and transcendent, and thus they make the ties that bind them to God the solid foundation and supreme criterion of their lives, both of that life which they live internally in the depths of their own souls and of that in which they are united to other men in society.

Attainment of the common good is the purpose of the public authority. . . .

Essential of the common good. . . .

For the common good since it is intimately bound up with human nature cannot therefore exist fully and completely unless the human person is taken into consideration and the essential nature and realization of the common good be kept in mind.

In the second place, the very nature of the common good requires that all members of the state be entitled to share in it, although in different ways according to each one's tasks, merits and circumstances. For this reason, every civil authority must take pains to promote the common good of all, without preference for any single citizen or civic group.

In this context, We judge that attention should be called to the fact that the common good touches the whole man, the needs both of his body and of his soul. Hence it follows that the civil authorities must undertake to effect the common good by ways and means that are proper to them; that is, while respecting the hierarchy of values, they should promote simultaneously both the material and the spiritual welfare of the citizens.

Responsibilities of the public authority, and rights and duties of individuals

It is agreed that in our time the common good is chiefly guaranteed when personal rights and duties are maintained. The chief concern of civil authorities must therefore be to ensure that these rights are acknowledged, respected, coordinated with other rights, defended and promoted, so that in this way each one may more easily carry out his duties.

This means that, if any government does not acknowledge the rights of man or violates them, it not only fails in its duty, but its orders completely lack juridical force.

Reconciliation and protection of rights and duties of individuals

One of the fundamental duties of civil authorities, therefore, is to coordinate social relations in such fashion that the exercise of one man's rights does not threaten others in the exercise of their own rights nor hinder them in the fulfillment of their duties. Finally, the rights of all should be effectively safeguarded and, if they have been violated, completely restored.

Duty of promoting the rights of individuals

It is therefore necessary that the administration give wholehearted and careful attention to the social as well as to the economic progress of the citizens, and to the development, in keeping with the development of the productive system, of such essential services as the building of roads, transportation, communications, water supply, housing, public health, education, facilitation of the practice of religion, and recreational facilities. It is necessary also that governments make efforts to see that insurance systems are made available to the citizens, so that, in case of misfortune or increased family responsibilities, no person will be without the necessary means to maintain a decent standard of living. The government should make similarly effective efforts to see that those who are able to work can find employment in keeping with their aptitudes, and that each worker receives a wage in keeping with the laws of justice and equity. It should be equally the concern of civil authorities to ensure that workers be allowed their proper responsibility in the work undertaken in industrial organization, and to facilitate the establishment of intermediate groups which will make social life richer and more effective. Finally, it should be possible for all the citizens to share as far as they are able in their country's cultural advantages.

Characteristics of the present day

From these considerations it becomes clear that in the juridical organization of states in our times the first requisite is that a charter of fundamental human rights be drawn up in clear and precise terms and that it be incorporated in its entirety in the constitution.

The second requisite is that the constitution of each state be drawn up, phrased in correct juridical terminology, which prescribes the manner of designating the public officials along with their mutual relations, the spheres of their competence, the forms and systems they are obliged to follow in the performance of their office.

The last requisite is that the relations between the government and the governed are then set forth in terms of rights and duties; and it is clearly laid down that the paramount task assigned to government officials is that of recognizing, respecting, reconciling, protecting and promoting the rights and duties of citizens.

It is of course impossible to accept the theory which professes to find the original and single source of civic rights and duties, of the binding force of the constitution, and of a government's right to command, in the mere will of human beings, individually or collectively.

The tendencies to which We have referred, however, do clearly show that the men of our time are becoming increasingly conscious of their dignity as human persons. This awareness prompts them to claim a share in the public administration of their country, while it also accounts for the demand that their own inalienable and inviolable rights be protected by law. It also requires that government officials be chosen in conformity with constitutional procedures, and perform their specific functions within the limits of law.

Subject of rights and duties

Our Predecessors have constantly maintained, and We join them in reasserting, that nations are reciprocally subjects of rights and duties. This means that their relationships also must be harmonized in truth, in justice, in a working solidarity, in liberty. The same natural law, which governs relations between individual human beings, serves also to regulate the relations of nations with one another.

This is readily clear to anyone if he would consider that the heads of states can in no way put aside their natural dignity while they represent their country and provide for its welfare, and that they are never allowed to depart from the natural law by which they are bound and which is the norm of their conduct.

Moreover, it is inconceivable that men because they are heads of government are forced to put aside their human endowments. On the contrary, they occupy this place of eminence for the very reason that they have earned a reputation as outstanding members of the body politic in view of their excellent intellectual endowments and accomplishments.

Indeed it follows from the moral order itself that authority is necessary for civil society, for civil society is ruled by authority; and that authority cannot be used to thwart the moral order without instantly collapsing because its foundation has been destroyed.

Lastly it is to be borne in mind that also in the regulating of relations between states, authority is to be exercised for the achievement of the common good, which constitutes the reason for its existence.

But a fundamental factor of the common good is acknowledgment of the moral order and exact observance of its commands.

In justice

Relations between nations are to be further regulated by justice. This implies, over and above recognition of their mutual rights, the fulfillment of their respective duties.

The treatment of minorities

Closely related to this point is the political trend which since the nineteenth century has gathered momentum and gained ground everywhere, namely, the striving of people of the same ethnic group to become independent and to form one nation. Since this cannot always be accomplished for various reasons, the result is that minorities often dwell within the territory of a people of another ethnic group, and this is the source of serious problems.

In the first place, it must be made clear that justice is seriously violated by whatever is done to limit the strength and numerical increase of these lesser peoples; the injustice is even more serious if vicious attempts of this kind are aimed at the very extinction of these groups.

It is especially in keeping with the principles of justice that effective measures be taken by the civil authorities to improve the lot of the citizens of an ethnic minority, particularly when that betterment concerns their language, the development of their natural gifts, their ancestral customs, and their accomplishments and endeavors in the economic order.

It should be noted, however, that these minority groups, either because of their present situation which they are forced to endure, or because of past experience, are often inclined to exalt beyond due measure anything proper to their own people, and to such a degree as to look down on things common to all mankind as if the welfare of the human family must yield to the good of their own ethnic group. Reason rather demands that these very people recognize also the advantages that accrue to them from their peculiar stances; for instance, no small contribution is made toward the development of their particular talents and spirit by their daily dealings with people who have grown up in a different culture since from this association they can gradually make their own the excellence which belongs to the other ethnic group. But this will happen only if the minorities through association with the people who live around them make an effort to share in their customs and institutions. Such, however, will not be the case if they sow discord which causes great damage and hinders progress.

Active solidarity

Since the mutual relations among nations must be regulated by the norm of truth and justice, they must also derive great advantage from an energetic union of mind, heart and resources. This can be effected at various levels by mutual cooperation in many ways, as is happening in our own time with beneficial results in the economic, social, political, educational, public health and sports spheres. We must remember that, of its very nature, civil authority exists, not to confine its people within the boundaries of their nation, but rather to protect, above all else, the common good of that particular civil society, which certainly cannot be divorced from the common good of the entire human family.

So it happens that civil societies in pursuing their interests not only must not harm others, but must join their plans and forces whenever the efforts of an individual government cannot achieve its desired goals; but in the execution of such common efforts, great care must be taken lest what helps some nations should injure others.

Furthermore, the universal common good requires that in every nation friendly relations be fostered in all fields between the citizens and their intermediate societies. Since in many parts of the world there are groups of people of varying ethnic backgrounds, we must be on our guard against isolating one ethnic group from its fellow men. This is clearly inconsistent with modern conditions since distances which separate people from each other have been almost wiped out. Neither are we to overlook the fact that men of every ethnic group, in addition to their own characteristic endowments by which they are distinguished from the rest of men, have other important gifts of nature in common with their fellow men by which they can make more and more progress and perfect themselves, particularly in matters that pertain to the spirit. They have the right and duty therefore to live in communion with one another.

The problem of political refugees

The sentiment of universal fatherhood which the Lord has placed in Our heart makes Us feel profound sadness in considering the phenomenon of political refugees: a phenomenon which has assumed large proportions and which always hides numberless and acute sufferings.

At this point it will not be superfluous to recall that such exiles are persons, and that all their rights as persons must be recognized, since they do not lose those rights on losing the citizenship of the states of which they are former members.

Now among the rights of a human person there must be included that by which a man may enter a political community where he hopes he can more fittingly provide a future for himself and his dependents. Wherefore, as far as the common good rightly understood permits, it is the duty of that state to accept such immigrants and to help to integrate them into itself as new members.

Wherefore, on this occasion, We publicly approve and commend every undertaking, founded on the principles of human solidarity and Christian charity, which aims at making migration of persons from one country to another less painful.

And We will be permitted to signal for the attention and gratitude of all right-minded persons the manifold work which specialized international agencies are carrying out in this very delicate field.

Disarmament

On the other hand, it is with deep sorrow that We note the enormous stocks of armaments that have been and still are being made in more economically developed countries, and a vast outlay of intellectual and economic resources. And it happens that, while the people of these countries are loaded with heavy burdens, other countries as a result are deprived of the collaboration they need in order to make economic and social progress.

The production of arms is allegedly justified on the grounds that in present-day conditions peace cannot be preserved without an equal balance of armaments. And so, if one country increases its armaments, others feel the need to do the same; and if one country is equipped with nuclear weapons, other countries must produce their own, equally destructive.

Consequently, people live in constant fear lest the storm that every moment threatens should break upon them with dreadful violence. And with good reason, for the arms of war are ready at hand. Even though it is difficult to believe that anyone would dare bring upon himself the appalling destruction and sorrow that war would bring in its train, it cannot be denied that the conflagration can be set off by some unexpected and unpremeditated act. And one must bear in mind that, even though the monstrous power of modern weapons acts as a deterrent, there is nevertheless reason to fear that the mere continuance of nuclear tests, undertaken with war in mind, can seriously jeopardize various kinds of life on earth.

Justice, then, right reason and consideration for human dignity and life urgently demand that the arms race should cease; that the stockpiles which exist in various countries should be reduced equally and simultaneously by the parties concerned; that nuclear weapons should be banned; and finally that all come to an agreement on a fitting program of disarmament, employing mutual and effective controls.

All must realize that there is no hope of putting an end to the building up of armaments, nor of reducing the present stocks, nor, still less — and this is the main point — of abolishing them altogether, unless the process is complete and thorough and unless it proceeds from inner conviction: unless, that is, everyone sincerely cooperates to banish the fear and anxious expectation of war with which men are oppressed. If this is to come about, the fundamental principle on which our present peace depends must be replaced by another, which declares that the true and solid peace of nations consists not in equality of arms but in mutual trust alone. We believe that this can be brought to pass, and we consider that, since it concerns a matter not only demanded by right reason but also eminently desirable in itself, it will prove to be the source of many benefits. . . .

In liberty

It has also to be borne in mind that relations between states should be based on freedom, that is to say, that no country may unjustly oppress others or unduly meddle in their affairs. On the contrary, all should help to develop in others a sense of responsibility, a spirit of enterprise, and an earnest desire to be the first to promote their own advancement in every field.

Signs of the times

Men are becoming more and more convinced that disputes which arise between states should not be resolved by recourse to arms, but rather by negotiation.

We grant indeed that this conviction is chiefly based on the terrible destructive force of modern weapons and a fear of the ties and frightful destruction which such weapons would cause. Therefore, in an age such as ours which prides itself on its atomic energy, it is contrary to reason to hold that war is now a suitable way to restore rights which have been violated.

Interdependence between political communities

The recent progress of science and technology, since it has profoundly influenced human conduct, is rousing men everywhere in the world to more and more cooperation and association with one another. Consequently, the close relations of individuals, families, intermediate associations belonging to different countries have become vastly more frequent and conferences between heads of states are held at shorter intervals. At the same time the interdependence of national economies has grown deeper, one becoming progressively more closely related to the other, so that they become, as it were, integral parts of the one world economy. Finally, the social progress, order, security and peace of each country are necessarily connected with the social progress, order, security and peace of all other countries.

In our time, relationships between states have changed greatly. On the one hand, the universal common good poses very serious questions which are difficult and which demand immediate solution especially because they are concerned with safeguarding the security and peace of the whole. On the other hand the heads of individual states, inasmuch as they are juridically equal, are not entirely successful no matter how often they meet or how hard they try to find more fitting juridical instruments. This is due not to lack of good will and initiative but to lack of adequate power to back up their authority.

Moreover, if we carefully consider the essential nature of the common good on the one hand, and the nature and function of public authority on the other, everyone sees that there is an intrinsic connection between the two. And, indeed, just as the moral order needs public authority to promote the common good in civil society, it likewise demands that public authority actually be able to attain it.

This public authority, having world-wide power and endowed with the proper means for the efficacious pursuit of its objective, which is the universal common good in concrete form, must be set up by common accord and not imposed by force.

Like the common good of individual states, so too the universal common good cannot be determined except by having regard for the human person. Therefore, the public and universal authority, too, must have as its fundamental objective the recognition, respect, safeguarding, and promotion of the rights of the human person: this can be done by direct action when required, or by creating on a world scale an environment in which leaders of the individual countries can suitably maintain their own functions.

Moreover, just as it is necessary in each state that relations which the public authority has with its citizens, families and intermediate associations be controlled and regulated by the principle of subsidiary, it is equally necessary that the relationships which exist between the worldwide public authority and the public authorities of individual nations be governed by the same principle.

The world-wide public authority is not intended to limit the sphere of action of the public authority of the individual state, much less to take its place. On the contrary, its purpose is to create, on a world basis, an environment in which the public authorities of each state, its citizens and immediate associations, can carry out their tasks, fulfill their duties and exercise their rights with greater security.

As is known, the United Nations Organization (U.N.O.) was established on June 26, 1945, and to it there were subsequently added specialized agencies consisting of members designated by the public authority of the various countries with important international tasks in the economic, social, cultural, educational and health fields. The United Nations Organization had as its essential purpose the maintenance and consolidation of peace between peoples, fostering between them friendly relations, based on the principles of equality, mutual respect, and varied forms of cooperation in every sector of human endeavor.

An act of the highest importance performed by the United Nations Organization was the Universal Declaration of Human Rights, approved in the General Assembly on December 10, 1948. In the preamble of that Declaration, the recognition and respect of those rights and respective liberties is proclaimed as a goal to be achieved by all peoples and all countries.

It is therefore our ardent desire that the United Nations Organization — in its structure and in its means — may become ever more equal to the magnitude and nobility of its tasks, and may the time come as quickly as possible when every human being will find therein an effective safeguard for the rights which derive directly from his dignity as a person, and which are therefore universal, inviolable and inalienable rights.

Once again We exhort Our children to take an active part in public life, and to contribute towards the attainment of the common good of the entire human family as well as to that of their own country. They should endeavor, therefore, in the light of the Faith and with the strength of love, to ensure that the various institutions — whether economic, social, cultural or political in purpose — should be such as not to create obstacles, but rather to facilitate or render less arduous man's perfecting of himself both in the natural order as well as in the supernatural.

In other words, it is necessary that human beings, in the intimacy of their own consciences, should so live and act in their temporal lives as to create a synthesis between scientific, technical and professional elements on the one hand, and spiritual values on the other.

It is no less clear that today, in traditionally Christian nations, secular institutions, although demonstrating a high degree of scientific and technical perfection, and efficiency in achieving their respective ends, not infrequently are but slightly affected by Christian motivation or inspiration.

How does one explain this? It is Our opinion that the explanation is to be found in an inconsistency in their minds between religious belief and their action in the temporal sphere.

It is Our opinion that the above-mentioned inconsistency between the religious faith in those who believe and their activities in the temporal sphere, results — in great part — from the lack of a solid Christian education.

It is indispensable, therefore, that in the training of youth, education should be complete and without interruption, namely, that in the minds of the young religious values should be cultivated and the moral conscience refined in a manner to keep pace with the continuous and ever more abundant assimilation of scientific and technical knowledge. And it is indispensable, too, that they be instructed regarding the proper way to carry out their actual tasks.

The doctrinal principles outlined in this document derive from both nature itself and the natural law. In putting these principles into practice it frequently happens that Catholics in many ways cooperate either with Christians separated from this Apostolic See, or with men of no Christian faith whatever, but who are endowed with reason and adorned with a natural uprightness of conduct.

In such relations let the faithful be careful to be always consistent in their actions, so that they may never come to any compromise in matters of religion and morals. At the same time, however, let them be, and show themselves to be, animated by a spirit of understanding and detachment, and disposed to work loyally in the pursuit of objectives which are of their nature good, or conducive to good.

However, one must never confuse error and the person who errs.

The person who errs is always and above all a human being, and he retains in every case his dignity as a human person; and he must be always regarded and treated in accordance with that lofty dignity.

It is, therefore, especially to the point to make a clear distinction between false philosophical teachings regarding the nature, origin, and destiny of the universe and of man, and movements which have a direct bearing either on economic and social questions, or cultural matters or on the organization of the state, even if these movements owe their origin and inspiration to these false tenets. Besides, who can deny that those movements, in so far as they conform to the dictates of right reason and are interpreters of the lawful aspirations of the human person, contain elements that are positive and deserving of approval?

Therefore, as far as Catholics are concerned, this decision rests primarily with those who live and work in the specific sectors of human society in which those problems arise, always, however, in accordance with the principles of the natural law, with the social doctrine of the church, and with the directives of ecclesiastical authorities. For it must not be forgotten that the Church has the right and the duty not only to safeguard the principles of ethics and religion, but also to intervene authoritatively with Her children in the temporal sphere, when there is a question of judging the application of those principles to concrete cases.

These words of Ours, which We have wished to dedicate to the problems that most beset the human family today and on the just solution of which the ordered progress of society depends, are dictated by a profound aspiration which We know is shared by all men of good will: the consolidation of peace in the world.

As a pledge of this peace, and with the ardent wish that it may shine forth on the Christian communities entrusted to your care, especially for the benefit of those who are most lowly and in the greatest need of help and defense, We are glad to impart to you, venerable brothers, to the priests both secular and religious, to the religious men and women and to the faithful of your dioceses, particularly to those who make every effort to put these exhortations of Ours into practice, Our Apostolic Blessing. Finally, upon all men of good will, to whom this encyclical letter is also addressed, We implore from Almighty God health and prosperity.

Given at Rome at St. Peter's, on Holy Thursday, the eleventh day of April, in the year 1963, the fifth of Our Pontificate.

※ POPE JOHN XXIII ※

Selections from

The Papal Encyclicals 1958-1981,

Claudia Carlen, I.H.M.,

A Consortium Book, McGratt Publishing Company, 1981

Chapter 64 • Pope Paul VI: *Credo, Humanae Vitae;* Vatican II: *Inter Mirifica, Unitatis Redintegratio, Gravissimum Educationis*

Born near Brescia in 1897, Giovanni Battista Montini (pope, 1963-1978) was the son of a well-known journalist. He studied in Rome and became recognized for his impressive learning and scholarship. While archbishop of Milan (1954-1963) he showed a deep concern for the poor and underprivileged. Elected pope on June 21, 1963, he took the name of Paul VI. The *Credo*, which he published on June 10, 1968, is a classic example of the fundamentals of Catholic teaching which have come down from the Apostles and have been repeated and reemphasized by representative church authorities in every period of the Church's development. Such a profession of faith comes at a very opportune time, when so many of the traditional teachings of the Catholic church have been challenged by what Maritain called the neo-modernists of our time. Paul VI is clear, forthright, unconfused, precise, and firm in his statement of the "one, holy, catholic, and apostolic faith." His exemplary courage is shown in the encyclical *Humanae Vitae*. It contains the traditional teaching of the Catholic Church on the subject of the transmission of life.

Vatican II was summoned by Pope John XXIII in 1962 to constitute a new Pentecost and a spiritual renewal that would "restore the church's energies" in the search for the means best adapted for the present-day needs of the Church. In 1963 he issued a series of documents urging that all pray for the success of the Council and laid down the rules to govern the conduct of the proceedings. Over two thousand church people took part in the many sessions. Pope John XXIII died in June 1963 and the results of the Council were promulgated by his successor Pope Paul VI.

The discussions of the role of the means of communication in economic, political, social, religious, and other aspects of human life resulted in the Decree on the Media of Social Communication, *Inter Mirifica*. At the same time the Constitution on the Sacred Liturgy, *Sacrosanctum Concilium,* was published. Both were approved by of Pope Paul VI.

About a year later two decrees were published, On Ecumenism, *Unitatis Redingratio,* and On the Catholic Churches of the Eastern Rite, *Orientalium Ecclesiarum*, and one constitution, On the Church, *Lumen Gentium*.

In 1965 were published six decrees: The Pastoral Office of Bishops in the Church *(Christus Dominus),* On the Adaptation and Renewal of the Religious Life (*Perfectae Caritatis*),

On Priestly Training (*Optatum Totius*), On the Apostolate of the Laity (*Apostolicam Actuositatem*), On Priestly Life and Ministry (*Presbyterorum Ordinis*), On the Missionary Activity of the Church (*Ad Gentes Divinitus*); two constitutions: On Divine Revelation (*Dei Verbum*), and On the Church in the Modern World (*Gaudium et Spes*); three declarations: On the Relation of the Church to Non-Christian Religions (*Nostra Aetate*), On Christian Education (*Gravissimum Educationis*), and On Religious Freedom (*Dignitatis Humanae*).

It is a fitting conclusion to this collection to present three of the publications of Vatican II, *Decree on the Media of Social Communication*, the *Decree on Ecumenism*, and *The Declaration On Christian Education*, and three short, joyful exclamations.

Credo

ROME, June 30, 1968 (Reuters)—Following, in an official Vatican translation into English, is the text of the Pope's message and credo today to mark the end of the Roman Catholic Church's Year of Faith.

Venerable brothers and beloved sons,

With this solemn liturgy we end the celebration of the 19th centenary of the martyrdom of the Holy Apostles Peter and Paul, and thus close the Year of Faith. We dedicated it to the commemoration of the Holy Apostles in order that we might give witness to our steadfast will to be faithful to the deposit of the faith which they transmitted to us, and that we might strengthen our desire to live by it in the historical circumstances in which the church finds herself in her pilgrimage in the midst of the world.

We feel it our duty to give public thanks to all who responded to our invitation by bestowing on the Year of Faith a splendid completeness through the deepening of their personal adhesion to the Word of God, through the renewal in various communities to the profession of faith, and through the testimony of a Christian life.

To our brothers in the episcopate especially, and to all the faithful of the Holy Catholic Church, we express our appreciation and we grant our blessing.

The Mandate of Peter

Likewise we deem that we must fulfill the mandate entrusted by Christ to Peter, whose successor we are, the last in merit, namely, to confirm our brothers in the faith. With the awareness, certainly, of our human weakness, yet with all the strength impressed on our spirit by such a command, we shall accordingly make a profession of faith, pronounce a creed which, without being strictly speaking a dogmatic definition, repeats in substance, with some developments called for by the spiritual condition of our time, the Creed of Nicaea, the creed of the immortal tradition of the Holy Church of God.

In making this profession, we are aware of the disquiet which agitates certain modern quarters with regard to the Faith. They do not escape the influence of a world being profoundly changed, in which so many certainties are being disputed or discussed. We see even Catholics allowing themselves to be seized by a kind of passion for change and novelty.

The Church most assuredly has always the duty to carry on the effort to study more deeply and to present in a manner ever better adapted to successive generations the unfathomable mysteries of God, rich for all in fruits of salvation. But at the same time the greatest care must be taken, while fulfilling the indispensable duty of research, to do no injury to the teachings of Christian doctrine. For that would be to give rise, as is unfortunately seen in these days, to disturbance and perplexity in many faithful souls.

Task of Interpretation

It is important in this respect to recall that, beyond scientifically verified phenomena, the intellect which God has given us reaches that which is, and not merely the subjective expression of the structures and development of consciousness, and, on the other hand, that the task of interpretation — of hermeneutics — is to try to understand and extricate, while respecting the word expressed, the sense conveyed by a text, and not to create, in some fashion, the sense in accordance with arbitrary hypotheses.

But above all, we place our unshakable confidence in the Holy Spirit, the soul of the Church, and in theological faith upon which rests the life of the Mystical Body. We know that souls await the word of the Vicar of Christ, and we respond to that expectation with the instructions which we regularly give. But today we are given an opportunity to make a more solemn utterance.

An Offering to God

On this day which is chosen to close the Year of Faith, on this feast of the Blessed Apostles Peter and Paul, we have wished to offer to the living God the homage of a profession of faith. And as once at Caesarea Philippi the Apostle Peter spoke on behalf of the twelve to make a true confession, beyond human opinions, of Christ as Son of the Living God, so today his humble successor, pastor of the Universal Church, raises his voice to give, on behalf of all the people of God, a firm witness to the divine truth entrusted to the church to be announced to all nations.

We have wished our profession of faith to be to a high degree complete and explicit in order that it may respond in a fitting way to the need of light felt by so many faithful souls, and by all those in the world, to whatever spiritual family they belong, who are in search of the truth.

To the glory of God most holy and of Our Lord Jesus Christ, trusting in the aid of the Blessed Virgin Mary and of the Holy Apostles, Peter and Paul, for the profit and edification of the Church, in the name of all the pastors and all the faithful, we now pronounce this profession of faith, in full spiritual communion with you all, beloved brothers and sons.

The Credo

We believe in one only God, Father, Son and Holy Spirit, creator of things visible such as this world in which our transient life passes, of things invisible such as the pure spirits which are also called angels, and creator in each man of his spiritual and immortal soul.

We believe that this only God is absolutely one in His infinitely holy essence as also in all His perfections, in His omnipotence, His infinite knowledge, His providence, His will and His love. He is He who is, as He revealed to Moses, and He is love, as the Apostle John teaches us: so that these two names, Being and Love, express ineffably the same divine reality of Him who has wished to make Himself known to us, and who "dwelling in light inaccessible," is in Himself above every name, above every thing and above every created intellect.

God alone can give us right and full knowledge of this reality by revealing Himself as Father, Son, and Holy Spirit, in whose eternal life we are by grace called to share, here below in the obscurity of faith and after death in eternal light.

Infinite Beyond Conception

The mutual bonds which eternally constitute the Three Persons, who are each one and the same divine being, are the blessed inmost life of God thrice holy, infinitely beyond all that we can conceive in human measure. We give thanks, however, to the divine goodness that very many believers can testify with us before men to the unity of God, even though they know not the mystery of the Most Holy Trinity.

We believe then in the Father who eternally begets the Son, in the Son, the Word of God, who is eternally begotten, in the Holy Spirit, the uncreated person who proceeds from the Father and the Son, as their eternal love. Thus in the three Divine Persons, *coaeternae sibi et coaequales*, the life and beatitude of God, perfectly one superabound and are consummated in the supreme excellence and glory proper to uncreated being, and always "there should be venerated Unity in the Trinity and Trinity in the Unity."

We believe in Our Lord Jesus Christ, who is the Son of God. He is the eternal Word, born of the Father before time began, and one in substance with the Father, *homoousios cum patri*, and through him all things were made.

Incarnate of Virgin Mary

He was incarnate of the Virgin Mary by the power of the Holy Spirit, and was made man: equal therefore to the Father according to His divinity,and inferior to the Father according to His humanity, and Himself one, not by some impossible confusion of His natures, but by the unity of His Person.

He dwelt among us, full of grace and truth. He proclaimed and established the Kingdom of God and made us know in Himself the Father. He gave us His new commandment to love one another as He loved us.

He taught us the way of the beatitude of the Gospel: Poverty in spirit meekness, suffering borne with patience, thirst after justice, mercy, purity of heart, will for peace, persecution suffered for justice's sake. Under Pontius Pilate He suffered, the Lamb of God bearing on Himself the sins of the world, and He died for us on the Cross, saving us by His redeeming blood.

He was buried, and, of His own power, rose the third day, raising us by His resurrection to that sharing in the divine life which is the life of grace. He ascended to Heaven and He will come again, this time in glory, to judge the living and the dead; each according to his merits — those who have responded to the love and pity of God going to eternal life, those who have refused them to the end going to the fire that will not extinguish.

And His Kingdom will have no end.

We believe in the Holy Spirit, Who is lord and giver of life, Who is adored and glorified together with the Father and the Son. He spoke to us by the prophets; He was sent by Christ after His Resurrection and His Ascension to the Father; He illuminates, vivifies, protects and guides the Church; He purifies the Church's members if they do not shun His grace. His action, which penetrates to the inmost of the soul, enables man to respond to the call of Jesus: be perfect as your Heavenly Father is perfect.

We believe that Mary is the mother, who remained ever a virgin, of the Incarnate Word, our God and Savior Jesus Christ, and that by reason of this singular election, she was, in consideration of the merits of her Son, redeemed in a more eminent manner, preserved from all stain of original sin and filled with the gift of grace more than all other creatures.

Assumption of the Virgin

Joined by a close and indissoluble bond to the mysteries of the incarnation and redemption, the Blessed Virgin, the immaculate, was at the end of her earthly life raised body and soul to heavenly glory and likened to her risen Son in anticipation of the future lot of all the just; and we believe that the Blessed Mother of God, the new Eve, Mother of the Church, continues in Heaven her maternal role with regard to Christ's members, cooperating with the birth and growth of divine life in the souls of the redeemed.

We believe that in Adam all have sinned, which means that the original offense committed by him caused human nature, common to all men, to fall to a state in which it bears the consequences of that offense, and which is not the state in which it was at first in our first-parents, established as they were in holiness and justice, and in which man know neither evil nor death.

It is human nature so fallen, stripped of the grace that clothed it, injured in its own natural powers and subjected to the dominion of death, that is transmitted to all men, and it is in this sense that every man is born in sin.

Cites Council of Trent

We therefore hold, with the Council of Trent, that original sin is transmitted with human nature, "not by imitation, but by propagation" and that it is thus "proper to everyone."

We believe that Our Lord Jesus Christ, by the sacrifice of the Cross, redeemed us from original sin and all the personal sins committed by each one of us, so that, in accordance with the word of the Apostle, "where sin abounded, grace did more abound."

We believe in one baptism instituted by Our Lord Jesus Christ for the remission of sins. Baptism should be administered even to little children who have not yet been able to be guilty of any personal sin, in order that, though born deprived of supernatural grace, they may be reborn "of water and the Holy Spirit" to the divine life in Christ Jesus.

Belief in the Church

We believe in One, Holy, Catholic, and Apostolic Church, built by Jesus Christ on that rock which is Peter. She is the Mystical Body of Christ, at the same time a visible society instituted with hierarchical organs, and a spiritual community, the Church on earth, the pilgrim people of God here below, and the Church filled with heavenly blessings, the germ and the first fruits of the Kingdom of God, through which the work and the sufferings of redemption are continued throughout human history, and which looks for its perfect accomplishment beyond time in glory.

In the course of time, the Lord Jesus forms His church by means of the sacraments emanating from His plenitude. By these she makes her members participants in the mystery of the death and resurrection of Christ, in the grace of the Holy Spirit who gives her life and movement. She is therefore holy, though she has sinners in her bosom, because she herself has no other life but that of grace: it is by living, by her life that her members are sanctified, it is by removing themselves from her life that they fall into sins and disorders that prevent the radiation of her Sanctity. This is why she suffers and does penance for these offenses, of which she has the power to heal her children through the Blood of Christ and the gift of the Holy Spirit.

Heiress of the divine promises and daughter of Abraham according to the spirit, through that Israel whose scriptures she lovingly guards, and whose patriarchs and prophets she venerates, founded upon the Apostles and handing on from century to century their ever-living word and their powers as pastors in the successor of Peter and the bishops in communion with him. Perpetually assisted by the Holy Spirit, she has the charge of guarding, teaching, explaining and spreading the truth which God revealed in a then-veiled manner by the Prophets, and fully by the Lord Jesus. We believe all that is contained in the word of God written or handed down, and that the Church proposes for belief as divinely revealed, whether by a solemn judgment or by the ordinary and universal magisterium.

Recognizing also the existence, outside the organism of the Church of Christ, of numerous elements of truth and sanctification which belong to her as her own and tend to Catholic unity, and believing in the action of the Holy Spirit Who stirs up in the heart of the disciples of Christ love of this unity, we entertain the hope that the Christians who are not yet in the full communion of the one only church will one day be reunited in one flock with one only shepherd.

We believe that the church is necessary for salvation, because Christ, Who is the sole mediator and way of salvation, renders Himself present for us in His Body which is the church. But the divine design of salvation embraces all men, and those who without fault on their part do not know the Gospel of Christ and His Church, but seek God sincerely, and under the influence of grace endeavor to do His will as recognized through the promptings of their conscience, they in a number known only to God, can obtain salvation.

Celebration of Mass

We believe that the Mass, celebrated by the priest representing the Person of Christ by virture of the power received through the sacrament of orders, and offered by him in the name of Christ and the members of His mystical body, is the sacrifice of Calvary rendered sacramentally present on our altars. We believe that as the bread and wine consecrated by the Lord at the Last Supper were changed into His Body and His Blood which were to be offered for us on the Cross, likewise the bread and wine consecrated by the priest are changed into the Body and Blood of Christ enthroned gloriously in Heaven, and we believe that the mysterious presence of the Lord, under what continues to appear to our senses as before, is a true, real and substantial presence.

Christ cannot be thus present in this sacrament except by the change into His Body of the reality itself of the bread and the change into His Blood of the reality itself of the wine, which our senses perceive. This mysterious change is very appropriately called by the church transubstantiation.

Doctrine of Eucharist

Every theological explanation which seeks some understanding of this mystery must, in order to be in accord with Catholic faith, maintain that in the reality itself, independently of our mind, the bread and wine have ceased to exist after the consecration, so that it is the adorable Body and Blood of the Lord Jesus that from then on are really before us under the sacramental species of bread and wine, as the Lord willed it, in order to give Himself to us as food and to associate us with the unity of His Mystical Body.

The unique and indivisible existence of the Lord Glorious in Heaven is not multiplied, but is rendered present by the sacrament in the many places on earth where mass is celebrated. And this existence remains present, after the sacrifice, in the Blessed Sacrament which is, in the tabernacle, the living heart of each of our churches. And it is our very sweet duty to honor and adore in the Blessed Host which our eyes see, the incarnate Word Whom they cannot see, and Who, without leaving Heaven, is made present before us.

We confess that the Kingdom of God begun here below in the Church of Christ is not of this world whose form is passing, and that its proper growth cannot be confounded with the progress of civilization, of science or of human technology, but that it consists in an ever more profound knowledge of the unfathomable riches of Christ, and ever stronger hope in eternal blessings, an ever more ardent response to the love of God, and an ever more generous bestowal of grace and holiness among men.

But it is this same love which induces the Church to concern herself constantly about the true temporal welfare of men. Without ceasing to recall to her children that they have not here a lasting dwelling, she also urges them to contribute, each according to his vocation and his means, to the welfare of their earthly city, to promote justice, peace and brotherhood among men, to give their aid freely to their brothers, especially to the poorest and most unfortunate.

The deep solicitude of the Church, the spouse of Christ, for the needs of men, for their joys and hopes, their griefs and efforts, is therefore nothing other than her great desire to present to them, in order to illuminate them with the light of Christ and to gather them all in Him, their only Savior. This solicitude can never mean that the Church conform herself to the things of this world, or that she lessen the ardor of her expectation of her Lord and of the eternal Kingdom.

We believe in the life eternal. We believe that the souls of all those who die in the grace of Christ, whether they must still be purified in Purgatory or whether from the moment they leave their bodies, Jesus takes them to Paradise as he did for the good thief, are the people of God in the eternity beyond death, which will be finally conquered on the day of the resurrection when these souls will be reunited with their bodies.

We believe that the multitude of those gathered around Jesus and Mary in Paradise forms the church of Heaven, where in eternal beatitude they see God as He is, and where they also, in different degrees, are associated with the holy angels in the divine rule exercised by Christ in glory interceding for us and helping our weakness by their brotherly care.

We believe in the communion of all the faithful of Christ, those who are pilgrims on earth, the dead who are attaining their purification, and the blessed in Heaven, all together forming one church, and we believe that in this communion the merciful love of God and of His saints is ever listening to our prayers, as Jesus told us: Ask and you will receive. Thus it is with faith and in hope that we look forward to the resurrection of the dead, and the life of the world to come.

Blessed be God thrice Holy. Amen.

Humanae Vitae

1. The most serious duty of transmitting human life, for which married persons are the free and responsible collaborators of God the Creator, has always been a source of great joy to them, even if sometimes accompanied by not a few difficulties and by distress.

At all times the fulfillment of this duty has posed grave problems to the conscience of married persons, but, with the recent evolution of society, changes have taken place that give rise to new questions which the Church could not ignore, having to do with a matter which so closely touches upon the life and happiness of men.

2. The changes which have taken place are in fact noteworthy and of varied kinds. In the first place, there is the rapid demographic development. Fear is shown by many that world population is growing more rapidly than the available resources, with growing distress to many families and developing countries, so that the temptation for authorities to counter this danger with radical measures is great. Moreover, working and lodging conditions, as well as increased exigencies both in the economic field and in that of education, often make the proper education of an elevated number of children difficult today. A change is also seen both in the manner of considering the person of woman and her place in society, and in the value to be attributed to conjugal love in marriage, and also in the appreciation to be made of the meaning of conjugal acts in relation to that love.

Finally and above all, man has made stupendous progress in the domination and rational organization of the forces of nature, such that he tends to extend this domination to his own total being: to the body, to psychical life, to social life and even to the laws which regulate the transmission of life.

3. This new state of things gives rise to new questions. Granted the conditions of life today, and granted the meaning which conjugal relations have with respect to the harmony between husband and wife and to their mutual fidelity,

would not a revision of the ethical norms, in force up to now, seem to be advisable, especially when it is considered that they cannot be observed without sacrifices, sometimes heroic sacrifices?

And again: by extending to this field the application of the so-called "principle of totality," could it not be admitted that the intention of a less abundant but more rationalized fecundity might transform a materially sterilizing intervention into a licit and wise control of birth? Could it not be admitted, that is, that the finality of procreation pertains to the ensemble of conjugal life, rather than to its single acts? It is also asked whether, in view of the increased sense of responsibility of modern man, the moment has not come for him to entrust to his reason and his will, rather than to the biological rhythms of his organism, the task of regulating birth.

4. Such questions required from the teaching authority of the Church a new and deeper reflection upon the principles of the moral teaching on marriage; a teaching founded on the natural law, illuminated and enriched by divine revelation.

No believer will wish to deny that the teaching authority of the Church is competent to interpret even the natural moral law. It is, in fact, indisputable, as our predecessors have many times declared that Jesus Christ, when communicating to Peter and to the Apostles His divine authority, and sending them to teach all nations His commandments, constituted them as guardians and authentic interpreters of all the moral law, not only, that is, of the law of the Gospel, but also of the natural law, which is also an expression of the will of God, the faithful fulfillment of which is equally necessary for salvation.

Comfortably to this mission of hers, the Church has always provided — and even more amply in recent times — a coherent teaching concerning both the nature of marriage and the correct use of conjugal rights and the duties of husband and wife.

Special Studies

5. The consciousness of that same mission induced us to confirm and enlarge the study commission which our predecessor Pope John XXIII of happy memory had instituted in March 1963. That commission which included, besides several experts in the various pertinent disciplines also married couples, had as its scope the gathering of opinions on the new questions regarding conjugal life, and in particular on the regulation of births, and of furnishing opportune elements of information so that the magisterium could give an ad-

equate reply to the expectation not only of the faithful, but also of world opinion.

The work of these experts, as well as the successive judgments and counsels spontaneously forwarded by or expressly requested from a good number of our brothers in the episcopate, have permitted us to measure more exactly all the aspects of this complex matter. Hence with all our heart we express to each of them our lively gratitude.

Reply of the Magisterium

6. The conclusions at which the commission arrived could not, nevertheless, be considered by us as definitive, nor dispense us from a personal examination of this serious question; and this also because, within the commission itself, no full concordance of judgments concerning the moral norms to be proposed had been reached, and above all because certain criteria of solutions had emerged which departed from the moral teaching on marriage proposed with constant firmness by the teaching authority of the Church.

Therefore, having attentively sifted the documentation laid before us, after mature reflection and assiduous prayers, we now intend, by virture of the mandate entrusted to us by Christ, to give our reply to these grave questions.

II. DOCTRINAL PRINCIPLES

A Total Vision of Man

7. The problem of birth, like every other problem regarding human life, is to be considered, beyond partial perspective — whether of the biological or psychological, demographic or sociological orders — in the light of an integral vision of man and of his vocation, not only his natural and earthly, but also his supernatural and eternal vocation. And since, in the attempt to justify artificial methods of birth control, many have appealed to the demands both of conjugal love and of "responsible parenthood" it is good to state very precisely the true concept of these two great realities of married life, referring principally to what was recently set forth in this regard, and in a highly authoritative form, by the Second Vatican Council in its pastoral constitution *Gaudium et Spes*.

Conjugal Love

8. Conjugal love reveals its true nature and nobility when it is considered in its supreme origin, God, who is love, "the Father, from whom every family in heaven and on earth is named."

Marriage is not, then, the effect of chance or the product of evolution of unconscious natural forces; it is the wise institution of the Creator to realize in mankind His design of love. By means of the reciprocal personal gift of self, proper and exclusive to them, husband and wife tend towards the communion of their beings in view of mutual personal perfection, to collaborate with God in the generation and education of new lives.

For baptized persons, moreover, marriage invests the dignity of a sacramental sign of grace, inasmuch as it represents the union of Christ and of the Church.

Its Characteristics

9. Under this light, there clearly appear the characteristic marks and demands of conjugal love, and it is of supreme importance to have an exact idea of these.

This love is first of all fully human, that is to say, of the senses and of the spirit at the same time. It is not, then, a simple transport of instinct and sentiment, but also, and principally, an act of the free will, intended to endure and to grow by means of the joys and sorrows of daily life, in such a way that husband and wife become one only heart and one only soul, and together attain their human perfection.

Then, this love is total, that is to say, it is a very special form of personal friendship, in which husband and wife generously share everything, without undue reservations or selfish calculations. Whoever truly loves his marriage partner loves not only for what he receives, but for the partner's self, rejoicing that he can enrich his partner with the gift of himself.

Again, this love is faithful and exclusive until death. Thus in fact do bride and groom conceive it to be on the day when they freely and in full awareness assume the duty of the marriage bond. A fidelity, this, which meritorious, as no one can deny. The example of so many married persons down through the centuries shows, not only that fidelity is according to the nature of marriage, but also that it is a source of profound and lasting happiness and finally, this love is fecund for it is not exhausted by the communion between husband and wife, but is destined to continue, raising up new lives. "Marriage and conjugal love are by their nature ordained toward the begetting and educating of children. Children are really the supreme gift of marriage and contribute very substantially to the welfare of their parents."

Responsible Parenthood

10. Hence conjugal love requires in husband and wife an awareness of their mission of "responsible parenthood," which today is rightly much insisted upon, and which also must be exactly understood. Consequently it is to be considered under different aspects which are legitimate and connected with one another.

In relation to the biological processes, responsible parenthood means the knowledge and respect of their functions human intellect discovers in the power of giving life biological laws which are part of the human person.

In relation to the tendencies of instinct or passion, responsible parenthood means that necessary dominion which reason and will must exercise over them.

In relation to physical, economic, psychological and social conditions, responsible parenthood is exercised, either by the deliberate and generous decision to raise a numerous family, or by the decision, made for grave motives and with due respect for the moral law, to avoid for the time being, or even for an indeterminate period, a new birth.

Responsible parenthood also and above all implies a more profound relationship to the objective moral order established by God, of which a right conscience is the faithful interpreter. The responsible exercise of parenthood implies, therefore, that husband and wife recognize fully their own duties towards God, towards themselves, towards the family and towards society, in a correct hierarchy of values.

In the task of transmitting life, therefore, they are not free to proceed completely at will, as if they could determine in a wholly autonomous way the honest path to follow; but they must conform their activity to the creative intention of God, expressed in the very nature of marriage and of its acts, and manifested by the constant teaching of the Church.

Respect for the Nature and Purpose of the Marriage Act

11. These acts, by which husband and wife are united in chaste intimacy, and by means of which human life is transmitted, are, as the council recalled, "noble and worthy" and they do not cease to be lawful if, for causes independent of the will of husband and wife, they are foreseen to be infecund, since they always remain ordained towards expressing and consolidating their union. In fact, as experience bears witness, not every conjugal act is followed by a new life. God has wisely disposed natural laws and rhythms of fecundity which, of themselves, cause a separation in the succession of births. Nonetheless the

church, calling men back to the observance of the norms of the natural law, as interpreted by their constant doctrine, teaches that each and every marriage act *(quilibet matrimonii usus)* must remain open to the transmission of life.

Two Inseparable Aspects: Union and Procreation

12. That teaching, often set forth by the magisterium, is founded upon the inseparable connection, willed by God and unable to be broken by man on his own initiative, between the two meanings of the conjugal act: the unitive meaning and the procreative meaning. Indeed, by its intimate structure, the conjugal act, while most closely uniting husband and wife, capacitates them for the generation of new lives, according to laws inscribed in the very being of man and of woman. By safeguarding both these essential aspects, the unitive and procreative, the conjugal act preserves in its fullness the sense of true mutual love and its ordination towards man's most high calling to parenthood. We believe that the men of our day are particularly capable of seizing the deeply reasonable and human character of this fundamental principle.

Faithfulness to God's Design

13. It is in fact justly observed that a conjugal act imposed upon one's partner without regard for his or her condition and lawful desires is not a true act of love, and therefore denies an exigency of right moral order in the relationships between husband and wife. Hence, one who reflects well must also recognize that a reciprocal act of love, which jeopardizes the responsibility to transmit life which God the Creator, according to particular laws, inserted therein, is in contradiction with the design constitutive of marriage, and with the will of the Author of life. To use this divine gift destroying, even if only partially, its meaning and its purpose is to contradict the nature both of man and of woman and of their most intimate relationship, and therefore it is to contradict also the plan of God and His will. On the other hand, to make use of the gift of conjugal love while respecting the laws of the generative process means to acknowledge oneself not to be the arbiter of the sources of human life, but rather the minister of the design established by the Creator. In fact, just as man does not have unlimited dominion over his body in general, so also with particular reason, he has no such dominion over his generative faculties as such, because of their intrinsic ordination towards raising up life, of which God is the principle. "Human life is sacred," Pope John XXIII recalled; "from its very inception it reveals the creating hand of God."

Illicit Ways of Regulating Birth

14. In conformity with these landmarks in the human and Christian vision of marriage, we must once again declare that the direct interruption of the generative process already begun, and, above all, directly willed and procured abortion, even if for therapeutic reasons, are to be absolutely excluded as licit means of regulating birth.

Equally to be excluded, as the teaching authority of the Church has frequently declared, is direct sterilization, whether perpetual or temporary, whether of the man or of the woman. Similarly excluded is every action which, either in anticipation of the conjugal act, or in its accomplishment, or in the development of its natural consequences, proposes, whether as an end or as a means, to render procreation impossible.

To justify conjugal acts made intentionally infecund, one cannot invoke as valid reasons the lesser evil, or the fact that such acts would constitute a whole together with the fecund acts already performed or to follow later, and hence would share in one and the same moral goodness. In truth, if it is sometimes licit to tolerate a lesser evil in order to avoid a greater evil or to promote a greater good it is not licit, even for the gravest reasons, to do evil so that good may follow therefrom, that is, to make into the object of a positive act of the will something which is intrinsically disorder, and hence unworthy of the human person, even when the intention is to safeguard or promote individual, family or social well-being. Consequently it is an error to think that a conjugal act which is deliberately made infecund and so is intrinsically dishonest could be made honest and right by the ensemble of a fecund conjugal life.

Licitness of Therapeutic Means

15. The Church, on the contrary, does not at all consider illicit the use of those therapeutic means truly necessary to cure diseases of the organism, even if an impediment to procreation, which may be foreseen, should result therefrom, provided such impediment is not, for whatever motive, directly willed.

Licitness of Recourse to Infecund Periods

16. To this teaching of the Church on conjugal morals, the objection is made today, as we observed earlier (no. 3), that it is the prerogative of the human intellect to dominate the energies offered by irrational nature and to orient them towards an end conformable to the good of man. Now, some may ask: in the present case, is it not reasonable in many circumstances to have

recourse to artificial birth control if, thereby, we secure the harmony and peace of the family, and better conditions for the education of the children already born? To this question it is necessary to reply with clarity: the Church is the first to praise and recommend the intervention of intelligence in a function which so closely associates the rational creature with his Creator; but she affirms that this must be done with respect for the order established by God.

If, then, there are serious motives to space out births, which derive from the physical or psychological conditions of husband and wife, or from external conditions, the Church teaches that it is then licit to take into account the natural rhythms immanent in the generative functions, for the use of marriage in the infecund periods only, and in this way to regulate birth without offending the moral principles which have been recalled earlier.

The Church is coherent with herself when she considers recourse to the infecund periods to be licit, while at the same time condemning as being always illicit, the use of means directly contrary to fecundation, even if such use is inspired by reasons which may appear honest and serious. In reality, there are essential differences between the two cases; in the former, the married couple make legitimate use of a natural disposition; in the later, they impede the development of natural processes. It is true that, in the one and the other case, the married couple are concordant in the positive will of avoiding children for plausible reasons, seeking the certainty that offspring will not arrive; but it is also true that only in the former case are they able to renounce the use of marriage in the fecund periods when, for just motives, procreation is not desirable, while making use of it during infecund periods to manifest their affection and to safeguard their mutual fidelity. By so doing, they give proof of a truly and integrally honest love.

Grave Consequences of Methods Of Artificial Birth Control

17. Upright men can even better convince themselves of the solid grounds on which the teaching of the Church in this field is based, if they care to reflect upon the consequences of methods of artificial birth control. Let them consider, first of all, how wide and easy a road would thus be opened up towards conjugal infidelity and the general lowering of morality. Not much experience is needed in order to know human weakness, and to understand that men — especially the young, who are so vulnerable on this point — have need of encouragement to be faithful to the moral law, so that they must not be offered some easy means of eluding its observance. It is also to be feared that the man, growing used to the employment of

anti-conceptive practices, may finally lose respect for the woman and, no longer caring for her physical and psychological equilibrium, may come to the point of considering her as a mere instrument of selfish enjoyment, and no longer as his respected and beloved companion.

Let it be considered also that a dangerous weapon would thus be placed in the hands of those public authorities who take no heed of moral exigencies. Who could blame a government for applying to the solution of the problems of the community those means acknowledged to be licit for married couples in the solution of a family problem? Who will stop rulers from favoring, from even imposing upon their peoples, if they were to consider it necessary, the method of contraception which they judge to be most efficacious? In such a way men, wishing to avoid individual, family, or social difficulties encountered in the observance of the divine law, would reach the point of placing at the mercy of the intervention of public authorities the most personal and most reserved sector of conjugal intimacy.

Consequently, if the mission of generating life is not to be exposed to the arbitrary will of men, one must necessarily recognize unsurmountable limits to the possibility of man's domination over his own body and its functions; limits which no man, whether a private individual or one invested with authority, may licitly surpass. And such limits cannot be determined otherwise than by the respect due to the integrity of the human organism and its functions, according to the principles recalled earlier, and also according to the correct understanding of the "principle of totality," illustrated by our predecessor Pope Pius XII.

The Church—Guarantor of True Human Values

18. It can be foreseen that this teaching will perhaps not be easily received by all: Too numerous are those voices — amplified by the modern means of propaganda — which are contrary to the voice of the Church. To tell the truth, the Church is not surprised to be made, like her divine founder, a "sign of contradiction," yet she does not because of this cease to proclaim with humble firmness the entire moral law, both natural and evangelical. Of such laws the Church was not the author, nor consequently can she be their arbiter; she is only their depositary and their interpreter, without ever being able to declare to be licit that which is not so by reason of its intimate and unchangeable opposition to the true good of man.

In defending conjugal morals in their integral wholeness, the Church knows that she contributes towards the establishment of a truly human civilization;

she engages man not to abdicate from his own responsibility in order to rely on technical means; by that very fact she defends the dignity of man and wife. Faithful to both the teaching and the example of the Savior, she shows herself to be the sincere and disinterested friend of men, whom she wishes to help, even during their earthly sojourn," to share as sons in the life of the living God, the Father of all men."

III. PASTORAL DIRECTIVES

The Church Mater et Magistra

19. Our words would not be an adequate expression of the thought and solicitude of the Church, mother and teacher of all peoples, if, after having recalled men to the observance and respect of the divine law regarding matrimony, we did not strengthen them in the path of honest regulation of birth, even amid the difficult conditions which today afflict families and peoples. The Church, in fact, cannot have a different conduct towards men than that of the Redeemer; she knows her weaknesses, has compassion on the crowd, receives sinners; but she cannot renounce the teaching of the law which is, in reality, that law proper to a human life restored to its original truth and conducted by the spirit of God. Though we are thinking also of all men of good will, we now address ourself particularly to our sons, from whom we expect a prompter and more generous adherence.

Possibility of Observing the Divine law

20. Teaching of the Church on the regulation of birth, which promulgates the divine law, will easily appear to many to be difficult or even impossible of actuation. And indeed, like all great beneficent realities, it demands serious engagement and much effort, individual, family and social effort. More than that, it would not be practicable without the help of God, who upholds and strengthens the good will of men. Yet, to anyone who reflects well, it cannot but be clear that such efforts ennoble man and are beneficial to the human community.

Mastery of Self

21. The honest practice of regulation of birth demands first of all that husband and wife acquire and possess solid convictions concerning the true values of life and of the family, and that they tend towards securing perfect self-mastery. To dominate instinct by means of one's reason and free will undoubt-

edly requires ascetical practices, so that the affective manifestations of conjugal life may observe the correct order, in particular with regard to the observance of periodic continence. Yet this discipline which is proper to the purity of married couples, far from harming conjugal love, rather confers on it a higher human value. It demands continual effort yet, thanks to its beneficent influence, husband and wife fully develop their personalities, being enriched with spiritual values. Such discipline bestows upon family life fruits of serenity and peace, and facilitates the solution of other problems: it favors attention for one's partner, helps both parties to drive out selfishness, the enemy of true love; and deepens their sense of responsibility. By its means, parents acquire the capacity of having a deeper and more efficacious influence in the education of their offspring; little children and youths grow up with a just appraisal of human values, and in the serene and harmonious development of their spiritual and sensitive faculties.

Creating an Atmosphere Favorable to Chastity

22. On this occasion, we wish to draw the attention of educators, and of all who perform duties or responsibility in regard to the common good of human society, to the need of creating an atmosphere favorable to education in chastity, that is, to the triumph of healthy liberty over license by means of respect for the moral order.

Everything in the modern media of social communications which leads to sense excitation and unbridled customs, as well as every form of pornography and licentious performances, must arouse the frank and unanimous reaction of all those who are solicitous for the progress of civilization and the defense of the good of the human spirit. Vainly would one seek to justify such depravation with the pretext of artistic or scientific exigencies, or to deduce an argument from the freedom allowed in this sector by the public authorities.

Appeal to Public Authorities

23. To Rulers, who are those principally responsible for the common good, and who can do so much to safeguard moral customs, we say: Do not allow the morality of your peoples to be degraded; do not permit that by legal means practices contrary to the natural and divine law be introduced into that fundamental cell, the family. Quite other is the way in which public authorities can and must contribute to the solution of the demographic problem: namely, the

way of a provident policy for the family, of a wise education of peoples in respect of moral law and the liberty of citizens.

We are well aware of the serious difficulties experienced by public authorities in this regard, especially in the developing countries. To their legitimate preoccupations we devoted our encyclical letter *Populorum Progressio*. But with our predecessor Pope John XXIII we repeat: no solution to these difficulties is acceptable "which does violence to man's essential dignity" and is based only on an utterly materialistic conception of man himself and of his life. The only possible solution to this question is one which envisages the social and economic progress both of individuals and of the whole of human society, and which respects and promotes true human values. Neither can one, without grave injustice, consider divine providence to be responsible for what depends, instead, on a lack of wisdom in government, on an insufficient sense of social justice, on selfish monopolization, or again on blameworthy indolence in confronting the efforts and the sacrifices necessary to ensure the raising of living standards of a people and of all its sons.

May all responsible public authorities — as some are already doing so laudably — generously revive their efforts. And may mutual aid between all the members of the great human family never cease to grow: This is an almost limitless field which thus opens up to the activity of the great international organizations.

To Men of Science

24. We wish now to express our encouragement to men of science, who "can considerably advance the welfare of marriage and the family, along with peace of conscience, if by pooling their efforts they labor to explain more thoroughly the various conditions favoring a proper regulation of births." It is particularly desirable that, according to the wish already expressed by Pope Pius XII, medical science succeed in providing a sufficiently secure basis for a regulation of birth, founded on that observance of natural rhythms. In this way, scientists and especially Catholic scientists will contribute to demonstrate in actual fact that, as the Church teaches, "a true contradiction cannot exist between the divine laws pertaining to the transmission of life and those pertaining to the fostering of authentic conjugal love."

To Christian Husbands and Wives

25. And now our words more directly address our own children, particularly those whom God calls to serve Him in marriage. The Church, while

teaching imperceptible demands of the divine law, announces the tidings of salvation, and by means of the sacraments opens up the paths of grace, which makes a man a new creature, capable of corresponding with love and true freedom to the design of his Creator and Savior, and of finding the yoke of Christ to be sweet.

Christian married couples, then, docile to her voice, must remember that their Christian vocation, which began at baptism, is further specified and reinforced by the sacrament of matrimony. By it husband and wife are strengthened and as it were consecrated for the faithful accomplishment of their proper duties, for the carrying out of their proper vocation even to perfection, and the Christian witness which is proper to them before the whole world. To them the Lord entrusts the task of making visible to men the holiness and sweetness of the law which unites the mutual love of husband and wife with their cooperation with the love of God, the author of human life.

We do not at all intend to hide the sometimes serious difficulties inherent in the life of Christian married persons; for them as for everyone else, "the gate is narrow and the way is hard, that leads to life." But the hope of that life must illuminate their way, as with courage they strive to live with wisdom, justice and piety in this present time, knowing that the figure of this world passes away.

Let married couples, then, face up to the efforts needed, supported by the faith and hope which "do not disappoint . . . because God's love has been poured into our hearts through the Holy Spirit, who has been given to us." Let them implore divine assistance by persevering prayer; above all, let them draw from the source of grace and charity in the Eucharist. And if sin should still keep its hold over them, let them not be discouraged, but rather have recourse with humble perseverance to the mercy of God, which is poured forth in the sacrament of Penance. In this way they will be enabled to achieve the fullness of conjugal life described by the Apostle: "Husbands, love your wives, as Christ loved the Church. . . Husbands should love their wives as their own bodies. He who loves his wife loves himself. For no man ever hates his own flesh, but nourishes and cherishes it, as Christ does the Church. . . This is a great mystery, and I mean in reference to Christ and the Church. However, let each one of you love his wife as himself, and let the wife see that she respects her husband."

Apostles in Homes

26. Among the fruits which ripen forth from a generous effort of fidelity to the divine law, one of the most precious is that married couples themselves not

infrequently feel the desire to communicate their experience to others. Thus there comes to be included in the vast pattern of the vocation of the laity a new and most noteworthy form of the apostolate of like to like; it is married couples themselves who become apostles and guides to other married couples. This is assuredly, among so many forms of apostolate, one of those which seem most opportune today.

To Doctors and Medical Personnel

27. We hold those physicians and medical personnel in the highest esteem who, in the exercise of their profession, value above every human interest the superior demands of their Christian vocation. Let them persevere, therefore, in promoting on every occasion the discovery of solutions inspired by faith and right reason, let them strive to arouse this conviction and this respect in their associates. Let them also consider as their proper professional duty the task of acquiring all the knowledge needed in this delicate sector, so as to be able to give to those married persons who consult them wise counsel and healthy direction, such as they have a right to expect.

To Priests

28. Beloved priest sons, by vocation you are the counselors and spiritual guides of individual persons and of families. We now turn to you with confidence. Your first task — especially in the case of those who teach moral theology — is to expound the Church's teaching on marriage without ambiguity. Be the first to give, in the exercise of your ministry, the example of loyal internal and external obedience to the teaching authority of the Church. That obedience, as you know well, obliges not only because of the reasons adduced, but rather because of the light of the Holy Spirit, which is given in a particular way to the pastors of the Church in order that they may illustrate the truth. You know, too, that it is of the utmost importance, for peace of consciences and for the unity of the Christian people, that in the field of morals as well as in that of dogma, all should attend to the magisterium of the Church, and all should speak the same language. Hence, with all our heart we renew to you the heartfelt plea of the great Apostle Paul: "I appeal to you, brethren, by the name of Our Lord Jesus Christ, that all of you agree and that there be no dissensions among you, but that you be united in the same mind and the same judgment."

29. To diminish in no way the saving teaching of Christ constitutes an

eminent form of charity for souls. But this must ever be accompanied by patience and goodness, such as the Lord Himself gave example of in dealing with men. Having come not to condemn but to save, he was indeed intransigent with evil, but merciful towards individuals.

In their difficulties, may married couples always find, in the words and in the heart of a priest, the echo of the voice and the love of the Redeemer.

To Bishops

30. Beloved and venerable brothers in the episcopate, with whom we most intimately share the solicitude of the spiritual good of the people of God, at the conclusion of this encyclical our reverent and affectionate thoughts turn to you. To all of you we extend an urgent invitation. At the head of the priests, your collaborators, and of your faithful, work ardently and incessantly for the safeguarding and the holiness of marriage, so that it may always be lived in its entire human and Christian fullness. Consider this mission as one of your most urgent responsibilities at the present time. As you know, it implies concerted pastoral action in all the fields of human activity, economic, cultural and social; for, in fact, only a simultaneous improvement in these various sectors will make it possible to render the life of parents and of children within their families not only tolerable, but easier and more joyous, to render the living together in human society more fraternal and peaceful, in faithfulness to God's design for the world.

Final Appeal

31. Venerable brothers, most beloved sons, and all men of good will, great indeed is the work of education, of progress and of love to which we call you, upon the foundation of the Church's teaching, of which the successor of Peter is, together with his brothers in the episcopate, the depositary and interpreter. Truly a great work, as we are deeply convinced, both for the world and for the Church, since man cannot find true happiness — towards which he aspires with all his being — other than in respect of the laws written by God in his very nature, laws which he must observe with intelligence and love. Upon this work, and upon all of you, and especially upon married couples, we invoke the abundant graces of the God of holiness and mercy, and in pledge thereof we impart to you all our apostolic blessing.

Given at Rome, from St. Peter's, this 25th day of July, feast of St. James the Apostle, in the year 1968, the sixth of our pontificate.

Vatican Council II
Inter Mirifica
Decree on the Media of Social Communications
Introduction

1. Among the wonderful technological discoveries which men of talent, especially in the present era, have made with God's help, the Church welcomes and promotes with special interest those which have a most direct relation to men's minds and which have uncovered new avenues of communicating most readily news, views and teachings of every sort. The most important of these inventions are those media which, such as the press, movies, radio, television and the like, can, of their very nature, reach and influence, not only individuals, but the very masses and the whole of human society, and thus can rightly be called the media of social communication.

2. The Church recognizes that these media, if properly utilized, can be of great service to mankind, since they greatly contribute to men's entertainment and instruction as well as to the spread and support of the kingdom of God. The Church recognizes, too, that men can employ these media contrary to the plan of the Creator and to their own loss. Indeed, the Church experiences maternal grief at the harm all too often done to society by their evil use.

Hence, this sacred Synod, attentive to the watchful concern manifested by the Supreme Ponfiffs and bishops in a matter of such great importance, judges it to be its duty to treat of the principal questions linked with the media of social communication. It trusts,moreover, that the teaching and regulations it thus sets forth will serve to promote, not only the eternal welfare of Christians, but also the progress of all mankind.

CHAPTER I
On the Teaching of the Church

3. The Catholic Church, since it was founded by Christ our Lord to bear salvation to all men and thus is obliged to preach the Gospel, considers it one of its duties to announce the Good News of salvation also with the help of the media of social communication and to instruct men in their proper use.

It is, therefore, an inherent right of the Church to have at its disposal and to employ any of these media insofar as they are necessary or useful for the instruction of Christians and all its efforts for the welfare of souls. It is the duty of Pastors to instruct and guide the faithful so that they, with the help of these same media, may further the salvation and perfection of themselves and of the entire family.

In addition, the laity especially must strive to instill a human and Christian spirit into these media, so that they may fully measure up to the great expectations of mankind and to God's design.

4. For the proper use of these media it is most necessary that all who imploy them be acquainted with the norms of morality and conscientiously put them into practice in this area. They must look, then, to the nature of what is communicated, given the special character of each of these media. At the same time they must take into consideration the entire situation or circumstances, namely, the persons, place, time and other conditions under which communication takes place and which can affect or totally change its propriety. Among these circumstances to be considered is the precise manner in which a given medium achieves it effect. For its influence can be so great that men, especially if they are unprepared, can scarcely become aware of it, govern its impact, or, if necessary, reject it.

5. It is, however, especially necessary that all parties concerned should adopt for themselves a proper moral outlook on the use of these media, especially with respect to certain questions that have been vigorously aired in our day.

The first question has to do with "information," as it is called, or the search for and reporting of the news. Now clearly this had become most useful and very often necessary for the progress of contemporary society and for achieving closer links among men. The prompt publication of affairs and events provides every individual with a fuller, continuing acquaintance with them, and thus all can contribute more effectively to the common good and more readily promote and advance the welfare of the entire civil society. Therefore, in society men have a right to information, in accord with the circumstances in each case, about matters concerning individuals or the community. The proper exercise of this right demands, however, that the news that is communicated should always be true and complete, within the bounds of justice and charity. In addition, the manner in which the news is communicated should be proper and decent. This means that in both the search for news and in reporting it, there must be full respect for the laws of morality and for the legitimate rights and dignity of the individual. For not all knowledge is helpful, but "it is charity that edifies."

6. The second question deals with the relationship between the rights, as

they are called, of art and the norms of morality. Since the mounting controversies in this area frequently take their rise from false teachings about ethics and esthetics, the Council proclaims that all must hold to the absolute primacy of the objective moral order, that is, this order by itself surpasses and fittingly coordinates all other spheres of human affairs — the arts not excepted — even though they be endowed with notable dignity. For man, who is endowed by God with the gift of reason and summoned to pursue a lofty destiny, is alone affected by the moral order in his entire being. And likewise, if man resolutely and faithfully upholds this order, he will be brought to the attainment of complete perfection and happiness.

7. Finally, the narration, description or portrayal of moral evil, even though the media of social communication, can indeed serve to bring about a deeper knowledge and study of humanity and, with the aid of appropriately heightened dramatic effects, can reveal and glorify the grand dimensions of truth and goodness. Nevertheless, such presentations ought always to be subject to moral restraint, lest they work to the harm rather than the benefit of souls, particularly when there is question of treating matters which deserve reverent handling or which, given the baneful effect of original sin in men, could quite readily arouse base desires in them.

8. Since public opinion exercises the greatest power and authority today in every sphere of life, both private and public, every member of society must fulfill the demands of justice and charity in this area. As a result, all must strive, through these media as well, to form and spread sound public opinion.

9. All who, of their own free choice, make use of these media of communications as readers, viewers or listeners have special obligations. For a proper choice demands that they fully favor those presentations that are outstanding for their moral goodness, their knowledge and their artistic or technical merit. They ought, however, to avoid those that may be a cause or occasion of spiritual harm to themselves, or that can lead others into danger through base example, or that hinder desirable presentations and promote those that are evil. To patronize such presentations, in most instances, would merely reward those who use these media only for profit.

In order that those who make use of these media may fulfill the moral code, they ought not to neglect to inform themselves in time about judgments passed by authorities competent in these matters. They ought also to follow such judgments according to the norms of an upright conscience. So that they may more easily resist improper inducements and rather encourage those that are desirable, let them take care to guide and instruct their consciences with suitable aids.

10. Those who make use of the media of communications, especially the young, should take steps to accustom themselves to moderation and self-control in their regard. They should, moreover, endeavor to deepen their understanding of what they see, hear or read. They should discuss these matters with their teachers and experts, and learn to pass sound judgments on them. Parents should remember that they have a most serious duty to guard carefully lest shows, publications and other things of this sort, which may be morally harmful, enter their homes or affect their children under other circumstances.

11. The principal moral responsibility for the proper use of the media of social communication falls on newsmen, writers, actors, designers, producers, displayers, distributors, operators and sellers, as well as critics and all others who play any part in the production and transmission of mass presentations. It is quite evident what gravely important responsibilities they have in the present day when they are in a position to lead the human race to good or to evil by informing or arousing mankind.

Thus, they must adjust their economic, political or artistic and technical aspects so as never to oppose the common good. For the purpose of better achieving this goal, they are to be commended when they join professional associations, which — even under a code, if necessary, of sound moral practice — oblige their members to show respect for morality in the duties and task of their craft.

They ought always to be mindful, however, that a great many of their readers and audience are young people, who need a press and entertainment that offer them decent amusement and cultural uplift. In addition, they should see to it that communications or presentations concerning religious matters are entrusted to worthy and experienced hands and are carried out with fitting reverence.

12. The public authority, in these matters, is bound by special responsibilities in view of the common good, to which these media are ordered. The same authority has, in virture of its office, the duty of protecting and safeguarding true and just freedom of information, a freedom that is totally necessary for the welfare of contemporary society, especially when it is a question of freedom of the press. It ought also to encourage spiritual values, culture and the fine arts and guarantee the rights of those who wish to use the media. Moreover, public authority has the duty of helping those projects which, though they are certainly most beneficial for young people, cannot otherwise be undertaken.

Lastly, the same public authority, which legitimately concerns itself with the health of the citizenry, is obliged, through the promulgation and careful enforcement of laws, to exercise a fitting and careful watch lest grave damage befall public morals and the welfare of society through the base use of these media. Such vigilance in no wise restricts the freedom of individuals or groups, especially where there is a lack of adequate precaution on the part of those who are professionally engaged in using these media.

Special care should be taken to safeguard young people from printed matter and performances which may be harmful at their age.

CHAPTER II

On the Pastoral Activity of the Church

13. All the children of the Church should join, without delay and with the greatest effort, in a common work to make effective use of the media of social communication in various apostolic endeavors, as circumstances and conditions demand. They should anticipate harmful developments, especially in regions where more urgent efforts to advance morality and religion are needed.

Pastors should hasten, therefore, to fulfill their duty in this respect, one which is intimately linked with their ordinary preaching responsibility. The laity, too, who have something to do with the use of these media, should endeavor to bear witness to Christ, first of all by carrying out their individual duties or office expertly and with an apostolic spirit, and further, by being of direct help in the pastoral activity of the Church — to the best of their ability — through their technical, economic, cultural and artistic talents.

14. First, a good press should be fostered. To instill a fully Christian spirit into readers, a truly Catholic press should be set up and encouraged. Such a press — whether immediately fostered and directed by ecclesiastical authorities or by Catholic laymen — should be edited with the clear purpose of forming, supporting and advancing public opinion in accord with natural law and Catholic teaching and precepts. It should disseminate and properly explain news concerning the life of tne Church. Moreover, the faithful ought to be advised of the necessity both to spread and read the Catholic press to formulate Christian judgments for themselves on all events.

The production and showing of films that have value as decent entertainment, humane culture or art, especially when they are designed for young people, ought to be encouraged and assured by every effective means. This can be done particularly by supporting and joining in projects and enterprises for the production and distribution of decent films, by encouraging worthwhile films through critical approval and awards, by patronizing or jointly sponsoring theaters operated by Catholic and responsible managers.

Similarly, effective support should be given to good radio and television programs, above all those that are suitable for families. Catholic programs should be promoted, in which listeners and viewers can be brought to share in the life of the Church and learn religious truths. An effort should also be made, where it may be necessary, to set up Catholic stations. In such instances, however, care must be taken that their programs are outstanding for their standards of excellence and achievement.

In addition, there should be an effort to see that the noble and ancient art of the drama, which now is diffused everywhere by the media of social communication, serves the cultural and moral betterment of audiences.

15. To provide for the needs just set forth, priests, religious and laymen who are equipped with the proper skills for adapting these media to the objective of the apostolate should be appointed promptly.

Importantly, laymen ought to be afforded technical, doctrinal and moral training. For this purpose, the number of school faculties and institutes should be increased, where newsmen, writers for screen, radio and television and all other interested parties can obtain a sound training that is imbued with the Christian spirit, especially with respect to the social teaching of the Church.

Finally, care must be taken to prepare literary, film, radio, television and other critics, who will be equipped with the best skills in their own crafts and trained and encouraged to render judgments which always put moral issues in their proper light.

16. Since the proper use of the media of social communications which are available to audiences of different cultural backgrounds and ages calls for instruction proper to their needs, programs which are suitable for this purpose — especially where they are designed for young people — should be encouraged, increased in numbers and organized according to Christian moral principles. This should be done in Catholic schools at every level, in seminaries and in lay apostolate groups. To speed this along catechetical manuals should present and explain Catholic teaching and regulations on this matter.

17. It is quite unbecoming for the Church's children idly to permit the message of salvation to be thwarted or impeded by the technical delays or expenses, however vast, which are encountered by the very nature of these media. Therefore, this sacred Synod advises them of the obligation they have

to maintain and assist Catholic newspapers, periodicals and film projects, radio and television programs and stations, whose principal objective is to spread and defend the truth and foster Christian influence in human society. At the same time, the Synod earnestly invites those organizations and individuals who possess financial and technical ability to support these media freely and generously with their resources and their skills, inasmuch as they contribute to genuine culture and the apostolate.

18. Moreover, that the varied apostolates of the Church with respect to the media of school communication may be strengthened effectively, each year in every diocese of the world, by the determination of the Bishops, there should be celebrated a day on which the faithful are instructed in their responsibilities in this regard. They should be invited to pray and contribute funds for this cause. Such funds are to be expended exclusively on the promotion, maintenance and development of institutes and undertakings of the Church in this area, according to the needs of the whole Catholic world.

19. In fulfilling his supreme control and charge with respect to the media of social communication, the Sovereign Pontiff has at hand a special office of the Holy See.

Moreover, the Fathers of the Council, freely acceding to the wish of the "Secretariat for the Supervision of Publications and Entertainment," reverently request that the Sovereign Pontiff extend the duties and competence of this office to include all media of social communication, including the press, and that experts from various countries be named to it, including laymen.

20. It will be the task of the Bishops, however, to watch over such works and undertakings in their own dioceses, to promote them and, as far as the public apostolate is concerned, to guide them, not excluding those that are under the direction of exempt religious.

21. Since an effective apostolate on a national scale calls for unity of planning and resources, this sacred Synod decrees and orders that national offices for affairs of the press, films, radio and television be established everywhere and given every aid. It will be the special task of these offices to see to it that the consciences of the faithful are properly instructed with respect to these media. Likewise they should foster and guide whatever is done by Catholics in these areas.

In each country the direction of such offices should be entrusted to a special committee of Bishops, or to a single Bishop. Moreover, laymen who are experts in Catholic teaching and in these arts or techniques should have a role in these offices.

22. Since the effectiveness of these media reaches beyond national boundaries and has an impact on individual members of the whole human family, national offices should co-operate among themselves on an international plane. The offices spoken of in Number 21 should assiduously work together with their own international Catholic associations. These Catholic international associations are legitimately approved by the Holy See alone and depend on it.

Appendices

23. So that the general principles and norms of this sacred Synod with respect to the media of social communications may be put into effect, by the express will of the Council, the office of the Holy See mentioned in Number 19 should undertake, with the assistance of experts from various countries, to issue a pastoral instruction.

25. As for the rest, this sacred Synod is confident that its issuance of these instructions and norms will be gladly accepted and religiously kept by all the Church's children. By using these helps they will experience no harm and, like salt and light,they will give savor to the earth and brighten the world. Moreover, the Synod invites all men of good will, especially those who have charge of these media, to strive to turn them solely to the good of society, whose fate depends more and more on their proper use. Thus, as was the case with ancient works of art, the name of the Lord may be glorified by these new discoveries in accordance with those words of the Apostle: "Jesus Christ, yesterday and today, and the same forever."

Unitatis Redintegratio
Decree on Ecumenism

Introduction

1. The RESTORATION OF UNITY among all Christians is one of the principal concerns of the Second Vatican Council. Christ the Lord founded one Church and one Church only. However, many Christian communions present themselves to men as the true inheritors of Jesus Christ; all indeed profess to be followers of the Lord but differ in mind and go their different ways, as if Christ Himself were divided. Such division openly contradicts the will of Christ, scandalizes the world, and damages the holy cause of preaching the Gospel to every creature.

But the Lord of Ages wisely and patiently follows out the plan of grace on our behalf, sinners that we are. In recent times more than ever before, He has been rousing divided Christians to remorse over their divisions and to a longing for unity. Everywhere large numbers have felt the impulse of this grace, and among our separated brethren also there increases from day to day the movement, fostered by the grace of the Holy Spirit, for the restoration of unity among all Christians. This movement toward unity is called "ecumenical." Those belong to it who invoke the Triune God and confess Jesus as Lord and Savior, doing this not merely as individuals but also as corporate bodies. For almost everyone regards the body in which he has heard the Gospel as his Church and indeed, God's Church. All however, though in different ways, long for the one visible Church of God, a Church truly universal and set forth into the world that the world may be converted to the Gospel and so be saved, to the glory of God.

The Sacred Council, gladly notes all this. It has already declared its teaching on the Church, and now, moved by a desire for the restoration of unity among all the followers of Christ, it wishes to set before all Catholics the ways and means by which they too can respond to this grace and to this divine call.

CHAPTER I

Catholic Principles On Ecumenism

2. What has revealed the love of God among us is that the Father has sent into the world His only-begotten Son, so that, being made man, He might by His redemption give new life to the entire human race and unify it. Before offering Himself up as a spotless victim upon the altar, Christ prayed to His Father for all who believe in him: "that they all may be one; even as thou, Father, art in me, and I in thee, that they also may be one in us, so that the world may believe that thou has sent me." In His Church He instituted the wonderful sacrament of the Eucharist by which the unity of His Church is both signified and made a reality. He gave His followers a new commandment to love one another, and promised the Spirit, their Advocate, who, as Lord and life-giver, should remain with them forever.

After being lifted up on the cross and glorified, the Lord Jesus poured forth His Spirit as He had promised, and through the Spirit He has called and gathered together the people of the New Covenant, who are the Church, into a unity of faith, hope, and charity, as the Apostle teaches us: "There is one body and one Spirit, just as you were called to the one hope of your calling; one Lord, one faith, one Baptism." For "all you who have been baptized into Christ have put on Christ . . . for you are all one in Christ Jesus." It is the Holy Spirit, dwelling in those who believe and pervading and ruling over the Church as a whole, who brings about that wonderful communion of the faithful. He brings them into intimate union with Christ, so that He is the principle of the Church's unity. The distribution of graces and offices is His work too, enriching the Church of Jesus Christ with different functions "in order to equip the saints for the work of service, so as to build up the body of Christ."

In order to establish this His holy Church everywhere in the world till the end of time, Christ entrusted to the College of the Twelve the task of teaching, ruling and sanctifying. Among their number He selected Peter, and after his confession of faith determined that on him He would build His Church. Also to Peter He promised the keys of the kingdom of heaven, and after His profession of love, entrusted all His sheep to him to be confirmed in faith and shepherded in perfect unity. Christ Jesus Himself was forever to remain the chief cornerstone and shepherd of our souls.

Jesus Christ, then, willed that the apostles and their successors — the bishops with Peter's successor at their head — should preach the Gospel faithfully, administer the sacraments, and rule the Church in love. It is thus, under the action of the Holy Spirit, that Christ wills His people to increase, and He perfects His people's fellowship in unity: in their confessing the one faith, celebrating divine worship in common, and keeping the fraternal harmony of the family of God.

The Church, then, is God's only flock; it is like a standard lifted high for the nations to see it: for it serves all mankind through the Gospel of peace as it makes its pilgrim way in hope towards the goal of the fatherland above.

This is the sacred mystery of the unity of the Church, in Christ and through Christ, the Holy Spirit energizing its various functions. It is a mystery that finds its highest exemplar and source in the unity of the Persons of the Trinity: the Father and the Son in the Holy Spirit one God.

3. Even in the beginnings of this one and only Church of God there arose certain rifts, which the Apostle strongly condemned. But in subsequent centuries much more serious dissensions made their appearance and quite large communities came to be separated from full communion with the Catholic Church — for which, often enough, men of both sides were to blame. The children who are born into these Communities and who grow up believing in Christ cannot be accused of the sin involved in the separation, and the Catholic Church embraces them as brothers, with respect and affection. For men who believe in Christ and have been truly baptized are in communion with the

Catholic Church even though this communion is imperfect. The differences that exist in varying degrees between them and the Catholic Church — whether in doctrine and sometimes in discipline, or concerning the structure of the Church — do indeed create many obstacles, sometimes serious ones, to full ecclesiastical communion. The ecumenical movement is striving to overcome these obstacles. But even in spite of them it remains true that all who have been justified by faith in Baptism are members of Christ's body, and have a right to be called Christian, and so are correctly accepted as brothers by the children of the Catholic Church.

Moreover, some and even very many of the significant elements and endowments which together go to build up and give life to the Church itself, can exist outside the visible boundaries of the Catholic Church: the written word of God; the life of grace; faith, hope and charity, with the other interior gifts of the Holy Spirit, and visible elements too. All of these, which come from Christ and lead back to Christ, belong by right to the one Church of Christ.

The brethren divided from us also use many liturgical actions of the Christian religion. These most certainly can truly engender a life of grace in ways that vary according to the condition of each Church or Community. These liturgical actions must be regarded as capable of giving access to the community of salvation.

If follows that the separated Churches and communities as such, though we believe them to be deficient in some respects, have been by no means deprived of significance and importance in the mystery of salvation. For the Spirit of Christ has not refrained from using them as means of salvation which derive their efficacy from the very fullness of grace and truth entrusted to the Church.

Nevertheless, our separated brethren, whether considered as individuals or as Communities and Churches, are not blessed with that unity which Jesus Christ wished to bestow on all those who through Him were born again into one body, and with Him quickened to newness of life — that unity which the Holy Scriptures and the ancient Tradition of the Church proclaim. For it is only though Christ's Catholic Church, which is "the all-embracing means of salvation," that they can benefit fully from the means of salvation. We believe that Our Lord entrusted all the blessings of the New Covenant to the apostolic college alone, of which Peter is the head, in order to establish the one Body of Christ on earth to which all should be fully incorporated who belong in any way to the people of God. This people of God, though still in its members liable to sin, is ever growing in Christ during the pilgrimage on earth, and is guided by God's gentle wisdom, according to His hidden designs, until it shall happily arrive at the fullness of eternal glory in the heavenly Jerusalem.

4. Today, in many parts of the world, under the inspiring grace of the Holy Spirit, many efforts are being made in prayer, word and action to attain that fullness of unity which Jesus Christ desires. The Sacred Council exhorts all the Catholic faithful to recognize the signs of the times and to take an active and intelligent part in the work of ecumenism.

The term "ecumenical movement" indicates the initiatives and activities planned and undertaken, according to the various needs of the Church and as opportunities offer, to promote Christian unity. These are: first, every effort to avoid expressions, judgments and actions which do not represent the condition of our separated brethren with truth and fairness and so make mutual relations with them more difficult; then, "dialogue" between competent experts from different Churches and Communities. At these meetings, which are organized in a religious spirit, each explains the teaching of his Communion in greater depth and brings out clearly its distinctive features. In such dialogue, everyone gains a truer knowledge and more just appreciation of the teaching and religious life of both Communions. In addition, the way is prepared for cooperation between them in the duties for the common good for humanity which are demanded by every Christian conscience; and, wherever this is allowed, there is prayer in common. Finally, all are led to examine their own faithfulness to Christ's will for the Church and accordingly to undertake with vigor the task of renewal and reform.

When such actions are undertaken prudently and patiently by the Catholic faithful, with the attentive guidance of their bishops, they promote justice and truth, concord and collaboration, as well as the spirit of brotherly love and unity. This is the way that, when the obstacles to perfect ecclesiastical communion have been gradually overcome, all Christians will at last, in a common celebration of the Eucharist, be gathered into the one and only Church in that unity which Christ bestowed on His Church from the beginning. We believe that this unity subsists in the Catholic Church as something she can never lose, and we hope that it will continue to increase until the end of time.

However, it is evident that, when individuals wish for full Catholic communion, their preparation and reconciliation is an undertaking which of its nature is distinct from ecumenical action. But there is no opposition between the two, since both proceed from the marvelous ways of God.

Catholics, in their ecumenical work, must assuredly be concerned for their separated brethren, praying for them, keeping them informed about the Church, making the first approaches toward them. But their primary duty is to make a careful and honest appraisal of whatever needs to be done or renewed in the Catholic household itself, in order that its life may bear witness more clearly and faithfully to the teachings and institutions which have come to it from Christ through the Apostles.

For although the Catholic Church has been endowed with all divinely revealed truth and with all means of grace, yet its members fail to live by them with all the fervor that they should, so that the radiance of the Church's image is less clear in the eyes of our separated brethren and of the world at large, and the growth of God's kingdom is delayed. All Catholics must therefore aim at Christian perfection and, each according to his station, play his part that the Church may daily be more purified and renewed. For the Church must bear in her own body the humility and dying of Jesus, against the day when Christ will present her to Himself in all her glory without spot or wrinkle.

All in the Church must preserve unity in essentials. But let all, according to the gifts they have received enjoy a proper freedom, in their various forms of spiritual life and discipline, in their different liturgical rites, and even in their theological elaborations of revealed truth. In all things let charity prevail. If they are true to this course of action, they will be giving ever better expression to the authentic catholicity and apostolicity of the Church.

On the other hand, Catholics must gladly acknowledge and esteem the truly Christian endowments from our common heritage which are to be found among our separated brethren. It is right and salutary to recognize the riches of Christ and virtuous works in the lives of others who are bearing witness to Christ, sometimes even to the shedding of their blood. For God is always wonderful in His works and worthy of all praise.

Nor should we forget that anything wrought by the grace of the Holy Spirit in the hearts of our separated brethren can be help to our own edification. Whatever is truly Christian is never contrary to what genuinely belongs to the faith; indeed, it can always bring a deeper realization of the mystery of Christ and the Church.

Nevertheless, the divisions among Christians prevent the Church from attaining the fullness of catholicity proper to her, in those of her sons who, though attached to her by Baptism, are yet separated from full communion with her. Furthermore, the Church herself finds it more difficult to express in actual life her full catholicity in all her bearings.

This Sacred Council is gratified to note that the participation by the Catholic faithful in ecumenical work is growing daily. It commends this work to the bishops everywhere in the world to be vigorously stimulated by them and guided with prudence.

Chapter II
The Practice of Ecumenism

5. The attainment of union is the concern of the whole Church, faithful and shepherds alike. This concern extends to everyone, according to his talent, whether it be exercised in his daily Christian life or in his theological and historical research. This concern itself reveals already to some extent the bond of brotherhood between all Christians and it helps towards that full and perfect unity which God in His kindness wills.

6. Every renewal of the Church is essentially grounded in an increase of fidelity to her own calling. Undoubtedly this is the basis of the movement toward unity.

Christ summons the Church to continual reformation as she sojourns here on earth. The Church is always in need of this, in so far as she is an institution of men here on earth. Thus if, in various times and circumstances, there have been deficiencies in moral conduct or in church discipline, or even in the way that church teaching has been formulated — to be carefully distinguished from the deposit of faith itself — these can and should be set right at the opportune moment.

Church renewal has therefore notable ecumenical importance. Already in various spheres of the Church's life, this renewal is taking place. The Biblical and liturgical movements, the preaching of the word of God and catechetics, the apostolate of the laity, new forms of religious life and the spirituality of married life, and the Church's social teaching and activity — all these should be considered as pledges and signs of the future progress of ecumenism.

7. There can be no ecumenism worthy of the name without a change of heart. For it is from renewal of the inner life or our minds, from self-denial and an unstinted love that desires of unity take their rise and develop in a mature way. We should therefore pray to the Holy Spirit for the grace to be genuinely self-denying, humble, gentle in the service of others, and to have an attitude of brotherly generosity towards them. St. Paul says: "I, therefore, a prisoner for the Lord, beg you to lead a life worthy of the calling to which you have been called, with all humility and meekness, with patience, forbearing

one another in love, eager to maintain the unity of the spirit in the bond of peace." This exhortation is directed especially to those raised to sacred Orders precisely that the work of Christ may be continued. He came among us "not to be served but to serve."

The words of St. John hold good about sins against unity: "If we say we have not sinned, we make him a liar, and his word is not in us." So we humbly beg pardon of God and of our separated brethren, just as we forgive them that trespass against us.

All the faithful should remember that the more effort they make to live holier lives according to the Gospels, the better will they further Christian unity and put it into practice. For the closer their union with the Father, the Word, and the Spirit, the more deeply and easily will they be able to grow in mutual brotherly love.

8. This change of heart and holiness of life, along with public and private prayer for the unity of Christians, should be regarded as the soul of the whole ecumenical movement, and merits the name, "spiritual ecumenism."

It is a recognized custom for Catholics to have frequent recourse to that prayer for the unity of the Church which the Savior Himself on the eve of His death so fervently appealed to His Father: "That they may all be one."

In certain special circumstances, such as the prescribed prayers "for unity," and during ecumenical gatherings, it is allowable, indeed desirable that Catholics should join in prayer with their separated brethren. Such prayers in common are certainly an effective means of obtaining the grace of unity, and they are a true expression of the ties which still bind Catholics to their separated brethren. "For where two or three are gathered together in my name, there am I in the midst of them."

Yet worship in common (*communicatio in sacris*) is not to be considered as a means to be used indiscriminately for the restoration of Christian unity. There are two main principles governing the practice of such common worship: first, the bearing witness to the unity of the Church, and second, the sharing in the means of grace. Witness to the unity of the Church very generally forbids common worship to Christians, but the grace to be had from it sometimes commends this practice. The course to be adopted, with due regard to all the circumstances of time, place, and persons, is to be decided by local episcopal authority, unless otherwise provided for by the Bishops' Conference according to its statues, or by the Holy See.

9. We must get to know the outlook of our separated brethren. To achieve

this purpose, study is of necessity required, and this must be pursued with a sense of realism and good will. Catholics, who already have a proper grounding, need to acquire a more adequate understanding of the respective doctrines of our separated brethren, their history, their spiritual and liturgical life, their religious psychology and general background. Most valuable for this purpose are meetings of the two sides — especially for discussion of theological problems — where each can treat with the other on an equal footing — provided that those who take part in them are truly competent and have the approval of the bishops. From such dialogue will emerge still more clearly what the situation of the Catholic Church really is. In this way too the outlook of our separated brethren will be better understood, and our own belief more aptly explained.

10. Sacred theology and other branches of knowledge, especially of an historical nature, must be taught with due regard for the ecumenical point of view, so that they may correspond more exactly with the facts.

It is most important that future shepherds and priests should have mastered a theology that has been carefully worked out in this way and not polemically, especially with regard to those aspects which concern the relations of separated brethren with the Catholic Church.

This importance is the greater because the instruction and spiritual formation of the faithful and of religious depends so largely on the formation which their priests have received.

Moreover, Catholics engaged in missionary work in the same territories as other Christians ought to know, particularly in these times, the problems and the benefits in their apostolate which derive from the ecumenical movement.

11. The way and method in which the Catholic faith is expressed should never become an obstacle to dialogue with our brethren. It is, of course, essentially that the doctrine should be clearly presented in its entirety. Nothing is so foreign to the spirit of ecumenism as a false irenicism, in which the purity of Catholic doctrine suffers loss and its genuine and certain meaning is clouded.

At the same time, the Catholic faith must be explained more profoundly and precisely, in such a way and in such terms as our separated brethren can also really understand.

Moreover, in ecumenical dialogue, Catholic theologies standing fast by the teaching of the Church and investigating the divine mysteries with the separated brethren must proceed with love for the truth, with charity, and with humility. When comparing doctrines with one another, they should remember that in Catholic doctrine there exists a "hierarchy" of faith. Thus the way will be opened by which through fraternal rivalry all will be stirred to a deeper understanding and a clearer presentation of the unfathomable riches of Christ.

12. Before the whole world let all Christians confess their faith in the Triune God, one and three in the incarnate Son of God, our Redeemer and Lord. United in their efforts, and with mutual respect, let them bear witness to our common hope which does not play us false. In these days when cooperation in social matters is so widespread, all men without exception are called to work together, with much greater reason all those who believe in God, but most of all, all Christians in that they bear the name of Christ. Cooperation among Christians vividly expresses the relationship which in fact already unites them, and it sets in clearer relief the features of Christ the Servant. This cooperation, which has already begun in many countries, should be developed more and more, particularly in regions where a social and technical evolution is taking place be it in a just evaluation of the dignity of the human person, the establishment of the blessings of peace, the application of Gospel principles to social life, the advancement of the arts and sciences in a truly Christian spirit, or also in the use of various remedies to relieve the afflictions of our times such as famine and natural disasters, illiteracy and poverty, housing shortage and the unequal distribution of wealth. All believers in Christ can, through this cooperation, be led to acquire a better knowledge and appreciation of one another, and so pave the way to Christian unity.

Chapter III

13. We now turn our attention to the two chief types of division as they affect the seamless robe of Christ.

The first divisions occurred in the East, when the dogmatic formulae of the Councils of Ephesus and Chalcedon were challenged, and later when ecclesiastical communion between the Eastern Patriarchates and the Roman See was dissolved.

Other divisions arose more than four centuries later in the West, stemming from the events which are usually referred to as "the Reformation." As a result, many Communions, national or confessional, were separated from the Roman See. Among those in which Catholic traditions and institutions in part continue to exist, the Anglican Communion occupies a special place.

These various divisions differ greatly from one another not only by reason of their origin, place and time, but especially in the nature and seriousness of questions bearing on faith and the structure of the Church. Therefore, without minimizing the differences between the various Christian bodies and without overlooking the bonds between them which exist in spite of divisions, this Holy Council decides to propose the following considerations for prudent ecumenical action.

I. The Special Consideration of the Eastern Churches

14. For many centuries the Church of the East and that of the West each followed their separate ways though linked in a brotherly union of faith and sacramental life; the Roman See by common consent acted as guide when disagreements arose between them over matters of faith or discipline. Among other matters of great importance, it is a pleasure for this Council to remind everyone that there flourish in the East many particular or local Churches, among which the Patriarchal Churches hold first place, and of these not a few pride themselves in tracing their origins back to the apostles themselves. Hence a matter of primary concern and care among the Easterns, in their local churches, has been, and still is, to preserve the family ties of common faith and charity which ought to exist between sister Churches.

Similarly, it must not be forgotten that from the beginning the Churches of the East have had a treasury from which the Western Church has drawn extensively — in liturgical practice, spiritual tradition, and law. Nor must we undervalue the fact that it was the ecumenical councils held in the East that defined the basic dogmas of the Christian faith, on the Trinity, on the Word of God Who took flesh of the Virgin Mary. To preserve this faith these Churches have suffered and still suffer much.

However, the heritage handed down by the apostles was received with differences of form and manner, so that from the earliest times of the Church it was explained variously in different places, owing to diversities of genius and conditions of life. All this, quite apart from external causes, prepared the way for divisions arising also from a lack of charity and mutual understanding.

For this reason the Holy Council urges all, but especially those who intend to devote themselves to the restoration of full communion hoped for between the Churches of the East and the Catholic Church, to give due consideration to this special feature of the origin and growth of the Eastern Churches, and to the character of the relations which obtained between them and the Roman See before separation. They must take full account of all these factors and, where this is done, it will greatly contribute to the dialogue that is looked for.

15. Everyone also knows with what great love the Christians of the East celebrate the sacred liturgy, especially the eucharistic celebration, source of the Church's life and pledge of future glory, in which the faithful, united with their bishop have access to God the Father through the Son, the Word made flesh, Who suffered and has been glorified, and so, in the outpouring of the Holy Spirit, they enter into communion with the most holy Trinity, being made "sharers of the divine nature." Hence, the Church of God is built up and grows in stature and through concelebration, their communion with one another is made manifest.

In this liturgical worship, the Christians of the East pay big tribute, in beautiful hymns of praise, to Mary ever Virgin, whom the ecumenical Council of Ephesus solemnly proclaimed to be the holy Mother of God, so that Christ might be acknowledged as being truly Son of God and Son of Man, according to the Scriptures. Many also are the saints whose praise they sing, among them the Fathers of the universal Church.

These Churches, although separated from us, yet possess true sacraments and above all, by apostolic succession, the priesthood and the Eucharist, whereby they are linked with us in closest intimacy. Therefore some worship in common (*communicatio in sacris*), given suitable circumstances and the approval of Church authority, is not only possible but to be encouraged.

Moreover, in the East are found the riches of those spiritual traditions which are given expression especially in monastic life. There from the glorious times of the holy Fathers, monastic spirituality flourished which then later flowed over into the Western world, and there provided the source from which Latin monastic life took its rise and has drawn fresh vigor ever since. Catholics therefore are earnestly recommended to avail themselves of the spiritual riches of the Eastern Fathers which lift up the whole man to the contemplation of the divine.

The very rich liturgical and spiritual heritage of the Eastern Churches should be known, venerated, preserved and cherished by all. They must recognize that this is of supreme importance for the faithful preservation of the fullness of Christian tradition, and for bringing about reconstruction between Eastern and Western Christians.

16. Already from the earliest times the Eastern Churches followed their own forms of ecclesiastical law and custom, which were sanctioned by the approval of the Fathers of the Church, of synods, and even of ecumenical councils. Far from being an obstacle to the church's unity a certain diversity of

customs and observances only adds to her splendor, and is of great help in carrying out her mission, as has already been stated. To remove, then, all shadow of doubt, this holy Council solemnly declares that the Churches of the East, while remembering the necessary unity of the whole Church, have the power to govern themselves according to the disciplines proper to them, since these are better suited to the character of their faithful, and more for the good of their souls. The perfect observance of this traditional principle not always indeed carried out in practice, is one of the essential prerequisites for any restoration of unity.

17. What has just been said about the lawful variety that can exist in the Church must also be taken to apply to the differences in theological expression of doctrine. In the study of revelation East and West have followed different methods, and have developed differently their understanding and confession of God's truth. It is hardly surprising, then, if from time to time one tradition has come nearer to a full appreciation of some aspects of a mystery of revelation than the other, or has expressed it to better advantage. In such cases, these various theological expressions are to be considered often as mutually complementary rather than conflicting. Where the authentic theological traditions of the Eastern Church are concerned, we must recognize the admirable way in which they have their roots in Holy Scripture, and how they are nurtured and given expression in the life of the liturgy. They derive their strength too from the living tradition of the apostles and from the works of the Fathers and spiritual writers of the Eastern Churches. Thus they promote the right ordering of Christian life and, indeed, pave the way to a full vision of Christian truth.

All this heritage of spirituality and liturgy, of discipline and theology, in its various traditions, this holy synod declares to belong to the full Catholic and apostolic character of the Church. We thank God that many Eastern children of the Catholic Church, who preserve this heritage, and wish to express it more faithfully and completely in their lives, are already living in full communion with their brethren who follow the tradition of the West.

18. After taking all these factors into consideration, this Sacred Council solemnly repeats the declaration of previous Councils and Roman Pontiffs, that for the restoration or the maintenance of unity and communion it is necessary "to impose no burden beyond what is essential." It is the Council's urgent desire that, in the various organizations and living activities of the Church, every effort should be made toward the gradual realization of this unity, espe-

cially by prayer, and for fraternal dialogue on points of doctrine and the more pressing pastoral problems of our time. Similarly, the Council commends to the shepherds and faithful of the Catholic Church to develop closer relations with those who are no longer living in the East but are far from home, so that friendly collaboration with them may increase, in the spirit of love, to the exclusion of all feeling of rivalry or strife. If this cause is wholeheartedly promoted, the Council hopes that the barrier dividing the Eastern Church and Western Church will be removed, and that at last there may be but the one dwelling, firmly established on Christ Jesus, the cornerstone, who will make both one.

II. Separated Churches and Ecclesial Communities in the West

19. In the great upheaval which began in the West toward the end of the Middle Ages, and in later times too, churches and ecclesial Communities came to be separated from the Apostolic See of Rome. Yet they have retained a particularly close affinity with the Catholic Church as a result of the long centuries in which all Christendom lived together in ecclesiastical communion.

However, since these Churches and ecclesial Communities, on account of their different origins, and different teachings in matters of doctrine on the spiritual life, vary considerably not only with us, but also among themselves, the task of describing them at all adequately is extremely difficult; and we have no intention of making such an attempt here.

Although the ecumenical movement and the desire for peace with the Catholic Church have not yet taken hold everywhere, it is our hope that ecumenical feeling and mutual esteem may gradually increase among all men.

It must however be admitted that in these Churches and ecclesial Communities there exist important differences from the Catholic Church, not only of an historical, sociological, psychological and cultural character, but especially in the interpretation of revealed truth. To make easier the ecumenical dialogue in spite of these differences, we wish to set down some considerations which can, and indeed should, serve as a basis and encouragement for such dialogue.

20. Our thoughts turn first to those Christians who make open confession of Jesus Christ as God and Lord and as the sole Mediator between God and men, to the glory of the one God, Father, Son and Holy Spirit. We are aware indeed that there exist considerable divergences from the doctrine of the Catholic Church concerning Christ Himself, the Word of God made flesh, the work of redemption, and consequently, concerning the mystery and ministry of the

Church, and the role of Mary in the plan of salvation. But we rejoice to see that our separated brethren look to Christ as the source and center of Church unity. Their longing for union with Christ inspires them to seek an ever closer unity, and also to bear witness to their faith among the peoples of the earth.

21. A love and reverence of Sacred Scriptures which might be described as devotion, leads our brethren to a constant meditative study of the sacred text. For the Gospel "is the power of God for salvation to every one who has faith, to the Jew first and then to the Greek."

While invoking the Holy Spirit, they seek in these very Scriptures God as it were speaking to them in Christ, Whom the prophets foretold, Who is the Word of God made flesh for us. They contemplate in the Scriptures the life of Christ and what the Divine Master taught and did for our salvation, especially the mysteries of His death and resurrection.

But while the Christians who are separated from us hold the divine authority of the Sacred Books, they differ from ours — some in one way, some in another — regarding the relationship between Scripture and the Church. For, according to Catholic belief, the authentic teaching authority of the Church has a special place in the interpretation and preaching of the written word of God.

But Sacred Scriptures provide for the work of dialogue an instrument of the highest value in the mighty hand of God for the attainment of that unity which the Savior holds out to all.

22. Whenever the Sacrament of Baptism is duly administered as Our Lord instituted it, and is received with the right dispositions, a person is truly incorporated into the crucified and glorified Christ, and reborn to a sharing of the divine life, as the Apostle says: "You were buried together with Him in Baptism, and in Him also rose again — through faith in the working of God, who raised Him from the dead."

Baptism therefore establishes a sacramental bond of unity which links all who have been reborn by it. But of itself Baptism is only a beginning, an inauguration wholly directed toward the fullness of life in Christ. Baptism, therefore envisages a complete profession of faith, complete incorporation in the system of salvation such as Christ willed it to be, and finally complete ingrafting in eucharistic communion.

Though the ecclesial Communities which are separated from us lack the fullness of unity with us flowing from Baptism, and though we believe they have not retained the proper reality of the eucharistic mystery in its fullness, especially because of the absence of the sacrament of Orders, nevertheless when they commemorate His death and resurrection in the Lord's Supper, they profess that it signifies life in communion with Christ and look forward to His coming in glory. Therefore the teaching concerning the Lord's Supper, the other sacraments, worship, the ministry of the Church, must be the subject of the dialogue.

23. The daily Christian life of these brethren is nourished by their faith in Christ and strengthened by the grace of Baptism and by hearing the word of God. This shows itself in their private prayer, their meditation on the Bible, in their Christian family life and in the worship of a community gathered together to praise God. Moreover, their form of worship sometimes displays notable features of the liturgy which they shared with us of old.

Their faith in Christ bears fruit in praise and thanksgiving for the blessings received from the hands of God. Among them, too, is a strong sense of justice and a true charity toward their neighbor. This active faith has been responsible for many organizations for the relief of spiritual and material distress, the furtherance of the education of youth, the improvement of the social conditions of life, and the promotion of peace throughout the world.

While it is true that many Christians understand the moral teaching of the Gospel differently from Catholics, and do not accept the same solutions to the more difficult problems of modern society, nevertheless they share our desire to stand by the words of Christ as the source of Christian virture, and to obey the command of the Apostle: "And whatever you do, in word or in work, do all in the name of the Lord Jesus Christ, giving thanks to God the Father through Him." For that reason an ecumenical dialogue might start with discussion of the application of the Gospel to moral conduct.

24. Now that we have briefly set out the conditions for ecumenical action and the principles by which it is to be directed, we look with confidence to the future. This Sacred Council exhorts the faithful to refrain from superficial and imprudent zeal, which can hinder real progress toward unity. Their ecumenical action must be fully and sincerely Catholic, that is to say, faithful to the truth which we have received from the apostles and Fathers of the Church, in harmony with the faith which the Catholic Church has always professed, and at the same time directed toward that fullness to which Our Lord wills His Body to grow in the course of time.

It is the urgent wish of this Holy Council that the measures undertaken by the sons of the Catholic Church should develop in conjunction with those of our separated brethren so that no obstacle be put in the ways of Divine Providence and no preconceived judgments impair the future inspirations of the Holy Spirit. The Council moreover professes its awareness that human powers and capacities cannot achieve this holy objective — the reconciling of all Christians in the unity of the one and only Church of Christ. It is because of this that the Council rests all its hope on the prayer of Christ for the Church, on our Father's love for us, and on the power of the Holy Spirit. "And hope does not disappoint, because God's love has been poured into our hearts through the Holy Spirit, Who has been given to us."

Each and all these matters which are set forth in this Decree have been favorably voted on by the Fathers of the Council. And We, by the apostolic authority given Us by Christ and in union with the Fathers, approve, decree and establish them in the Holy Spirit and command that they be promulgated for the glory of God.

Given in Rome at St. Peter's, November 21, 1964.

Gravissimum Educationis
Declaration on Christian Education

The Sacred Ecumenical Council has considered with care how extremely important education is in the life of man and how its influence ever grows in the social progress of this age.

1. (*The Meaning of the Universal Right to an Education*)

All men of every race, condition and age, since they enjoy the dignity of a human being, have an inalienable right to an education that is in keeping with their ultimate goal, their ability, their sex, and the culture and tradition of their country, and also in harmony with their fraternal association with other peoples in the fostering of true unity and peace on earth. For a true education aims at the formation of the human person in the pursuit of his ultimate end and of the good of the societies of which, as man, he is a member, and in whose obligations, as an adult, he will share.

Therefore children and young people must be helped, with the aid of the latest advances in psychology and the arts and science of teaching, to develop harmoniously their physical, moral and intellectual endowments so that they may gradually acquire a mature sense of responsibility in striving endlessly to form their own lives properly and in pursuing true freedom as they surmount the vicissitudes of life with courage and constancy. Let them be given also, as they advance in years, a positive and prudent sexual education. Moreover, they should be so trained to take their part in social life that properly instructed in the necessary and opportune skills they can become actively involved in various community organizations, open to discourse with others and willing to do their best to promote the common good.

This Sacred Synod likewise declares that children and young people have a right to be motivated to appraise moral values with a right conscience, to embrace them with a personal adherence, together with a deeper knowledge and love of God. Consequently it earnestly entreats all those who hold a position of public authority or who are in charge of education to see to it that youth is never deprived of this sacred right. It further exhorts the sons of the Church to give their attention with generosity to the entire field of education, having especially in mind the need of extending very soon the benefits of a suitable education and training to everyone in all parts of the world.

2. *(Christian Education)*

Since all Christians have become by rebirth of water and the Holy Spirit new creatures so that they should be called and should be children of God, they have a right to a Christian education. A Christian education does not merely strive for the maturing of a human person as just now described, but has as principal purpose this goal: that the baptized, while they are gradually introduced to the knowledge of the mystery of salvation, become ever more aware of the gift of Faith they have received, and that they learn in addition how to worship God the Father in spirit and truth (cf. *John* 4, 23), especially in liturgical action, and be conformed in their personal lives according to the new man created in justice and holiness of truth (*Eph.* 4,22-24); also that they develop into perfect manhood, to the mature measure of the fullness of Christ (cf. *Eph.* 4,13) and strive for the growth of the Mystical Body; moreover, that aware of their calling, they learn not only how to bear witness to the hope that is in them (cf. 1 *Peter* 3,15) but also how to help in the Christian formation of the world that takes place when natural powers viewed in the full consideration of man redeemed by Christ contribute to the good of the whole of society. Wherefore this Sacred Synod recalls to pastors of souls their most serious obligation to see to it that all the faithful, but especially the youth who are the hope of the Church, enjoy this Christian education.

3. (*The Authors of Education*)

Since parents have given children their life, they are bound by the most serious obligation to educate their offspring and therefore must be recognized as the primary and principal educators. This role in education is so important that only with difficulty can it be supplied where it is lacking. Parents are the ones who must create a family atmosphere animated by love and respect for God and man, in which the well-rounded personal and social education of children is fostered. Hence the family is the first school of social virtues that every society needs. It is particularly in the Christian family, enriched by the grace and office of the sacrament of matrimony, that children should be taught from their early years to have a knowledge of God according to the faith received in baptism, to worship Him, and to love their neighbor. Here too they find their fist experience of a wholesome human society and of the Church. Finally, it is through the family that they are gradually led to a companionship with their fellow men and with the People of God. Let parents, then, recognize the inestimable importance a truly Christian family has for the life and progress of God's own People.

The family which has the primary duty of imparting education needs the help of the whole community. In addition, therefore, to the rights of parents and others' to whom the parents entrust a share in work of education, certain rights and duties belong indeed to civil society, whose role is to direct what is required for the common temporal good. Its function is to promote the education of youth in many ways, namely: to protect the duties and rights of parents and others who share in education and to give them aid; according to the principal subsidiarity, when the endeavors of parents and other societies are lacking, to carry out the work of education in accordance with the wishes of the parents; and, moreover, as the common good demands, to build schools and institutions.

Finally, in a special way, the duty of educating belongs to the Church, not merely because it must be recognized as a human society capable of educating, but especially because it has the responsibility of announcing the way of salvation to all men, of communicating the life of Christ to those who believe, and, in her unfailing solicitude, of assisting men to be able to come to the fullness of this life. The Church is bound as a mother to give to these children of hers an education by which their whole life can be imbued with the spirit of Christ and at the same time do all she can to promote for all peoples the complete perfection of the human person, the good of earthly society and the building of a world that is more human.

4. (*Various Aids to Christian Education*)

In fulfilling its educational role, the Church, eager to employ all suitable aids, is concerned especially about those which are her very own. Foremost among these is catechetical instruction, which enlightens and strengthens the faith, nourishes life according to the spirit of Christ, leads to intelligent and active participation in the liturgical mystery and gives motivation for apostolic activity. The Church esteems highly and seeks to penetrate and ennoble with her own spirit also other aids which belong to the general heritage of man and which are of great influence in forming souls and molding men, such as the media of communication, various groups for mental and physical development, youth associations, and, in particular, schools.

5. (*The Importance of Schools*)

Among all educational instruments the school has a special importance. It is designed not only to develop with special care the intellectual facilities but also to form the ability to judge rightly, to hand on the cultural legacy of previous generations, to foster a sense of values, to prepare for professional life. Between pupils of different talents and backgrounds it promotes friendly relations and fosters a spirit of mutual understanding; and it establishes as it were a center whose work and progress must be shared together by families, teachers, associations of various types that foster cultural, civic and religious life, as well as by civil society and the entire human community.

Beautiful indeed and of great importance is the vocation of all those who aid parents in fulfilling their duties and who, as representatives of the human community, undertake the task of education in schools. This vocation demands special qualities of mind and heart, very careful preparation, and continuing readiness to renew and to adapt.

6. (*The Duties and Rights of Parents*)

Parents who have the primary and inalienable right and duty to educate their children must enjoy true liberty in their choice of schools. Consequently, the public power, which has the obligation to protect and defend the rights of citizens, must see to it, in its concern for distributive justice, that public subsidies are paid out in such a way that parents are truly free to choose according to their conscience the schools they want for their children.

In addition it is the task of the state to see to it that all citizens are able to come to a suitable share in culture and are properly prepared to exercise their civic duties and rights. Therefore, the state must protect the right of children to an adequate school education, check on the ability of teachers and the excellence of their training, look after the health of the pupils and in general, promote the whole school project. But it must always keep in mind the principle of subsidiarity so that there is no kind of school monopoly, for this is opposed to the native rights of the human person, to the development and spread of culture, to the peaceful association of citizens and to the pluralism that exists today in ever so many societies.

Therefore this Sacred Synod exhorts the faithful to assist to their utmost in finding suitable methods of education and programs of study and in forming teachers who can give youth a true education. Through the associations of parents in particular they should further with their assistance all the work of the school but especially the moral education it must impart.

7. (*Moral and Religious Education in All Schools*)

Feeling very keenly the weighty responsibility of diligently caring for the moral and religious education of all her children, the Church must be present with her own special affection and help for the great number who are being trained in schools that are not Catholic. This is possible by the witness of the lives of those who teach and direct them, by the apostolic action of their fellow-students, but especially by the ministry of priests and laymen who give them the doctrine of salvation in a way suited to their age and circumstances and provide spiritual aid in every way the times and conditions allow.

The Church reminds parents of the duty that is theirs to arrange and even demand that their children be able to enjoy these aids and advance in their Christian formation to a degree that is abreast of their development in secular subjects. Therefore the Church esteems highly those civil authorities and societies which, bearing in mind the pluralism of contemporary society and respecting religious freedom, assist families so that the education of their children can be imparted in all schools according to the individual moral and religious principles of the families.

8. (*Catholic Schools*)

The influence of the Church in the field of education is shown in a special manner by the Catholic school. No less than other schools does the Catholic school pursue cultural goals and the human formation of youth. But its proper function is to create for the school community a special atmosphere animated by the Gospel spirit of freedom and charity, to help youth grow according to the new creatures they were made through Baptism as they develop their own personalities, and finally to order the whole of human culture to the news of salvation so that the knowledge the students gradually acquire of the world, life and man is illumined by faith. So indeed the Catholic school, while it is open, as it must be, to the situation of the contemporary world, leads its students to promote efficaciously the good of the earthly city and also prepares them for service in the spread of the Kingdom of God, so that by leading an exemplary apostolic life they become, as it were, a saving leaven in the human community.

Since, therefore, the Catholic school can be such an aid to the fulfillment of the mission of the People of God and to the fostering of the dialogue between the Church and mankind, to the benefit of both, it retains even in our present circumstances the utmost importance. Consequently this Sacred Synod proclaims anew what has already been taught in several documents of the magisterium, namely: the right of the Church freely to establish and to conduct schools of every type and level. And the Council calls to mind that the exercise of a right of this kind contributes in the highest degree to the protection of freedom and conscience, the rights of parents, as well as to the betterment of culture itself.

But let teachers recognize that the Catholic school depends upon them almost entirely for the accomplishment of its goals and programs. They should therefore be very carefully prepared so that both in secular and religious knowledge they are equipped with suitable qualifications and also with a pedagogical skill that is in keeping with the findings of the contemporary world. Intimately linked in charity to one another and to their students and endowed with an apostolic spirit, may teachers by their life as much as by their instruction bear witness to Christ the unique Teacher. Let them work as partners with parents and together with them in every phase of education give due consideration to the difference of sex and the proper ends Divine Providence assigns to each sex in the family and in society. Let them do all they can to stimulate their students to act for themselves and even after graduation to continue to assist them with advice, friendship and by establishing special associations imbued with the true spirit of the Church. The work of these teachers, this Sacred Synod declares, is in the real sense of the word an apostolate most suited to and necessary for our times and at once a true service offered to society. The Council also reminds Catholic parents of the duty of entrusting their children to Catholic schools wherever it is possible and of supporting these schools to the best of their ability and of cooperating with them for the education of their children.

9. (*Different Types of Catholic Schools*)

To this concept of a Catholic school all schools that are in any way dependent on the Church must conform as far as possible, though the Catholic school is to take on different forms in keeping with local circumstances. Thus the Church considers very dear to her heart those Catholic schools, found especially in the areas of the new churches, which are attended also by students who are not Catholic.

Attention should be paid to the needs of today in establishing and directing Catholic schools. Therefore, although primary and secondary schools, the foundation of education, must still be fostered, great importance is to be attached to those which are required in a particular way by contemporary conditions, such as professional and technical schools, centers for educating adults and promoting social welfare, of for the retarded in need of special care, and also schools for preparing teachers for religious instruction and other types of education.

This Sacred Council of the Church earnestly entreats pastors and all the faithful to spare no sacrifice in helping Catholic schools fulfill their function in a continually more perfect way, and especially in caring for the needs of those who are poor in the goods of this world or who are deprived of the assistance and affection of a family or who are strangers to the gift of faith.

10. (*Catholic Colleges and Universities*)

The Church is concerned also with schools of a higher level, especially colleges and universities. In those schools dependent on her she intends that by their very constitution individual subjects be pursued according to their own principles, method, and liberty of scientific inquiry, in such a way that an ever deeper understanding in these fields will be obtained and that, as questions that are new and current are raised and investigations carefully made according to the example of the Doctors of the Church and especially of St. Thomas Aquinas, there may be a deeper realization of the harmony of faith and science. Thus there is accomplished a public, enduring and pervasive influence of the Christian mind in the furtherance of culture, and the students of these institutions are molded into men truly outstanding in their training, ready to undertake weighty responsibilities in society and witness to the faith in the world.

In Catholic universities where there is no faculty of sacred theology there should be established an institute or chair of sacred theology in which there should be lectures suited to lay students. Since science advances by means of the investigations peculiar to higher scientific studies, special attention should be given in Catholic universities and colleges to institutes that serve primarily the development of scientific research.

The Sacred Synod heartily recommends that Catholic colleges and universities be conveniently located in different parts of the world, but in such a way that they are outstanding not for their numbers but for their pursuit of knowledge. Matriculation should be readily available to students of real promise, even though they be of slender means, especially to students from the newly emerging nations.

Since the destiny of society and of the Church itself is intimately linked with the progress of young people pursuing higher studies, the pastors of the Church are to expend their energies not only on the spiritual life of students who attend Catholic universities, but, with solicitude for the spiritual formation of all their children, they must see to it, after consultations between bishops, that even at universities that are not Catholic there should be associations and university centers under Catholic auspices in which priests, religious and laity, carefully selected and prepared, should give abiding spiritual and intellectual assistance to the youth of the university. Whether in Catholic universities or others, young people of greater ability who seem suited for teaching or research should be specially helped and encouraged to undertake a teaching career.

11. *(Faculties of Sacred Sciences)*

The Church expects much from the zealous endeavors of the faculties of the sacred sciences. For to them she entrusts the very serious responsibility of preparing her own students not only for the priestly ministry, but especially for teaching in the seats of higher ecclesiastical studies or for promoting learning on their own or for undertaking the work of a more rigorous intellectual apostolate. Likewise, it is the role of these very faculties to make more penetrating inquiry into the various aspects of the sacred sciences so that an ever-deepening undertaking of sacred revelation is obtained, the legacy of Christian wisdom handed down by our forefathers is more fully developed, the dialogue with our separated brethren and with non-Christians is fostered, and answers are given to questions arising from the development of doctrine.

Therefore ecclesiastical faculties should reappraise their own laws so that they can better promote the sacred sciences and those linked with them and, by employing up-to-date methods and aids, lead their students to more penetrating inquiry.

12. (Coordination to be Fostered in Scholastic Matters)

Cooperation is the order of the day. It increases more and more to supply the demand on a diocesan, national and international level. Since it is altogether necessary in scholastic matters, every means should be employed to foster suitable cooperation between Catholic schools, and between these and other schools that collaboration should be developed which the good of all mankind requires.

From greater coordination and cooperative endeavor greater fruits will be derived particularly in the area of academic institutions. Therefore in every university let the various faculties work mutually to this end, insofar as their goal will permit. In addition, let the universities also endeavor to work together by promoting international gatherings, by sharing scientific inquiries with one another, by communicating their discoveries to one another, by having exchange of professors for a time and by promoting all else that is conducive to greater assistance.

The Sacred Synod earnestly entreats young people themselves to become aware of the importance of the work of education and to prepare themselves to take it up, especially where because of a shortage of teachers the education of youth is in jeopardy.

This same Sacred Synod, while professing its gratitude to the priests, Religious men and women, and the laity who by their evangelical self-dedication are devoted to the noble work of education and of schools of every type and level, exhorts them to persevere generously in the work they have undertaken and, imbuing their students with the Spirit of Christ, to strive to excel in pedagogy and the pursuit of knowledge in such a way that they not merely advance the internal renewal of the Church but preserve and enhance its beneficent influence upon today's world, especially the intellectual world.

The entire text and all the individual elements which have been set forth in this Declaration have pleased the Fathers. And by the Apostolic power conferred on us by Christ, we, together with the Venerable Fathers, in the Holy Spirit, approve, decree and enact them; and we order that what has been thus enacted in Council be promulgated, to the glory of God.

Rome, at St. Peter's, 28 October, 1965.

I, PAUL, Bishop of the Catholic Church

There follow the signatures of the Fathers.

Praise God from Whom all blessings flow,
Praise Him All creatures here below;
Praise Him all ye Heavenly Hosts,
Praise Father, Son, and Holy Ghost.

Glory be to the Father, the Son, and the Holy Spirit, as it was in the beginning, is now and forever, Amen.

For Thine is the Kingdom and
the Power, and the Glory
now and forever,
Amen.

Chapter 65 • Pope John Paul II: *Veritatis Splendor*

Pope John Paul II in this document gives a detailed explanation of what has been the official teachings of the Catholic Church regarding the essentials of human beliefs and practices as they came from the Gospels, are found in the documents of the Early Fathers and Doctors of the Catholic Church, and in the theologians and philosophers who have defended them in every age. This encyclical is an outstanding companion to the materials selected to present *The Heart of Catholicism*.

Veritatis Splendor
The Splendor of Truth

3. The Church's Pastors, in communion with the Successor of Peter, are close to the faithful in this effort; they guide and accompany them by their authoritative teaching, finding ever new ways of speaking with love and mercy not only to believers but to all people of good will. The Second Vatican Council remains an extraordinary witness of this attitude on the part of the Church which, as an "expert in humanity,"[1] places herself at the service of every individual and of the whole world.[2]

The Church knows that the issue of morality is one which deeply touches every person; it involves all people, even those who do not know Christ and his Gospel or God himself. She knows that it is precisely *on the path of the moral life that the way of salvation is open to all*. The Second Vatican Council clearly recalled this when it stated that "those who without any fault do not know anything about Christ or his Church, yet who search for God with a sincere heart and under the influence of grace, try to put into effect the will of God as known to them through the dictate of conscience . . . can obtain eternal salvation." The Council added: "Nor does divine Providence deny the helps that are necessary for salvation to those who, through no fault of their own have not yet attained to the express recognition of God, yet who strive, not without divine grace, to lead an upright life. For whatever goodness and truth is found in them is considered by the Church as a preparation for the Gospel and bestowed by him who enlightens everyone that they may in the end have life."[3]

The Purpose of the Present Encyclical

4. At all times, but particularly in the last two centuries, the Popes, whether individually or together with the College of Bishops, have developed and proposed a moral teaching regarding the *many different spheres of human life*. In Christ's name and with his authority they have exhorted, passed judgment and explained. In their efforts on behalf of humanity, in fidelity to their mission, they have confirmed, supported and consoled. With the guarantee of assistance from the Spirit of truth they have contributed to a better understanding of moral demands in the areas of human sexuality, the family, and social, economic and political life. In the tradition of the Church and in the history of humanity, their teaching represents a constant deepening of knowledge with regard to morality.[4]

Today, however, it seems *necessary to reflect on the whole of the Church's moral teaching*, with the precise goal of recalling certain fundamental truths of Catholic doctrine which, in the present circumstances, risk being distorted or denied. In fact, a new situation has come *about within the Christian community itself,* which has experienced the spread of numerous doubts and objections of a human and psychological, social and cultural, religious and even properly theological nature, with regard to the Church's moral teachings. It is no longer a matter of limited and occasional dissent, but of an overall and systematic calling into question of traditional moral doctrine, on the basis of certain anthropological and ethical presuppositions. At the root of these presuppositions is the more or less obvious influence of currents of thought which end by detaching human freedom from its essential and constitutive relationship to truth. Thus the traditional doctrine regarding the natural law, and the universality and the permanent validity of its precepts, is rejected; certain of the Church's moral teachings are found simply unacceptable; and the Magisterium itself is considered capable of intervening in matters of morality only in order to "exhort consciences" and to "propose values," in the light of which each individual will independently make his or her decisions and life choices.

In particular, note should be taken of the *lack of harmony between the traditional response of the Church and certain theological positions*, encountered even in Seminaries and in Faculties of Theology, *with regard to questions of the greatest importance* for the Church and for the life of faith of Christians, as well as for the life of society itself. In particular, the question is asked: do the commandments of God, which are written on the human heart and are part of the Covenant, really have the capacity to clarify the daily decisions of individuals and entire societies? Is it possible to obey God and thus love God and neighbour, without respecting these commandments in all circumstances? Also, an opinion is frequently heard which questions the intrinsic and unbreakable bond between faith and morality, as if membership in the Church and her internal unity were to be decided on the basis of faith alone, while in the sphere of morality a pluralism of opinions and of kinds of behaviour could be tolerated, these being left to the judgment of the individual subjective conscience or to the diversity of social and cultural contexts.

5. Given these circumstances, which still exist, I came to the decision — as I announced in my Apostolic Letter *Spiritus Domini*, issued on 1 August 1987 on the second centenary of the death of Saint Alphonsus Maria de' Liguori — to write an Encyclical with the aim of treating "more fully and more deeply the issues regarding the very foundations of moral theology",[5] foundations which are being undermined by certain present-day tendencies.

I address myself to you, Venerable Brothers in the Episcopate, who share with me the responsibility of safeguarding "sound teaching" (*2 Tim 4:3*), with the intention of *clearly setting forth certain aspects of doctrine which are of crucial importance in facing what is certainly a genuine crisis*, since the difficulties which it engenders have most serious implications for the moral life of the faithful and for communion in the Church, as well as for a just and fraternal social life.

If this Encyclical, so long awaited, is being published only now, one of the reasons is that it seemed fitting for it to be preceded by the *Catechism of the Catholic Church*, which contains a complete and systematic exposition of Christian moral teaching. The Catechism presents the moral life of believers in its fundamental elements and in its many aspects as the life of the "children of God": "Recognizing in the faith their new dignity, Christians are called to lead henceforth a life `worthy of the Gospel of Christ' (*Phil* 1:27). Through the sacraments and prayer they receive the grace of Christ and the gifts of his Spirit which make them capable of such a life."[6] Consequently, while referring back to the Catechism "as a sure and authentic reference text for teaching Catholic doctrine,"[7] the Encyclical will limit itself to dealing with *certain fundamental questions regarding the Church's moral teaching*, taking the form of a necessary discernment about issues being debated by ethicists and moral theologians. The specific purpose of the present Encyclical is this: to set forth, with regard to the problems being discussed, the principles of a moral teaching based upon Sacred Scripture and the living Apostolic Tradition,[8] and at the same time to shed light on the presuppositions and consequences of the dissent which that teaching has met.

It is our common duty, and even before that our common grace, as Pastors and Bishops of the Church, to teach the faithful the things which lead them to God, just as the Lord Jesus did with the young man in the Gospel. Replying to the question: "What good must I do to have eternal life?", Jesus referred the young man to God, the Lord of creation and of the Covenant. He reminded him of the moral commandments already revealed in the Old Testament and he indicated their spirit and deepest meaning by inviting the young man to follow him in poverty, humility and love: "Come, follow me!" The truth of this teaching was sealed on the Cross in the Blood of Christ: in the Holy Spirit, it has become the new law of the Church and of every Christian.

This "answer" to the question about morality has been entrusted by Jesus Christ in a particular way to us, the Pastors of the Church; we have been called to make it the object of our preaching, in the fulfilment of our *munus propheticum*. At the same time, our responsibility as Pastors with regard to Christian moral teaching must also be exercised as part of the *munus sacerdotale*: this happens when we dispense to the faithful the gifts of grace and sanctification as an effective means for obeying God's holy law, and when with our constant and confident prayers we support believers in their efforts to be faithful to the demands of the faith and to live in accordance with the Gospel (cf. *Col* 1:9-12). Especially today, Christian moral teaching must be one of the chief areas in which we exercise our pastoral vigilance, in carrying out our *munus regale*.

115. This is the first time, in fact, that the Magisterium of the Church has set forth in detail the fundamental elements of this teaching, and presented the principles for the pastoral discernment necessary in practical and cultural situations which are complex and even crucial.

In the light of Revelation and of the Church's constant teaching, especially that of the Second Vatican Council, I have briefly recalled the essential characteristics of freedom, as well as the fundamental values connected with the dignity of the person and the truth of his acts, so as to be able to discern in obedience to the moral law a grace and a sign of our adoption in the one Son (cf. *Eph* 1:4-6). Specifically, this Encyclical has evaluated certain trends in moral theology today. I now pass this evaluation on to you, in obedience to the word of the Lord who entrusted to Peter the task of strengthening his brethren (cf. Lk 22:32), in order to clarify and aid our common discernment.

Each of us knows how important is the teaching which represents the central theme of this Encyclical and which is today being restated with the authority of the Successor of Peter. Each of us can see the seriousness of what is involved, not only for individuals but also for the whole of society, with the *reaffirmation of the universality and immutability of the moral commandments*, particularly those which prohibit always and without exception *intrinsically evil acts*.

In acknowledging these commandments, Christian hearts and our pastoral charity listen to the call of the One who "first loved us" (1 *Jn* 4:19). God asks us to be holy as he is holy (cf. *Lev* 19:2), to be — in Christ — perfect as he is perfect (cf. *Mt* 5:48). The unwavering demands of that commandment are based upon God's infinitely merciful love (cf. *Lk* 6:36), and the purpose of that commandment is to lead us, by the grace of Christ, on the path of that fullness of life proper to the children of God.

116. We have the duty, as Bishops, to *be vigilant that the word of God is faithfully taught*. My Brothers in the Episcopate, it is part of our pastoral ministry to see to it that this moral teaching is faithfully handed down and to have recourse to appropriate measures to ensure that the faithful are guarded from every doctrine and theory contrary to it. In carrying out this task we are all assisted by theologians; even so, theological opinions constitute neither the rule nor the norm of our teaching. Its authority is derived, by the assistance of the Holy Spirit and in communion *cum Petro et sub Petro*, from our fidelity to the Catholic faith which comes from the Apostles. As Bishops, we have the grave obligation to be *personally* vigilant that the "sound doctrine" (1 *Tim* 1:10) of faith and morals is taught in our Dioceses.

A particular responsibility is incumbent upon Bishops with regard to *Catholic institutions*. Whether these are agencies for the pastoral care of the family or for social work, or institutions dedicated to teaching or health care, Bishops can canonically erect and recognize these structures and delegate certain responsibilities to them. Nevertheless, Bishops are never relieved of their own personal obligations. It falls to them, in communion with the Holy See, both to grant the title "Catholic" to Church-related schools,[9] universities,[10] health-care facilities and counselling services, and, in cases of a serious failure to live up to that title, to take it away.

117. In the heart of every Christian, in the inmost depths of each person,

there is always an echo of the question which the young man in the Gospel once asked Jesus: "Teacher, what good must I do to have eternal life?" (*Mt* 19:16). Everyone, however, needs to address this question to the "Good Teacher", since he is the only one who can answer in the fullness of truth, in all situations, in the most varied of circumstances. And when Christians ask him the question which rises from their conscience, the Lord replies in the words of the New Covenant which have been entrusted to his Church. As the Apostle Paul said of himself, we have been sent "to preach the Gospel, and not with eloquent wisdom, lest the Cross of Christ be emptied of its power" (1 1 *Cor* 1:17). The Church's answer to man's question contains the wisdom and power of Christ Crucified, the Truth which gives of itself.

When people ask the Church the questions raised by their consciences, when the faithful in the Church turn to their Bishops and Pastors, *the Church's reply contains the voice of Jesus Christ, the voice of the truth about good and evil.* In the words spoken by the Church there resounds, in people's inmost being, the voice of God who "alone is good" (cf. *Mt* 19:17), who alone "is love" (1 *Jn* 4:8,16).

Through the *anointing of the Spirit* this gentle but challenging word becomes light and life for man. Again the Apostle Paul invites us to have confidence, because "our competence is from God, who has made us competent to be ministers of a new covenant, not in a written code but in the Spirit. . . The Lord is the Spirit, and where the Spirit of the Lord is, there is freedom. And all of us, with unveiled faces, reflecting the glory of the Lord, are being changed into his likeness from one degree of glory to another; for this comes from the Lord, the Spirit" (2 *Cor* 3:5-6,17-18).

Conclusion
Mary, Mother of Mercy

118. At the end of these considerations, let us entrust ourselves, the sufferings and the joys of our life, the moral life of believers and people of good will, and the research of moralists, to Mary, Mother of God and Mother of Mercy.

Mary is Mother of Mercy because her Son, Jesus Christ, was sent by the Father as the revelation of God's mercy (cf. *Jn* 3:16-18). Christ came not to condemn but to forgive, to show mercy (cf. *Mt* 9:13). And the greatest mercy of all is found in his being in our midst and calling us to meet him and to confess, with Peter, that he is "the Son of the living God" (*Mt* 16:16). No human sin can erase the mercy of God, or prevent him from unleashing all his triumphant power, if we only call upon him. Indeed, sin itself makes even more radiant the love of the Father who, in order to ransom a slave, sacrificed his Son:[11] his mercy towards us is Redemption. This mercy reaches its fullness in the gift of the Spirit who bestows new life and demands that it be lived. No matter how many and great the obstacles put in his way by human frailty and sin, the Spirit, who renews the face of the earth (cf. *Ps* 104:30), makes possible the miracle of the perfect accomplishment of the good. This renewal, which gives the ability to do what is good, noble, beautiful, pleasing to God and in conformity with his will, is in some way the flowering of the gift of mercy, which offers liberation from the slavery of evil and gives the strength to sin in no more. Through the gift of new life, Jesus makes us sharers in his love and leads us to the Father in the Spirit.

119. Such is the consoling certainty of Christian faith, the source of its profound humanity and *extraordinary simplicity*. At times, in the discussions about new and complex moral problems, it can seem that Christian morality is in itself too demanding, difficult to understand and almost impossible to practice. This is untrue, since Christian morality consists, in the simplicity of the Gospel, in *following Jesus Christ*, in abandoning oneself to him, in letting oneself be transformed by his grace and renewed by his mercy, gifts which come to us in the living communion of his Church. Saint Augustine reminds us that "he who would live has a place to live, and has everything needed to live. Let him draw near, let him believe, let him become part of the body, that he may have life. Let him not shrink from the unity of the members".[12] By the light of the Holy Spirit, the living essence of Christian morality can be understood by everyone, even the least learned, but particularly those who are able to preserve an "undivided heart" (*Ps* 86:11). On the other hand, this evangelical simplicity does not exempt one from facing reality in its complexity; rather it can lead to a more genuine understanding of reality, inasmuch as following Christ will gradually bring out the distinctive character of authentic Christian morality, while providing the vital energy needed to carry it out. It is the task of the Church's Magisterium to see that the dynamic process of following Christ develops in an organic manner, without the falsification or obscuring of its moral demands, with all their consequences. The one who loves Christ keeps his commandments (cf. *Jn* 14:15).

120. Mary is also Mother of Mercy because it is to her that Jesus entrusts his Church and all humanity. At the foot of the Cross, when she accepts John

as her son, when she asks, together with Christ, forgiveness from the Father for those who do not know what they do (cf. *Lk* 23:34), Mary experiences, in perfect docility to the Spirit, the richness and the universality of God's love, which opens her heart and enables it to embrace the entire human race. Thus Mary becomes Mother of each and every one of us, the Mother who obtains for us divine mercy.

Mary is the radiant sign and inviting model of the moral life. As Saint Ambrose put it, "The life of this one person can serve as a model for everyone,"[13] and while speaking specifically to virgins but within a context open to all, he affirmed: "The first stimulus to learning is the nobility of the teacher. Who can be more noble than the Mother of God? Who can be more glorious than the one chosen by Glory Itself?"[14] Mary lived and exercised her freedom precisely by giving herself to God and accepting God's gift within herself. Until the time of his birth, she sheltered in her womb the Son of God who became man; she raised him and enabled him to grow, and she accompanied him in that supreme act of freedom which is the complete sacrifice of his own life. By the gift of herself, Mary entered fully into the plan of God who gives himself to the world. By accepting and pondering in her heart events which she did not always understand (cf. *Lk* 2:19), she became the model of all those who hear the word of God and keep it (cf. *Lk* 11:28), and merited the title of "Seat of Wisdom." This Wisdom is Jesus Christ himself, the Eternal Word of God, who perfectly reveals and accomplishes the will of the Father (cf. *Heb* 10:5-10). Mary invites everyone to accept this Wisdom. To us too she addresses the command she gave to the servants at Cana in Galilee during the marriage feast: "Do whatever he tells you" (*Jn* 2:5).

Mary shares our human condition, but in complete openness to the grace of God. Not having known sin, she is able to have compassion on every kind of weakness. She understands sinful man and loves him with a Mother's love. Precisely for this reason she is on the side of truth and shares the Church's burden in recalling always and to everyone the demands of morality. Nor does she permit sinful man to be deceived by those who claim to love him by justifying his sin, for she knows that the sacrifice of Christ her Son would thus be emptied of its power. No absolution offered by beguiling doctrines, even in the areas of philosophy and theology, can make man truly happy: only the Cross and the glory of the Risen Christ can grant peace to his conscience and salvation to his life.

O Mary,

Mother of Mercy,
watch over all people,
that the Cross of Christ
may not be emptied of its power,
that man may not stray
from the path of the good
or become blind to sin,
but may put his hope ever more fully in God
who is "rich in mercy" (*Eph* 2:4).
May he carry out the good works prepared
by God beforehand (cf. *Eph* 2:10)
and so live completely
"for the praise of his glory" (*Eph* 1:12).

Given in Rome, at Saint Peter's, on 6 August, Feast of the Transfiguration of the Lord, in the year 1993, the fifteenth of my Pontificate.

Notes

1. Paul VI, *Address* to the General Assembly of the United Nations (4 October 1965), 1: *AAS* 57 (1965), 878; cf. Encyclical Letter *Populorum Progressio* (26 March 1967), 13: *AAS* 59 (1967), 263-264.

2. Cf. Second Vatican Ecumenical Council, Pastoral Consitution on the Church in the Modern World *Gaudium et Spes*, 16.

3. Dogmatic Constitution on the Church *Lumen Gentium*, 16.

4. Pius XII had already pointed out this doctrinal development: cf. *Radio Message* for the Fiftieth Anniversary of the Encyclical Letter *Rerum Novarum* of Leo XIII (1 June 1941): *AAS* 33 (1941), 195-205. Also JOHN XXIII, Encyclical Letter *Mater et Magistra* (15 May 1961): *AAS* 53 (1961), 410-413.

5. Apostolic Letter *Spiritus Domini* (1 August 1987): *AAS* 79 (1987), 1374.

6. *Catechism of the Catholic Church*, No. 1692.

7. Apostolic Constitution Fidei Depositum (11 October 1992), 4.

8. Cf. Second Vatican Ecumenical Council, Dogmatic Constitution on Divine Revelation *Die Verbum*, 10.

9. Cf. *Code of Canon Law*, Canon 803, 3.

10. Cf. *Code of Canon Law*, Canon 808.

11. "O inaestimabilis dilectio caritatis: ut servum redimeres, Filium tradidisti!": *Missale Romanum, In Resurrectione Domini, Praeconium Paschale*.

12. *In Iohannis Evangelium Tractatus*, 26, 13: CCL, 36, 266.

13. *De Virginibus*, Bk. II, Chap. II, 15: *PL* 16, 222.

14. *Ibid.*, Bk. II, Chap. II, 7: *PL* 16, 220.

Index

A

B

C

D

E

F

G

I

J

K

L

M

N

O

P

Q

R

S

T

X

Y

Z